TRUCKLOAD TRANSPORTATION:
ECONOMICS, PRICING & ANALYSIS

Leo J. Lazarus, M.B.A.

Monument Press
Memphis, TN

Truckload Transportation: Economics, Pricing & Analysis

Copyright ©2010 by Leo J. Lazarus, M.B.A.

ISBN: 978-0-9827848-1-5

Library of Congress Control Number : 2010934769

All rights reserved. Printed in the United States of America. No part of this book may be reproduced in any manner whatsoever without written permission except in the case of brief quotations embodied in critical articles and reviews.

For information, contact the publisher.
Visit the author's web site at:
www.truckloadtransportation.com

monument
PRESS

Monument Press
P.O. Box 752384, Memphis, TN, 38175
901.328.7206
www.monumentpress.com
publish@monumentpress.com

TRUCKLOAD TRANSPORTATION: ECONOMICS, PRICING & ANALYSIS

CONTENTS

Section 1: Introduction to Truckload Transportation

Chapter 1	Introduction to Truckload Transportation	1
Chapter 2	The Trucking Business Model	29

Section 2: One-Way Pricing and Network Analysis

Chapter 3	Introduction to One-Way Pricing	51
Chapter 4	Core Concepts in One-Way Pricing	71
Chapter 5	Advanced Concepts in One-Way Pricing	97
Chapter 6	Network Management and Optimization	123
Chapter 7	Operations and Profitability Analysis	139

Section 3: Dedicated Fleet Pricing and Design

Chapter 8	Introduction to Dedicated Fleet Pricing	169
Chapter 9	Dedicated Pricing and Cost Forecasting	193
Chapter 10	Establishing the Proper Profit Margin for a Dedicated Fleet	219
Chapter 11	Special Topics in Dedicated Pricing	263
Chapter 12	Semi-Dedicated Pricing and Design	291

Section 4: Bid Response and Analysis

Chapter 13	Bid Analysis and Response	337
Chapter 14	Case Studies in Bid Response Analysis	377

Section 5: Key Concepts for Shippers

Chapter 15	Key Concepts for Shippers	431

CONTENTS

Section 1: Introduction to Truckload Transportation

CHAPTER 1
Introduction to Truckload Transportation 1

Introduction 1
The Trucking Business Cycle 2
The Organizational Structure of a Truckload Carrier 4
Carrier Measurements and Key Performance Indicators 7
    Mileage Measurements 7
    Revenue Types and Measurements 9
    Key Operating Measurements and Statistics 11
Types of Truckload Operations 13
    Linehaul Operations 14
    Regional Operations 15
    Short Haul and Local Operations 16
    Dedicated Fleets 17
    Specialized Carriers and Trailer Equipment 18
Driver Turnover 20
Driver Hours of Service Regulations 21
Owner-Operators 22
Primary Truckload Operating Cost Components 23
    Variable Costs 23
    Fixed Costs 26

CHAPTER 2
The Trucking Business Model 29

Truckload Economics 29
    Introduction 29
    Individual Truck Business Model 30
    Operating Ratio 32
    Utilization Analysis 33
    Loaded Revenue Per Mile Analysis 37
    Empty Mile Percentage Analysis 39
    Break-even Point Utilization 42
Primary Cost Drivers for Carriers 43
    Total Cost Driver: Booking Loads 43
    Total Cost Driver: Driving Miles 43
    Total Cost Driver: Owning / Leasing Tractors and Trailers 44
Activity-Based Costing 45
    Developing a Simple Activity-Based Cost Model 45
    Application of the Activity-Based Costing Model 48
Revenue Per Day and Asset Productivity 50

CONTENTS

Section 2: One-Way Pricing and Network Analysis

CHAPTER 3
Introduction to One-Way Pricing 51

Lanes 51
Sample Contract 52
Accessorial Charges 56
The Pricing Matrix 66
    Backup Matrix 66
    Guideline Pricing Matrix 67
    Pricing Regions 68

CHAPTER 4
Core Concepts in One-Way Pricing 71

Cycle Time 72
    Cycle Time Illustrations 74
    Buffer Time 76
    Dwell Time 79
Length of Haul 80
    Other Length of Haul Statistics 85
    Empty Miles and Net Revenue Per Mile 88
Assigning Empty Miles to Load Activity 90
Profitability Optimization 91
    Critical Profitability Factors 91
    Business Models by Utilization Level 92
Utilization Maximization 94
Revenue Per Truck Per Week 96

CHAPTER 5
Advanced Concepts in One-Way Pricing 97

The One-Way Pricing Process 97
    Lane and Customer Analysis 97
    The Preliminary One-Way Rate 100
    Pricing Adjustments 102
Network Capacity and Balance 103
    Real-Time Capacity and Balance 103
    Capacity and Balance and Pricing Strategy 104
Headhaul and Backhaul Markets 106
    Common Factors that Create Headhaul or Backhaul Markets 108
    Theoretical Pricing from Market Type to Market Type 109
    Demand Shifts and Market Pricing 110
    Supply Shifts and Market Pricing 111
    Case Study: The Florida Backhaul Market 112
    Market Type and Length of Haul 114
Seasonality 116
Round Trip Pricing 121

CONTENTS

Section 2: One-Way Pricing and Network Analysis (cont'd)

CHAPTER 6
Network Management and Optimization 123

Network Capacity and Balance 123
    Freight Solicitation 124
    Truck Repositioning 125
Exchanging Loads from One Driver to Another 126
    Carrier Reasons for Load Swaps 126
    Shipper Reasons for Load Swaps 128
    Other Swap Considerations 129
Customer Diversification and the Portfolio Concept 130
The Tractor and Load Assignment Problem 132
    The Optimization Model 133
    The Optimization Solution 135

CHAPTER 7
Operations and Profitability Analysis 139

Carrier Analysis Reports 139
    Fleet Level Analysis 140
    Customer Level Analysis 144
    Market Level Analysis 152
    Lane Level Analysis 157
Other Analysis and Reporting Considerations 160
    Carrier Income Statements 160
    On-time Service Reporting 163
    Operating Reports 165

CONTENTS

Section 3: Dedicated Fleet Pricing and Design

CHAPTER 8
Introduction to Dedicated Fleet Pricing 169

Common Types of Dedicated Fleets 169
    Multi-Stop Retail Distribution 169
    Short Haul Regional Distribution 170
    Over-the-Road High Utilization 171
Common Dedicated Contract Structures 172
    Utilization Scale Pricing 173
    Over-Under Pricing 175
    Fixed-Variable Pricing 178
    Backhaul Revenue Sharing 180
Dedicated Fleet Contract 182
Dedicated Fleet Invoice 183
The Steps in Dedicated Pricing 184
    Step 1: Define the Operating Characteristics of the Fleet 184
    Step 2: Estimate Costs for the Operation 188
    Step 3: Determine the Pricing and Margin for the Fleet 190
    The Pro-forma Income Statement 191

CHAPTER 9
Dedicated Pricing and Cost Forecasting 193

Basic Cost Assumptions 193
Basic Dedicated Fleet Example 195
    Carrier Decision Variables for Dedicated Pricing 196
    Revenue and Cost Calculations and Line Items 201
Basic Dedicated Fleet Pricing Example 204
    Fixed-Variable Pricing Format 207
    Over-Under Pricing Format 210
    Utilization Scale Pricing Format 213
Revenue Validation and Consistency by Contract Type 215
Handling On-site Costs and Other Fixed Overhead 216

CHAPTER 10
Establishing the Proper Profit Margin for a Dedicated Fleet 219

The Risks of Operating Ratio Based Pricing 219
    The Hidden Weakness of Operating Ratio 221
    Utilization and Trailer Ratio Scenario Analysis 228
Investment Analysis Approach to Dedicated Pricing 239
    Review of Capital Budgeting (NPV and IRR) 239
Cash Flow / Investment Analysis Pricing Techniques 241
    The Steps in Investment Analysis Dedicated Fleet Pricing 241
    Additional Considerations for Investment-Based Pricing 255
Pricing for Lease Equipment or Owner-Operators 258

CONTENTS

Section 3: Dedicated Fleet Pricing and Design (cont'd)

CHAPTER 11
Special Topics in Dedicated Pricing 263

Estimating Backhaul Revenues 263
    Backhaul Revenue by Destination 263
    Secondary Backhaul Considerations 266
    Other Backhaul Revenue Share Considerations 267
    Partially Completed Backhaul Loads 269
    The Backhaul Funnel 271
Customizing the Driver Compensation Program 271
    Fixed Weekly Salary 274
    Hourly Pay 275
    Per Mile Pay 277
    Activity-Based Pay 278
    Modified Mileage Pay 280
Matching the Driver Pay Program to Revenues 281
Measuring the Efficiency of Dedicated Fleets 286
    Fleet Design and Actual Performance 286
    Tractor Utilization Charts 288

CHAPTER 12
Semi-Dedicated Pricing and Design 291

Short Haul Dedicated Fleets 292
Shuttle / Extreme Short Haul Pricing 294
    Slip-Seat Fleet 296
    Example Inbound Automotive Parts Fleet 297
Mileage Band Pricing Contracts 299
    Determining the Mileage Band Rates 300
    Shipper Network Operating Characteristics 302
    Basic Fleet Size Model Operating Assumptions 303
    Basic Short Haul Fleet Size Model 304
    Applying Dedicated Pricing to the Mileage Band Rates 309
    Sensitivity Analysis – Dedicated Pricing 311
    Allocation of Dedicated Revenues to Mileage Bands 312
    Mileage Bands with Secondary Coverage 316
    Advanced Simulation and Fleet Size Sensitivity Analysis 323

CONTENTS

Section 4: Bid Response and Analysis

CHAPTER 13
Bid Analysis and Response 337

Request for Proposal (RFP) 337
RFP and Bid Contents 339
Sample Bid Analysis 340
    Before Pricing the Bid 341
    Summary Analysis of Bid Contents 344
    Developing a Strategy and Pricing the Bid 348
    Bid Strategy by Carrier 348
Bid Optimization Tools and Strategies 351
    Decision Variables for the Carrier 351
    Decision Variables for the Shipper 355
"Packaged" Bid Responses 357
    Bid Strategy and Packaged Bids 358
    Packaged Bid Strategy: Additional Considerations 364
Shipper Network Data in RFPs 365
    Summary Load Volumes 365
    Discrete Shipment History 367
    Shipment Data for Multi-Stop Designs 368

CHAPTER 14
Case Studies in Bid Response Analysis 377

Case 1: Traditional One-Way Bid 377
    The Case 377
    Carrier Analysis 378
    Carrier Solution Design 380
    Carrier Pricing and Proposal 385
Case 2: One-Way Bid with Packaging and Optimization 386
    The Case 386
    Carrier Analysis 388
    Carrier Solution Design 391
    Carrier Pricing and Proposal 403
Case 3: Regional Distribution Bid 405
    The Case 405
    Carrier Analysis 406
    Carrier Solution Design 408
    Carrier Pricing and Proposal 413
Case 4: Dedicated Fleet with Fixed-Variable Pricing 417
    The Case 417
    Carrier Analysis 419
    Carrier Solution Design 421
    Carrier Pricing and Proposal 429

CONTENTS

Section 5: Key Concepts for Shippers

CHAPTER 15
Key Concepts for Shippers 431

Shipper Transportation Cost Measurements 431
    Cost Per Mile 432
    Cost Per Unit of Product 435
Flexible Budgeting and Transportation Cost Analysis 440
Transportation Cost Allocations 445
    Cost Allocation Models 445
    Applying Cost Allocations 448
Dedicated Fleets and Marginal Cost Analysis 450
Shipper Cost Strategies for Short Haul Pricing 452
    Time-of-Day Information 452
    Seasonal Shipping Patterns 454
    Mileage Band Destinations 455
Diseconomies of Scale in One Way Pricing 457
Volume-based One-Way Pricing 461
Outsourcing Private Fleets to Dedicated Carriers 462
Summary 464

! Technical Tips

Matrix Rate "Look Up" Spreadsheet Design (VLOOKUP) 70
Linear Programming (Solver) Spreadsheet Feature 138
Creating Basic Reports with Microsoft Access 166
Calculations with Date and Time Information 168
Net Present Value (NPV) and Internal Rate of Return (IRR) Spreadsheet Functions 261
Monte Carlo Simulation Spreadsheet Design 329
Sensitivity Analysis and the "Table" Spreadsheet Feature 334
Using Spreadsheet "Pivot" Tables 371
Spreadsheet Text Tips and Techniques 375

How To Use This Book

Truckload transportation pricing is a complex topic with many variables and considerations. This book is organized so that a novice can learn the basics of truckload transportation then move into the more advanced concepts involved with one-way pricing, dedicated pricing, and bid response analysis. However, it is highly recommended that even experienced readers start from the beginning of the book. A sound understanding and review of the basic principles of truckload transportation provides the necessary foundation for fully comprehending the more advanced concepts that are presented later in the book.

While the book is written primarily for the benefit of truckload carriers, shippers and related parties will also gain valuable insight into truckload transportation by reading the entire book. While Chapter 15 focuses specifically on shipper issues, it is important that shippers read the entire book to get the maximum benefit from this chapter. The topics covered throughout the book will provide shippers with a much deeper understanding of the truckload carrier's business model, cost structure, and operating strategy. By having a greater understanding of the needs of their carriers, shippers can become better partners and potentially enjoy improved service and lower transportation costs as a result.

Throughout this book, readers will see operating cost information and specific rates and prices. While most costs and rates are historically accurate for the time this book was written, this information is shown for illustration purposes only. Truckload rates and operating costs change over time based on market conditions, fuel prices, driver wage expectations, equipment costs, and many other factors. Unless otherwise indicated, consider all cost and price figures shown in this book as only examples and not specific facts or pricing recommendations.

In some circumstances, there will be real-world exceptions to the general concepts in this book. However, a thorough understanding of the concepts presented in this book will provide the ability to identify and interpret any exceptions to the general rule. While this book cannot possibly address every unique situation a carrier or shipper will face, it does provide a solid foundation of general theory and specific analytical techniques to properly approach almost any pricing and analysis challenge.

Technical Tips
The book includes a number of "Technical Tips" that provide detailed explanations of the application of spreadsheet and database software to several of the analysis examples presented in the book. The tips provide no new information about a particular topic other than the programming details around the solution. Unless the reader has a specific interest in the technical details of a particular topic, these "Technical Tips" can safely be disregarded.

On-line Resources
Certain lengthy technical tips are not covered in complete detail within the book but are available for download online at no cost. Please visit www.TruckloadTransportation.com to access these expanded technical tips. In addition, the full spreadsheet models for many of the analysis and pricing techniques presented in this book are available for purchase at the website, including the full dedicated fleet pricing model.

About the Author

Leo Lazarus has over 15 years of experience as a financial analyst, pricing analyst, transportation consultant, and adjunct professor of business. As a part-time college instructor, Leo taught courses including Corporate Finance, Management Accounting, Economics, Business Statistics, Management, Marketing, and Operations Management.

In the truckload transportation field, Leo worked for Memphis-based M.S. Carriers from 1995 to 2002, primarily as a senior pricing analyst for both dedicated and one-way truckload transportation. While at M.S. Carriers, Leo was highly involved with the most sophisticated and complex distribution networks for many of the nation's largest shippers. Since 2002, Leo has been an independent consultant in the truckload transportation field, serving the analysis, pricing and training needs of several Fortune 500 shippers and carriers of all sizes.

Leo has an M.B.A. from The University of Mississippi and a B.B.A. in Management, also from The University of Mississippi.

CHAPTER 1: Introduction to Truckload Transportation

Introduction

On the surface, full-truckload transportation appears to be a fairly simple business. For a predetermined charge, a truck picks up a full truckload for a customer at Point A and delivers the load to Point B. Next, the truck picks up a load for a different customer at Point C and delivers the load to Point D. Basically, this cycle continues constantly for every truck and every driver in a carrier's network. As this cycle continues, well-managed trucking companies have many challenges. In the short run, carrier management must answer such questions as:

1. How much should we charge customers moving loads from Point A to Point B?
2. How much should we charge customers moving loads from Point B to Point A?
3. Is the company making a profit while moving loads between Points A and B?
4. Are some customers and some loads more profitable than others? If so, why?
5. Should some customers be charged more than others for the same trip?
6. Should we increase rates with certain customers to improve profitability? Should we decrease rates with certain customers to attract additional business?
7. Within our network, should we increase business with certain customers? Should we decrease or eliminate business with certain customers?

In the long run, the carrier's management team must determine profitable growth strategies for the company. Strategic considerations for the carrier include:

1. What services should be offered to our customers?
2. Should our services be expanded into new types of truckload transportation?
3. Should our current services be expanded into new geographic areas?
4. Should our fleet of tractors and trailers be expanded? Should we expand with new types of equipment or new services?
5. How will the charges and prices for these new services be determined? How will profits be measured for these new services?

The overall goal of this book is to provide trucking managers with the tools and techniques to successfully answer these and other tactical and strategic questions. The book provides a general overview of trucking companies, including the organizational structure, cost structure, and basic profitability strategies ideal for anyone wishing to better understand the truckload transportation industry. In addition, the book provides an excellent resource that will allow shippers to better understand how their expectations, requirements, and restrictions impact the costs, profitability, and revenue needs of their carriers. By having a greater understanding of the needs of their carriers, shippers can become better partners and potentially enjoy improved service and lower transportation costs as a result.

In some circumstances, there will be real-world exceptions to the general concepts in this book. However, a thorough understanding of the concepts in this book will provide the ability to identify and interpret any exceptions to the general rule. While this book cannot possibly address every unique situation a carrier or shipper will face, it does provide a solid foundation of general theory and specific analytical techniques to properly approach almost any pricing and analysis challenge.

Truckload pricing, especially on a one-way basis, is as much of an art as it is a science. For example, if several experienced pricing managers from different carriers were asked to provide a truckload rate per mile from Columbus, OH to Dallas, TX, the rates provided by those experts would likely vary significantly. However, the internal and external factors that are considered by those pricing managers to determine the rate per mile are the same. This book provides a detailed explanation of these factors and how the factors interact to influence the pricing decision. After learning these basic concepts, readers will understand why the rate per mile in the Columbus to Dallas example could vary noticeably among different carriers.

Throughout this book, readers will see operating cost information and specific rates and prices. While most costs and rates are historically accurate for the time this book was written, this information is shown for illustration purposes only. Truckload rates and operating costs change over time based on market conditions, fuel prices, driver wage expectations, equipment costs, and many other factors. Unless otherwise indicated, consider all cost and price figures shown in this book as only examples and not specific facts or pricing recommendations.

The Trucking Business Cycle

The core business model of a trucking company is similar to most common businesses. Each truck serves as a moving "factory" and the miles driven by the truck represent the product that is produced by the factory. The table below compares the trucking business model to the models of General Motors and McDonald's.

Business Model Comparison

Company	Facility	Unit of Output
General Motors	Plant	Cars
McDonald's	Restaurant	Hamburgers
Truckload Carrier	Truck	Miles

Trucking companies produce miles in much the same way that General Motors produces cars or McDonald's produces hamburgers. Keep this relationship in mind throughout the discussion of fixed and variable costs and the various economic models that follow.

Each truck moves continuously throughout the carrier's network in a semi-random pattern from load to load and customer to customer. The timeline in the table below illustrates the work flows for a truck and driver over a three day period.

Three Day Driver Work Cycle

Day and Time	Activity / Event
Sunday 5:00 pm	**Home awaiting dispatch.** The driver is at home in West Memphis, AR waiting to receive his next load assignment from his dispatcher. At 5 pm, the driver receives his dispatch. He must pick up his next load at ABC Express in Memphis, TN at 7 am on Monday. He must deliver the load to Houston, TX by 2 pm on Tuesday.
Monday 6:45 am	**Arrival at Origin for Pick-up.** The driver arrives at ABC Express in Memphis. After hooking to the pre-loaded trailer and receiving the paperwork for the load, the driver is ready to depart for Houston, TX.
Monday 7:22 am	**Departure from Origin.** The driver departs ABC Express in Memphis, TN and begins the 650 mile trip to Houston, TX.
Monday 6:05 pm	**Rest Break.** After approximately 11 hours of driving, the driver stops at a truck stop about 120 miles from Houston, TX to take a legally required rest break for 10 hours.
Tuesday 5:10 am	**Drive to Destination.** After the mandatory rest break required by U.S. Department of Transportation safety regulations, the driver continues on the final portion of the trip to Houston, TX.
Tuesday 7:14 am	**Final Delivery.** The driver arrives at the destination in Houston, TX. After dropping the trailer and completing the paperwork, the driver is ready for his next load.
Tuesday 7:53 am	**Meal and fuel awaiting dispatch.** The driver goes to a nearby truck stop to eat breakfast, fill the truck with fuel, and wait for his headquarters to assign him to a new load.
Tuesday 8:55 am	**Dispatch.** The driver receives his next load assignment from his dispatcher. He must drive 22 empty miles to Sugar Land, TX to pick up his next load going to Dallas, TX.
Tuesday 10:15 am	**Load Pick-up.** The driver arrives in Sugar Land, TX for his next load. After receiving the paperwork for the load, the driver is ready to depart on the 260 mile trip to Dallas, TX.
Tuesday 3:37 pm	**Load Delivery.** The driver arrives at the destination in Dallas, TX. After dropping the trailer and completing the paperwork, the driver is ready for his next load.
Tuesday 4:45 pm	**Awaiting Dispatch.** After delivering his load, the driver goes to his carrier's terminal and maintenance facility in nearby Garland, TX. While at the terminal, the driver takes a required rest break and again waits for his dispatcher to assign him to his next load.

Truck drivers operate in a cycle very similar to the above example at all times. Since most drivers are paid by the mile, time management is critical to the driver's income. In most cases, drivers prefer to be assigned to a new load as soon as possible after completing the previous load. The carrier's revenues are also usually earned on a mileage basis, so time management and driver productivity is critically important to the carrier's goals as well.

The driver work cycle shown above is typical of most over-the-road carriers. Carriers and drivers must work together to maximize the efficiency of the work cycle and the carrier's customer network. This book will discuss and analyze each of the primary operating variables and how those variables affect the carrier's productivity and profitability. The book will also discuss how each operating variable impacts the carrier's pricing, rate structure, and operating strategy.

The Organizational Structure of a Truckload Carrier

The core organizational structure of a trucking company includes two major groups, operations management and general support staff. The operations group recruits, hires, and manages the truck drivers, communicates with customers, and maintains the fleet of trucks and trailers. The support group includes key areas such as sales, marketing, human resources, and accounting. The organizational chart below reflects the primary departments within most trucking companies. With smaller carriers, a single individual may perform several of the roles described below.

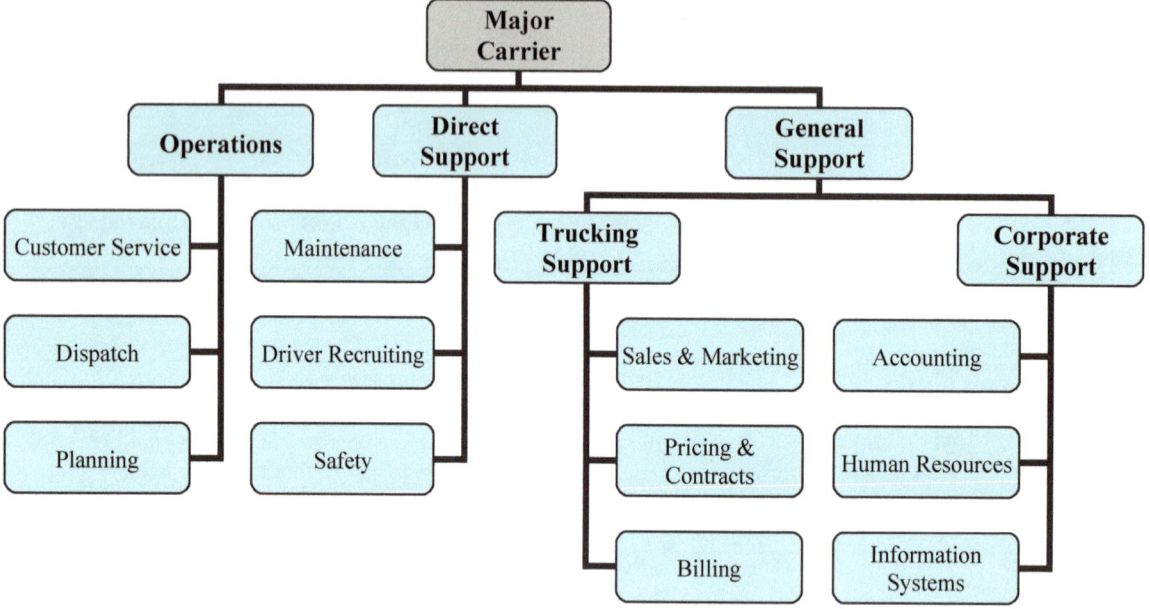

Operations

Customer Service

Customer service representatives serve as the primary day-to-day contact for customers. Customer service representatives are usually assigned responsibility for the customers in a specific geographic area or a specialized group of related customers. Customer service representatives are responsible for determining which customer loads are accepted and which loads are declined. Through internal and external communication, the customer service group must balance the needs of the customer with the needs of the trucking company and its drivers.

Customer service representatives receive the critical load information from the customer. The basic load information includes the origin and destination, the pick-up and delivery dates and times, and trailer numbers. The pick-up and delivery dates and times may be negotiated to fit the needs of the carrier without disrupting the delivery needs of the customer. The customer service representative will also contact the customer if any problems occur with a load, especially issues that will cause the load to be delivered late, such as weather, accidents, traffic delays, or driver errors.

Customer service representatives also manage the trailers at each customer location. The customer service group makes sure that customers have an adequate number of trailers at each location while also making sure that customers unload trailers in a timely fashion.

Dispatch

Dispatchers serve as the manager and primary contact person for a group of truck drivers. Dispatchers are in constant contact with their drivers to make sure that both the driver's needs and the company's needs are being met. The driver's needs include securing adequate miles (income), maintaining log books, and honoring the driver's need to get home on a regular basis. Dispatchers also focus closely on company objectives including safety, on-time delivery, and driver productivity.

Planning

Planners are responsible for assigning available trucks to available customer loads. The goals of the planner in creating load assignments include insuring on-time delivery, minimizing empty miles between loads, and meeting driver needs. Planners may be assigned to a specific fleet of trucks or all available trucks within a specific geographic region. Many trucking companies utilize computer-based optimization technology that assists the planner with recommendations on the complex decision of which trucks to assign to which loads.[1]

Direct Support Departments

Maintenance

The maintenance department is responsible for the repair and routine preventative maintenance of the company's tractors and trailers. The maintenance department may also provide input into what types of equipment the company will purchase. Large trucking companies will often have company-owned maintenance facilities in multiple locations throughout their service area. Smaller trucking companies may have one central maintenance facility and subcontract a portion of maintenance activities to equipment dealerships and other third party maintenance providers. The computer systems of many carriers will track activity for all equipment and provide alerts to the carrier when equipment is due for routine maintenance.

Driver Recruiting

The driver recruiting department is responsible for attracting and hiring the team of truck drivers for the carrier. Because driving a truck is a difficult and stressful career, driver turnover is a very serious problem for all trucking companies. Many trucking companies experience driver turnover rates in excess of 100% per year and, as a result, carriers must constantly recruit, hire and train new drivers. Since the company will not be able to satisfy customer needs without drivers, the role of the driver recruiter is critical to the success of trucking companies.

---

[1] A future chapter provides a more detailed discussion of network management and network optimization software programs.

Common activities performed by the driver recruiting department include developing and placing advertisements for drivers, carefully screening and interviewing new applicants, and measuring driver turnover and related items such as the causes of driver turnover. The driver recruiting department can help with the driver turnover problem by establishing employment policies and hiring practices to hire only the best candidates for driver job openings.

Safety

The carrier's safety department is responsible for the management of the company's safety programs and initiatives. The safety performance of all carriers is constantly monitored by the United States Department of Transportation (D.O.T.) to ensure the safety of all vehicles on the nation's highways and interstates. The carrier's safety department must be certain that the company is in compliance with all D.O.T. regulations. The safety department organizes and performs many critical activities including training drivers, investigating accidents, and reviewing driver logs and hours-of-service compliance.[2]

The safety department or an insurance-related operations group will oversee the management of shipment issues related to over, short, or damaged shipments and freight claims by shippers.[3] Shipper issues will commonly arise as a result of accidents, improper loading, inaccurate paperwork, or even driver theft. The department will investigate each incident and provide the appropriate compensation to shippers in cases where the loss was caused by the carrier.

Trucking Support Departments

Sales and Marketing

While the customer service team provides the day-to-day contact with the shipper, the sales department is the primary strategic contact between the shipper and carrier. The sales department will negotiate pricing with the shipper and provide the shipper's transportation management team with information on available capacity and the markets the carrier would like to serve for the shipper. The sales department provides the link between the shipper and the carrier's customer service and operations team. The sales department must constantly be certain that the carrier is meeting the shipper's expectations for capacity and service. If the customer fails to meet commitments made to the carrier, the salesman will contact the customer to address any outstanding issues.

Trucking companies of all size have a sales department. In a small carrier, the owner or president is often the primary salesperson. Most large carriers employ national sales forces with sales representatives strategically located across the country in every major

---

[2] The D.O.T. has very strict regulations governing the amount of time a driver can spend behind the wheel driving each day and each week. These regulations and their impact on carriers will be discussed in detail throughout this book.

[3] Over, short, and damaged is commonly referred to as O S & D.

market that the carrier serves. Large carriers may also have specialized national account sales managers that serve major shippers in large industries such as retail distribution or automobile production. The national account managers work closely with regional sales managers to meet needs and address problems.

Pricing and Contracts

The pricing department is responsible for setting company pricing and managing contracts with customers. The pricing department will work closely with the sales group during the process of setting prices, negotiating contracts, and identifying desirable business opportunities. The pricing department may also perform various types of profitability studies to identify pricing deficiencies and evaluate the profitability of individual customers and geographic markets.

Carriers must maintain accurate and up-to-date files on customer contracts and rate agreements. Large carriers will often have an extensive department to manage pricing and contracts. In smaller carriers, a salesman or administrative person might also perform the majority of the duties for the pricing and contracts function.

Billing and Revenue Management

The revenue management department is responsible for the billing and collection of the company's revenues based on rates and contracts provided by the pricing department. The department prepares and submits invoices to customers and makes collection calls to customers that fail to pay invoices in a timely manner. This group may also provide the shipper with important paperwork such as signed bills of lading and other important shipment documentation. The carrier maintains these documents in order to provide "proof of delivery" when required.

Carrier Measurements and Key Performance Indicators

This section provides a brief introduction to several major definitions and measurements that are critical to all truckload carriers. Each item is a key component of the truckload business model. The relationships between the measures and their impact on pricing and profitability will be explained in detail throughout this book.

Mileage Measurements

In much the same way as a manufacturer produces a product, truckload carriers produce miles. A large portion of a carrier's costs are incurred as miles are driven by the carrier's trucks. Also, most loads are charged to the customer on a rate-per-mile basis. As a result, carriers must measure and manage miles closely to control costs and maintain a profitable network. The key mileage types are described below.

Billed Miles

Billed miles are the standardized miles that appear on the customer's invoice for trucking services. Billed miles represent a predefined standard number of miles between Point A and Point B, not necessarily the actual miles driven by the carrier to deliver the load. The standard miles are commonly determined through a published third-party source such as Rand-McNally or PC-Miler.[4] Since mileages vary slightly based on the particular reference source, the carrier and the shipper will agree upon a predetermined third-party mileage source as a standard part of the contract.

Loaded Miles

All miles driven when the truck is loaded with customer freight are considered loaded miles. Loaded miles may occasionally differ slightly from billed miles when the driver takes a different route while moving a load from Point A to Point B. For example, a truck moving a customer load with 600 billed miles may be routed through a carrier terminal for preventive maintenance and incur 25 out-of-route loaded miles. In this case, the load would include 600 billed miles and 625 loaded miles.

Empty Miles

Empty miles occur when a truck is not loaded with any freight and the carrier receives no compensation from a customer. Empty miles are usually incurred either when positioning a truck from one customer location to another or returning the truck to a terminal. Minimizing empty miles is a critical element of overall profitability and network efficiency for the carrier.[5]

Total Miles

All miles driven by the truck are included in total miles. Total miles include all loaded miles and all empty miles. Total miles drive all variable costs for the carrier. For every mile driven, the carrier will incur variable operating costs such as fuel, maintenance and driver compensation. The load-level detail report below shows each of the different mileage types for six truckloads.

Load Detail Report

Load Number	Billed Miles	Loaded Miles	Empty Miles	Total Miles	Empty Percent	OOR Miles
59841	752	752	82	834	9.8%	0
59842	611	611	45	656	6.9%	0
59843	452	477	70	547	12.8%	25
59844	1,021	1,056	106	1,162	9.1%	35
59845	547	547	130	677	19.2%	0
59846	865	865	93	958	9.7%	0
Totals:	4,248	4,308	526	4,834	10.9%	60

6 total loads

| Averages: | 708 | 718 | 88 | 806 | 10.9% | 10 |

---

[4] Rand-McNally and PC Miler are third-party companies that provide software products and databases that contain the mileage information for any point-to-point combination.
[5] Empty miles also occur when the tractor moves from point to point without a trailer. A tractor operating without a trailer is often referred to as "bobtailing" in industry jargon.

Out-of-Route (OOR) Miles

Out-of-route miles are loaded miles driven beyond the practical, standard route from Point A to Point B. For example, a truck might drive out of route so that a driver may visit his home or a terminal location for maintenance or fuel. Out-of-route miles are a necessary part of normal operations but are generally only a minor concern for most carriers. However, measures should be taken to minimize out-of-route miles as much as possible to avoid unnecessary variable costs.

Revenue Types and Measurements

Gross revenue levels and revenue per mile are critical operating measures for all carriers. This section describes the different types of carrier revenues and the key per-mile revenue measurements. The load detail report below includes the miles and revenues for six truckloads. Refer back to this table as the various revenue types are discussed in the sections that follow.

Load Detail Report

Load Number	Billed Miles	Loaded Miles	Empty Miles	Total Miles	Empty Percent	Billed Rate Per Mile	Linehaul Revenue	Revenue Per Mile Loaded	Revenue Per Mile Net
59841	752	752	82	834	9.8%	$ 1.62	$ 1,218.24	$ 1.62	$ 1.46
59842	611	611	45	656	6.9%	$ 1.44	$ 879.84	$ 1.44	$ 1.34
59843	452	477	70	547	12.8%	$ 1.90	$ 858.80	$ 1.80	$ 1.57
59844	1,021	1,056	106	1,162	9.1%	$ 1.33	$ 1,357.93	$ 1.29	$ 1.17
59845	547	547	130	677	19.2%	$ 1.71	$ 935.37	$ 1.71	$ 1.38
59846	865	865	93	958	9.7%	$ 1.55	$ 1,340.75	$ 1.55	$ 1.40
Totals:	4,248	4,308	526	4,834	10.9%	$ 1.55	$ 6,590.93	$ 1.53	$ 1.36

6 total loads									
Averages:	708	718	88	806	10.9%	$ 1.55	$ 1,098.49	$ 1.53	$ 1.36

Linehaul Revenue

Linehaul revenue is the revenue paid by the shipper for the pure transportation or mileage portion of the service. In other words, linehaul revenue is the compensation the carrier receives for moving the load from Point A to Point B. The rate will be quoted to the customer as either a rate per mile or a flat charge per load. In most cases, longer distance loads are charged at a per-mile rate and shorter distance loads are charged based on a flat charge per load.

Accessorial Revenue

Accessorial revenues cover all services beyond the linehaul charges paid by the shipper for the basic transportation service. For example, the customer may require that the carrier's driver unload the trailer at the final destination. In addition to the basic linehaul revenue, the carrier will also charge an accessorial amount (perhaps $100) as an additional charge for the unloading service. Most accessorial charges are flat fees for each service regardless of the number of billed miles for the load. Many other common accessorial charges, such as stop charges and fuel surcharges, are discussed in detail in later chapters.

Billed Revenue Per Mile

Billed revenue per mile represents the average amount of linehaul revenue per billed mile and is unrelated to actual loaded and empty miles. All other things being equal, the carrier's goal is to maximize billed revenue per mile relative to other key statistics such as utilization and length of haul.

$$\frac{\text{Billed Revenue}}{\text{Per Mile}} = \frac{\text{Linehaul Revenue}}{\text{Total Billed Miles}} = \frac{\$6,590.93}{4,248 \text{ miles}} = \$1.55 \text{ per loaded mile}$$

Billed miles represent the "standard" number of miles from Point A to Point B. Billed miles are used for invoicing purposes to determine the linehaul charges for each load. Because the actual physical miles driven on a load cannot be standardized, the actual miles driven by the carrier are not used in determining a customer's charges.

Loaded Revenue Per Mile

Loaded revenue per mile is closely related to billed revenue per mile. In the absence of any out-of-route miles, loaded revenue per mile and billed revenue per mile will be exactly the same.

$$\frac{\text{Loaded Revenue}}{\text{Per Mile}} = \frac{\text{Linehaul Revenue}}{\text{Total Loaded Miles}} = \frac{\$6,590.93}{4,308 \text{ miles}} = \$1.53 \text{ per loaded mile}$$

Since out-of-route miles occurred on two loads, the revenue per loaded mile is slightly less than the revenue per billed mile. All other things being equal, the carrier's goal is to maximize loaded revenue per mile relative to other key statistics such as utilization, length of haul, and out-of-route miles.

Net Revenue Per Mile

Net revenue per mile represents total linehaul revenue on a total-miles basis. It is the most important revenue per mile performance indicator for any carrier.

$$\frac{\text{Net Revenue}}{\text{Per Mile}} = \frac{\text{Linehaul Revenue}}{\text{Total Miles}} = \frac{\$6,590.93}{4,834 \text{ miles}} = \$1.36 \text{ per mile}$$

Net revenue per mile spreads the loaded revenue per mile over the empty miles to create a "bottom line" revenue amount for all miles. All other things being equal, the carrier's goal is to maximize net revenue per mile relative to other key statistics such as empty miles, utilization, and length of haul.

To avoid any potentially misleading information, it is generally correct to exclude any accessorial revenue from each of these "per mile" measurements. The events that generate accessorial revenue do not occur on all loads or for all customers. Also, the accessorial events and charges do not fluctuate from load to load based on distance, so including accessorial revenue can easily distort revenue per mile measurements.[6]

---

[6] The only exception to this rule is fuel surcharges. Total fuel surcharges for a load increase in direct proportion to the number of billed miles for the load.

Key Operating Measurements and Statistics

All carriers closely measure the operating statistics of each fleet of trucks. Each measurement is a critical component of developing and managing a profitable network. The key operating measurements are described below. These measurements are described in greater detail throughout this book.

Utilization

Utilization is the primary asset productivity measurement for all carriers. Utilization is the total number of miles (loaded miles plus empty miles) a tractor produces in a given period, usually one week. A one week period is a good standard for measuring utilization, especially since a weekly period is reasonably consistent with the D.O.T. hours of service regulations for drivers. The example report below shows the weekly utilization and summary of activity for a fleet of 7 trucks.

Weekly Fleet Utilization Report

Tractor Number	Load Count	Loaded Miles	Empty Miles	Total Miles	Empty Percent	Average LOH
104	4	1,858	245	2,103	11.7%	465
105	3	1,701	282	1,983	14.2%	567
110	3	2,471	312	2,783	11.2%	824
114	5	2,199	283	2,482	11.4%	440
115	2	1,578	188	1,766	10.6%	789
118	5	2,210	201	2,411	8.3%	442
120	3	1,988	310	2,298	13.5%	663
Fleet Totals:	25	14,005	1,821	15,826	11.5%	560
Fleet Averages:	3.57	2,001	260	2,261	11.5%	560

The utilization for tractor 104 was 2,103 miles. The average utilization for the entire fleet was 2,261 miles.

$$\text{Utilization} = \frac{\text{Total Miles}}{\text{Number of Trucks}} = \frac{15,826 \text{ miles}}{7 \text{ trucks}} = 2,261 \text{ miles per truck}$$

Trucking companies focus very closely on the average utilization for their entire fleet each week. If all other key measures remain constant, an increase in utilization results in an increase in revenue and profitability for the trucking company.

Utilization goals are different from carrier to carrier and operation to operation. As a general rule, all carriers seek to maximize utilization for their fleet. However, carriers will not always seek additional utilization at the expense of other key statistics such as revenue per mile and the empty mile percentage.

Average Length of Haul (LOH)

Average length of haul is the average number of billed miles (or loaded miles) per load for a specific group of loads. In the example report above, the average length of haul for the fleet was 560 miles.

$$\text{Average Length of Haul} = \frac{\text{Total Loaded Miles}}{\text{Number of Loads}} = \frac{14{,}005 \text{ miles}}{25 \text{ loads}} = 560 \text{ miles per load}$$

Tractor 110 had an average length of haul of 824 miles while Tractor 114 had an average length of haul of only 440 miles. In linehaul operations, the goal of most carriers is to increase the average length of haul or maintain a desirable average length of haul. In short haul operations, length of haul is important but is not as critical as it is for long haul or regional operations.

Empty Mile Percentage

The empty mile percentage is the percentage of total miles that are empty and without any form of customer compensation. In industry jargon, the empty mile percentage is also commonly referred to as the "deadhead" percentage. In the previous sample report, the empty mile percentage for the fleet is 11.5%.

$$\text{Empty Mile Percentage} = \frac{\text{Total Empty Miles}}{\text{Total Miles}} = \frac{1{,}821 \text{ miles}}{15{,}826 \text{ miles}} = 0.115 \text{ or } 11.5\%$$

Much like utilization goals, empty mile percentage goals will also differ from carrier to carrier. Carriers with a very long average length of haul will have a much lower empty mile percentage than carriers with a very short length of haul. The empty mile percentage goal for each operation must be reasonable in relation to other key operating statistics such as utilization, length of haul, and loaded revenue per mile.

Another way to measure empty miles is in terms of the average empty miles per load. Viewing empty miles only in terms of the empty mile percentage can sometimes hide potential problems and opportunities. For example, a load with a length of haul of 1,800 miles and empty miles of 200 will have an empty mile percentage of 10.0%. While the 10% empty percentage may appear reasonable, the 200 empty miles associated with the load may be considered excessive.

Empty miles are a normal part of a trucking operation and cannot be completely avoided. Carriers use a variety of tools and tactics to minimize empty miles while not disrupting normal operations or affecting customer service. Technologically advanced carriers also use real-time optimization tools to identify cost-efficient load assignment solutions.[7] Empty miles are a critical component of one-way pricing strategy and will be discussed in greater detail in the chapters covering one-way pricing.

---

[7] These optimization tools are discussed in greater detail in a future chapter.

Types of Truckload Operations

Truckload operations can be divided into several different categories depending on the type of service to be provided and the type of contractual relationship with the customer. For the purposes of this book, each type of service is defined in terms of how pricing strategy must be adjusted for the different operating characteristics of the network. The major types of truckload operations include linehaul, regional, short haul, and dedicated fleets. Each type of operation is described in the sections below.

Carrier Specialization

While each individual trucking company has its own unique size, network and operating characteristics, the core operating environment of most carriers is the same. Some carriers specialize in a particular strength or market niche. Specialization allows carriers to focus on one particular network, minimize risk, and maximize profits. Several examples of specialization are listed below.

Carrier Specialization Examples

- A Chicago-based carrier providing full-truckload service only in the Chicago metro area.
- An Atlanta-based regional carrier providing full-truckload service only within a 500 mile radius of Atlanta, Georgia.
- A large carrier operating an irregular route network only in the Eastern two-thirds of the United States.
- A carrier using only teams[8] to provide service on extremely long haul, coast-to-coast type loads.

Regardless of the type and degree of specialization, all carriers face many of the same challenges. The specific types of specialization and scope of services offered influences the carrier's pricing strategy and operating objectives. To fully meet customer needs, large and medium sized trucking companies often provide services that include several types of operations. While different trucking organizations might call these types of operations by different names, the operating characteristics and profitability strategies described below are essentially the same.

---

[8] A team is when two drivers share one truck. Usually one driver sleeps in the bunk while the second is driving, allowing for high productivity and faster transit times.

Linehaul Operations

Irregular route linehaul operations are the core service provided by most full truckload carriers. Trucks provide service for semi-random customers throughout a wide geographic service area. The average length of haul for a linehaul operation can range between 500 and 1,200 miles per load, perhaps even more for specialized carriers. The major goals of a profitable linehaul operation are listed below.

Primary Carrier Operating Goals
Maximize Net Revenue Per Mile
Minimize Empty Miles
Maximize Asset Productivity (Utilization)
Optimize Length of Haul

The two most important goals for a linehaul carrier are maximizing productivity (utilization) and minimizing empty miles. These goals sometimes conflict with one another, so trucking managers must make intelligent decisions regarding the tradeoffs among conflicting goals. For example, increasing length of haul will usually cause an increase in tractor utilization but will also result in a decline in loaded revenue per mile. If these tradeoffs are not evaluated correctly, profitability will decline despite the fact that some key measurements are improving. These goals and their interaction with one another will be presented in detail in future sections and chapters.

The table below displays the typical type of activity that would be served by a normal linehaul operation.

Typical Linehaul Lanes		
Origin	Destination	Miles
Jacksonville, FL	Chicago, IL	1,070
Memphis, TN	Newark, NJ	1,087
Charlotte, NC	St. Louis, MO	730
Columbus, OH	Boston, MA	765
Kansas City, MO	Los Angeles, CA	1,617
Chicago, IL	Memphis, TN	533

Team Linehaul Operations: Team operations are a special type of linehaul service where two drivers share the driving responsibilities for one truck, allowing for nearly double the weekly miles of a single driver. The goals of the team operation are the same as those for a linehaul operation, but the average length of haul is often much longer. Since fixed operating costs are spread over a larger number of miles, team operations typically benefit from a lower cost per mile than single driver units.

Regional Operations

Regional operations are irregular-route networks much like linehaul operations. The only major difference is that regional operations focus on a smaller service area, perhaps operating within a 300 to 500 mile radius of a base terminal location. Trucks spend the vast majority of their time operating within the pre-defined service area and return to the base terminal every few days or at least every weekend. The map below illustrates a regional service area based in Atlanta, Georgia.[9]

Regional Service Area

Empty miles as a percentage of total miles for regional fleets are usually higher than linehaul fleets. The empty mile percentage is higher mainly because the length of haul is much shorter for a regional fleet compared to a linehaul fleet. The average length of haul in a regional operation will often be between approximately 200 and 450 miles. The table below displays the type of activity that would be served by a regional operation.

Typical Regional Lanes		
Origin	Destination	Miles
Atlanta, GA	Mobile, AL	328
Birmingham, AL	Atlanta, GA	146
Charlotte, NC	Tifton, GA	408

While utilization is a key measurement for regional operations, time management, scheduling, and revenue productivity are also critically important. Because of the shorter length of haul, the carrier must minimize the time between loads in order to maximize revenues and productivity. Pure revenue productivity, even at the expense of lower utilization, is a key element of a profitable regional fleet strategy.

---

[9] Unless otherwise indicated, all maps in this book were created using Microsoft MapPoint® software.

Short Haul and Local Operations

Short haul operations are random, multi-customer networks that operate within a very small geographic region. The operations are often based in a major metropolitan area or transportation center and typically focus on a radius of no more than 250 miles from the base of operations. The map below illustrates both a short haul service area and a local service area based in Atlanta, Georgia.

Short Haul and Local Service Area

Short haul operations are needed by many different industries. Some of the more common needs are listed below.

Common Needs Met by Short Haul Fleets
Beverage Distribution and Delivery
Automotive Manufacturing (Inbound Shipments)
Retail Distribution to Stores
Facility to Facility Shuttles

Total miles and weekly utilization are not as important in short haul operations as they are in regional and linehaul fleets. The minimization of empty miles is also not a major area of focus. Revenue per truck per week, however, is probably the most important measurement for success. Trucks and drivers must be managed so that their time is used in a productive manner in order to maximize revenue each day. Skillful, knowledgeable customer service managers and dispatchers must aggressively manage customer appointment times and driver hours of service to maximize productivity.

The compensation structure for short haul truck drivers is typically designed around the dynamics of the operation. Unlike linehaul and regional operations, pay per mile is typically only a small portion of the driver compensation package. The short haul pay package often includes a flat fee for shorter loads in addition to per-mile pay.[10]

Dedicated Fleets

Dedicated fleets are a specialized group of tractors and drivers custom-designed to provide transportation services for a single customer. One unique characteristic of a dedicated fleet is a contractual relationship between the carrier and the shipper under which the shipper has *exclusive* use of a set number of tractors, trailers, and drivers to transport only the shipper's products.

Shippers that require dedicated fleets usually have specialized transportation needs that are best met with customized services. Several examples of special shipper needs often served by dedicated fleets are listed below.

Common Reasons for Dedicated Fleets
Specialized trailer needs
Intensive driver labor requirements
Excessive stop-off deliveries
Challenging service expectations
Heavy activity under 150 miles

Dedicated fleets are attractive to trucking companies because they generally involve less operating uncertainty than traditional trucking operations. Dedicated fleets also typically offer less financial uncertainty because of the detailed dedicated contract relationship. Most dedicated fleets also offer very attractive jobs for truck drivers. Most fleets offer consistent and predictable activity as well as above average home time for the driver. Driver turnover and driver-related problems are often reduced in dedicated fleets compared to typical over-the-road operations such as linehaul and regional fleets.

Dedicated fleets are attractive to shippers because of the guaranteed capacity and excellent service performance. Dedicated fleets can also meet difficult shipper needs that cannot be met in a cost effective manner with typical trucking services. In certain operations, well-designed, correctly priced fleets can also offer shippers significant savings over traditional one-way services. The analysis, design, and pricing of dedicated fleets will be discussed in much greater detail in later chapters.

---

[10] Various types of driver pay structures are presented in detail in future sections and chapters.

Specialized Carriers and Trailer Equipment

Most carriers specialize in the use of a particular type of trailer. In some cases, larger carriers may offer more than one type of trailer equipment. Carriers may also choose to utilize a variety of trailer types within a dedicated fleet environment. The sections below describe several of the most common trailer types.

Standard "Dry Van" Trailer

The standard "dry van" trailer is the type of trailer used in the transportation of most general commodities. This type of trailer will typically transport any product that does not require a more specialized trailer.

Standard "Dry Van" Trailer[11]

The majority of the strategies and concepts presented in this book are based on operations that use the standard "dry van" trailer.

Temperature-Controlled Trailer

The temperature-controlled or "reefer" trailer is used to transport commodities that must be protected from heat or cold (usually heat). This type of trailer is often used to transport food, beverages, medical supplies, or other heat-sensitive materials. Because of the refrigeration unit, these trailers are far more costly to own and operate than standard "dry van" trailers.

Temperature-Controlled Trailer[11]

Standard Flat-Bed Trailer

The flat-bed trailer is a specialized trailer used to serve commodities that cannot be easily transported in a standard trailer. Flat-bed trailers are often used to transport awkward, heavy items that cannot be easily loaded and unloaded when using a standard "dry van" trailer. A flat-bed trailer may also be used when the pick-up or delivery location is unable to safely load or unload a standard "dry van" trailer.

Flat-Bed Trailer[11]

While the tools and strategies in this book are intended primarily for "dry van" carriers, many of the concepts can also be applied to carriers with specialized trailer equipment such as temperature-controlled carriers and flat-bed carriers.

Other Specialized Trailers

A number of highly specialized trailers exist far beyond the examples shown here. As trailer specialization increases, the pricing strategy for the equipment also becomes very specialized. While many of the pricing concepts and variables presented in this book apply to all trucking operations, this book does not specifically address pricing strategy for special equipment. However, the concepts and techniques regarding dedicated fleet pricing do apply to any type of trailer equipment when operating under a dedicated fleet contract arrangement.

---

[11] All trailer photos courtesy of Wabash National Corporation. For more information, please visit www.wabashnational.com and www.transcraft.com.

Driver Turnover

Driver turnover continues to be one the most critical issues facing all trucking companies today. Driver turnover is simply the percentage of the total driver workforce that quits and must be replaced during a 12-month period. To the surprise of many outside the industry, the driver turnover for most carriers can range from 80% to 130% or more each year, indicating that each company must, in effect, hire an entirely new staff of drivers every year.

Both the direct cost and the opportunity cost of this problem are extremely detrimental to the stability, growth and profitability of any carrier. The primary direct cost that results from driver turnover is the cost to recruit, screen, hire and train new drivers. Many large carriers maintain an entire department of driver recruiters to manage and meet driver staffing needs. Carriers incur significant costs to place newspaper advertisements, perform background checks on potential candidates, and provide training to new drivers.

A second direct cost of driver turnover occurs in the recovery of the carrier's tractor after a driver quits. Often when a driver quits, the tractor is abandoned at a truck stop, customer facility, or other obscure location. Carriers must incur significant costs just to recover the tractor and return it to service with the next driver. In fact, some large carriers even have a small team of employees whose sole responsibility it is to locate abandoned tractors and return them to a carrier facility.

The primary opportunity cost that results from driver turnover is the revenues and profits that are lost while expensive tractors sit idle without drivers. A carrier with tractors that don't run because of a shortage of drivers is similar to a manufacturer whose plants are temporarily shut down and don't produce any products. Carriers continue to incur significant equipment ownership costs without generating any revenue from the inactive tractor equipment.

Driver turnover also affects carriers in the area of customer service. Idle tractors reduce the amount of capacity available to customers. Even worse, drivers may decide to quit while hauling an important load for a customer, leaving the carrier with the challenge of trying to recover the load with a second driver to still provide on-time delivery.

Carriers must constantly take driver turnover into account as they make many critical decisions, including pricing and network decisions. Shippers can also help carriers with the driver turnover problem in many ways as well. Throughout this book, the impact of driver turnover will be discussed in detail, along with many ways carriers and shippers can work together to prevent and minimize driver turnover and provide a more cost-efficient truckload transportation network.

Driver Hours of Service Regulations

The United States Department of Transportation and the Federal Motor Carrier Safety Administration have established detailed rules and regulations that govern the amount of time a driver is allowed to drive a truck before being required by law to stop and take a mandatory rest break.[12] The primary purpose of the regulations is to restrict fatigued drivers from operating vehicles in order to prevent accidents and traffic fatalities.

The key components of the regulations place a limit on how many hours a driver may drive and be on-duty during a 24-hour period. As of 2010, the regulations limit a driver to 14 hours on duty in a 24-hour period. Only 11 of the 14 on-duty hours can be spent driving. After 14 hours on duty or 11 hours of driving, the driver must a take a full 10 hour break before returning to work. The regulations also restrict how many hours a driver can cumulatively work and drive during any continuous 7 day or 8 day period.

The table below includes the primary hours of service regulations established by the U.S. Department of Transportation in 2003.

	Hours of Service Regulations (Revised 2003)
Daily	Maximum of 11 driving hours per day (24-hour period)
	Maximum of 14 on-duty hours per day (24-hour period)
	10 consecutive hours off duty
Extended	Maximum of 60 driving hours in a 7 day period
	Maximum of 70 driving hours in an 8 day period
	34 consecutive off duty hours resets 7 day / 8 day period

The hours of service restrictions are a critical factor in how carriers set prices and establish driver pay rates. The hours of service restrictions are also a key factor in assigning available drivers to available loads. The specific impact of the hours of service regulations on carrier strategies and pricing analysis will be described in much greater detail throughout this book.

---

[12] For detailed information on these rules and regulations, please consult the Federal Motor Carrier Safety Administration and Department of Transportation website at www.fmsca.dot.gov.

Owner-Operators

The primary fleet for most carriers includes company-owned trucks and company-employed drivers. In addition to company assets, some carriers will choose to expand capacity through the use of owner-operators. Owner-operators are independent contractors that own their own truck and lease the tractor and driver to the carrier. With owner-operators, the carrier is able to expand capacity and increase revenues without investing in additional tractor equipment or hiring additional drivers. In most cases, the owner-operator provides only a truck and driver while the carrier provides all necessary trailer equipment.

The owner-operator is usually paid a fixed rate per mile for all miles traveled. The fixed rate per mile will vary from carrier to carrier based on the expected utilization level for the owner-operator. With the revenue earned from the carrier, the owner-operator must pay all operating expenses associated with the use of the tractor including fuel, maintenance, legalization, insurance, and tractor costs. If the driver is also the owner of the tractor, the amount remaining after expenses is the income for the owner operator. If the driver is not the owner, the driver must be paid by the owner.

The benefit for the owner-operator of leasing with an established carrier is that the carrier will provide the owner-operator with all load activity. Fully independent owner-operators often have a difficult time securing loads. These owner-operators will work through brokers, web-sites and other resources to find work on a load-by-load basis. Working with an established carrier provides the owner-operator with consistent loads at a fixed revenue level with fewer hassles.

The primary benefit to the carrier of owner-operators is the ability to expand capacity without investing in tractor equipment or hiring additional drivers. Owner-operators are also easier to terminate when capacity must be reduced during slow shipping periods. Most carriers that utilize owner-operators will limit owner-operators to a certain percentage of available capacity to protect the interests of company drivers and to protect against service issues.

Owner-operators are not employees of the carrier and must operate under different dispatch rules than company-employed drivers. As independent contractors, owner-operators have the right to refuse a load and cannot be forced to take a load. As a result, the carrier is always at risk of service disruptions should an available owner-operator refuse to serve a load. If an individual owner-operator refuses loads on a consistent basis, the carrier may choose to terminate the relationship with the unreliable owner-operator.

Carriers usually approach pricing the same way regardless of whether a load will be served by a company driver or an owner-operator. Specialized one-way pricing is rarely designed specifically for owner-operators because the carrier cannot accurately predict the loads that will be served with owner-operators.

Primary Truckload Operating Cost Components

The principals and concepts in this book require a sound understanding of the operating costs experienced by all carriers. This section provides a basic overview of each major cost. In the chapters to come, these costs will be explained in greater detail and applied to each pricing and analysis concept.

Truckload transportation costs can be broken down into four major variable components and three major fixed components. The variable components include driver compensation, fuel, maintenance, and insurance. The fixed components include tractor and trailer ownership costs, equipment legalization costs, and overhead costs. Overhead costs include computer systems, offices and terminals, and administrative support such as customer service, sales, recruiting, executives, and other support personnel. In some dedicated and specialized operations, certain cost items may change between fixed and variable cost behavior based on the specific characteristics of the operation. The cost definitions that follow are based on a traditional linehaul or regional operation.

Variable Costs

Variable costs are costs that change in total with each unit of output, but do not change on a per-unit basis. The primary unit of variable output for a carrier is a mile. For example, if truck drivers are paid 35 cents per mile, driver pay is a variable cost. The 35 cents per mile remains constant regardless of the number of miles driven. The table below illustrates the behavior of driver pay as a variable cost.

Variable Cost: Driver Pay		
Miles Driven	Driver Pay Per Mile	Total Cost
500	$ 0.35	$ 175.00
750	$ 0.35	$ 262.50
1,000	$ 0.35	$ 350.00
1,250	$ 0.35	$ 437.50
1,500	$ 0.35	$ 525.00
1,750	$ 0.35	$ 612.50
2,000	$ 0.35	$ 700.00
2,250	$ 0.35	$ 787.50
2,500	$ 0.35	$ 875.00
2,750	$ 0.35	$ 962.50
3,000	$ 0.35	$ 1,050.00

Notice that total cost increases by $0.35 per mile for every additional mile. Total cost continues to increase, but the $0.35 rate of pay per mile remains constant.

Trucking companies incur variable expenses for every mile driven, empty or loaded. Some expenses listed below as variable costs may not truly occur for every mile driven, but a per-mile basis is the best activity base for estimating and managing these expenses.

Driver Compensation

The most common method for compensating drivers is to pay a fixed amount per mile for every mile driven, empty or loaded. The actual rate of pay a driver receives will depend on many factors including:

- Years of driving experience
- Years of service with their current employer
- Safety and service record
- Potential for the driver to spend time at home
- Expected number of weekly miles to be driven (utilization)

Expected utilization is a key factor in determining the rate per mile a driver will be paid. For instance, in a certain market the average driver may need to earn at least $900 per week to be satisfied in a truck driving job, regardless of the number of miles he or she will drive. The table below illustrates what this driver might expect to earn per mile depending on the trucking company's expected utilization in the operation.

Driver Pay Per Mile

Expected Utilization	Desired Income	Pay Per Mile
1,600	$ 900	$ 0.56
1,800	$ 900	$ 0.50
2,000	$ 900	$ 0.45
2,200	$ 900	$ 0.41
2,400	$ 900	$ 0.38
2,600	$ 900	$ 0.35
2,800	$ 900	$ 0.32

Utilization and income for an average weekly period.

Cost Behavior: In normal linehaul and regional operations, driver pay is a per-mile variable cost. For every mile driven, the driver will earn his base rate of pay per mile.

Driver Fringe Benefits

Fringe benefits for drivers, much like any employee, include costs such as employment taxes, vacation pay, health insurance, and employer-funded retirement plans. These costs are directly related to the driver's income, usually on a percentage basis. While this type of expense is not directly related to any other business activity, it is easily estimated as a percentage of driver pay. Depending on the level of fringe benefits provided by the carrier, this percentage could range anywhere from 15% to 35% of driver earnings.

Cost Behavior: Since many of the fringe benefit cost items are based on a percentage of driver compensation, which is primarily per mile, these expenses are generally considered to be incurred on a per-mile basis concurrent with variable driver pay.

Fuel

Fuel is a major cost component for all trucking companies. Trucks consume fuel both while driving and while idling.[13] Idling occurs as drivers take mandatory rest breaks in their trucks and leave the truck running for comfort. This "idle time" must be managed carefully to avoid the excessive use of fuel during driver breaks.

Cost Behavior: Fuel is purely a per-mile expense. The cost of idle time will average out over all the miles driven, so the fuel expense is incurred on a per-mile basis. Fuel cost per mile will vary significantly depending on the price of fuel, the fuel economy of the tractor, and the driving conditions.

Carriers manage the risk of changes in the cost of fuel through a fuel surcharge agreement with customers. The fuel surcharge agreement establishes the "fuel peg" as the base cost of fuel. If the actual price of fuel is higher than the fuel peg, the customer incurs an additional charge for the higher cost of fuel. If the actual fuel price is lower than the fuel peg, the carrier will discount the customer's invoice relative to the price of fuel. The fuel surcharge process is presented in greater detail in an upcoming chapter.

Equipment Maintenance

Equipment maintenance includes such items as oil changes, new tires, tune-ups, brake jobs, replacement parts, and all types of preventive maintenance and repairs. Replacement tires and tire repairs comprise a large portion of maintenance costs for both tractors and trailers.

Cost Behavior: Since tire wear and other maintenance needs occur naturally on every mile, maintenance costs are incurred primarily on a per-mile basis.

While most maintenance costs are directly related to miles, some costs of maintenance such as facilities, management, tools and equipment might be considered fixed overhead costs because they do not change based on the number of miles driven.

---

[13] Idling is the act of running a truck's engine while the trucking is not in motion. Often, when the driver is taking a rest break, the truck will continue to run in order to provide heat or air conditioning for the driver.

Insurance

Insurance is a major cost for a carrier of any size. In recent years, the cost of liability and cargo insurance has soared, placing a financial strain on many carriers. Because of the risk of catastrophic accidents, all carriers must carry the required legal amounts of insurance. The cost structure and cost behavior for different types of insurance policies will vary from carrier to carrier.

> *Cost Behavior:* The cost of these insurance premiums is based on many factors, with expected total miles in a given period playing a key role in costs. Miles and utilization are key factors in how the insurance provider determines insurance premiums. For this reason, insurance is generally considered a per-mile cost even though the insurance premiums may be fixed for a short period, regardless of actual miles. Exposure to potential accidents also increases in proportion to the number of miles driven.

Fixed Costs

Fixed costs are those costs that do not change with total output but will vary on a per-unit of output basis. For example, one major fixed cost for a carrier is the fleet of tractors. The cost of each tractor is fixed regardless of the amount of miles the truck generates each week. However, as the truck runs more and more miles, the tractor cost per mile declines as the fixed cost is spread over an increasing number of miles. Spreading fixed costs over a large number of miles (units of activity) is a key profitability goal of almost all truckload carriers.

Tractor Equipment

The cost of tractors is a major fixed expense item for all carriers. While most carriers purchase and own their fleet of trucks, some choose to lease a fleet of tractors instead. Carriers that own their trucks will depreciate them over the expected useful life of the equipment. Equipment depreciation or lease expense is a fixed cost.

> *Cost Behavior:* In the short run, tractor depreciation or lease expense is a fixed cost on a per-tractor basis. In the long run, carriers can reduce the size of the fleet if necessary in order to reduce the overall fixed cost burden.

Tractors are often equipped with satellite tracking and sophisticated on-board computer systems. The cost of the tracking equipment is usually handled in much the same way as the base tractor costs.

Trailer Equipment

The cost of trailers is a major fixed expense item for all carriers. While most carriers purchase and own their fleet of trailers, some choose to lease trailers instead. Carriers that own their trailers will depreciate them over the expected useful life of the equipment. Equipment depreciation or lease expense is a fixed cost.

> *Cost Behavior:* In the short run, trailer depreciation or lease expense is a fixed cost on a per-trailer basis. In the long run, carriers can reduce the size of the trailer fleet if necessary in order to reduce the overall fixed cost burden.

Equipment Legalization

All tractors and trailers must be registered with state or local authorities each year. The majority of this cost is for tractor and trailer registration and legalization.

> *Cost Behavior:* Equipment legalization is a fixed cost on a per-tractor and per-trailer basis in the short run. As the fleet size changes, total legalization costs will increase or decrease in relation to changes in the fleet size.

Driver Recruiting Overhead

Because of the enormous problem of driver turnover, large trucking companies employ a staff of driver recruiters and advertise driver job openings aggressively in newspapers, on billboards, through employment services, and on the internet. Smaller carriers will often utilize outside driver recruiting firms and word-of-mouth to meet driver hiring needs.

> *Cost Behavior:* The salaries of the recruiters and the advertising expenses are true fixed costs. As trucking companies grow, the need for recruiters and advertising will likely increase, but in contrast to equipment legalization above, this cost will not typically change on a direct, per-truck basis.

Direct Support Staffing

The direct support staff includes all those employees directly involved in the process of booking and dispatching loads such as customer service personnel and dispatchers. The salaries for these staff members comprise a large portion of the fixed overhead costs.

> *Cost Behavior:* The base support staff is a fixed cost for the organization. As the company grows and adds new trucks, the cost of new personnel that will need to be added to support growth is a step cost.[14] The salary of each new employee represents a "step" in cost.

---

[14] Step-pattern costs are costs that increase or decrease in total over a range of activity greater than a unit-by-unit basis. Step-pattern costs are fixed over a small range of activity but variable over a large range of activity. For example, suppose a dispatcher can manage a maximum of 40 drivers. The carrier would need only one dispatcher until the company grows to 41 drivers. At that point, a "step" increase in cost will occur as the company hires a second dispatcher to handle the growing workload.

Corporate Overhead

Corporate overhead includes many of the costs associated with any company, regardless of industry. Typical corporate overhead includes such costs as executive salaries, advertising, and office expenses. Corporate overhead also includes the staffing and other costs in such departments as accounting, marketing, human resources, and management information systems.

> *Cost Behavior:* Corporate overhead is a pure fixed cost on an annual basis. In a trucking company, these costs will change very little in total even if the number of trucks or number of miles changes significantly. One exception is when a carrier's operating software provider charges a variable fee for each truck or driver that is managed within the system.

In large carriers, corporate overhead can be significant in terms of total costs. In small carriers, overhead costs are usually kept relatively low. Regardless of the size of the carrier, the goal is to expand the fleet and increase utilization to reduce the overhead cost per mile.

CHAPTER 2: The Trucking Business Model

The goal of this chapter is to describe the basic business model of a carrier. A sound understanding of the basic carrier business model will provide a vital foundation for the pricing and strategy concepts covered in future chapters. The business model presented here is based on common linehaul and regional operations where trucks typically generate between 1,500 and 2,800 miles per week. Short haul and local operations that average less than 1,500 miles per week operate under a slightly different business model.

Truckload Economics

Introduction

Trucks and drivers are the carrier's mobile factories for mileage production. Trucks move continuously in a semi-random pattern from load to load and customer to customer throughout the carrier's network. Most customers are charged on a rate-per-mile basis. In addition, a large portion of operating expenses such as fuel, maintenance, and driver pay are incurred primarily on a per-mile basis. Trucking companies must measure mileages closely to control costs and evaluate the efficiency of their operations.

In order to develop and maintain a profitable network, carriers have several key goals and performance measurements that interact to achieve profitability. The primary goals of a truckload carrier are listed below.

Primary Truckload Carrier Operating Goals
Maximize Net Revenue Per Mile
Minimize Empty Miles
Maximize Asset Productivity (Utilization)
Optimize Length of Haul

The overall objective of the carrier is to maximize profits while balancing the complex tradeoffs among these primary operating goals. Because an increase in one goal can potentially result in a corresponding decline in another goal, the carrier must carefully evaluate the impact of each decision. The complex relationships between the primary goals and operating variables will be presented throughout this book, primarily in the chapters covering one-way pricing strategy.

Individual Truck Business Model

The basic day-to-day business model of a carrier is based on the semi-random interaction of customer shipping activity and the carrier's fleet of trucks and drivers. The example that follows assumes a carrier with only one truck and driver.[15] The tractor movement report below summarizes the activity for the truck and driver for a one week period.

Tractor Movement Report							Week Ending: October 5
Load Number	Customer Name	Trip Origin	Trip Destination	Movement Type	Miles Loaded	Miles Empty	Total Miles
1	General Motors	Columbus, OH	Rockford, IL	Loaded	439	-	439
	Empty Move	Rockford, IL	Chicago, IL	Empty	-	85	85
2	McDonald's	Chicago, IL	Hammond, LA	Loaded	872	-	872
	Empty Move	Hammond, LA	New Orleans, LA	Empty	-	57	57
3	Best Co.	New Orleans, LA	Cincinnati, OH	Loaded	802	-	802
	Empty Move	Cincinnati, OH	Columbus, OH	Empty	-	106	106
Totals:		3 loads			2,113	248	2,361
				% of Total Miles:	89.5%	10.5%	

The tractor movement report shows that the truck completed three loads and ran a total of 2,361 miles. The 2,361 miles represent the truck's asset utilization for the week.[16] Of the 2,361 total miles, 2,113 were loaded miles and 248 were empty miles. The truck had an empty mile percentage of 10.5% for the week.

The tractor revenue report below reflects the revenue earned by the carrier for the customer activity performed during the week.

Tractor Revenue Report					Week Ending: October 5		
Load Number	Customer Name	Trip	Billed Miles	Rate Per Mile	Revenue Linehaul	Revenue Accessorial	Total Revenue
1	General Motors	Col, OH to Roc, IL	439	$ 1.95	$ 856.05	$ -	$ 856.05
2	McDonald's	Chi, IL, to Ham, LA	872	$ 1.57	$ 1,369.04	$ -	$ 1,369.04
3	Best Co.	NO, LA to Cin, OH	802	$ 1.33	$ 1,066.66	$ -	$ 1,066.66
Totals:		3 loads	2,113	$ 1.56	$ 3,291.75	$ -	$ 3,291.75

The tractor revenue report shows that the truck generated a total of $3,291.75 in revenue for the three loads. The rate per mile for each load is multiplied by the billed miles to determine the linehaul revenue. Linehaul revenue represents the carrier's revenue for moving the load. Accessorial revenue, discussed in detail in a later chapter, represents the revenue for secondary services such as unloading or stop-offs. The average revenue per loaded mile for all loads was $1.56 per mile.

Notice that the carrier is paid for only 2,113 miles even though total utilization was 2,361 miles. Each shipper is responsible for paying the carrier for only the billed miles associated with each load, not the empty miles. The cost of the empty miles is a normal

---

[15] The carrier's network is considered to be only "semi-random" since many shippers have consistent, predictable network activity. Some shippers even have specific weekly shipping schedules that allow carriers to be aware of a large portion of future shipping activity days or even weeks in advance.

[16] Most carriers measure and benchmark utilization and other operating activity on a weekly basis. A weekly focus provides a common frame of reference and is also generally consistent with the D.O.T. driver hours of service regulations.

operating expense of the carrier. Minimizing empty miles and the cost of moving the truck from one customer to the next is a critical element of the carrier's real-time operating strategy.

Estimated Income Statement

The table below shows the estimated profit (or loss) generated by this truck during the week. This simplified income statement applies some basic fixed and variable cost assumptions to determine the estimated profit.

Estimated Weekly Profit and Loss Statement

Fleet Activity Summary			
Loaded Miles		2,113	
Empty Miles		248	
Total Miles (Utilization)		2,361	
Gross Linehaul Revenue	$	3,291.75	Calculations:
Loaded Revenue Per Mile	$	1.558	(Gross Revenue / Loaded Miles)
Net Revenue Per Mile (NRPM)	$	1.394	(Gross Revenue / Total Miles)

Estimated Profit and Loss			Per Mile	Tractor Total
Linehaul Revenue (NRPM)			$ 1.394	$ 3,291.75
Variable Costs	ASSUMPTIONS			
Driver Wages	$	0.36	$ 0.360	$ 849.96
Fringe Benefits (% of wages)		25.0%	$ 0.090	$ 212.49
Fuel	$	0.40	$ 0.400	$ 944.40
Maintenance	$	0.11	$ 0.110	$ 259.71
Insurance	$	0.10	$ 0.100	$ 236.10
Total Variable Costs			$ 1.060	$ 2,502.66
Fixed Costs	PER WEEK			
Tractor Depreciation	$	230.77	$ 0.098	$ 230.77
Trailer Depreciation	$	38.46	$ 0.016	$ 38.46
Legalization/Recruiting/Admin	$	192.31	$ 0.081	$ 192.31
Corporate Overhead	$	115.38	$ 0.049	$ 115.38
Total Fixed Costs	$	576.92	$ 0.244	$ 576.92
Grand Total Cost			$ 1.304	$ 3,079.58
Operating Profit			$ 0.090	$ 212.17
Operating Ratio			93.6%	93.6%
Profit Margin			6.4%	6.4%

Each fixed cost is estimated as a simple amount per truck per week. All variable costs other than driver fringe benefits are simply the estimated cost per mile multiplied by the total miles driven for the week. Driver fringe benefits are calculated as a percentage of the estimated driver wages.

Operating Ratio

Operating ratio, shown at the bottom of the profit and loss statement, is a very common profitability indicator used by practically all truckload carriers. Operating ratio is the ratio of operating expenses to operating revenues expressed as a percentage. Operating ratio and profit margin provide the same information with respect to financial performance. For example, a 95% operating ratio provides the exact same information as a 5% operating profit margin.

Historically, typical truckload carriers have targeted an operating ratio between 85% and 92%. However, as fuel costs and other costs rise, operating ratio targets must be revised to reflect the changing cost structures. Also, operating ratio targets may be higher or lower than average for carriers who provide specialized services or operate under a different business model than the typical truckload carrier.

While operating ratio is a primary area of focus for most carriers, focusing only on operating ratio as the key indicator of financial performance is very dangerous and potentially inaccurate. Other common measures of financial performance such as return on assets and return on investment should also be critical components of performance evaluation. The pitfalls of focusing exclusively on operating ratio are discussed in detail in the chapters covering dedicating pricing strategies.

Sensitivity Analysis

The estimated profit and loss in this example provides the basic format for determining the profitability of an individual truck or a large fleet of trucks. The truck in the example earned an operating profit of $212.17 for the week. The ongoing challenge for the carrier is to identify ways to improve the profitability of the truck by improving the key operating statistics that drive carrier profitability.

Key Operating Statistics for Profitability
Asset Utilization (Miles Per Truck Per Week)
Empty Mile Percentage
Loaded Revenue Per Mile

The table above indicates the three areas the carrier must manage to improve profitability. Another related statistic, net revenue per mile, is driven by the relationship between loaded revenue per mile and the empty mile percentage. Using the previous example as a baseline, the sections that follow illustrate how a change in each one of these key statistics impacts the carrier's profitability.

Utilization Sensitivity Analysis

The table below recreates the profit and loss statement for the example week by leaving all operating factors unchanged other than utilization. The loaded revenue per mile is constant at $1.558 and the empty mile percentage is constant at 10.5%. The analysis illustrates the impact of both positive and negative changes in utilization of 100 and 200 miles. Based on the 10.5% empty mile percentage, loaded miles and empty miles both change proportionally as utilization changes.

Utilization Sensitivity Analysis			Utilization Scenario				
			- 200	- 100	Baseline	+ 100	+ 200
Loaded Miles			1,934	2,024	2,113	2,202	2,292
Empty Miles			227	237	248	259	269
Total Miles (Utilization)			2,161	2,261	2,361	2,461	2,561
Empty Miles Percentage			*10.5%*	*10.5%*	*10.5%*	*10.5%*	*10.5%*
Gross Linehaul Revenue			$ 3,012.91	$ 3,152.33	$ 3,291.75	$ 3,431.17	$ 3,570.59
Loaded Revenue Per Mile			$ 1.558	$ 1.558	$ 1.558	$ 1.558	$ 1.558
Net Revenue Per Mile (NRPM)			$ 1.394	$ 1.394	$ 1.394	$ 1.394	$ 1.394
Estimated Profit and Loss			- 200	- 100	Baseline	+ 100	+ 200
Linehaul Revenue			$ 3,012.91	$ 3,152.33	$ 3,291.75	$ 3,431.17	$ 3,570.59
Variable Costs	ASSUMPTIONS						
Driver Wages	$	0.36	$ 777.96	$ 813.96	$ 849.96	$ 885.96	$ 921.96
Fringe Benefits (% of wages)		25.0%	$ 194.49	$ 203.49	$ 212.49	$ 221.49	$ 230.49
Fuel	$	0.40	$ 864.40	$ 904.40	$ 944.40	$ 984.40	$ 1,024.40
Maintenance	$	0.11	$ 237.71	$ 248.71	$ 259.71	$ 270.71	$ 281.71
Insurance	$	0.10	$ 216.10	$ 226.10	$ 236.10	$ 246.10	$ 256.10
Total Variable Costs			$ 2,290.66	$ 2,396.66	$ 2,502.66	$ 2,608.66	$ 2,714.66
Fixed Costs	PER WEEK						
Tractor Depreciation	$	230.77	$ 230.77	$ 230.77	$ 230.77	$ 230.77	$ 230.77
Trailer Depreciation	$	38.46	$ 38.46	$ 38.46	$ 38.46	$ 38.46	$ 38.46
Legalization/Recruiting/Admin	$	192.31	$ 192.31	$ 192.31	$ 192.31	$ 192.31	$ 192.31
Corporate Overhead	$	115.38	$ 115.38	$ 115.38	$ 115.38	$ 115.38	$ 115.38
Total Fixed Costs	$	576.92	$ 576.92	$ 576.92	$ 576.92	$ 576.92	$ 576.92
Grand Total Cost			$ 2,867.58	$ 2,973.58	$ 3,079.58	$ 3,185.58	$ 3,291.58
Operating Profit			$ 145.32	$ 178.75	$ 212.17	$ 245.59	$ 279.01
Operating Ratio			95.2%	94.3%	93.6%	92.8%	92.2%
Profit Margin			4.8%	5.7%	6.4%	7.2%	7.8%

Variable costs move up and down in direct proportion to each utilization change. Fixed costs remain constant at $576.92 per week regardless of utilization. As utilization increases, revenue and operating profit also increase. As utilization falls, total revenue and operating profit also fall. Both operating ratio and profit margin improve as utilization increases.

The graph below illustrates the relationship between utilization and profitability as shown in the utilization sensitivity analysis.

Utilization Sensitivity Analysis

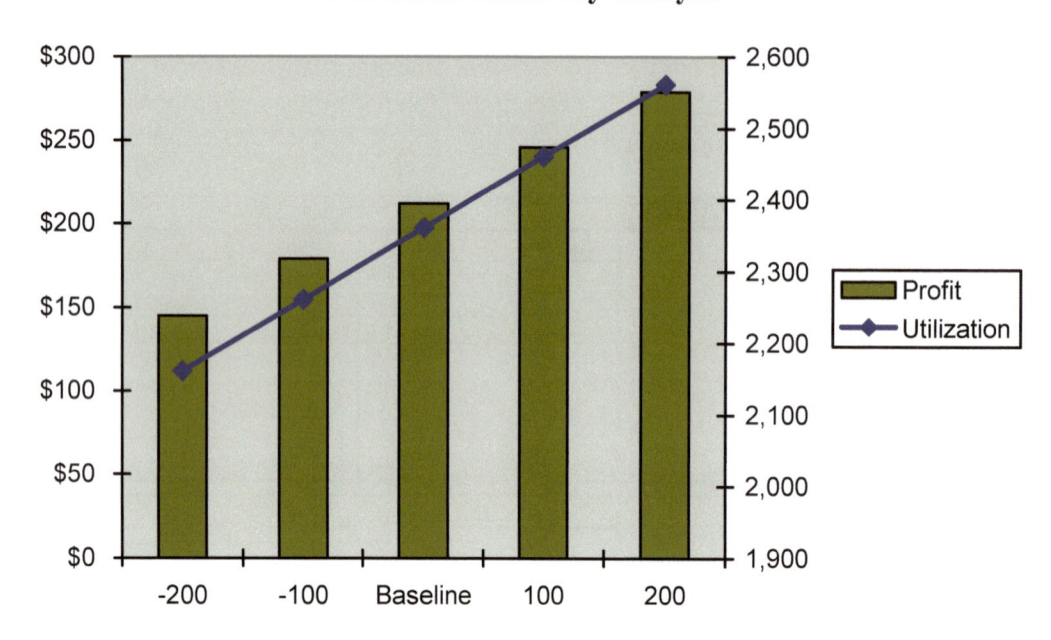

As the graph illustrates, profitability increases as utilization increases. Because of the relationship between utilization and profitability, carriers implement a number of tactics in an effort to increase utilization. A carrier with 1,000 trucks that can create a 50 mile per week increase in utilization across all trucks will enjoy dramatic growth in revenues and profits. However, achieving such an increase is very difficult and requires careful planning and analysis.

Carriers are also very aggressive in managing existing utilization levels to prevent potential lost utilization. Just as increases in utilization produce positive financial results, utilization loses can have even more dramatic negative results. Customer service managers, dispatchers and planners work closely with customers and drivers to prevent or correct situations that have a negative impact on utilization.

Key Truckload Economic Concept: All other things being equal, as utilization increases, profitability increases.

Utilization, Operating Leverage and Cost Per Mile. The reason that profitability improves as utilization increases is operating leverage. Most carriers have a large amount of fixed operating costs including tractor equipment, trailer equipment, maintenance facilities, and other support overhead. These fixed costs remain in place regardless of tractor utilization levels. Since the fixed cost burden is so high and the range of potential utilization levels (output) is so wide, carriers operate under a high degree of operating leverage. As a result, increases in utilization provide the carrier with significant decreases in total cost per mile.

Continuing with the costs in the baseline example, the table below illustrates the impact of increasing utilization on total cost per mile.

Utilization Levels and Total Cost Per Mile

Utilization	Variable Cost Per Mile	Weekly Variable Cost	Weekly Fixed Cost	Fixed Cost Per Mile	Total Cost	Total Cost Per Mile
1,200	$ 1.06	$ 1,272.00	$ 576.92	$ 0.481	$ 1,849	**$ 1.541**
1,400	$ 1.06	$ 1,484.00	$ 576.92	$ 0.412	$ 2,061	**$ 1.472**
1,600	$ 1.06	$ 1,696.00	$ 576.92	$ 0.361	$ 2,273	**$ 1.421**
1,800	$ 1.06	$ 1,908.00	$ 576.92	$ 0.321	$ 2,485	**$ 1.381**
1,900	$ 1.06	$ 2,014.00	$ 576.92	$ 0.304	$ 2,591	**$ 1.364**
2,000	$ 1.06	$ 2,120.00	$ 576.92	$ 0.288	$ 2,697	**$ 1.348**
2,100	$ 1.06	$ 2,226.00	$ 576.92	$ 0.275	$ 2,803	**$ 1.335**
2,200	$ 1.06	$ 2,332.00	$ 576.92	$ 0.262	$ 2,909	**$ 1.322**
2,300	$ 1.06	$ 2,438.00	$ 576.92	$ 0.251	$ 3,015	**$ 1.311**
2,361	$ 1.06	$ 2,502.66	$ 576.92	$ 0.244	$ 3,080	**$ 1.304**
2,400	$ 1.06	$ 2,544.00	$ 576.92	$ 0.240	$ 3,121	**$ 1.300**
2,500	$ 1.06	$ 2,650.00	$ 576.92	$ 0.231	$ 3,227	**$ 1.291**
2,600	$ 1.06	$ 2,756.00	$ 576.92	$ 0.222	$ 3,333	**$ 1.282**
2,700	$ 1.06	$ 2,862.00	$ 576.92	$ 0.214	$ 3,439	**$ 1.274**
2,800	$ 1.06	$ 2,968.00	$ 576.92	$ 0.206	$ 3,545	**$ 1.266**

The chart is based on achievable utilization levels between 1,200 and 2,800 miles per week. If the example was expanded to a wider range of utilization levels, the cost per mile impact would be even more dramatic.

A simple increase in utilization of 100 to 300 miles per week is critical for the average linehaul or regional carrier. An increase in utilization from 2,000 to 2,300 miles results in a reduction in cost of 2.7% or 3.7 cents per mile. A change of this magnitude will have a significant impact on the carrier's overall profitability.

The graph below provides additional insight into the relationship between utilization and total cost per mile.

Utilization and Cost Per Mile

Both fixed cost per mile and total cost per mile decline as utilization increases. The incremental decrease in cost per mile becomes smaller and smaller as utilization increases. Variable cost per mile remains constant at all levels of utilization.[17] A 3 cent reduction in cost per mile as the result of a utilization increase is as valuable to the carrier as a 3 cent increase in net revenue per mile.

In summary, increases in utilization provide the carrier with two key benefits. First, increases in utilization generate an increase in revenue. Second, increases in utilization reduce the carrier's overall cost per mile. The combined effect of these two factors is the reason that utilization maximization is a major goal of every carrier.

---

[17] Since the variable cost per mile in this example is based strictly on mileage pay for the driver, at lower utilization levels the driver would not be able to achieve a satisfactory level of income. In reality, the variable cost per mile at low utilization levels would be higher than shown here because the driver's rate of pay per mile would need to be raised to be consistent with the level of utilization and the driver's income expectations.

Loaded Revenue Per Mile Sensitivity Analysis

The table below recreates the profit and loss statement for the example week by leaving all operating factors unchanged other than loaded revenue per mile. Utilization is constant at 2,361 miles and the empty mile percentage is constant at 10.5%. The analysis illustrates the impact of both positive and negative changes in loaded revenue per mile of 5 cents and 10 cents. Total revenue and net revenue per mile change proportionally as loaded revenue per mile changes.

Revenue Per Mile Sensitivity Analysis			Loaded Rate Per Mile Scenario				
			- $.10	- $.05	Baseline	+ $.05	+ $.10
Loaded Miles			2,113	2,113	2,113	2,113	2,113
Empty Miles			248	248	248	248	248
Total Miles (Utilization)			2,361	2,361	2,361	2,361	2,361
Empty Miles Percentage			*10.5%*	*10.5%*	*10.5%*	*10.5%*	*10.5%*
Gross Linehaul Revenue			$ 3,080.45	$ 3,186.10	$ 3,291.75	$ 3,397.40	$ 3,503.05
Loaded Revenue Per Mile			$ 1.458	$ 1.508	$ 1.558	$ 1.608	$ 1.658
Net Revenue Per Mile (NRPM)			$ 1.305	$ 1.349	$ 1.394	$ 1.439	$ 1.484
Estimated Profit and Loss			- $.10	- $.05	Baseline	+ $.05	+ $.10
Linehaul Revenue			$ 3,080.45	$ 3,186.10	$ 3,291.75	$ 3,397.40	$ 3,503.05
Variable Costs	ASSUMPTIONS						
Driver Wages	$	0.36	$ 849.96	$ 849.96	$ 849.96	$ 849.96	$ 849.96
Fringe Benefits (% of wages)		25.0%	$ 212.49	$ 212.49	$ 212.49	$ 212.49	$ 212.49
Fuel	$	0.40	$ 944.40	$ 944.40	$ 944.40	$ 944.40	$ 944.40
Maintenance	$	0.11	$ 259.71	$ 259.71	$ 259.71	$ 259.71	$ 259.71
Insurance	$	0.10	$ 236.10	$ 236.10	$ 236.10	$ 236.10	$ 236.10
Total Variable Costs			$ 2,502.66	$ 2,502.66	$ 2,502.66	$ 2,502.66	$ 2,502.66
Fixed Costs	PER WEEK						
Tractor Depreciation	$	230.77	$ 230.77	$ 230.77	$ 230.77	$ 230.77	$ 230.77
Trailer Depreciation	$	38.46	$ 38.46	$ 38.46	$ 38.46	$ 38.46	$ 38.46
Legalization/Recruiting/Admin	$	192.31	$ 192.31	$ 192.31	$ 192.31	$ 192.31	$ 192.31
Corporate Overhead	$	115.38	$ 115.38	$ 115.38	$ 115.38	$ 115.38	$ 115.38
Total Fixed Costs	$	576.92	$ 576.92	$ 576.92	$ 576.92	$ 576.92	$ 576.92
Grand Total Cost			$ 3,079.58	$ 3,079.58	$ 3,079.58	$ 3,079.58	$ 3,079.58
Operating Profit			$ 0.87	$ 106.52	$ 212.17	$ 317.82	$ 423.47
Operating Ratio			100.0%	96.7%	93.6%	90.6%	87.9%
Profit Margin			0.0%	3.3%	6.4%	9.4%	12.1%

Total variable costs remain constant since utilization does not change. Fixed costs remain constant at $576.92 per week. As loaded revenue per mile increases, revenue and operating profit also increase. As loaded revenue per mile falls, total revenue and profit margin also fall.

The relationship between revenue changes and profitability illustrated in this example is obvious. The important point in this example is the degree to which small changes in loaded revenue per mile have on overall profitability. A seemingly small 5 cent increase or decrease in loaded revenue per mile has a dramatic impact on operating profits.

The graph below illustrates the relationship between loaded revenue per mile and profitability.

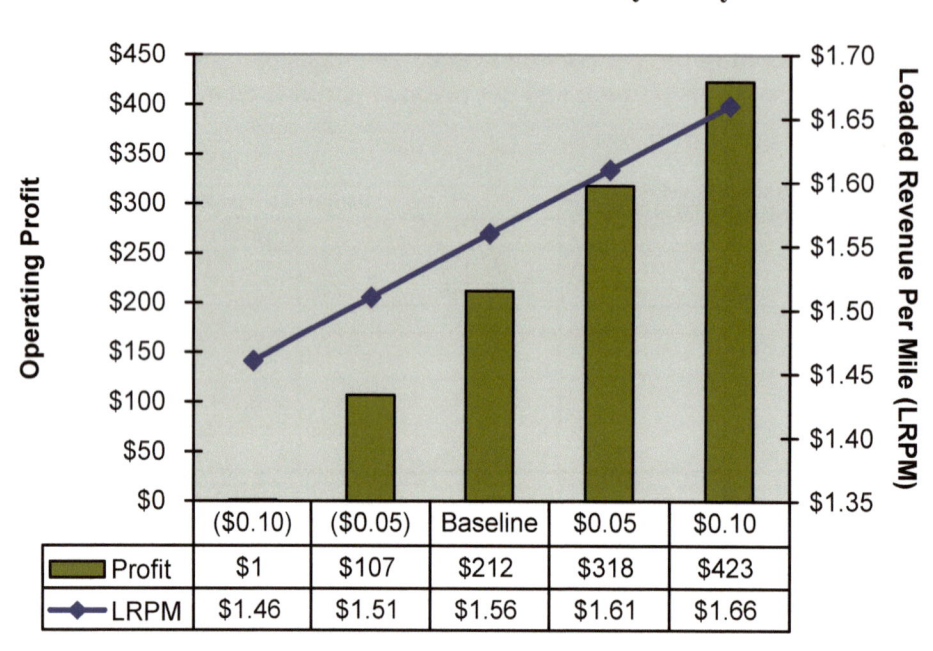

Loaded Revenue Per Mile Sensitivity Analysis

	($0.10)	($0.05)	Baseline	$0.05	$0.10
Profit	$1	$107	$212	$318	$423
LRPM	$1.46	$1.51	$1.56	$1.61	$1.66

All other things being equal, as loaded revenue per mile increases, profits also increase. Operating ratio and profit margins also improve as loaded revenue per mile increases.

While carriers seek to increase loaded revenue per mile, those increases are not easily achieved. Carriers are very reluctant to ask customers for rate increases. If the carrier were to insist on a rate increase, the customer could shift the activity to a different carrier with lower rates and the original carrier would lose the business entirely.

Carriers can also increase loaded revenue per mile by introducing new customers into their network at higher rates than existing customers. If the carrier has limited capacity, the carrier might even take available trucks away from existing customers and provide the trucks to the new customers with higher rates.

Key Truckload Economic Concept: All other things being equal, as loaded revenue per mile increases, profitability increases. Operating profits are extremely sensitive to even small changes in loaded revenue per mile.

Empty Mile Percentage Sensitivity Analysis

The table below recreates the profit and loss statement for the example week by leaving all operating factors unchanged other than the empty mile percentage. Utilization is constant at 2,361 miles and loaded revenue per mile is constant at $1.558. The analysis illustrates the impact of both positive and negative changes in the empty mile percentage of 1% and 2%. Loaded miles, empty miles, total revenue, and net revenue per mile change proportionally as the empty mile percentage changes.

Empty Miles Sensitivity Analysis			Empty Mile Percentage Scenario				
			-2%	-1%	**Baseline**	+1%	+2%
Loaded Miles			2,160	2,137	**2,113**	2,089	2,066
Empty Miles			201	224	**248**	272	295
Total Miles (Utilization)			2,361	2,361	**2,361**	2,361	2,361
Empty Miles Percentage			*8.5%*	*9.5%*	***10.5%***	*11.5%*	*12.5%*
Gross Linehaul Revenue			$ 3,365.46	$ 3,328.68	**$ 3,291.75**	$ 3,255.12	$ 3,218.34
Loaded Revenue Per Mile			$ 1.558	$ 1.558	**$ 1.558**	$ 1.558	$ 1.558
Net Revenue Per Mile (NRPM)			$ 1.425	$ 1.410	**$ 1.394**	$ 1.379	$ 1.363
Estimated Profit and Loss			-2%	-1%	**Baseline**	+1%	+2%
Linehaul Revenue			$ 3,365.46	$ 3,328.68	**$ 3,291.75**	$ 3,255.12	$ 3,218.34
Variable Costs	ASSUMPTIONS						
Driver Wages	$	0.36	$ 849.96	$ 849.96	**$ 849.96**	$ 849.96	$ 849.96
Fringe Benefits (% of wages)		25.0%	$ 212.49	$ 212.49	**$ 212.49**	$ 212.49	$ 212.49
Fuel	$	0.40	$ 944.40	$ 944.40	**$ 944.40**	$ 944.40	$ 944.40
Maintenance	$	0.11	$ 259.71	$ 259.71	**$ 259.71**	$ 259.71	$ 259.71
Insurance	$	0.10	$ 236.10	$ 236.10	**$ 236.10**	$ 236.10	$ 236.10
Total Variable Costs			$ 2,502.66	$ 2,502.66	**$ 2,502.66**	$ 2,502.66	$ 2,502.66
Fixed Costs	PER WEEK						
Tractor Depreciation	$	230.77	$ 230.77	$ 230.77	**$ 230.77**	$ 230.77	$ 230.77
Trailer Depreciation	$	38.46	$ 38.46	$ 38.46	**$ 38.46**	$ 38.46	$ 38.46
Legalization/Recruiting/Admin	$	192.31	$ 192.31	$ 192.31	**$ 192.31**	$ 192.31	$ 192.31
Corporate Overhead	$	115.38	$ 115.38	$ 115.38	**$ 115.38**	$ 115.38	$ 115.38
Total Fixed Costs	$	576.92	$ 576.92	$ 576.92	**$ 576.92**	$ 576.92	$ 576.92
Grand Total Cost			$ 3,079.58	$ 3,079.58	**$ 3,079.58**	$ 3,079.58	$ 3,079.58
Operating Profit			**$ 285.88**	**$ 249.10**	**$ 212.17**	**$ 175.53**	**$ 138.75**
Operating Ratio			91.5%	92.5%	**93.6%**	94.6%	95.7%
Profit Margin			8.5%	7.5%	**6.4%**	5.4%	4.3%

Utilization remains constant at 2,361 miles per week in each scenario. As the empty mile percentage increases, the total empty miles increase and the total loaded miles decrease. Notice that the operating ratio and profit margin both improve by roughly 1% for each decline of 1% in the empty mile percentage. As the empty mile percentage decreases, operating profits increase significantly. Likewise, as the empty mile percentage increases, profits decline.

The graph below illustrates the relationship between the empty mile percentage and profitability. Profits increase as the empty mile percentage decreases.

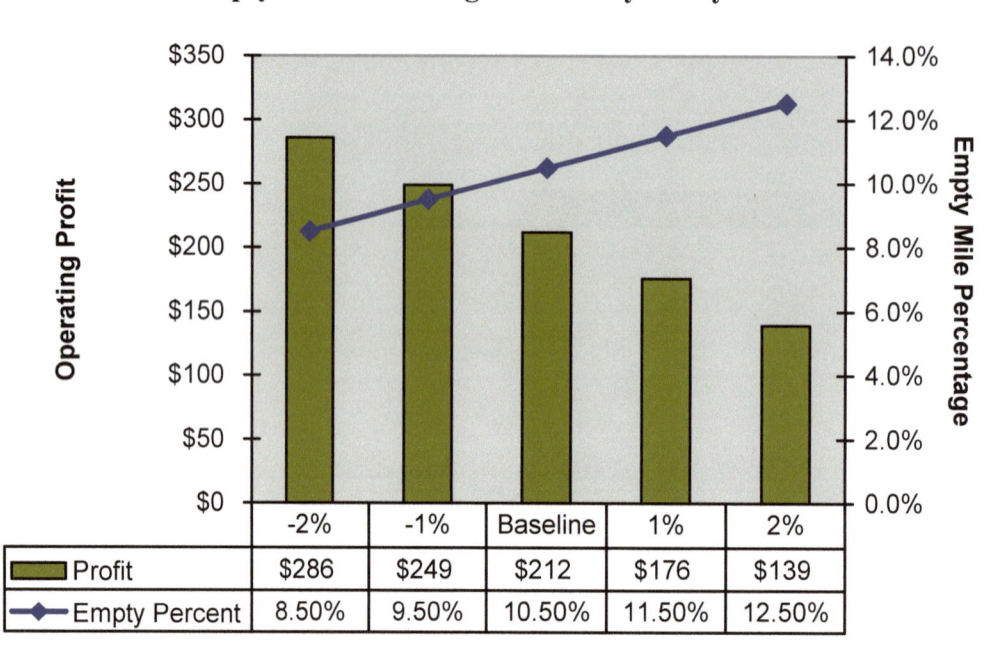

Empty Mile Percentage Sensitivity Analysis

	-2%	-1%	Baseline	1%	2%
Profit	$286	$249	$212	$176	$139
Empty Percent	8.50%	9.50%	10.50%	11.50%	12.50%

Clearly, as empty miles increase as a percentage of total miles, profits decline dramatically. Carriers cannot avoid empty miles completely, but must develop strategies to minimize empty miles as much as possible. A variety of strategies for minimizing empty miles are included throughout the chapters on one-way pricing.

Key Truckload Economic Concept: All other things being equal, as the empty mile percentage increases, profitability decreases. As the empty mile percentage decreases, profitability increases.

Empty Mile Percentage and Net Revenue Per Mile

One of the most critical relationships in trucking economics is the impact of the empty mile percentage on net revenue per mile. As the empty mile percentage decreases, net revenue per mile increases. Likewise, as the empty mile percentage increases, net revenue per mile decreases. This relationship, along with the direct variable cost of the empty miles, is the reason that minimizing empty miles is a key profitability initiative of all carriers.

The graph below, based on the example with a loaded revenue per mile of $1.558, illustrates the relationship between the empty mile percentage and net revenue per mile.

Empty Mile Percentage and Revenue Per Mile

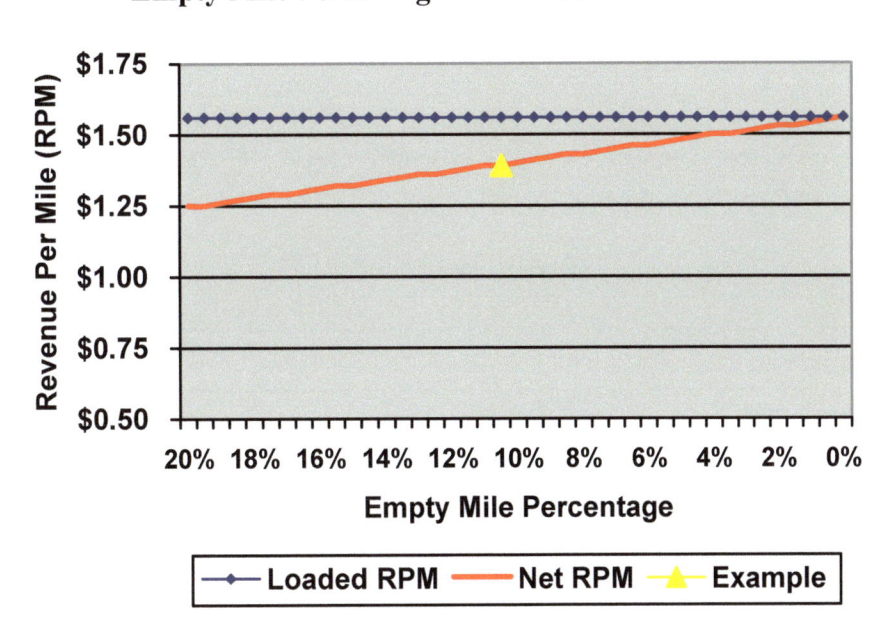

Notice that loaded revenue per mile is constant and is not affected by the empty mile percentage. However, net revenue per mile increases as the empty mile percentage decreases. As the empty mile percentage approaches 0%, net revenue per mile and loaded revenue per mile would be equal. In this example, every 1% decrease in the empty mile percentage creates an increase in net revenue per mile of between 1 and 2 cents.

> **Key Truckload Economic Concept:** All other things being equal, as the empty mile percentage decreases, net revenue per mile increases. Likewise, as the empty mile percentage increases, net revenue per mile decreases.

Break-Even Point Utilization

The sensitivity scenarios in this example can be extended to include a break-even point analysis to determine the utilization level at which the truck would achieve an operating profit of exactly $0, the break-even point. The traditional break-even point formula is shown below.

$$\text{Break-Even Point (in units)} = \frac{\text{Fixed Cost}}{\text{Selling Price - Variable Cost}}$$

Adjusting the basic break-even formula to the trucking cost structure, net revenue per mile would represent the selling price and variable cost per mile would represent the variable cost component as shown below.

$$\text{Break-Even Point (Utilization)} = \frac{\text{Fixed Costs}}{\text{Net RPM - Var. Cost Per Mile}}$$

For simplification, the formula as shown assumes loaded revenue per mile and the empty mile percentage remain constant over any utilization level. The graph below illustrates the break-even analysis for the example.

Break-Even Analysis

The point at which total revenue and total cost are equal represents the break-even point in utilization.

The break-even point in utilization in this example is 1,726 miles per week. The calculation is shown below.

$$\text{Break-Even Point (Utilization)} = \frac{\$576.92}{\$1.394 - \$1.06} = \frac{\$576.92}{\$0.334} = 1{,}726 \text{ miles}$$

The break-even point can also be expressed in terms of total revenue by multiplying the break-even utilization level by the net revenue per mile.

$$\text{Break-Even Revenue} = 1{,}726 \text{ miles} \times \$1.394 = \$2{,}406.68$$

The break-even point analysis provides the carrier with a reference point to evaluate potential risk within the operation. An operation that requires an unreasonably high utilization level just to break-even creates a high degree of risk for the carrier. A much more common occurrence is for utilization to be lower than expected instead of higher than expected, so carriers must identify the break-even utilization level in order to reduce exposure to high risk operations.

Primary Cost Drivers for Carriers

Cost drivers are the events that directly create cost or consume the limited available productive time of fixed resources. The primary events that directly drive overall costs within a trucking company are described below.

Total Cost Driver: Booking Loads

Each load creates both direct operating cost and direct administrative costs. On the administrative side, each load must be entered into the computer system, communicated to the driver, and billed to the customer. On the operations side, each load will require loaded miles to be driven and utilize the productive time of a driver, tractor and trailer in the delivery of the load. Each load, regardless of the length of haul, will also involve other normal operating events such as empty miles and dock time at the beginning and end of each load.

Total Cost Driver: Driving Miles

For every mile driven, empty or loaded, carriers incur variable mileage-based expenses. These variable expenses include such costs as driver pay, fuel, maintenance and insurance. If a truck is idle, no mileage expenses are incurred. However, for each mile of driving activity, all variable mileage expenses are incurred.

Total Cost Driver: Owning / Leasing Tractors and Trailers

As part of the planning process each year, the carrier must determine the number of tractors and trailers to be included in the overall fleet. The carrier's decision to expand the fleet of tractors or trailers will create new costs. The ownership costs of new equipment will also add depreciation expenses or lease expenses. In addition to ownership costs, the new equipment will incur registration costs and must be moved into position to begin operations.[18] The carrier may also choose to reduce the size of the tractor and trailer fleet and reduce overall equipment ownership costs.

Core Activities that Drive Total Carrier Costs	
Cost Driver	**Cost Events**
Book a Load	Empty miles before and after the load.
	Dock time to pick up and deliver the load.
	Order entry and customer service.
	Dispatching and driver communication.
	Creating and sending invoice. Collection of charges.
Drive a Mile	Driver compensation on a per-mile basis.
	Driver fringe benefits as a percentage of per-mile pay.
	Fuel costs.
	Variable maintenance costs.
	Insurance costs.
Tractor and Trailer Equipment	Tractor ownership or leasing costs.
	Trailer ownership or leasing costs.
	Equipment legalization costs.
	Driver hiring and recruiting costs.
	Terminals, drop yards and other facility costs.

These cost elements reflect the basic short term and long term decisions made by a carrier and how those decisions influence the total cost pool. The actual cost structure will be slightly different from carrier to carrier. However, these basic decisions and cost drivers will remain relatively consistent for all carriers.

---

[18] In many equipment purchase agreements, the cost of moving the trailer from the point of origin to the carrier's facility or customer location is included in the purchase price of the equipment.

Activity-Based Costing

Activity-based costing is a costing model that assigns cost to each product or service based on the resources consumed in the production of the product or service.[19] An activity-based costing approach allows carriers to estimate profitability for different layers of activity such as by fleet, by customer, and by load. This section utilizes a simple activity-based costing approach designed to assign cost and determine estimated profitability on a load-by-load basis. The primary objective of this activity-based approach is to provide a deeper understanding of the various trucking events that directly create cost. The approach also illustrates the critical role of time management in relation to the carrier's revenue producing assets, which include drivers, tractors and trailers.

To better understand the importance of activity-based costing in the trucking model, think of a carrier's trucks and drivers as being much a like hotel rooms. If a hotel is unable to rent out a portion of its available rooms on a given night, the revenue opportunity for the unsold rooms is lost forever. The hotel cannot save unsold rooms in inventory for a future date when demand exceeds available capacity. A truckload carrier's trucks and drivers operate under these same conditions. The available work time of the truck and driver is a highly perishable item. Any time spent by the truck and driver in non-revenue producing activity cannot be recovered and is effectively lost forever.

Developing a Simple Activity-Based Cost Model

The purpose of this section is to develop a simple activity-based costing model to illustrate the primary cost drivers for a carrier. The model is based on the 2,361 mile utilization model presented throughout this chapter. The model assumes this same activity takes place with a fleet of 100 trucks as shown in the activity summary below.

Fleet Activity Summary	Per Truck	Total Fleet
Fleet Size	1 Truck	100 Trucks
Loaded Miles	2,113	211,300
Empty Miles	248	24,800
Total Miles (Utilization)	2,361	236,100
Gross Linehaul Revenue	$ 3,291.75	$ 329,175
Loaded Revenue Per Mile	$ 1.558	$ 1.558
Net Revenue Per Mile (NRPM)	$ 1.394	$ 1.394

Notice that both the loaded revenue per mile and net revenue per mile for the total fleet are the same as the single truck average. The per-truck column represents the average truck in the 100 truck fleet.

---

[19] For a more detailed review of activity-based costing, consult a Management Accounting textbook or other similar reference source. Activity-based costing is most often used for the allocation of manufacturing overhead costs to the product level.

The activity summary is extended into an estimated profit and loss statement as shown in the table below.

Profit & Loss Statement

Fleet Activity Summary		Per Truck	Total Fleet
Fleet Size		1 Truck	100 Trucks
Loaded Miles		2,113	211,300
Empty Miles		248	24,800
Total Miles (Utilization)		2,361	236,100
Gross Linehaul Revenue		$ 3,291.75	$ 329,175
Loaded Revenue Per Mile		$ 1.558	$ 1.558
Net Revenue Per Mile (NRPM)		$ 1.394	$ 1.394

Estimated Profit and Loss			Per Mile	Per Truck	Total Fleet
Linehaul Revenue (NRPM)			$ 1.394	$ 3,291.75	$ 329,175
Variable Costs	ASSUMPTIONS				
Driver Wages	$ 0.36		$ 0.360	$ 849.96	$ 84,996
Fringe Benefits (% of wages)	25.0%		$ 0.090	$ 212.49	$ 21,249
Fuel	$ 0.40		$ 0.400	$ 944.40	$ 94,440
Maintenance	$ 0.11		$ 0.110	$ 259.71	$ 25,971
Insurance	$ 0.10		$ 0.100	$ 236.10	$ 23,610
Total Variable Costs			$ 1.060	$ 2,502.66	$ 250,266
Fixed Costs	PER WEEK				
Tractor Depreciation	$ 230.77		$ 0.098	$ 230.77	$ 23,077
Trailer Depreciation	$ 38.46		$ 0.016	$ 38.46	$ 3,846
Legalization/Recruiting/Admin	$ 192.31		$ 0.081	$ 192.31	$ 19,231
Corporate Overhead	$ 115.38		$ 0.049	$ 115.38	$ 11,538
Total Fixed Costs	$ 576.92		$ 0.244	$ 576.92	$ 57,692
Grand Total Cost			$ 1.304	$ 3,079.58	$ 307,958
Operating Profit			$ 0.090	$ 212.17	$ 21,217
Operating Ratio			93.6%	93.6%	93.6%
Profit Margin			6.4%	6.4%	6.4%

The total fleet column will be used as the cost basis to determine the actual estimated cost for each carrier cost driver. Along with total costs, the carrier must also identify the total amount of activity for each cost driver that directly corresponds to the total cost information shown above. The table below lists the actual activity levels that correspond to the cost activity shown on the profit and loss statement. The hours shown represent the total on-duty work hours for all drivers in the fleet.

Activity by Cost Driver

Summary of Activity	Miles	Loads	Hours
Actual Activity Volume for Period	236,100	300	5,500

The load, mile and hour activity provides the basis for allocating costs and establishing the activity-based costing rates. The total hours are based on driver on-duty time of 55 hours per truck per week, which does not include the time the driver spends on required rest breaks.[20]

The table below illustrates how each cost is assigned to an activity and carrier cost driver.

Assignment of Activity-Based Costs

Activity-Based Costing Model			Per Mile	Per Load	Per Hour
Activity Component:			Miles	Loads	Hours
Actual Activity Volume for Period			236,100	300	5,500
Cost Allocation to Cost Drivers					
Cost Item	Detail Cost	Total Cost		Allocated Rate	
Variable Mileage Costs		$ 250,266	$ 1.06		
Tractor Depreciation		$ 23,077			$ 4.20
Trailer Depreciation		$ 3,846			$ 0.70
Legalization/Recruiting/Admin		$ 19,231			
Legalization	$ 4,481				$ 0.81
Recruiting	$ 6,150				$ 1.12
Customer Service	$ 3,175			$ 10.58	
Dispatch & Planning	$ 3,600			$ 12.00	
Billing & Collections	$ 1,825			$ 6.08	
Corporate Overhead		$ 11,538			
Computer Systems	$ 1,622			$ 5.41	
Maintenance	$ 3,750				$ 0.68
Sales	$ 4,041				$ 0.73
General Admin.	$ 2,125				$ 0.39
Totals		$ 307,958	$ 1.06	$ 34.07	$ 8.63

Verification of Costing Model	Total Cost	Per Mile	Per Load	Per Hour
Actual Activity Volume		236,100	300	5,500
Rate Per Activity Unit		$ 1.06	$ 34.07	$ 8.63
Rate Per Activity Unit x Activity	$ 307,958	$ 250,266	$ 10,222	$ 47,470

The activity-based rates are established at $1.06 per mile, $34.07 per load and $8.63 per hour.[21] In the last section of the table, the costing model is validated by multiplying each activity-based rate times the activity level for each cost driver. The result is equal to the total cost to be allocated and thus verifies the allocation rate design.

---

[20] Utilizing only on-duty time allows for a simplified costing model. In actual practice, some carriers may utilize a more sophisticated and detailed approach.
[21] These activity-based rates are strictly theoretical and do not represent recommended rates or costs.

Application of the Activity-Based Costing Model

The activity-based costing model can now be applied to an actual load to determine the approximate cost of moving the load. In order to apply the model, the number of miles and the number of hours associated with the load must be identified. The per-load costs are transaction-based and applied directly to each load regardless of total miles or total hours. The table below illustrates the application of the activity-based costs to two example loads.

Application of Costing Model	Per Mile	Per Load	Per Hour	Total Cost
Costing Rate Per Unit of Activity	$ 1.060	$ 34.073	$ 8.631	
Load 101				
Loaded Miles	875			
Empty Miles	77			
Actual Activity Volume	952	1	26.5	
Applied Costs	$ 1,009.12	$ 34.07	$ 228.72	$ 1,271.91
	Estimated Profit:		Per Mile	Total Load
	Total Revenue		$ 1.48	$ 1,408.96
	Total Cost		$ 1.34	$ 1,271.91
	Estimated Profit Load 101		$ 0.14	$ 137.05
	Estimated Operating Ratio		90.3%	90.3%
Load 102				
Loaded Miles	450			
Empty Miles	102			
Actual Activity Volume	552	1	14.0	
Applied Costs	$ 585.12	$ 34.07	$ 120.83	$ 740.03
	Estimated Profit:		Per Mile	Total Load
	Total Revenue		$ 1.52	$ 839.04
	Total Cost		$ 1.34	$ 740.03
	Estimated Profit Load 102		$ 0.18	$ 99.01
	Estimated Operating Ratio		88.2%	88.2%

The miles for each load include both the loaded and empty miles associated with the load. The hours as shown include only the direct working hours and not the hours associated with the driver's break time, consistent with the original design of the activity-based costing model.

The profitability shown for each load is only an estimate. Carriers are generally not concerned with the profitability of any one specific load. The goal for the carrier is the maximization of profits for the entire network of loads and trucks. This activity-based approach could be applied to a larger group of loads to determine the approximate profitability of any segment of the carrier's network.

Cost Per Mile and Length of Haul. The activity-based costing model is also useful in illustrating the critical relationship between length of haul and cost per mile. The table below applies the activity-based cost model to loads of various length of haul levels.

Cost Per Mile and Length of Haul

Activity-Based Costs: Per Mile $1.06 | Per Load $34.07 | Per Hour $8.63

Length of Haul	Miles Per Hour	Transit Hours	Dock Time Hours	Total Activity Based Costs Per Mile	Per Load	Per Hour	Total Trip Cost	Cost Per Mile
100	40	2.50	1.50	$106.00	$34.07	$34.52	$174.59	$1.75
300	45	6.67	1.50	$318.00	$34.07	$70.48	$422.55	$1.41
500	45	11.11	1.50	$530.00	$34.07	$108.83	$672.90	$1.35
700	50	14.00	1.50	$742.00	$34.07	$133.77	$909.84	$1.30
900	50	18.00	1.50	$954.00	$34.07	$168.29	$1,156.36	$1.28
1,200	55	21.82	1.50	$1,272.00	$34.07	$201.24	$1,507.31	$1.26
1,500	55	27.27	1.50	$1,590.00	$34.07	$248.31	$1,872.38	$1.25

The application of cost assumes that miles per hour increases as length of haul increases, a basic concept of length of haul efficiencies. The model also assumes that the dock time to pick up and deliver the load is the same regardless of the length of haul. The fixed cost per load of $34.07 remains constant regardless of the length of haul. The graph below illustrates the reduction in cost per mile as length of haul increases.

Length of Haul and Cost Per Mile

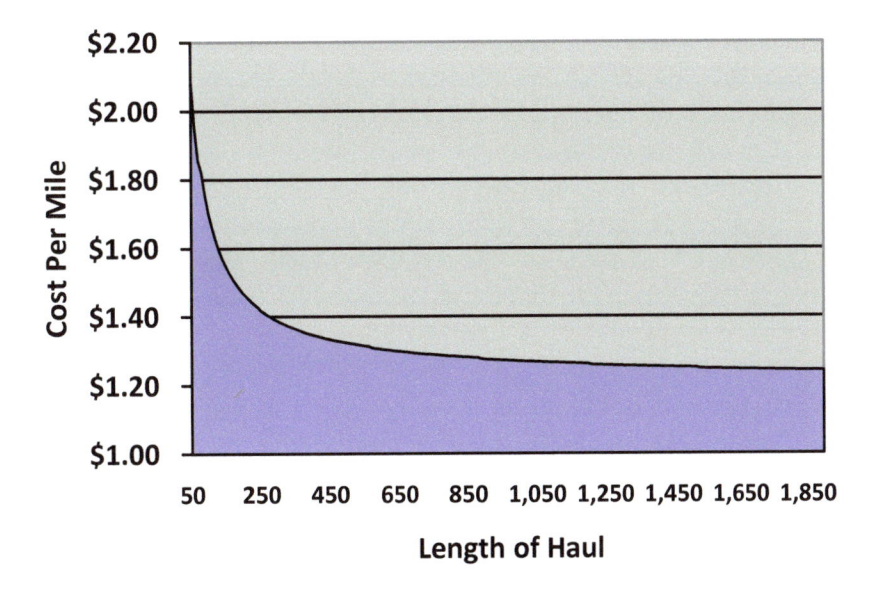

At a certain length of haul, perhaps around 1,000 miles, the bulk of the length of haul efficiencies are represented in the cost per mile so that very little reduction in cost per mile occurs beyond that point. This relationship between length of haul and cost per mile is a key element in the pricing concepts presented in future chapters.

Revenue Per Day and Asset Productivity

While weekly utilization is a critical productivity measure for regional and short haul operations, a potentially more important goal is the maximization of revenue. Instead of focusing only on an operating plan that maximizes utilization, successful carriers also focus on organizing load activity into a plan that maximizes revenues regardless of relatively low utilization levels. The table below illustrates how this important principle results in increased revenues and profitability.

Maximizing Revenue Per Day

Load Option	Miles Loaded	Miles Empty	Miles Total	Empty Miles %	Total Revenue	Revenue Per Mile Loaded	Revenue Per Mile Net
Single Load							
Memphis to New Orleans	405	50	455	11.0%	$ 650	$ 1.60	$ 1.43
Daily Total	405	50	455	11.0%	$ 650	$ 1.60	$ 1.43
Multiple Loads							
Memphis to Tupelo, MS	100	100	200	50.0%	$ 400	$ 4.00	$ 2.00
Memphis to West Memphis, AR	30	30	60	50.0%	$ 300	$ 10.00	$ 5.00
Daily Total	130	130	260	50.0%	$ 700	$ 4.00	$ 2.69

Notice that the single load option will result in much higher utilization than the multiple load option. However, the multiple load option results in higher total revenue while also requiring fewer miles. The multiple load scenario provides very profitable results compared to the single load option. Even though the multiple load option has a higher empty miles percentage, the carrier is compensated for these empty miles through a much higher loaded and net revenue per mile.

The primary cost item that may change behavior in the single and multiple load scenario comparison is driver pay. In the multiple load option, the total miles for the day are much less than the single load scenario. As a result of the lower miles, the driver pay program may require adjustment so that the driver receives a suitable income relative to the lower number of miles available for compensation.

One other minor cost impact of the multiple load strategy, based on the activity-based costing model, is per-load costs. In the multiple load option, the carrier will incur transaction costs such as dispatching and invoicing for two loads instead of one load. The carrier may also have additional trailers deployed in the network to serve multiple customers. Despite these extra costs, the multiple load option results in the higher level of profitability in the majority of cases.

CHAPTER 3: Introduction to One-Way Pricing

A one-way truckload rate is simply the charge to move a load from Point A to Point B. The shipper's obligation begins when the load is picked up at Point A and ends once the load is delivered to Point B. After delivery, the carrier is responsible for locating the next customer and load for the available truck. The topic of one-way pricing covers both the linehaul charges and accessorial charges for basic trucking services. This chapter covers the basic components of one-way pricing as well as accessorial charges. Future chapters will cover one-way pricing strategy and network analysis in greater detail.

Lanes

One-way prices are generally quoted and organized on a "lane" basis. A lane is any unique pairing of an origin point and a destination point. Most often, one-way lanes are based on a city-to-city pair, but other geographic definitions may also be used. A few examples of common lane definitions are listed below.

Common Lane Types	
Lane Type	**Lane Example**
Point-to-Point	Franklin, TN to Newark, NJ
Point-to-State	Franklin, TN to New Jersey
State-to-State	Tennessee to New Jersey
State-to-Point	Tennessee to Newark, NJ
Zip-to-Zip	38655 to 39206
3-Digit Zip to 3-Digit Zip	386 to 392

Obviously, there are millions of possible lanes that could be identified. The lanes for a specific shipper are based on that shipper's freight network. One shipper may have less than 20 lanes while another shipper may have well over 1,000 lanes.

Most contracts between a shipper and a carrier will include lane-specific, point-to-point rates for the most common lanes in the shipper's network. Most contracts will also include backup rates to cover any other shipments that are not specifically covered by the point-to-point rates. Backup rates are commonly based on broad geographic areas such as a simple state-to-state matrix.

The more geographically specific a lane is, the more precise the rate on the lane will be. For example, when developing a point-to-point rate, the carrier knows the exact length of haul and the exact origin and destination points. The carrier can set the rate accordingly based on the specific information. On the other hand, a state-to-state rate would apply to a load moving from any point in State A to any point in State B. When the carrier sets the rate, the carrier does not know the exact length of haul or the exact origin and destination points. As a result, the carrier must set the rate high enough to cover all the various scenarios for loads that could move under the rate.

Sample Contract

The example contract below illustrates the basic components of a one-way pricing agreement between a carrier and a shipper.

Sample Contract

Customer Name: ABC Electronics		Rates Expire: 12/31/2010

Point-to-Point Rates
From: St. Louis, MO

To:	Rate Per Mile	Minimum Charge
Los Angeles, CA	$ 1.36	
Chicago, IL	$ 1.95	
Columbus, OH	$ 1.82	
St. Louis, MO	$ 2.05	$475
Springfield, MO	$ 2.05	$650
Memphis, TN	$ 1.47	

Backup Rates
From: St. Louis, MO

To:	Rate Per Mile	Minimum Charge
CA	$ 1.38	$750
IA	$ 1.55	$700
IL	$ 2.05	$675
MO	$ 2.05	$550
OH	$ 1.90	$725
OK	$ 1.65	$650
TN	$ 1.55	$650

All miles to be based on practical miles as stated in Rand McNally Version 20.

Accessorial Charges

Stopoffs	$60	per occurrence
Unloading	$120	per occurrence
Truck Order Not Used	$350	per occurrence
Layover	$400	per occurrence
Pallet Jack	$75	per occurrence
Tractor Detention	$50	per hour after 2 hours
Trailer Detention	$30	per day after 3 business days

The sample contract includes point-to-point rates from St. Louis, MO to several different cities. The sample contract also includes point-to-state backup rates from St. Louis, MO (point) to several different states.[22] The contract also includes basic accessorial charges for secondary services. Accessorial items will be discussed in detail later in this chapter.

Notice that the point-to-point rates are lower than the corresponding point-to-state backup rates. If a point-to-point rate was higher than the corresponding point-to-state rate, a rate conflict would exist. The lower point-to-state rate would override the higher point-to-point rate and the shipper would be charged the lower rate.

Conflicting Rates

The table below illustrates a basic rate contract proposal between a shipper and carrier for transportation from Atlanta, GA to Florida, Alabama, Tennessee and Mississippi. The proposal includes point-to-point rates for high volume lanes and a backup scale that will apply to all other activity not specifically included in the point-to-point lane rates.

Example Contract Proposal Containing Rate Conflicts

Origin: Atlanta, GA

Point-to-Point Lane Rates			Point-to-State Rates		
Destination City	Rate Per Mile	Flat Charge	Destination State	Rate Per Mile	Flat Charge
Memphis, TN	$ 1.90		AL	$ 2.25	$ 700.00
Nashville, TN		$ 775.00	FL	$ 2.95	$ 850.00
Jacksonville, FL		$ 925.00	MS	$ 1.90	$ 700.00
Fort Lauderdale, FL	$ 2.20		TN	$ 1.95	$ 700.00
Miami, FL	$ 2.90				
Mobile, AL	$ 2.15				
Montgomery, AL		$ 725.00			
Jackson, MS	$ 1.88				
McComb, MS	$ 2.05				

Before the contract is executed, carrier pricing managers, as well as transportation managers for shippers, must review the contract rates carefully to identify any potential rate conflicts. Rate conflicts occur when a rate in one portion of the contract is inconsistent with rates in another portion of the contract. For illustration purposes, the example contract above contains two critical rate conflicts.

Conflicts Between Point-to-Point and Backup Rates

The first conflict exists between a lane rate to Mississippi and the point-to-state backup rate to Mississippi. Keeping in mind that the rates in the point-to-state backup matrix apply to all points in Mississippi, the conflict exists with the lane rate to McComb, MS of $2.05 and the backup rate of $1.90 to *any point* in Mississippi. In order to avoid conflicts of this type, the point-to-state backup rate per-mile should be at least as high as the highest per-mile lane rate to the state.

---

[22] The sample contract is scaled down for illustration purposes. In actual practice, the contract would likely include far more point-to-point rates and the backup rates could include all 48 contiguous U.S. states.

Conflicts Among Lane Rates

The second conflict exists between two of the lane rates to Florida. The rate to Fort Lauderdale is $2.20 per mile while the rate to Miami is $2.90 per mile. Since Fort Lauderdale and Miami are only a few miles apart, the difference in the two rates is unreasonable. All other service requirements being equal, two destinations so close together should usually have the same or very similar per-mile rates. In some cases, there may be exceptions to this rule. For example, if a significant toll charge is incurred to reach one location and not the other, the higher rate to the market with the toll expense would be reasonable.

Practical Miles

Unless otherwise stated in the contract, the "billed miles" are usually based on the most practical and reasonable routing from Point A to Point B. The "practical route" usually includes major roads and interstates and avoids secondary roads and high traffic metropolitan areas. The example below shows two possible routes from Memphis, TN to Meridian, MS.

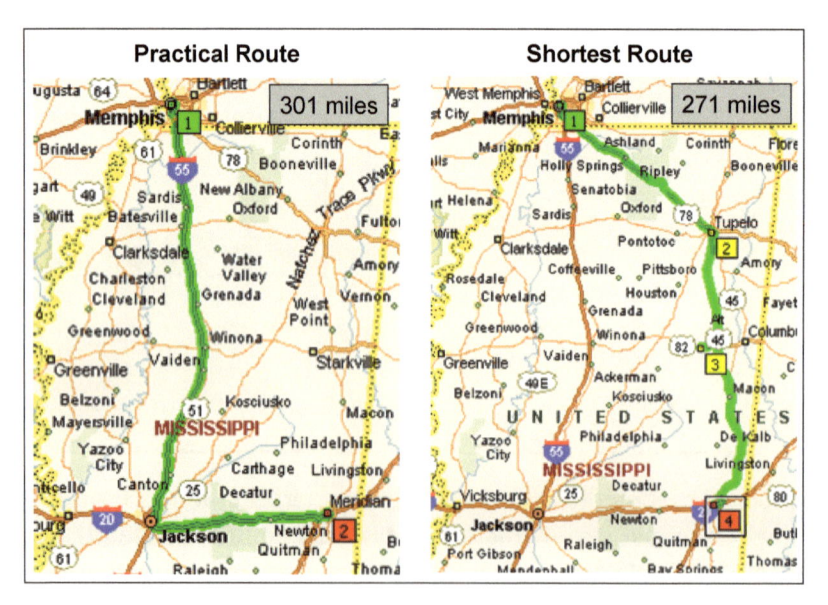

The shortest route minimizes the number of miles for the trip but also routes the trip through small towns, poor roads, and slow speed limits. The practical route utilizes the much safer interstate system with a much higher speed limit. Even though the practical route is longer, the practical route is much safer and often faster than the shortest route.

The practical route may even be more fuel efficient regardless of the extra miles because the trip would avoid the "stop and start" driving associated with the shortest route. Since practical miles are the standard, the common industry practice is that the carrier is paid based on practical miles regardless of the actual route the carrier or driver chooses for the trip. Most carriers also pay per-mile compensation to the driver based on practical miles regardless of the actual route chosen by the individual driver.

County Qualifiers

As strange as it may seem, many states have more than one city with the exact same city name. For example, in the state of Pennsylvania, there are four different cities named Middletown. The four Middletown, PA city locations are shown in the map below.

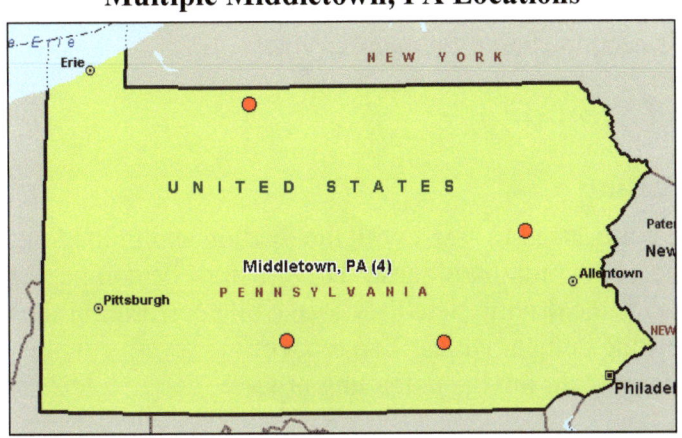

Multiple Middletown, PA Locations

When lane pricing in a contract is based on a city-to-city format, it is impossible to determine which of the four city locations is referenced in the pricing without the presence of additional geographic information. Consider the lane below.

City to City Lane: Columbus, OH to Middletown, PA: $1.95 per mile

To correctly identify the intended destination city in this situation, a county qualifier is often applied. The county qualifier provides additional geographic information by indicating the county in which the city is located.

Counties for Each Middletown, PA Location

City	State	County	City with County Qualifier
Middletown	PA	Dauphin	Middletown, DA
Middletown	PA	Huntingdon	Middletown, HU
Middletown	PA	Luzerne	Middletown, LU
Middletown	PA	Mckean	Middletown, MC

Within the contract, the lane would list the city along with the county qualifier to avoid any confusion as to which Middletown location is referenced in the contract.

Revised Lane: Columbus, OH to Middletown, HU, PA: $1.95 per mile

Not only is the county qualifier used to apply the correct rate, it is also used by the carrier in the pricing process to determine the correct miles for the lane as well. If a carrier were to price the lane using an inaccurate number of miles, the carrier may price the lane incorrectly.[23]

---

[23] Five-digit zip codes could also be used to identify the specific city location.

Accessorial Charges

The base one-way linehaul rates charged to a customer only cover the movement of the load from Point A to Point B. If the customer requires additional services, the charges for these services are known as accessorial (accessory) charges. The two most commonly occurring accessorial items are stop-offs and driver unloading services. This section provides a brief explanation of each of the common accessorial charges and the reasoning behind the carrier's need to charge for each service.

Unloading and Stop-offs

Loading / Unloading

On occasion, drivers are asked to assist with the loading and unloading of the trailer, with unloading being the most common request. Drivers must be compensated for performing this extra labor and for the driving time they lose while performing the unloading service. In addition, the trucking company must also recover the revenue that is lost while the driver and tractor are idle during the unloading process.

In the majority of cases, both carriers and drivers view the loading/unloading request as undesirable. As a result, the charge for this service will not only cover the time and labor costs, but may also serve to discourage the shipper from requesting this service. Carriers will commonly charge as much as $150 or more per request for loading or unloading. Carriers may charge even higher rates for the loading and unloading of undesirable or difficult-to-handle products such as automobile tires. Unloading is sometimes charged as a per-piece or per-pound rate instead of a flat fee per occurrence.

The potential for work-related injuries as a result of strenuous loading and unloading is another reason carriers generally try to avoid or discourage loads that require driver labor services. Insurance claims, medical bills, and lost driver productivity are very costly to the carrier if a driver is injured on the job. Injuries, or the risk of injury, due to unloading may also cause drivers to quit their job and further compound driver turnover challenges faced by the carrier.[24]

Stop-offs

Stop-offs occur when the driver must deliver a single truckload to more than one customer location. For example, it is very common for major retailers to ship a full truckload that is shared among several of its retail stores. The truck will stop at each store and deliver a portion of the load until the trailer is completely empty after the final store on the route.

Each stop-off consumes valuable time and productivity from the truck and driver. Because of this lost productivity, both the driver and trucking company must receive

---

[24] Carriers will sometimes pay a third-party "lumper" service to perform the unloading labor instead of having the driver do the actual unloading. The carrier may even charge the shipper for a "lumper" charge instead of a loading or unloading charge.

suitable compensation. The primary reasons that stop-offs result in lost utilization and lost productivity are listed below.

Time Consuming Factors of Stop-offs
Extra city driving at reduced speeds
Wait/dock time at the stop-off location
Unloading time at the stop-off location
Time to position trailer to dock at the stop-off location
Driver may lose available driving hours due to time spent at stop-off location

The stop-off charge will apply only to the additional stops above and beyond the final delivery. A stop-off charge is almost never applied to the final delivery or the pick-up at the origin.[25] For example, a load with two total deliveries will be charged with one stop charge. A load with three total deliveries will be charged with two stop charges. Stop charges would also apply in cases where a load has multiple pick-ups. For example, a load with two pick-ups and one delivery would be charged with one stop charge for the extra pick-up.

Even though the trucking company is compensated for the stop-offs, the stops are generally considered to be undesirable in most cases. In order to discourage loads with excessive stop-offs, carriers may include escalating stop charges in the customer's contract. The graphic below illustrates this type of contract provision.

Escalating Stop Charges

First Stop	$75
Second Stop	$75
Third Stop	$100
Additional	$125

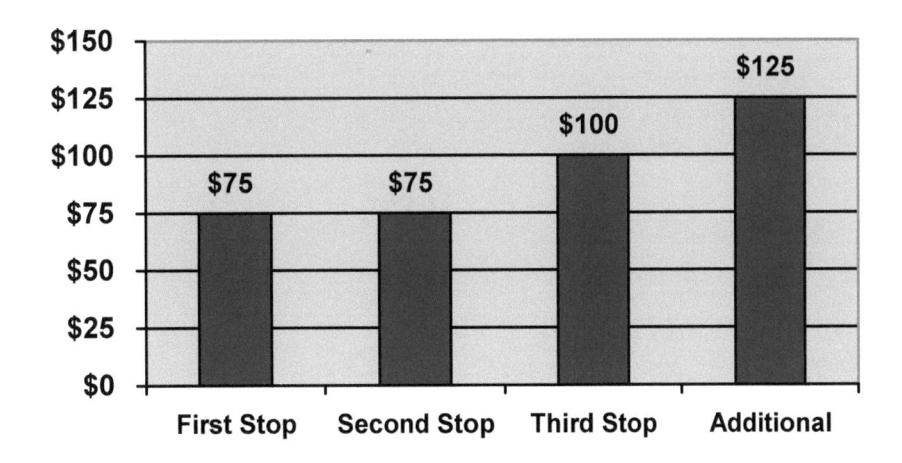

Trucking companies use the escalating stop charges to discourage excessive stop-offs for two main reasons. First, the stop-offs waste valuable time and cause the truck and driver to lose utilization. Second, the majority of drivers don't like stop-offs for many reasons. If a driver is consistently assigned to loads with excessive stops, the driver will be more likely to quit his job, further compounding the driver turnover issue for the carrier.

---

[25] Certain types of specialized pricing formats may apply stop charges to all deliveries, including the final delivery, but this exception is not common.

A portion of the stop charge is used to provide drivers with compensation for each stop. The rate of pay per stop can vary significantly from carrier to carrier. Internally, a carrier may also have several different rates of pay for stop-offs for different customers, fleet types, or operations.

Other Common Accessorial Charges

Shrink Wrap

A shrink wrap charge is applicable when the driver is required to perform shrink wrapping of the pallets for the shipper. The purpose of the shrink wrap is to secure boxes and cargo on a pallet to prevent the product from shifting or falling during shipping. In the vast majority of cases, the shipper will provide the shrink wrap materials to the driver. The charge is generally less than a standard loading or unloading charge since the labor is less strenuous and the time required to complete the shrink wrapping is usually less than typical loading or unloading.

Pallet Jack

A pallet jack charge is applicable when the driver is required to perform unloading or loading labor with a pallet jack instead of manually. The charge is generally less than a standard unloading charge since the labor is not as strenuous and the time required to complete the pallet jack unloading is usually less than standard unloading labor. In the vast majority of cases, the customer location will provide the pallet jack to the driver.

Layovers

A layover occurs when a truck and driver are required to wait in a location for an extended period, usually overnight. The most common reason to layover a truck and driver is to provide additional capacity for the next day in the driver's current location. Carriers will usually provide extra pay to the driver for the layover to compensate for the income the driver loses during the layover period. If a shipper has requested a layover from the carrier, the shipper will be charged a layover accessorial fee to compensate the carrier for the layover pay to the driver and the lost productivity for the truck during the layover period.

Truck Order Not Used (TONU)

A truck order not used charge occurs when a shipper has requested truckload service from a carrier then later cancels the request after a predetermined grace period expires.[26] The specific charges and cancellation rules will be clearly defined in the carrier's contract with the shipper. The carrier must charge a TONU to protect itself from the costs incurred to begin the process to pick up a load. The main direct cost is the empty miles driven to position the truck for pick-up. There is also an opportunity cost (lost revenue) because the truck may have to wait an extended period to find a new load to replace the load canceled at the last minute.

---

[26] Cancellation grace periods to avoid a truck order not used charge generally range from 24 hours to a few hours before the actual scheduled pick-up time.

Power Detention

Power detention is charged to a customer when the customer fails to unload or release a truck and driver in a timely fashion when making a pick-up or delivery. Detention charges during delivery are generally more common. The contract between the shipper and the carrier will contain very specific rules for determining any detention charges. For example, the contract may allow for three hours of free time from the time the driver arrives at the facility. After the three hour period, a per-hour charge will begin to accrue.

The example below illustrates the calculation of a power detention charge. The example is based on three free hours and a power detention charge of $60 per hour after 3 hours.

Example Power Detention Charge

Power Detention Contract Provisions:
3 Free Hours After Delivery Appointment (Carrier must arrive on time)
$60 Per Hour After 3 Hours (Billed at $15 per 15 minute increment or fraction thereof)

Example Power Detention Charge:			
Time	Event / Status	Billable Event?	Amount
10:00 am	Driver arrives for delivery at scheduled 10 am appointment time.		
11:00 am	Driver waits for available dock door to begin unloading.	Free hour	$ -
12:00 pm	Driver places trailer at dock door for unloading.	Free hour	$ -
1:00 pm	Receiver continues unloading trailer. 3 Free Hours Expired.	Free hour	$ -
2:00 pm	Receiver continues unloading trailer.	1 Billable Hour (1pm-2pm)	$ 60.00
3:00 pm	Receiver continues unloading trailer.	1 Billable Hour (2pm - 3pm)	$ 60.00
3:28 pm	Receiver completes trailer unloading. Driver released.	Two 15 min increments	$ 30.00
		Total Power Detention Charge:	$ 150.00

The driver arrives at 10:00 am as scheduled. The driver waits 2 hours before the receiver begins unloading the trailer at 12:00 pm. The receiver completes the unloading of the trailer at 3:28 pm. The unit "goes into detention" at 1:00 pm, meaning that from 1:00 pm and beyond detention charges will accrue until the tractor and driver are released. The receiver was charged a total of $150 for 2.5 hours of detention for the period of 1:00 pm until 3:28 pm.

Carriers must carefully document the timing of events in order to substantiate any detention charges. In most cases, if the carrier is late for a scheduled delivery, the carrier is not entitled to charge detention. If the carrier is late for the delivery appointment and must wait to make delivery as a result, the detention is considered to be the fault of the carrier and not the receiving location.

Detention charges are important to the carrier because of the downstream effects of the lost productivity. During detention, both the tractor and driver lose valuable productivity and revenue opportunities. Also, using the example above, the driver stuck in detention may have been scheduled to pick up a load at 2 pm. Since the driver is unable to make the scheduled 2 pm pick-up, the carrier must locate a different driver to make the scheduled pick-up or face a service issue with the 2 pm pick-up.

Trailer Detention

Trailer detention is charged to a customer when the customer fails to release or unload a trailer within a predetermined time limit. For example, the contract may allow for three free days from the day of delivery to release the trailer. After three days, a per-day charge will begin to accrue. In most contracts, weekend days are not included in the free days before trailer detention charges begin to accrue.

A basic example of a trailer detention charge is shown below.

Example Trailer Detention Charge

Trailer Detention Contract Provisions:
3 Free Days After Delivery Day
$50 Per Day Trailer Detention
Weekends - No Charge

Example Trailer Detention Charge:				
Date	Day	Event / Trailer Status	Billable Event?	Amount
6/24/2009	Wednesday	Loaded trailer is delivered at 1:00 pm.		
6/25/2009	Thursday	Trailer remains loaded at customer facility.	Day 1 - Free	$ -
6/26/2009	Friday	Trailer remains loaded at customer facility.	Day 2 - Free	$ -
6/27/2009	Saturday	Trailer remains loaded at customer facility.	Weekend - Free	$ -
6/28/2009	Sunday	Trailer remains loaded at customer facility.	Weekend - Free	$ -
6/29/2009	Monday	Trailer remains loaded at customer facility.	Day 3 - Free	$ -
6/30/2009	Tuesday	Trailer remains loaded at customer facility.	Day 4 - $50	$ 50.00
7/1/2009	Wednesday	Trailer remains loaded at customer facility.	Day 5 - $50	$ 50.00
7/2/2009	Thursday	Trailer is unloaded by customer.	No charge.	$ -
			Total Trailer Detention Charge:	$ 100.00

According to the contract, the customer is allowed three days to unload the trailer with no charge for weekend days. After the three free days, a charge of $50 per day will accrue. In the above example, the trailer is delivered on a Wednesday, but is not unloaded and released until eight days later on the following Thursday. During this time, the customer is charged $100 for two days of trailer detention. Since weekend days are excluded, the trailer detention charges do not begin to accrue until the Tuesday after delivery.

Trailer detention charges are important to the carrier for two reasons. First, if the trailer is not released in a timely manner, the carrier will not be able to use the trailer on other loads to generate revenue. Second, the carrier must continually have empty trailers available for all of its customers. Any trailers that are not released by customers in a timely manner reduce the number of trailers that the carrier has available to meet customer trailer needs. The reduction in available empty trailers causes the carrier to incur otherwise unnecessary operating costs to locate available trailers and transfer those trailers to locations where empty trailers are needed.

Requested Empty Move (Deadhead)

During peak business periods, shippers may have an unusually high need for truck capacity beyond what is normally available in their general area or customarily provided by their carriers. In these extreme cases, the shipper may agree to pay carriers for the empty miles incurred by the carrier to source trucks to meet the shipper's needs. Without this compensation, carriers would be unwilling to move additional trucks into the area at their own expense to meet the shipper's demand. The primary reason for this reluctance by the carrier to provide additional trucks at no charge is that the trucks must be sourced from too far away and at too great a cost.

New York City (Boroughs) Charges

The delivery of a load into the five boroughs of New York City presents several issues and challenges to the carrier. The primary challenges and issues are listed below.

Major New York City Issues
Tolls. Depending on the entry route, trucks can be charged tolls ranging from $50 to $150 dollars or more. Additional tolls costs may also be incurred while exiting New York City.
Traffic. Traffic is a serious issue in and around New York City. As a result, the tractor and driver can expect to experience traffic delays and lose valuable productive time as a result.
Safety and Accidents. Minor accidents are very common when delivering into New York City because of traffic, very tight spaces for delivery, and similar complications.
Equipment Restrictions. Many customers may require special tractor or trailer equipment to make deliveries to their location because of bridge heights, out-of-date buildings, or limited space for maneuvering the trailer into the location.

As a result of these issues, carriers will typically charge an additional fee of $200 or more to deliver a load into the five boroughs of New York City. Again, both carriers and drivers prefer to avoid deliveries into this region, so a portion of the charge is intended to discourage shippers from sending the carrier into New York City.

Circuitous Miles

In cases where a load has an out-of-route stop-off, the contract may call for a circuitous miles rate to apply to a portion of the cost of the load. Circuitous miles are the net additional billed miles created as a result of a stop-off. Consider the example below.

Load with Circuitous Miles

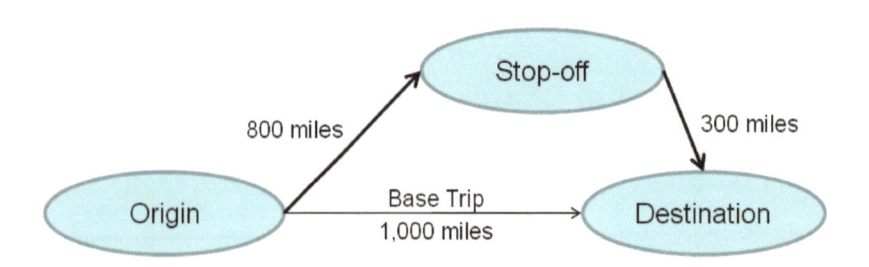

In the above example, the base trip has 1,000 billed miles. However, when the stop-off is added, the new trip has 800 + 300 = 1,100 billed miles. The additional 100 miles represent the circuitous miles. Because one-way rates are often influenced by many external market factors and are not a pure reflection of the direct operating cost to serve the load, the circuitous miles rate is applied to these additional miles. For example, the one-way rate per mile from Atlanta, GA to Miami, FL might be $2.40 per mile while the rate from Miami, FL to Atlanta, GA is $0.90 per mile. The example below applies these rates to the above example assuming a circuitous miles rate of $1.50 per mile.

The circuitous mileage rate equally protects the interests of both the carrier and the shipper. When the base rate is high, the shipper is protected. When the base rate is especially low, the carrier is protected.

The circuitous miles rate should reflect only the carrier's average or standard cost per mile plus a reasonable profit and disregard market rate implications.

Circuitous Miles Charges	Atlanta, GA to Miami, FL	Miami, FL to Atlanta, GA
Base Trip		
Billed Miles	1,000	1,000
One-Way Rate Per Mile	$ 2.40	$ 0.90
Base Charge	$ 2,400.00	$ 900.00
Trip with Stop Off		
Based Trip Billed Miles	1,000	1,000
One-Way Rate Per Mile	$ 2.40	$ 0.90
Base Charge	$ 2,400.00	$ 900.00
Circuitous Miles	100	100
Circuitous Miles Rate	$ 1.50	$ 1.50
Circuitous Miles Charge	$ 150.00	$ 150.00
Total Trip Billed Miles	1,100	1,100
Total Trip Charges	$ 2,550.00	$ 1,050.00
Total Trip Cost Per Mile	**$ 2.32**	**$ 0.95**

Fuel Surcharge

Fuel represents a significant portion of every carrier's operating costs. Over time, fuel costs per gallon move up and down significantly due to a variety of economic factors. Most carrier contracts include a fuel surcharge provision to provide a mechanism to pass the additional fuel costs above a predetermined level along to the shipper in the form of a fuel surcharge. The fuel provision also provides for a fuel discount or rebate to the shipper when fuel prices fall below the predetermined base level.

Example Fuel Surcharge Table:

Price of Fuel From	Price of Fuel To	Surcharge (Rebate)
$ 2.000	$ 2.069	$ (0.06)
$ 2.070	$ 2.129	$ (0.05)
$ 2.130	$ 2.189	$ (0.04)
$ 2.190	$ 2.249	$ (0.03)
$ 2.250	$ 2.309	$ (0.02)
$ 2.310	$ 2.369	$ (0.01)
$ 2.370	$ 2.429	$ -
$ 2.430	$ 2.489	$ 0.01
$ 2.490	$ 2.549	$ 0.02
$ 2.550	$ 2.609	$ 0.03
$ 2.610	$ 2.669	$ 0.04
$ 2.670	$ 2.729	$ 0.05
$ 2.730	$ 2.789	$ 0.06
$ 2.790	$ 2.849	$ 0.07
$ 2.850	$ 2.909	$ 0.08
$ 2.910	$ 2.969	$ 0.09
$ 2.970	$ 3.029	$ 0.10
$ 3.030	$ 3.089	$ 0.11
$ 3.090	$ 3.149	$ 0.12
$ 3.150	$ 3.209	$ 0.13
$ 3.210	$ 3.269	$ 0.14
$ 3.270	$ 3.329	$ 0.15
$ 3.330	$ 3.389	$ 0.16
$ 3.390	$ 3.449	$ 0.17
$ 3.450	$ 3.509	$ 0.18
$ 3.510	$ 3.569	$ 0.19
$ 3.570	$ 3.629	$ 0.20
$ 3.630	$ 3.689	$ 0.21
$ 3.690	$ 3.749	$ 0.22
$ 3.750	$ 3.809	$ 0.23

The predetermined cost per gallon in the contract is commonly referred to as the "fuel peg." The fuel peg represents the base cost per gallon for fuel upon which the contract pricing is based. The fuel cost per gallon is converted to a fuel adjustment amount per mile. The table to the left illustrates a common format for a fuel surcharge agreement based on a fuel peg of $2.37 per gallon.

The fuel peg may be established by either the shipper or the carrier. If the fuel peg is defined by the shipper, the carrier must adjust standard pricing up or down to match the cost of the fuel dictated by the shipper's predefined fuel peg.

The fuel surcharge on the invoice is based on the billed miles for the trip multiplied by the applicable cents per mile surcharge (or rebate) for the billing period. For example, if the average fuel price for the applicable index was $3.010 per gallon, the fuel surcharge per billed mile would be $0.10 per mile. For a load with 200 billed miles, the fuel surcharge would be $20.00 (200 miles x $0.10 per mile).

To determine the applicable fuel surcharge amount for invoicing, the fuel peg is compared to a predefined standard that is specified in the contract. The most common standard is the Department of Energy (DOE) index. The table below shows the Department of Energy fuel information for the week of June 16, 2008.[27]

---

[27] Source: Energy Information Administration / U.S. Department of Energy. (www.eia.doe.gov) The data for the Diesel Fuel Cost Per Gallon graph is also from this same source.

Department of Energy Fuel Price Index
(in cents per gallon)

By Area	5/12/2008	5/19/2008	5/26/2008	6/2/2008	6/9/2008	6/16/2008
U.S.	372.2	379.1	393.7	397.6	403.9	408.2
East Coast (PADD 1)	371.3	379.5	393.7	397.0	401.9	405.2
New England (PADD 1A)	375.0	383.8	397.4	402.8	408.9	413.1
Central Atlantic (PADD 1B)	372.9	382.4	394.8	400.1	405.8	410.3
Lower Atlantic (PADD 1C)	369.0	375.9	391.8	392.9	396.9	399.0
Midwest (PADD 2)	373.6	379.9	395.1	395.2	398.2	399.7
Gulf Coast (PADD 3)	361.6	368.9	382.9	384.6	390.9	393.7
Rocky Mountain (PADD 4)	360.9	368.6	385.1	389.0	394.1	399.4
West Coast (PADD 5)	383.3	388.3	402.9	416.6	432.5	445.2
West Coast less California	368.5	376.3	390.9	403.5	413.7	421.7

The most common standard is the "U.S." average price. In some cases, one of the other regional measures may be applied as the standard. For example, a dedicated fleet that operates only in California and Nevada might use the "West Coast" average instead of the national average.

Fuel is one of the largest operating expenses for carriers. The fuel surcharge is necessary to protect the carrier from inflation in the cost of fuel. The graph below illustrates the trend in fuel prices from 1994 through 2008.

1994 – 2008 Diesel Fuel Cost Per Gallon
(by month)

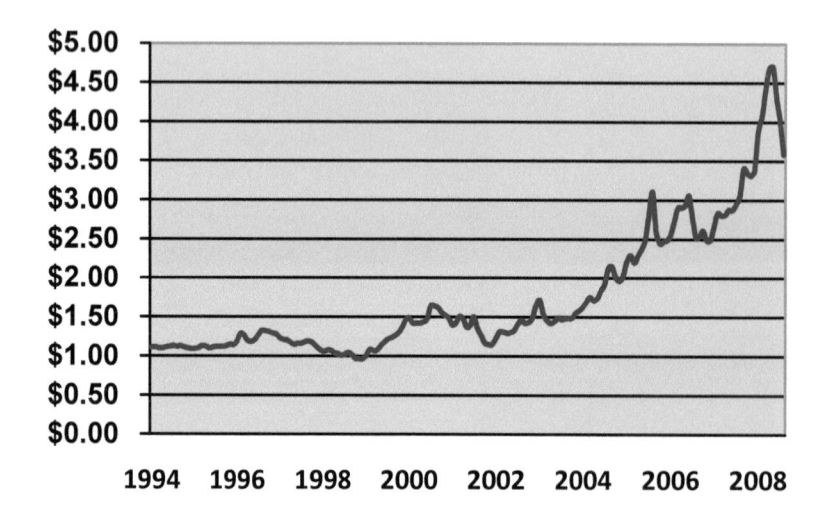

The protection offered by the fuel surcharge contract provision also benefits the shipper as well. Since the carrier is protected from fuel price inflation, the carrier does not have to speculate on the future price of fuel when determining the pricing and rates for the shipper. As a result, shippers should enjoy lower rates that more accurately reflect the carrier's actual operating costs.

Dilution of Fuel Surcharge Revenues. In almost all cases, fuel surcharges are only billable on the billed miles associated with each load. As a part of normal operations, the carrier incurs empty miles and out-of-route miles above and beyond billed miles. As a result, the effectiveness of the fuel surcharge revenues intended to offset rising fuel costs is reduced when these additional miles are introduced. The table below illustrates the dilution of fuel revenues across total miles.

Dilution of Fuel Surcharge Revenue

Dilution of Fuel Surcharge Revenues	Actual Miles			
	Billed	Out of Route	Empty	Total
Actual Mileage Activity	785,874	9,587	122,875	918,336
% of Total Miles	*85.58%*	*1.04%*	*13.38%*	
Fuel Surcharge Revenues	$ 48,724.19			
Fuel Revenue Per Mile				
Per Billed Mile	$ 0.062			
Per Loaded Mile		$ 0.061		
Per Total Mile				$ 0.0531

In the above example, the carrier collected 6.2 cents per billed mile in fuel surcharge revenues. After introducing out-of-route and empty miles, the carrier received a net of 5.31 cents per mile in fuel revenue. The actual dilution level is dependent primarily upon the empty mile percentage for the carrier. The higher the empty mile percentage, the greater the dilution of fuel surcharge revenues will be.

The dilution impact is also dependent on the actual price of fuel relative to the fuel peg in each customer contract. As the gap between the actual fuel price and the fuel peg increases, the greater the dilution becomes. Carriers must examine the structure of fuel surcharge provisions closely and adjust pricing as necessary to account for any gaps in the fuel surcharge structure.

The Pricing Matrix

Backup Matrix

The pricing matrix provides a simple format for establishing one-way pricing between a large number of locations. A simple, standard pricing matrix will contain pricing from one state or region to another. An abbreviated state-to-state pricing matrix is shown below. A full matrix might include the 48 contiguous states, the District of Columbia, and perhaps even destinations in Mexico and Canada.

State-to-State Pricing Matrix

Origin	\\ Destination (Minimum Charge = $575.00)										
	AL	AR	AZ	CA	CO	CT	DC	DE	FL	GA	IA
AL	$ 1.90	$ 1.50	$ 1.56	$ 1.24	$ 1.58	$ 1.56	$ 1.61	$ 1.56	$ 2.37	$ 1.81	$ 1.36
AR	$ 1.51	$ 1.90	$ 1.56	$ 1.30	$ 1.81	$ 1.54	$ 1.54	$ 1.54	$ 1.87	$ 1.41	$ 1.34
AZ	$ 1.04	$ 1.04	$ 1.95	$ 1.06	$ 1.60	$ 1.20	$ 1.18	$ 1.18	$ 1.30	$ 1.06	$ 1.06
CA	$ 1.10	$ 1.10	$ 1.91	$ 1.80	$ 1.64	$ 1.22	$ 1.20	$ 1.20	$ 1.36	$ 1.12	$ 1.10
CO	$ 0.98	$ 0.98	$ 1.31	$ 1.01	$ 2.16	$ 1.13	$ 1.13	$ 1.13	$ 1.32	$ 1.01	$ 0.96
CT	$ 0.92	$ 0.92	$ 1.32	$ 1.12	$ 1.51	$ 2.00	$ 1.51	$ 1.81	$ 1.52	$ 0.91	$ 0.93
DC	$ 1.01	$ 1.01	$ 1.37	$ 1.12	$ 1.51	$ 2.06	$ 2.69	$ 1.90	$ 1.58	$ 1.01	$ 0.98
DE	$ 0.95	$ 0.95	$ 1.37	$ 1.12	$ 1.51	$ 2.06	$ 1.90	$ 2.00	$ 1.58	$ 0.96	$ 0.98
FL	$ 0.96	$ 0.94	$ 1.31	$ 1.16	$ 1.34	$ 1.31	$ 1.31	$ 1.31	$ 2.02	$ 0.91	$ 1.01
GA	$ 1.52	$ 1.33	$ 1.48	$ 1.21	$ 1.56	$ 1.56	$ 1.56	$ 1.56	$ 2.28	$ 1.90	$ 1.24
IA	$ 1.52	$ 1.62	$ 1.58	$ 1.37	$ 2.21	$ 1.81	$ 1.81	$ 1.81	$ 1.99	$ 1.51	$ 1.90

The origin states are listed down the left and the destination states are listed across the top. In this matrix, the per-mile rate from Alabama to California is $1.24 per mile. This rate per mile is applicable for any city in Alabama to any city in California. The rate from California to Alabama is $1.10 per mile. This rate per mile is applicable for any city in California to any city in Alabama.

At the top of the matrix, a minimum charge of $575 per load is indicated. This rate will apply to any situation where the billed miles multiplied by the rate per mile does not total at least $575. For example, the rate per mile from Alabama to Georgia is $1.81 per mile. If there was a 100 mile load from Alabama to Georgia, the matrix rate of $1.81 would result in a charge of only $181.00 for the load. In this case, the minimum flat charge would supercede the per-mile charge and the customer would pay $575.00 for this load. If needed, the carrier and customer could also establish a second pricing matrix that provided a specific minimum charge for each state-to-state combination.

The pricing matrix is most often used as a backup to more specific pricing such as point-to-point lane pricing. The backup matrix pricing is applied only when a more specific rate is not available. The backup pricing matrix establishes a contract rate for every possible lane combination so that load acceptance and invoicing are not delayed because there is no contract rate established for a load.

Rates on the backup pricing matrix should always be higher than or equal to any other more specific pricing, otherwise there will be a conflict in the pricing agreement. For example, the example matrix shows a rate of $1.24 from Alabama to California. If there was a point-to-point rate of $1.28 per mile on loads from Birmingham, AL to Fresno, CA, this rate would conflict with the matrix. Under contract, the carrier would be required to honor the backup rate of $1.24 in place of the $1.28 point-to-point rate for the loads from Birmingham to Fresno.

The point-to-state matrix is another common format for backup pricing. The point-to-state format allows for more specific pricing than a state-to-state matrix since a specific origin location is defined in the matrix. A sample point-to-state matrix is shown below for loads originating in St. Louis, MO.

Point-to-State Pricing Matrix

From: St. Louis, MO		
To:	Rate Per Mile	Minimum Charge
CA	$ 1.38	$750
IA	$ 1.55	$700
IL	$ 2.05	$675
MO	$ 2.05	$550
OH	$ 1.90	$725
OK	$ 1.65	$650
TN	$ 1.55	$650

The origin point is listed at the top and the destination states are listed down the left. A unique minimum charge is also included for each destination state in the matrix. A minimum charge should be included in all backup pricing formats. This format could be converted into a state-to-point matrix to organize inbound pricing for a specific destination location.

Guideline Pricing Matrix

Many carriers choose to develop a guideline pricing matrix to establish an internal rate per mile on any possible lane combination. The guideline pricing is created with input from the sales team and pricing group. Once created, the guideline matrix can be used as a starting point for pricing new lanes and new business opportunities. In general, the guideline rates would be slightly higher than normal rates then adjusted for the characteristics of each new business opportunity.

In most cases, guideline rates would be established based on carrier-defined pricing zones where states are split into strategic regions. Each region would have certain market characteristics that dictate the need for unique rate levels. The regions will be defined differently from carrier to carrier. The format of the guideline pricing matrix and carrier-defined pricing regions are discussed in greater detail in the next section.

Pricing Regions

In some contracts, the carrier or shipper may request that the backup matrix be based on geographic areas smaller than entire states. A common format would involve most states being divided into two or three smaller regions within the state. Smaller pricing regions allow the carrier to provide more accurate rates and perhaps even reduce total transportation costs for the shipper.

The smaller zones are usually based on a group of contiguous zip codes. The map below illustrates how the state of Tennessee might be broken down into three pricing zones.

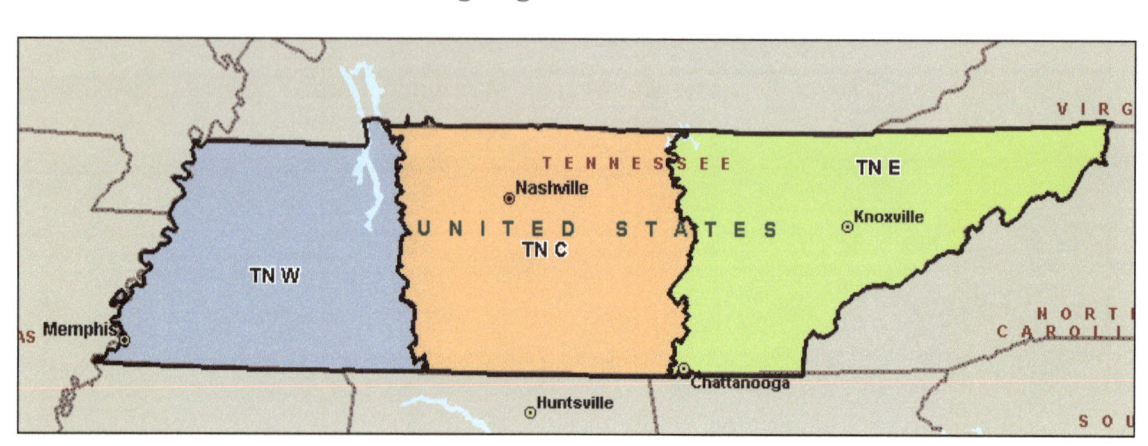

Pricing Regions for Tennessee

In this example, Tennessee is broken down into three zones, West (TN W), Central (TN C), and East (TN E). Each zone has distinct pricing characteristics that would dictate a unique price between each zone and most other pricing zones. For example, pricing from the three Tennessee zones as shown would likely be different to nearby states like Arkansas or Virginia. However, each of the three zones might have the same pricing to longer haul markets such as Oregon or Arizona.

Pricing zones such as these are valuable for most states, especially for large states such as Texas, California and Florida. The zones are rarely necessary for smaller states such as Massachusetts, Vermont, New Hampshire, or Rhode Island. These states are already so small that no distinct pricing characteristics exist from one part of the state to another.

Within a contract based on pricing zones, the specific geography for the zones is most often based on zip code definitions. The table below illustrates the zip codes as assigned to the three Tennessee pricing zones.[28]

5-digit Zip Assignments by Pricing Zone

Zone	Zips
TN E	37401 to 37450; 37601 to 37998; 37032; 38589 38541; 38542; 38543; 38579
TN C	37010 to 37057; 37059 to 37077; 37098 to 37133 37186 to 37301
TN W	37058; 37078; 37096; 37097; 38001 to 38392

Zip codes provide an excellent reference for rates since each load will be entered into the carrier's computer system with zip code information. The carrier's system can automatically identify the applicable rates based on the origin and destination zip codes.

Pricing zones can be inserted into a pricing matrix as primary pricing or for backup pricing purposes. The pricing matrix below includes the three example regions for the split of the state of Tennessee.

Matrix with Pricing Zones/Regions

Origin	AL	AR	AZ	CA	CO	CT	DC	DE	TNC	TNE	TNW
AL	$1.90	$1.50	$1.56	$1.24	$1.58	$1.56	$1.61	$1.56	$2.35	$2.25	$2.35
AR	$1.51	$1.90	$1.56	$1.30	$1.81	$1.54	$1.54	$1.54	$1.55	$1.45	$1.75
AZ	$1.04	$1.04	$1.95	$1.06	$1.60	$1.20	$1.18	$1.18	$1.18	$1.18	$1.18
CA	$1.10	$1.10	$1.91	$1.80	$1.64	$1.22	$1.20	$1.20	$1.15	$1.15	$1.15
CO	$0.98	$0.98	$1.31	$1.01	$2.16	$1.13	$1.13	$1.13	$1.12	$1.12	$1.12
CT	$0.92	$0.92	$1.32	$1.12	$1.51	$2.00	$1.51	$1.81	$1.15	$1.15	$1.12
DC	$1.01	$1.01	$1.37	$1.12	$1.51	$2.06	$2.69	$1.90	$1.15	$1.15	$1.12
DE	$0.95	$0.95	$1.37	$1.12	$1.51	$2.06	$1.90	$2.00	$1.15	$1.15	$1.12
FL	$0.96	$0.94	$1.31	$1.16	$1.34	$1.31	$1.31	$1.31	$1.05	$1.05	$1.00
GA	$1.52	$1.33	$1.48	$1.21	$1.56	$1.56	$1.56	$1.56	$1.90	$1.90	$1.40
IA	$1.52	$1.62	$1.58	$1.37	$2.21	$1.81	$1.81	$1.81	$1.45	$1.45	$1.38

Destination (Minimum Charge = $575.00)

The actual pricing to the Tennessee zones varies significantly based on the origin zone's proximity to Tennessee and each individual Tennessee zone. Notice that the pricing is the same for states such as Colorado and Arizona that are a great distance from Tennessee. Also notice that the pricing is much different on a zone basis for states that are near Tennessee such as Arkansas and Georgia. The pricing zones could be included in any other similar pricing formats as well.

---

[28] For simplification and space considerations, not all applicable zip codes are shown in this table.

! *Technical Tip* – Matrix Rate Lookup Spreadsheet Design

The pricing matrix can quickly be reformatted to allow the user to easily perform rate "lookups" using the powerful spreadsheet lookup functions known as "V" lookups and "H" lookups.[29] A carrier might use the "lookup" feature to automatically apply pricing to each lane in a bid based on the rates already established in an existing pricing matrix.

The previous pricing matrix has been reformatted below by adding the lookup "key" rows and columns to facilitate the lookup process. The lookup keys are needed because to look up a rate on the matrix is a two step process to locate the rate for an origin-destination pair.

"Lookup" Formula Design

	B	C	D	E	F	G	H	I	J	K
2		Destination	(Minimum Charge = $575.00)							
3			AL	AZ	CA	CO	CT	DE	FL	GA
4	Origin	Key	3	4	5	6	7	8	9	10
5	AL	3	$ 1.90	$ 1.56	$ 1.24	$ 1.58	$ 1.56	$ 1.56	$ 2.37	$ 1.81
6	AR	4	$ 1.51	$ 1.56	$ 1.30	$ 1.81	$ 1.54	$ 1.54	$ 1.87	$ 1.41
7	AZ	5	$ 1.04	$ 1.95	$ 1.06	$ 1.60	$ 1.20	$ 1.18	$ 1.30	$ 1.06
8	CA	6	$ 1.10	$ 1.91	$ 1.80	$ 1.64	$ 1.22	$ 1.20	$ 1.36	$ 1.12
9	CO	7	$ 0.98	$ 1.31	$ 1.01	$ 2.16	$ 1.13	$ 1.13	$ 1.32	$ 1.01
10	CT	8	$ 0.92	$ 1.32	$ 1.12	$ 1.51	$ 2.00	$ 1.81	$ 1.52	$ 0.91
11	DC	9	$ 1.01	$ 1.37	$ 1.12	$ 1.51	$ 2.06	$ 1.90	$ 1.58	$ 1.01
12	DE	10	$ 0.95	$ 1.37	$ 1.12	$ 1.51	$ 2.06	$ 2.00	$ 1.58	$ 0.96
13	FL	11	$ 0.96	$ 1.31	$ 1.16	$ 1.34	$ 1.31	$ 1.31	$ 2.02	$ 0.91
14	GA	12	$ 1.52	$ 1.48	$ 1.21	$ 1.56	$ 1.56	$ 1.56	$ 2.28	$ 1.90
15	IA	13	$ 1.52	$ 1.58	$ 1.37	$ 2.21	$ 1.81	$ 1.81	$ 1.99	$ 1.51

Row	Bid Response / Automatic Matrix Lookup Example:	Origin City	ST	Destination City	ST	Destination Lookup Key	Rate Per Mile
20		Miami	FL	Atlanta	GA	10	$ 0.91
21		Denver	CO	Orlando	FL	9	$ 1.32
22		Atlanta	GA	Phoenix	AZ	4	$ 1.48
23		Mobile	AL	Hartford	CT	7	$ 1.56

Lookup Formulas: =HLOOKUP(H23,$D$3:$K$4,2,FALSE)

=VLOOKUP(F23,$B$5:$K$15,I23)

The values in the key column represent the relative position of the destination state to the corresponding origin state column where the origin column is column 1. As an alternative to using the two step lookup key approach, the hlookup formula could be embedded within the vlookup formula.

---

[29] A "V" lookup is a "Vertical" lookup and an "H" lookup is a horizontal lookup.

CHAPTER 4: Core Concepts in One-Way Pricing

One-way pricing requires a thorough understanding of the cost behavior and operating characteristics of a trucking operation, along with an understanding of the dynamics of supply and demand in the trucking marketplace. This chapter and the next will explore all the key operating variables that must be evaluated in the development of a sound one-way pricing strategy. After defining the core concepts in one-way pricing, the chapter will review how these factors interact to impact a carrier's pricing strategy.

The critical factors in one-way pricing are displayed in the graphic below.

Critical Factors in One-Way Pricing

One-Way Pricing factors: Cycle Time, Capacity & Balance, Seasonal Activity, Stops & Unloading, Empty Miles, Length of Haul, Market Types.

All of the factors shown above must be taken into account in the development of profitable one-way pricing. Length of haul, empty miles, and market type influence virtually all one way pricing, while seasonality may become a major factor only in certain situations. Cycle time is universal to all loads and will be discussed first as a framework for introducing the other one-way pricing factors. Capacity and balance issues are unique to each carrier and, as a result, will impact the specific pricing strategy of each individual carrier differently.

Cycle Time

Cycle time represents the total time a tractor and driver spend involved in the pick-up and delivery of a single load. An understanding of cycle time and each of the underlying load events in the order cycle is critical to all elements of one-way pricing. The key events in the basic order cycle are illustrated in the graphic below.

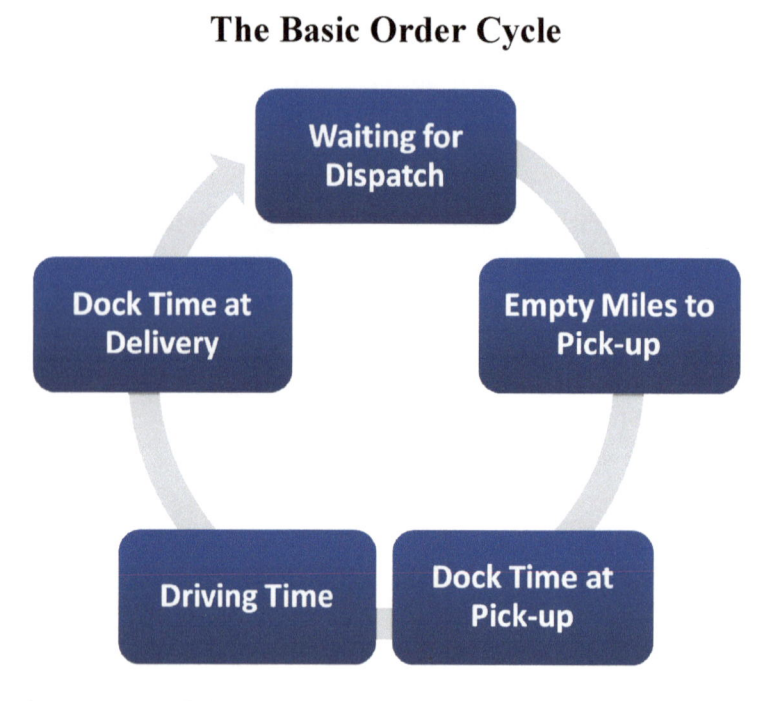

The Basic Order Cycle

- Waiting for Dispatch
- Empty Miles to Pick-up
- Dock Time at Pick-up
- Driving Time
- Dock Time at Delivery

An increase in the amount of time required to complete any segment in the load cycle will result in an increase in the cycle time and increase the possibility of lost utilization. Each segment of the basic order cycle is described in detail below.

Waiting for Dispatch (Dwell Time)

Dwell time is the time the tractor and driver spend after one load is completed and before the next load cycle begins. At the time the driver comes on duty for work, the carrier may not have a load available or perhaps the driver's dispatcher has not yet identified and selected the best load for the driver. The dwell time stage ends when the driver has been dispatched on a load and begins traveling to pick up the load at the customer's location.

Empty Miles to Pick-Up

The time the tractor and driver spend moving to the customer pick-up location is the first active step in the order cycle. The amount of time in this segment is dependent on the distance from the driver's beginning location to the customer's shipping facility. Ideally, the tractor and driver will be in close proximity to the customer's facility, minimizing the use of the driver's available on-duty work time and drive time in this non-revenue-producing activity.

Dock Time – Pick-Up

Pick-up dock time is the time spent by the tractor and driver at the customer's facility to pick up the load. The time needed to pick up a load will usually range from 30 minutes to 1 hour. However, in situations where the shipper does a live load of the truck, the pick-up can sometimes take much longer.[30] Some shippers may require that the driver arrive at a specific appointment time, which may add to the wait time for the driver during the load pick-up process. For example, if the load has a 10:00 am pick-up appointment and the driver arrives at 8:00 am, the driver will often be required to wait two hours then begin the pick-up process at the scheduled 10:00 am appointment time.[31]

Transit Time

Transit time for each load consists of two time components, drive time and break time. The drive time is simply the time the driver spends actually driving from the origin to the destination. The average miles per hour for the trip will usually increase as length of haul increases. For a 1,000 mile trip at 50 miles per hour, the drive time will be 20 hours.

Break time is the portion of the transit time when the driver is required to take a mandatory hours-of-service rest break. On most loads of approximately 500 miles or more, the driver will need to take one or more mandatory 10-hour breaks as part of the transit time. For a 1,000 mile trip, a driver who begins the load fully-rested (14 hours available to work and 11 hours available to drive) would be required to take at least one mandatory 10-hour break during the load. For this 1,000 mile load, 20 hours of drive time plus 10 hours of break time equates to a total minimum transit time of approximately 30 hours.

Dock Time – Delivery

Delivery dock time is the time spent by the tractor and driver at the customer's facility to deliver the load. The time needed to deliver a load will usually range from 30 minutes to 1 hour. However, in situations where the shipper performs a live unload of the inbound trailers, deliveries can take much longer.[32] If the receiving customer is busy unloading other loads, the driver may have to wait for an available slot to get unloaded. Some receivers have a "first-come first-served" receiving process where trucks are unloaded in the order they arrive. During busy periods, drivers can wait for several hours or longer to get unloaded.

---

[30] A live load is when the driver arrives with an empty trailer and backs up to the dock and waits while the shipper loads the trailer. Carriers often prefer to drop empty trailers at the customer location so that these trailers can be pre-loaded prior to the driver's arrival.

[31] The carrier's customer service representative may call to notify the shipper that the driver has arrived early in the hope that the shipper will begin the loading process early.

[32] A live unload is when the driver arrives with a load that is immediately unloaded by the shipper. The driver must wait for the shipper to complete the unloading. In some cases, the driver may actually assist in the unloading process.

Cycle Time Illustrations

As a general rule, the goal of the carrier is to minimize cycle times as much as possible. Efficient cycle times save the driver's valuable time and maximize asset utilization as well as revenues, profits, and the driver's income. The two examples below illustrate the expected cycle times for a 400 mile load and a 1,000 mile load.

Cycle Time – 400 Mile Load

The example below reflects a reasonable cycle time for a 400 mile load with a fully-rested driver. The cycle time includes the time associated with the 80 empty miles before the load. The load has a firm pick-up appointment of 2 pm on Day 1. The load has a generous delivery window of 6 am to 6 pm on Day 2. Delivery can be made at any time during the window based on the time that works best for the carrier. The cycle time assumes 1 hour of dock time during pick-up and 1 hour of dock time during delivery.

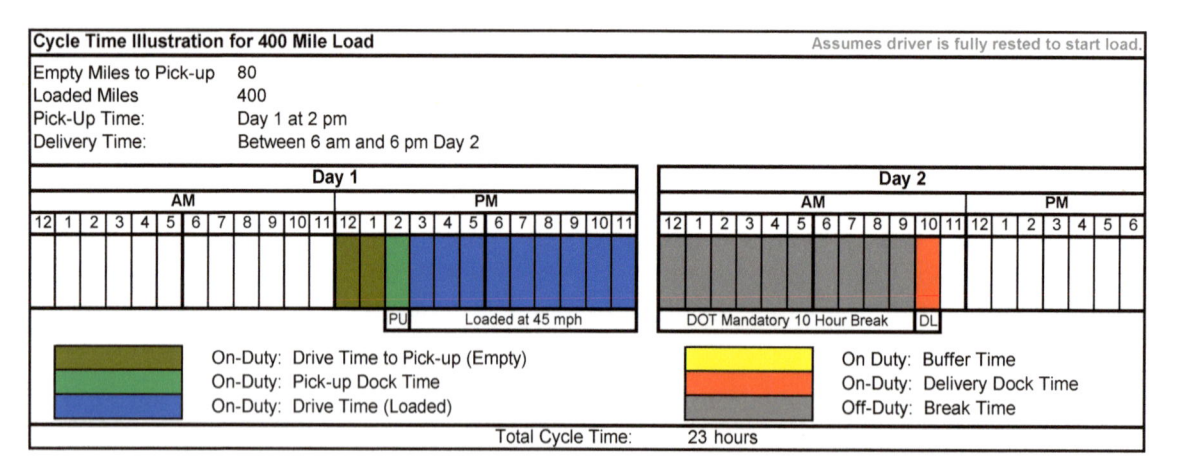

Cycle Time Illustration for 400 Mile Load		Assumes driver is fully rested to start load.
Empty Miles to Pick-up	80	
Loaded Miles	400	
Pick-Up Time:	Day 1 at 2 pm	
Delivery Time:	Between 6 am and 6 pm Day 2	

Legend:
- On-Duty: Drive Time to Pick-up (Empty)
- On-Duty: Pick-up Dock Time
- On-Duty: Drive Time (Loaded)
- On Duty: Buffer Time
- On-Duty: Delivery Dock Time
- Off-Duty: Break Time

Total Cycle Time: 23 hours

The drive time on Day 1 is based on an average speed of 45 miles per hour, resulting in approximately 9 hours of drive time. The 9 hours of loaded drive time plus the 2 hours of empty drive time total 11 hours. The 11 driving hours exhausts the driver's available hours and requires the driver to take a 10 hour break beginning at midnight on Day 2. After the required break, the driver is able to deliver the load at 10 am.

Cycle Time: 400 Mile Load		
Cycle Time Component	On-Duty Hours	Total Hours
Drive Time to Pick-up (Empty)	2.0	2.0
Pick-up Dock Time	1.0	1.0
Drive Time (Loaded)	9.0	9.0
Buffer Time	-	-
Delivery Dock Time	1.0	1.0
Break Time		10.0
Total Hours	13.0	23.0

The total cycle time for this load is 23 hours. The total time includes 13 on-duty hours and 10 hours of break time. The on-duty time is isolated to identify the portion of the driver's available hours for the entire week consumed by this load.

Cycle Time – 1,000 Mile Load

The example below reflects the normal cycle time for a 1,000 mile load with a fully-rested driver. The cycle time includes the time associated with the 35 empty miles before the load. The load has a pick-up window of between 1 am and 6 am on Day 1. The load has a generous delivery window of 6 am to 6 pm on Day 2. Wide pick-up and delivery windows allow the carrier significant flexibility in the scheduling of trucks and drivers, allowing for potential improvements in utilization and efficiency. The cycle time assumes 1 hour of dock time during pick-up and 1 hour of dock time during delivery.

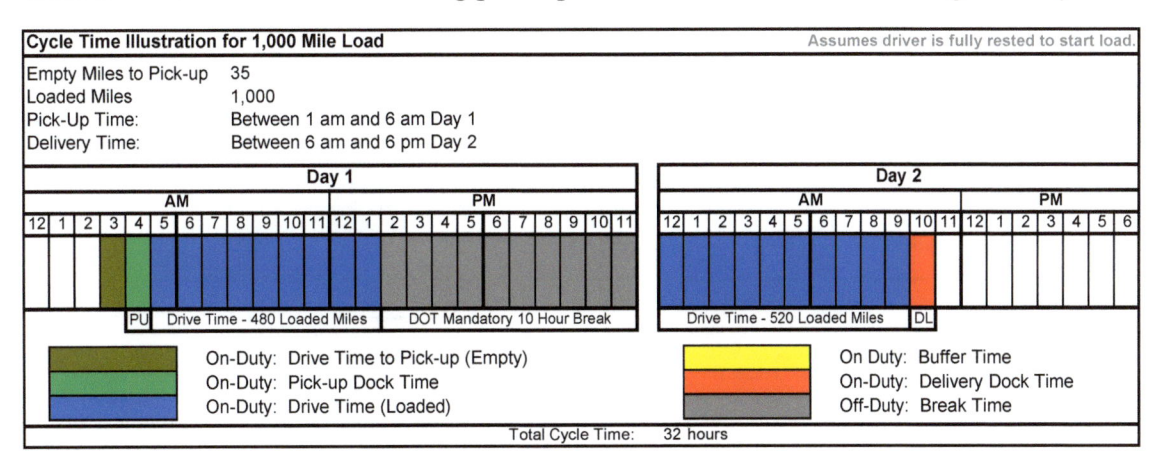

Cycle Time Illustration for 1,000 Mile Load	Assumes driver is fully rested to start load.
Empty Miles to Pick-up: 35	
Loaded Miles: 1,000	
Pick-Up Time: Between 1 am and 6 am Day 1	
Delivery Time: Between 6 am and 6 pm Day 2	

Day 1: PU, Drive Time - 480 Loaded Miles, DOT Mandatory 10 Hour Break
Day 2: Drive Time - 520 Loaded Miles, DL

- On-Duty: Drive Time to Pick-up (Empty)
- On-Duty: Pick-up Dock Time
- On-Duty: Drive Time (Loaded)
- On Duty: Buffer Time
- On-Duty: Delivery Dock Time
- Off-Duty: Break Time

Total Cycle Time: 32 hours

The drive time on Day 1 is based on an average speed of 53 miles per hour, resulting in approximately 9 hours of drive time. The driver is able to drive 480 of the 1,000 total miles before stopping for a meal. At that point, the driver decides to take a 10 hour rest break beginning at 2 pm on Day 2. After the required break time, the driver is able to begin driving again at 12 am on Day 2. After driving the final 520 miles, the load is delivered at 10 am. After delivery, the driver has utilized most of the available on-duty time for the day, so the driver must take another mandatory break soon after delivery.

Cycle Time: 1,000 Mile Load		
Cycle Time Component	On-Duty Hours	Total Hours
Drive Time to Pick-up (Empty)	1.0	1.0
Pick-up Dock Time	1.0	1.0
Drive Time (Loaded)	19.0	19.0
Buffer Time	-	-
Delivery Dock Time	1.0	1.0
Break Time		10.0

The total cycle time for this load is 32 hours, including 22 total on-duty hours and 10 hours of break time. The subsequent break that will occur shortly after this load is not included in the cycle time for this load. The cycle time ends once the load is delivered.

Buffer Time

Buffer time represents extra, unnecessary time the truck and driver must spend with a load. Buffer time is often caused by specific pick-up and delivery appointments that significantly conflict with the normal transit time for a load. Excess buffer time will cause the load cycle time to increase and often result in the loss of asset utilization.

The 400 mile load below is exactly the same as the 400 mile load in the previous example other than the pick-up and delivery times. In this example, the load has a firm pick-up appointment set at 2 pm on Day 1. The load also has a firm delivery appointment at 3 pm on Day 2. The cycle time chart below illustrates the impact of these seemingly minor time changes.

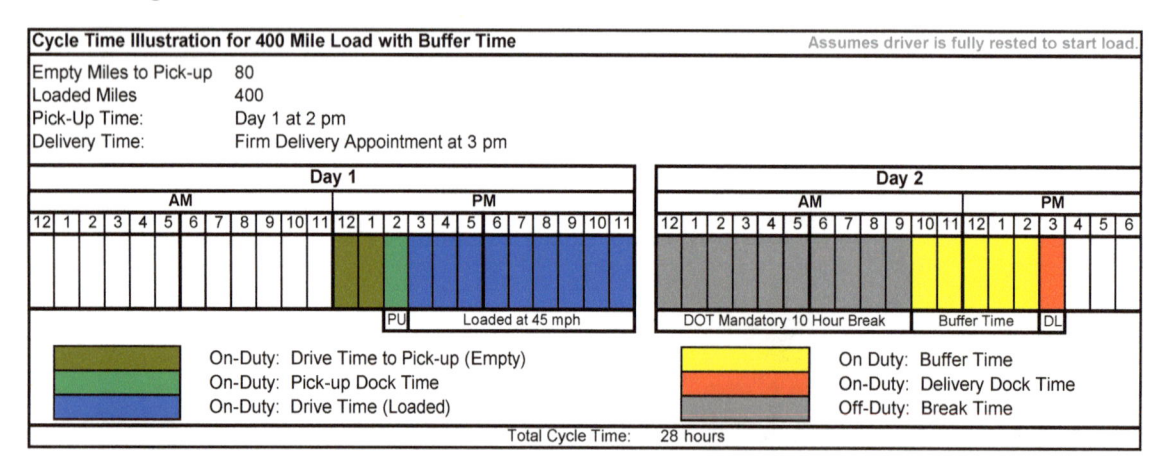

Cycle Time Illustration for 400 Mile Load with Buffer Time	Assumes driver is fully rested to start load.
Empty Miles to Pick-up: 80	
Loaded Miles: 400	
Pick-Up Time: Day 1 at 2 pm	
Delivery Time: Firm Delivery Appointment at 3 pm	

On-Duty: Drive Time to Pick-up (Empty)
On-Duty: Pick-up Dock Time
On-Duty: Drive Time (Loaded)
On Duty: Buffer Time
On-Duty: Delivery Dock Time
Off-Duty: Break Time

Total Cycle Time: 28 hours

The expected drive time for the load is the same at 9 hours. However, since the driver cannot deliver the load until 3 pm, 5 hours of buffer time are created. The 5 hours of buffer time reduce the driver's potential productivity and utilization for the day and for the week.

Cycle Time: 400 Mile Load with Buffer Time		
Cycle Time Component	On-Duty Hours	Total Hours
Drive Time to Pick-up (Empty)	2.0	2.0
Pick-up Dock Time	1.0	1.0
Drive Time (Loaded)	9.0	9.0
Buffer Time	5.0	5.0
Delivery Dock Time	1.0	1.0
Break Time		10.0
Total Hours	18.0	28.0

The 5 hours of buffer time increases the cycle time for the trip from 23 hours to 28 hours. The on-duty hours also increase from 13 hours to 18 hours. This increase in cycle time has a potentially devastating effect on the carrier's utilization, productivity and service. Carrier customer service representatives are responsible for negotiating suitable appointment times with shippers to reduce buffer time as much as possible.

Buffer Time and Lost Utilization. Excess buffer time has a significant financial impact on both the carrier and the driver. When buffer time occurs, carriers lose the opportunity to generate revenues and drivers lose the opportunity to earn income.[33] The impact to both the carrier and the driver is seen in terms of lost utilization.

Hours of service regulations limit drivers to 60 hours of driving over a 7 day period. As a result, the average driver is able to engage in productive activities such as driving and dock time for approximately 50 to 60 hours per week.[34] Based on the 400 mile load example with various buffer times, the table below illustrates the potential utilization for a driver that achieves an average on-duty time of 60 hours per week.

Buffer Time and Potential Utilization

Cycle Time Component	Cycle Time: 400 Mile Load with Buffer Time								
	-	1.0	2.0	3.0	4.0	5.0	6.0	7.0	8.0
Drive Time to Pick-up (Empty)	2.0	2.0	2.0	2.0	2.0	2.0	2.0	2.0	2.0
Pick-up Dock Time	1.0	1.0	1.0	1.0	1.0	1.0	1.0	1.0	1.0
Drive Time (Loaded)	9.0	9.0	9.0	9.0	9.0	9.0	9.0	9.0	9.0
Buffer Time	-	1.0	2.0	3.0	4.0	5.0	6.0	7.0	8.0
Delivery Dock Time	1.0	1.0	1.0	1.0	1.0	1.0	1.0	1.0	1.0
On-Duty Cycle Time	13.0	14.0	15.0	16.0	17.0	18.0	19.0	20.0	21.0
Weekly On-Duty Hours	60.0	60.0	60.0	60.0	60.0	60.0	60.0	60.0	60.0
Loads per Week (Activity)	4.6	4.3	4.0	3.8	3.5	3.3	3.2	3.0	2.9
Total Miles Per Load	480	480	480	480	480	480	480	480	480
Weekly Utilization	**2,215**	**2,057**	**1,920**	**1,800**	**1,694**	**1,600**	**1,516**	**1,440**	**1,371**

While the potential utilization levels shown in this example are simplified and theoretical, the utilizations shown accurately reflect the truck's relative productivity level under each buffer time scenario as measured by potential weekly utilization.

Another relative productivity measure for each buffer time scenario is miles per hour. The table below compares the miles per hour for each of the buffer time scenarios.

Activity	Miles Per Hour: 400 Mile Load with Buffer Time								
	-	1.0	2.0	3.0	4.0	5.0	6.0	7.0	8.0
On-Duty Cycle Time	13.0	14.0	15.0	16.0	17.0	18.0	19.0	20.0	21.0
Total Miles Per Load	480	480	480	480	480	480	480	480	480
Miles Per Hour (On-Duty Hours)	**36.9**	**34.3**	**32.0**	**30.0**	**28.2**	**26.7**	**25.3**	**24.0**	**22.9**

Just like utilization, the effective miles per hour declines as buffer time increases, reducing the tractor's relative productivity level.

---

[33] The primary source of income for a driver is per-mile pay. Any non-productive time represents a lost income opportunity.
[34] On average, a driver can only utilize a reasonable portion of the 14 hours of on-duty time each day, usually 10 to 12 hours per day or 50 to 60 hours per week.

The graph below further illustrates the relationship between cycle time and expected weekly utilization levels.

Cycle Time Impact on Utilization

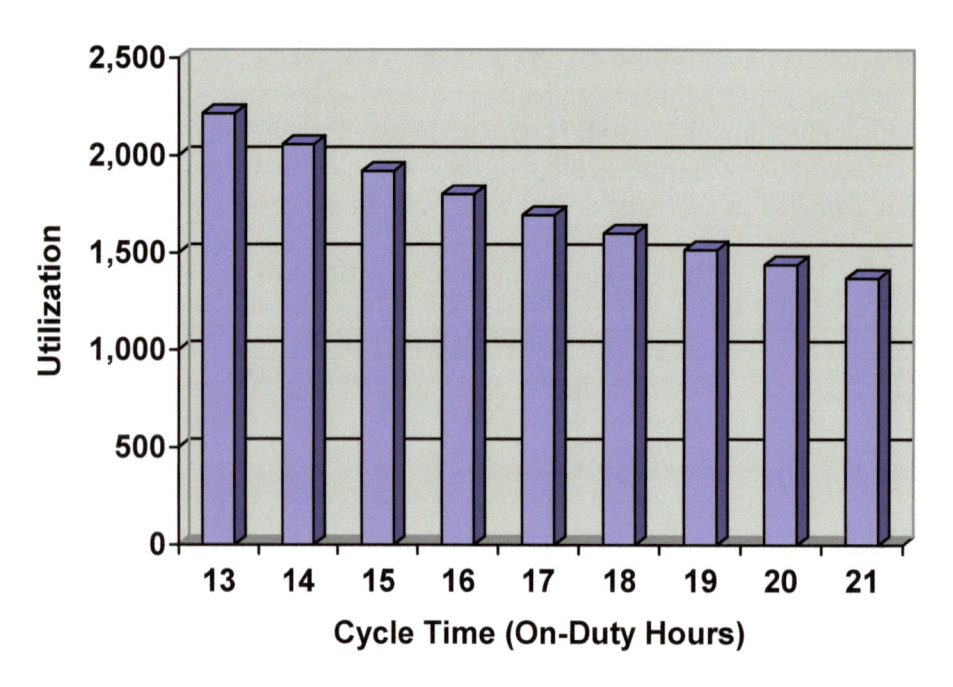

Generally speaking, one of a carrier's main goals is to maximize utilization. Effective management of cycle times is a key component in utilization maximization. The carrier's management team will implement aggressive strategies that reduce dock times, eliminate buffer time, and minimize transit times. However, quality carriers will not implement any cycle time improvement policies that introduce any type of safety risk. Examples of risky safety policies that potentially increase asset utilization include violating driver hours of service regulations or simply driving at unsafe speeds.

Driver Income. Driver income is also affected by excessive cycle times and buffer times. The table below depicts a driver's estimated income levels from mileage pay at the projected utilization levels for the buffer time scenarios.

	\multicolumn{9}{c}{Driver Income Levels: 400 Mile Load with Buffer Time}
	\multicolumn{9}{c}{Hours of Buffer Time}
Activity	-	1.0	2.0	3.0	4.0	5.0	6.0	7.0	8.0
Expected Utilization	2,215	2,057	1,920	1,800	1,694	1,600	1,516	1,440	1,371
Pay Rate Per Mile	$ 0.38	$ 0.38	$ 0.38	$ 0.38	$ 0.38	$ 0.38	$ 0.38	$ 0.38	$ 0.38
Gross Income Per Week	$ 842	$ 782	$ 730	$ 684	$ 644	$ 608	$ 576	$ 547	$ 521
Gross Income Per Year (000)	$ 44	$ 41	$ 38	$ 36	$ 33	$ 32	$ 30	$ 28	$ 27

At some level of inadequate utilization, the driver will become dissatisfied with his income level. A dissatisfied driver will either perform poorly or quit his driving job altogether, causing additional driver turnover problems for the carrier.

Dwell Time

Dwell time represents the time the tractor and driver spend waiting from one load to the next. A dwell time period may include a combination of on-duty time and break time, the most critical of which is inactive on-duty time. A reasonable amount of dwell time between loads is normal and virtually impossible to prevent. However, the carrier must work diligently to maintain a network of available loads in order to minimize dwell time.

The chart below illustrates how dwell time fits into the driver's schedule from one load to the next.

Dwell Time Illustration

The driver experiences 4 hours of dwell time on Day 2 from 11 am to 3 pm. During the dwell time period, the carrier's customer service and network management team is likely searching for a load for this driver or deciding which available load is the best fit for the driver. It is also possible that the next load was identified well in advance but has a firm 3 pm pick-up appointment that cannot be changed. In this case, the driver must simply wait until 3 pm to pick up the load.

Like buffer time, excess dwell time can have a significant impact on utilization. After completion of the previous load, the goal of the carrier is to minimize dwell time by planning and dispatching the driver on his next load as soon as possible. In fact, some carriers may plan load assignments in advance and have the driver's next load already selected and assigned before the driver even completes his current load.

Length of Haul (LOH)

The average length of haul is simply the average number of billed miles for a given group of loads. Average length of haul is a very important measurement for any carrier. The average length of haul is usually computed for all loads over a specific period of time using the formula and example below.[35]

$$\frac{\text{Average}}{\text{Length of Haul}} = \frac{\text{Total Billed Miles}}{\text{Number of Loads}} = \frac{677{,}206 \text{ miles}}{1{,}142 \text{ loads}} = 593 \text{ miles}$$

Average length of haul levels are different from carrier to carrier and network to network. An individual carrier's length of haul is a function of the lanes and load volumes within the unique network of customers it serves. As a result, each individual carrier must identify strategies and execute policies and procedures that match each unique length of haul with the appropriate revenue streams.

Length of haul is a critical element of a utilization maximization and network optimization strategy, especially for carriers whose business model is based on high utilization. The basic goal is not to purely maximize length of haul, but to optimize the mix of length of haul, utilization, empty miles, and loaded revenue per mile. The focus of the carrier is on achieving the utilization level that is appropriate for the underlying length of haul. At the same time, the carrier must establish pricing levels that generate a revenue stream appropriate for the expected average length of haul and utilization levels.

A longer length of haul allows carriers to increase utilization in two ways. The first benefit of a longer length of haul is that the average velocity (miles per hour) of the tractor will most likely be higher as length of haul increases, allowing for greater potential utilization. The second benefit is an overall reduction in the proportion of the driver's time that is spent in non-driving activities such as dock time and dwell time. With a longer length of haul, the driver spends less time stopping and starting to pick up and deliver loads and spends more time driving. The sections that follow explain these relationships in greater detail.

Length of Haul and Cost Per Mile

All other things being equal, the longer the length of haul, the lower the cost per mile will be for a load. The first reason for this efficiency is associated with the higher utilization and economies of scale created by longer length of haul loads. The second reason for the cost efficiency is the result of transaction-based per-load costs being spread over a larger number of billed miles.[36]

---

[35] Average length of haul may also be computed based on loaded miles as well as billed miles.
[36] These costs relationships are discussed in detail in Chapter 2.

Economies of Scale

The first reason for the cost efficiency of length of haul is simple economies of scale. As a general rule, the greater the length of haul, the higher the utilization level will be. As a result, the carrier's fixed costs, including tractors, trailers and general overhead, are spread over a greater number of miles, thereby reducing the overall cost per mile. Direct variable costs such as fuel, maintenance and driver pay will remain constant on a per-mile basis, regardless of utilization. Based on the cost assumptions from a previous chapter, the table below illustrates the decline in cost per mile as utilization increases.

Cost Per Mile as Utilization Increases

Utilization	Variable Cost Per Mile	Weekly Variable Cost	Weekly Fixed Cost	Fixed Cost Per Mile	Total Cost	Total Cost Per Mile
1,400	$ 1.06	$ 1,484.00	$ 576.92	$ 0.412	$ 2,061	$ 1.472
1,500	$ 1.06	$ 1,590.00	$ 576.92	$ 0.385	$ 2,167	$ 1.445
1,600	$ 1.06	$ 1,696.00	$ 576.92	$ 0.361	$ 2,273	$ 1.421
1,700	$ 1.06	$ 1,802.00	$ 576.92	$ 0.339	$ 2,379	$ 1.399
1,800	$ 1.06	$ 1,908.00	$ 576.92	$ 0.321	$ 2,485	$ 1.381
1,900	$ 1.06	$ 2,014.00	$ 576.92	$ 0.304	$ 2,591	$ 1.364
2,000	$ 1.06	$ 2,120.00	$ 576.92	$ 0.288	$ 2,697	$ 1.348
2,100	$ 1.06	$ 2,226.00	$ 576.92	$ 0.275	$ 2,803	$ 1.335
2,200	$ 1.06	$ 2,332.00	$ 576.92	$ 0.262	$ 2,909	$ 1.322
2,300	$ 1.06	$ 2,438.00	$ 576.92	$ 0.251	$ 3,015	$ 1.311
2,400	$ 1.06	$ 2,544.00	$ 576.92	$ 0.240	$ 3,121	$ 1.300
2,500	$ 1.06	$ 2,650.00	$ 576.92	$ 0.231	$ 3,227	$ 1.291
2,600	$ 1.06	$ 2,756.00	$ 576.92	$ 0.222	$ 3,333	$ 1.282
2,700	$ 1.06	$ 2,862.00	$ 576.92	$ 0.214	$ 3,439	$ 1.274
2,800	$ 1.06	$ 2,968.00	$ 576.92	$ 0.206	$ 3,545	$ 1.266

The incremental reduction in cost per mile diminishes at higher utilization levels. This occurs for two reasons. First, at higher utilization levels, variable costs become a larger percentage of total cost, thereby reducing the impact of the fixed cost efficiencies. Second, as utilization increases, the cost efficiency created by each incremental mile of utilization is relatively less significant on a percentage basis. Since a longer length of haul generally leads to higher utilization, a portion of these utilization cost efficiencies are also attributable to the effects of a longer length of haul.

While a longer length of haul does lead to higher utilization, the goal of every carrier is not simply to maximize length of haul. With proper pricing and execution, carriers can make substantial profits serving networks and customers with any length of haul level. The importance of length of haul is ultimately in its relationship to the carrier's pricing decision. The revenue and price for any load must be appropriate for the length of haul of the specific trip and the expected productivity (utilization / cycle time) the driver and tractor will experience while serving the load.

The impact of length of haul on utilization also has a diminishing return as length of haul increases. For example, an increase in length of haul from 600 to 800 miles (a 200 mile increase) will often translate into a significant increase in utilization. However, a 200 mile increase from 1,000 to 1,200 miles will have less upward impact on utilization.

Per Load Transaction & Event Costs

A second reason for the cost and utilization efficiency of length of haul is related to the various events that occur for every load, regardless of length of haul. These events include dwell time, empty miles, and dock time. Longer length of haul loads offer more billed miles to absorb these per-load fixed costs. In addition, longer length of haul loads allow the driver to spend a larger percentage of available work time in productive driving time as opposed to non-productive activities such as dwell time and dock time.

To illustrate this point, consider a driver that averages 56 hours of on-duty time per week. The table below illustrates how the driver will utilize this on-duty time based on average length of haul levels of 400 miles, 800 miles, and 1,200 miles.

Estimated Utilization based on Average Length of Haul	Average Length of Haul		
	400	800	1,200
Loaded Driving:			
Length of Haul	400	800	1,200
Miles Per Hour	50	53	56
Drive Time Per Load (hrs)	8.0	15.1	21.4
Empty Miles Per Load	75	75	75
Per Load Events:			
Drive Time for Empty Miles	2.0	2.0	2.0
Pick-up Dock Time	0.5	0.5	0.5
Delivery Dock Time	0.5	0.5	0.5
Dwell Time Per Load (On-Duty)	2.0	2.0	2.0
Total Non-driving Hours per Load	5.0	5.0	5.0
Total Cycle Time Per Load	13.0	20.1	26.4
Driver On-duty Hours (Weekly)	56.0	56.0	56.0
Expected Trips Per Week	4.31	2.79	2.12
Expected Utilization:			
Loaded Miles	1,723	2,229	2,543
Empty Miles	323	209	159
Total Utilization	**2,046**	**2,438**	**2,702**

The above analysis assumes that the driver spends 5.0 hours per load in activities such as driving empty miles, dock time, and dwell time. These events will all occur on practically every load regardless of the actual length of haul. Expected utilization increases as length of haul increases because a larger proportion of the driver's time is spent driving instead of in these non-revenue producing events.

Based on this same example, the table below illustrates the proportion of the driver's on-duty time associated with each activity.

Distribution of Work Time	Hours by Work Type Average Length of Haul			% of On-duty Hours Average Length of Haul		
Time Segment/Work Type	400	800	1,200	400	800	1,200
Drive Time for Loaded Miles	34.5	42.1	45.4	61.5%	75.1%	81.1%
Drive Time for Empty Miles	8.6	5.6	4.2	15.4%	10.0%	7.6%
Pick-up Dock Time	2.2	1.4	1.1	3.8%	2.5%	1.9%
Delivery Dock Time	2.2	1.4	1.1	3.8%	2.5%	1.9%
Dwell Time (On-duty)	8.6	5.6	4.2	15.4%	10.0%	7.6%
Total On-duty Hours	56.0	56.0	56.0	100.0%	100.0%	100.0%

At a 400 mile length of haul, the driver spends 61.5 % of available on-duty time driving loaded miles. At a 1,200 mile length of the haul, the driver spends 81.1% of available on-duty time driving loaded miles.[37] The graph below also illustrates how a driver's time is distributed between driving and other activity as length of haul increases.

Consumption of On-Duty Time

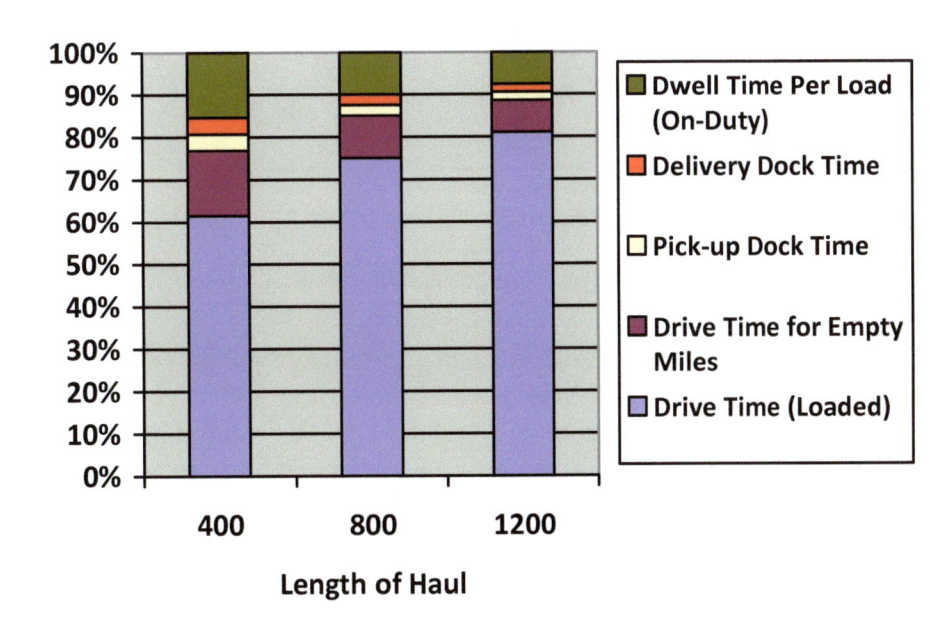

Clearly, all other things being equal, as length of haul increases, utilization increases. However, many other factors will also influence utilization levels. Carriers must also manage other key variables such as buffer times, pick-up and delivery windows, dock times, driver availability, and network balance. If these variables are not managed effectively, utilization will suffer regardless of the length of haul.

---

[37] These percentages are estimated based on the theoretical model. Actual percentages will vary slightly from network to network.

Diminishing Effect of Length of Haul on Cost Per Mile

As has been shown, a basic assumption of one-way pricing is that as length of haul increases, cost per mile decreases. An important extended concept is that this cost per mile efficiency offers diminishing returns as the length of haul continues to increase. The graph below reflects the basic cost per mile curve as length of haul increases.

Length of Haul and Cost Per Mile

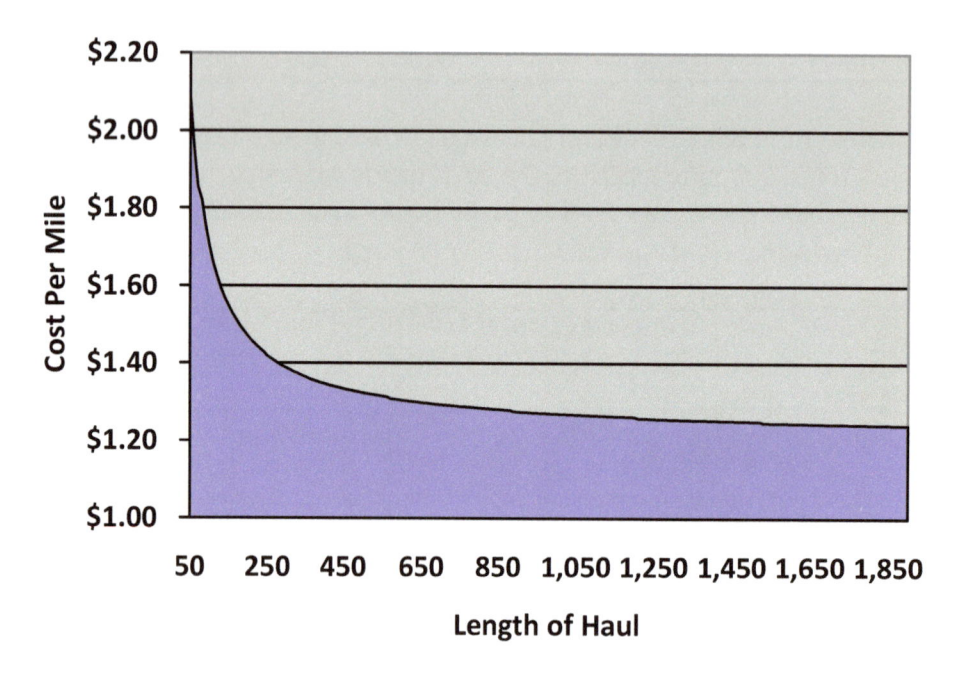

Notice that the cost per mile line flattens out at approximately the 1,000 mile length of haul level. At these high length of haul levels, almost all cost efficiencies have been absorbed by the longer length of haul. Beyond the 1,000 to 1,200 mile length of haul level, very little additional cost efficiencies are experienced through any further increase in the length of haul.

The cost and utilization efficiencies of length of haul shown here are just one key element in the overall development of a one-way pricing strategy. Many other internal and external factors must also be taken into account before setting a particular one-way price. However, all other factors being equal, longer length of haul loads will generally have a lower price per mile than shorter length of haul loads.

Other Length of Haul Statistics

The average length of haul measurement provides a simple statistic to represent the type of loads in a carrier's network. However, focusing only on average length of haul without a more detailed understanding of the underlying network could cause a carrier to fail to identify many key problems and opportunities.

Carriers should also evaluate the distribution of loads over different length of haul levels to determine the specific length of haul levels that make up the overall average length of haul. Consider the chart below that illustrates the average length of haul for three different truckload carriers. For simplification, the analysis assumes each carrier serves only 12 lanes.

Length of Haul (LOH) Distribution Analysis by Carrier

	Carrier A			Carrier B			Carrier C		
Lane:	LOH	Loads	Total Miles	LOH	Loads	Total Miles	LOH	Loads	Total Miles
Lane 1	380	148	56,240	245	41	10,045	115	73	8,395
Lane 2	392	281	110,152	268	37	9,916	156	256	39,936
Lane 3	401	85	34,085	346	138	47,748	159	210	33,390
Lane 4	421	110	46,310	385	77	29,645	178	312	55,536
Lane 5	445	188	83,660	440	103	45,320	225	90	20,250
Lane 6	456	224	102,144	442	95	41,990	345	219	75,555
Lane 7	467	252	117,684	461	90	41,490	378	77	29,106
Lane 8	471	324	152,604	491	210	103,110	455	47	21,385
Lane 9	518	84	43,512	524	218	114,232	687	109	74,883
Lane 10	554	64	35,456	545	77	41,965	729	389	283,581
Lane 11	571	120	68,520	621	122	75,762	864	145	125,280
Lane 12	587	275	161,425	714	28	19,992	977	272	265,744
Avg/Totals:	470	2,155	1,011,792	470	1,236	581,215	470	2,199	1,033,041

Average LOH	470	470	470
Shortest Lane	380	245	115
Longest Lane	587	714	977
LOH Range	207	469	862

While each carrier has an average length of haul of 470 miles, each carrier has a very unique distribution of activity over of a variety of length of haul levels. Carrier A has a length of haul range of only 207 miles while Carrier C has a much wider length of haul range of 862 miles. The formula for the length of haul range is shown below.

Length of Haul Range = LOH for Longest Lane - LOH for Shortest Lane

The length of haul range indicates the degree to which the carrier engages in a wide variety of length of haul activity. Carrier A serves only loads between 300 and 600 miles while Carrier C serves both very short loads under 200 miles and relatively long loads over 800 miles. Carrier B serves a wider range of loads, but avoids loads less than 200 miles and over 800 miles.

The graph below reflects the relative frequency distribution of loads over various length of haul groups for Carrier A.

Load Count by Length of Haul – Carrier A

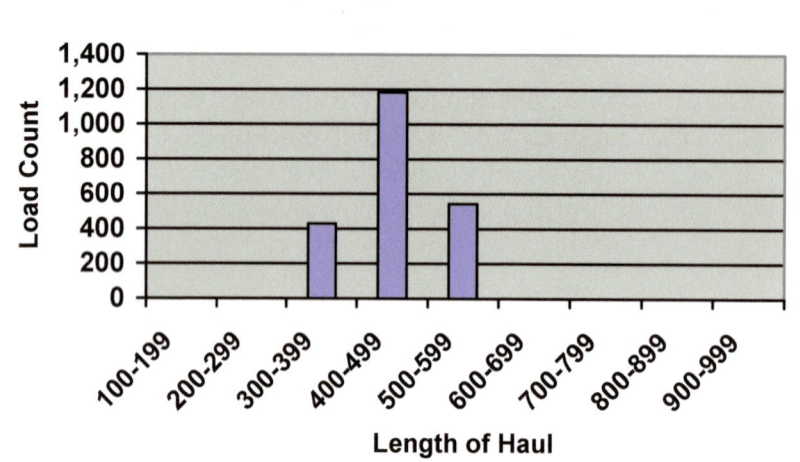

Notice that Carrier A only operates loads between 300 and 600 miles. As a result, the 470 mile average length of haul is very indicative of the type of freight served by this carrier.

The graph below reflects the relative frequency distribution of loads over various length of haul groups for Carrier B.

Load Count by Length of Haul – Carrier B

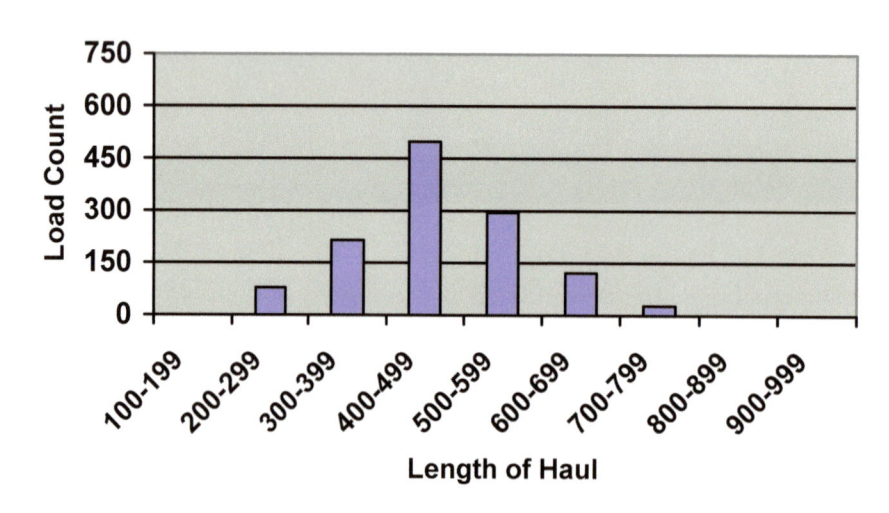

Notice that Carrier B operates loads between 200 and 800 miles, with the majority of loads ranging from 300 to 600 miles. The average length of haul of 470 miles for Carrier B is a fairly accurate reflection of the type of freight served by the carrier, but the average length of haul statistic does not tell the entire story of the carrier's network.

The graph below reflects the frequency distribution of loads over various length of haul groups for Carrier C.

Load Count by Length of Haul – Carrier C

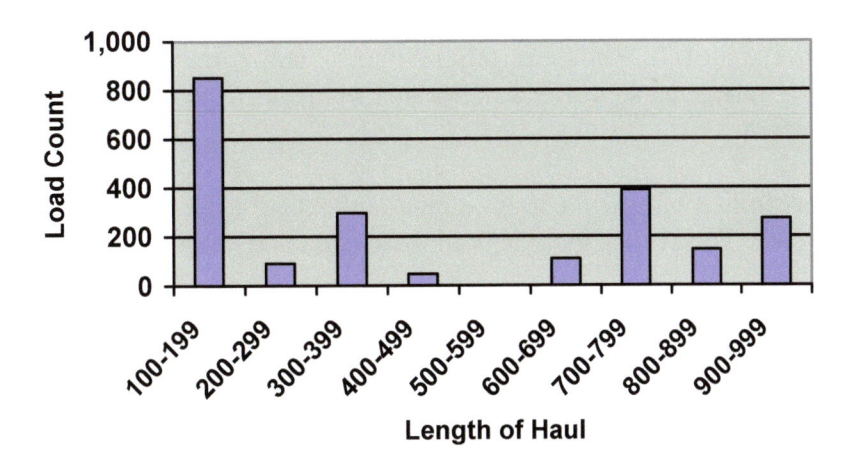

Notice that the load activity for Carrier C is spread out among a variety of length of haul levels. Despite the fact that Carrier C has an average length of haul of 470 miles, the carrier's largest mileage group is between 100 and 199 miles. Very little of the carrier's activity is between 400 and 599 miles, so the 470 mile length of haul, while accurate, is not a good indication of the type of freight served by Carrier C. The very short lanes and the very long lanes average out at 470 miles, but the 470 mile average length of haul is not meaningful in the case of this carrier's network. As illustrated here, just a few long length of haul loads can skew the average length of haul for a carrier's network.

Because the three carriers in this example have the same average length of haul, the general expectation would be that the carriers would also have very similar utilization levels and loaded revenue per mile levels. However, after a deeper analysis of the distribution of length of haul activity for each carrier, it is reasonable to expect that each carrier will have unique utilization and loaded revenue per mile levels.

In addition to average length of haul, the carrier can also focus length of haul analysis on other statistical measures such as the median and standard deviation. The median would represent the length of haul where half the carrier's loads are less than the median length of haul and half are higher than the median length of haul. The standard deviation of length of haul measures the dispersion of length of haul activity similar to the range and graphical analysis shown above. In the previous example, Carrier A would have the lowest standard deviation and Carrier C would have the highest standard deviation.

Empty Miles and Net Revenue Per Mile

Empty miles represent a major challenge and a major cost for all truckload carriers. Empty miles occur as a truck moves from the destination point of one load to the origin point of the next load. While customers pay the carrier for billed miles, customers do not pay for the empty miles.[38] While a certain number of empty miles are unavoidable, excessive empty miles can seriously deteriorate the carrier's net revenue per mile and overall profitability.

Net revenue per mile is simply the total linehaul revenue for the load divided by the total miles for the load. Total miles include both the loaded and empty miles associated with the load.

$$\text{Net Revenue Per Mile} = \frac{\text{Linehaul Revenue}}{\text{Loaded Miles} + \text{Empty Miles}}$$

Empty miles are a major operating risk for every carrier. Prior to establishing pricing, carriers must estimate the amount of empty miles per load that will be required to supply capacity to a customer location. The example below shows the net revenue per mile scenarios for a 750 mile load priced at $1.70 per mile.

Impact of Empty Miles on Net Revenue Per Mile

Length of Haul (Billed Miles)	750	Pricing Design:	
Loaded Rate Per Mile	x $ 1.70	Expected Empty Miles	80
Linehaul Revenue	= $1,275.00	Expected Net Revenue Per Mile	$ 1.54

| Total Trip Miles ||| Empty Mile % | Linehaul Revenue | Revenue Per Mile ||
Empty Miles	Loaded Miles	Total Miles			Loaded	Net
0	750	750	0.0%	$ 1,275	$ 1.70	$ 1.70
20	750	770	2.6%	$ 1,275	$ 1.70	$ 1.66
40	750	790	5.1%	$ 1,275	$ 1.70	$ 1.61
60	750	810	7.4%	$ 1,275	$ 1.70	$ 1.57
80	**750**	**830**	**9.6%**	**$ 1,275**	**$ 1.70**	**$ 1.54**
100	750	850	11.8%	$ 1,275	$ 1.70	$ 1.50
120	750	870	13.8%	$ 1,275	$ 1.70	$ 1.47
140	750	890	15.7%	$ 1,275	$ 1.70	$ 1.43
160	750	910	17.6%	$ 1,275	$ 1.70	$ 1.40
180	750	930	19.4%	$ 1,275	$ 1.70	$ 1.37
200	750	950	21.1%	$ 1,275	$ 1.70	$ 1.34
220	750	970	22.7%	$ 1,275	$ 1.70	$ 1.31
240	750	990	24.2%	$ 1,275	$ 1.70	$ 1.29
260	750	1,010	25.7%	$ 1,275	$ 1.70	$ 1.26
280	750	1,030	27.2%	$ 1,275	$ 1.70	$ 1.24
300	750	1,050	28.6%	$ 1,275	$ 1.70	$ 1.21

---

[38] In rare circumstances, shippers may agree to pay for empty miles. The most common reason a shipper would agree to pay for empty miles is during peak shipping periods when large amounts of capacity are needed to meet above average transportation demands.

Based on the previous table, the graph below illustrates the impact of increasing empty miles on net revenue per mile. The planned empty mile expectation of 80 miles per load is highlighted.

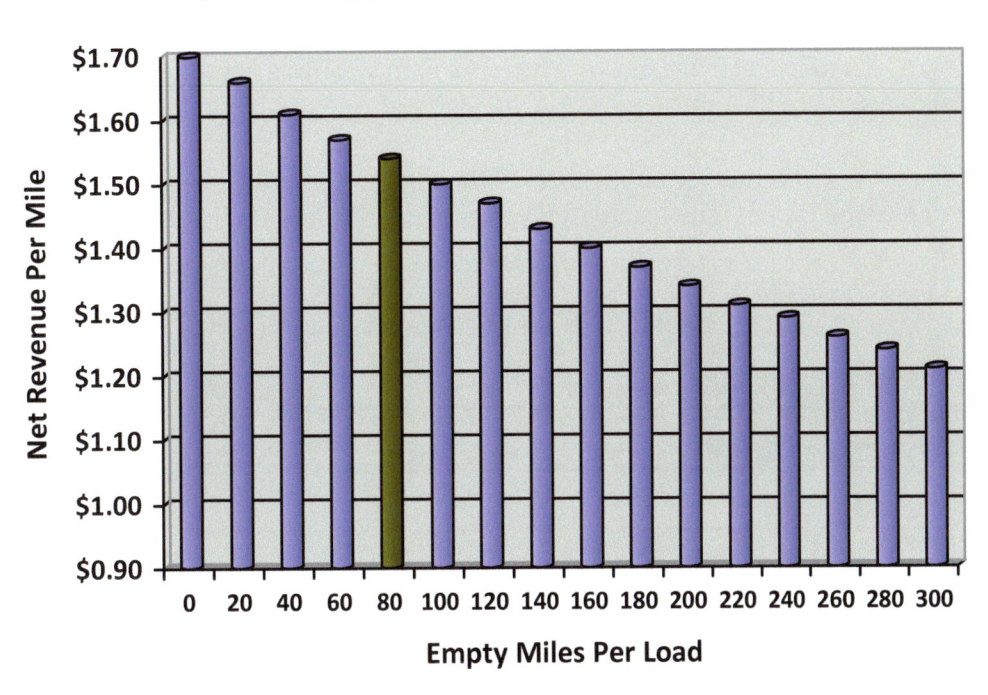

Impact of Empty Miles on Net Revenue Per Mile

If the carrier is able to manage the network efficiently, empty miles will be minimized and net revenue per mile and profits will be maximized. However, if excess empty miles are incurred, net revenue per mile and profits will be much lower than planned.

Accessorial Revenues and Revenue Per Mile. Accessorial revenues such as unloading, stop charges, and fuel surcharges are usually not included in the total revenue for revenue per mile analysis calculations. Accessorial revenues such as stop charges and unloading can skew revenue per mile figures because these revenue items occur on a per-event or per-load basis. For this reason, accessorial revenues should usually be excluded from any revenue per mile information used for analysis or comparison purposes.

Assigning Empty Miles to Load Activity

Empty miles occur both before and after almost every load. For most analysis purposes, the empty miles before a load are associated with the load for net revenue per mile calculations. It would also be correct for certain types of analysis to apply 50% of the empty miles before the load and 50% of the empty miles after the load as the empty miles for the load. There are also situations where the empty miles after the load would be considered instead of the empty miles before the load.

The table below illustrates the application of the different approaches for applying empty miles to a 680 mile load. The load had 88 empty miles before the load and 140 empty miles after the load.

Empty Mile Application Scenarios

Allocation of Empty Miles	Actual Load Events	100% Empty Before		50% Before 50% After		100% Empty After	
Allocation of Empty Miles							
Loaded Miles	680						
Empty Miles Before Pick-up	88	100%	88.0	50%	44.0	0%	-
Empty Miles After Delivery	140	0%	-	50%	70.0	100%	140.0
Allocated Empty Miles			88.0		114.0		140.0
Allocation Method Comparison							
Loaded Miles			680.0		680.0		680.0
Allocated Empty Miles			88.0		114.0		140.0
Total Miles			768.0		794.0		820.0
Empty Miles Percentage			11.5%		14.4%		17.1%
Impact on Net Revenue Per Mile							
Linehaul Revenue	$ 1,169.60		$ 1,169.60		$ 1,169.60		$ 1,169.60
Loaded Revenue Per Mile	$ 1.72		$ 1.72		$ 1.72		$ 1.72
Net Revenue Per Mile			$ 1.52		$ 1.47		$ 1.43

Depending on the nature of the analysis, any of the empty mile application methods could be used. Notice that the allocation method has a significant impact on the empty mile percentage and the net revenue per mile at the load level. However, regardless of how empty miles are assigned at the load level, the total empty miles and empty mile percentage for the carrier network remain constant. The carrier's overall net revenue per mile remains constant as well.

Profitability Optimization

Critical Profitability Factors

In order to create and sustain a profitable one-way operation, carriers must optimize the three critical profitability factors of asset utilization, loaded revenue per mile, and the empty mile percentage. Different carriers with different types of operations can all develop a profitable network through successful integration of these factors.

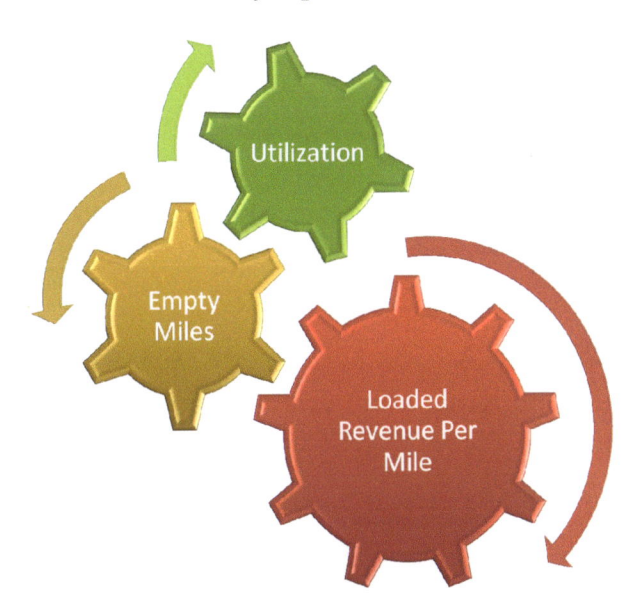

Critical Profitability Optimization Factors

Different types of profitable operations will display significantly different results for each key factor. For certain specialized operations, a shortfall in one key profitability factor will be offset by a very high level of performance in a different profitability factor. For example, a profitable operation based on extremely low utilization will display very high loaded revenue per mile levels.

Carriers must have a strong understanding of the expected utilization and empty mile percentage of their network as they determine the loaded revenue per mile that must be charged to each customer. The next section provides an overview of the business models for carriers with very different length of haul and utilization levels. Despite the operational differences, each carrier has the ability to achieve profitable results as long as the pricing levels are appropriate for each unique operation.

Business Models by Utilization Level

Different carriers and fleets will have a variety of different goals and targets based on the type of network that the carrier serves. Short haul and regional carriers will have a shorter length of haul, so their goals will be based on lower utilization, a higher empty mile percentage, and a higher loaded rate per mile. A long haul carrier's goals will be based on high utilization, a low empty miles percentage, and a relatively low loaded rate per mile. The table below illustrates what these key goals and operating statistics might look like by carrier type.

Weekly Goals and Key Operating Statistics by Carrier Type

Goals and Statistics	Shorthaul	Regional	Intermediate	Long Haul
Average Length of Haul	120	275	650	1,100
Goals:				
Utilization	1,250	1,850	2,300	2,700
Empty Miles Percentage	37.0%	20.0%	12.0%	9.0%
Revenue Per Loaded Mile	$ 3.35	$ 2.05	$ 1.58	$ 1.40
Resulting Operating Statistics:				
Net Revenue Per Mile	$ 2.11	$ 1.64	$ 1.39	$ 1.27
Empty Miles	463	370	276	243
Loaded Miles	788	1,480	2,024	2,457
Total Miles (Utilization)	1,250	1,850	2,300	2,700
Total Revenue Per Truck	$ 2,638	$ 3,034	$ 3,198	$ 3,440

Comparing the goals and operating statistics of the four carrier types shown reflects all of the key truckload economics concepts and principals. Each carrier, regardless of utilization or length of haul, can create and maintain a profitable network. Each of these carriers will focus heavily on utilization maximization and empty mile minimization. All other things being equal, as utilization and empty mile performance improves, profitability increases for each of the carriers in this example.

The key factor for each carrier is to generate the revenue level necessary to compensate for the unique characteristics of each network. The loaded and net revenue per mile for the short haul carrier is much greater than the long haul carrier. The short haul carrier must charge a higher rate per loaded mile to compensate for the lower utilization and higher empty mile percentage that is caused by the very short average length of haul. The graph below illustrates this key relationship between utilization and loaded revenue per mile.

Utilization and Loaded Revenue Per Mile Goals by Carrier Type

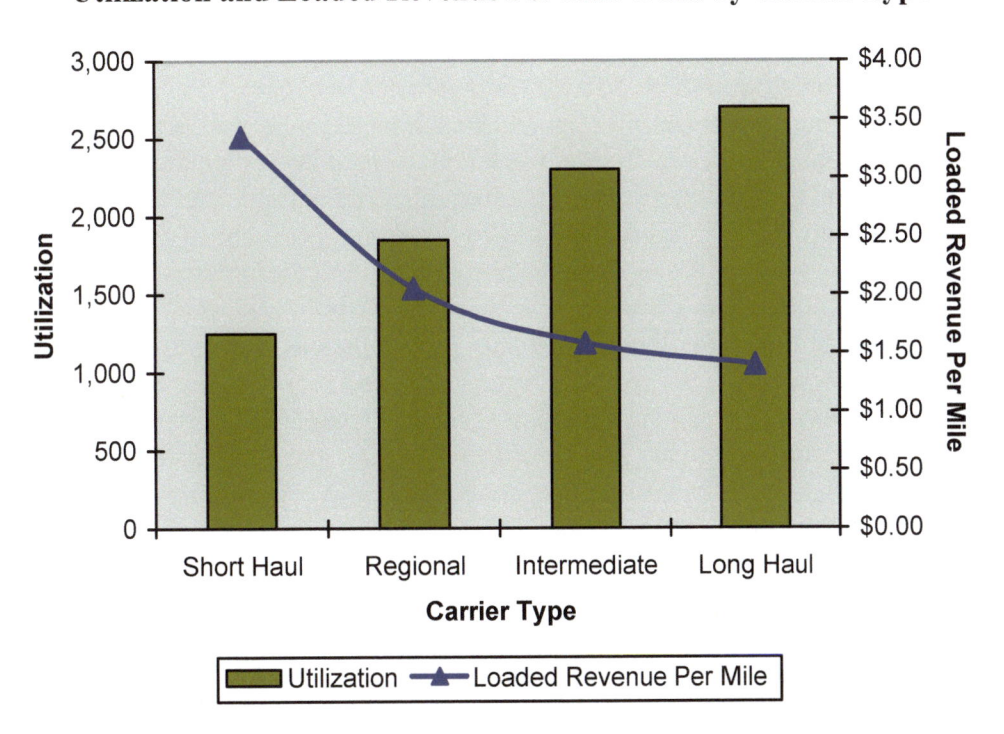

By correctly associating the appropriate revenue level with each utilization and business model scenario, an efficient carrier can enjoy suitable profitability regardless of utilization, length of haul, or empty mile levels. However, pricing alone cannot compensate for a poorly managed network with inadequate utilization or an inefficient empty mile percentage. The pricing required to overcome these deficiencies is very likely to be uncompetitive in the marketplace. Shippers can simply choose a more efficient carrier with reasonable and competitive pricing.

At the lower utilization levels of the short haul and regional carrier, utilization becomes a less important measure of productivity for the business model. Instead of focusing only on maximizing utilization in miles, carriers attempt to maximize revenue levels through scheduling efficiency and attractive pricing, especially in extreme short haul networks. Regardless of actual utilization in miles, pure revenue productivity increases in importance and the empty mile percentage becomes less critical.

Utilization Maximization

Utilization maximization is one of the most important goals for any carrier. Not only does high utilization maximize carrier revenues, it also maximizes driver incomes.[39] While there are many operating strategies and tactics for utilization maximization, the focus here will be on the basic strategies and measurements that contribute to utilization maximization and the overall impact of utilization on the carrier's profitability.

Utilization Expectations

Because each carrier manages a unique network of loads and customers, utilization maximization expectations will be different from carrier to carrier. The goal is not to simply maximize the number of miles per truck each week. The goal is to maximize utilization levels and revenues relative to the length of haul and other freight characteristics in the carrier's network. The optimal combination of revenues and utilization relative to length of haul is the key to maximum profitability, not purely utilization alone.

Length of haul and expected utilization are only part of the basic pricing strategy. The carrier must also incorporate the specific expectations and requirements of each customer. For example, certain customers may require fixed-appointment deliveries that increase cycle time and negatively impact utilization. The carrier must usually price this customer's business higher than normal because of the delivery appointment requirement. The utilization maximization goal for this carrier will be lower than the utilization goal for a different carrier that serves customers with more efficient requirements or longer average length of haul levels.

Another important consideration in utilization maximization is empty miles. Empty miles are included in the miles per week that comprise the utilization measurement. However, empty miles also cost the carrier money and reduce the carrier's overall profitability. Utilization maximization strategies should seek to increase and maximize only loaded miles per week and revenue. Increasing utilization only by increasing empty miles is counter-productive and only serves to reduce the carrier's profitability.

---

[39] Since most drivers are paid on a per-mile basis, higher utilization results in higher income levels for productive drivers.

Utilization Maximization Strategies

Many of the utilization maximization strategies used by carriers are covered in detail in the various sections throughout this book. These maximization strategies also serve to protect existing utilization while attempting to increase utilization. The table below summarizes the most common variables that impact utilization.

Utilization Maximization Strategies			
Network Variable	**Utilization Impact**		
	Variable Behavior:	Increases	Decreases
Length of Haul	A longer length of haul generally leads to higher utilization.	Increases	Decreases
Cycle Time	Carriers seek to minimize cycle time for every load by setting optimal appointments and choosing the best route for each trip.	Decreases	Increases
Dwell Time	Carriers seek to minimize dwell time while also meeting the needs of drivers and customers.	Decreases	Increases
Drop Trailers	The use of drop trailers reduces cycle time by allowing drop-and-hook pick-ups and deliveries.	Extensive Use of Drop Trailers	Limited Use of Drop Trailers
Driver Pay Structure	In utilization-based networks, per-mile driver pay programs are intended to give drivers significant incentive to maximize utilization.	Per Mile Rate Encourages Utilization	Pay Program Discourages Utilization
Accessorial Charges	Carriers utilize accessorial charges to discourage certain unproductive activities, especially stops and driver unloading. When these events take place, the tractor is idle and valuable utilization is lost. Even though the carrier and driver are often compensated for these activities, the revenue earned from greater utilization is preferred to the accessorial revenues.		

Cycle time minimization is one of the most critical elements of utilization maximization. Carriers utilize a variety of strategies to minimize cycle time. The best routes are chosen to minimize drive time. Carriers also negotiate efficient pick-up and delivery times with customers to minimize buffer time. Whenever possible and cost effective, drop trailers are deployed to allow for drop-and-hook deliveries, reducing dock time delays.

The driver pay program is also a key element of utilization maximization. A per-mile driver pay program provides the driver with a significant incentive to maximize utilization. As utilization increases, the driver's gross income also increases. A variable pay program of this type encourages drivers to complete each load as quickly as possible. In addition, the variable pay program encourages the driver to make optimal use of available driving hours and total work time each week.

Every carrier must develop a set of strategies to maximize utilization in terms of the individual network. Some carrier networks are more dependent on efficient cycle times and less dependent on length of haul to maximize utilization. Regardless of the network, protecting and maximizing utilization is a primary objective of every carrier.

Revenue Per Truck Per Week

Revenue per truck per week is a secondary measure of asset productivity similar to utilization. The measurement serves as an excellent benchmark for profitability and efficient operations. Revenue per truck per week is directly related to utilization and simply represents the total revenue generated by a truck during a seven day period or the average revenue generated by a group of trucks over a seven day period. The goal is to maximize revenue per week while maintaining consistent performance in other key areas.

The expectations for the revenue per truck per week benchmark must be adjusted relative to weekly utilization, loaded revenue per mile, and the empty mile percentage of the network. Managers should not automatically assume that a truck with $3,250 in revenue per week is more profitable than a truck with $2,750 in revenue per week. If the second truck generated the $2,750 in revenue on 500 less miles than the higher revenue truck, the lower revenue truck is likely to be much more profitable than the truck with the higher revenue per week.

The analysis to the right shows how the truck with only $2,750 in revenue can be significantly more profitable. Because of lower total miles, the variable costs for the low utilization scenario are significantly less.

The most valuable use of revenue per truck per week in pricing design is to quickly validate proposed pricing and avoid critical mistakes. The revenue per week standard helps to insure that revenue levels are adequate for covering operating costs, especially fixed costs and overhead.

Revenue Per Truck Per Week and Profitability			Utilization Scenario		
			High		Low
Loaded Miles			2,255		1,608
Empty Miles			328		368
Total Miles (Utilization)			**2,583**		**1,976**
Empty Miles Percentage			12.7%		18.6%
Gross Linehaul Revenue		$	3,250.00	$	2,750.00
Loaded Revenue Per Mile		$	1.441	$	1.710
Net Revenue Per Mile (NRPM)		$	1.258	$	1.392
Estimated Profit and Loss					
Linehaul Revenue Per Truck Per Week		$	3,250.00	$	2,750.00
Variable Costs	ASSUMPTIONS				
Driver Wages	$ 0.38	$	981.54	$	750.88
Fringe Benefits (% of wages)	25.0%	$	245.39	$	187.72
Fuel	$ 0.23	$	594.09	$	454.48
Maintenance	$ 0.11	$	284.13	$	217.36
Insurance	$ 0.10	$	258.30	$	197.60
Total Variable Costs		$	2,363.45	$	1,808.04
Fixed Costs	PER WEEK				
Tractor Depreciation	$ 230.77	$	230.77	$	230.77
Trailer Depreciation	$ 38.46	$	38.46	$	38.46
Legalization/Recruiting/Admin	$ 192.31	$	192.31	$	192.31
Corporate Overhead	$ 115.38	$	115.38	$	115.38
Total Fixed Costs	$ 576.92	$	576.92	$	576.92
Grand Total Cost		$	2,940.37	$	2,384.96
Operating Profit		$	309.63	$	365.04
Operating Ratio			90.5%		86.7%

Some carriers also use revenue per truck per day in much the same way as revenue per truck per week. While revenue per truck per day is sometimes easier to interpret, both measures are effectively the same. Both measures are best used only for general pricing validation and not for estimating or comparing profitability levels.

CHAPTER 5: Advanced Concepts in One-Way Pricing

In the majority of one-way pricing situations, other factors beyond length-of-haul, empty miles, utilization, and operating costs influence pricing strategy and pricing decisions. Two of the most important considerations include local market supply and demand conditions and the carrier's available capacity in each market region. Customer seasonality, shipping patterns and related characteristics will also influence the pricing strategy. A thorough understanding of the concepts in this chapter will allow carriers to correctly account for these special situations and avoid serving unusual or difficult shipper requirements without the appropriate revenue levels.

The One-Way Pricing Process

As has been emphasized, the one-way pricing process is as much of an art as it is a science. Every carrier and every pricing manager has a unique approach and thought process for determining one-way rates. The objective of this section is to tie together all the key concepts associated with one-way pricing. While it is impossible to explain the exact thought process of any individual pricing manager, this section will define the key items considered by a pricing manager and provide a general model for the one-way pricing analysis process.

Lane and Customer Analysis

The most important step in one-way pricing is gathering information about the lane, the shipper, and the impact of the potential lane on the carrier's existing network. The sections that follow outline the most common questions for pricing a one-way lane. While each potential lane and customer will have unique issues, the questions below provide a general framework for evaluating any one-way lane.

External Lane-Specific Questions

External, lane-specific questions relate directly to the general parameters of the lane without specifically considering the carrier or the shipper. The issues addressed include such factors as length of haul, toll costs, road conditions, and transit times.

External Lane-Specific Pricing Strategy Questions

Lane-Specific Questions	
Component	Questions
General Lane Elements	What are the origin and destination points for the lane?
	What is the loaded mile and billed mile length of haul for the lane?
Operating Costs	Will any toll costs be incurred on the lane? If so, what are the costs?
	Is reasonably priced fuel readily available on the trip?
Transit Time	What types of roads will be traveled on the trip? Two-lane? Interstate?
	What is the average miles-per-hour and transit time for the trip?

The answers to these questions provide the carrier with a general overview of the lane. The answers will also be important as the carrier's network and the shipper's key requirements are introduced into the pricing analysis.

Internal Carrier-Related Questions

Carrier-related questions focus on the carrier's existing network and how the potential new customer and lane will fit with current activity. These questions help the carrier determine if the lane merits consideration for a rate proposal.

Internal Carrier-Related Pricing Strategy Questions

Component	Questions
General Strategy	Do the parameters of this lane meet the existing business model?
	Does this lane offer the opportunity to profitably expand the network?
	Is the current network in need of additional freight?
	Does this lane flow through existing company maintenance facilities?
	Is this a new lane or customer with significant future growth potential?
Capacity & Balance	How many trucks per week are currently available in the origin market?
	If capacity is not available, how will trucks be sourced to this customer?
	Is any additional capacity needed in or near the destination market?
	How will trucks be used once they reach the destination market?
Existing Customers	What rates are being charged to current customers on this lane?
	Do any current customers have substandard rates on this lane?
	Is this lane currently profitable with existing customers?
Market Conditions	Is the origin a headhaul, backhaul or intermediate pricing market?
	Is the destination a headhaul, backhaul or intermediate pricing market?
Empty Miles	How many empty miles will be incurred to pick up these loads?
	How many empty miles will be incurred after the delivery?
Driver Satisfaction	Does this lane facilitate the need to get drivers home?
	Will this lane provide reasonable income and productivity for the driver?

A key element the carrier must always consider is a lane's fit with the carrier's general strategy and business model. If a lane does not fit the carrier's model, the carrier may decline to price the lane or may price the lane very high as a result of the poor fit. In some cases, a new lane or new customer will provide the carrier with the opportunity to profitably expand the existing network and customer base. If the customer represents a major growth opportunity, the carrier may price the lane very aggressively in the hope of establishing a long-term working relationship with the new customer.

Strategic factors such as capacity and balance, market conditions, and empty miles are explained in detail throughout the chapters covering one-way pricing. These sections explain the pricing implications of each operating variable. However, since all carriers operate unique networks, each of these factors potentially affects each carrier's pricing differently. Certain lanes and markets are a better fit for some carriers than others. If a carrier has an excellent network fit or business model for a given lane, that carrier is likely to propose much lower pricing than carriers that do not have a good network fit for the lane in question.

External Shipper-Related Questions

All pricing must be carefully adjusted based on the shipper's expectations and service platform. Shipper-related questions focus on the shipper's general requirements, service expectations, and operating model. These questions allow the carrier to identify the key issues that will dictate any customer-specific adjustments to the pricing.

External Shipper-Related Pricing Strategy Questions

Component	Questions
Operating Costs	What will be the fuel surcharge peg for this customer?
	What are the trailer equipment requirements for this lane?
Load Pick-Up	Are outbound trailers pre-loaded or is a live pick-up required?
	Is there an open window for pick-up or is an appointment required?
	How much dock time is typically required for the pick-up?
Load Delivery	Is there an open window for delivery or is an appointment required?
	If an appointment is required, how wide is the delivery window?
	If using a drop delivery, how quickly are inbound trailers unloaded?
	How much dock time is typically required for the delivery?
Seasonality	Are load volumes reasonably consistent on a daily basis?
	Are there any end-of-month or end-of-quarter spikes in shipment levels?
Service	How does the shipper measure on-time service?
	What level of on-time service does the customer require?
	Are any special services required to meet transit time expectations?
Load Tendering	How will load information be communicated? Email? Phone? Fax?
	How much advanced notice is provided for load pick-up times?
Driver Satisfaction	Is any driver unloading or similar labor service required on this lane?
	Does this lane ever involve multi-stop deliveries? How often?

All these questions are critical for the carrier's pricing design. Even a detail such as the amount of advanced notice on load tendering is important to the pricing design. If the shipper consistently tenders loads to the carrier only a few hours before the required pick-up time, the carrier will have a limited window for efficient planning and incur additional costs as a result. On the other hand, if the shipper communicates load information with plenty of advanced notice, the carrier can efficiently plan the network and minimize the costs to serve the customer.

Service requirements and expectations are also an important consideration in the pricing design. Shippers with very high service requirements or very rapid transit time requirements can cost much more for the carrier to serve. The pick-up and delivery time requirements can dictate a very demanding transit time expectation. Tight transit times limit the carrier's ability to assign available drivers to a load. If the shipper's transit time does not allow enough time for the driver to take a mandatory rest break, the carrier will incur additional costs to meet the demanding transit time requirement.

The impact of other key factors such as seasonality, operating costs, appointment windows, and dock times are discussed in detail throughout this book. These factors all interact in the adjustments necessary for the carrier to establish accurate pricing levels.

The Preliminary One-Way Rate

The one-way pricing process always starts with a preliminary rate. The preliminary rate is usually based on market expertise and experience, cost analysis, or a reference source such as a guideline pricing matrix. Seasoned pricing managers are able to identify an accurate preliminary rate directly from experience and market expertise. Those less experienced with one-way pricing will often refer to a guideline rate reference or costing model. The graphic below summarizes the general application of these common pricing references.

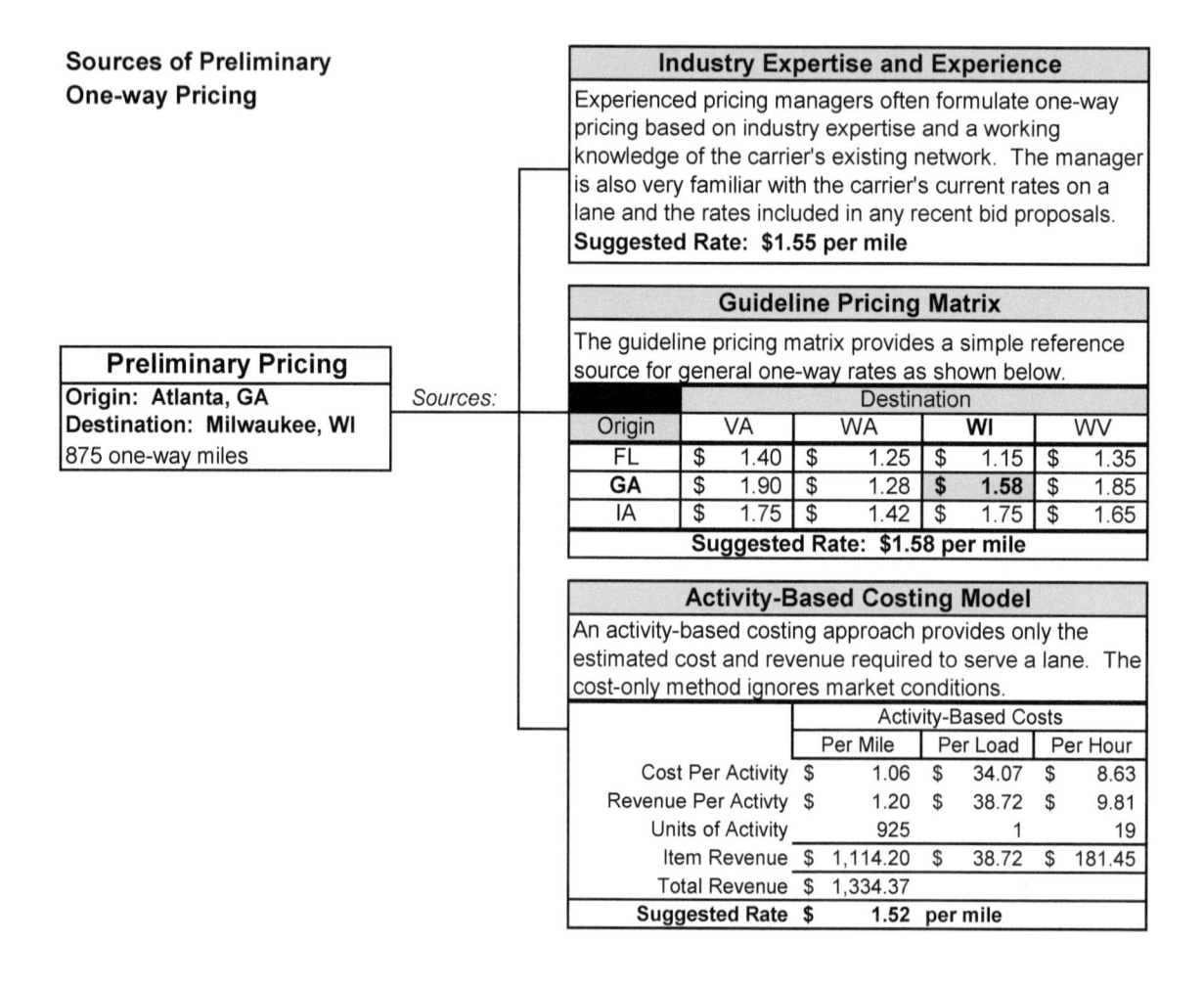

Sources of Preliminary One-way Pricing

Preliminary Pricing
Origin: Atlanta, GA
Destination: Milwaukee, WI
875 one-way miles

Sources:

Industry Expertise and Experience
Experienced pricing managers often formulate one-way pricing based on industry expertise and a working knowledge of the carrier's existing network. The manager is also very familiar with the carrier's current rates on a lane and the rates included in any recent bid proposals.
Suggested Rate: $1.55 per mile

Guideline Pricing Matrix
The guideline pricing matrix provides a simple reference source for general one-way rates as shown below.

	Destination			
Origin	VA	WA	WI	WV
FL	$ 1.40	$ 1.25	$ 1.15	$ 1.35
GA	$ 1.90	$ 1.28	**$ 1.58**	$ 1.85
IA	$ 1.75	$ 1.42	$ 1.75	$ 1.65

Suggested Rate: $1.58 per mile

Activity-Based Costing Model
An activity-based costing approach provides only the estimated cost and revenue required to serve a lane. The cost-only method ignores market conditions.

	Activity-Based Costs		
	Per Mile	Per Load	Per Hour
Cost Per Activity	$ 1.06	$ 34.07	$ 8.63
Revenue Per Activty	$ 1.20	$ 38.72	$ 9.81
Units of Activity	925	1	19
Item Revenue	$ 1,114.20	$ 38.72	$ 181.45
Total Revenue	$ 1,334.37		
Suggested Rate	$ 1.52 per mile		

Industry Expertise and Experience

Pricing managers with years of experience and industry knowledge rely on this expertise to formulate preliminary pricing. The carrier will draw upon that expertise to evaluate the key pricing strategy questions about the lane, the carrier's situation as it relates to the lane, and the shipper's requirements and parameters. These experienced pricing managers can inherently integrate all the various pricing variables and quickly determine an appropriate preliminary rate for any lane.

Guideline Pricing

Guideline pricing provides an excellent resource for those without pricing experience or experience with pricing a particular lane or market. The carrier's guideline pricing is usually created by the carrier's most experienced pricing personnel. Typically, the guideline pricing is used only as a starting point or general standard for one-way pricing. Depending on the actual freight characteristics, most of the carrier's actual rates will be slightly lower than guideline standards.

Guideline pricing is usually organized in a state-to-state or zone-to-zone matrix similar to the abbreviated state-to-state format shown below.

Abbreviated Guideline Pricing Matrix

Origin \ Destination (Minimum Charge = $575.00)	AL	AR	AZ	CA	CO	CT	DC	DE	FL	GA	IA
AL	$ 1.90	$ 1.50	$ 1.56	$ 1.24	$ 1.58	$ 1.56	$ 1.61	$ 1.56	$ 2.37	$ 1.81	$ 1.36
AR	$ 1.51	$ 1.90	$ 1.56	$ 1.30	$ 1.81	$ 1.54	$ 1.54	$ 1.54	$ 1.87	$ 1.41	$ 1.34
AZ	$ 1.04	$ 1.04	$ 1.95	$ 1.06	$ 1.60	$ 1.20	$ 1.18	$ 1.18	$ 1.30	$ 1.06	$ 1.06
CA	$ 1.10	$ 1.10	$ 1.91	$ 1.80	$ 1.64	$ 1.22	$ 1.20	$ 1.20	$ 1.36	$ 1.12	$ 1.10
CO	$ 0.98	$ 0.98	$ 1.31	$ 1.01	$ 2.16	$ 1.13	$ 1.13	$ 1.13	$ 1.32	$ 1.01	$ 0.96
CT	$ 0.92	$ 0.92	$ 1.32	$ 1.12	$ 1.51	$ 2.00	$ 1.51	$ 1.81	$ 1.52	$ 0.91	$ 0.93
DC	$ 1.01	$ 1.01	$ 1.37	$ 1.12	$ 1.51	$ 2.06	$ 2.69	$ 1.90	$ 1.58	$ 1.01	$ 0.98
DE	$ 0.95	$ 0.95	$ 1.37	$ 1.12	$ 1.51	$ 2.06	$ 1.90	$ 2.00	$ 1.58	$ 0.96	$ 0.98
FL	$ 0.96	$ 0.94	$ 1.31	$ 1.16	$ 1.34	$ 1.31	$ 1.31	$ 1.31	$ 2.02	$ 0.91	$ 1.01
GA	$ 1.52	$ 1.33	$ 1.48	$ 1.21	$ 1.56	$ 1.56	$ 1.56	$ 1.56	$ 2.28	$ 1.90	$ 1.24
IA	$ 1.52	$ 1.62	$ 1.58	$ 1.37	$ 2.21	$ 1.81	$ 1.81	$ 1.81	$ 1.99	$ 1.51	$ 1.90

A format of this type allows the carrier to organize a large number of lane combinations in a manageable structure. The carrier must also update the pricing periodically to reflect internal strategy, changing costs, and evolving market conditions.

Activity-Based Costing

A pure activity-based costing model provides a method for identifying the pure cost and revenue required for a one-way lane. The weakness of the approach is that it does not reflect market conditions or the carrier's current capacity and balance situation. However, the model does provide a sound baseline for later adjusting the activity-based rate relative to market and carrier conditions. The activity-based approach would most often be used when a rate is not readily available from another source.

Well-designed activity-based costing provides an excellent method for estimating actual operating costs on any length of haul lane.[40] Since most one-way pricing is based on a combination of length of haul, capacity and balance, market conditions, empty miles, and other factors, true operating cost is only a small factor in the lane-level pricing design. An accurate estimate of true operating costs, along with the key operating factors, provides the carrier with a complete picture of the profit potential for any lane.

---

[40] Most activity-based costing models will only be valid over appropriate length of haul levels. A costing model for long length of haul lanes may not be accurate for short length of haul lanes primarily because of different utilization levels and driver pay structures.

Pricing Adjustments

Once the preliminary lane pricing is established, the rate must be adjusted as necessary to meet the specific requirements of the customer. At this stage, critical pricing factors such as empty miles, length of haul, dock times, and cycle times enter the process. The table below illustrates how a carrier might adjust pricing to account for the impact of these critical pricing variables. The preliminary rate in this example is based on the activity-based costing approach.

One-Way Pricing Design and Adjustments

One-Way Pricing Design and Adjustments		Activity-Based Costs			Suggested Pricing		Final Rate
		Per Mile	Per Load	Per Hour	Per Load	Per Mile	Per Mile
Activity-Based Cost Per Unit of Activity		$ 1.060	$ 34.073	$ 8.631			
Revenue Per Unit of Activity (88.0% O.R.)		$ 1.205	$ 38.720	$ 9.808			
Step 1: Baseline Cost-Plus Pricing Based on Length of Haul	Loaded Miles	875					
	Empty Miles (8% standard)	76					
	Actual Units of Activity	951	1.00	19.02			
	Applied Revenue	$ 1,145.52	$ 38.72	$ 186.55	$ 1,370.79	$ 1.57	$ 1.57
Step 2: Adjustments to Empty Miles Expectations	Actual Empty Mile %	6.4%					
	Actual Empty Miles	60					
	Difference to Standard	(16)					
	Applied Revenue	$ (19.27)	Discount for lower empty miles.		$ (19.27)	$ (0.02)	$ 1.54
Step 3: Cycle Time Adjustments	Hours Per Load	Standard	Expectation	Adjustment			
	Total Dock Time (PU & Del)	1.75	1.25	(0.50)			
	Transit Time	19.02	24.00	4.98			
	Total Adjusted Hours			4.48			
	Applied Revenue			$ 43.94	$ 43.94	$ 0.05	$ 1.59
Step 4: Special Customer-Specific Adjustments	Adjustments	Per Mile	Per Load	Total			
	Insurance Requirements	$ 0.02		17.50			
	Trailer Requirements		$ 17.00	17.00			
	Other Special Requirements		$ 10.00	10.00			
	Total Revenue Adjustments		$ 44.50	$ 44.50	$ 0.05	$ **1.65**

The analysis above illustrates several of the most common items considered in one-way pricing strategy, particularly empty miles and customer cycle time. After all adjustments, the final rate is set at $1.65 per mile.

The objective of the pricing design table is to provide a general format for how these factors impact pricing adjustments. Any number of additional factors may also need to be considered by a carrier on a lane-by-lane basis. Each individual carrier will handle these factors using slightly different methods and approaches. However, all carriers take these and related factors into consideration in the development of one-way pricing.

Keep the one-way pricing process and key strategy questions in mind throughout the advanced pricing concepts contained in this chapter. All the pricing concepts and analysis techniques work closely together to determine the carrier's ultimate pricing strategy and rate per mile.

Network Capacity and Balance

Capacity and balance represents the net amount of available trucks and available loads for a carrier in a geographic region. A market area is considered to be "balanced" when the number of available trucks equals the number of available loads at a given point in time. A geographic region can be out of balance in two ways. When the carrier has more available trucks than available loads, the carrier has excess capacity. If the carrier has more available loads than available trucks, the carrier has excess demand. Capacity and balance is a critical factor in both pricing strategy and real-time tactical decision making. The sections that follow address how carriers are affected by balance problems and the strategies used to correct and prevent balance issues.

Real-Time Capacity and Balance

In a real-time scenario, the carrier must actively manage customers and trucks to balance each market on a daily basis. A major component of the ultimate solution to the balance problem will involve shifting capacity between markets and regions. Trucks will move from a market that has excess capacity into a market that has excess demand. The movement of available trucks will require a significant number of empty miles and cause the carrier to incur a major variable expense. Where possible, the carrier will also work with customers to adjust the required pick-up or delivery times for the excess loads. By adjusting appointment times, the carrier is then able to pick up loads at a later time when more trucks naturally enter the region and become available.

The table below provides an example of a real-time capacity and balance analysis for a regional carrier based in Birmingham, Alabama.

Capacity & Balance as of 8:15 am				
Planning Region	Available Trucks	Available Loads	Net Balance
AL - North	32	40	(8)
AL - South	15	11	4
GA - North	41	38	3
GA - South	27	15	12
MS - North	18	22	(4)
MS - South	11	7	4
TN - East	21	21	-
TN - Central	21	15	6
TN - West	22	35	(13)
Network Totals	**208**	**204**	**4**

The network totals indicate a reasonable net balance of available trucks and loads across the network. However, several planning regions are extremely unbalanced with either excess trucks or excess loads. A negative net balance value indicates a region with excess loads. A positive net balance indicates a region with available trucks.

The carrier's planners and customer service team must find loads for available trucks as quickly as possible. Also, if trucks are to be moved from one region to another to balance the network, the carrier's planners must make this decision quickly as well. If the carrier utilizes a network optimization system, the system will assist the planners in determining the exact assignment of trucks to loads and any specific network shifts needed to balance the network.

The carrier may also utilize a variety of mapping tools to visualize the capacity and balance situation. The map below illustrates the 8:15 am capacity and balance situation across the carrier's operating region.

Real-time Capacity & Balance

The map reflects the fact that one corner of the network is in need of trucks while the other areas of the network have available trucks. The TN E region is perfectly balanced, but all other regions are out of balance. Maps, optimization software, and a team of experience planners allow carriers to resolve real-time capacity and balance problems as quickly as possible. In a later chapter, additional tactical strategies will be presented on how the carrier manages the real-time capacity and balance problem.

Capacity and Balance and Pricing Strategy

From a strategic perspective, capacity and balance plays a major role in the development of one-way pricing strategy. Serious capacity and balance problems cause the carrier to incur significant empty miles and waste the valuable time of both the driver and tractor. Key measures such as net revenue per mile and utilization will also suffer. The carrier may also experience service problems with key customers as loads are picked up or delivered late.

At the strategic planning level for the network, the carrier must utilize a variety of strategies to correct capacity and balance issues as quickly as possible. The capacity and balance solution will involve the collective efforts of the sales team, the customer service team, and the pricing department. When a region consistently has an excess capacity of trucks, the carrier will emphasize the search for new customers in the area and provide aggressive pricing when appropriate. The carrier will also solicit existing customers in the area for additional load volumes.

In addition to searching for additional outbound loads, the carrier may use pricing strategies to address the capacity and balance issue. The carrier may offer reduced rates to existing customers to attract incremental load activity. The carrier may offer attractive pricing to potential new customers as well. The carrier may even choose to increase pricing on lanes into the unbalanced market in an effort to reduce demand for inbound activity or provide additional compensation for serving loads into the unbalanced destination market.

The long-term summary below represents the net capacity and balance of actual load activity for a one-month period.

Capacity & Balance Summary			
Planning Region	Inbound Loads	Outbound Loads	Net Balance
AL - North	338	410	(72)
AL - South	261	215	46
GA - North	544	598	(54)
GA - South	380	315	65
MS - North	225	190	35
MS - South	310	251	59
TN - East	205	165	40
TN - Central	418	450	(32)
TN - West	433	520	(87)
Network Totals	**3,114**	**3,114**	**0**

The two planning regions most in need of trucks are AL-North and TN-West. The two planning regions with the most available capacity include GA-South and MS-South. Assuming this network balance trend will continue, the carrier's marketing team should focus on lanes from the regions with available trucks to the regions in need of trucks. Regardless of actual operating costs, the carrier may offer particularly aggressive pricing to attract the load volumes needed to properly balance the network. By creating a highly balanced network, the carrier is likely to enjoy many potential benefits including reduced empty miles, reduced dwell time, higher utilization, increased driver satisfaction, and improved customer service.

Headhaul and Backhaul Markets

In a given geographic market, both the supply of available trucks from all carriers and the cumulative market demand for truck capacity from all shippers play a major role in determining actual one-way pricing. Over time, pricing on both inbound and outbound lanes slowly adjusts to the aggregate capacity and balance situation in a market region. The economic principles of supply and demand certainly hold true in this situation. When demand for trucks exceeds supply in a market, the outbound equilibrium price will eventually increase. Likewise, when the supply of trucks exceeds demand, the equilibrium outbound price will be driven downward.

The graph below illustrates the supply and demand principles applied to a one-way pricing environment. In this theoretical case, the equilibrium price represents the average price of all outbound lanes from a market, not any one particular lane or price.

The Impact of Supply and Demand on Outbound One-Way Pricing

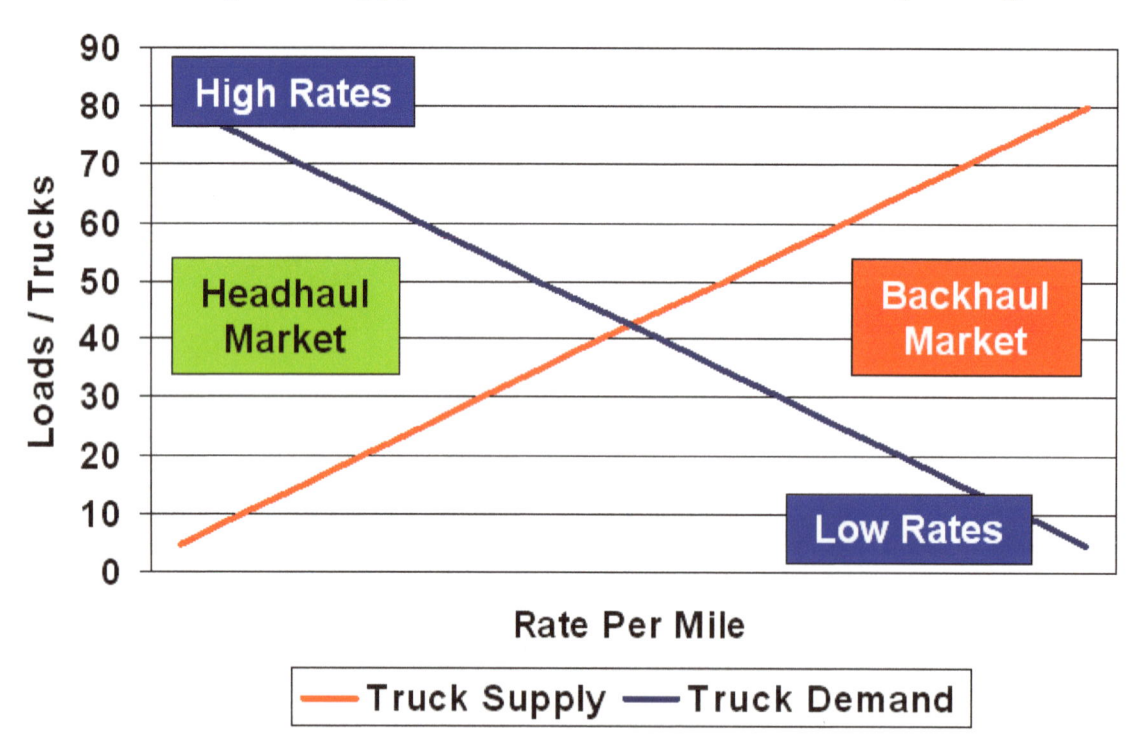

The basic principles of supply and demand also apply because, given typical shipper requirements, trucking services are basically a commodity item. In other words, the basic service provided by one carrier is effectively the same as the service provided by all other carriers. When this is the case, cost becomes a primary decision variable in the shipper's carrier selection process. While trucking is not a commodity item in all situations, this concept is still applicable to how supply and demand will impact pricing in each individual geographic market. Regardless of shipper requirements, supply and demand conditions still influence all pricing in a market.

Headhaul Markets

The outbound pricing for a headhaul market is generally higher than average because the demand for trucks exceeds the supply of available trucks. However, the pricing is actually driven up to serve these markets because of the true operating costs incurred by the carriers. Because demand exceeds supply, carriers must move trucks into the market to serve the shippers, incurring a significant cost for the associated empty miles in the process. The cost of these empty miles requires carriers to increase rates to cover the above average cost of sourcing the required amount of capacity to the market.

To minimize empty miles and provide capacity to shippers, carriers will also discount rates from other markets into desirable headhaul markets. To make up for the revenue lost on the inbound trip, carriers must increase revenue on the outbound trip from the headhaul market. Either way, the cost to provide capacity is higher regardless of whether the capacity is provided by reduced inbound pricing or additional empty miles.

In some cases, certain carriers may define their base of operations as their "headhaul" market or primary origin point. In this context, "headhaul" refers only to the carrier's base of operations, not necessarily the true market pricing characteristics of the location. For the purposes of this discussion on market conditions, headhaul and backhaul markets refer to the general market pricing conditions and how those conditions affect the pricing of all carriers operating in the market.

Backhaul Markets

The outbound pricing for a backhaul market is generally lower than average because the demand for trucks is far less than the supply of available trucks. Since the demand for trucks is very low, trucks that are not able to secure loads out of a backhaul market must move to another market to secure an available load. Carriers that are able to secure loads out of a backhaul market provide very aggressive, very low pricing because, all other factors being equal, any revenue is better than no revenue. The carrier is able to offset miles that would otherwise be empty with a minimal amount of revenue.

Carriers are very aware of the costs and risks associated with sending trucks into a backhaul market, so pricing inbound to a backhaul market is very high in the majority of cases. Carriers provide higher than average pricing into a backhaul market because the carrier will either incur significant empty miles to move the truck to its next load or provide severely discounted pricing on the truck's next load out of the backhaul market. In certain circumstances or market conditions, some carriers will even go as far as to refuse service into extremely undesirable backhaul markets.

Before moving any further, it should be noted that length of haul is an important part of headhaul and backhaul markets. This market discussion applies primarily to loads in excess of 400 to 500 miles or more. On loads of around 250 miles or less, headhaul and backhaul conditions become less relevant. Since the truck has not moved a significant distance away from the origin point, the option of returning empty to the origin is still feasible. If the outbound pricing assumes the carrier will return empty to the origin market, the actual destination market characteristics are not a significant factor in the pricing decision. Length of haul and its relationship to market conditions is discussed in greater detail in a future section.

Common Factors that Create Headhaul or Backhaul Markets

A number of factors interact to create headhaul and backhaul market environments. The most common and influential factors are discussed below.

\	Common Market Variables
Variable	**Impact of Variable**
Geography	Markets in isolated areas can become backhaul markets as a result of the limited nearby options for carriers to find shippers and loads. Because of their location on the Atlantic Ocean, Miami, FL and Boston, MA are good examples of backhaul markets influenced by geographic location. Likewise, markets in centralized locations like Memphis, TN or Columbus, OH tend to exhibit headhaul characteristics. Shippers are likely to establish distribution or manufacturing operations in these centrally-located markets to minimize the distance to and from customers and suppliers.
Population Density	Markets with a very high population tend to show backhaul market characteristics. Because of the high population, consumption of goods in these areas is often much greater than production. As a result, many more goods are shipped into the market relative to the amount of goods that are produced and shipped out of the market. This imbalance causes the supply of available trucks to exceed the demand for trucks, creating backhaul market conditions.
Industry	Markets with highly specialized or extremely limited industry will often display backhaul market characteristics. For example, the major industry in central and south Florida is agriculture and citrus products. Shipments of citrus products are highly seasonal. In addition, most of the citrus products require specialized, temperature-controlled trailer equipment. The combination of these factors contributes to Florida's severe backhaul market situation, especially for traditional dry-van carriers.

Boston, MA provides an excellent example of a backhaul market that displays each of these common characteristics. Boston is certainly in an isolated location geographically, which limits outbound options for carriers that deliver into the area. The highly populated Boston area is dominated by service-oriented industries such as law firms, consulting groups, and academic institutions. As a result, the production of goods requiring outbound transportation service is very low relative to the amount of goods that must be delivered into the market. The combination of all these factors leads to very high pricing on loads into the Boston area and very low pricing on the few scarce loads out of the Boston region.

Theoretical Pricing from Market Type to Market Type

The table below illustrates how one-way rates change based on the origin and destination market characteristics. The table assumes an 800 mile length of haul and an average billed rate of $1.50 per mile excluding fuel surcharges and accessorial revenues.

	\multicolumn{5}{c}{**Impact of Market Type on Billed Rate Per Mile**}	
	\multicolumn{5}{c}{**Destination Market Type**}	Network
Origin Market Type	Headhaul Strong	Headhaul Normal	Intermediate	Backhaul Normal	Backhaul Severe	Average Rate
Headhaul Strong	$ 1.50	$ 1.60	$ 1.80	$ 1.95	$ 2.25	$ 1.82
Headhaul Normal	$ 1.40	$ 1.50	$ 1.65	$ 1.75	$ 2.00	$ 1.66
Intermediate	$ 1.20	$ 1.35	$ 1.50	$ 1.65	$ 1.80	$ 1.50
Backhaul Normal	$ 1.05	$ 1.15	$ 1.35	$ 1.50	$ 1.65	$ 1.34
Backhaul Severe	$ 0.90	$ 1.05	$ 1.20	$ 1.35	$ 1.50	$ 1.20
Network Average Rate	$ 1.21	$ 1.33	$ 1.50	$ 1.64	$ 1.84	$ 1.50

Rates shown are not suggested rates. This chart is purely theoretical and intended only to illustrate the relative relationships between market types and corresponding one-way rates.

Notice that the rate per mile from each market type to the same market type equals the base rate of $1.50 per mile. In each case, the truck's market situation has not been impacted either positively or negatively, so the rate should, theoretically, stay at the standard rate of $1.50 per mile.[41] Also notice that rates increase for each origin market as the quality of the destination market deteriorates. The need to increase rates as the destination market quality deteriorates is true for each origin market type, even backhaul origin markets.

Also notice that the average rate per mile back and forth between any two corresponding market types is very close to $1.50 per mile. For example, the rate from Headhaul Normal to Intermediate is $1.65 and the rate from Intermediate to Headhaul Normal is $1.35 per mile. The average of these two rates is exactly $1.50 per mile. This concept doesn't always hold true in reality, but does provide a good benchmark for measuring and explaining rates back and forth between any two points.

The average rate for all the various market combinations is exactly $1.50, the same as the established baseline rate for this example. The concept illustrated here is that a carrier needs to build a network of freight that is priced to yield the desired loaded rate per mile over all loaded miles. The appropriate mix of headhaul and backhaul lanes, along with accurate pricing, provides the foundation for a profitable network. Strategies for maximizing asset utilization and minimizing empty miles are also critical elements of an overall profitable network.

---

[41] This statement is theoretically correct, but not always the case in actual pricing, especially when severe backhaul markets are involved.

Demand Shifts and Market Pricing

As market conditions evolve over time, the demand for trucks will increase or decrease in response to changing market conditions. For example, suppose a major company opens a new distribution center in a market that increases the net demand for trucks in the market by 8 loads per day. Net demand represents the net number of trucks this shipper demands from the market after any inbound trucks the shipper brings into the market. For example, this shipper may have 28 outbound loads per day and 20 inbound loads per day, creating a net demand for 8 trucks. Over time, this shift in the demand for trucks will drive up outbound pricing in this market. The theoretical graphic below illustrates the upward shift in demand for this example.

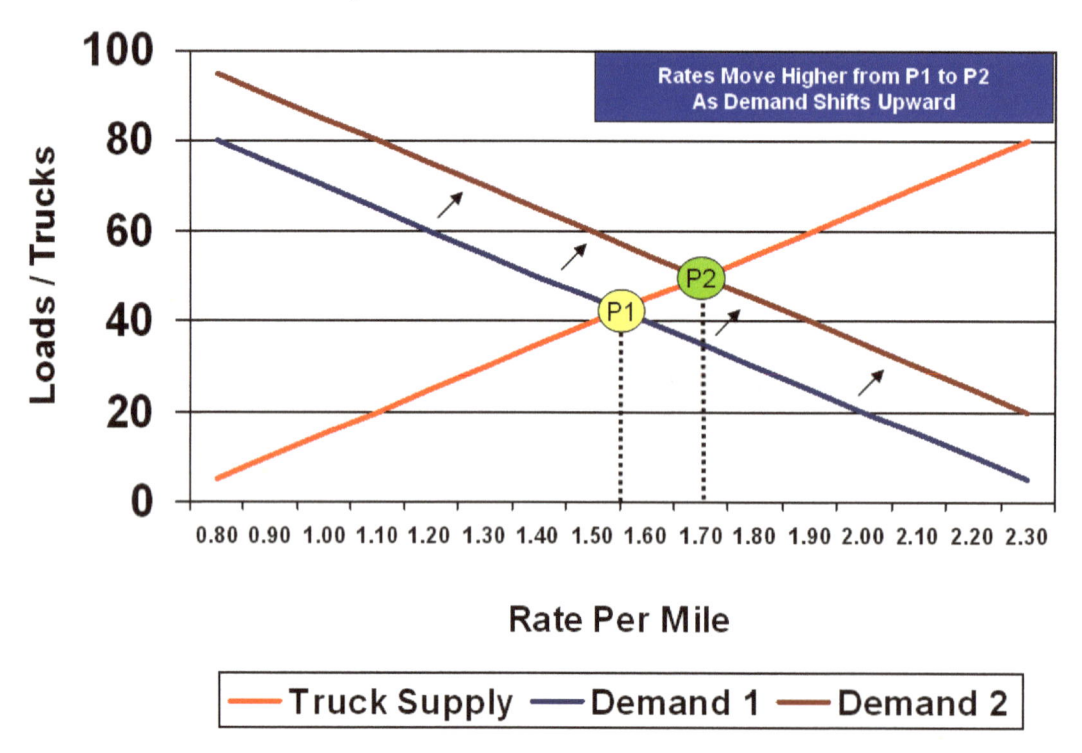

An Upward Shift in the Demand for Trucks

The result of the upward shift in demand is a move in the market equilibrium price from P1 to P2. The theoretical average market price has increased from $1.55 per mile to $1.70 per mile. The equilibrium load volume has increased from 42 to 50 loads per day. This pricing shift does not occur right away. The pricing changes occur slowly over time as carriers adjust rates to compensate for prevailing market conditions.

Supply Shifts and Market Pricing

Just as demand changes, the supply of trucks in a market will change as the result of many potential factors. For example, the population in an area may decline over time and cause a decrease in the demand for products being shipped into the area. This shift will cause a corresponding decrease in the amount of inbound trucks for the market. A change of this type would represent a "downward" shift in the supply of available trucks.

Along the same lines, if a large company in the market were to begin receiving a significantly larger volume of inbound shipments without a similar corresponding increase in outbound shipments, the supply of available trucks in the market would increase. A change of this type would represent an "upward" shift in the supply of trucks. The chart below illustrates the downward impact of this shift on the average market price.

An Upward Shift in the Supply of Trucks

The result of the upward shift in supply shown above is a move in the market equilibrium price from P1 to P2. The average market price has decreased from $1.55 per mile to $1.40 per mile. The equilibrium load volume has increased from 42 to 50 loads per day. Since the prevailing market rate is lower, certain shippers may begin to utilize truckload transportation as a cost-efficient or service-efficient substitute for other modes of transportation such as less-than-truckload (LTL) or intermodal (Rail), thereby creating a higher equilibrium load volume level for the market.

Case Study: The Florida Backhaul Market

Historically, the most challenging backhaul market in the United States is the state of Florida, especially central and south Florida. The state exhibits all of the key characteristics of a backhaul market. The most influential backhaul characteristics of the state include a high population, limited industry, and restrictive geography.

The high population and unique demographics of Florida each play a key role in the backhaul nature of the state. The Miami metro area is one of the most densely populated areas in the United States, as are the Orlando and Tampa areas. These highly populated areas create a tremendous demand for products to be shipped into the area.

Another factor is the demographic makeup of this large population. A larger than normal percentage of the Florida population is comprised of retired individuals and families. Since this portion of the population does not work, there is no offsetting production of outbound goods to balance with the inbound goods they consume. This imbalance creates a situation of far more trucks coming into the market relative to the amount of goods being shipped out of the market.

While industry and population are major backhaul factors in Florida, the isolated geography of Florida significantly increases the severity of the backhaul conditions. The map below illustrates the relative severity of the Florida backhaul market by region. In effect, the further south a truck travels into Florida, the more limited the options for a nearby load become.

General Florida Backhaul Regions

The fact that Florida is a peninsula only makes the problem worse. The only option for a truck in south Florida is to travel north to find an available load. The nearby load options for a truck in Florida are much more limited than trucks in centrally located markets such as Memphis, TN or Columbus, OH. The closest reasonable market to the Florida area is Georgia, primarily the Atlanta area. Atlanta is about 340 miles from Jacksonville, 440 miles from Orlando, and 650 miles from Miami. Carriers could also move trucks to Savannah, Georgia or Mobile, Alabama, both of which are also a great distance from the central and south Florida backhaul markets.

The lack of industry in Florida also contributes to the backhaul situation. The primary industry in central and south Florida is agriculture and citrus products. Not only is shipping for the citrus industry highly seasonal, but these goods often require temperature-controlled trailers for shipping. The combination of these factors means that a large number of trucks are bringing products into this market and very few outbound loads are available to move trucks out of the state, especially for traditional dry-van truckload carriers.

As a result of these factors, truckload rates into central and south Florida have traditionally been extremely high. Likewise, rates on the relatively small amount of loads out of Florida are extremely low. Carriers offer very lower rates to attract a portion of the scarce customers and loads. In fact, backhaul conditions in Florida have been so poor at times that some carriers have refused to haul loads into Florida for any customers other than a few top strategic accounts.

The carriers that do haul into Florida charge rates high enough to provide compensation for moving the truck empty back to a more reasonable location such as Atlanta, GA. The example below shows how a carrier might determine a one-way rate per mile from Memphis, TN to Miami, FL based on expected empty miles.

Pricing from Memphis, TN to Miami, FL	
Desired Net Revenue Per Mile	$ 1.50
Loaded Miles (Memphis to Miami)	1,052
Empty Miles (Miami to Atlanta)	670
Total Trip Miles	1,722
Total Desired Revenue	$ 2,583.00
Billed Miles Per Trip	1,052
Suggested Revenue Per Billed Mile	**$ 2.46**

Using this method, the carrier includes the loaded miles from Memphis to Miami, as well as the empty miles from Miami to Atlanta, to determine the total desired revenue for the trip. The total trip miles are multiplied by the desired net revenue per mile to determine the total desired revenue (1,722 total miles x $1.50 per mile). This adjustment is necessary to provide the carrier with the appropriate revenue level for serving an extreme backhaul market such as south Florida.

Market Type and Length of Haul

While market types are always an important factor, the relative significance of the backhaul and headhaul market characteristics changes over different length of haul levels. Origin and destination market characteristics become less important in both very short length of haul ranges and very long length of haul ranges. The purely theoretical scale below shows that market characteristics are usually most important on loads with a length of haul between 500 and 1,500 miles.[42] The graph is based on a scale of 1 to 10, with 10 representing the highest relevance of market type to one-way pricing strategy.

Significance of Market Type at Different Length of Haul Levels

Short Length of Haul

Headhaul and backhaul market characteristics are not of great significance in pricing on short length of haul loads for several reasons. First, on very short loads up to about 200 miles, it is not uncommon for trucks to simply return to the origin point without securing a return load. The shorter the load, the more likely it is that the truck will just return empty to the origin market for its next load. In these cases, the characteristics of both the origin and destination markets are irrelevant. However, as distance increases, the characteristics of both the origin and destination market increase in importance.

On loads between 200 and 400 miles, market characteristics increase in importance compared to shorter loads, but are not always a major factor in the pricing decision. The most important pricing factors for these loads are length of haul, expected empty miles,

---

[42] This is a theoretical statement to illustrate how length of haul generally impacts pricing between different market types. In actual practice, there are notable exceptions to this rule.

and cycle time. Regardless of other factors, as distance increases beyond the extreme short haul range, the characteristics of both the origin and destination market increase in importance, especially in more extreme headhaul and backhaul markets.

Long Length of Haul

As the length of haul increases over approximately 1,300 to 1,500 miles, market characteristics begin to become increasingly less significant. Market significance declines because the pricing impact of a change in market type is spread over a greater and greater number of miles. At these high mileages, length of haul, velocity, and asset utilization become the main factors in the pricing decision. Market characteristics are still a factor, but rate levels and market conditions will appear to "even out" over longer and longer length of haul levels.

Consider the following example of pricing from Memphis, TN, a strong headhaul market, to three similar backhaul markets with very different length of haul levels.

Origin	Destination	Miles	Rate
Memphis, TN	Richmond, VA	824	$ 1.95
Memphis, TN	Albuquerque, NM	1,008	$ 1.85
Memphis, TN	Portland, OR	2,339	$ 1.65

The three destination markets are all similar backhaul markets, but as length of haul increases, the rate per mile decreases. On the much longer Portland, OR lane, it is not necessary to charge $1.95 per mile for the entire trip like the shorter Richmond, VA destination. The compensation needed by the carrier for sending the truck into a backhaul market is captured in the first 700 to 1,000 miles of the trip. The revenue for the miles beyond that point can be at normal rates. The table below illustrates this concept by breaking the Portland trip down into two segments.

Long Length of Haul Backhaul Market Pricing by Trip Segment

Mileage Segment	Miles	Rate	Total Cost
First 800 Miles	800	$ 1.95	$ 1,560.00
All Other Miles	1,539	$ 1.50	$ 2,308.50
Total Trip	2,339	$ 1.65	$ 3,868.50

The rate per mile of $1.65 for the trip can be broken down into two segments. The first 800 miles of the trip is charged at $1.95 to capture the revenue needed for moving the truck into a backhaul market. The last 1,539 miles are charged at a standard rate of $1.50 per mile.[43] The net result is the actual rate of $1.65 per billed mile. This theoretical segment example is presented to provide an explanation of the $1.65 rate at this length of haul compared to higher rates for similar shorter length of haul lanes. This example is not intended to be a specific technique for pricing these lanes.

---

[43] The $1.50 per mile rate is used as a general baseline average rate per mile for illustration purposes only. The rate is not meant to be indicative of any actual or suggested one-way pricing.

Seasonality

Seasonal shipping patterns are an important consideration in developing a pricing strategy for a customer. Seasonal shipping patterns can occur within a variety of time segments. Common seasonal patterns are often observed by day of week, weekly or monthly. Some shippers also have unique seasonal patterns or special shipping needs such as end-of-month and end-of-quarter spikes in shipping activity.

End-of-Month Spikes

The graph below illustrates monthly seasonality during the year along with end-of-quarter spikes in shipping volumes. For this shipper, the average monthly volume increases from the beginning of the year to the end of the year. This type of pattern is common for shippers in many different industries.

Average Load Volume by Month

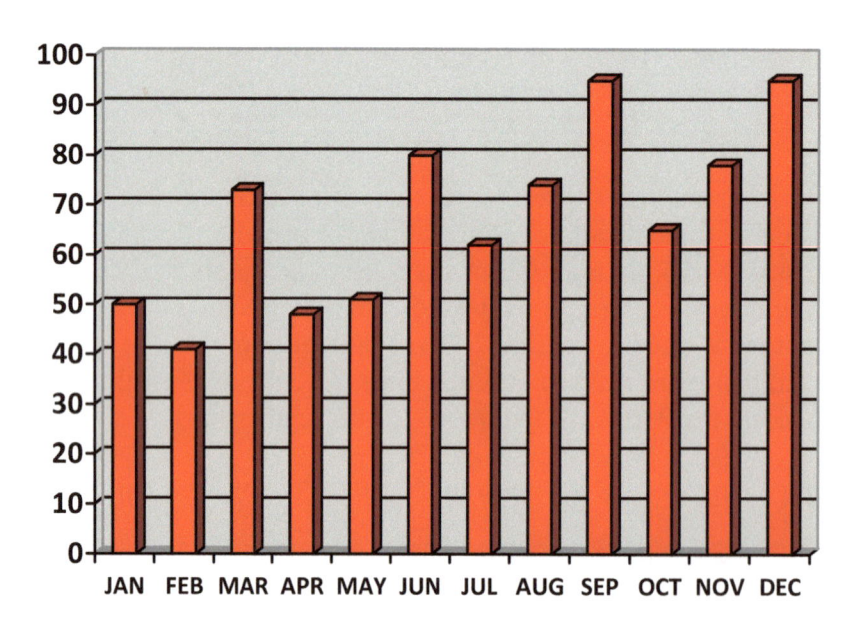

The end-of-quarter spikes in volume are also common for many shippers. In many cases, the reason for the spikes is due to the accounting system and measurement programs in place by the shipper's corporate management. The accounting treatment of end-of-quarter shipments allows shippers to reduce inventory and appear to increase sales for the ending quarter, thus improving (or appearing to improve) financial performance for the ending quarter.

Day-of-Week Seasonality

The graph below illustrates seasonality from day to day during the typical shipping week for a customer location. Ignoring weekends, loads fluctuate from a low of 9 loads on Wednesday to a high of 18 loads on Friday.

Load Volume by Day of Week

Day	Loads
SUN	4
MON	15
TUE	10
WED	9
THU	14
FRI	18
SAT	3

Significant day-to-day fluctuations in load volume put intense pressure on the carrier to make operating adjustments to provide the necessary capacity for the shipper on a daily basis. Suppose the carrier plans to provide 13 trucks each day for this shipper. On days when this shipper's volumes are down, the carrier will potentially have trucks without an available load. Likewise, when load volumes are higher than expected, the carrier will need to locate additional trucks.

On high volume days, one option for providing capacity is to take trucks away from other customers in the area. This reallocation of available capacity could create service problems for customers that don't receive adequate capacity.[44] A second option is to move trucks into the market for the shipper, potentially from excessive distances, causing the carrier to incur costly empty miles and in turn reduce the net revenue per mile and profitability for this customer.[45] Carriers must take these potential seasonal fluctuations into account and price appropriately as shown in the examples that follow.

---

[44] When the demand for trucks exceeds available capacity, carriers must make difficult decisions when determining which customers receive available trucks and which customers do not.

[45] For more information on the impact of shifting capacity, refer to the section on capacity and balance.

Adjusting Empty Mile Estimates for Seasonal Business

In order to correctly price seasonal business, carriers must adjust pricing based on the expected number of empty miles that will occur as a result of the network adjustments necessary to serve the seasonal shipment volumes. As a baseline, consider a situation where a shipper has 50 loads per week in a very steady pattern of 10 loads per day, Monday through Friday. In this case, no adjustment in empty miles is necessary. The pricing manager can assume a normal amount of empty miles and price the opportunity accordingly. The table below illustrates the empty miles analysis for this network.

Expected Empty Miles – Steady Volumes

Average Expected Weekly Activity Day	Loads	Average Length of Haul	Expected Empty Miles	Total Trip Miles	Empty Miles %	Loaded Miles	Empty Miles	Total Miles
Monday	10	800	90.0	890	10.1%	8,000	900	8,900
Tuesday	10	800	90.0	890	10.1%	8,000	900	8,900
Wednesday	10	800	90.0	890	10.1%	8,000	900	8,900
Thursday	10	800	90.0	890	10.1%	8,000	900	8,900
Friday	10	800	90.0	890	10.1%	8,000	900	8,900
Weekly Totals	**50**	**800**	**90.0**	**890**	**10.1%**	**40,000**	**4,500**	**44,500**

In this case, an expected empty mile level of 90 miles per load is applied to all loads in the network, resulting in a reasonable empty miles percentage of 10.1% for this balanced customer network.[46]

Now consider a situation that also consists of 50 loads per week, but because of the shipper's needs, the shipment levels are much higher on Monday and Friday and much lower on Tuesday, Wednesday, and Thursday. The table below illustrates how empty miles might be incurred on both the high volume and low volume days.

Expected Empty Miles – Seasonal Volumes

Average Expected Weekly Activity Day	Loads	Average Length of Haul	Expected Empty Miles	Total Trip Miles	Empty Miles %	Loaded Miles	Empty Miles	Total Miles
Monday	17	800	140.0	940	14.9%	13,600	2,380	15,980
Tuesday	6	800	75.0	875	8.6%	4,800	450	5,250
Wednesday	6	800	80.0	880	9.1%	4,800	480	5,280
Thursday	6	800	75.0	875	8.6%	4,800	450	5,250
Friday	15	800	125.8	925.8	13.6%	12,000	1,887	13,887
Weekly Totals	**50**	**800**	**112.9**	**912.94**	**12.4%**	**40,000**	**5,647**	**45,647**

Notice that the average empty miles per trip have increased from 90.0 to 112.9 in the seasonal scenario. Also notice that the expected empty miles increased dramatically on the heavy shipping days of Monday and Friday while actually decreasing on the lower volume days.

---

[46] A "reasonable" empty miles percentage varies depending on many factors such as length of haul, origin market location, and capacity and balance levels.

The changes in expected empty miles are directly related to the distance each incremental truck must travel to reach the customer's shipping location. The first few trucks assigned to this customer will likely be very close to the customer's facility, perhaps less than 50 miles away. Each additional truck will be sourced from further and further from the customer's facility, causing empty miles to continue to increase.[47] For this reason, empty miles are higher on a per-load basis on heavy shipping days and lower on lighter shipping days. The table below illustrates the impact of the empty miles generated as each incremental truck is sourced to the customer.

Incremental Empty Miles as Real-Time Truck Needs Increase

Friday			
Estimated Empty Miles			
Truck	Empty Miles		
1	41		
2	55		
3	66		
4	72		
5	77		
6	92		
7	97		
8	115		
9	135		
10	150	90.0	Average for first 10 Trucks
11	175		
12	187		
13	190		
14	210		
15	225	125.8	Average for all 15 Trucks

The average empty miles for the first 10 trucks of 90 miles matches the previous steady volume illustration. The 125.8 average empty miles for 15 total trucks matches the seasonal volume illustration for Friday. The table indicates that each incremental truck is sourced from further and further away from the customer's shipping location.

An additional challenge for the carrier during peak periods is the fact that often these extra trucks take valuable capacity away from other customers in the carrier's network. On the other hand, during low volume periods, the carrier may struggle to find loads for available trucks that would otherwise be utilized by the seasonal shipper.

Suppose this customer's facility is located in Greenville, TX, a suburb of Dallas, TX. The map that follows illustrates where the first 10 trucks and last 5 trucks might be located prior to being assigned to this customer. The first 10 trucks are sourced from the Dallas metropolitan area. The final 5 trucks must come from as far away as Shreveport,

---

[47] This statement is generally true, but is oversimplified for the illustration in this theoretical example. In actual practice, empty miles, along with many other factors, will influence the decision of how each truck is assigned to a load.

LA and Abilene, TX. Any additional trucks needed by this shipper would, theoretically, be sourced from further and further away.

Sourcing Incremental Trucks to Greenville, TX

Rate Per Mile Adjustment. The carrier must adjust pricing to compensate for the additional empty miles that will be required by this shipper. The table below illustrates the calculation of the adjustment to the pricing assuming the carrier wishes to earn a net revenue per mile of $1.28 per mile.

Adjustments to Rate Per Mile	Shipping Pattern	
	Steady	**Seasonal**
Desired Net Revenue Per Mile	$ 1.28	$ 1.28
Loaded Miles	800.0	800.0
Empty Miles	90.0	112.9
Total Trip Miles	890.0	912.9
Total Desired Revenue	$ 1,139.20	$ 1,168.51
Billed Miles Per Trip	800.0	800.0
Suggested Revenue Per Billed Mile	**$ 1.42**	**$ 1.46**

The total desired trip revenue is computed as the $1.28 desired net revenue per mile multiplied by the total trip miles, including empty miles. The resulting total revenue is then divided by the billed miles of 800 miles per trip to determine the rate per billed mile. Based on this example, the seasonal business requires an additional 4 cents per billed mile to compensate for the empty miles created by the customer's seasonal demands.

While in this example the seasonal approach has been applied to a day-of-week situation, the same approach could be adapted and applied to other seasonal timeframes such as weekly, monthly, or end-of-quarter peak demands. Intelligent carriers may be able to adapt their network to fit seasonal customer requirements of this type. However, in order to do so, they may need to offer attractive pricing to other customers that provide the flexibility needed to consistently source trucks into the Dallas market for this customer.

Carriers may also use operational and customer diversification strategies to accommodate seasonal shippers. One strategy is to find other shippers with complementary shipment volumes that fit well with the original seasonal shipper's patterns. This approach is discussed in detail in a later chapter.

Round Trip Pricing

Round-trip pricing applies to loads that are pre-arranged to originate at Point A, move to Point B, then return to Point A, all as part of a single trip. For example, automobile manufacturers often require moves of this type when parts are shipped from a supplier (Point A) into an assembly plant (Point B) on special racks. After the parts delivery, a load of empty racks is then returned back to the supplier's origin location (Point A) by the carrier.

Cost-Plus Round Trip Pricing

In round-trip pricing, headhaul and backhaul markets are not a consideration since the truck will return to the origin point with the same customer and without incurring any empty or unpaid miles. As a result, operating costs provide the basis for establishing round-trip pricing. Carriers often use an activity-based costing model or similar costing model to forecast costs and determine round trip rates. An activity-based model, such as the one shown below, provides an accurate method for determining round-trip pricing.[48]

Calculation of Round Trip Pricing

Round Trip Pricing Using Activity Based Costing Model									
				Per Mile	Per Load	Per Hour			
	Activity-Based Costs:			$ 1.06	$ 34.07	$ 8.63			

Based on One-way Length of Haul Desired Operating Ratio: 87.0%

Length of Haul	Miles Per Hour	Transit Hours	Dock Hours	Total Activity Based Costs			Total Trip Cost	Target Revenue	RT Rate Per Mile
				Per Mile	Per Load	Per Hour			
300	50	6.00	1.50	$ 318.00	$ 34.07	$ 64.73	$ 416.80	$ 479.07	$ 1.60
400	50	8.00	1.50	$ 424.00	$ 34.07	$ 81.99	$ 540.06	$ 620.75	$ 1.55
500	55	9.09	1.50	$ 530.00	$ 34.07	$ 91.40	$ 655.47	$ 753.41	$ 1.51
600	55	10.91	1.50	$ 636.00	$ 34.07	$ 107.09	$ 777.16	$ 893.29	$ 1.49
700	55	12.73	1.50	$ 742.00	$ 34.07	$ 122.78	$ 898.85	$ 1,033.16	$ 1.48
800	57	14.04	1.50	$ 848.00	$ 34.07	$ 134.07	$ 1,016.14	$ 1,167.97	$ 1.46
900	57	15.79	1.50	$ 954.00	$ 34.07	$ 149.21	$ 1,137.28	$ 1,307.22	$ 1.45
1,000	57	17.54	1.50	$ 1,060.00	$ 34.07	$ 164.35	$ 1,258.42	$ 1,446.46	$ 1.45
1,100	57	19.30	1.50	$ 1,166.00	$ 34.07	$ 179.49	$ 1,379.56	$ 1,585.70	$ 1.44
1,200	57	21.05	1.50	$ 1,272.00	$ 34.07	$ 194.63	$ 1,500.70	$ 1,724.94	$ 1.44

The goal of the calculations is to determine the rate per mile for the round-trip. For accuracy and simplification, the model determines the cost based on the one-way distance. Basing the round-trip rate per mile on the one-way distance is more accurate because the round trip is, in terms of cycle time, two one-way trips with no empty miles. This method avoids overestimating the efficiency of the round-trip by using the one-way distance instead of the full round-trip distance.

---

[48] Refer to Chapter 2 on truckload economics for a detailed review of how these activity-based cost standards were established.

The round-trip pricing format above forecasts the cost of each trip based on three cost drivers: miles, loads and time. The model computes the transit time based on standard velocity (miles per hour) for each length of haul segment. The total costs include a flat charge per load, a variable charge per mile, and a variable charge per hour.

To determine the price to the customer, the carrier must add a profit margin. One simple method for computing the profit margin is to establish a standard operating ratio and apply this operating ratio standard to compute the margin and revenue. Total revenue is computed as total cost divided by the target operating ratio.

Once the rate calculations are completed, the round-trip rates are ready to be added to the contract. The table below illustrates a standard round-trip rate agreement that might be included in the contract between the carrier and the shipper.

Round Trip Pricing Agreement		
Origin: Dallas, TX		
Minimum Charge: $650		
Standard fuel surcharge applies.		
Miles		Rate
One-Way	Round Trip	Per Mile
Under 300	Under 600	$ 1.75
300 - 399	600 - 799	$ 1.60
400 - 499	800 - 999	$ 1.55
500 - 599	1,000 - 1,199	$ 1.51
600 - 699	1,200 - 1,399	$ 1.49
700 - 799	1,400 - 1,599	$ 1.48
800 - 899	1,600 - 1,799	$ 1.46
900 - 999	1,800 - 1,999	$ 1.45
Over 1,000	Over 2,000	$ 1.44

The contract includes a minimum charge of $650 as well as the per-mile round-trip rates. All trips over 2,000 miles are charged at the same rate per mile. Effectively, all cost efficiencies of length of haul have been absorbed in the rate beyond the 2,000 mile level, so no further rate reduction is appropriate beyond this mileage level.

Round-trip rates also assume that the shipper will provide the return trip to the carrier in a timely manner. The carrier can't hold the tractor and driver for an excessive amount of time waiting for the return trip from the shipper. The round-trip rate agreement should include a provision for the amount of time the carrier allows the shipper for reloading the truck with the return trip. If the grace period expires before the return load is provided, the cost for the trip may revert back to one-way pricing and the round-trip pricing will no longer apply. The contract may also include applicable detention charges if the return trip is not provided in a timely manner.

CHAPTER 6: Network Management and Optimization

Accurate one-way pricing is only part of the challenge for a successful carrier. After the pricing is in place and the shipper begins to utilize the carrier, the carrier must then optimize the trucks, loads and customers into an efficient, profitable network. These goals must be accomplished while also successfully meeting each shipper's unique service expectations.

Successful carriers utilize a combination of well-trained, detail-oriented staff and sophisticated computer systems to manage and evaluate their freight network. The two major network challenges for a carrier are 1) how to maintain a balance between customer loads and available tractors in each market and 2) how to assign each tractor to each load. This chapter provides an overview of various carrier methods for addressing these critical real-time challenges.

Network Capacity and Balance

Network capacity and balance is a critical element of a carrier's daily and weekly operating environment. The carrier's goal is to balance the number of trucks in a market with the number of available customer loads. A well-balanced network allows the carrier to minimize empty miles, maximize utilization, and avoid capacity-related service issues. The table below, presented in a previous chapter, provides an example of a real-time capacity and balance situation for a regional carrier based in Birmingham, Alabama.

Capacity & Balance as of 8:15 am			
Planning Region	Available Trucks	Available Loads	Net Balance
AL - North	32	40	(8)
AL - South	15	11	4
GA - North	41	38	3
GA - South	27	15	12
MS - North	18	22	(4)
MS - South	11	7	4
TN - East	21	21	-
TN - Central	21	15	6
TN - West	22	35	(13)
Network Totals	**208**	**204**	**4**

The network totals indicate a reasonable net balance of available trucks and available loads across the network. However, several planning regions are extremely unbalanced with either excess trucks or excess loads. A negative net balance value indicates a region with excess loads. A positive net balance indicates a region with available trucks.

The carrier must constantly work to correct the capacity and balance situation in each market. Both situations, excess trucks and excess loads, are equally important for the carrier to rectify. Markets with excess loads are at risk of loads not being picked up or delivered according to customer requirements. Markets with excess trucks are at risk of having trucks and drivers that are underutilized. The carrier's revenue and utilization could potentially suffer. Another important implication of lost utilization is driver satisfaction. Drivers that wait long periods of time for an available load will experience high levels of dissatisfaction, causing the carrier to face a potential increase in driver turnover problems.

The carrier will utilize a variety of strategies to alleviate capacity and balance issues. A previous chapter focused on the marketing and pricing approach to address the problem in the long run. A bid response case study in a future chapter also provides additional examples of the influence of capacity and balance on the carrier's pricing strategy. The strategies presented in the sections that follow focus on the daily and weekly operational solution to the capacity and balance challenge.

Freight Solicitation

Real-Time Freight Solicitation

One critical function of the carrier's customer service and network management team is freight solicitation. Freight solicitation is the process of contacting customers and requesting freight to fill specific carrier inbound or outbound needs. For example, as a result of temporary network imbalances on a given day, the carrier may have an excess number of trucks in a geographic market. In order to secure additional loads for the excess trucks and drivers, the customer service team will urgently call customers within this market and request additional outbound loads.

Carriers will also use freight solicitation to secure loads to meet excess demand for trucks in a particular market. For example, on Friday morning, a major customer in the Atlanta market may inform the carrier that their outbound shipping needs on the following Monday will increase from 20 loads to 40 loads. After reviewing expected capacity and balance for Monday in the Atlanta market, the carrier determines that additional capacity will be needed to meet the anticipated outbound demand. The customer service team would then use freight solicitation to call shippers around the region and request extra loads into the Atlanta market that deliver on or before the following Monday.

Yield Management and Freight Solicitation

Sophisticated carriers utilize optimization programs or yield management systems to optimize the freight solicitation process. The optimization and analysis process provides recommendations on the most profitable customers to solicit on a particular lane or in a particular market. The recommendations are based on a variety of factors such as revenue per mile, operational efficiency, and overall customer and lane profitability. This information is determined from the detailed load history present in the carrier's computer system. The process may also recommend those customers that are most likely to have available freight so that the customer service team does not waste valuable time soliciting customers that are unlikely to have freight available.

The yield management system will provide the carrier's customer service team with a list of customers to call and the specific lanes to request from the customer. In the previous example for the regional carrier based in Birmingham, AL, a yield management system will first attempt to recommend lanes that address the capacity and balance problems in both markets with a single load. For example, the south Alabama region has excess trucks and the north Alabama region is in need of trucks. The yield management system will search for customers with loads that move from south Alabama into north Alabama. The yield management recommendations may also include a ranking of the best lanes to request from the customer.

Truck Repositioning

In order to balance the network and continuously provide tractor capacity to customers, carriers must move available equipment from one area to another by incurring empty miles. Not only do carriers incur the direct variable costs such as fuel and maintenance when moving the truck, but the time spent by the driver also takes away from the driver's hours available to drive, so valuable productivity is lost. In fact, the driver's empty trip may require so much time that the driver may run out of available driving time and be forced to take a mandatory break after arriving for the pick-up of the next load.

One strategy a carrier might use in repositioning equipment is to assign trucks to loads so that the empty miles and lost driving hours are spread among different trucks. This tactic is especially applicable when moving equipment out of severe backhaul markets. The example below illustrates this tactic assuming the two loads and two trucks shown here represent the only loads and trucks in the area for the carrier.

Rolling Capacity to Available Loads

The carrier has two alternatives for assigning each truck to one of the available loads. Despite the fact that Truck 6 is already very close to Load A, the carrier may choose to assign Truck 6 to Load B. By doing so, Truck 4 would then be assigned to Load A. This tactic splits the empty miles among the two available drivers and minimizes the wait time for picking up Load B. Many other operating variables may also influence the assignment decision, especially the required pick-up times for each load and the number of driving hours each of the two drivers has available. For example, if Load A must be picked up in 45 minutes and Load B can be picked up the next day, the carrier would assign Truck 6 to Load A in order to meet the pick-up time requirement for Load A.

Exchanging Loads from One Driver to Another

For many reasons, carriers may elect to have two drivers meet in-transit and exchange loads with one another. Similarly, the carrier may have a driver temporarily drop a load at a secure location and later assign a different driver to pick up the dropped load and deliver it to the final destination. This tactic is often called a "t-call" or terminal-call. The carrier will utilize these tactics for many reasons including utilization maximization, service recovery, and driver satisfaction. Several specific situations are described in the table and sections below.

Common Reasons for Swapping Loads	
Stakeholder	**Reason**
Carrier	Maximize driver home time
	Minimize the impact of buffer time
	Transfer a load to the appropriate fleet
	Adhere to driver "comfort zones"
Shipper	Service recovery to prevent a late delivery
	Meet transit time requirements
	Meet pick-up time expectations

The most common of these reasons are discussed in the sections below.

Carrier Reasons for Load Swaps

Buffer Time Avoidance

Buffer time occurs when a load has required pick-up and delivery times that significantly exceed the necessary transit time for a load. For example, suppose a 400 mile load is required to be picked up on a Friday morning and cannot be delivered until Monday morning. The carrier must manage the load for three days but the 400 mile distance requires no more than one day to complete. The extra two days represent unnecessary buffer time. To avoid lost utilization and driver dissatisfaction, the carrier might choose to utilize a terminal call and let the load sit in a secure location during the two days of buffer time.[49] Once the buffer time has expired, the carrier will assign an available truck to the waiting load to complete the final delivery.

---

[49] The average driver would be very unhappy if he were stuck with this inefficient load for three days. The driver would experience very poor productivity and lost income opportunities.

Driver Get Home

The carrier's ability to provide drivers with consistent home-time is critical to driver satisfaction and driver retention. Whenever possible, quality carriers will search for opportunities to get drivers home on a regular basis without significantly impacting empty mile costs and profitability. Identifying and executing strategic swaps can increase home-time opportunities without a significant cost. Consider the scenario outlined below.

Swap Opportunity	Driver A	Driver B
Home Location	Dallas, TX	Chicago, IL
Load Assignment	New Orleans, LA to Chicago, IL	Nashville, TN to Dallas, TX

Provided that the transit times and delivery schedules will allow an efficient swap, the two drivers could meet in Memphis, TN and swap loads.[50] The driver from Dallas would deliver the load to Dallas and the Chicago driver would deliver the load to Chicago, allowing both drivers the opportunity for home time that otherwise would not have been available without a swap.

Fleet Type Switch

Large carriers will often have several different fleet types that specialize in serving different types of loads, especially loads of different distances or within certain geographic regions. As part of the network optimization process, these carriers will utilize swaps to switch loads from the unintended fleet type to the correct fleet type. For example, a carrier might have an Atlanta-based "Regional" truck pick up a "Linehaul" load in Jacksonville, FL that is going to Chicago, IL.[51] The regional truck just happened to be available in Jacksonville and needed a load back to Atlanta. The "Regional" truck will make the pick-up in Jacksonville and drop the load in Atlanta. The carrier will then assign a "Linehaul" truck to carry the load from Atlanta to the final destination in Chicago, Illinois.

Comfort Zones

As a method to improve driver satisfaction and prevent turnover, some carriers implement "Comfort Zones" to limit a driver's operating territory to a certain mileage radius around the home terminal. The goal of this strategy is to increase opportunities for the driver to enjoy valuable home time. In order to respect these zones, the carrier will use strategic swaps to keep each driver within these predefined regions. The typical swap scenario would be very similar to the example in the fleet type switch section above.

---

[50] Both loads route through Memphis, TN on the way to each final destination.
[51] Regional trucks typically serve shorter length of haul loads within a particular region. Linehaul trucks typically serve longer length of haul loads and are not limited to a specific service region.

Shipper Reasons for Load Swaps

Service Recovery

As circumstances dictate, carriers will utilize a load swap to recover a load that would otherwise be late without executing the swap. For example, suppose Driver A picks up an 800 mile load on Monday morning and must make delivery on Wednesday at noon. Based on the hours-of-service regulations, Driver A has enough time to complete the trip safely and legally. However, on Monday evening, Driver A's tractor has a mechanical problem that cannot be fixed until Wednesday, which would cause the load to be delivered late. To prevent a late delivery, the carrier would quickly locate a second truck and driver to take the load from Driver A and complete the final delivery on time.

Transit Time Requirements

Certain shippers may require transit times on some shipments that cannot be completed legally by a single driver due to hours-of-service regulations. For example, the shipper may request a transit time of 24 hours on a 1,000 mile load. If the carrier has a team available, the transit time is rarely a problem. However, a single driver would require at least 30 to 38 hours to complete the 1,000 mile load while properly conforming to the hours-of-service regulations.

The carrier can complete the load within the required transit time by utilizing two single drivers and a load swap tactic. The first driver will pick up the load and drive about 500 miles, at which point the driver will require a mandatory break. A fully-rested second driver will meet the first driver at the 500 mile point, secure the trailer and drive the next 500 miles to make the final delivery. This strategy is effective to meet transit times but does create additional cost for the carrier. The same load with a normal transit time requirement is far less costly for the carrier to manage.

Pick-up Time Expectations

Shippers sometimes request that carriers arrive to pick up a load on a certain date and time even if the pick-up time is much sooner than what is needed to deliver the load on time. For example, the shipper may request that the carrier pick up a 500 mile load on Friday afternoon, but the load cannot be delivered until the following Wednesday. The transit time on the load should take only about 1 day, but the carrier is left to manage the load for five days. This extra buffer time is very inefficient for the carrier and driver. In order to protect and maximize utilization, the carrier will often choose to have the driver that picks up the load drop it at a secure location in-route to the final destination. At the appropriate time, the carrier will dispatch a new driver to pick up the dropped load and complete the final delivery. This strategy allows the carrier to avoid the buffer time inefficiency, but it does create additional costs to execute the load swap tactic.

Other Swap Considerations

Cost of Out-of-Route Miles

For most potential swap situations, each of the two drivers will be required to deviate from the normal route for any load involved in a swap. This deviation will cause the loaded miles for each load to exceed the billed miles for the load, thereby increasing the direct cost to serve both loads.[52] While the carrier must consider the cost of the swap, in most cases, the carrier expects the benefits of the swap to exceed the cost of the extra miles and the time consumed by both drivers during the execution of the swap.

Load Swap Optimization Technology

The operating systems for some carriers include an optimization module for identifying opportunities to execute value-added load swaps. The optimization system can include specific rules (constraints) for conforming to carrier requirements such as comfort zones, service performance, transit times, and buffer time avoidance. The system will weigh the benefits of the potential swap with the operating costs associated with the proposed swap. In cases where the benefits exceed the cost, the optimization system will recommend a swap. The swap recommendation will identify the optimal drivers and loads to be included as well as the actual swap location.

Driver Satisfaction

The carrier must consider the impact of every operating decision on the satisfaction of the drivers involved. In some swap situations, the drivers may feel that the swap is a waste of time and counterproductive. On the other hand, strategic swaps are often executed to allow one or both of the drivers involved to get home on or before a specific date. Carriers must use swaps wisely to add the most value while minimizing the potential negative impact of swaps on driver morale and productivity.

---

[52] Billed miles represent the base miles for the trip and the miles the customer will pay for, regardless of the actual route chosen by the driver and the carrier.

Customer Diversification and the Portfolio Concept

Investment experts recommend that investors "not put all their eggs in one basket." Instead, investors should reduce investment risk through diversification by investing in many different stocks in many different industries. Following the same concept, intelligent carriers can reduce risk by applying the same principles to the development and management of their one-way customer base and freight network.

Far too often, smaller carriers become extremely dependent on a particular industry, or even worse, on one individual customer. If this industry or customer should experience a significant drop in business or shipping activity, the carrier's revenue and profitability will suffer. By establishing significant business relationships with multiple customers in a variety of industries, the carrier can protect itself against a downturn in any particular industry or customer.

Diversification of the customer base can also protect the carrier against seasonal business fluctuations. In fact, the carrier may be able to establish relationships with various customers with complementary season patterns. For example, a carrier with significant freight volumes from a customer that manufactures soup might seek out a new customer to complement the seasonal shipping pattern of the soup customer.

The graph below illustrates the seasonal shipping pattern a carrier might experience with a major soup shipper.

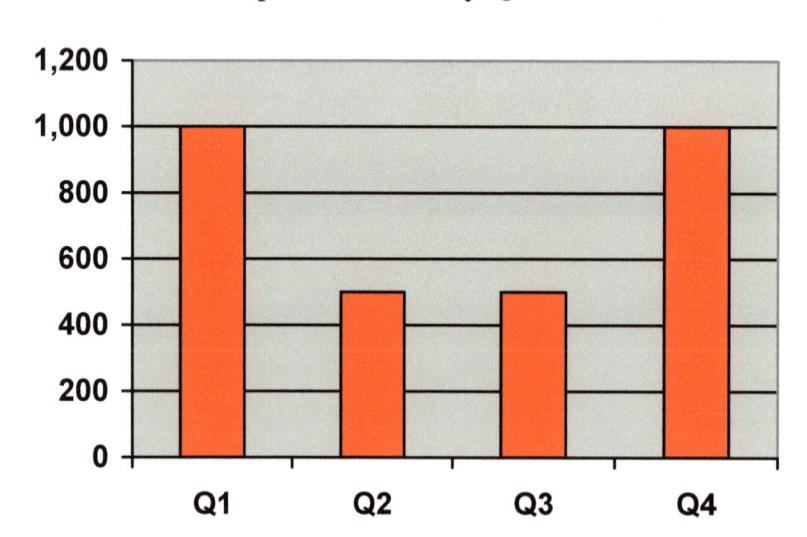

Soup Load Count by Quarter

Quarter	Load Count
Q1	1,000
Q2	500
Q3	500
Q4	1,000

Since soup ships heavily during the colder periods of Q1 and Q4, the carrier might seek out relationships with shippers of products that peak during warmer periods.

Consider the seasonal shipping pattern below for a manufacturer of consumer grills.

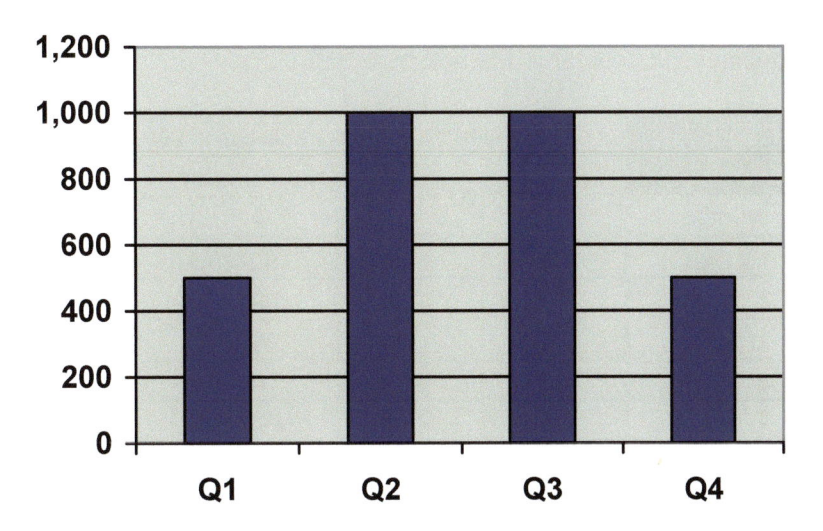

Grill Load Count by Quarter

If the carrier is successful in gaining a significant volume of freight from the grill manufacturer, the two seasonal customers will effectively balance each other out and the carrier's network should become more efficient. The graph below illustrates the combined network of both the grill shipper and soup shipper.

Combined Soup & Grill Load Count by Quarter

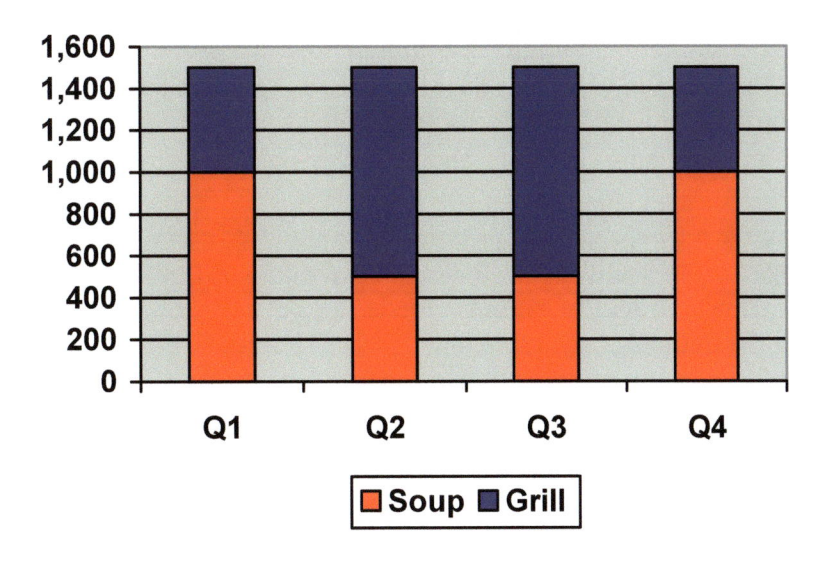

This theoretical example illustrates the potential benefit to the carrier of creating a network of customers that are complimentary in seasonality, industry and relative share of the carrier's total network.

The Tractor and Load Assignment Problem

Carriers constantly face the critical decision of determining which available trucks to assign to the pool of available customer loads. Consider the simple network of five available tractors and five available loads shown below.

Current Network Tractor Number	Empty Miles from Tractor Location to Load Pick-up Location					
	Load Number				
	A	B	C	D	E
1	95	150	60	77	123
2	210	160	140	110	190
3	41	15	79	101	40
4	88	91	115	62	55
5	350	210	140	120	105

The carrier has five available loads (A, B, C, D, and E) and five available trucks (1, 2, 3, 4, and 5). The values in the table represent the number of empty miles that each truck must travel to pick up each available load. For example, Truck 1 must drive 95 empty miles from its current location to pick up Load A at the customer location.

The carrier's planners must determine which truck to assign to each load while also minimizing the total empty miles. While the minimization of the empty miles is the primary objective, the assignment plan must also take into consideration many other factors. Other key factors include the driver's need to get home, the driver's available hours of service, customer pick-up times, and each load's required transit time. Including these factors in the decision will often dictate a load assignment solution where empty miles are not fully minimized. However, empty miles are minimized while also allowing other important network considerations and company objectives to be met.

In order to solve the load assignment problem and minimize costs, many carriers utilize sophisticated optimization software that allows them to identify the optimal (lowest cost) assignment of available trucks to available loads. The primary objective in the development of the optimal assignment plan is to minimize the empty miles of the network. In addition, many of the optimization systems also take into consideration many of the other variables such as driver hours of service, customer requirements, and expected transit times.

The network optimization software utilizes a common approach to this type of problem known as Linear Programming. While the model to solve the entire problem and account for all variables is very complex, the basic model presented in this section is designed only to minimize empty miles.

For the purposes of this example, the model below is simplified and represents a network involving only five tractors (1, 2, 3, 4, and 5) and five available customer loads (A, B, C, D, and E). The goal of the optimization model is to decide how each of the five available trucks should be assigned to each of the five available loads in order to minimize total empty miles for the network.

The Optimization Model

Decision Variables

Each of these decision variables represents a possible tractor and load combination. Each variable will be assigned a value "1" if the tractor is assigned to the load or a value of "0" if the tractor is not assigned to the load. For example, if Truck 3 is assigned to Load A, then $X_{3A}=1$. Otherwise, $X_{3A}=0$.

X_{1A} = Truck 1 assigned to Load A
X_{1B} = Truck 1 assigned to Load B
X_{1C} = Truck 1 assigned to Load C
X_{1D} = Truck 1 assigned to Load D
X_{1E} = Truck 1 assigned to Load E

X_{2A} = Truck 2 assigned to Load A
X_{2B} = Truck 2 assigned to Load B
X_{2C} = Truck 2 assigned to Load C
X_{2D} = Truck 2 assigned to Load D
X_{2E} = Truck 2 assigned to Load E

X_{3A} = Truck 3 assigned to Load A
X_{3B} = Truck 3 assigned to Load B
X_{3C} = Truck 3 assigned to Load C
X_{3D} = Truck 3 assigned to Load D
X_{3E} = Truck 3 assigned to Load E

X_{4A} = Truck 4 assigned to Load A
X_{4B} = Truck 4 assigned to Load B
X_{4C} = Truck 4 assigned to Load C
X_{4D} = Truck 4 assigned to Load D
X_{4E} = Truck 4 assigned to Load E

X_{5A} = Truck 5 assigned to Load A
X_{5B} = Truck 5 assigned to Load B
X_{5C} = Truck 5 assigned to Load C
X_{5D} = Truck 5 assigned to Load D
X_{5E} = Truck 5 assigned to Load E

The Objective Equation

$$\begin{aligned}
\text{Minimize:} \quad & 95X_{1A} + 150X_{1B} + 60X_{1C} + 77X_{1D} + 123X_{1E} \\
+ & 210X_{2A} + 160X_{2B} + 140X_{2C} + 110X_{2D} + 190X_{2E} \\
+ & 41X_{3A} + 15X_{3B} + 79X_{3C} + 101X_{3D} + 40X_{3E} \\
+ & 88X_{4A} + 91X_{4B} + 115X_{4C} + 62X_{4D} + 55X_{4E} \\
+ & 350X_{5A} + 210X_{5B} + 140X_{5C} + 120X_{5D} + 105X_{5E}
\end{aligned}$$

The coefficients for each decision variable are taken from the original chart showing the distance each truck must travel to pick up each load. For example, Truck 1 must travel 95 miles to pick up Load A, 150 miles to pick up Load B, and so forth.

Truck Availability / Capacity Constraints:

```
Truck 1 Capacity:   X_1A + X_1B + X_1C + X_1D + X_1E = 1
Truck 2 Capacity:   X_2A + X_2B + X_2C + X_2D + X_2E = 1
Truck 3 Capacity:   X_3A + X_3B + X_3C + X_3D + X_3E = 1
Truck 4 Capacity:   X_4A + X_4B + X_4C + X_4D + X_4E = 1
Truck 5 Capacity:   X_5A + X_5B + X_5C + X_5D + X_5E = 1
```

Load Availability / Demand Constraints:

```
Load A Availability: X_1A + X_2A + X_3A + X_4A + X_5A = 1
Load B Availability: X_1B + X_2B + X_3B + X_4B + X_5B = 1
Load C Availability: X_1C + X_2C + X_3C + X_4C + X_5C = 1
Load D Availability: X_1D + X_2D + X_3D + X_4D + X_5D = 1
Load E Availability: X_1E + X_2E + X_3E + X_4E + X_5E = 1
```

Decision Variable Constraints:

```
Non-Negativity:        X_1A  X_2A  X_3A . . . X_5E  ≥ 0
Maximum Value of 1:    X_1A  X_2A  X_3A . . . X_5E  ≤ 1
Integer Requirement:   X_1A  X_2A  X_3A . . . X_5E  = Integer
```

Each type of constraint is explained in detail in the next section.

Overview of Decision Variables, Objective Equation and Constraints

Decision Variables: Through the application of the various constraints, each decision variable will take on a value of either "0" or "1." For example, if $X_{3A}=0$, this indicates that Truck 3 is not assigned to Load A. If $X_{3A}=1$, this indicates that Truck 3 is assigned to Load A. This assignment will continue for each truck and load until all trucks are assigned to an available load.

The Objective Equation: The objective equation is designed to compute the total number of empty miles to be incurred based on the proposed optimization solution. For this type of optimization, the goal is to minimize the result of the objective equation. In other words, the primary goal is to minimize the total number of empty miles to be driven to pick up all five loads.

Decision Variable Constraints: These constraints work together to force each decision variable to take on a value of either "0" or "1" in the final solution. Without these constraints, the optimization software could assign unrealistic or negative values to the decision variables. For example, it would be unrealistic to assign 0.40 trucks to a load or to assign -1 loads to a truck. These constraints force the decision variables to take on an integer value of either "0" for not assigned or "1" for assigned.

Truck Availability / Capacity Constraints: These constraints represent the fact that each available truck can be assigned to one and only one available load. The non-negativity constraint and the integer constraint are also necessary for the capacity constraints to function correctly. Based on the design of the constraints, each decision variable can only take on an integer value of "0" or "1." The constraint equation must equal exactly "1" so that each truck receives exactly one load assignment.

Load Availability Constraints: These constraints represent the fact that each load can only be assigned to one and only one truck. The non-negativity constraint and the integer constraint are also necessary for the capacity constraints to function correctly. Based on the design of the constraints, each decision variable can only take on an integer value of "0" or "1." The sum of the constraint equation must equal exactly "1" so that each load is assigned to exactly one truck.

The Optimization Solution

The truck availability constraints, load availability constraints, and other constraints work together to guarantee that no type of double assignment is recommended in the solution. Closely review the example solution below, which has not been optimized. This solution is provided to demonstrate the format of the solution and the calculation of the total empty miles returned by the example solution.

Example Solution	Load Assignments					Total Truck Assignments
Tractor Number	A	B	C	D	E	
1	$X_{1A} = 1$	$X_{1B} = 0$	$X_{1C} = 0$	$X_{1D} = 0$	$X_{1E} = 0$	1
2	$X_{2A} = 0$	$X_{2B} = 1$	$X_{2C} = 0$	$X_{2D} = 0$	$X_{2E} = 0$	1
3	$X_{3A} = 0$	$X_{3B} = 0$	$X_{3C} = 1$	$X_{3D} = 0$	$X_{3E} = 0$	1
4	$X_{4A} = 0$	$X_{4B} = 0$	$X_{4C} = 0$	$X_{4D} = 1$	$X_{4E} = 0$	1
5	$X_{5A} = 0$	$X_{5B} = 0$	$X_{5C} = 0$	$X_{5D} = 0$	$X_{5E} = 1$	1
Load Assignments	1	1	1	1	1	5

The preliminary example solution has assigned Load A to Truck 1, Load B to Truck 2, Load C to Truck 3, Load D to Truck 4, and Load E to Truck 5.

The empty miles can be computed by plugging the solution above into the objective equation. The empty miles calculation for the Tractor 1 portion of the objective equation is shown below.

$$\text{Tractor A Empty Miles} = 95X_{1A} + 150X_{1B} + 60X_{1C} + 77X_{1D} + 123X_{1E}$$

$$\text{Tractor A Empty Miles} = \mathbf{95(1)} + 150(0) + 60(0) + 77(0) + 123(0) = 95 \text{ miles}$$

Instead of showing the previous substitution for the entire objective equation, the table below shows the total empty miles for each truck and for the total assignment solution after plugging the solution into the objective equation. The table format is much simpler to review and summarize than plugging into the actual objective equation.

Proposed Solution	Total Empty Miles					Total Empty Miles
Tractor Number	A	B	C	D	E	
1	95	-	-	-	-	95
2	-	160	-	-	-	160
3	-	-	79	-	-	79
4	-	-	-	62	-	62
5	-	-	-	-	105	105
Miles	95	160	79	62	105	**501**

Since Tractor 1 was assigned to Load A, the empty miles for Tractor 1 and Load A will be 95 miles. Tractor 2 will incur 160 empty miles to pick up load B and so forth for tractors 3, 4, and 5. The total empty miles for all five trucks in this preliminary solution is 501 miles.

While the preliminary solution shown above will get the five loads picked up and delivered, it does not represent the low-cost, optimized solution. Also keep in mind that carriers must constantly solve this problem for fleets of hundreds of trucks or more, thereby making the problem much more complex and impossible to solve by hand. By applying the linear programming optimization model, the true low-cost solution can be quickly identified, regardless of the number of tractors and loads involved.

As a reference, the table below again shows the empty miles each tractor must travel to each available load.

Current Network	Empty Miles from Tractor Location to Load Pick-up Location				
Tractor Number	A	B	C	D	E
1	95	150	60	77	123
2	210	160	140	110	190
3	41	15	79	101	40
4	88	91	115	62	55
5	350	210	140	120	105

The next table shows the optimized, low-cost solution provided by the optimization software package.

Final Optimized Solution

Optimized Solution	Load Assignments					Total Truck Assignments
	Load Number					
Tractor Number	A	B	C	D	E	
1	0	0	0	1	0	1
2	0	1	0	0	0	1
3	1	0	0	0	0	1
4	0	0	0	0	1	1
5	0	0	1	0	0	1
Load Assignments	1	1	1	1	1	5

In this optimized solution, Tractor 1 has been assigned to Load C and Tractor 2 has been assigned to Load B. Notice that all columns and all rows sum to a value of "1" so that each constraint is met. Each tractor has been assigned to only one load and each load has been assigned to only one tractor.

The final table below computes the total empty miles created with the optimization solution. This table is the equivalent of plugging the load assignment solution into the objective equation.

Solution Results	Total Empty Miles					Total Empty Miles
	Load Number					
Tractor Number	A	B	C	D	E	
1	-	-	-	77	-	77
2	-	160	-	-	-	160
3	41	-	-	-	-	41
4	-	-	-	-	55	55
5	-	-	140	-	-	140
Miles	41	160	140	77	55	**473**

Notice that the total empty miles in the solution have been reduced from 501 miles to 473 miles. While 28 miles may not seem like much, it represents a savings of 5.60 miles per load. If a carrier with 500 truck assignments per day were to apply this technology, the carrier could save over 2,500 miles per day and approximately 600,000 miles per year. For most carriers utilizing this approach, the actual savings is very often much greater than 5.6 miles per load.

The model and solution presented here really only solves the core objective of minimizing empty miles. The set-up of this problem becomes much more complex in situations when a carrier has more available trucks than available loads or when more loads are available than the carrier has available trucks. The problem also becomes more complex as other considerations such as available driver hours, pick-up windows, and transit times are introduced into the model.

! *Technical Tip* – Linear Programming (Solver) Spreadsheet Feature

The solution to the simple truck and load assignment problem presented in this chapter was developed using the "Solver" spreadsheet feature. In Microsoft Excel® 2003, the "Solver" feature is located in the "Tools" menu as shown in the screenshot below.

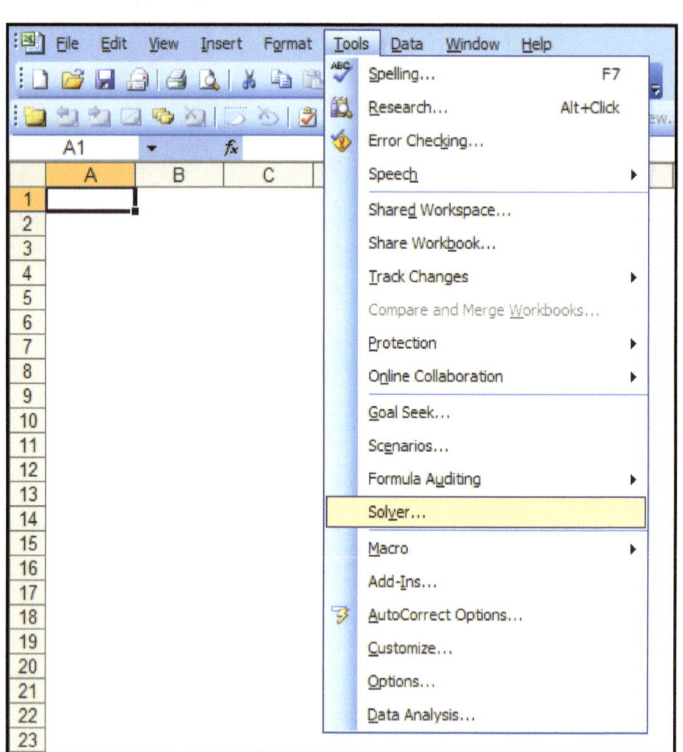

Accessing the Solver Function in Excel®

In some installations of Excel®, the Solver feature may not be immediately available. The Solver may need to be set up using "Add-Ins" or a custom installation. Consult the Excel® help feature for more information.

Please visit www.TruckloadTransportation.com to download a no-cost copy of this highly detailed technical tip. The full technical tip includes the initial spreadsheet design, the definition of the constraints within the Solver, and the steps required to use the Solver to determine the optimized solution.

CHAPTER 7: Operations and Profitability Analysis

Carrier freight and customer networks are extremely complex and unpredictable. Managers at medium and large carriers cannot possibly keep track of each load, each driver, and each customer, especially in the largest carrier networks. In order to properly manage the network, carriers must develop measurements and management reports to accurately estimate the performance of each fleet of trucks, each customer, and each lane of traffic. These reports should extend far beyond the reports provided for accounting and tax purposes. Analysis reports should cover all areas of operations, especially those not included in traditional accounting reports. This chapter provides a variety of example reports covering all major areas of carrier operations and analysis.

Carrier Analysis Reports

The key reports and measurements can be broken down into the groups outlined below. The primary groups include Fleet Level Analysis, Customer Efficiency Analysis, Market Level Analysis, and Lane Level Analysis.

Key Carrier Analysis Groups

Reporting Group	Key Measurements
Fleet Level Analysis	Utilization Empty Miles Percentage Loaded Revenue Per Mile Net Revenue Per Mile
Customer Efficiency	Cycle Times and Dock Times Revenue Per Mile Seasonality Empty Miles
Market Level Analysis	Capacity and Balance Empty Miles Length of Haul Lane by Lane Profitability Comparison
Lane Level Analysis	Relative Customer Pricing and Profitability Revenue Per Hour by Customer Empty Miles at Destination

This chapter provides detailed examples of many different reports and analysis methods carriers might use to measure internal performance. Certain reports are dependent on the availability of certain information within the carrier's information systems. While not all reports are relevant to every carrier, these examples provide a general framework for the most important areas of internal network analysis.

For simplification purposes, all reports are based on a fictional carrier based in Memphis, TN that operates a small 4 truck fleet. The carrier serves one primary customer, ABC Express, outbound from Memphis, TN to several destinations around the Southeast. The carrier has developed a variety of different customers to reposition the fleet back to Memphis for future outbound loads. The data used in the reports represents a four week period of load activity.

Fleet Level Analysis

Fleet level analysis focuses on key operating measurements such as utilization, empty miles, length of haul, and revenue per mile. The goal of these reports is to identify areas of poor performance and determine strategies to improve performance.

Tractor Movement Report

The summary report below details the load activity of an individual tractor for a one week period. The report includes key measurements such as the empty mile percentage, length of haul, utilization, and revenue per mile.

Weekly Tractor Movement Report 01/04/09 to 01/10/09

Pick-Up Date	Customer	Origin	Destination	Loaded	Empty	Total	Empty %	Loaded	Net
Tractor 101									
1/4/2009	ABC Express	Memphis, TN	Atlanta, GA	380	44	424	10.38%	$ 1.91	$ 1.71
1/5/2009	Ellis Inc.	Dunwoody, GA	Millington, TN	408	27	435	6.21%	$ 1.35	$ 1.26
1/6/2009	ABC Express	Memphis, TN	Dallas, TX	453	17	470	3.62%	$ 2.04	$ 1.97
1/7/2009	TexArk Industries	Texarkana, AR	W. Memphis, AR	268	180	448	40.18%	$ 2.05	$ 1.23
1/8/2009	ABC Express	Memphis, TN	New Orleans, LA	393	9	402	2.24%	$ 2.10	$ 2.05
1/9/2009	Smiley Stores	Brookhaven, MS	Bartlett, TN	276	132	408	32.35%	$ 2.12	$ 1.43
TOTALS:				2,178	409	2,587	15.81%	$ 1.91	$ 1.61

Summary Statistics		Revenue Summary	
Total Loads	6	Linehaul	$ 4,161
Avg LOH	363	Fuel Surcharges	$ 242
Utilization	2,587	Accessorials	$ 75
		Total	$ 4,478

The report provides a quick glance at the tractor's movement throughout the week. The carrier can identify any unusual events such as excess empty miles or loads with inadequate revenue. The week shown in this report appears to be reasonably efficient and productive. The utilization of 2,587 miles and the linehaul revenue of $4,161 both represent excellent productivity levels for this carrier.

The empty miles percentage of 15.81% for this tractor is excellent for this carrier's network. The carrier's network typically averages 17 to 20% empty miles. The empty miles shown on this report and all future reports represent the empty miles before the pick-up of the load. Unless otherwise indicated, all empty miles represent empty miles before pick-up.

Revenue Analysis by Tractor

The report below summarizes four weeks of activity by tractor. The report includes key measurements such as load count, empty mile percentage, length of haul, utilization, and net revenue per mile.

Revenue Analysis by Tractor 01/04/09 to 01/31/09

Tractor Number	Total Loads	Loaded	Empty	Total	Empty %	LOH	Utilization	Total Revenue	Linehaul Revenue	Loaded	Net
101	24	8,959	1,617	10,576	15.29%	373	2,644	$18,019	$16,895	$1.89	$1.60
102	22	8,469	1,524	9,993	15.25%	385	2,498	$16,402	$15,495	$1.83	$1.55
103	23	7,752	2,798	10,550	26.52%	337	2,638	$17,238	$15,980	$2.06	$1.51
104	23	8,050	2,123	10,173	20.87%	350	2,543	$16,934	$15,810	$1.96	$1.55
Totals:	92	33,230	8,062	41,292	19.52%	361	2,581	$68,593	$64,180	$1.93	$1.55

The report shows that the performance of each tractor is reasonably consistent with the fleet averages. The report below shows the previous information by tractor broken down on a week-by-week basis for the four week period.

Revenue Analysis by Tractor by Week 01/04/09 to 01/31/09

Tractor / Week	Total Loads	Loaded	Empty	Total	Empty %	LOH	Utilization	Total Revenue	Linehaul Revenue	Loaded	Net
101	24	8,959	1,617	10,576	15.29%	373	2,644	$18,019	$16,895	$1.89	$1.60
1/10/2009	6	2,178	409	2,587	15.81%	363	2,587	$4,477	$4,160	$1.91	$1.61
1/17/2009	6	2,421	253	2,674	9.46%	404	2,674	$4,502	$4,250	$1.76	$1.59
1/24/2009	6	2,122	527	2,649	19.89%	354	2,649	$4,623	$4,310	$2.03	$1.63
1/31/2009	6	2,238	428	2,666	16.05%	373	2,666	$4,416	$4,175	$1.87	$1.57
102	22	8,469	1,524	9,993	15.25%	385	2,498	$16,402	$15,495	$1.83	$1.55
1/10/2009	6	2,421	247	2,668	9.26%	404	2,668	$4,502	$4,250	$1.76	$1.59
1/17/2009	6	2,238	428	2,666	16.05%	373	2,666	$4,416	$4,175	$1.87	$1.57
1/24/2009	5	1,723	755	2,478	30.47%	345	2,478	$3,689	$3,500	$2.03	$1.41
1/31/2009	5	2,087	94	2,181	4.31%	417	2,181	$3,795	$3,570	$1.71	$1.64
103	23	7,752	2,798	10,550	26.52%	337	2,638	$17,238	$15,980	$2.06	$1.51
1/10/2009	5	1,739	827	2,566	32.23%	348	2,566	$3,900	$3,675	$2.11	$1.43
1/17/2009	6	2,059	841	2,900	29.00%	343	2,900	$4,374	$4,060	$1.97	$1.40
1/24/2009	6	2,011	480	2,491	19.27%	335	2,491	$4,401	$4,060	$2.02	$1.63
1/31/2009	6	1,943	650	2,593	25.07%	324	2,593	$4,563	$4,185	$2.15	$1.61
104	23	8,050	2,123	10,173	20.87%	350	2,543	$16,934	$15,810	$1.96	$1.55
1/10/2009	6	2,364	207	2,571	8.05%	394	2,571	$4,563	$4,235	$1.79	$1.65
1/17/2009	6	2,134	579	2,713	21.34%	356	2,713	$4,386	$4,100	$1.92	$1.51
1/24/2009	5	1,548	450	1,998	22.52%	310	1,998	$3,596	$3,335	$2.15	$1.67
1/31/2009	6	2,004	887	2,891	30.68%	334	2,891	$4,388	$4,140	$2.07	$1.43
Totals:	92	33,230	8,062	41,292	19.52%	361	2,581	$68,593	$64,180	$1.93	$1.55

The addition of the weekly reporting layer provides additional insight into each tractor's activity. The carrier can look for weeks with poor performance and research further to determine the underlying causes of poor performance. The tractor movement report shown previously might be used for further research. The revenue analysis by customer shown in the next section might also be used to identify revenue-related problems.

Tractor Revenue Analysis by Customer

The revenue analysis by tractor by customer provides a summary view of the customers served during the period, along with the associated miles and revenues.

Revenue Analysis by Tractor by Customer 01/04/09 to 01/31/09

Tractor / Customer	Total Loads	Loaded	Empty	Total	Empty %	LOH	Total Revenue	Linehaul Revenue	Rev/Mile Loaded	Rev/Mile Net
101	**24**	**8,959**	**1,617**	**10,576**	**15.3%**	**373**	**$ 18,019**	**$ 16,895**	**$ 1.89**	**$ 1.60**
ABC Express	12	4,914	206	5,120	4.0%	410	$ 10,665	$ 10,075	$ 2.05	$ 1.97
Ellis Inc.	6	2,235	591	2,826	20.9%	373	$ 3,554	$ 3,375	$ 1.51	$ 1.19
MLS Logistics	1	451	16	467	3.4%	451	$ 670	$ 625	$ 1.39	$ 1.34
Smiley Stores	2	555	264	819	32.2%	278	$ 1,376	$ 1,170	$ 2.11	$ 1.43
TexArk Industries	3	804	540	1,344	40.2%	268	$ 1,755	$ 1,650	$ 2.05	$ 1.23
102	**22**	**8,469**	**1,524**	**9,993**	**15.3%**	**385**	**$ 16,402**	**$ 15,495**	**$ 1.83**	**$ 1.55**
ABC Express	12	4,841	537	5,378	10.0%	403	$ 10,456	$ 9,875	$ 2.04	$ 1.84
Ellis Inc.	6	2,235	591	2,826	20.9%	373	$ 3,554	$ 3,375	$ 1.51	$ 1.19
MLS Logistics	2	917	32	949	3.4%	459	$ 1,362	$ 1,270	$ 1.38	$ 1.34
TexArk Industries	1	268	180	448	40.2%	268	$ 585	$ 550	$ 2.05	$ 1.23
Tyler Chicken	1	208	184	392	46.9%	208	$ 446	$ 425	$ 2.04	$ 1.08
103	**23**	**7,752**	**2,798**	**10,550**	**26.5%**	**337**	**$ 17,238**	**$ 15,980**	**$ 2.06**	**$ 1.51**
ABC Express	12	4,867	934	5,801	16.1%	406	$ 10,659	$ 10,075	$ 2.07	$ 1.74
BD Electronics	1	233	146	379	38.5%	233	$ 572	$ 500	$ 2.15	$ 1.32
BMI Computers	1	136	320	456	70.2%	136	$ 539	$ 450	$ 3.31	$ 0.99
Ellis Inc.	1	337	170	507	33.5%	337	$ 602	$ 575	$ 1.71	$ 1.13
HC Logistics	2	336	541	877	61.7%	168	$ 960	$ 900	$ 2.68	$ 1.03
MLS Logistics	1	451	16	467	3.4%	451	$ 670	$ 625	$ 1.39	$ 1.34
Smiley Stores	3	831	396	1,227	32.3%	277	$ 2,063	$ 1,755	$ 2.11	$ 1.43
TexArk Industries	2	561	275	836	32.9%	281	$ 1,173	$ 1,100	$ 1.96	$ 1.32
104	**23**	**8,050**	**2,123**	**10,173**	**20.9%**	**350**	**$ 16,934**	**$ 15,810**	**$ 1.96**	**$ 1.55**
ABC Express	12	4,855	609	5,464	11.1%	405	$ 10,533	$ 9,950	$ 2.05	$ 1.82
BD Electronics	1	233	259	492	52.6%	233	$ 572	$ 500	$ 2.15	$ 1.02
Ellis Inc.	2	816	54	870	6.2%	408	$ 1,165	$ 1,100	$ 1.35	$ 1.26
HC Logistics	1	103	282	385	73.2%	103	$ 394	$ 375	$ 3.64	$ 0.97
MLS Logistics	1	451	16	467	3.4%	451	$ 670	$ 625	$ 1.39	$ 1.34
Smiley Stores	2	558	264	822	32.1%	279	$ 1,376	$ 1,170	$ 2.10	$ 1.42
TexArk Industries	4	1,034	639	1,673	38.2%	259	$ 2,224	$ 2,090	$ 2.02	$ 1.25
Totals	**92**	**33,230**	**8,062**	**41,292**	**19.5%**	**361**	**$ 68,593**	**$ 64,180**	**$ 1.93**	**$ 1.55**

Based on this information, the carrier can identify any customers that may have contributed to below average performance. The utilization column is not shown in this report since utilization is not applicable at the customer level.

Tractor Revenue Analysis by Lane

The revenue analysis by tractor by lane provides a more detailed view of the customers and lanes served by a tractor over a period of time. The report below summarizes the various lanes served by tractor 101 during the analysis period.

Tractor Revenue Analysis by Lane 01/04/09 to 01/31/09

Tractor / Customer / Lane	Total Loads	Loaded	Empty	Total	Empty %	LOH	Total Revenue	Linehaul Revenue	Loaded	Net
101	24	8,959	1,617	10,576	15.3%	373	$ 18,019	$ 16,895	$ 1.89	$ 1.60
ABC Express	12	4,914	206	5,120	4.02%	410	$ 10,665	$ 10,075	$ 2.05	$ 1.97
Memphis, TN	12	4,914	206	5,120	4.02%	410	$ 10,665	$ 10,075	$ 2.05	$ 1.97
to: Atlanta, GA	3	1,140	69	1,209	5.71%	380	$ 2,312	$ 2,175	$ 1.91	$ 1.80
to: Dallas, TX	4	1,812	68	1,880	3.62%	453	$ 3,917	$ 3,700	$ 2.04	$ 1.97
to: Mobile, AL	3	1,176	43	1,219	3.53%	392	$ 2,691	$ 2,550	$ 2.17	$ 2.09
to: New Orleans, LA	2	786	26	812	3.20%	393	$ 1,744	$ 1,650	$ 2.10	$ 2.03
Ellis Inc.	6	2,235	591	2,826	20.91%	373	$ 3,554	$ 3,375	$ 1.51	$ 1.19
Dunwoody, GA	3	1,224	81	1,305	6.21%	408	$ 1,748	$ 1,650	$ 1.35	$ 1.26
to: Millington, TN	3	1,224	81	1,305	6.21%	408	$ 1,748	$ 1,650	$ 1.35	$ 1.26
Montgomery, AL	3	1,011	510	1,521	33.53%	337	$ 1,806	$ 1,725	$ 1.71	$ 1.13
to: Millington, TN	3	1,011	510	1,521	33.53%	337	$ 1,806	$ 1,725	$ 1.71	$ 1.13
MLS Logistics	1	451	16	467	3.43%	451	$ 670	$ 625	$ 1.39	$ 1.34
Garland, TX	1	451	16	467	3.43%	451	$ 670	$ 625	$ 1.39	$ 1.34
to: Memphis, TN	1	451	16	467	3.43%	451	$ 670	$ 625	$ 1.39	$ 1.34
Smiley Stores	2	555	264	819	32.23%	278	$ 1,376	$ 1,170	$ 2.11	$ 1.43
Brookhaven, MS	2	555	264	819	32.23%	278	$ 1,376	$ 1,170	$ 2.11	$ 1.43
to: Bartlett, TN	1	276	132	408	32.35%	276	$ 688	$ 585	$ 2.12	$ 1.43
to: Cordova, TN	1	279	132	411	32.12%	279	$ 688	$ 585	$ 2.10	$ 1.42
TexArk Industries	3	804	540	1,344	40.18%	268	$ 1,755	$ 1,650	$ 2.05	$ 1.23
Texarkana, AR	3	804	540	1,344	40.18%	268	$ 1,755	$ 1,650	$ 2.05	$ 1.23
to: W. Memphis, AR	3	804	540	1,344	40.18%	268	$ 1,755	$ 1,650	$ 2.05	$ 1.23

The report shows the tractor served four outbound lanes for the carrier's primary customer, ABC Express. The tractor served inbound lanes for four different customers across six different lanes. The loaded and net revenue per mile is much higher for the outbound loads for ABC Express than for the inbound loads for the other customers. This difference in inbound and outbound revenue per mile is expected since Memphis is the primary outbound market for this carrier.

The report indicates that the empty miles percentage to serve the ABC Express loads out of Memphis is very efficient at only 4.02%. However, the empty miles percentage associated with the return loads is very high, with several lanes over 30%. Where possible, the carrier may look to secure backhaul loads in more efficient locations. Additional lane and market reports will reveal further information on any specific opportunities to reduce empty miles.

Customer Level Analysis

Customer level analysis focuses on operating measurements such as length of haul, empty miles, loaded revenue per mile, net revenue per mile, and cycle time. The goal of these reports is to identify underperforming customers or lanes and determine strategies to improve performance. Many of these reports are excellent for face-to-face meetings between shippers and carriers. Carriers can demonstrate and quantify problems areas and work with the shipper to improve performance.

Revenue Summary by Customer

The revenue summary by customer provides an overview of the miles and revenue for each customer. The carrier can quickly see the top revenue customers as well as other important customer statistics such as length of haul, empty miles, and revenue per mile.

Revenue Summary by Customer   01/04/09 to 01/31/09

Customer Name	Total Loads	Loaded	Empty	Total	Empty %	LOH	Total Revenue	Linehaul Revenue	Revenue Per Mile Loaded	Net
ABC Express	48	19,477	2,286	21,763	10.50%	406	$ 42,312	$ 39,975	$ 2.05	$ 1.84
BD Electronics	2	466	405	871	46.50%	233	$ 1,144	$ 1,000	$ 2.15	$ 1.15
BMI Computers	1	136	320	456	70.18%	136	$ 539	$ 450	$ 3.31	$ 0.99
Ellis Inc.	15	5,623	1,406	7,029	20.00%	375	$ 8,875	$ 8,425	$ 1.50	$ 1.20
HC Logistics	3	439	823	1,262	65.21%	146	$ 1,354	$ 1,275	$ 2.90	$ 1.01
MLS Logistics	5	2,270	80	2,350	3.40%	454	$ 3,372	$ 3,145	$ 1.39	$ 1.34
Smiley Stores	7	1,944	924	2,868	32.22%	278	$ 4,814	$ 4,095	$ 2.11	$ 1.43
TexArk Industries	10	2,667	1,634	4,301	37.99%	267	$ 5,737	$ 5,390	$ 2.02	$ 1.25
Tyler Chicken	1	208	184	392	46.94%	208	$ 446	$ 425	$ 2.04	$ 1.08
Totals	**92**	**33,230**	**8,062**	**41,292**	**19.52%**	**361**	**$ 68,593**	**$ 64,180**	**$ 1.93**	**$ 1.55**

The report could also be reformatted to rank all customers by total revenue as shown below. Ranking by revenue allows the carrier to focus attention on the customers with the largest amount of load and revenue activity. From time to time, the carrier may find unexpected customers moving higher and higher in the revenue rankings.

Revenue Ranking by Customer   01/04/09 to 01/31/09

Customer Name	Total Loads	Loaded	Empty	Total	Empty %	LOH	Total Revenue	Linehaul Revenue	Revenue Per Mile Loaded	Net
ABC Express	48	19,477	2,286	21,763	10.50%	406	$ 42,312	$ 39,975	$ 2.05	$ 1.84
Ellis Inc.	15	5,623	1,406	7,029	20.00%	375	$ 8,875	$ 8,425	$ 1.50	$ 1.20
TexArk Industries	10	2,667	1,634	4,301	37.99%	267	$ 5,737	$ 5,390	$ 2.02	$ 1.25
Smiley Stores	7	1,944	924	2,868	32.22%	278	$ 4,814	$ 4,095	$ 2.11	$ 1.43
MLS Logistics	5	2,270	80	2,350	3.40%	454	$ 3,372	$ 3,145	$ 1.39	$ 1.34
HC Logistics	3	439	823	1,262	65.21%	146	$ 1,354	$ 1,275	$ 2.90	$ 1.01
BD Electronics	2	466	405	871	46.50%	233	$ 1,144	$ 1,000	$ 2.15	$ 1.15
BMI Computers	1	136	320	456	70.18%	136	$ 539	$ 450	$ 3.31	$ 0.99
Tyler Chicken	1	208	184	392	46.94%	208	$ 446	$ 425	$ 2.04	$ 1.08
Totals	**92**	**33,230**	**8,062**	**41,292**	**19.52%**	**361**	**$ 68,593**	**$ 64,180**	**$ 1.93**	**$ 1.55**

Customer Revenue Analysis by Lane

The customer revenue analysis by lane provides a detailed review of operating efficiency and revenue per mile for each customer lane. The carrier can use this report to identify any lanes with poor operating or revenue performance.

Customer Revenue Analysis by Lane 01/04/09 to 01/31/09

Customer / Lane	Total Loads	Loaded (Miles)	Empty (Miles)	Total (Miles)	Empty %	LOH	Total Revenue	Linehaul Revenue	RPM Loaded	RPM Net
ABC Express	48	19,477	2,286	21,763	10.50%	406	$42,312	$39,975	$2.05	$1.84
Memphis, TN	48	19,477	2,286	21,763	10.50%	406	$42,312	$39,975	$2.05	$1.84
to: Atlanta, GA	12	4,560	578	5,138	11.25%	380	$9,247	$8,700	$1.91	$1.69
to: Dallas, TX	13	5,889	647	6,536	9.90%	453	$12,732	$12,025	$2.04	$1.84
to: Mobile, AL	11	4,312	582	4,894	11.89%	392	$9,867	$9,350	$2.17	$1.91
to: New Orleans, LA	12	4,716	479	5,195	9.22%	393	$10,466	$9,900	$2.10	$1.91
BD Electronics	2	466	405	871	46.50%	233	$1,144	$1,000	$2.15	$1.15
Birmingham, AL	2	466	405	871	46.50%	233	$1,144	$1,000	$2.15	$1.15
to: Jackson, TN	2	466	405	871	46.50%	233	$1,144	$1,000	$2.15	$1.15
BMI Computers	1	136	320	456	70.18%	136	$539	$450	$3.31	$0.99
Little Rock, AR	1	136	320	456	70.18%	136	$539	$450	$3.31	$0.99
to: Memphis, TN	1	136	320	456	70.18%	136	$539	$450	$3.31	$0.99
Ellis Inc.	15	5,623	1,406	7,029	20.00%	375	$8,875	$8,425	$1.50	$1.20
Dunwoody, GA	8	3,264	216	3,480	6.21%	408	$4,661	$4,400	$1.35	$1.26
to: Millington, TN	8	3,264	216	3,480	6.21%	408	$4,661	$4,400	$1.35	$1.26
Montgomery, AL	7	2,359	1,190	3,549	33.53%	337	$4,214	$4,025	$1.71	$1.13
to: Millington, TN	7	2,359	1,190	3,549	33.53%	337	$4,214	$4,025	$1.71	$1.13
HC Logistics	3	439	823	1,262	65.21%	146	$1,354	$1,275	$2.90	$1.01
Birmingham, AL	1	233	259	492	52.64%	233	$567	$525	$2.25	$1.07
to: Memphis, TN	1	233	259	492	52.64%	233	$567	$525	$2.25	$1.07
Tupelo, MS	2	206	564	770	73.25%	103	$787	$750	$3.64	$0.97
to: Memphis, TN	2	206	564	770	73.25%	103	$787	$750	$3.64	$0.97
MLS Logistics	5	2,270	80	2,350	3.40%	454	$3,372	$3,145	$1.39	$1.34
Garland, TX	5	2,270	80	2,350	3.40%	454	$3,372	$3,145	$1.39	$1.34
to: Memphis, TN	4	1,804	64	1,868	3.43%	451	$2,680	$2,500	$1.39	$1.34
to: Millington, TN	1	466	16	482	3.32%	466	$692	$645	$1.38	$1.34

One common application for this report is lane analysis and review. Managers can quickly see all the lanes served for each customer. In certain cases, managers may identify a lane that has been served that should not have been served. Along those same lines, managers may see that a lane has a volume level that is much different than the planned volume for the customer. Managers might also use this report to identify any pricing discrepancies or billing errors.

Customer Cycle Time Analysis by Lane

The "customer cycle time analysis by lane" provides critical information about the time efficiency of each lane. The carrier's goal is to minimize the cycle time for each lane and avoid excess buffer time. In this report, the cycle time includes empty mile drive time to the pick-up, pick-up dock time, transit drive time, and delivery dock time.

Cycle Time Analysis by Customer by Lane 01/04/09 to 01/31/09

Customer / Lane	Total Loads	Avg Miles Loaded	Avg Miles Empty	Avg Miles Total	MT Drive	PU Dock	Transit	Del Dock	Total	Buffer Time	Transit MPH
ABC Express	48	406	48	453	1.57	1.35	9.48	1.83	14.23	0.5	42.8
Memphis, TN	48	406	48	453	1.57	1.35	9.48	1.83	14.23	0.5	42.8
to: Atlanta, GA	12	380	48	428	1.69	1.55	8.80	1.97	14.02	0.4	43.2
to: Dallas, TX	13	453	50	503	1.68	1.25	10.74	1.57	15.25	0.7	42.2
to: Mobile, AL	11	392	53	445	1.67	1.09	9.12	2.13	14.00	0.4	43.0
to: New Orleans, LA	12	393	40	433	1.25	1.51	9.11	1.68	13.55	0.4	43.1
BD Electronics	2	233	203	436	5.67	1.19	6.80	0.82	14.48	1.6	34.3
Birmingham, AL	2	233	203	436	5.67	1.19	6.80	0.82	14.48	1.6	34.3
to: Jackson, TN	2	233	203	436	5.67	1.19	6.80	0.82	14.48	1.6	34.3
BMI Computers	1	136	320	456	8.00	1.56	3.81	1.40	14.77	0.8	35.7
Little Rock, AR	1	136	320	456	8.00	1.56	3.81	1.40	14.77	0.8	35.7
to: Memphis, TN	1	136	320	456	8.00	1.56	3.81	1.40	14.77	0.8	35.7
Ellis Inc.	15	375	94	469	3.13	1.22	9.85	1.73	15.93	1.5	38.1
Dunwoody, GA	8	408	27	435	1.21	1.04	10.50	1.96	14.70	1.4	38.9
to: Millington, TN	8	408	27	435	1.21	1.04	10.50	1.96	14.70	1.4	38.9
Montgomery, AL	7	337	170	507	5.32	1.43	9.10	1.48	17.34	1.6	37.0
to: Millington, TN	7	337	170	507	5.32	1.43	9.10	1.48	17.34	1.6	37.0
HC Logistics	3	146	274	421	6.78	1.25	4.52	1.16	13.70	1.3	32.4
Birmingham, AL	1	233	259	492	6.48	0.42	6.89	0.92	14.71	1.7	33.8
to: Memphis, TN	1	233	259	492	6.48	0.42	6.89	0.92	14.71	1.7	33.8
Tupelo, MS	2	103	282	385	6.93	1.67	3.34	1.27	13.20	1.0	30.9
to: Memphis, TN	2	103	282	385	6.93	1.67	3.34	1.27	13.20	1.0	30.9
MLS Logistics	5	454	16	470	1.09	1.91	11.42	2.41	16.83	1.3	39.8
Garland, TX	5	454	16	470	1.09	1.91	11.42	2.41	16.83	1.3	39.8
to: Memphis, TN	4	451	16	467	1.10	1.71	11.38	2.27	16.45	1.4	39.6
to: Millington, TN	1	466	16	482	1.07	2.75	11.58	2.98	18.37	1.2	40.2

Buffer time represents the difference between a "standard" transit time and the actual transit time for each lane. A reasonable amount of buffer time is unavoidable. However, excess buffer time will result in lost utilization and poor productivity. This report allows managers to identify customers and lanes with excess buffer time. This report can be used to document problems for customers and facilitate discussions to resolve buffer time, dock time, and other cycle time issues.

The report also includes the miles per hour (MPH) for each lane. Miles per hour measures the velocity of each lane as a critical measure of time efficiency. Interpreting the miles per hour measurement should be based in large part on the length of haul. In general, the longer the length of the haul, the greater the miles per hour (velocity) of the lane should be.

Customer Lane Cycle Time Analysis Detail

The customer cycle time analysis detail report provides event-specific information about the efficiency of each lane. The report includes each individual load so that cycle time issues can be further evaluated at the event level.

Cycle Time Detail Analysis by Customer by Lane 01/04/09 to 01/31/09

Customer / Lane / Delivery Date	Total Loads	Loaded	Empty	Total	MT Drive	PU Dock	Transit	Del Dock	Total	Buffer Time	Transit MPH
Ellis Inc.	**15**	**94**	**375**	**469**	**3.13**	**1.22**	**9.85**	**1.73**	**15.93**	**1.50**	**38.1**
Dunwoody, GA	8	27	408	435	1.21	1.04	10.50	1.96	14.70	1.40	38.9
To: Millington, TN	8	27	408	435	1.21	1.04	10.50	1.96	14.70	1.40	38.9
1/5/2009		27	408	435	1.22	1.12	9.85	2.40	14.59	0.80	41.4
1/5/2009		27	408	435	1.05	1.88	9.55	3.19	15.67	0.50	42.7
1/7/2009		27	408	435	1.55	0.65	13.00	1.89	17.08	3.90	31.4
1/14/2009		27	408	435	1.41	1.11	14.60	1.17	18.29	5.50	27.9
1/14/2009		27	408	435	1.28	0.63	9.40	1.61	12.91	0.30	43.4
1/16/2009		27	408	435	0.97	1.29	8.90	1.39	12.55	-	45.8
1/28/2009		27	408	435	1.34	0.83	9.62	2.40	14.19	0.60	42.4
1/29/2009		27	408	435	0.88	0.81	9.05	1.60	12.35	-	45.1
Montgomery, AL	7	170	337	507	5.32	1.43	9.10	1.48	17.34	1.60	37.0
To: Millington, TN	7	170	337	507	5.32	1.43	9.10	1.48	17.34	1.60	37.0
1/9/2009		170	337	507	5.44	0.64	11.20	0.93	18.20	3.70	30.1
1/12/2009		170	337	507	5.22	2.73	8.60	2.41	18.96	1.10	39.2
1/16/2009		170	337	507	4.65	0.82	7.79	0.71	13.97	0.30	43.3
1/19/2009		170	337	507	5.67	0.64	8.51	1.15	15.97	1.00	39.6
1/23/2009		170	337	507	5.68	0.81	7.50	1.16	15.15	-	44.9
1/23/2009		170	337	507	4.89	3.05	11.22	1.60	20.76	3.70	30.0
1/26/2009		170	337	507	5.72	1.34	8.91	2.40	18.37	1.40	37.8

This detailed analysis allows managers to determine if dock time and buffer time issues are related to a small number of problem loads or a consistent problem across the majority of loads. For example, the excessive buffer time for this customer appears to be associated with a small number of isolated events. The first load from Dunwoody to Millington on 1/14/09 had 5.5 hours of buffer time. Most other loads on this lane show reasonable levels of buffer time.

As the cycle time for each load is averaged across different origins for a customer, the cycle time information becomes less meaningful. Cycle time is best measured on a specific lane for a customer. However, if the average buffer time or dock time is excessive for a customer network, a cycle time problem is likely to exist. The carrier must break down the cycle times by lane to isolate the causes of the problem.

Customer Revenue Summary Analysis

The customer revenue analysis report provides a summary of the revenue performance for each customer. The revenue is broken down into key components including linehaul revenue, accessorial revenue, and fuel surcharges. A sample report is shown below.

Customer Revenue Summary Analysis 01/04/09 to 01/31/09

Customer / Origin	Total Loads	Linehaul	Access.	Fuel	Total	Linehaul	Access.	Fuel	Total
ABC Express	48	$ 39,975	$ -	$ 2,337	$ 42,312	$ 2.05	$ -	$ 0.12	$ 2.17
Memphis, TN	48	$ 39,975	$ -	$ 2,337	$ 42,312	$ 2.05	$ -	$ 0.12	$ 2.17
BD Electronics	2	$ 1,000	$ 100	$ 44	$ 1,144	$ 2.15	$ 0.21	$ 0.09	$ 2.45
Birmingham, AL	2	$ 1,000	$ 100	$ 44	$ 1,144	$ 2.15	$ 0.21	$ 0.09	$ 2.45
BMI Computers	1	$ 450	$ 75	$ 14	$ 539	$ 3.31	$ 0.55	$ 0.10	$ 3.96
Little Rock, AR	1	$ 450	$ 75	$ 14	$ 539	$ 3.31	$ 0.55	$ 0.10	$ 3.96
Ellis Inc.	15	$ 8,425	$ -	$ 450	$ 8,875	$ 1.50	$ -	$ 0.08	$ 1.58
Dunwoody, GA	8	$ 4,400	$ -	$ 261	$ 4,661	$ 1.35	$ -	$ 0.08	$ 1.43
Montgomery, AL	7	$ 4,025	$ -	$ 189	$ 4,214	$ 1.71	$ -	$ 0.08	$ 1.79
HC Logistics	3	$ 1,275	$ -	$ 79	$ 1,354	$ 2.90	$ -	$ 0.18	$ 3.08
Birmingham, AL	1	$ 525	$ -	$ 42	$ 567	$ 2.25	$ -	$ 0.18	$ 2.43
Tupelo, MS	2	$ 750	$ -	$ 37	$ 787	$ 3.64	$ -	$ 0.18	$ 3.82
MLS Logistics	5	$ 3,145	$ -	$ 227	$ 3,372	$ 1.39	$ -	$ 0.10	$ 1.49
Garland, TX	5	$ 3,145	$ -	$ 227	$ 3,372	$ 1.39	$ -	$ 0.10	$ 1.49
Smiley Stores	7	$ 4,095	$ 525	$ 194	$ 4,814	$ 2.11	$ 0.27	$ 0.10	$ 2.48
Brookhaven, MS	7	$ 4,095	$ 525	$ 194	$ 4,814	$ 2.11	$ 0.27	$ 0.10	$ 2.48
TexArk Industries	10	$ 5,390	$ -	$ 347	$ 5,737	$ 2.02	$ -	$ 0.13	$ 2.15
Hattiesburg, MS	2	$ 1,100	$ -	$ 76	$ 1,176	$ 1.88	$ -	$ 0.13	$ 2.01
Jackson, MS	1	$ 440	$ -	$ 27	$ 467	$ 2.15	$ -	$ 0.13	$ 2.28
Texarkana, AR	7	$ 3,850	$ -	$ 244	$ 4,094	$ 2.05	$ -	$ 0.13	$ 2.18
Tyler Chicken	1	$ 425	$ -	$ 21	$ 446	$ 2.04	$ -	$ 0.10	$ 2.14
Jackson, MS	1	$ 425	$ -	$ 21	$ 446	$ 2.04	$ -	$ 0.10	$ 2.14
Totals	92	$ 64,180	$ 700	$ 3,713	$ 68,593	$ 1.93	$ 0.02	$ 0.11	$ 2.06

This report provides the carrier with a summary view of the revenue components for each customer. The carrier can verify that customers are being charged a fuel surcharge and accessorial fees when applicable. If the carrier was expecting to see accessorial charges on a certain customer but did not, the potential billing issue could be investigated.

The report could also be broken down into more detail to include the specific accessorial charges for items such as stop-offs, unloading, tolls and other common charges. The report could also be expanded to include empty miles and net revenue per mile.

Customer Lane Network Map

The customer lane network map provides carriers with a summary view of all the lanes served for a customer over a particular time period. The map should also reflect the load volumes over the period for each destination point. A lane map for ABC Express is shown below.

Outbound Customer Lane Network
(4 Weeks)

Based on this information, carrier management can determine if the shipper is meeting the load volume expectations for the carrier. The carrier can also identify if any lanes are being served for the shipper that the carrier sales team has not authorized. In some cases, the carrier's customer service group may agree to serve lanes for the shipper that were not included in the planned lanes. The sales group may need to establish pricing for the new lanes or instruct the carrier customer service group to discontinue accepting loads on these lanes.

The customer network map also provides the carrier with information on where trucks are landing throughout the network. This information provides managers with a mental picture of the existing network. As new sales opportunities appear, the carrier's sales team will be able to recognize any potential lanes that provide a substantial fit with the existing network.

Customer Origin Empty Miles Before Analysis

The "customer origin empty miles before analysis" provides a summary of the empty miles required to position trucks to each customer origin location. The report extends beyond the average number of empty miles to include the distribution of empty mile events by distance. A sample report is shown below.

Empty Miles Before Pick-up Analysis by Origin 01/04/09 to 01/31/09

Customer / Origin	Total Loads	Loaded	Empty	Total	0 to 25	26 to 50	51 to 100	101 to 150	151 to 250	Over 250
ABC Express	48	406	48	453	41	1	2	-	-	4
Memphis, TN	48	406	48	453	41	1	2	-	-	4
BD Electronics	2	233	203	436	-	-	-	1	-	1
Birmingham, AL	2	233	203	436	-	-	-	1	-	1
BMI Computers	1	136	320	456	-	-	-	-	-	1
Little Rock, AR	1	136	320	456	-	-	-	-	-	1
Ellis Inc.	15	375	94	469	-	8	-	-	7	-
Dunwoody, GA	8	408	27	435	-	8	-	-	-	-
Montgomery, AL	7	337	170	507	-	-	-	-	7	-
HC Logistics	3	146	274	421	-	-	-	-	-	3
Birmingham, AL	1	233	259	492	-	-	-	-	-	1
Tupelo, MS	2	103	282	385	-	-	-	-	-	2
MLS Logistics	5	454	16	470	5	-	-	-	-	-
Garland, TX	5	454	16	470	5	-	-	-	-	-
Smiley Stores	7	278	132	410	-	-	-	7	-	-
Brookhaven, MS	7	278	132	410	-	-	-	7	-	-
TexArk Industries	10	267	163	430	-	-	2	-	8	-
Hattiesburg, MS	2	293	95	388	-	-	2	-	-	-
Jackson, MS	1	205	184	389	-	-	-	-	1	-
Texarkana, AR	7	268	180	448	-	-	-	-	7	-
Tyler Chicken	1	208	184	392	-	-	-	-	1	-
Jackson, MS	1	208	184	392	-	-	-	-	1	-

The report includes the average empty miles for each origin as well as the distribution of empty events by distance. For example, ABC Express in Memphis, TN had 41 loads with actual empty miles of 25 miles or less. Most notably for ABC Express, there were 4 event mile events over 250 miles. These four events could represent a serious problem. The carrier might dig deeper to determine exactly what occurred to cause these excessive empty mile events. Once the problems are identified, the carrier can take action to correct major problems and reduce the total number of empty miles in the network. The excess empty miles could be caused by a number of issues including delivery times, lack of nearby customers, or excess load volumes to the destination market. Reducing empty miles will improve net revenue per mile and profitability.

Customer Destination Empty Miles After Analysis

The "customer empty miles after analysis" provides a summary of the empty miles that occur after a load is delivered to a particular destination. The report extends beyond the average number of empty miles to include the distribution of empty mile events by distance. A sample report is shown below.

Empty Miles After Delivery Analysis by Customer Destination   01/04/09 to 01/31/09

Customer / Lane	Total Loads	Average Miles Loaded	Average Miles Empty	Average Miles Total	0 to 25	26 to 50	51 to 100	101 to 150	151 to 250	Over 250
ABC Express	48	406	148	453	4	8	4	8	16	8
Memphis, TN	48	406	148	453	4	8	4	8	16	8
to: Atlanta, GA	12	380	84	428	-	8	1	1	-	2
to: Dallas, TX	13	453	132	503	4	-	1	-	7	1
to: Mobile, AL	11	392	173	445	-	-	2	-	7	2
to: New Orleans, LA	12	393	206	433	-	-	-	7	2	3
BD Electronics	2	233	85	436	-	-	2	-	-	-
Birmingham, AL	2	233	85	436	-	-	2	-	-	-
to: Jackson, TN	2	233	85	436	-	-	2	-	-	-
BMI Computers	1	136	-	456	1	-	-	-	-	-
Little Rock, AR	1	136	-	456	1	-	-	-	-	-
to: Memphis, TN	1	136	-	456	1	-	-	-	-	-
Ellis Inc.	15	375	17	469	15	-	-	-	-	-
Dunwoody, GA	8	408	17	435	8	-	-	-	-	-
to: Millington, TN	8	408	17	435	8	-	-	-	-	-
Montgomery, AL	7	337	17	507	7	-	-	-	-	-
to: Millington, TN	7	337	17	507	7	-	-	-	-	-

This report indicates the empty miles that occur after the load is delivered instead of before the load is picked up. The empty miles in the report demonstrate the carrier's ability to efficiently reload trucks in or near each destination market. The carrier can quickly see that for the major customer, ABC Express, the empty miles after delivery represent a major portion of the empty miles for the entire network.

For ABC Express, the two worst empty mile destinations are Mobile, AL and New Orleans, LA. For Mobile, 9 of the 11 loads to the market had an empty mile move of 150 miles or more. For New Orleans, all 12 loads had an empty mile move of at least 101 miles. Clearly, the carrier has no local customers in New Orleans or Mobile to reload the trucks that land in these markets. The carrier may be able to find a more efficient network of customers in these markets to reduce the empty miles.

The empty mile report as shown above does not include net revenue per mile. For some lanes, the net revenue per mile may be acceptable despite what appears to be excessive empty miles. Regardless, the carrier may be able to improve profitability by reducing empty miles and increasing net revenue per mile in these problem markets.

Market Level Analysis

Market level analysis focuses on operating measurements such as capacity and balance, length of haul, empty miles, and revenue per mile. The goal of these reports is to identify underperforming markets and determine strategies to improve performance. Another benefit of these reports is to identify the most attractive and unattractive markets. Knowledge of each market helps the carrier determine the optimal pricing and network strategy by avoiding poor markets and exploiting the best markets.

Market Revenue Analysis by Origin Zone

The market revenue analysis reports reflect key operating statistics such as empty miles, length of haul, and revenue per mile for carrier-defined geographic markets. In this case, the carrier has established analysis regions such as AL NOR. AL NOR represents the northern half of Alabama. The carrier's home market region of the Memphis, TN metropolitan area is represented by zone TN MEM. The report below includes an analysis by state and a breakdown of each zone within the state.

Market Revenue Analysis by Origin Zone 01/04/09 to 01/31/09

Origin ST / Zone	Total Loads	Loaded	Empty	Total	Empty %	LOH	Total Revenue	Linehaul Revenue	Loaded	Net
AL	10	3,058	1,854	4,912	37.74%	306	5,925	5,550	$ 1.81	$ 1.13
AL NOR	3	699	664	1,363	48.72%	233	1,711	1,525	$ 2.18	$ 1.12
AL STH	7	2,359	1,190	3,549	33.53%	337	4,214	4,025	$ 1.71	$ 1.13
AR	8	2,012	1,580	3,592	43.99%	252	4,632	4,300	$ 2.14	$ 1.20
AR CEN	1	136	320	456	70.18%	136	539	450	$ 3.31	$ 0.99
AR WEST	7	1,876	1,260	3,136	40.18%	268	4,094	3,850	$ 2.05	$ 1.23
GA	8	3,264	216	3,480	6.21%	408	4,661	4,400	$ 1.35	$ 1.26
GA ATL	8	3,264	216	3,480	6.21%	408	4,661	4,400	$ 1.35	$ 1.26
MS	13	3,149	2,046	5,195	39.38%	242	7,690	6,810	$ 2.16	$ 1.31
MS CEN	11	2,943	1,482	4,425	33.49%	268	6,903	6,060	$ 2.06	$ 1.37
MS NOR	2	206	564	770	73.25%	103	787	750	$ 3.64	$ 0.97
TN	48	19,477	2,286	21,763	10.50%	406	42,312	39,975	$ 2.05	$ 1.84
TN MEM	48	19,477	2,286	21,763	10.50%	406	42,312	39,975	$ 2.05	$ 1.84
TX	5	2,270	80	2,350	3.40%	454	3,372	3,145	$ 1.39	$ 1.34
TX DFW	5	2,270	80	2,350	3.40%	454	3,372	3,145	$ 1.39	$ 1.34
Totals	92	33,230	8,062	41,292	19.5%	361	68,592	64,180	$ 1.93	$ 1.55

This report allows the carrier to quickly evaluate length of haul, empty miles, and revenue per mile by geographic region. The carrier can identify any markets that are performing below expectations and take action to improve performance for those markets. The carrier can also identify any markets that are exceeding expectations and identify ways in which activity in the top performing markets can be expanded.

Market Revenue Analysis by Destination Zone

The market revenue analysis reports reflect key operating statistics such as empty miles, length of haul, and revenue per mile for pre-defined geographic markets. The report below is based on the same format as the previous origin zone report but groups the information by destination zone.

Market Revenue Analysis by Destination Zone 01/04/09 to 01/31/09

Dest ST / Zone	Total Loads	Loaded	Empty	Total	Empty %	LOH	Total Revenue	Linehaul Revenue	Loaded	Net
AL	11	4,312	582	4,894	11.89%	392	9,867	9,350	$ 2.17	$ 1.91
AL STH	11	4,312	582	4,894	11.89%	392	9,867	9,350	$ 2.17	$ 1.91
AR	7	1,876	1,260	3,136	40.18%	268	4,094	3,850	$ 2.05	$ 1.23
TN MEM	7	1,876	1,260	3,136	40.18%	268	4,094	3,850	$ 2.05	$ 1.23
GA	12	4,560	578	5,138	11.25%	380	9,247	8,700	$ 1.91	$ 1.69
GA ATL	12	4,560	578	5,138	11.25%	380	9,247	8,700	$ 1.91	$ 1.69
LA	12	4,716	479	5,195	9.22%	393	10,466	9,900	$ 2.10	$ 1.91
LA STH	12	4,716	479	5,195	9.22%	393	10,466	9,900	$ 2.10	$ 1.91
MS	3	791	374	1,165	32.10%	264	1,643	1,540	$ 1.95	$ 1.32
TN MEM	3	791	374	1,165	32.10%	264	1,643	1,540	$ 1.95	$ 1.32
TN	34	11,086	4,142	15,228	27.20%	326	20,544	18,815	$ 1.70	$ 1.24
TN MEM	34	11,086	4,142	15,228	27.20%	326	20,544	18,815	$ 1.70	$ 1.24
TX	13	5,889	647	6,536	9.90%	453	12,732	12,025	$ 2.04	$ 1.84
TX DFW	13	5,889	647	6,536	9.90%	453	12,732	12,025	$ 2.04	$ 1.84
Totals	92	33,230	8,062	41,292	19.52%	361	$ 68,593	$ 64,180	$ 1.93	$ 1.55

The report groups the information by the destination state as well as by the destination geographic zone. The state summary provides a consolidated evaluation of each state regardless of the zones within each state.

Much like the origin zone report, this report allows the carrier to quickly evaluate length of haul, empty miles, and revenue per mile by geographic region. The carrier can identify any markets that are performing below expectations and take action to improve performance for those markets. The carrier can also identify any markets that are exceeding expectations and identify ways in which the top performing markets can be profitably expanded.

Market Inbound and Outbound Analysis by Zone

The market inbound and outbound analysis compares key operating statistics such as capacity and balance, revenue per mile, and length of haul for all load activity that flows through each analysis zone. A sample report is shown below. The "OB" columns represent outbound activity and the "IB" columns represent inbound activity.

Zone Inbound / Outbound Analysis 01/04/09 to 01/31/09

Zone	Total Loads OB	IB	Balance	Length of Haul OB	IB	Loaded Rev / Mile OB	IB	Net Rev / Mile OB	IB	Empty Mile % OB	IB
AL NOR	3	-	(3)	233		$2.18		$1.12		48.7%	0.0%
AL STH	7	11	4	337	392	$1.71	$2.17	$1.13	$1.91	33.5%	11.9%
AR CEN	1	-	(1)	136		$3.31		$0.99		70.2%	0.0%
AR WEST	7	-	(7)	268		$2.05		$1.23		40.2%	0.0%
GA ATL	8	12	4	408	380	$1.35	$1.91	$1.26	$1.69	6.2%	11.2%
LA STH	-	12	12		393		$2.10		$1.91	0.0%	9.2%
MS CEN	11	-	(11)	268		$2.06		$1.37		33.5%	0.0%
MS NOR	2	-	(2)	103		$3.64		$0.97		73.2%	0.0%
TN MEM	48	44	(4)	406	313	$2.05	$1.76	$1.84	$1.24	10.5%	29.6%
TX DFW	5	13	8	454	453	$1.39	$2.04	$1.34	$1.84	3.40%	9.90%
Totals	**92**	**92**		**361**	**361**	**$ 1.93**	**$ 1.93**	**$ 1.55**	**$ 1.55**	**19.5%**	**19.5%**

The report provides a summary of the capacity and balance situation for each zone for the period. For markets that are out of the balance, the carrier can evaluate the length of haul and net revenue per mile to determine if revenue levels provide adequate compensation for the empty miles associated with zone balance problems.

This report is also useful in evaluating the overall inbound and outbound revenue per mile performance of each zone. For strong headhaul markets, the outbound rate per mile should be significantly higher than the inbound rate per mile in most cases. Backhaul markets would be just the opposite, with a relatively low outbound rate per mile. For backhaul markets, the inbound rate per mile should be significantly higher than the outbound rate per mile. The capacity and balance situation should also be taken into account when evaluating rate levels for backhaul markets. The greater the amount of excess capacity in a backhaul market, the lower the outbound rates may be.

For reports of this type that focus heavily on capacity and balance and revenue per mile, the reports should exclude very short length of haul loads, especially those typically served on an out and back basis. Loads of this type are not part of the true market-to-market operating network and can skew balance figures and revenue per mile statistics.

Market Customer Outbound Summary

The market customer outbound summary report provides key operating statistics for every customer that ships loads out of a zone. A sample report is shown below.

Outbound Revenue Analysis by Customer 01/04/09 to 01/31/09

Origin Zone / Customer	Total Loads	Loaded	Empty	Total	Empty %	LOH	Total Revenue	Linehaul Revenue	Rev/Mile Loaded	Rev/Mile Net
AL NOR	3	699	664	1,363	48.72%	233	$ 1,711	$ 1,525	$ 2.18	$ 1.12
BD Electronics	2	466	405	871	46.50%	233	$ 1,144	$ 1,000	$ 2.15	$ 1.15
HC Logistics	1	233	259	492	52.64%	233	$ 567	$ 525	$ 2.25	$ 1.07
AL STH	7	2,359	1,190	3,549	33.53%	337	$ 4,214	$ 4,025	$ 1.71	$ 1.13
Ellis Inc.	7	2,359	1,190	3,549	33.53%	337	$ 4,214	$ 4,025	$ 1.71	$ 1.13
AR CEN	1	136	320	456	70.18%	136	$ 539	$ 450	$ 3.31	$ 0.99
BMI Computers	1	136	320	456	70.18%	136	$ 539	$ 450	$ 3.31	$ 0.99
AR WEST	7	1,876	1,260	3,136	40.18%	268	$ 4,094	$ 3,850	$ 2.05	$ 1.23
TexArk Industries	7	1,876	1,260	3,136	40.18%	268	$ 4,094	$ 3,850	$ 2.05	$ 1.23
GA ATL	8	3,264	216	3,480	6.21%	408	$ 4,661	$ 4,400	$ 1.35	$ 1.26
Ellis Inc.	8	3,264	216	3,480	6.21%	408	$ 4,661	$ 4,400	$ 1.35	$ 1.26
MS CEN	11	2,943	1,482	4,425	33.49%	268	$ 6,903	$ 6,060	$ 2.06	$ 1.37
Smiley Stores	7	1,944	924	2,868	32.22%	278	$ 4,814	$ 4,095	$ 2.11	$ 1.43
TexArk Industries	3	791	374	1,165	32.10%	264	$ 1,643	$ 1,540	$ 1.95	$ 1.32
Tyler Chicken	1	208	184	392	46.94%	208	$ 446	$ 425	$ 2.04	$ 1.08
MS NOR	2	206	564	770	73.25%	103	$ 787	$ 750	$ 3.64	$ 0.97
HC Logistics	2	206	564	770	73.25%	103	$ 787	$ 750	$ 3.64	$ 0.97
TN MEM	48	19,477	2,286	21,763	10.50%	406	$ 42,312	$ 39,975	$ 2.05	$ 1.84
ABC Express	48	19,477	2,286	21,763	10.50%	406	$ 42,312	$ 39,975	$ 2.05	$ 1.84
TX DFW	5	2,270	80	2,350	3.40%	454	$ 3,372	$ 3,145	$ 1.39	$ 1.34
MLS Logistics	5	2,270	80	2,350	3.40%	454	$ 3,372	$ 3,145	$ 1.39	$ 1.34
Totals	**92**	**33,230**	**8,062**	**41,292**	**19.52%**	**361**	**$ 68,593**	**$ 64,180**	**$ 1.93**	**$ 1.55**

The report provides a quick summary of every customer that ships loads out of a zone. Each customer can be evaluated in terms of length of haul, revenue per mile, and other key statistics. This report format could be broken down into a more detailed report that displayed every lane for every customer out of a market.

Sales managers can also evaluate total customer load volumes and compare volumes to expected activity levels for the customer. Each regional sales manager could be provided this report for his territory in order to evaluate rate levels, empty miles, lane mix, and other key statistics. The regional sales manager would then seek out customers that offer potential lanes that fit network needs. The sales manager may also seek rate increases or other action with underperforming lanes and customers.

Market Customer Inbound Summary

The market customer inbound summary report provides key operating statistics for every customer that ships loads into a zone. A sample report is shown below.

Inbound Revenue Analysis by Customer 01/04/09 to 01/31/09

Origin Zone / Customer	Total Loads	Loaded	Empty	Total	Empty %	LOH	Total Revenue	Linehaul Revenue	Loaded	Net
AL STH	11	4,312	582	4,894	11.89%	392	$ 9,867	$ 9,350	$ 2.17	$ 1.91
ABC Express	11	4,312	582	4,894	11.89%	392	$ 9,867	$ 9,350	$ 2.17	$ 1.91
GA ATL	12	4,560	578	5,138	11.25%	380	$ 9,247	$ 8,700	$ 1.91	$ 1.69
ABC Express	12	4,560	578	5,138	11.25%	380	$ 9,247	$ 8,700	$ 1.91	$ 1.69
LA STH	12	4,716	479	5,195	9.22%	393	$ 10,466	$ 9,900	$ 2.10	$ 1.91
ABC Express	12	4,716	479	5,195	9.22%	393	$ 10,466	$ 9,900	$ 2.10	$ 1.91
TN MEM	44	13,753	5,776	19,529	29.58%	313	$ 26,280	$ 24,205	$ 1.76	$ 1.24
BD Electronics	2	466	405	871	46.50%	233	$ 1,144	$ 1,000	$ 2.15	$ 1.15
BMI Computers	1	136	320	456	70.18%	136	$ 539	$ 450	$ 3.31	$ 0.99
Ellis Inc.	15	5,623	1,406	7,029	20.00%	375	$ 8,875	$ 8,425	$ 1.50	$ 1.20
HC Logistics	3	439	823	1,262	65.21%	146	$ 1,354	$ 1,275	$ 2.90	$ 1.01
MLS Logistics	5	2,270	80	2,350	3.40%	454	$ 3,372	$ 3,145	$ 1.39	$ 1.34
Smiley Stores	7	1,944	924	2,868	32.22%	278	$ 4,814	$ 4,095	$ 2.11	$ 1.43
TexArk Industries	10	2,667	1,634	4,301	37.99%	267	$ 5,737	$ 5,390	$ 2.02	$ 1.25
Tyler Chicken	1	208	184	392	46.94%	208	$ 446	$ 425	$ 2.04	$ 1.08
TX DFW	13	5,889	647	6,536	9.90%	453	$ 12,732	$ 12,025	$ 2.04	$ 1.84
ABC Express	13	5,889	647	6,536	9.90%	453	$ 12,732	$ 12,025	$ 2.04	$ 1.84
Totals	92	33,230	8,062	41,292	19.52%	361	$ 68,592	$ 64,180	$ 1.93	$ 1.55

The report provides a quick summary of every customer that ships loads into a zone. Each customer can be evaluated in terms of length of haul, revenue per mile, and other key statistics. This report could be broken down into a more detailed format that displayed every lane for every customer into each market.

Sales managers for a region are very interested in the rates, length of haul, and customers that deliver into their service area. If a particular territory has too many inbound trucks flowing into the region, the sales manager may ask the managers of other regions to reduce volumes into the area or increase rates on loads into the area. While the loads may appear very profitable for the origin region, the excess loads may have a negative impact on the destination region. The destination region may be incurring excessive empty miles or reducing outbound rates significantly to keep the inbound capacity flowing back out of the region. A report of this type, especially at the lane level, gives the regional sales manager the information needed to manage the inbound capacity for his sales territory.

Lane Level Analysis

Lane level analysis focuses on operating measurements such as cycle time, revenue per hour, length of haul, empty miles, and revenue per mile. The goal of these reports is to identify underperforming lanes and customers and determine strategies to improve performance. Another benefit of these reports is the ability to identify the most attractive and unattractive lanes. Knowledge of each lane helps the carrier determine the optimal pricing and network strategy by avoiding poor lanes and expanding business on the most profitable lanes.

Revenue Analysis by Lane

The revenue analysis by lane report is an extension of the market level analysis reports. Key operating statistics can be evaluated in greater detail to identify lane-specific problems with rates, empty miles, and other key statistics.

Revenue Analysis by Lane 01/04/09 to 01/31/09

Lane	Total Loads	Loaded	Empty	Total	Empty %	LOH	Total Revenue	Linehaul Revenue	Rev/Mile Loaded	Rev/Mile Net
Inbound	**44**	**13,753**	**5,776**	**19,529**	**29.58%**	**313**	**$ 26,280**	**$ 24,205**	**$ 1.76**	**$ 1.24**
AL NOR	3	699	664	1,363	48.72%	233	$ 1,711	$ 1,525	$ 2.18	$ 1.12
to: TN MEM	3	699	664	1,363	48.72%	233	$ 1,711	$ 1,525	$ 2.18	$ 1.12
AL STH	7	2,359	1,190	3,549	33.53%	337	$ 4,214	$ 4,025	$ 1.71	$ 1.13
to: TN MEM	7	2,359	1,190	3,549	33.53%	337	$ 4,214	$ 4,025	$ 1.71	$ 1.13
AR CEN	1	136	320	456	70.18%	136	$ 539	$ 450	$ 3.31	$ 0.99
to: TN MEM	1	136	320	456	70.18%	136	$ 539	$ 450	$ 3.31	$ 0.99
AR WEST	7	1,876	1,260	3,136	40.18%	268	$ 4,094	$ 3,850	$ 2.05	$ 1.23
to: TN MEM	7	1,876	1,260	3,136	40.18%	268	$ 4,094	$ 3,850	$ 2.05	$ 1.23
GA ATL	8	3,264	216	3,480	6.21%	408	$ 4,661	$ 4,400	$ 1.35	$ 1.26
to: TN MEM	8	3,264	216	3,480	6.21%	408	$ 4,661	$ 4,400	$ 1.35	$ 1.26
MS CEN	11	2,943	1,482	4,425	33.49%	268	$ 6,903	$ 6,060	$ 2.06	$ 1.37
to: TN MEM	11	2,943	1,482	4,425	33.49%	268	$ 6,903	$ 6,060	$ 2.06	$ 1.37
MS NOR	2	206	564	770	73.25%	103	$ 787	$ 750	$ 3.64	$ 0.97
to: TN MEM	2	206	564	770	73.25%	103	$ 787	$ 750	$ 3.64	$ 0.97
TX DFW	5	2,270	80	2,350	3.40%	454	$ 3,372	$ 3,145	$ 1.39	$ 1.34
to: TN MEM	5	2,270	80	2,350	3.40%	454	$ 3,372	$ 3,145	$ 1.39	$ 1.34
Outbound	**48**	**19,477**	**2,286**	**21,763**	**10.50%**	**406**	**$ 42,312**	**$ 39,975**	**$ 2.05**	**$ 1.84**
TN MEM	48	19,477	2,286	21,763	10.50%	406	$ 42,312	$ 39,975	$ 2.05	$ 1.84
to: AL STH	11	4,312	582	4,894	11.89%	392	$ 9,867	$ 9,350	$ 2.17	$ 1.91
to: GA ATL	12	4,560	578	5,138	11.25%	380	$ 9,247	$ 8,700	$ 1.91	$ 1.69
to: LA STH	12	4,716	479	5,195	9.22%	393	$ 10,466	$ 9,900	$ 2.10	$ 1.91
to: TX DFW	13	5,889	647	6,536	9.90%	453	$ 12,732	$ 12,025	$ 2.04	$ 1.84
Totals	92	33,230	8,062	41,292	19.52%	361	$ 68,592	$ 64,180	$ 1.93	$ 1.55

Because this carrier only serves lanes into and out of Memphis, TN, the revenue analysis by lane is broken down into inbound and outbound lanes. The carrier can quickly identify any lanes with poor performance in revenue per mile or empty miles. The format of this report should be modified to meet the particular analysis needs of the individual carrier network.

Lane Cycle Time Analysis by Customer

The customer cycle time analysis report compares transit times, dock times, and cycle times for every customer on a given lane. A sample report is shown below.

Lane Cycle Time Analysis by Customer 01/04/09 to 01/31/09

Lane / Customer	Total Loads	Average Miles Loaded	Average Miles Empty	Average Miles Total	MT Drive	PU Dock	Transit	Del Dock	Total	Buffer Time	Transit MPH
AL NOR to TN MEM	3	233	221	454	5.94	0.94	6.83	0.85	14.56	1.7	34.1
BD Electronics	2	233	203	436	5.67	1.19	6.80	0.82	14.48	1.6	34.3
HC Logistics	1	233	259	492	6.48	0.42	6.89	0.92	14.71	1.7	33.8
AL STH to TN MEM	7	337	170	507	5.32	1.43	9.10	1.48	17.34	1.6	37.0
Ellis Inc.	7	337	170	507	5.32	1.43	9.10	1.48	17.34	1.6	37.0
GA ATL to TN MEM	8	408	27	435	1.21	1.04	10.50	1.96	14.70	1.4	38.9
Ellis Inc.	8	408	27	435	1.21	1.04	10.50	1.96	14.70	1.4	38.9
MS CEN to TN MEM	11	268	135	402	4.44	1.21	7.10	1.73	14.48	1.2	37.7
Smiley Stores	7	278	132	410	4.33	1.19	7.37	1.95	14.84	1.2	37.7
TexArk Industries	3	264	125	388	4.16	1.29	7.07	1.39	13.91	1.2	37.3
Tyler Chicken	1	208	184	392	6.13	1.12	5.29	1.16	13.70	0.7	39.3
MS NOR to TN MEM	2	103	282	385	6.93	1.67	3.34	1.27	13.20	1.0	30.9
HC Logistics	2	103	282	385	6.93	1.67	3.34	1.27	13.20	1.0	30.9
TN MEM to AL STH	11	392	53	445	1.67	1.09	9.12	2.13	14.00	0.4	43.0
ABC Express	11	392	53	445	1.67	1.09	9.12	2.13	14.00	0.4	43.0
TN MEM to GA ATL	12	380	48	428	1.69	1.55	8.80	1.97	14.02	0.4	43.2
ABC Express	12	380	48	428	1.69	1.55	8.80	1.97	14.02	0.4	43.2
TN MEM to LA STH	12	393	40	433	1.25	1.51	9.11	1.68	13.55	0.4	43.1
ABC Express	12	393	40	433	1.25	1.51	9.11	1.68	13.55	0.4	43.1
TN MEM to TX DFW	13	453	50	503	1.68	1.25	10.74	1.57	15.25	0.7	42.2
ABC Express	13	453	50	503	1.68	1.25	10.74	1.57	15.25	0.7	42.2
TX DFW to TN MEM	5	454	16	470	1.09	1.91	11.42	2.41	16.83	1.3	39.8
MLS Logistics	5	454	16	470	1.09	1.91	11.42	2.41	16.83	1.3	39.8

The areas of emphasis for this report are transit time and loaded revenue per mile. A carrier must identify the best customers on each lane in order to make profitable decisions on the allocation of available capacity. Shippers that perform poorly may face rate increases or other corrective action from the carrier.

One minor issue on this report is present on the MS CEN to TN MEM lane. The cycle time for Smiley Stores is about 1 hour longer than the cycle time for other customers on the lane. Part of the reason for the longer cycle time is the slightly longer length of haul. However, the delivery dock time also looks high for this customer on this lane. The carrier may choose to investigate further to determine if any action is available to improve the cycle time for this customer.

Customer Cycle Time and Revenue Analysis by Lane

The customer lane analysis report is focused on comparing transit times, dock times, and cycle times for every customer on a given lane. A sample report is shown below.

Lane Cycle Time Analysis by Customer 01/04/09 to 01/31/09

Lane / Customer	Total Loads	Average Miles Loaded	Average Miles Empty	Average Miles Total	MT Drive	PU Dock	Transit	Del Dock	Total	Buffer Time	Transit MPH
AL NOR to TN MEM	3	233	221	454	5.94	0.94	6.83	0.85	14.56	1.7	34.1
BD Electronics	2	233	203	436	5.67	1.19	6.80	0.82	14.48	1.6	34.3
HC Logistics	1	233	259	492	6.48	0.42	6.89	0.92	14.71	1.7	33.8
AL STH to TN MEM	7	337	170	507	5.32	1.43	9.10	1.48	17.34	1.6	37.0
Ellis Inc.	7	337	170	507	5.32	1.43	9.10	1.48	17.34	1.6	37.0
GA ATL to TN MEM	8	408	27	435	1.21	1.04	10.50	1.96	14.70	1.4	38.9
Ellis Inc.	8	408	27	435	1.21	1.04	10.50	1.96	14.70	1.4	38.9
MS CEN to TN MEM	11	268	135	402	4.44	1.21	7.10	1.73	14.48	1.2	37.7
Smiley Stores	7	278	132	410	4.33	1.19	7.37	1.95	14.84	1.2	37.7
TexArk Industries	3	264	125	388	4.16	1.29	7.07	1.39	13.91	1.2	37.3
Tyler Chicken	1	208	184	392	6.13	1.12	5.29	1.16	13.70	0.7	39.3

Each customer on each lane can be compared to identify the most time-efficient customers. The customers with the shortest cycle time and highest transit miles-per-hour are likely providing the most productive and highest utilization loads on the lane. The lane analysis should also include a review of revenue levels including revenue per mile and revenue per hour. The revenue analysis is shown below.

Lane Revenue Analysis by Customer 01/04/09 to 01/31/09

Lane / Customer	Total Loads	Loaded	Empty	Total	Transit	Total	Total	Loaded	Net	LH Rev Per Hr	Transit MPH
AL NOR to TN MEM	3	233	221	454	6.83	14.56	$ 508	$ 2.18	$ 1.12	$ 34.91	34.1
BD Electronics	2	233	203	436	6.8	14.48	$ 500	$ 2.15	$ 1.15	$ 34.52	34.3
HC Logistics	1	233	259	492	6.89	14.71	$ 525	$ 2.25	$ 1.07	$ 35.68	33.8
AL STH to TN MEM	7	337	170	507	9.1	17.34	$ 575	$ 1.71	$ 1.13	$ 33.16	37.0
Ellis Inc.	7	337	170	507	9.1	17.34	$ 575	$ 1.71	$ 1.13	$ 33.16	37.0
GA ATL to TN MEM	8	408	27	435	10.5	14.7	$ 550	$ 1.35	$ 1.26	$ 37.40	38.9
Ellis Inc.	8	408	27	435	10.5	14.7	$ 550	$ 1.35	$ 1.26	$ 37.40	38.9
MS CEN to TN MEM	11	268	135	402	7.1	14.48	$ 551	$ 2.06	$ 1.37	$ 38.04	37.7
Smiley Stores	7	278	132	410	7.37	14.84	$ 585	$ 2.11	$ 1.43	$ 39.43	37.7
TexArk Industries	3	264	125	388	7.07	13.91	$ 513	$ 1.95	$ 1.32	$ 36.91	37.3
Tyler Chicken	1	208	184	392	5.29	13.7	$ 425	$ 2.04	$ 1.08	$ 31.02	39.3

In actual practice, the revenue and cycle time reports may be included on one detailed lane analysis report. The two are separated in this example in part due to space limitations and presentation considerations.

Other Analysis and Reporting Considerations

Carrier Income Statements

In order to manage individual fleets and operations, carriers must develop internal accounting measurements to accurately evaluate each segment of the company. The most important step is to separate segments of the company with different operating characteristics and cost structures. Individual income statements for each segment allow the carrier to accurately evaluate the performance of each business unit. The individual measurements also allow the carrier to avoid potential confusion or misinterpretation of results by having all operating segments blended into only a summary income statement.

Consider a large national carrier that operates a national linehaul operation and three regional operations in Dallas, TX, Atlanta, GA and Columbus, OH. The linehaul operation has a long average length of haul and high utilization. The regional fleets have a relatively short length of haul and lower utilization.

The income statement to the right reflects the performance of the entire company, including both regional and linehaul operations. The company's goal is to achieve an operating ratio of less than 90%. Based only on that goal, the company had a successful year.

The weakness of this income statement is that the performance of each individual business unit is not reflected. In addition, the revenue per mile information represents blended activity from all operations. Based on this format, the carrier is unable to evaluate and interpret the performance of each individual business segment. The income statement format could be improved by expanding it to include a detailed breakdown of each unique fleet of trucks.

Annual Income Statement	Total Company
Revenues	
Linehaul Revenue	$ 69,264,876
Accessorial Revenue	$ 1,439,654
Fuel Surcharge Revenue	$ 938,160
Grand Total Revenue	**$ 71,642,690**
Revenue Per Loaded Mile	
Linehaul Revenue Per Mile	$ 1.65
Accessorial Revenue Per Mile	$ 0.03
Fuel Revenue Per Mile	$ 0.02
Total Revenue Per Mile	$ 1.70
Revenue Per Total Mile	
Linehaul Revenue Per Mile	$ 1.42
Accessorial Revenue Per Mile	$ 0.03
Fuel Revenue Per Mile	$ 0.02
Total Revenue Per Mile	$ 1.47
Expenses	
Driver Wages	$ 19,118,927
Fringe Benefits	$ 4,779,732
Fuel	$ 15,306,832
Maintenance	$ 5,485,477
Insurance	$ 4,997,093
Tractor Depreciation	$ 6,633,000
Trailer Depreciation	$ 2,384,800
Corporate Overhead	$ 3,216,000
Other Costs	$ 2,412,000
Total Costs	**$ 64,333,860**
Operating Profit	**$ 7,308,830**
Operating Ratio	89.8%

The income statement below has been reformatted to include the detailed performance of each independent operating unit. The income statement also includes the key operating statistics for each fleet.

Segmented Income Statement

Annual Income Statement	Regional Fleet Atlanta	Regional Fleet Columbus	Regional Fleet Dallas	Total Regional	Linehaul	Total Company
Operating Statistics						
Total Loads	11,351	10,965	9,502	31,818	40,561	72,379
Total Trucks	42	37	35	114	288	402
Loaded Miles	3,303,141	2,883,795	2,898,110	9,085,046	32,935,532	42,020,578
Empty Miles	854,690	681,944	702,987	2,239,621	4,578,260	6,817,881
Total Miles	4,157,831	3,565,739	3,601,097	11,324,667	37,513,792	48,838,459
Empty Miles Percentage	20.6%	19.1%	19.5%	19.8%	12.2%	14.0%
Utilization	1,904	1,853	1,979	1,910	2,505	2,336
Average Length of Haul	291	263	305	286	812	581
Revenues						
Linehaul Revenue	$ 7,068,722	$ 6,055,970	$ 5,419,466	$ 18,544,157	$ 50,720,719	$ 69,264,876
Accessorial Revenue	$ 251,913	$ 288,955	$ 210,044	$ 750,912	$ 688,742	$ 1,439,654
Fuel Surcharge Revenue	$ 96,718	$ 63,098	$ 62,984	$ 222,800	$ 715,360	$ 938,160
Grand Total Revenue	$ 7,417,353	$ 6,408,023	$ 5,692,494	$ 19,517,869	$ 52,124,821	$ 71,642,690
Revenue Per Loaded Mile						
Linehaul Revenue Per Mile	$ 2.14	$ 2.10	$ 1.87	$ 2.04	$ 1.54	$ 1.65
Accessorial Revenue Per Mile	$ 0.08	$ 0.10	$ 0.07	$ 0.08	$ 0.02	$ 0.03
Fuel Revenue Per Mile	$ 0.03	$ 0.02	$ 0.02	$ 0.02	$ 0.02	$ 0.02
Total Revenue Per Mile	$ 2.25	$ 2.22	$ 1.96	$ 2.15	$ 1.58	$ 1.70
Revenue Per Total Mile						
Linehaul Revenue Per Mile	$ 1.70	$ 1.70	$ 1.50	$ 1.64	$ 1.35	$ 1.42
Accessorial Revenue Per Mile	$ 0.06	$ 0.08	$ 0.06	$ 0.07	$ 0.02	$ 0.03
Fuel Revenue Per Mile	$ 0.02	$ 0.02	$ 0.02	$ 0.02	$ 0.02	$ 0.02
Total Revenue Per Mile	$ 1.78	$ 1.80	$ 1.58	$ 1.72	$ 1.39	$ 1.47
Expenses						
Driver Wages	$ 1,746,289	$ 1,568,925	$ 1,548,472	$ 4,863,686	$ 14,255,241	$ 19,118,927
Fringe Benefits	$ 436,572	$ 392,231	$ 387,118	$ 1,215,921	$ 3,563,810	$ 4,779,732
Fuel	$ 1,330,506	$ 1,176,694	$ 1,170,357	$ 3,677,556	$ 11,629,276	$ 15,306,832
Maintenance	$ 498,940	$ 427,889	$ 432,132	$ 1,358,960	$ 4,126,517	$ 5,485,477
Insurance	$ 457,361	$ 392,231	$ 396,121	$ 1,245,713	$ 3,751,379	$ 4,997,093
Tractor Depreciation	$ 693,000	$ 610,500	$ 577,500	$ 1,881,000	$ 4,752,000	$ 6,633,000
Trailer Depreciation	$ 286,000	$ 235,400	$ 215,600	$ 737,000	$ 1,647,800	$ 2,384,800
Corporate Overhead	$ 336,000	$ 296,000	$ 280,000	$ 912,000	$ 2,304,000	$ 3,216,000
Other Costs	$ 252,000	$ 222,000	$ 210,000	$ 684,000	$ 1,728,000	$ 2,412,000
Total Costs	$ 6,036,668	$ 5,321,870	$ 5,217,298	$ 16,575,837	$ 47,758,023	$ 64,333,860
Operating Profit	$ 1,380,684	$ 1,086,152	$ 475,195	$ 2,942,032	$ 4,366,798	$ 7,308,830
Operating Ratio	81.4%	83.1%	91.7%	84.9%	91.6%	89.8%

The detailed breakdown of the individual performance of each fleet reveals several important items. The Atlanta and Columbus regional fleets have performed very well. However, the Dallas regional fleet and the linehaul fleet both have operating ratios above the company goal of 90%. Without the breakdown by fleet, the information might not otherwise be available.

Given the poor performance of the two divisions, the segmented income statement also allows the carrier to review the operating statistics to identify potential issues for the underperforming fleets. Certain key operating statistics such as revenue per mile, utilization, and the empty mile percentage may be to blame for the poor performance of the divisions in question.

A close review of the operating statistics for the Dallas regional fleet indicates that utilization, length of haul, and the empty mile percentage are fairly consistent with the other regional fleets. However, the loaded revenue per mile for the Dallas fleet at $1.87 per mile is far below the other two regional fleets. Part of the reason for the lower loaded revenue per mile is reflected in the fact that Dallas has a slightly longer length of haul. However, it appears clear that insufficient pricing is a major cause of the poor financial performance of this regional fleet.

The linehaul fleet, with an operating ratio of 91.6%, has also failed to meet the company's 90% operating ratio goal. The most significant operating statistic is the empty mile percentage. The company's goal for the linehaul fleet is 10%. However, the actual empty mile percentage for the linehaul fleet was 12.2%. The poor empty mile performance appears to be a primary cause of the inadequate financial results. The carrier might also compare this year's performance and statistics with prior period results to identify other potential issues.

The segmented income statement is highly dependent on tracking expenses and allocating certain costs accurately to each fleet. If cost allocations are inaccurate, the value of the segmented income statement is minimized. In addition, inaccurate allocations may cause the carrier to reach incorrect conclusions about the financial performance of each fleet. The carrier must have accurate cost tracking and allocation processes in place to support the segmented income statement approach.

On-time Service Reporting

Shippers often require carriers to provide accurate and timely reports regarding on-time service performance. Carriers must develop reporting systems to capture and report service information to shippers. The reporting process may include both on-time pick-up and on-time delivery or focus only on on-time delivery. For most shippers, on-time delivery is considered the most important service measurement.

The reporting process for the carrier can become complicated because every customer may have unique on-time service expectations. For example, Customer A may consider a load to be on time if delivered within 30 minutes of the scheduled delivery appointment. Meanwhile, Customer B may consider a load to be on time only if delivered within 5 minutes of the scheduled delivery appointment. The carrier must develop a measurement system that is able to recognize the requirements of each customer and measure against those requirements. The sample report below reflects service by destination and codes each late delivery by the party that caused the late delivery.

On-Time Service by Destination 01/04/09 to 01/31/09

Customer	Total Loads	Carrier Failures	Carrier On-Time %	Shipper Failures	Shipper On-Time %	Total Failures	Total On-Time %
ABC Express	48	3	93.80%	1	97.90%	4	91.70%
Memphis, TN	48	3	93.80%	1	97.90%	4	91.70%
to: Atlanta, GA	12	2	83.30%	0	100.00%	2	83.30%
to: Dallas, TX	13	1	92.30%	0	100.00%	1	92.30%
to: Mobile, AL	11	0	100.00%	0	100.00%	0	100.00%
to: New Orleans, LA	12	0	100.00%	1	91.70%	1	91.70%

The carrier may also provide detailed on-time service reports that not only show the number of late loads, but also include the relative lateness of each late delivery. The sample report below provides the details for each late load event.

Service Failure Detail Report 01/04/09 to 01/31/09

Customer: ABC Express

Delivery Date	Shipment Number	Origin	Destination	Scheduled	Actual	Minutes Late	Late Reason
1/4/2009	ABC849341	Memphis, TN	Atlanta, GA	10:15	10:26	11	Driver Error
1/4/2009	ABC849284	Memphis, TN	Atlanta, GA	12:30	12:37	7	Driver Error
1/11/2009	ABC849271	Memphis, TN	Dallas, TX	8:00	8:32	32	Dispatch
1/8/2009	ABC849355	Memphis, TN	New Orleans, LA	11:45	12:31	46	Shipper

The report shows that the two late deliveries to the Atlanta location were only 11 minutes and 7 minutes late. The late delivery to Dallas was much later at 32 minutes past the scheduled delivery time. The degree of lateness information provides the shipper with additional insight into the relative impact of each late delivery.

As part of the reports, the carrier should provide reason codes to identify the cause of each late delivery. Each late delivery will be coded as shipper-related or carrier-related. The carrier will also provide reason codes for each late delivery. A sample on-time service report with reason codes is shown below.

On-Time Service Summary Report

Quarterly On-Time Service Report	Month April	Month May	Month June	Total Quarter	
Total Deliveries	628	597	658	**1,883**	
Total Service Failures	6	5	12	**23**	
On-time Deliveries	622	592	646	**1,860**	
Carrier On-Time Percentage	99.2%	99.2%	98.5%	**98.9%**	
Total On-time Percentage	99.0%	99.2%	98.2%	**98.8%**	
Late Delivery Reason Codes					
Carrier Related Failures					% of Events
Driver-Related	3	2	5	10	43.5%
Maintenance	1	1	3	5	21.7%
Dispatch	0	1	1	2	8.7%
Customer Service	1	1	0	2	8.7%
Other	0	0	1	1	4.3%
Total Carrier Related	5	5	10	20	87.0%
Other Failures					
Shipper-Related	1	0	1	2	8.7%
Force Majeure	0	0	1	1	4.3%
Total Service Failures	6	5	12	23	100.0%

The report measures on-time service in two ways. The first is the carrier on-time percentage. The carrier on-time percentage represents only the late deliveries caused by carrier error. The typical reasons for a late delivery caused by the carrier include driver error, maintenance problems, or management error. The report also details how many carrier failures were caused by each reason code.

The second measure is the total or shipper on-time percentage. The total on-time percentage includes all late deliveries to represent the effective total on-time service for the shipper. Shipper-related failures include items such as delays in trailer loading or paperwork errors. Force majeure failures are caused by extraordinary events or "Acts of God" that are beyond the control of both the carrier and shipper. Force majeure events include such items as an earthquake, a flood, a riot, a war, or other event beyond the reasonable control of either the carrier or the shipper.

Operating Reports

Carriers may also extend reporting beyond the reports shown previously covering fleet, customer and market activity. For many carriers, each tractor includes satellite tracking and on-board computer systems that track important driver-specific items such as idle time, miles per gallon, out-of-route miles, and many other technical metrics. While the detailed formats and contents of these technical reports are beyond the scope of this book, several of these measurements are critical to the overall profitability of the carrier, particularly fuel efficiency.

Miles Per Gallon

Fuel is a major cost component for all carriers. In order to minimize fuel costs, carriers can use on-board computer systems to measure miles per gallon for each tractor and driver. The driving habits of the individual driver have a significant impact on fuel consumption. Driving variables such as average speeds, rpm's, shifting, and idle time all factor into miles per gallon. All these variables are monitored by on-board computers and can provide important analysis information for each driver. Based on these reports, drivers that consistently perform poorly in miles per gallon performance can be counseled or receive follow-up training in driving habits that maximize fuel efficiency.

Idle Time

Idle time is the time a tractor spends with the engine on while not engaged in actual driving. Most idle time occurs during the time the driver is taking a mandatory DOT rest break. Quite often, the driver will sleep in the bunk area of the truck with the engine running to provide heat or air conditioning for the driver's comfort.

As a general rule of thumb, a tractor will consume about one gallon of fuel per hour of idle time. While this secondary fuel consumption may seem insignificant, when converted into a cost per mile amount, the costs can be very significant. The table below provides an estimated cost per mile of idle time for various weekly utilization and idle time scenarios.

Idle Time Cost Per Mile		Weekly Utilization					
		1,800	2,000	2,200	2,400	2,600	2,800
Idle Time Hours Per Week	25	$ 0.035	$ 0.031	$ 0.028	$ 0.026	$ 0.024	$ 0.022
	30	$ 0.042	$ 0.038	$ 0.034	$ 0.031	$ 0.029	$ 0.027
	35	$ 0.049	$ 0.044	$ 0.040	$ 0.036	$ 0.034	$ 0.031
	40	$ 0.056	$ 0.050	$ 0.045	$ 0.042	$ 0.038	$ 0.036
	45	$ 0.063	$ 0.056	$ 0.051	$ 0.047	$ 0.043	$ 0.040
	50	$ 0.069	$ 0.063	$ 0.057	$ 0.052	$ 0.048	$ 0.045
Assumptions: Fuel Cost of $2.50 per gallon. 1 gallon per hour of idle time.							

Based on this example, idle time has a cost of between 2 and 7 cents per mile. Because of the significance of this cost, carriers must measure idle time closely for each driver. Some carriers may even provide special financial incentives for those drivers that are able to minimize idle time and improve fuel efficiency.

> **! *Technical Tip* – Creating Basics Reports with Microsoft Access®**

Microsoft Access® database software provides an excellent tool for creating basic reports and analysis. The majority of the analysis reports included in this chapter were created using a single Access database. Creating reports in Access is similar to the logic of working with pivot tables in spreadsheets. The benefit of the database approach is that data can easily "flow" through the database to predefined reports with little or no manipulation. Raw data from a spreadsheet, text file, or other format can be imported into Access and quickly integrated into the predefined reports. An abbreviated spreadsheet data table is shown below.

Sample Spreadsheet Data Table for Import into Access

Date	Tractor	Customer Name	Origin City	Origin ST	Destination City	Dest ST	Dest Name	Loaded Miles	Empty Miles
1/4/2009	101	ABC Express	Memphis	TN	Atlanta	GA	Store 503	380	44
1/5/2009	101	Ellis Inc.	Dunwoody	GA	Millington	TN	Jiffy Stores, Inc.	408	27
1/6/2009	101	ABC Express	Memphis	TN	Dallas	TX	Store 460	453	17
1/7/2009	101	TexArk Industries	Texarkana	AR	W. Memphis	AR	AA Warehouse	268	180
1/8/2009	101	ABC Express	Memphis	TN	New Orleans	LA	Store 375	393	9
1/9/2009	101	Smiley Stores	Brookhaven	MS	Bartlett	TN	Store 1566	276	132
1/11/2009	101	ABC Express	Memphis	TN	Dallas	TX	Store 460	453	15

Once imported, reports can be created in Access® that source data from the imported spreadsheet table. A sample report design screen is shown below.[53]

Report Design in Microsoft Access®

One major benefit of Access® is that once a report format is created as shown above, the reporting layers or "headers" can quickly be changed to perform the same analysis on different fields in the data table. The "Customer Name Header" in the above report could be changed to Tractor, Origin State, Origin Zone, or any other field and a new report would quickly be created. While a full discussion of database design is beyond the scope of this book, once mastered, the reporting and time saving analysis possibilities are virtually unlimited.

---

[53] Microsoft® product screen shot reprinted with permission from Microsoft® Corporation.

Reporting Dashboard. In an Access® database, customized forms can be created to allow for drill-down analysis by any number of criteria. A report management form created in Microsoft Access® is shown below.

Report Management Form

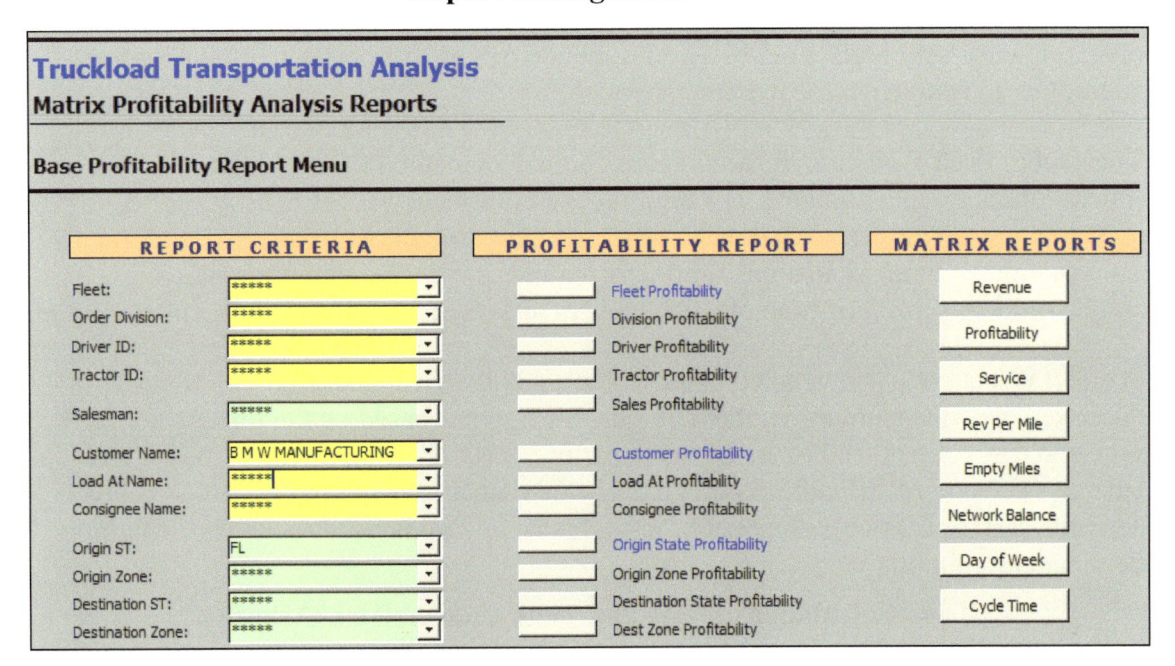

The form allows users to select from a variety of criteria to create customized reports. Once a report format is created, a matrix of reporting options can be created so that analysis can be performed on many different grouping combinations as shown below.

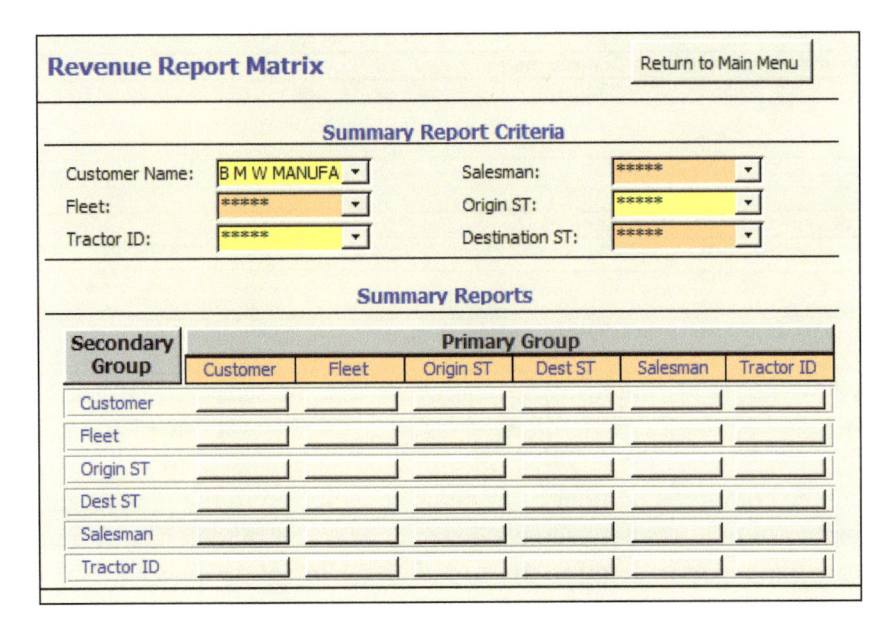

The matrix of reports provides users with 36 different grouping combinations for the same report, providing an applicable report for just about any analysis need.

! *Technical Tip* – Calculations with Date & Time Information

Many of the critical efficiency measurements such as dock time, transit time, and cycle time are computed with time-based information, primarily the dates and times provided by the truck driver as pick-up and delivery activity takes place. As the carrier accesses operating data for reports, time-based information can be difficult to work with when attempting to compute these measurements.

The goal of this calculation illustration is to provide a method for converting the date and time information into minutes. The minute-level information is then easily applied to compute the various time-based measurements. The example below illustrates the dock time and transit time calculations for the basic order cycle. The times are based on simple military time. For example, the delivery arrival time of 13:45 represents 1:45 p.m.

While it is relatively simple to compare a single set of arrival and departure times with the naked eye, it is more difficult to compute the minutes based on the information in the time and date format. If the arrival and departure occur on different days, the calculation becomes even more difficult. Based on the serial date information, the method below converts each of the time components, days, hours, and minutes, into the least common denominator of minutes.

Time Calculations: Date and Time Conversion to Minutes

	Basic Order Cycle			
	Pick Up Dock Time		**Transit Time**	**Delivery Dock Time**	
	Arrival	Departure		Arrival	Departure
Date	5/1/2008	5/1/2008		5/2/2008	5/2/2008
Time	08:15	09:10		13:45	14:52

Identification and Isolation of Time Components				
Days	39,569	39,569	39,570	39,570
Hours	8	9	13	14
Minutes	15	10	45	52

Conversion of Time Components to Minutes				
Days (1,440)	56,979,360	56,979,360	56,980,800	56,980,800
Hours (60)	480	540	780	840
Minutes (1)	15	10	45	52
Total	56,979,855	56,979,910	56,981,625	56,981,692

Final Time Components	Pick Up Dock Time	Transit Time	Delivery Dock Time
	55 minutes	1,715 minutes	67 minutes
	0.92 hours	28.58 hours	1.12 hours

By comparing the computed number of minutes at each step in the pick-up and delivery cycle, the number of minutes between each step can be computed. The formulas and calculations are explained in detail in the complete technical tip available for no charge at www.TruckloadTransportation.com.[54]

---

[54] The complete detail and full spreadsheet design for this technical tip can be downloaded at no cost from the website www.TruckloadTransportation.com.

CHAPTER 8: Introduction to Dedicated Fleet Pricing

Dedicated fleets are customer-specific operations where the customer has exclusive use of a fleet of trucks, trailers, and drivers for the movement of their products. Dedicated fleets are sometimes referred to as "Dedicated Contract Carriage." Shippers that require dedicated fleets usually have specialized transportation needs that are best met with customized services instead of standard one-way truckload transportation. Several examples of special shipper needs often served by dedicated fleets are listed below.

Common Reasons for Dedicated Fleets
Specialized trailer and/or tractor equipment
Intense driver labor requirements, especially unloading
Excessive number of stop-off deliveries
Heavy volumes of traffic under 200 miles
Shipper need for extraordinary on-time delivery service

Dedicated fleets are attractive to trucking companies because they generally involve less operating uncertainty than traditional one-way trucking operations. Dedicated fleets also offer less financial uncertainty because of the detailed dedicated contract relationship. The terms and parameters of the contract reduce the overall risk for the carrier. In most situations, the majority of risk is effectively shared with the dedicated shipper.

In its simplest form, the pricing for a dedicated fleet is basically a cost-plus decision. However, this book will discuss pricing methods that are much more sophisticated (and accurate) than a simple cost-plus approach. Several common methods of structuring dedicated pricing contracts and the advantages and disadvantages of each approach will also be discussed.

Common Types of Dedicated Fleets

Dedicated fleets are implemented to serve many specialized and unique transportation needs. Each fleet is custom-designed for the network and shipper it will serve. Described below are a few general needs that are commonly served by dedicated fleets, along with specific examples of actual dedicated fleets.

Multi-Stop Retail Distribution

A retail distribution fleet is designed to meet the needs of a retailer to deliver products to a group of retail stores. The customized solution might include multi-stop peddle runs, an on-site manager, and load-building optimization technology.[55] While making deliveries, drivers follow specific procedures for the unloading process such as handling products, obtaining signatures, and reporting cargo claims.

---

[55] Peddle runs are full truckloads that combine small shipments to multiple destinations into one truckload. The truckload is delivered by making brief stops at each destination or "consignee" location on the route.

Networks with a high number of stops per load are often served with dedicated fleets because most one-way carriers prefer to avoid loads with a large number of stops. The excess stops waste valuable time and cause the carrier to lose asset utilization. The number of stops will often cause dissatisfaction for typical over-the-road drivers because they generally prefer driving much more than making stop-off deliveries. With a dedicated fleet solution, drivers are hired to join the fleet and are made aware of the stops and other requirements during the hiring process.

Example Fleet: Several major retailers use a multi-stop retail distribution dedicated fleet to deliver tires to their retail locations within a specific geographic area. Each retail store receives one or two tire deliveries each week, depending upon sales volume. Each trailer can hold approximately 1,500 tires and the average tire delivery ranges from 100 to 350 tires per store. Therefore, an efficiently loaded outbound trailer will contain enough tires to make multi-stop deliveries to between 3 and 7 stores.

In order to save miles and reduce cost, the retailer or the carrier uses a transportation optimization software package to identify the most efficient routing of stores for each day's shipping. The optimization software will identify the routing solution that minimizes the total number of miles and total cost. This solution is achieved by loading the stores into the fewest number of trailers and by identifying the most efficient delivery route for each load.

The drivers for this type of fleet must usually assist with unloading the tires at each store. The unloading process is physically demanding, so not just any truck driver is capable of handling this workload. The unloading demands, along with the high number of stops, make a dedicated fleet essential for the success of this operation. The typical linehaul truck driver would be very unhappy if assigned to a load with these difficult stop-off and labor requirements. The retailers also have a high need for exceptional on-time delivery service, furthering the need for a specialized dedicated fleet.

Short Haul Regional Distribution

A short haul regional distribution fleet is designed to meet the needs of a shipper that ships a large number of loads within a small geographic area, usually from a single distribution center. In many cases, tractors will perform multiple outbound loads each day and return empty to the distribution center after each load in order to quickly be available for the day's next outbound load.

In some networks, the shipper may also have nearby vendor shipments that need to be delivered into the distribution center. Whenever possible, outbound trucks will pick up these vendor loads as they return to the distribution center. The ability to pick up some or all of these inbound loads can make the fleet very cost effective for the dedicated shipper.

Example Fleet. Many major beverage producers use short haul regional fleets to ship finished goods to local distributors who make the final delivery to grocery stores and other retail outlets. In some cases, totes and packaging materials must be returned to the plant. The fleet might also pick up manufacturing materials such as bottles, cans, and product packaging from local vendors.

A dedicated fleet is a common solution for this network because of the large volume of very short loads in a small geographic area. The shipper may choose a dedicated carrier that also operates additional truck capacity and services in the same area. A carrier with a local, short haul, or regional fleet based in the same area is ideal. The carrier's other operations can provide additional local capacity during peak shipping periods for the beverage manufacturer.

Because the beverage products are very heavy and don't fully utilize the space inside a normal trailer, carriers may provide beverage shippers with customized, light-weight trailers that allow the shipper to legally load additional weight and product on each trailer. The tractors used in the fleet might also be customized with light-weight features to allow the shipper to place even more weight and product on the trailer.[56] The use of specialized equipment of this type would dictate the need for a dedicated fleet in order to keep the equipment captive in the shipper's dedicated network.

Over-the-Road High Utilization

High utilization services provide a fleet of trucks to provide transportation for semi-random, long haul loads within the shipper's network. Shippers often use fleets of this type not only to save on transportation costs, but also to "guarantee" that trucks will be available to transport their products. These fleets are often priced on a per-mile basis using a mileage scale or a fixed-variable contract structure. These and other contract structures are presented in detail later in this chapter.

Example Fleet. One major retailer uses a high utilization fleet to transport vendor shipments and inventory from one regional distribution center to another. The retailer has a large network of regional distribution centers around the country. After the retailer's private fleet from Distribution Center A makes deliveries to retail stores, those same private fleet trucks will stop at nearby vendors to pick up products to be returned to the distribution center. However, the products that are picked up may actually be needed by Distribution Center B in another part of the county. Meanwhile, a truck from Distribution Center B may pick up a vendor load ultimately destined for Distribution Center A.

As these vendor pick-ups happen all over the country, the high utilization fleet transports these vendor loads from the distribution center that made the original pick-up to the distribution center that needs the actual product. As the high utilization truck arrives at

---

[56] Current regulations allow the total tractor-trailer unit to weigh a maximum of 80,000 lbs. This weight includes the equipment, fuel and cargo.

the destination distribution center, a new load is immediately ready for the truck to take to the next distribution center. The fleet saves the retailer money through very high utilization and an extremely low empty miles percentage. If dedicated lane imbalances occur, the carrier may also attempt to fill empty lanes with third-party backhaul loads to reposition equipment for the dedicated shipper and further reduce costs.

These are just a few examples of common dedicated fleet solutions. Every dedicated fleet is customized to meet the needs of the individual shipper, so each fleet will display specialized design and operating characteristics. Additional examples are presented in the upcoming discussions of dedicated fleet pricing and design in future chapters.

Common Dedicated Contract Structures

Dedicated fleet contracts require specific commitments on the part of both the carrier and the shipper. The parameters of each contract are customized based on the expected operating characteristics of the shipper's network and other requirements established by the shipper. In most cases, the contract parameters allow the shipper to realize most of the financial benefits of an efficient network. However, the shipper also assumes a majority of the operating risk. If the fleet is not efficient, the shipper's costs may increase considerably. The carrier's revenue and profitability will likely suffer as well.

While each dedicated fleet contract is often customized, most contracts are based on one of several common base structures. These common contract structures are listed in the table below.

Common Dedicated Fleet Contract Structures
Fixed-Variable
Utilization Scale
Over-Under
Optional Feature: Backhaul Revenue Sharing

The particular contract structure for a given fleet will depend on the shipper's preference. The shipper's choice of contract structure will depend on factors such as average miles per truck per week, week-to-week variability in miles per truck per week, and week-to-week variability in total shipping volumes. In the end, the shipper may simply choose a familiar format that has been used with success in the past.

Regardless of the contract format and rate structure, the contract will usually specify the exact number of trucks, drivers, and trailers to be provided by the carrier. The risk for the shipper is the agreement to pay for the entire fleet of trucks, trailers, and drivers regardless of the number of miles driven each week or the amount of value-added work performed by the fleet. Depending on the contract language, the carrier may be guaranteed a minimum level of revenue, thereby further reducing the level of financial risk for the carrier.

Utilization Scale Pricing

A dedicated contract based on a utilization scale format is fairly straightforward. The rate per mile is determined by the average weekly utilization of the fleet for each billing period. The table below illustrates pricing in a simple utilization scale format.[57]

Utilization Ranges	Rate Per Mile
1,000 - 1,100	$ 2.28
1,101 - 1,200	$ 2.14
1,201 - 1,300	$ 2.02
1,301 - 1,400	$ 1.92
1,401 - 1,500	$ 1.84
1,501 - 1,600	$ 1.76
1,601 - 1,700	$ 1.69
1,701 - 1,800	$ 1.63
1,801 - 1,900	$ 1.58
1,901 - 2,000	$ 1.54
2,001 - 2,100	$ 1.49
2,101 - 2,200	$ 1.45
2,201 - 2,300	$ 1.42
2,301 - 2,400	$ 1.39
2,401 - 2,500	$ 1.36
2,501 - 2,600	$ 1.33
2,601 - 2,700	$ 1.31
2,701 - 2,800	$ 1.28
2,801 - 2,900	$ 1.26
2,901 - 3,000	$ 1.24

At the end of each week (or other billing period), the average utilization for the fleet is computed. The rate per mile that corresponds with the average utilization will be charged for all miles. For example, if the average utilization was 2,344 miles, the applicable rate would be $1.39 per mile.

This format provides the carrier with revenue protection at low levels of utilization while also providing the shipper with significant cost-saving rate reductions as utilization increases.

While this format is very simple and easy to manage, it does provide one fundamental problem for the carrier, the utilization scale revenue gap, discussed in detail in the next section.

The Utilization Scale Revenue Gap. One weakness of the common utilization scale format is the gap in revenue that occurs in the shift from one utilization level to the next. This quirk exists because the rate per mile declines as utilization increases, but only at specific increments within the structure. In this example, the rate per mile declines at specific increments at each utilization increase of 100 miles. The table below illustrates the total revenue earned by the carrier as the utilization shifts from one range to the next.

The Revenue Gap			
Utilization	Rate Per Mile	Total Revenue	Change in Revenue
1,999	1.54	$ 3,078.46	
2,000	1.54	$ 3,080.00	$ 1.54
2,001	**1.49**	**$ 2,981.49**	**$ (98.51)**
2,002	1.49	$ 2,982.98	$ 1.49
2,003	1.49	$ 2,984.47	$ 1.49

The table above shows that, at the 2,001 mile level, the carrier receives $98.51 less in total revenue while driving more miles and incurring more cost. In fact, utilization must increase to 2,067 miles ($3,080.00 ÷ $1.49 per mile) to achieve the same revenue that was earned at the 2,000 mile level. While this revenue quirk should balance out over the term of the contract, it still represents a risk for the carrier.

---

[57] The utilization ranges shown in the rate table represent the average miles per truck per week.

The graph below illustrates the total revenue received by the carrier as weekly tractor utilization increases.

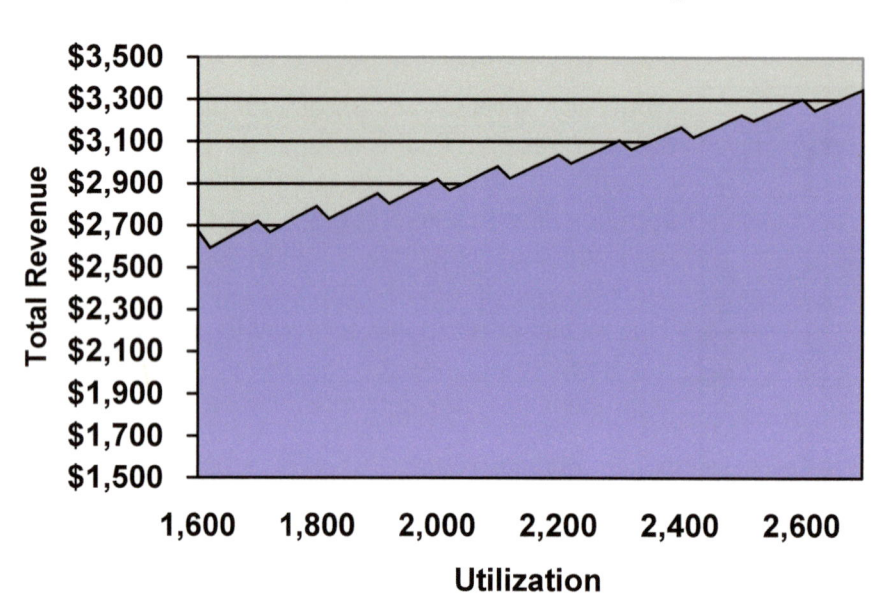

The Utilization Scale Revenue Gap

[Chart: Total Revenue vs. Utilization, ranging from 1,600 to 2,600 on x-axis and $1,500 to $3,500 on y-axis, showing a sawtooth pattern rising from approximately $2,600 to $3,300]

Because of the revenue gap, carriers should only agree to the format in 100 mile increments for fleets that will average high levels of utilization, perhaps 2,400 miles per week or more. The impact of the revenue gap is reduced as the average utilization increases because the spread between the two per-mile rates is not as great. At lower expected utilization levels, the carrier should suggest smaller utilization increments such as 25 or 50 miles. Smaller rate increments minimize the revenue gap and are ultimately in the best interest of both the shipper and the carrier.

Utilization Scale Pricing - Advantages and Disadvantages

Utilization Scale	*Carrier*	*Shipper*
Advantages	• Absorbs minimal utilization and efficiency risk. • Assumes little financial risk as rate scales lock in profit at every pricing level.	• Enjoys the majority of the financial benefits of higher utilization levels.
Disadvantages	• Enjoys a smaller portion of financial benefits of higher utilization levels. • Less revenue at higher mileages when bands switch to lower rate per mile (Revenue Gap).	• Costs increase dramatically during periods of low utilization. • Difficult for carriers to always provide accurate utilization statistics. • Absorbs the majority of utilization risk.

Over-Under Pricing

An over-under dedicated pricing agreement generally contains four components that determine the rate to be charged. The components are listed below.

Over-Under Pricing Components
Base weekly utilization level
Rate per mile at base utilization level
Rate per mile for miles above the base utilization level
Rate per mile for miles not used below the base utilization level

A typical over-under agreement might call for a base utilization of 2,000 miles per truck per week at a base rate of $1.60 per mile. For the miles over the 2,000 mile level, a rate of $0.73 per mile will be charged. If the average utilization were to fall below 2,000 miles, a rate of $0.88 per mile will be charged for "deficit" miles not utilized by the shipper. These contract provisions are summarized in the table below.

Example Over / Under Contract Provisions	
Base Weekly Utilization (Per Tractor)	2,000
Base Rate Per Mile	$ 1.60
Over Rate Per Mile	$ 0.73
Under Rate Per Mile	$ 0.88

Base Utilization Level

The applicable rates and total cost per week will be determined by the actual utilization level. The chart below demonstrates the charges when the actual utilization level meets the base utilization level as stated in the contract.

Sample Charges – At Standard Utilization

Fleet Activity	Standard	Actual	Over (Under)
Weekly Utilization Level	2,000	2,000	-

Actual Charges	Miles	Rate Per Mile	Total Charge
Base Mileage	2,000	$ 1.60	$ 3,200.00
Over Base Miles	-	$ 0.73	$ -
Under Base Miles	-	$ 0.88	$ -
Totals - All Miles	2,000	$ 1.60	$ 3,200.00

Since the base utilization level of 2,000 miles per week is met exactly without going over or under, the customer is charged the base mileage rate of $1.60 for 2,000 miles. Neither the over or under rates are applicable in this particular week.

Over the Base Utilization Level

The chart below demonstrates the charges when the actual utilization level exceeds the base utilization level as stated in the contract.

Sample Charges – Over Base Utilization

Fleet Activity	Standard	Actual	Over (Under)
Weekly Utilization Level	2,000	2,200	200

Actual Charges	Miles	Rate Per Mile	Total Charge
Base Mileage	2,000	$ 1.60	$ 3,200.00
Over Base Miles	200	$ 0.73	$ 146.00
Under Base Miles	-	$ 0.88	$ -
Totals - All Miles	2,200	$ 1.52	$ 3,346.00

During this week, the actual utilization exceeded the base utilization by 200 miles per truck per week. In this scenario, the first 2,000 miles are charged at $1.60 per mile and the 200 miles over the base utilization are charged at $0.73 per mile. The net result is a total charge of $3,346.00 per truck per week or $1.52 per mile. The overall rate per mile is reduced from $1.60 per mile to $1.52 per mile as a result of the 200 "over" miles being charged at only $0.73 per mile. The under rate is not relevant in this example since the utilization was over the base level.

Under the Base Utilization Level

The chart below demonstrates the applicable charges when the actual utilization level fails to reach the base utilization level stated in the contract.

Sample Charges – Under Base Utilization

Fleet Activity	Standard	Actual	Over (Under)
Weekly Utilization Level	2,000	1,800	(200)

Actual Charges	Miles	Rate Per Mile	Total Charge
Base Mileage	1,800	$ 1.60	$ 2,880.00
Over Base Miles	-	$ 0.73	$ -
Under Base Miles	200	$ 0.88	$ 176.00
Totals - All Miles	1,800	$ 1.70	$ 3,056.00

During this week, the actual utilization fell below the base utilization level. In this scenario, the actual 1,800 miles are charged at the base rate of $1.60 per mile. However, the rate of $1.60 was based on 2,000 miles per week, so the carrier has a revenue shortfall as a result of the low utilization level. To correct for the revenue shortfall, the carrier will also charge $0.88 per mile for the 200 miles that *were not used* by the shipper. This charge allows the carrier to recoup any fixed costs included in the base rate. The result is an effective rate of $1.70 per mile. The $1.70 per actual mile is greater than the base $1.60 per mile as a result of the charges for the under (deficit) miles.

Over-Under Pricing - Advantages and Disadvantages

Over - Under	*Carrier*	*Shipper*
Advantages	• Absorbs minimal utilization and efficiency risk. • Assumes little financial risk as over/under rates lock in profit at every utilization level.	• Enjoys the majority of the financial benefits of higher utilization levels.
Disadvantages	• Enjoys a smaller portion of the financial benefits of higher utilization levels. • Shippers may be displeased when faced with deficit mileage charges when the base utilization level is not reached.	• Costs increase dramatically during periods of low utilization. • Difficult for carriers to always provide accurate utilization statistics. • Charges for deficit miles that may be unexpected or not included in shipper budgets.

The most significant disadvantage of the over-under contract structure occurs when the actual utilization is below the base utilization. When this occurs, carriers are forced to invoice the shipper for miles that the shipper did not actually use. Even though these charges are clearly stated in the contract and agreed upon by the shipper, these charges can often cause a strain in the relationship between the carrier and shipper. In fact, the carrier may even have a difficult time collecting payment from the shipper for these "under" charges.

The "under" charges are necessary to allow the carrier to collect the unrealized portion of the revenue per mile needed to cover the fixed costs of tractors, trailers and overhead. The "under" rate may also include revenues needed to cover a minimum pay level for the drivers. The carrier's design process for the actual rates in an over-under contract agreement is presented in a later section.

Fixed-Variable Pricing

A fixed-variable pricing agreement generally contains two pricing components, a fixed charge per tractor per week and a variable charge per mile. The variable charge per mile is constant regardless of the number of miles driven. For example, the contract may call for the rates shown below.

Fixed-Variable Rate Structure

- **Fixed Charge:** $1,600 per truck per week
- **Variable Charge:** $0.62 per mile

Based on information provided by the shipper, the carrier must estimate the expected weekly utilization for the fleet in order to determine the appropriate cost and rate structure for the operation. The carrier, perhaps with the help of the shipper, will also determine the number of trucks, drivers, and trailers needed by the operation.

A primary consideration in the pricing design is the treatment of driver compensation and how the cost of wages and fringe benefits should be split between the fixed and variable rate components. Regardless of the fleet's weekly utilization level, the carrier must be sure that enough revenue is generated to cover driver wage expenses. This decision will be discussed in greater detail as specific dedicated pricing examples are presented in future sections and chapters.

Fixed-Variable Pricing - Advantages and Disadvantages

Fixed - Variable	*Carrier*	*Shipper*
Advantages	<ul><li>Absorbs no utilization and efficiency risk.</li><li>Earns a small incremental profit on each additional mile.</li></ul>	<ul><li>Enjoys the majority of the financial benefits of higher utilization levels.</li></ul>
Disadvantages	<ul><li>Little or no opportunity for above average profits.</li><li>Pricing must be accurate so that profits exist at any utilization level.</li></ul>	<ul><li>Costs increase dramatically during periods of low utilization.</li><li>May be difficult to accurately identify the exact fleet size for fixed charges.</li><li>Exact transportation cost is not known on a load-by-load basis.</li></ul>

Fixed-variable pricing is often used in networks with below average utilization levels where the shipper may have the opportunity to improve the utilization of the fleet over time. If the shipper is able to increase utilization (get more loads delivered) with the existing fleet, the only charge for the incremental utilization is the variable mileage rate. This arrangement provides the shipper with cost leverage and the incentive necessary to identify and execute on opportunities to improve utilization and productivity.

A major benefit of a fixed-variable dedicated fleet for shippers is the potential cost savings available in the efficient use of the fleet. As fleet productivity increases, the shipper's costs fall significantly. Consider the example below.

Fixed-Variable Rate Structure

- **Fixed Charge:** $1,600 per truck per week
- **Variable Charge:** $0.62 per mile

Because the fixed weekly charge per truck is paid regardless of the number of miles driven, the shipper is in a unique position to minimize per-load costs by maximizing the utilization of the dedicated fleet.

Consider a simple network where the shipper has only one customer that is 40 miles away. The shipper contracts for a 1 truck dedicated fleet at the rates shown above. The truck/driver is capable of performing up to 5 round trip customer loads per day based on DOT hours of service restrictions. The actual number of loads will fluctuate each day based on customer demand. The table below summarizes the shipper's cost per load depending on the average number of loads delivered each day.

Fixed-Variable Pricing Cost Per Load Analysis		Utilization Scenarios (Loads Per Day)				
Number of Loads Per Day		1	2	3	4	5
Number of Loads Per Week (5 days)		5	10	15	20	25
Round Trip Miles Per Load		80	80	80	80	80
Total Daily Miles		80	160	240	320	400
Total Weekly Miles		400	800	1,200	1,600	2,000
Total Weekly Costs:	Rates:					
Fixed Tractor Charge	$ 1,600.00	$1,600.00	$1,600.00	$1,600.00	$1,600.00	$1,600.00
Variable Mileage Charge	$ 0.62	$ 248.00	$ 496.00	$ 744.00	$ 992.00	$1,240.00
Total Weekly Costs		$1,848.00	$2,096.00	$2,344.00	$2,592.00	$2,840.00
Average Cost Per Load		$ 369.60	$ 209.60	$ 156.27	$ 129.60	$ 113.60

The fixed-variable pricing structure creates a situation where, as more loads are served by the dedicated truck, the lower and lower the shipper's cost per load becomes. If the shipper only averages one load per day, the cost per load is $369.60. However, if the shipper is able to average 4 loads per day, the cost per load drops to $129.60 per load.[58]

---

[58] This example is presented in greater detail in the "Key Concepts for Shippers" chapter.

Backhaul Revenue Sharing

A backhaul revenue sharing provision could be added as an option in almost any dedicated contract. Backhaul loads are loads secured by the dedicated carrier from a third party customer. The loads serve to return the dedicated customer's outbound truck to the origin region with extra revenue from a third-party shipper. The revenue from the third-party shipper for the backhaul loads allows the dedicated customer to offset the cost of empty miles and reduce the dedicated shipper's total transportation costs.

The contract provision for backhauls will provide the rate at which the backhaul revenue will be shared between the dedicated customer (who is usually paying for all miles) and the dedicated carrier that secured the backhaul load. Most contracts call for 70% to 80% of the revenue to be given as a credit to the dedicated customer. The carrier will keep 20% to 30% of the revenue to cover direct load costs and provide a small, incremental operating profit.

The shared revenue should include only the linehaul (base) portion of the revenue. Accessorial revenues such as unloading and stop charges should not be shared with the dedicated customer. In most cases, backhaul fuel surcharges should be shared with the dedicated customer if the dedicated customer is being charged a fuel surcharge on the backhaul miles portion of the trip. The relationship between backhaul revenue sharing and fuel surcharges is presented in greater detail in a future chapter.

Determining the Percentage of the Backhaul Revenue to be Shared. The carrier must consider several factors when determining the appropriate percentage of the revenue to share with the dedicated customer. First, the carrier must recover the direct per-load costs incurred to secure and manage the load. The direct per-load costs include such items as sales, customer service, dispatch, billing, collections, and electronic transactions. The majority of these costs are fixed on a per-load basis, so as a percentage of revenue, these costs represent a higher percentage of revenue on shorter length of haul loads than longer length of haul loads. As a result, the carrier must reduce the percentage of the revenue that is shared with the dedicated customer when the length of haul for backhauls is relatively short.

A second consideration is the average revenue per mile that is expected to be charged to the third-party customer on the backhaul loads. The average revenue per mile should be based on the expected average length of haul of the backhaul loads. If the average revenue per mile of the backhaul loads will be less than average, the percentage that is shared with the dedicated customer must be reduced. On the other hand, if the expected revenue per mile will be higher than average, the percentage could be increased, which may give the carrier an excellent competitive advantage and selling point when making a proposal to a potential dedicated customer.

Carriers must also carefully consider the impact that these revenue-share backhaul loads will have on the carrier's normal, one-way network of freight. In some cases, if loads are used as backhauls for the dedicated fleet and the other fleets for which those loads were originally secured are subsequently left without enough loads to meet their own utilization objectives, the overall profitability of the trucking company may be negatively impacted. Trucking companies must be careful to not cannibalize the core network by committing too much valuable network freight to dedicated customers as backhaul loads.

One complication in a backhaul revenue sharing agreement is the tracking of the backhaul activity and the application of the shared revenue to the customer's invoice. Before agreeing to a backhaul revenue sharing arrangement, the shipper and carrier should be certain of the carrier's ability to accurately track and administer the program.

Despite the potential complications, there are several potential benefits of a backhaul revenue share agreement. The key advantages and disadvantages of a backhaul revenue sharing program are listed below.

Backhaul Revenue Sharing - Advantages and Disadvantages

Backhaul Sharing	*Carrier*	*Shipper*
Advantages	• Fleet earns a secondary profit margin on each backhaul load. • Attractive selling feature and potential cost/rate advantage.	• Transportation costs are reduced by the amount of the backhaul revenue credits.
Disadvantages	• Backhaul loads reduce the freight that is available for the carrier's one-way network. • Administration of the program is difficult, as determination of backhaul credits is sometimes complex and time consuming.	• Minimal direct benefit to carrier for providing backhaul loads. • Carrier may fail to meet expected level of backhaul revenue. • Dedicated trucks may expend too much time and effort on backhaul loads and reduce the number of trucks available for the dedicated shipper's loads.

The base backhaul revenue share calculation is typically very simple. The backhaul revenue share percentage is multiplied by the gross linehaul revenue for the dedicated backhaul load as shown below.

Backhaul Revenue Share Calculation

Linehaul Revenue		$ 700.00
Revenue Share %	x	80%
Backhaul Share to Shipper		**$ 560.00**

The calculation in this basic format assumes that the dedicated truck provides 100% of the transportation service for the load. In certain cases, the revenue share calculation can become much more complex. Several of these scenarios are presented in a later chapter.

Dedicated Fleet Contract

The illustration below provides a general summary of the standard provisions of a dedicated fleet contract. The contract shown below is for a 10 truck fleet with a fixed-variable contract structure.

ABC Carriers
Dedicated Fleet Contract

Effective: 1/1/2010
Contract Expires: 12/31/2012

Overview:

ABC Carriers will provide a dedicated fleet as described below to transport household goods as directed by the shipper, XYZ Products. The fleet will provide round trip transportation from the XYZ facility located in Dallas, Texas. Tractors are expected to achieve a utilization of 1,300 to 1,600 miles per tractor per week. Pricing is based on a fixed-variable contract structure and the rates shown below.

Fleet Details:

Tractors:	10 units	
Drivers:	10 units	
Trailers:	40 units	53 foot swing-door trailers

Pricing:

Fixed Charge Per Tractor Per Week	$ 1,600.00	(includes tractor and driver)
Variable Mileage Charge	$ 0.62	(per mile - all miles)
On-site Manager	$ 1,450.00	flat charge per week
Stopoffs	$ 75.00	per occurrence
Driver Assist Loading / Unloading	$ 75.00	per occurrence
Additional Trailers	$ 85.00	per trailer per week
Tolls	Treated as a pass-through expense	

Backhauls:

ABC Carriers will make a "good faith" effort to offset shipper's transportation costs by securing third-party backhaul loads through the carrier's existing one-way customer network. ABC Carriers will share 80% of the linehaul revenue with the dedicated shipper. ABC Carriers will retain 20% of the linehaul revenue for each backhaul load to cover direct transaction-related costs. The dedicated shipper will pay for all out-of-route miles associated with the pick-up and delivery of each backhaul load based on the variable mileage charge shown above.

Fuel Surcharge:

The standard fuel surcharge of XYZ Products will apply, with the fuel peg (base) set at $1.40 per gallon.

In reality, the contract would contain a number of legal provisions and related items. This example simply serves to define the specific items associated with the dedicated fleet as well as the pricing and rate levels.

Dedicated Fleet Invoice

The illustration below displays a simple weekly invoice for a fixed-variable dedicated fleet with backhaul revenue credits. The rates and other provisions are based on the dedicated contract in the previous section.

Fixed-Variable Dedicated Fleet Invoice with Backhaul Revenue Credits

ABC Carriers
Dedicated Fleet Invoice — Week Ending: 5/11/2009

Item	Rate	Units	Total Cost
Tractors	$ 1,600.00	10	$ 16,000.00
Loaded Miles	$ 0.62	9,815	$ 6,085.30
Empty Miles	$ 0.62	8,277	$ 5,131.74
On-site Management Fee	$ 1,450.00	1	$ 1,450.00
Base Dedicated Charges			**$ 28,667.04**
Fuel Surcharge	$ 0.22	18,092	$ 3,980.24
Gross Total Charges			**$ 32,647.28**

Less: Backhaul Revenue Credits

Backhaul Details	Gross	% Shared	Revenue Share
5/10/09 483722 Houston to Dallas	$ 550.00	80%	$ 440.00
5/09/09 483791 Shreveport to Dallas	$ 625.00	80%	$ 500.00
5/09/09 483682 Austin to Dallas	$ 525.00	80%	$ 420.00
5/07/09 483822 Houston to Dallas	$ 550.00	80%	$ 440.00
5/08/09 483745 Tulsa to Dallas	$ 710.00	80%	$ 568.00
Total Backhaul Revenue Credit			$ 2,368.00
Net Total Dedicated Charges			**$ 30,279.28**

During this week, the dedicated carrier was able to secure five third-party backhaul loads. The revenue for each backhaul is split between the dedicated shipper and the carrier. The shipper received a credit for 80% of the revenue and the remaining 20% is retained by the carrier. The net result of the backhaul activity for the week is a $2,368 savings for the dedicated shipper.

The Steps in Dedicated Pricing

While every carrier has their own approach to dedicated pricing and cost forecasting, the basic steps in the process are always the same. The key elements of dedicated pricing can be grouped into three primary steps.

Dedicated Pricing Steps

1. Define the Operating Characteristics of the Fleet

2. Estimate Operating Costs for the Fleet

3. Determine the Pricing and Estimated Margin for the Fleet

In most cases, these steps should be completed in the order shown. Each step is discussed in the sections that follow.

Step 1: Define the Operating Characteristics of the Fleet

In order to accurately price a dedicated fleet, a number of operating characteristics and cost elements must be identified or estimated. For most dedicated fleets, identifying or estimating the operating characteristics is the most important step in the pricing process. Trucking companies want to propose a price and total cost to a potential customer that is both competitive for the shipper and reasonably profitable for the carrier. Depending on how the operating risk is shared in the proposed contract structure, this step will be the primary determining factor for success for the trucking company. In this case, "success" for the trucking company would be winning the bid for the dedicated fleet.

The operating characteristics of a dedicated fleet must be carefully evaluated and accurately estimated. In some cases, these statistics and assumptions may be provided by the requirements listed by the shipper as part of a dedicated fleet bid. If the shipper does not provide the requirements and parameters, the carrier must estimate these items through modeling, general experience, or other method. Listed below are the major items that must be identified before determining pricing for a dedicated fleet.

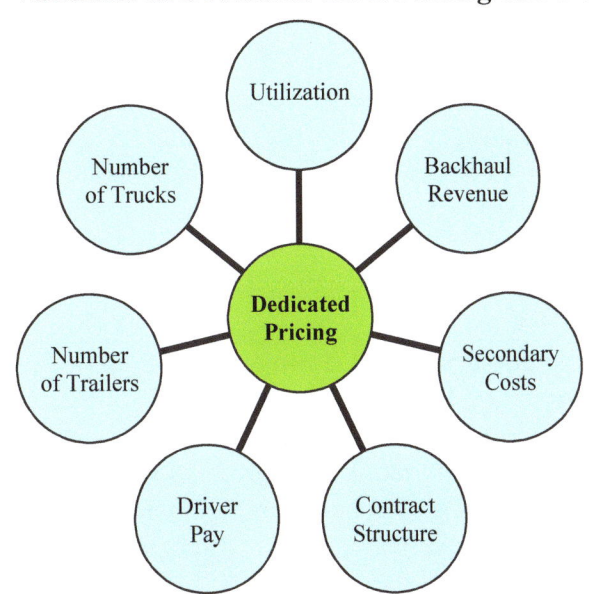

Key Variables in Dedicated Fleet Pricing and Design

Diagram: Dedicated Pricing (center) connected to: Utilization, Backhaul Revenue, Secondary Costs, Contract Structure, Driver Pay, Number of Trailers, Number of Trucks.

Not all of the items shown above will be part of every dedicated fleet opportunity. However, the carrier must consider each item as part of the due diligence on any potential deal. The carrier must determine the resources and activities that will drive costs for the operation. Accurate estimates should be made for each of the items described below.

Utilization

Utilization represents the average miles per truck per week for the fleet, based on all miles, both loaded and empty. The shipper will provide an estimate of utilization as a part of some dedicated bids. Otherwise, utilization will be estimated based on detailed shipment information provided by the shipper. If not specifically stated by the shipper, the carrier should ask the shipper how many weeks per year the fleet will operate at the expected utilization based on facility holidays and vacation schedules. Without specific guidance from the shipper, carriers should usually determine the annual utilization by assuming 50 active weeks per year, allowing the equivalent of 2 weeks of down time for holidays, weather problems, and similar events.

Number of Trucks

The number of trucks needed for a dedicated fleet will either be stated by the shipper's request or determined through an analysis of the shipper's network by the carrier. The analysis process for determining the fleet size will be presented in a future chapter. In the interim, the examples in this chapter will assume the fleet size is provided by the shipper.

Number of Trailers

Much like the number of trucks, the number of trailers needed for a dedicated fleet will either be stated by the shipper or determined through an analysis by the carrier. The number of trailers will usually be stated as a discrete number of trailers or in terms of a trailer to tractor ratio. For example, a 3:1 trailer ratio indicates the need for 3 trailers for each tractor in the fleet.

In the absence of specific guidance from the shipper, estimating the number of trailers needed for a fleet based on shipper data is a difficult task and not an exact science. The number of trailers needed will depend on many variables including origin facility behavior, destination facility behavior, and drop and hook opportunities. The modeling of trailer needs will be covered in more detail in future chapters.

Driver Compensation

Perhaps the most flexible element of cost estimation for each dedicated opportunity is determining how much to pay drivers and how to structure the compensation program. Carriers must structure a compensation program that allows for a competitive price and allows the carrier to attract and retain qualified drivers that are capable of meeting the shipper's expectations. The factors that should be taken into account in establishing the driver compensation plan are listed below.

Driver Compensation Considerations
Driver income expectations in the local market.
Experience and skill requirements.
Customer-specific labor requirements, especially stop-offs and unloading.
Expected weekly miles per driver.
Amount of home-time a driver can expect in the operation.

Many dedicated fleets offer drivers the opportunity for much more time at home than traditional linehaul and regional driving jobs. Carriers may be able to pay drivers less than market income levels when employed in fleets offering significant time at home.

Shipper's Note: If possible, when asking carriers to submit proposals for dedicated fleets, shippers should provide specific driver qualification requirements and minimum income expectations. Carriers will base dedicated pricing on a wide range of driver income assumptions which will significantly impact the proposed cost of each quote. The carrier with the low-cost proposal may plan to hire an inferior driver pool that is not qualified to successfully meet the unique needs of the shipper. The inferior drivers will often cause the low cost carrier's service or cost performance to fail to meet the shipper's needs.

Secondary Costs

Some dedicated fleets will require additional costs beyond the standard operating costs of trucking. Shippers should specifically list many of these requirements in each request for proposal. However, some items, such as tolls, must be identified by the carrier. A few common secondary costs are described below.

On-Site Management. Certain dedicated fleets will dictate the need for one or more on-site carrier employees to oversee the day-to-day operation. The on-site staff will manage drivers, communicate with customer shipping personnel, maintain trailer pools, organize paperwork, and perform other daily functions. The major costs of the staff will include hiring costs, base salaries, bonuses and fringe benefits. Other costs of on-site management might include training, office expenses, phone and communication costs, and travel expenses.

Special Equipment. Dedicated fleet shippers will occasionally have the need for specialized equipment or other requirements that will create additional costs in the operation. Often this type of special equipment will involve protecting or securing each load with straps, tarps, load locks or other equipment. Carriers must estimate the initial cost of the equipment and the ongoing costs such as maintenance and any equipment replacements.

Tolls. Certain areas in the United States are notorious for excessive toll charges, especially areas in the Northeast like Ohio, Pennsylvania, New Jersey, and New York. If the toll charges are to be included in the dedicated pricing, the carrier must estimate the toll costs and include the cost of tolls in the pricing. Ignoring or underestimating toll costs could cause a dedicated fleet that would otherwise be profitable to achieve below average profitability. In some cases, toll costs may be treated as a "pass through" expense. In a "pass through" arrangement, the carrier records the actual toll costs then invoices the shipper an amount equal to the actual toll cost expense.

Contract Structure

Key elements of the contract structure can have a significant impact on the dedicated pricing strategy. These elements include the contract length, the pricing structure, and payment terms. The impact of these items will be discussed in greater detail in future chapters covering dedicated pricing.

Backhaul Revenues

Backhaul revenue for a dedicated fleet represents additional revenue generated by the fleet with third-party customers outside of the primary dedicated shipper. Backhaul revenues can be used to offset the transportation costs for the dedicated shipper in several ways. The shipper and carrier may structure the contract with backhauls as upfront dedicated rate reductions or ongoing backhaul revenue credits. Also, in some dedicated networks, third-party backhauls are not a feasible part of the design solution and will be excluded from consideration in the contract and the pricing design.

Shipper-Specific Considerations

As part of the design process, the carrier should also make note of unique shipper operating needs such as a shut-down schedule for holidays and vacations. Some major manufacturers shut down their operations for vacations during a certain time of year. For example, many auto producers have a scheduled, two-week shut down period in the summer during which *all* employees take vacations. During the shut-down period, the dedicated fleet would also be shut down, so carriers must take this period of inactivity into account in estimating costs and average weekly utilization. Drivers in the operation might also be required to take their vacation during this same period.

Step 2: Estimate Costs for the Operation

The total cost of the operation will be based on the projected operating activities of the fleet. The primary cost-producing activities include tractors, trailers, drivers and miles. Each fleet must also bear administrative costs and corporate overhead allocations. Beyond these normal operating costs, each deal may have some additional operating costs such as on-site management, special equipment, and tolls that must also be taken into consideration.

Cost Adjustments

While the carrier will likely have previously established cost assumptions for each of the key cost components, the cost model for each fleet must account for any unique needs of the fleet that may not be accurately reflected in the standard cost assumptions. Several examples of special cost situations are listed below.

Special Cost Considerations	
Variable	**Impact of Variable**
Special Equipment	Special tractor or trailer equipment may cause maintenance expenses to be greater than normal. The carrier must also determine where and how the equipment maintenance will be performed. If the fleet location dictates that the carrier use a third-party maintenance service, maintenance costs could be higher than usual.
Driver Pay Requirements	Driver pay should reflect the nature of the work to be performed and the difficulty of the workload. The carrier should provide appropriate pay for more difficult work in order to attract and retain quality drivers. Driver pay needs will vary from one hiring location to the next. Driver pay programs must meet local competitive standards in order to attract the quality of driver needed for the fleet.
Fuel Costs	The carrier must determine how and where the fleet will obtain fuel. If fuel must be purchased from a third-party such as a truck stop, fuel costs may be higher than normal. Also, certain portions of the country historically have significantly higher fuel costs than others. Further, when using a fuel peg provided by the shipper in place of the carrier's standard fuel peg, the fuel cost per mile assumption must be adjusted to reflect the shipper's fuel peg.

The items listed above are a few common examples of special cost considerations. Each new fleet opportunity should be carefully evaluated to identify exceptions of this type prior to establishing specific costs assumptions for the fleet cost model and submitting proposed pricing to the shipper.

Dedicated Fleet Pricing Example

Suppose a shipper has asked a carrier to provide a pricing proposal for a new dedicated fleet consisting of 10 trucks, 10 drivers, and 20 trailers. The fleet is expected to achieve a utilization level of 100,000 miles per year or 2,000 miles per week (based on 50 active weeks) over the four year contract term. The carrier expects to purchase the tractors for $80,000 each and the trailers for $20,000 each. The cost of trucks and trailers is expensed as depreciation. For this fleet, the depreciation expense, based on the straight-line method, will be $12,000 per tractor per year and $2,000 per trailer per year. Annual administrative expenses, legalization costs, and other overhead expenses are estimated to be $18,000 per tractor per year.

In order to attract qualified drivers, the carrier has decided to pay 42 cent per mile to the drivers. Fringe benefits and payroll taxes for the drivers are expected to cost 25% of gross pay. The fuel surcharge peg for this account will be set at $2.40 per gallon. The $2.40 per gallon peg divided by 6 miles per gallon gives a projected fuel cost of $0.40 per mile. Maintenance is expected to cost 11 cents per mile and insurance 10 cents per mile. This account is not expected to incur any additional costs for tolls, on-site management, or other expenses.

Fleet Cost Projections

Fleet Design Summary

Miles Per Tractor Per Week	2,000	Number of Trucks	10
Active Weeks Per Year	50	Number of Drivers	10
Total Annual Miles Per Tractor	100,000	Number of Trailers	20
Total Fleet Annual Miles	1,000,000	On-site Manager	None

Projected Annual Costs	Assumptions	Per Mile	Total Fleet	Per Tractor
Variable Costs				
Driver Wages	$ 0.42	$ 0.420	$ 420,000	$ 42,000
Fringe Benefits (% of wages)	25.0%	$ 0.105	$ 105,000	$ 10,500
Fuel	$ 0.40	$ 0.400	$ 400,000	$ 40,000
Maintenance	$ 0.11	$ 0.110	$ 110,000	$ 11,000
Insurance	$ 0.10	$ 0.100	$ 100,000	$ 10,000
Total Variable Costs		$ 1.135	$ 1,135,000	$ 113,500
Fixed Costs				
Tractor Depreciation	$ 12,000	$ 0.120	$ 120,000	$ 12,000
Trailer Depreciation	$ 2,000	$ 0.040	$ 40,000	$ 4,000
Legalization/Recruiting/Admin	$ 18,000	$ 0.180	$ 180,000	$ 18,000
On-Site Manager	$ -	$ -	$ -	$ -
Start Up /Special Equipment	$ -	$ -	$ -	$ -
Total Fixed Costs		$ 0.340	$ 340,000	$ 34,000
Grand Total Cost		$ 1.475	$ 1,475,000	$ 147,500

The cost projections above show a total cost of $1,475,000 or $1.475 per mile to operate the fleet. Based on this information, the carrier must now determine the profit margin for the fleet and the customer's proposed rate per mile.

Step 3: Determine the Pricing and Margin for the Fleet

Once total costs have been identified, the carrier must now add a profit margin to the estimated operating costs to determine the total revenue requirement and final rate per mile. Different carriers have different methods and policies for establishing the required margin and margin percentage for a dedicated fleet. Many carriers use a simple cost-plus rule to establish the margin, such as a minimum margin of 12% or a minimum operating ratio of 88%.[59] Others use more sophisticated financial and investment criteria to evaluate opportunities. To simplify the initial presentation of dedicated pricing, an 88% operating ratio requirement will be used. In a later chapter, a more sophisticated and more accurate investment-based approach will be presented for determining the appropriate gross margin and operating ratio.

Based on the previous total annual cost projections, the table below adds the margin to the total cost of the fleet based on a target operating ratio of 88.0%.

Identification of Revenue Requirement

Revenue Requirements	Per Mile	Total Fleet	Per Tractor
Grand Total Cost	$ 1.475	$ 1,475,000	$ 147,500
Desired Operating Ratio		88.0%	
Target Gross Revenue	**$ 1.676**	**$ 1,676,136**	**$ 167,614**

The formula shown below is applied to compute the revenue requirement based on operating costs and the minimum operating ratio requirement.

$$\text{Desired Revenue} = \frac{\text{Total Annual Cost}}{\text{Desired Operating Ratio}} = \frac{\$1,475,000}{0.88} = \$1,676,136$$

The same relationship could also be applied to determine the desired rate per mile based on a target operating ratio.

$$\text{Desired Rate Per Mile} = \frac{\text{Total Cost Per Mile}}{\text{Desired Operating Ratio}} = \frac{\$1.475}{0.88} = \$1.676$$

In actual practice, the carrier will almost always round the per-mile rate of $1.676 to either $1.670 or $1.680 for the actual quote to the potential dedicated customer.

---

[59] The target operating ratio of 88% is a common historical target for many carriers.

The Pro-forma Income Statement

The cost projections and revenue requirements can now be tied together in the form of a pro-forma, or projected, income statement as shown below.

Pro-forma Income Statement

Fleet Design Summary			
Miles Per Tractor Per Week	2,000	Number of Trucks	10
Active Weeks Per Year	50	Number of Drivers	10
Total Annual Miles Per Tractor	100,000	Number of Trailers	20
Total Fleet Annual Miles	1,000,000	On-site Manager	None

Pro-forma Income Statement			Per Mile	Total Fleet	Per Tractor
Target Gross Revenue			$ 1.676	$ 1,676,136	$ 167,614
Variable Costs	ASSUMPTIONS				
Driver Wages	$	0.42	$ 0.420	$ 420,000	$ 42,000
Fringe Benefits (% of wages)		25.0%	$ 0.105	$ 105,000	$ 10,500
Fuel	$	0.40	$ 0.400	$ 400,000	$ 40,000
Maintenance	$	0.11	$ 0.110	$ 110,000	$ 11,000
Insurance	$	0.10	$ 0.100	$ 100,000	$ 10,000
Total Variable Costs			$ 1.135	$ 1,135,000	$ 113,500
Fixed Costs					
Tractor Depreciation	$	12,000	$ 0.120	$ 120,000	$ 12,000
Trailer Depreciation	$	2,000	$ 0.040	$ 40,000	$ 4,000
Legalization/Recruiting/Admin	$	18,000	$ 0.180	$ 180,000	$ 18,000
On-Site Manager	$	-	$ -	$ -	$ -
Start Up /Special Equipment	$	-	$ -	$ -	$ -
Total Fixed Costs			$ 0.340	$ 340,000	$ 34,000
Grand Total Cost			$ 1.475	$ 1,475,000	$ 147,500
Operating Profit			$ 0.201	$ 201,136	$ 20,114
Operating Ratio			88.0%	88.0%	88.0%
Profit Margin			12.0%	12.0%	12.0%

The pro-forma income statement allows the carrier to review and validate the underlying assumptions for the fleet. The income statement also facilitates a review of the projected overall profitability as well as the profitability on a per-mile and per-truck basis. Should the carrier be awarded the fleet, the per-mile and per-truck projections will provide valuable benchmarks as the carrier attempts to evaluate the operating performance and profitability of the fleet in actual operation. The dedicated fleet pricing process will be presented in much greater detail in the chapters that follow.

CHAPTER 9: Dedicated Pricing and Cost Forecasting

The first critical step in the dedicating pricing process is the design phase. The purpose of the design phase is to determine the fleet operating characteristics such as weekly utilization, the number of trucks and the number of trailers. The focus of this chapter is on the second critical dedicated pricing step of cost forecasting and the third step of the final pricing design. Future chapters and case studies will provide examples and techniques for the design of a dedicated fleet. For the examples in this chapter, the dedicated fleet design will be provided.

Basic Cost Assumptions

The carrier must forecast the cost of providing the fleet and determine a price for the shipper that meets the carrier's operating requirements and profitability expectations. In the process, the carrier must estimate the cost of key items such as driver pay, tractors, trailers, fuel, maintenance, and insurance. Most carriers will estimate these costs based on historical information and future cost expectations. The table below outlines the basic cost assumptions for each of the major cost categories.

Basic Fleet Cost Assumptions

Equipment Depreciation and Values	
Tractors	
Initial Cost	$100,000
Expected Salvage / Trade Value	$50,000
Depreciation Term (Years)	3.00
Annual Depreciation Per Unit	**$16,667**
Monthly Depreciation Per Unit	$ 1,389

Other Operating Costs	
Fuel Costs	
Cost Per Gallon	$1.200
Miles Per Gallon	6.0
Fuel Tax	$ 0.008
Fuel Cost Per Mile	**$0.208**

Equipment Depreciation and Values	
Trailers	
Initial Cost	$21,600
Expected Salvage / Trade Value	$15,000
Depreciation Term (Years)	3.00
Annual Depreciation Per Unit	**$2,200**
Monthly Depreciation Per Unit	$ 183

Other Operating Costs	
Insurance Cost Per Mile	$0.100
Maintenance Cost Per Mile	$0.110
Fringe Benefits (% of Driver Pay)	25.0%

Equipment selection and cost is also a key factor in the cost of a dedicated proposal. Based in large part on shipper requirements, the carrier must determine what types of tractor and trailer equipment are needed and the expected cost of the equipment. To determine the annual depreciation cost, the carrier must select a depreciation method and estimate the expected value of the equipment at the end of the dedicated contract term. In this example, the annual depreciation expense for tractors and trailers is computed based on the straight-line method.

The cost of maintenance should be estimated based on the final equipment selection. Typically, both used tractor and used trailer equipment will have a higher maintenance cost than new equipment. The estimated maintenance cost per mile should be based on the specific type of equipment to be used in the dedicated fleet. In this example, maintenance and insurance are simple per-mile assumptions. Most maintenance costs, especially tires and preventive maintenance, are the direct result of miles driven.

The fuel cost per mile is computed based on the contracted fuel surcharge "peg" and the expected miles per gallon for the fleet. The fuel cost per mile is computed based on the formula shown below.

$$\frac{\text{Fuel Cost}}{\text{Per Mile}} = \frac{\text{Fuel Cost (Peg) Per Gallon}}{\text{Miles Per Gallon}} = \frac{\$1.20}{6.0} = \$0.20 \text{ per mile}$$

Any fuel taxes or other related costs could also be added to the final fuel cost per mile. The carrier may also choose to adjust the final fuel cost per mile by a factor for any unrecorded out-of-route miles.

The miles per gallon in the fuel cost per mile calculation should be based on applicable carrier "book" miles for accounting and reporting purposes. "Book" miles represent the miles the carrier records as part of normal operations. For example, the "book" miles for a load may be 820 miles, while the truck may actually drive 836 odometer or "hub" miles on the trip.

Insurance cost behavior can vary significantly by carrier, so for the purposes of this model, insurance is assumed to be a simple per-mile expense. While most insurance expenses are not incurred directly on a per-mile basis like maintenance and fuel, a per-mile basis is a simple and reasonable method for estimating insurance costs. When modeling insurance costs, each individual carrier should adjust the model to best reflect the cost dynamics of the carrier's insurance program.

A creative, accurate, and competitive driver compensation program is often a critical factor in the relative cost competitiveness of a carrier's dedicated fleet proposal. The carrier must first determine the amount of income that is necessary to attract and retain a group of quality drivers in the market where the fleet is to be located. The carrier must also determine how the compensation program will be structured in terms of fixed salary, per-mile pay, hourly pay, accessorial pay, and any other considerations. Specific strategies for the design of the driver pay program will be discussed in greater detail throughout the discussion of dedicated pricing.

In this example, the assumption for driver fringe benefits is a simple 25% of gross driver wages. This cost assumption covers items such as vacation pay, retirement plan contributions, health benefits, and payroll taxes. The actual percentage applied from carrier to carrier will fluctuate based on the overall package of fringe benefits offered by each individual organization.

Basic Dedicated Fleet Example

Suppose a shipper has asked a carrier to provide a dedicated fleet consisting of 10 trucks, 10 drivers, and 20 trailers. The fleet is expected to achieve a utilization level of 105,000 miles per year or 2,100 miles per week (50 active weeks per year) over the three year contract term. The carrier expects to purchase the tractors for $100,000 per unit and the trailers for $22,000 per unit.

Because of the repetitive cost and pricing calculations, many carriers choose to develop a spreadsheet model to assist in the cost forecast and revenue analysis. The model presented here has been simplified for demonstration purposes, but is still very effective and accurate for dedicated pricing. The main screen of the dedicated pricing spreadsheet is shown below.[60]

Dedicated Pricing Model

Customer Name:	Chapter 9	Fleet Description:	Basic Example

Fleet Parameters

Number of Tractors	10.00
Backup Tractors	0.00
Number of Drivers	10.00
Utilization (Miles per Tractor per Active Week)	2,100
Active Fleet Weeks Per Year (max = 52 weeks)	50.0
Total Fleet Annual Miles	1,050,000
Number of Trailers	20.00
Trailer/Tractor Ratio	2.00

Overhead Costs

Tractor Legalization/Taxes	$ 2,000
Driver Recruiting Costs	$ 3,000
Administration Expenses	$ 5,000
Total Overhead (per tractor per year)	$ 10,000
Direct Staffing (On-site CSR / Offices / Etc.)	$ -
Other Annual Expenses (Total Fleet)	$ 5,000
Initial Start-Up Costs (Total)	$ 10,000

Other Parameters

Driver Rate of Pay (Per Mile or Annual Gross)	$ 0.40
Duration of Deal/Contract (in months)	36.0
Average Collection Period (in days)	30.0

Pricing and Analysis

Suggested Rate Per Mile (all miles)	$ 1.3600
Operating Ratio	89.84%
Profit Margin	10.16%

Pro-Forma Income Statement		Fleet Totals		Per Tractor	
		Per Mile	Annual	Weekly	Annual
Total Fleet Miles			1,050,000	2,019	105,000
Total Revenue		$1.360	$1,428,000	$2,746	$142,800
Variable Costs	Assumptions				
Driver Wages	$0.40	$0.400	$420,000	$808	$42,000
Fringe Benefits (% of wages)	25.0%	0.100	105,000	202	10,500
Fuel	$0.208	0.208	218,400	420	21,840
Maintenance	$0.110	0.110	115,500	222	11,550
Insurance	$0.100	0.100	105,000	202	10,500
Total Variable Costs		0.918	963,900	1,854	96,390
Fixed Costs	Assumptions				
Tractor Depreciation	$ 16,667	0.159	166,667	$321	$16,667
Trailer Depreciation	$ 2,200	0.042	44,000	85	4,400
Legalization/Recruiting/Admin	$ 10,000	0.095	100,000	192	10,000
On-Site Manager	$ -	0.000	0	0	0
Start Up /Special Equipment	$ 8,333	0.008	8,333	16	833
Total Fixed Costs		0.304	319,000	613	31,900
Total Cost		1.222	1,282,900	2,467	128,290
Operating Profit		$0.14	$145,100	$279	$14,510
Operating Ratio		89.84%	89.84%	89.84%	89.84%

---

[60] The dedicated fleet pricing model spreadsheet presented throughout this book is available for purchase at www.TruckloadTransportation.com. The model includes all the various features presented in this book.

Each shaded cell is an "input" cell where information about the parameters of the fleet is entered. Each of these "input" cells is briefly discussed below. Some input items will be derived from the fleet design and others will be determined based on internal carrier cost estimates or standard assumptions.

Carrier Decision Variables for Dedicated Pricing

Fleet Parameters

Number of Tractors: This parameter represents the average number of trucks to be actively used in the fleet during a one year period. The number of trucks will usually be based on a specific number of tractors requested by the shipper or the results of a fleet size analysis performed by the carrier.

In most cases, dedicated fleet sizes will remain constant or fluctuate only slightly over the entire year. However, some shippers may ask that the fleet size be adjusted to meet seasonal shipping needs. For example, a shipper may need 20 trucks for the first six months of the year and 30 trucks for the last six months of the year. For this request, the average fleet size would be 25 trucks (see example that follows).

Backup Tractors: This parameter represents any additional tractors that are to be included in the cost of this fleet that are not actively involved in the operation. The tractors are provided only as backup equipment in the case of breakdowns, accidents, or other service disruption. Backup tractors will not be included in all dedicated fleets, but may be common when a fleet is fairly large or located in an isolated location away from the carrier's normal operating area. Carriers may also choose to deploy backup tractors but *not* include the cost of the tractors in the customer's dedicated fleet pricing.

Number of Trailers: This parameter represents the average number of trailers to be actively used in the fleet during a one year period. The number of trailers will usually be based on a specific number of trailers requested by the shipper or the results of a fleet size analysis performed by the carrier. If for any reason the number of trailers will fluctuate during the year, this cell should usually represent the average number of trailers in the fleet. Depending on the fleet location and specific trailer type, the carrier may be able to temporarily shift dedicated trailers for use by nearby customers. However, if the excess trailers can't be utilized with other customers, the fleet pricing should be based on the maximum number of trailers instead of the average number of trailers.

Trailer to Tractor Ratio: This value is a calculation that measures the ratio of trailers to tractors. The calculation is simply the number of trailers divided by the number of tractors. Most normal fleets will have a trailer to tractor ratio of 2.0 to 4.0, depending on many factors. In some special cases, the shipper may require trailer ratios of 6.0, 7.0 or even higher. Some shippers will also provide their own trailers at their own expense, in which case the trailer ratio would be 0.0 for pricing purposes.

Important Note on the Average Number of Tractors and Trailers. Suppose the shipper has asked the carrier to provide the seasonal fleet of tractors and trailers as shown below.

Period	Tractors	Trailers
January - June	20.0	50.0
July - December	30.0	76.0
Weighted Average	**25.0**	**63.0**

The average fleet sizes should be based on a weighted average of the time each fleet size is to be in place. In most cases, the dedicated pricing should be based on the computed weighted-average fleet sizes, however, there are several potential situations in which the average fleet size would not be appropriate and instead the maximum number of tractors and trailers should be used to price the fleet (30 tractors and 76 trailers in this example).

Special Situations for Pricing Fleet at Peak Size	
Special Equipment	If the tractors or trailers must be customized with special equipment or unique features that don't allow the equipment to be easily used by other customers, the shipper's fleet must be priced at the maximum fleet size instead of the weighted-average fleet size.
Duration of Reduced Fleet Size	Suppose in the above example that the shipper needed the reduced fleet of 20 tractors and 50 trailers only during January and February. The full fleet of 30 tractors and 76 trailers would be needed during the rest of the year. In extreme cases such as this, the carrier will rarely be able to efficiently redeploy the equipment, so the dedicated fleet should be priced at the maximum fleet size instead of the weighted-average fleet size.
Fleet Location	If the dedicated fleet is located in a market that does not allow the equipment to be easily converted to support other customers, the dedicated fleet should be priced at the maximum fleet size.

The carrier must have a thorough understanding of its network and customer needs to determine the extent to which dedicated equipment can be used periodically in other operations. Each individual carrier's assessment of the network will dictate the appropriate cost strategy for each dedicated fleet opportunity.

Active Weeks Per Year: This parameter represents the number of weeks during the year that the fleet and the trucks will be operating. Because of driver vacations, shipper facility vacations, weather issues, and similar factors, most fleets are likely to only operate between 49 and 51 weeks per year. In the absence of specific information, it is generally best to assume the fleet will operate 50 weeks per year at the expected utilization level.

Utilization: This parameter represents the average miles per truck per week during active weeks. This value should include all miles, empty and loaded. This parameter should not be adjusted for inactive weeks. For example, if a fleet design calls for 2,000 miles per week for 50 weeks, the tractor will drive 100,000 miles per year, which is actually 1,923 miles per week over a 52 week period. The entry for weekly utilization should be consistent with the entry for active weeks per year so that the annual miles per tractor per year figure is computed correctly.

Total Fleet Annual Miles: This value is calculated from the inputs of number of tractors, operating weeks per year, and weekly utilization. The result of multiplying the operating weeks times the utilization times the number of tractors is the total annual miles for the entire fleet. It is imperative that this total number of miles be accurate because the fixed costs of the fleet will be spread over these miles and ultimately into the rate per mile. If the total miles are overstated, the resulting rate per mile will be too low and the dedicated fleet will not be as profitable as indicated in the model. Preventing the overstatement of total annual fleet miles is a key reason for using only 50 weeks, as opposed to 52 weeks, for the operating weeks per year.

Other Parameters

Driver Rate of Pay: This parameter represents the base budget for driver compensation. In this model, the pay should be entered as either a fixed amount per mile or a fixed gross income on an annual or weekly basis. For example, enter 0.40 to pay the driver 40 cents for every mile or $42,000 as the budget for the annual income level for each driver.

Based on the specific dedicated operation, the carrier must use good judgment when planning the gross amount to pay the driver. The carrier must also design the specifics of exactly how driver earnings will be computed once actual operations begin. Since actual driver compensation programs can take many forms, the objective of the pricing model is only to budget enough money to provide the drivers with the necessary amount of total compensation. The intent of the pricing model at this stage is not to determine the specific structure of the actual driver payroll program.

When pricing a fleet, the safe approach is to enter a total weekly or annual gross income for the driver instead of a rate of pay per mile. For example, if a rate of pay of $0.40 per mile is entered into the model for a fleet where the tractors achieve only 1,000 miles per tractor per week, the model would budget only $400 per week or $20,800 per year for driver compensation, which is far less than what is necessary. While pricing fleets, carriers must be very aware of expected driver income levels at different levels of utilization. Various scenarios involving the design of driver pay programs will be addressed in more detail as specific fleet pricing examples are presented in future sections and chapters.

Duration of the Contract: This parameter should reflect the expected length of the dedicated contract in months. The duration of the contract plays a critical role in the financial calculations that drive the outputs of the model. The model can handle a maximum duration of 5 years or 60 months. Virtually any deal that may last more than 5 years can be safely priced based on a 5 year term. A dedicated contract with a guaranteed duration over 5 years is very uncommon. Most contracts will call for a 2 to 4 year term.

Carriers should also keep in mind that, even though a dedicated contract may call for a term of 4 or more years, there is still no guarantee that the contract will actually last for the full term of the agreement. Many dedicated contracts are terminated early due to many factors such as poor carrier performance or unexpected changes in shipper distribution patterns.

Average Collection Period (Days Sales Outstanding): This parameter should reflect the average number of days that it will take the customer to pay each invoice. The parameter is used to compute the working capital investment in the accounts receivable balance associated with the fleet. The estimated accounts receivable balance becomes a part of the upfront investment in working capital associated with the fleet and plays a key role in the discounted cash flow calculations presented in the next chapter. If the customer's payment terms are not known, 25 to 40 days, or a carrier average, would be a reasonable assumption as the standard value for this parameter.

While the average collection period does not play a major role in the pricing, it does allow the carrier to quantify the customer's payment terms in the pricing. All other things being equal, a customer that pays in 10 days should be offered a slightly lower rate per mile than a customer that pays in 45 days. The impact of the average collection period is not reflected in the operating ratio measurement, but will be fully reflected in a more advanced approach to dedicated pricing presented in the next chapter.

Overhead Costs

Initial Start-up Costs: This operating cost parameter should reflect the total start-up expenses associated with this fleet. The amount entered here should be a one-time, lump sum total cost for the project. For pricing purposes, this cost will be amortized over the term of the dedicated fleet contract. Common start-up costs include tractor positioning, trailer positioning, travel expenses, and initial driver recruiting. Highly specialized fleets may require additional start-up costs.

Tractor Legalization / Taxes: This operating cost parameter should reflect all annual vehicle registration costs and estimated fuel, use, and other taxes on a per truck per year basis. These costs will vary slightly from carrier to carrier and fleet to fleet depending upon their locations, types of equipment, and routes served. In the absence of more specific information, the carrier's company average for these types of cost should suffice when pricing most dedicated fleets.

Driver Recruiting Costs: This operating cost parameter should reflect the cost per tractor per year of attracting, training, and hiring a new driver for the operation. Most carriers should have a company standard amount for this cost that can be applied here. However, if this particular operation is expected to be particularly attractive and result in below average driver turnover rates, a cost slightly less than the company standard could be applied. Likewise, if this driving job is relatively difficult and could result in above average driver turnover rates, a higher amount should be used to reflect the additional hiring activity that will be associated with the proposed dedicated fleet.

Administration Expenses (Per Tractor): This operating cost parameter should reflect all other indirect operating costs not specifically outlined elsewhere in the model. The bulk of these costs should represent general corporate overhead and cost allocations that are not directly associated with any individual fleet or customer. Common administrative cost items include computer systems, corporate overhead, and executive salaries.

Other Annual Expenses: This operating cost parameter should reflect any unusual direct operating costs beyond the normal costs listed elsewhere in the model. The amount entered should be a total annual cost for the entire fleet. A common item included here would be toll expenses based on the specific routes to be run by the fleet. Other common items might include load straps, load bars, or a drop lot near the customer's location for parking empty trailers.

Direct Staffing: This operating cost parameter should reflect the direct expenses associated with the management of this fleet, particularly those associated with direct employees and local offices established specifically for the management of the proposed dedicated fleet. The amount entered should be a total annual cost for the entire fleet. The most common items included here are salaries and benefits for on-site employees and any general office expenses such as rent, utilities, computers, telephones and supplies.

Pricing and Analysis

Suggested Rate Per Mile: This revenue parameter should reflect the rate per mile to be charged on all miles incurred by the fleet, both empty and loaded. This rate will flow through the model and be compared to the cost parameters to determine the estimated profitability of the fleet. The rate per mile can continually be adjusted until the desired level of profitability is reached.

Operating Ratio: Operating ratio is a common measure of profitability. Operating ratio is computed as the ratio of operating costs to total revenue. Acceptable operating ratios vary by carrier and operation. However, target operating ratios for most dedicated fleet operations generally range between 80% and 90%.

Profit Margin: Profit margin is a common measure of profitability. Profit margin is computed by dividing operating profit into total revenues. Profit margin is directly related to operating ratio. For example, if the profit margin is 10.0%, the operating ratio is 90.0%.

Revenue and Cost Calculations and Line Items[61]

Revenues

Revenue and Cost Columns: The revenues and costs will be shown within the model in four different columns, per mile, annual fleet totals, per tractor per week, and per tractor per year. The "Annual Fleet Totals" column represents the grand totals for all miles and all trucks in the fleet. The "Per Mile" column represents the total fleet amounts divided by the total miles. The "Annual Per Tractor" column represents the total fleet amounts divided by the number of tractors. The "Weekly Per Tractor" column represents the "Annual Per Tractor" column divided over 52 weeks per year. The "Per Mile" column and both "Per Tractor" columns allow the carrier to review the assumptions and quickly identify any possible problems or errors in the cost and operating assumptions.

Total Fleet Miles: The total miles for the fleet are shown in the "Annual Totals" column. The miles are also shown on a per-tractor basis in the weekly and annual per tractor columns. The weekly miles per tractor shown in this line item is always based on 52 weeks and, as a result, will not match the utilization assumption for the fleet when the active fleet weeks assumption is less than 52 weeks.

Total Revenue: The total annual revenue is computed as the rate per mile on all miles (as set by the carrier) multiplied by the total annual miles for the fleet. This line item also shows the revenue on a per-tractor basis as well.

Variable Costs

Variable costs are those costs that will, in most cases, be incurred on a per-mile basis, regardless of the number of trucks or trailers. A common exception to the per-mile assumption is seen in cases where the driver pay is entered as a gross earnings amount instead of a rate of pay per mile. For example, if the driver rate of pay field contains an entry of $42,500 per year, the driver pay will be a fixed cost and remain at $42,500 per driver per year, regardless of the actual number of miles per driver.

Driver Wages: For costing purposes, the model requires that the carrier estimate driver income on either a per-mile rate of pay or a fixed annual or fixed weekly income amount. If wages are based on a per-mile amount, the total annual cost of driver wages is the driver rate of pay per mile multiplied by the total annual miles of the fleet. If driver wages are based on a fixed annual income, the total annual cost of driver wages is the budgeted annual pay per driver multiplied by the number of drivers in the fleet.

Fringe Benefits (% of driver wages): Fringe benefits are a simple calculation based on a percentage of gross driver wages. Fringe benefits include such items as payroll taxes, unemployment taxes, vacation time, insurance benefits, and retirement benefits. Each company should establish their own internal standard when setting the percentage based

---

[61] As necessary, refer back to the discussion of specific cost behaviors for more information about each cost item.

on the particular benefits that are offered. Most fringe benefit percentages will range between 15% and 32%. The fringe benefits cost will be computed as the percentage multiplied by the gross driver wages.

Fuel: The fuel expense is very straightforward since fuel cost is directly related to total miles driven. Before estimating fuel costs, the carrier must be aware of the exact specifications of the fuel surcharge agreement associated with this customer and fleet.[62] The fuel surcharge agreement will provide a base cost per gallon of fuel that the pricing should be based upon. The basic formula for fuel cost per mile is shown below.

$$\frac{\text{Fuel Cost}}{\text{Per Mile}} = \frac{\text{Fuel Cost Per Gallon}}{\text{Miles Per Gallon}}$$

For example, if the carrier expects a fuel cost per gallon of $1.20 and 6.0 miles per gallon, the estimated fuel cost would equal $0.20 per mile. The fuel cost per mile is applied to all miles, both empty and loaded.

Maintenance: Maintenance expenses are very straightforward since maintenance costs are directly related to total miles driven. The primary maintenance costs include tires and general preventive maintenance. Carriers should base the cost per mile for maintenance on the historical cost and expected future cost of these items. If the equipment is specialized and requires non-standard maintenance costs, the maintenance cost assumptions should be adjusted accordingly.

Insurance: Insurance is probably the most difficult expense to estimate on an individual fleet basis. Over the years, insurance costs for trucking companies have skyrocketed and become very difficult to predict for future years. Each carrier should define an approach for modeling insurance costs that fits the carrier's cost model. For the purposes of this book, insurance costs will be assumed to occur on a simple per-mile basis.

Total Variable Costs: This amount is the sum of all the variable costs for each column.

Fixed Costs

Fixed costs are those costs that will remain constant as an annual cost and do not change as a result of miles driven. For example, tractor and trailer costs are fixed on a per-unit basis but will change in total depending on the number of tractors and trailers used in the dedicated fleet. The fixed cost of tractors and trailers will remain constant regardless of the number of miles driven.

Tractor Depreciation: The total tractor depreciation expense is computed as the per-tractor annual depreciation expense multiplied by the number of tractors in the fleet.

---

[62] A fuel surcharge agreement states the additional charges or discounts associated with significant changes in actual fuel costs above or below the base fuel cost per gallon upon which the pricing is based.

Each carrier will establish their own specific depreciation method and assumptions. In the example model, simple straight-line depreciation expense is used.

$$\text{Annual Tractor Depreciation Expense} = \frac{\text{Net Tractor Cost - Expected Salvage (Trade) Value}}{\text{Depreciable Life (Years)}}$$

Trailer Depreciation: The trailer depreciation expense is computed as the per-trailer annual depreciation expense multiplied by the number of trailers in the fleet. Each carrier will establish their own specific depreciation method and assumptions. In the example model, a simple straight-line depreciation expense is used. The formula for the straight-line depreciation method is shown below.

$$\text{Annual Trailer Depreciation Expense} = \frac{\text{Net Trailer Cost - Expected Salvage (Trade) Value}}{\text{Depreciable Life (Years)}}$$

Legalization / Recruiting / Administration: The total annual cost in this line item is the annual cost per truck per year multiplied by the number of trucks in the fleet. The per-mile and per-truck amounts are simply the total annual costs divided by the number of miles and number of trucks respectively.

On-Site Manager: This line item cost will represent the annual costs as entered in the direct staffing cost parameter. The per-mile and per-truck amounts are simply the total annual costs divided by the number of miles and number of trucks respectively.

Start-up / Special Equipment: This cost will represent the annual costs as entered in the start-up cost and other expense input cells. The per-mile and per-truck amounts are simply the total annual costs divided by the number of miles and number of trucks respectively. The annual start-up costs are computed as the total lump sum amount amortized over the duration of the contract.

Operating Profits

Operating Profit: Operating profit is computed as total revenue minus total cost. This amount is based on the direct operating figures only and is before interest, taxes and other financial considerations.

Operating Ratio: Operating ratio is a common measure of profitability for carriers. Operating ratio is computed as the ratio of operating costs to total revenue. Dedicated fleet operating ratios can vary dramatically from fleet to fleet. For most dedicated fleets, operating ratios range between 80% and 90%.

Basic Dedicated Fleet Pricing Example

The basic dedicated pricing example below will demonstrate how to model the cost and margins of a dedicated fleet. The example will demonstrate the use of the dedicated pricing model. This demonstration will also provide an overview of the various outputs of the model and how those outputs are computed.

> **Example Dedicated Fleet.** A major retail shipper would like a dedicated fleet to provide weekly deliveries to each of its retail locations within a 600 mile radius of a major distribution center in Nashville, TN. After an internal analysis of historical shipment volumes, the retailer has requested dedicated pricing on a fleet of 20 trucks, 20 drivers, and 60 trailers. Each truck and driver can expect to run an average of 2,200 miles per week. However, due to seasonal business demands, actual utilization is expected to fluctuate from week to week between 1,800 and 2,500 miles. The fleet will operate 51 weeks per year after adjusting for the distribution center's scheduled holidays.
>
> The shipper's need for the dedicated fleet is dictated by the fact that the drivers must assist in the unloading of loose boxes at each store. Since the freight will not be palletized,[63] the trucks will also carry special roller equipment to be used by the driver to roll the boxes off the back of the trailer to store personnel on the ground. As part of the fleet, the carrier must provide and maintain the roller equipment. The customer also requires that the trucking company provide an on-site manager to manage the fleet from inside the customer's facility and to actively participate in daily transportation meetings and related communications.
>
> The customer has asked carriers to submit pricing proposals in each of the three common formats for fleets of this type: 1) Fixed-Variable; 2) Utilization Mileage Scale; and 3) Over-Under Pricing.

For this example, the basic operating parameters of the fleets are predefined, including the fleet size, the number of drivers, and the expected weekly utilization. Next, the carrier must determine the appropriate level of driver pay, along with other secondary factors such as special equipment costs and start-up costs. Once this information is complete, the fleet is ready to be priced using the dedicated pricing model spreadsheet.

Before pricing the fleet, the carrier must determine the amount of pay for the driver. The driver pay level must be high enough to attract and retain quality drivers for the fleet without adding excessive cost. For this example, the carrier will assume that the average driver should earn $42,000 per year.

The carrier must also identify the cost of the secondary requirements of the fleet, particularly the on-site manager costs and the costs of the roller equipment for unloading. For this proposal, the model will assume a total cost of $70,000 per year for the on-site manager. This amount includes a base salary of $56,000 plus fringe benefits of $14,000 or 25% of the base salary. The model will assume a cost of $25,000 per year for the roller equipment. The model will also assume $10,000 in start-up costs to get the fleet up and running.

---

[63] Palletized freight is shipped on pallets for quick and easy loading and unloading, usually with a forklift or pallet jack.

The basic cost assumptions for the carrier are shown below. These amounts are generally standard from deal to deal, so these assumptions are usually consistent for each fleet. The equipment costs and maintenance costs may change if special equipment is required. The cost per gallon of fuel will change based on the "fuel peg" stated in the fuel surcharge agreement for the fleet.

Base Cost Assumptions

Equipment Depreciation and Values

Tractors

Initial Cost	$100,000
Expected Salvage / Trade Value	$50,000
Depreciation Term (Years)	3.00
Annual Depreciation Per Unit	**$16,667**
Monthly Depreciation Per Unit	$ 1,389

Trailers

Initial Cost	$21,600
Expected Salvage / Trade Value	$15,000
Depreciation Term (Years)	3.00
Annual Depreciation Per Unit	**$2,200**
Monthly Depreciation Per Unit	$ 183

Other Operating Costs

Fuel Costs

Cost Per Gallon	$1.200
Miles Per Gallon	6.0
Fuel Tax	$ 0.008
Fuel Cost Per Mile	**$0.208**

Other Operating Costs

Insurance Cost Per Mile	$0.100
Maintenance Cost Per Mile	$0.110
Fringe Benefits (% of Driver Pay)	25.0%

The key variables that change often from deal to deal are included in the primary pricing section of the spreadsheet model shown below.

Dedicated Pricing Model

Customer Name:	Chapter 9	Fleet Description:	Nashville Example

Fleet Parameters

Number of Tractors	20.00
Backup Tractors	0.00
Number of Drivers	20.00
Utilization (Miles per Tractor per Active Week)	2,200
Active Fleet Weeks Per Year (max = 52 weeks)	51.0
Total Fleet Annual Miles	2,244,000
Number of Trailers	60.00
Trailer/Tractor Ratio	3.00

Other Parameters

Driver Rate of Pay (Per Mile or Annual Gross)	$ 42,000.00
Duration of Deal/Contract (in months)	36.0
Average Collection Period (in days)	30.0

Overhead Costs

Tractor Legalization/Taxes	$ 2,000
Driver Recruiting Costs	$ 3,000
Administration Expenses	$ 5,000
Total Overhead (per tractor per year)	$ 10,000
Direct Staffing (On-site CSR / Offices / Etc.)	$ 70,000
Other Annual Expenses (Total Fleet)	$ 25,000
Initial Start-Up Costs (Total)	$ 10,000

Pricing and Analysis

Suggested Rate Per Mile (all miles)	$ 1.3800
Operating Ratio	88.86%
Profit Margin	11.14%

Each "input cell" above has been updated with the specific assumptions for this fleet. The number of tractors, drivers, and trailers reflects the correct fleet size. The active fleet weeks is set to 51 to match the shipper's holiday schedule. Driver pay is set to $42,000 per year and direct staffing is set to $70,000 per year for the on-site manager. The other annual expenses entry is set to $25,000 for the roller equipment and the initial start-up costs entry is set to $10,000.

The full pricing model and pro-forma income statement are shown below. The carrier has chosen to price the fleet at $1.38 per mile as shown in the "Suggested Rate Per Mile" cell. This revenue level results in an operating ratio of 88.86% for the fleet. The carrier bases all dedicated pricing on operating ratio with a minimum operating ratio expectation of 89.0%.

Dedicated Pricing Model

Customer Name:	Chapter 9	Fleet Description:	Nashville Example

Fleet Parameters

Number of Tractors	20.00
Backup Tractors	0.00
Number of Drivers	20.00
Utilization (Miles per Tractor per Active Week)	2,200
Active Fleet Weeks Per Year (max = 52 weeks)	51.0
Total Fleet Annual Miles	2,244,000
Number of Trailers	60.00
Trailer/Tractor Ratio	3.00

Overhead Costs

Tractor Legalization/Taxes	$ 2,000
Driver Recruiting Costs	$ 3,000
Administration Expenses	$ 5,000
Total Overhead (per tractor per year)	$ 10,000
Direct Staffing (On-site CSR / Offices / Etc.)	$ 70,000
Other Annual Expenses (Total Fleet)	$ 25,000
Initial Start-Up Costs (Total)	$ 10,000

Other Parameters

Driver Rate of Pay (Per Mile or Annual Gross)	$ 42,000.00
Duration of Deal/Contract (in months)	36.0
Average Collection Period (in days)	30.0

Pricing and Analysis

Suggested Rate Per Mile (all miles)	$ 1.3800
Operating Ratio	88.86%
Profit Margin	11.14%

Pro-Forma Income Statement

		Fleet Totals Per Mile	Fleet Totals Annual	Per Tractor Weekly	Per Tractor Annual
Total Fleet Miles			2,244,000	2,158	112,200
Total Revenue		$1.380	$3,096,720	$2,978	$154,836
Variable Costs	Assumptions				
Driver Wages	$42,000.00	$0.374	$840,000	$808	$42,000
Fringe Benefits (% of wages)	25.0%	0.094	210,000	202	10,500
Fuel	$0.208	0.208	466,752	449	23,338
Maintenance	$0.110	0.110	246,840	237	12,342
Insurance	$0.100	0.100	224,400	216	11,220
Total Variable Costs		0.886	1,987,992	1,912	99,400
Fixed Costs	Assumptions				
Tractor Depreciation	$ 16,667	0.149	333,333	$321	$16,667
Trailer Depreciation	$ 2,200	0.059	132,000	127	6,600
Legalization/Recruiting/Admin	$ 10,000	0.089	200,000	192	10,000
On-Site Manager	$ 70,000	0.031	70,000	67	3,500
Start Up /Special Equipment	$ 28,333	0.013	28,333	27	1,417
Total Fixed Costs		0.340	763,667	734	38,183
Total Cost		1.226	2,751,659	2,646	137,583
Operating Profit		$0.15	$345,061	$332	$17,253
Operating Ratio		88.86%	88.86%	88.86%	88.86%

Once the carrier has finalized the pricing and determined the total annual revenue needed for the fleet, the pricing must be reformatted to meet the rate structures requested by the shipper. For this fleet, the shipper has requested pricing in three formats including fixed-variable, over-under, and a utilization scale.

Fixed-Variable Pricing Format

The table below illustrates the calculations to place the annual revenue into the fixed-variable pricing format. Because the fixed-variable pricing format applies to any utilization level, a highly critical element of the fixed-variable pricing design is determining how to split revenues into the fixed rate per tractor per week and the variable rate per mile. While each individual carrier may have a certain preference on how to split the revenues, certain standard rules of thumb should generally apply.

First, pure variable costs such as fuel and maintenance should be included in the variable component. Likewise, pure fixed cost components such as tractors, trailers, and other overhead items should be included in the fixed component. Depending on the carrier's preference, insurance could be applied to either the variable component or the fixed component or allocated among both components.

Dedicated Pricing Model *Fixed / Variable Pricing* Chapter 9 - Nashville Example	Enter a percentage in the yellow cells to indicate the portion of each item to allocate to each pricing component.		
	Allocation	Variable	Fixed
	Driver Wages	35%	65%
	Operating Profit	45%	55%

	Total Revenue Allocation			Fixed / Variable Pricing		
	Fleet	Variable	Fixed	Variable	Fixed Per Truck	
Revenue/Cost Components	Totals	Rate	Rate	Per Mile	Per Year	Per Week
Driver Wages	$ 840,000	$ 294,000	$ 546,000	$ 0.131	$ 27,300	$ 525
Fringe Benefits (% of wages)	$ 210,000	$ 73,500	$ 136,500	$ 0.033	$ 6,825	$ 131
Fuel	$ 466,752	$ 466,752	$ -	$ 0.208	$ -	$ -
Maintenance	$ 246,840	$ 246,840	$ -	$ 0.110	$ -	$ -
Insurance	$ 224,400	$ 224,400	$ -	$ 0.100	$ -	$ -
Total Variable Costs	$ 1,987,992	$ 1,305,492	$ 682,500	$ 0.582	$ 34,125	$ 656
Tractor Depreciation	$ 333,333	$ -	$ 333,333	$ -	$ 16,667	$ 321
Trailer Depreciation	$ 132,000	$ -	$ 132,000	$ -	$ 6,600	$ 127
Legalization/Recruiting/Admin	$ 200,000	$ -	$ 200,000	$ -	$ 10,000	$ 192
On-Site Manager	$ 70,000	$ -	$ 70,000	$ -	$ 3,500	$ 67
Start Up /Special Equipment	$ 28,333	$ -	$ 28,333	$ -	$ 1,417	$ 27
Total Fixed Costs	$ 763,667	$ -	$ 763,667	$ -	$ 38,183	$ 734
Operating Profit	$ 345,061	$ 155,278	$ 189,784	$ 0.069	$ 9,489	$ 182
Total Desired Revenue	$ 3,096,720	$ 1,460,770	$ 1,635,950	$ 0.651	$81,798	$1,573

Minimum Weekly Charge	Annual	Per Truck Per Week		Final Rates:	
Base Fixed Charge		$ 1,573		Fixed:	$ 1,573
Plus: Variable Driver Wages	$ 367,500	$ 353		Variable:	$ 0.651
Plus: Profit on Driver Wages	$ 43,711	$ 42			
Minimum Charge Per Truck Per Week		$ 1,968			

Revenue Verification	Rate	Annual Units	Annual Revenue
Fixed Charge Per Tractor Per Week	$ 1,573	1,040	$ 1,635,950
Variable Charge Per Mile	$ 0.651	2,244,000	$ 1,460,770
Total Annual Revenue			$ 3,096,720

The remaining revenue and cost items include driver compensation (pay plus fringes) and the operating profit. These two items provide the greatest challenge in the fixed-variable pricing design. The model provides two input cells for these items at the top of the design table, one for driver pay and one for operating profit. These cells provide the means to allocate a percentage of each item to the variable component. The balance of each item is then allocated to the fixed component.

Because the drivers must earn a reasonable income regardless of the level of utilization, the carrier must protect itself from having inadequate revenues to fund driver pay in low utilization scenarios. Even though driver pay is generally considered a variable expense, placing 100% of the revenue for driver pay in the variable component is very risky for the carrier. If the utilization of the fleet is lower than expected, revenues will fall below expectations and the carrier may not have enough revenue to pay the drivers and still achieve the desired level of profitability.

In this example, 35% of the driver pay is applied to the variable charge and 65% is applied to the fixed charge. As a result, $525 of revenue to fund driver pay is included in the fixed revenue component and 13.1 cents per mile is included in the variable component. This allocation assures the carrier of $525 of revenue to fund driver pay regardless of utilization, plus any additional revenues generated from the variable component. The table below shows the expected revenues for driver compensation at different levels of utilization.

Driver Pay Scenarios	Total Revenues		
	Fixed	Variable	Total
Rate:	$ 525	$ 0.131	
Utilization:			
1,000	$ 525	$ 131	$ 656
1,100	$ 525	$ 144	$ 669
1,200	$ 525	$ 157	$ 682
1,300	$ 525	$ 170	$ 695
1,400	$ 525	$ 183	$ 708
1,500	$ 525	$ 197	$ 722
1,600	$ 525	$ 210	$ 735
1,700	$ 525	$ 223	$ 748
1,800	$ 525	$ 236	$ 761
1,900	$ 525	$ 249	$ 774
2,000	$ 525	$ 262	$ 787
2,100	$ 525	$ 275	$ 800
2,200	**$ 525**	**$ 288**	**$ 813**
2,300	$ 525	$ 301	$ 826
2,400	$ 525	$ 314	$ 839
2,500	$ 525	$ 328	$ 853
2,600	$ 525	$ 341	$ 866

Based around the planned utilization level of 2,200 miles per week, the table above assumes that utilization will be no lower than 1,000 miles per week. At 1,000 miles per week, $656 of revenue is generated towards driver compensation. Had driver pay been modeled 100% in the variable component, the revenue for driver compensation would have been only $374 (1,000 miles x $0.374 per mile), creating a very serious revenue and profitability gap for the carrier.

The tremendous advantage for the carrier inherent in the fixed-variable pricing structure is the fixed charge component. The fixed component eliminates the majority of the operating risk for the carrier. By properly leveraging the fixed charge, the carrier can "lock in" enough revenue to cover fixed costs, a portion of driver wages, and a portion of the profit margin. This reduction in the carrier's risk should also benefit the shipper in the form of lower rates since the shipper assumes much of the utilization risk.

The revenue-utilization curve for the fixed-variable pricing of the example fleet is shown in the graph below. The proposed fixed-variable pricing includes a fixed charge of $1,573 per tractor per week and a variable charge of $0.651 per mile.

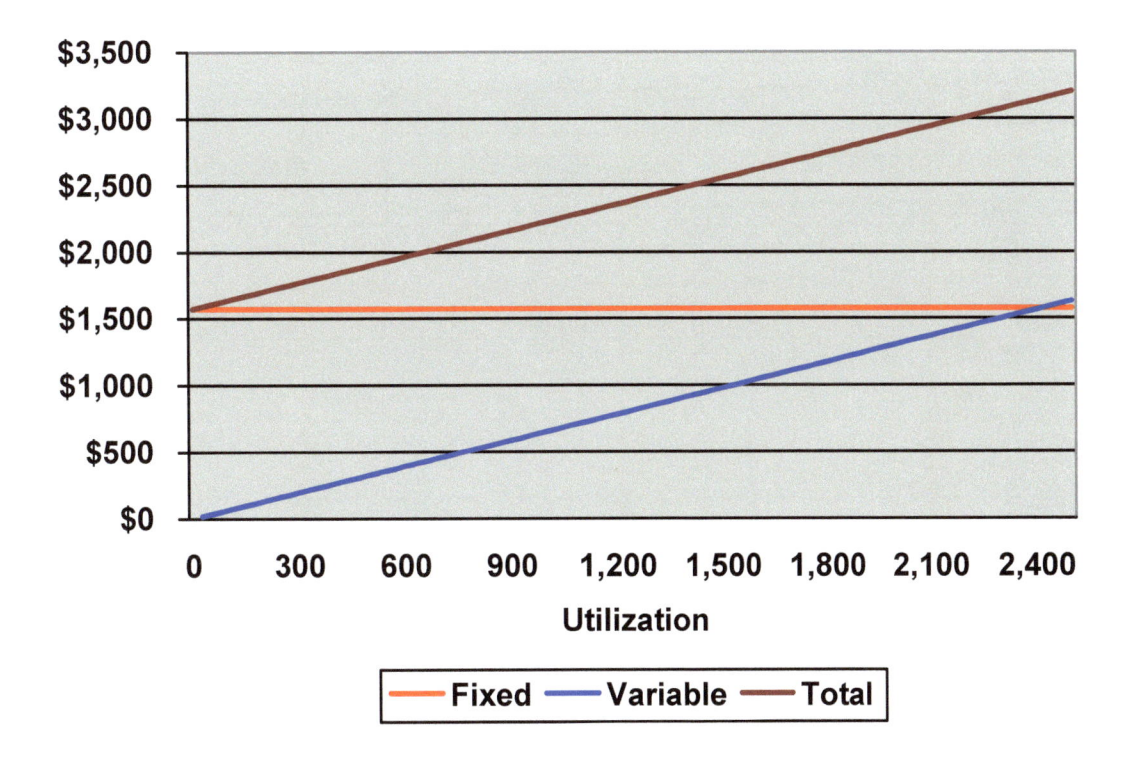

Fixed-Variable Revenues Per Tractor Per Week

The fixed revenue amount of $1,573 per tractor per week is earned regardless of utilization. Variable revenue and total revenue increase at the same rate as weekly utilization increases.

Over-Under Pricing Format

Step 1: Preliminary Fixed-Variable Design

The table below illustrates the calculations to place the annual revenue into an over-under pricing format. The model is very similar to the fixed-variable model in terms of the allocation of driver wages and operating profits. The allocation of these two items influences the degree to which revenues are placed in the "over" and "under" rate components. When using the pricing model, the fixed-variable pricing should be defined prior to beginning the over-under design. Once established, the fixed-variable rates are used to compute the over-under rate components.

Over-Under Pricing Design

Dedicated Pricing Model	Allocation	Variable	Fixed	
Over / Under Pricing	Driver Wages	35%	65%	Allocations entries from the Fixed / Variable Tab
Chapter 9 - Nashville Example	Operating Profit	45%	55%	

	Total Revenue Allocation			Fixed / Variable Pricing		
	Fleet	Variable	Fixed	Variable	Fixed Per Truck	
Revenue/Cost Components	Totals	Rate	Rate	Per Mile	Per Year	Per Week
Driver Wages	$ 840,000	$ 294,000	$ 546,000	$ 0.131	$ 27,300	$ 525
Fringe Benefits (% of wages)	$ 210,000	$ 73,500	$ 136,500	$ 0.033	$ 6,825	$ 131
Fuel	$ 466,752	$ 466,752	$ -	$ 0.208	$ -	$ -
Maintenance	$ 246,840	$ 246,840	$ -	$ 0.110	$ -	$ -
Insurance	$ 224,400	$ 224,400	$ -	$ 0.100	$ -	$ -
Total Variable Costs	$ 1,987,992	$ 1,305,492	$ 682,500	$ 0.582	$ 34,125	$ 656
Tractor Depreciation	$ 333,333	$ -	$ 333,333	$ -	$ 16,667	$ 321
Trailer Depreciation	$ 132,000	$ -	$ 132,000	$ -	$ 6,600	$ 127
Legalization/Recruiting/Admin	$ 200,000	$ -	$ 200,000	$ -	$ 10,000	$ 192
On-Site Manager	$ 70,000	$ -	$ 70,000	$ -	$ 3,500	$ 67
Start Up /Special Equipment	$ 28,333	$ -	$ 28,333	$ -	$ 1,417	$ 27
Total Fixed Costs	$ 763,667	$ -	$ 763,667	$ -	$ 38,183	$ 734
Operating Profit	$ 345,061	$ 155,278	$ 189,784	$ 0.069	$ 9,489	$ 182
Total Desired Revenue	$3,096,720	$1,460,770	$1,635,950	$ 0.651	$81,798	$1,573

The shaded rates in the total desired revenue line represent the recommended fixed-variable rates based on the model and allocations of driver pay and operating profit shown previously. The over-under pricing structure will be computed based on these fixed-variable rates. Using this basis, the over-under pricing structure will generate the same revenue as a fixed-variable structure at any level of utilization. Since the over-under format poses the same driver compensation revenue risks as a fixed-variable rate structure, an accurate fixed-variable design provides the safest foundation for computing the over-under rate components.

Step 2: Design the Over-Under Rate Components

Over Rate. The "over" rate is computed the same way as the variable rate in a fixed-variable pricing structure. The "over" rate should always include all variable costs such as fuel, maintenance and insurance.[64] The "over" rate should also include an allocated portion of driver wages and operating profits. In this example, the "over" rate is set at $0.651 per mile, the same as the variable rate in the fixed-variable pricing structure.

Under Rate. The "under" rate is derived directly from the fixed weekly charge from the fixed-variable pricing structure. The formula for the "under" rate is shown below.

$$\text{"Under" Rate Per Mile} = \frac{\text{Fixed Weekly Charge}}{\text{Planned Utilization Level}} = \frac{\$1,573}{2,200 \text{ miles}} = \$0.715 \text{ per mile}$$

The "under" rate serves to effectively guarantee the carrier a weekly revenue level of $1,573 per truck per week regardless of actual utilization.

$$\text{Minimum Revenue} = \text{Planned (Base) Utilization Level} \times \text{"Under" Rate Per Mile}$$

Base Rate. The base rate of $1.366 is the over rate plus the under rate. The calculations from the pricing spreadsheet are shown below.

Over-Under Calculations and Validation

Rate Determination:	Per Week	Total	Per Mile
Base Utilization Level	2,200		
Fixed Charge		$ 1,573	$ 0.715
Variable Charge		$ 1,432	$ 0.651
Total		$ 3,005	$ 1.366

Pricing Utilization Analysis:									
A	B	C	D	E = A x C	F = D x B	G = E + F	H = G / A	I	I / H
Utilization	Over (Under)	Base Rate	O / U Rate	Base Charge	O/U Charge	Total Charge	Rate Per Mile	Cost Per Mile	Operating Ratio
1,900	(300)	$ 1.366	$ 0.715	$ 2,595.36	$ 214.50	$ 2,809.87	$ 1.48	$ 1.31	88.83%
2,000	(200)	$ 1.366	$ 0.715	$ 2,731.96	$ 143.00	$ 2,874.96	$ 1.44	$ 1.28	88.84%
2,100	(100)	$ 1.366	$ 0.715	$ 2,868.56	$ 71.50	$ 2,940.06	$ 1.40	$ 1.24	88.85%
2,200	0	$ 1.366	$ -	$ 3,005.16	$ -	$ 3,005.16	$ 1.37	$ 1.21	88.86%
2,300	100	$ 1.366	$ 0.651	$ 3,005.16	$ 65.10	$ 3,070.25	$ 1.33	$ 1.19	88.87%
2,400	200	$ 1.366	$ 0.651	$ 3,005.16	$ 130.19	$ 3,135.35	$ 1.31	$ 1.16	88.88%
2,500	300	$ 1.366	$ 0.651	$ 3,005.16	$ 195.29	$ 3,200.45	$ 1.28	$ 1.14	88.89%

The pricing utilization analysis section computes the revenues, costs and operating ratio across a range of utilization levels around the planned utilization of 2,200 miles per week. With accurate pricing, the operating ratio will remain steady and within an acceptable range across these potential utilization levels. Sensitivity analysis on the pricing design allows the carrier to evaluate risk and identify any possible gaps in the dedicated pricing design and rate structure.

---

[64] Some carriers may prefer to treat insurance as a fixed expense. In these examples, insurance is treated as a per-mile variable expense.

The table below illustrates the revenues by component for various utilization levels between 0 and 2,500 miles.

Over-Under Revenues Per Tractor Per Week

Rates:	$ 1.366	$ 0.651	$ 0.715		Base Utilization:		2,200
	Billable Miles			Revenues			Total
Actual Utilization	Base	Over	Under	Base	Over	Under	Revenue
0	0	0	2,200	$ 0	$ -	$ 1,573	$ 1,573
500	500	0	1,700	$ 683	$ -	$ 1,216	$ 1,899
1,000	1,000	0	1,200	$ 1,366	$ -	$ 858	$ 2,224
1,500	1,500	0	700	$ 2,049	$ -	$ 501	$ 2,550
2,000	2,000	0	200	$ 2,732	$ -	$ 143	$ 2,875
2,100	2,100	0	100	$ 2,869	$ -	$ 72	$ 2,940
2,200	2,200	0	-	$ 3,005	$ -	$ -	$ 3,005
2,300	2,200	100	-	$ 3,005	$ 65	$ -	$ 3,070
2,400	2,200	200	-	$ 3,005	$ 130	$ -	$ 3,135
2,500	2,200	300	-	$ 3,005	$ 195	$ -	$ 3,201

The graph below illustrates the revenue curves between 0 and 2,500 miles per week.

Over-Under Revenues Per Tractor Per Week

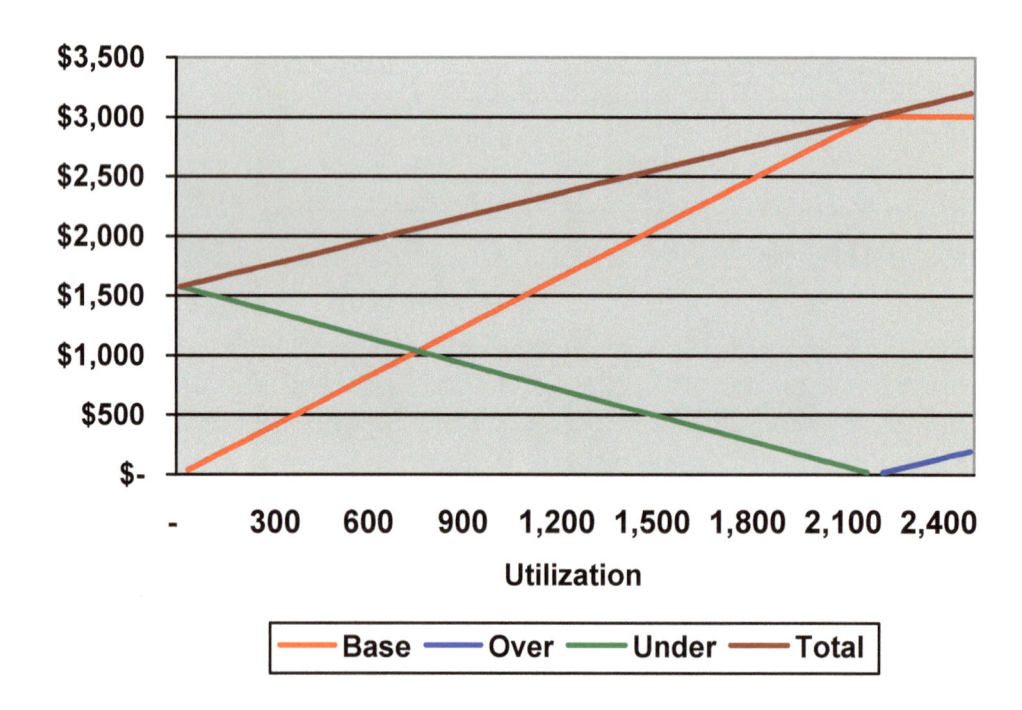

At the planned utilization level, the total revenue is made up of only base revenues. At levels less than the planned level, total revenue is made up of base revenues plus "under" revenues. At utilization levels above the planned level, total revenue is made up of base revenues plus "over" revenues. Also notice that base revenues flatten out at the planned utilization level and remain constant at $3,005 per week above the planned level.

Utilization Scale Pricing Format

The table below illustrates the calculations to place the annual target revenue into a utilization scale pricing format. The fixed-variable rates should be established before populating the utilization scale pricing format. The calculated scale rates at each potential utilization level are based directly on the fixed-variable rates.

Utilization Scale Pricing

	Pricing Base:	0%					
Utilization Ranges	**Modeled Utilization**	**Fixed Rate**	**Variable Rate**	**Gross Revenue**	**Minimum Revenue**	**Applied Revenue**	**Rate Per Mile**
1,000 - 1,099	1,000	$1,573	$ 0.651	$ 2,224	$ 1,968	$ 2,224	$ 2.22
1,100 - 1,199	1,100	$1,573	$ 0.651	$ 2,289	$ 1,968	$ 2,289	$ 2.08
1,200 - 1,299	1,200	$1,573	$ 0.651	$ 2,354	$ 1,968	$ 2,354	$ 1.96
1,300 - 1,399	1,300	$1,573	$ 0.651	$ 2,419	$ 1,968	$ 2,419	$ 1.86
1,400 - 1,499	1,400	$1,573	$ 0.651	$ 2,484	$ 1,968	$ 2,484	$ 1.77
1,500 - 1,599	1,500	$1,573	$ 0.651	$ 2,549	$ 1,968	$ 2,549	$ 1.70
1,600 - 1,699	1,600	$1,573	$ 0.651	$ 2,615	$ 1,968	$ 2,615	$ 1.63
1,700 - 1,799	1,700	$1,573	$ 0.651	$ 2,680	$ 1,968	$ 2,680	$ 1.58
1,800 - 1,899	1,800	$1,573	$ 0.651	$ 2,745	$ 1,968	$ 2,745	$ 1.52
1,900 - 1,999	1,900	$1,573	$ 0.651	$ 2,810	$ 1,968	$ 2,810	$ 1.48
2,000 - 2,099	2,000	$1,573	$ 0.651	$ 2,875	$ 1,968	$ 2,875	$ 1.44
2,100 - 2,199	2,100	$1,573	$ 0.651	$ 2,940	$ 1,968	$ 2,940	$ 1.40
2,200 - 2,299	2,200	$1,573	$ 0.651	$ 3,005	$ 1,968	$ 3,005	$ 1.37
2,300 - 2,399	2,300	$1,573	$ 0.651	$ 3,070	$ 1,968	$ 3,070	$ 1.33
2,400 - 2,499	2,400	$1,573	$ 0.651	$ 3,135	$ 1,968	$ 3,135	$ 1.31
2,500 - 2,599	2,500	$1,573	$ 0.651	$ 3,200	$ 1,968	$ 3,200	$ 1.28
2,600 - 2,699	2,600	$1,573	$ 0.651	$ 3,266	$ 1,968	$ 3,266	$ 1.26
2,700 - 2,799	2,700	$1,573	$ 0.651	$ 3,331	$ 1,968	$ 3,331	$ 1.23
2,800 - 2,899	2,800	$1,573	$ 0.651	$ 3,396	$ 1,968	$ 3,396	$ 1.21
2,900 - 2,999	2,900	$1,573	$ 0.651	$ 3,461	$ 1,968	$ 3,461	$ 1.19

The utilization ranges should represent a relevant range around the planned utilization. The modeled utilization is computed from the pricing base of 0% where the percentage represents the point within each utilization range to base the revenue and rate level. In this example, the pricing base of 0% sets the modeled utilization at the starting point of the utilization range. The primary reason for setting the base at 0% in this example is because the planned utilization level of 2,200 falls at the beginning of its utilization range. Raising the pricing base will lower the rate per mile outputs as the fixed charges are then spread over a slightly larger number of miles. In general, setting the base at 0% is the safest assumption.

Once the base utilization level is set, the fixed-variable rates are applied to determine the target revenue for each utilization level. This revenue level is represented in the gross revenue column. The minimum revenue column was computed as part of the fixed-variable pricing. The applied revenue column represents the greatest value from either the gross revenue column or the minimum revenue column. The rate per mile is simply the applied revenue divided by the modeled utilization.

Revenue Verification. The revenue verification box below computes the total revenue for the deal based on the rates as populated in the utilization scale.

Revenue Verification:	
Planned Utilization	2,200
Planned Annual Miles	2,244,000
Scale Rate Per Mile	$ 1.37
Annual Revenue	$ 3,074,280 per scale
Check Figure:	
Proforma Revenue	$ 3,096,720

The revenue computed from the scale at the target utilization level should be reasonably close to the desired annual revenue from the pro-forma income statement in the pricing model. In this example, the projected revenue is slightly short of the pro-forma revenue because of the "revenue gap" of the utilization scale structure. Rounding of the per-mile rates is also a factor in some cases.

The revenue at 2,200 miles per week falls short because the planned utilization of 2,200 miles falls at the beginning of a 100-mile pricing range. In reality, when weekly utilization falls into this range, a variety of actual utilization levels will occur around the target utilization level of 2,200 miles per week. The table below shows that the average fleet annual revenue will "average out" and match closely to the target revenue level when utilization levels around the target utilization are considered.

Intra-Range Revenue Scenarios

Utilization Scenario	Scale Rate Per Mile	Per Truck Weekly	Fleet Annual Revenue
2,150	$ 1.40	$ 3,010	$ 3,070,200
2,160	$ 1.40	$ 3,024	$ 3,084,480
2,170	$ 1.40	$ 3,038	$ 3,098,760
2,180	$ 1.40	$ 3,052	$ 3,113,040
2,190	$ 1.40	$ 3,066	$ 3,127,320
2,200	$ 1.37	$ 3,014	$ 3,074,280
2,210	$ 1.37	$ 3,028	$ 3,088,254
2,220	$ 1.37	$ 3,041	$ 3,102,228
2,230	$ 1.37	$ 3,055	$ 3,116,202
2,240	$ 1.37	$ 3,069	$ 3,130,176
2,250	$ 1.37	$ 3,083	$ 3,144,150
Average Fleet Annual Revenue			**$ 3,104,463**

Check Figure:
Proforma Revenue $ 3,096,720

Over the term of the contract, the revenue "shortfall" will average out as random weekly utilization levels occur. However, the existence of the revenue gap is a serious weakness of the utilization scale format and puts both the shipper and carrier at a moderate risk.

Revenue Validation and Consistency by Contract Type

When each pricing format is based on the same pre-established fixed-variable rate design, each of the three standard dedicated pricing contract types should generate approximately the same level of revenue for the carrier at any level of utilization. The table below computes the revenue levels for the three contract types based on a relevant range of utilization levels around the 2,200 mile per week expectation.

Dedicated Revenue Validation by Contract Type

Dedicated Revenue Validation	Rate	\\ Actual Utilization \\ 1,750	1,900	2,050	**2,200**	2,350	2,500	2,650
Fixed - Variable								
Fixed Component	$1,573	$ 1,573	$ 1,573	$ 1,573	$ 1,573	$ 1,573	$ 1,573	$ 1,573
Variable Component	$ 0.651	$ 1,139	$ 1,237	$ 1,334	$ 1,432	$ 1,530	$ 1,627	$ 1,725
Total Revenue: Fixed-Variable		$ 2,712	$ 2,810	$ 2,908	$ 3,005	$ 3,103	$ 3,200	$ 3,298
Utilization Scale								
Rate Per Mile	From Scale:	$ 1.576	$ 1.479	$ 1.437	$ 1.366	$ 1.335	$ 1.280	$ 1.256
Total Revenue: Utilization Scale		$ 2,758	$ 2,810	$ 2,947	$ 3,005	$ 3,137	$ 3,200	$ 3,328
Over - Under								
Base Miles	Base Rate	1,750	1,900	2,050	2,200	2,200	2,200	2,200
Over (Under) Miles	Over or Under	(450)	(300)	(150)	0	150	300	450
Base Rate Charges	$ 1.366	$ 2,390	$ 2,595	$ 2,800	$ 3,005	$ 3,005	$ 3,005	$ 3,005
Over Charges	$ 0.651	$ -	$ -	$ -	$ -	$ 98	$ 195	$ 293
Under Charges	$ 0.715	$ 322	$ 215	$ 107	$ -	$ -	$ -	$ -
Total Revenue: Over-Under		$ 2,712	$ 2,810	$ 2,908	$ 3,005	$ 3,103	$ 3,200	$ 3,298

For the purpose of this analysis, the utilization scale rates are not rounded to the actual contract rates. For example, at 2,200 miles, the rate applied is $1.366 instead of the proposed contract rate of $1.37.

Since the utilization scale pricing base was set at 0%, all three pricing formats match at the 2,200 mile utilization level, as well as the 1,900 mile level and the 2,500 mile level. The utilization scale pricing does not match at the other levels such as 2,050 because of the revenue gap problem presented previously. However, the fixed-variable and over-under dedicated revenues should match at any utilization level as shown here.

The point of the revenue validation exercise is to show that the shipper's dedicated fleet cost should not be materially different purely as a result of the pricing and contract format. A carrier may view one contract structure as more risky than another and adjust pricing accordingly based purely on risk. However, the carrier's underlying cost structure does not change based on the contract or pricing design. Therefore, in the absence of any specific risk, the total transportation cost to the shipper should be approximately the same for any of the three contract types and pricing formats.

Handling On-site Costs and Other Fleet Overhead

The costs of on-site management and other lump-sum fixed overhead cost items associated with a fleet are fixed costs that do not change as the actual fleet size changes. Too often, these costs are included in the per-mile dedicated rates or the fixed-variable dedicated rates. Embedding these costs in the base dedicated rate structure is equally risky for both the shipper and the carrier.

Regardless of the actual rate structure, fleet-specific cost items that are independent of fleet size, particularly an on-site manager, should be removed from the dedicated pricing structure and treated as an independent accessorial charge. This separation prevents the shipper from incurring excess costs when the fleet size grows and protects the carrier's revenues when the fleet size is reduced. Otherwise, these costs are embedded into the base dedicated rates and become difficult to adjust after the pricing is implemented.

As an example, the fixed-variable pricing from earlier in this chapter shown below will be used to illustrate the issue with fleet-level fixed costs such as an on-site manager.

Dedicated Pricing Model
Fixed / Variable Pricing
Chapter 9 - Nashville Example

Enter a percentage in the yellow cells to indicate the portion of each item to allocate to each pricing component.

Allocation	Variable	Fixed
Driver Wages	35%	65%
Operating Profit	45%	55%

Revenue/Cost Components	Fleet Totals	Variable Rate	Fixed Rate	Variable Per Mile	Fixed Per Truck Per Year	Fixed Per Truck Per Week
Driver Wages	$ 840,000	$ 294,000	$ 546,000	$ 0.131	$ 27,300	$ 525
Fringe Benefits (% of wages)	$ 210,000	$ 73,500	$ 136,500	$ 0.033	$ 6,825	$ 131
Fuel	$ 466,752	$ 466,752	$ -	$ 0.208	$ -	$ -
Maintenance	$ 246,840	$ 246,840	$ -	$ 0.110	$ -	$ -
Insurance	$ 224,400	$ 224,400	$ -	$ 0.100	$ -	$ -
Total Variable Costs	**$ 1,987,992**	**$ 1,305,492**	**$ 682,500**	**$ 0.582**	**$ 34,125**	**$ 656**
Tractor Depreciation	$ 333,333	$ -	$ 333,333	$ -	$ 16,667	$ 321
Trailer Depreciation	$ 132,000	$ -	$ 132,000	$ -	$ 6,600	$ 127
Legalization/Recruiting/Admin	$ 200,000	$ -	$ 200,000	$ -	$ 10,000	$ 192
On-Site Manager	$ 70,000	$ -	$ 70,000	$ -	$ 3,500	$ 67
Start Up /Special Equipment	$ 28,333	$ -	$ 28,333	$ -	$ 1,417	$ 27
Total Fixed Costs	**$ 763,667**	**$ -**	**$ 763,667**	**$ -**	**$ 38,183**	**$ 734**
Operating Profit	$ 345,061	$ 155,278	$ 189,784	$ 0.069	$ 9,489	$ 182
Total Desired Revenue	**$ 3,096,720**	**$ 1,460,770**	**$ 1,635,950**	**$ 0.651**	**$81,798**	**$1,573**

Minimum Weekly Charge	Annual	Per Truck Per Week
Base Fixed Charge		$ 1,573
Plus: Variable Driver Wages	$ 367,500	$ 353
Plus: Profit on Driver Wages	$ 43,711	$ 42
Minimum Charge Per Truck Per Week		**$ 1,968**

Final Rates:	
Fixed:	$ 1,573
Variable:	$ 0.651

Revenue Verification	Rate	Annual Units	Annual Revenue
Fixed Charge Per Tractor Per Week	$ 1,573	1,040	$ 1,635,950
Variable Charge Per Mile	$ 0.651	2,244,000	$ 1,460,770
Total Annual Revenue			**$ 3,096,720**

Notice that the on-site manager row has an annual cost of $70,000 for the entire fleet and a cost of $67.31 per truck per week. The $67.31 per week cost is included in the fixed charge per tractor per week of $1,573. The table below illustrates the cost and revenue impact of changes in the fleet size to both the shipper and the carrier.

Impact of Embedded On-Site Manager Costs						
Actual Fleet Size	On-Site Manager Charges			Actual Carrier Cost	Excess (Deficit) Amount	Impact
	Per Truck Per Week	Per Truck Per Year	Actual Annual Revenue			
10	$ 67.31	$ 3,500	$ 35,000	$ 70,000	$ (35,000)	
12	$ 67.31	$ 3,500	$ 42,000	$ 70,000	$ (28,000)	Carrier has
14	$ 67.31	$ 3,500	$ 49,000	$ 70,000	$ (21,000)	a revenue
16	$ 67.31	$ 3,500	$ 56,000	$ 70,000	$ (14,000)	shortfall
18	$ 67.31	$ 3,500	$ 63,000	$ 70,000	$ (7,000)	
20	**$ 67.31**	**$ 3,500**	**$ 70,000**	**$ 70,000**	**$ -**	**No Impact**
22	$ 67.31	$ 3,500	$ 77,000	$ 70,000	$ 7,000	
24	$ 67.31	$ 3,500	$ 84,000	$ 70,000	$ 14,000	Shipper pays
26	$ 67.31	$ 3,500	$ 91,000	$ 70,000	$ 21,000	more than
28	$ 67.31	$ 3,500	$ 98,000	$ 70,000	$ 28,000	necessary
30	$ 67.31	$ 3,500	$ 105,000	$ 70,000	$ 35,000	

If the fleet size increases, the shipper will pay more than what is necessary for the on-site manager. If the fleet size decreases, the carrier will not receive the planned amount of revenue needed to fund the cost of the on-site manager. To correct this problem, the on-site manager cost should be removed from the fixed charge per truck per week and handled as a separate item as shown below.

Revised Pricing Structure	
Fixed Charge Per Truck Per Week	$ 1,573.03
Cost of On-site Manager	$ (67.31)
Revised Fixed Charge Per Truck Per Week	$ 1,505.72
Annual On-Site Manager Cost	$ 70,000
Weeks Per Year	÷ 52
Weekly On-Site Manager Charge	$ 1,346.15

Using the revised structure, the carrier's revenue to fund the cost of the on-site manager will always be $70,000 per year, regardless of the fleet size. This adjustment protects the carrier from a revenue shortfall in the event of a fleet size reduction. The change also prevents the shipper from paying too much when the fleet size increases. Also, should the need for an on-site manager no longer exist, the cost can be easily removed from the pricing without having to revisit the existing fixed and variable charges.[65] Similar overhead costs could be handled in much the same way.

---

[65] A fixed-variable pricing structure was used in this example because it provides a clear illustration of the issue. The same issue still exists with any other pricing structure and can also be resolved by treating the fixed fleet overhead as a stand-alone accessorial charge.

CHAPTER 10: Establishing the Proper Profit Margin for a Dedicated Fleet

In the previous chapter, dedicated fleet margin was determined based on a target operating ratio requirement such as a standard of 88.0%. While this method is very easy to apply, operating ratio fails to account for all of the necessary variables for establishing proper margin levels and accurate pricing. A standard operating ratio pricing rule is fairly accurate for fleets where there are no unusual equipment requirements and where the expected utilization falls into a typical range of 1,900 to 2,500 miles per truck per week. However, even on some "typical" deals, the standard operating ratio method is not entirely accurate.

Many dedicated fleets are specialized solutions that often contain unusual equipment requirements or extreme utilization levels.[66] Pricing that is based purely on a standard operating ratio or cost-plus approach does not fully capture the financial and investment implications of the unusual requirements. The standard operating ratio approach also fails to fully account for the efficiencies of high utilization and the inefficiencies of low utilization. This chapter demonstrates the weaknesses of the operating ratio method and provides a more sophisticated approach based on the application of common financial analysis tools for evaluating capital investment decisions.

Note: The concepts presented in this chapter assume that the carrier purchases and owns the fleet of trucks and trailers. In arrangements where the carrier utilizes owner-operator tractors or leased equipment, the analysis process is much different and certain concepts shown here will not necessarily apply. The key financial and pricing considerations in these types of non-ownership of equipment arrangements will be discussed at the end of the chapter.

The Risks of Operating Ratio Based Pricing

Dedicated pricing that is based purely on the operating ratio method represents a simple cost-plus pricing approach. A cost-plus approach is often appropriate for an on-going business such as a new product line for a retail store or a new menu item at a restaurant. However, a cost-plus approach is not always appropriate for a new, incremental investment such as a new fleet of trucks and trailers. The key difference is that the purchase of the incremental group of trucks and trailers requires the carrier to make a substantial capital investment in the new equipment. The fleet will also have unique operating characteristics, particularly utilization, that must also be taken into account within the pricing strategy and analysis.

In order for the proposed dedicated fleet to be profitable, revenues must exceed operating cost. However, for the *capital investment* to be profitable and justifiable, profits and cash flows from the investment must meet or exceed a minimum required return on the invested funds. As will be illustrated in this chapter, an operating ratio of 88% (or any

---

[66] Specialized deals may require 10 trailers per tractor, utilization of only 900 miles per week, or utilization of 5,000 miles per week. Deals of this type require special margin considerations.

static operating ratio level) does not always result in an acceptable return on investment. In other cases, an 88% operating ratio can also result in a return on investment that is far too high, resulting in unnecessarily high pricing.

Using a static operating ratio level to price every fleet will often result in one of two critical pricing mistakes. The first and most costly mistake occurs when a carrier prices an undesirable opportunity too low. The most common mistake of this type would involve a low utilization fleet that requires a high number of trailers per tractor being priced too low. Not only is the fleet potentially unprofitable, but because of the low pricing mistake, the carrier also stands a good chance of being awarded a fleet that produces poor financial results.

The second mistake occurs when a carrier prices a very attractive opportunity too high and fails to provide competitive pricing for the business opportunity. A common mistake of this type might occur when the shipper requests a fleet of dedicated trucks and drivers but the entire trailer fleet is provided by the shipper. Carriers that do not adjust pricing and margin downward by the appropriate amount will be priced too high and miss out on this financially attractive opportunity. The most critical mistakes are outlined below.

Critical Operating Ratio Pricing Mistakes	
Under-pricing a Less Desirable Dedicated Fleet Opportunity	**Over-pricing a Highly Attractive Dedicated Fleet Opportunity**
The most critical error is to price a dedicated opportunity too low by not properly adjusting for extremely low utilization levels or extremely high investment requirements such as a high trailer-to-tractor ratio. Operating ratio does not consider the significant capital investment required by a fleet with an above average trailer-to-tractor ratio. Inaccurate, low pricing could result in the carrier being awarded the potentially unprofitable dedicated fleet. In reality, the fleet is actually not as profitable as it may appear when the evaluation of financial performance is based only on operating ratio.	In opportunities that offer above average utilization or below average equipment (trailer) requirements, an operating ratio pricing approach will often result in a price that is too high and not competitive. The operating ratio approach does not fully adjust for the benefits of the high utilization or reduced trailer investment levels. Over-pricing will result in an uncompetitive proposal and the loss of an otherwise profitable opportunity. In the long run, over-pricing may also cause the carrier to be excluded from future opportunities with a shipper because of past pricing being consistently too high.

This chapter provides the tools for avoiding these mistakes by creating dedicated pricing using an investment-based approach. The next section illustrates the basic weaknesses of the operating ratio approach. Later sections will outline a more suitable, investment-based analysis approach to facilitate accurate, competitive and profitable pricing.

The Hidden Weakness of Operating Ratio

To illustrate the hidden weaknesses of operating ratio, consider the three dedicated fleet opportunities available to a carrier shown below. Also assume that the carrier can only accept one fleet opportunity because fleets A, B, and C are available from three rival shippers who each prefer that their carriers not provide service for their competitors. For simplification, each deal is initially presented as mutually exclusive, 1 truck fleets as shown in the table below. The carrier has already agreed upon the pricing with each potential shipper.

Mutually Exclusive Fleet Opportunities	Fleet Opportunity A	Fleet Opportunity B	Fleet Opportunity C
Fleet Summary:			
Tractors	1	1	1
Trailers	6	3	None
Utilization (Weekly Miles)	2,050	2,500	2,390
Rate Per Mile (All Miles)	$1.77	$1.56	$1.46
Expected Operating Ratio	**86.00%**	**89.00%**	**92.00%**
Profit Margin	*14.00%*	*11.00%*	*8.00%*

Profit Margin by Opportunity

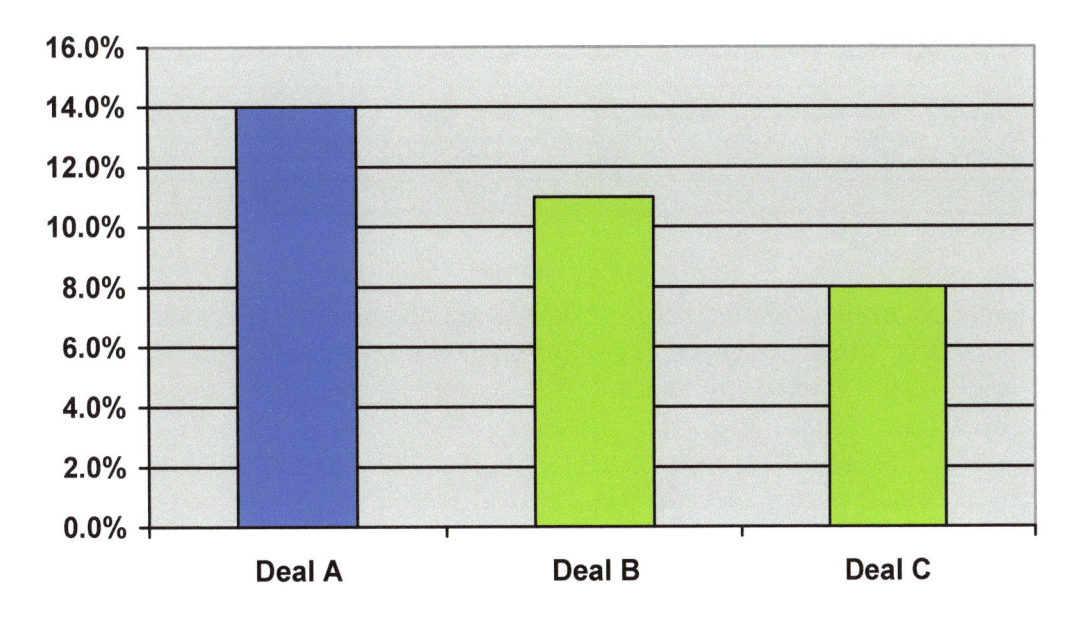

Deal	Profit Margin
Deal A	14.0%
Deal B	11.0%
Deal C	8.0%

Which deal should be chosen based on this information? Many carriers would immediately select Deal A because it offers the lowest (best) operating ratio at 86% and the highest profit margin of 14%. Other carriers might select Deal B since the utilization is much higher than Deal A and the operating ratio is reasonable at 89%. Very few carriers would select Deal C because of the expected operating ratio of 92% and the rate of $1.46 per mile.

To accurately determine the best choice, a deeper financial analysis is necessary. The table below estimates the costs and revenues associated with each opportunity. Driver pay is based on $0.38 per mile and a minimum weekly pay of $700 per week.

Projected Income Statements		Fleet Opportunity A	Fleet Opportunity B	Fleet Opportunity C
Fleet Summary:				
Tractors		1	1	1
Trailers		6	3	-
Utilization (Weekly Miles)		2,050	2,500	2,390
Variable Costs	Per Mile			
Driver Pay (Min = $700)	$ 0.38	$ 40,508	$ 49,400	$ 47,226
Fringe Benefits	25.0%	$ 10,127	$ 12,350	$ 11,807
Fuel ($2.52 per gallon)	$ 0.42	$ 44,772	$ 54,600	$ 52,198
Maintenance	$ 0.10	$ 10,660	$ 13,000	$ 12,428
Insurance	$ 0.10	$ 10,660	$ 13,000	$ 12,428
Total Variable Costs		$ 116,727	$ 142,350	$ 136,087
Fixed Costs	Annual			
Tractor Depreciation	$ 13,000	$ 13,000	$ 13,000	$ 13,000
Trailer Depreciation	$ 2,500	$ 15,000	$ 7,500	-
Legalization/Recruiting/Adm	$ 17,500	$ 17,500	$ 17,500	$ 17,500
Total Fixed Costs		$ 45,500	$ 38,000	$ 30,500
Total Annual Costs		$ 162,227	$ 180,350	$ 166,587
Expected Operating Ratio		86.0%	89.0%	92.0%
Desired Gross Revenue		$ 188,636	$ 202,640	$ 181,072
Less: Total Annual Costs		$ 162,227	$ 180,350	$ 166,587
Operating Income		$ 26,409	$ 22,290	$ 14,486
Operating Ratio		86.0%	89.0%	92.0%

Deal A has the lowest operating ratio and the highest operating income on a per truck basis. Deal C has the highest operating ratio and the lowest operating income on a per truck basis. Deal B is relatively standard with three trailers per tractor and an operating ratio of 89.0%.

The cost model correctly reflects the fact that Deal A requires six trailers, Deal B requires three trailers, and Deal C requires no trailers.[67] However, the above analysis does not take into consideration the overall upfront investment in tractors and trailers associated with each deal on a per-tractor basis. To complete the analysis, the investment side of each opportunity must be included in the evaluation.

---

[67] For some fleets, shippers may choose to provide their own trailers. Shippers may already own a fleet of trailers or have specialized equipment needs that dictate that the trailers be owned by the shipper.

The table below introduces the initial investment required for each deal, assuming equipment costs of $80,000 per tractor and $20,000 per trailer.

Total Equipment Investment	Fleet Opportunity A	B	C
Investment Summary			
Tractor Cost Per Unit	$ 80,000	$ 80,000	$ 80,000
Trailer Cost Per Unit	$ 20,000	$ 20,000	$ 20,000
Total Tractor Investment	$ 80,000	$ 80,000	$ 80,000
Total Trailer Investment	$ 120,000	$ 60,000	$ -
Grand Total Investment/Assets	**$ 200,000**	**$ 140,000**	**$ 80,000**

Total Investment Per Tractor

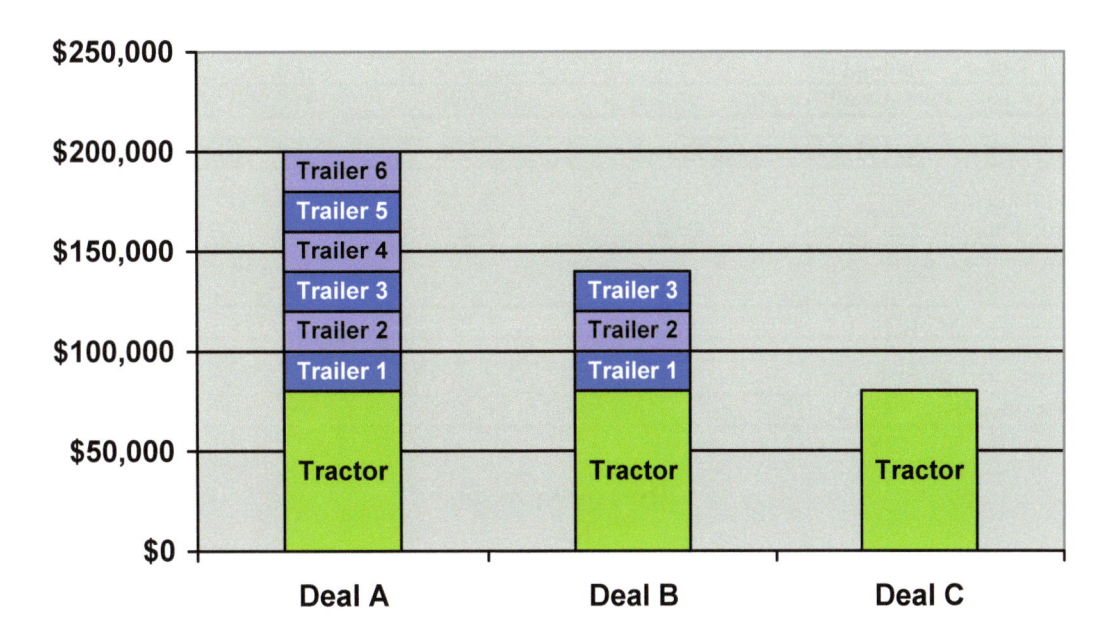

[Bar chart showing Deal A at $200,000 (Tractor + Trailers 1-6), Deal B at $140,000 (Tractor + Trailers 1-3), and Deal C at $80,000 (Tractor only).]

Notice that the total investment in Deal A is $200,000 because of the $120,000 investment in the six required trailers per tractor. The total investment for Deal B is only $140,000 because this opportunity only requires three trailers per tractor. Deal C requires a much smaller total investment, only $80,000 for the tractor, because this opportunity does not require the carrier to provide trailers. **These three different investment levels must be accounted for in the analysis and pricing process.**

To correctly introduce the impact of the investment requirements of each deal into the analysis, a return on assets or return on investment approach should be applied. Return on assets is simply the ratio of net income to total assets. Return on assets measures how efficiently assets are being managed to create profits. Return on assets takes into account revenues, expenses, taxes, and total assets while operating ratio only takes into account revenue and operating expenses. The table below computes the return on assets for each deal assuming 75% of the investment capital must be borrowed at 9.5% interest. The analysis also assumes a marginal tax rate of 36.0%.

Return on Assets by Fleet		Fleet Opportunity A	Fleet Opportunity B	Fleet Opportunity C
Investment Summary				
Tractor Cost Per Unit		$ 80,000	$ 80,000	$ 80,000
Trailer Cost Per Unit		$ 20,000	$ 20,000	$ 20,000
Total Tractor Investment		$ 80,000	$ 80,000	$ 80,000
Total Trailer Investment		$ 120,000	$ 60,000	$ -
Grand Total Investment/Assets		**$ 200,000**	**$ 140,000**	**$ 80,000**
Borrowing to Finance Equipment Purchase		$ 150,000	$ 105,000	$ 60,000
Operating Income		$ 26,409	$ 22,290	$ 14,486
Less: Interest Expense	9.50%	$ 14,250	$ 9,975	$ 5,700
Earnings Before Tax		$ 12,159	$ 12,315	$ 8,786
Less: Taxes	36.0%	$ 4,377	$ 4,434	$ 3,163
Earnings After Tax		**$ 7,782**	**$ 7,882**	**$ 5,623**
Return on Assets		**3.89%**	**5.63%**	**7.03%**
Operating Ratio		**86.00%**	**89.00%**	**92.00%**

Return on Assets

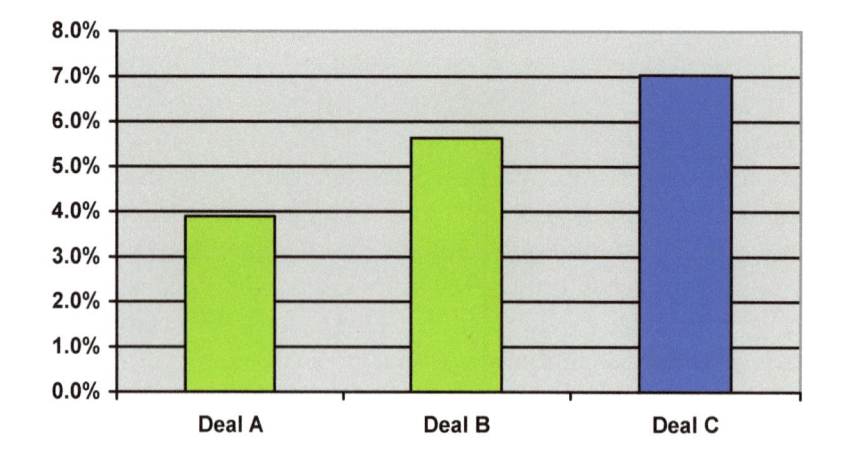

Deal	Return on Assets
Deal A	~3.89%
Deal B	~5.63%
Deal C	~7.03%

Perhaps surprisingly, and despite a 92% operating ratio, Deal C offers a much higher return on assets than either Deal A or Deal B. **Deal C is actually the best choice of the three opportunities because it offers the highest return on assets.**

To further illustrate why Deal C is the best choice, assume the carrier has a maximum of $2,000,000 in capital available to invest in a fleet expansion. Also assume that each of the shippers offering the possible deals has a tremendous need for dedicated capacity and offers each carrier the opportunity to provide as many as 50 trucks under the proposed terms of the contract. The carrier can now determine the size of the potential fleet for each shipper after investing the entire $2,000,000 in tractors and trailers. The table below outlines these calculations.

Potential Fleet Size with $2,000,000 Investment	Fleet Opportunity A	Fleet Opportunity B	Fleet Opportunity C
Investment Capital Available	$ 2,000,000	$ 2,000,000	$ 2,000,000
Tractors	1	1	1
Trailers	6	3	-
Investment Summary			
Tractor Cost Per Unit	$ 80,000	$ 80,000	$ 80,000
Trailer Cost Per Unit	$ 20,000	$ 20,000	$ 20,000
Total Tractor Investment	$ 80,000	$ 80,000	$ 80,000
Total Trailer Investment	$ 120,000	$ 60,000	$ -
Total Investment Per Tractor	$ 200,000	$ 140,000	$ 80,000
Potential Fleet Size			
Tractors	10.00	14.29	25.00
Trailers	60.00	42.86	-
Equipment Purchases			
Tractors	$ 800,000	$ 1,142,857	$ 2,000,000
Trailers	$ 1,200,000	$ 857,143	$ -
Total Investment	$ 2,000,000	$ 2,000,000	$ 2,000,000

Maximum Fleet Size (Tractors) with $2,000,000 Investment

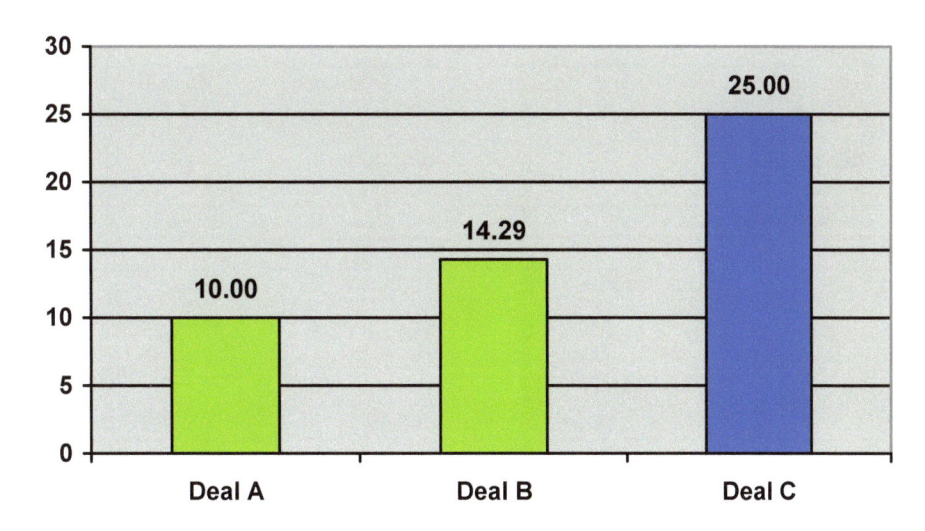

- Deal A: 10.00
- Deal B: 14.29
- Deal C: 25.00

For Deal A, $800,000 is invested in 10 tractors and $1,200,000 is invested in the required 60 trailers. For Deal C, the entire $2,000,000 is invested only in tractors, allowing the carrier to create a 25 truck fleet with the same amount of capital. The table below shows the total revenue, operating income, and earnings after tax that each fleet would generate after the $2,000,000 investment in the maximum fleet size.

Projected Income Statements at Maximum Fleet Size			Fleet Opportunity A	Fleet Opportunity B	Fleet Opportunity C
Fleet Summary:					
Tractors			10	14	25
Trailers			60	43	-
Utilization (Weekly Miles)			2,050	2,500	2,390
Total Annual Fleet Miles			1,066,000	1,857,143	3,107,000
Expected Operating Ratio			86.0%	89.0%	92.0%
Desired Gross Revenue			$ 1,886,360	$ 2,894,864	$ 4,526,810
Variable Costs	Per Mile				
Driver Pay (Min = $700)	$ 0.38	$	405,080	$ 705,714	$ 1,180,660
Fringe Benefits	25.0%	$	101,270	$ 176,429	$ 295,165
Fuel ($2.52 per gallon)	$ 0.42	$	447,720	$ 780,000	$ 1,304,940
Maintenance	$ 0.10	$	106,600	$ 185,714	$ 310,700
Insurance	$ 0.10	$	106,600	$ 185,714	$ 310,700
Total Variable Costs		$	1,167,270	$ 2,033,571	$ 3,402,165
Fixed Costs	Annual				
Tractor Depreciation	$ 13,000	$	130,000	$ 185,714	$ 325,000
Trailer Depreciation	$ 2,500	$	150,000	$ 107,143	-
Legalization/Recruiting/Adm	$ 17,500	$	175,000	$ 250,000	$ 437,500
Total Fixed Costs		$	455,000	$ 542,857	$ 762,500
Total Annual Costs		$	1,622,270	$ 2,576,429	$ 4,164,665
Operating Income		$	264,090	$ 318,435	$ 362,145
Operating Ratio			86.0%	89.0%	92.0%
Investment Summary					
Tractor Cost Per Unit		$	80,000	$ 80,000	$ 80,000
Trailer Cost Per Unit		$	20,000	$ 20,000	$ 20,000
Total Tractor Investment		$	800,000	$ 1,142,857	$ 2,000,000
Total Trailer Investment		$	1,200,000	$ 857,143	-
Grand Total Investment/Assets		$	2,000,000	$ 2,000,000	$ 2,000,000
Borrowing to Finance Equipment Purchase		$	1,500,000	$ 1,500,000	$ 1,500,000
Operating Income		$	264,090	$ 318,435	$ 362,145
Less: Interest Expense	9.50%	$	142,500	$ 142,500	$ 142,500
Earnings Before Tax		$	121,590	$ 175,935	$ 219,645
Less: Taxes	36.0%	$	43,773	$ 63,337	$ 79,072
Earnings After Tax		$	77,818	$ 112,598	$ 140,573
Return on Assets			3.89%	5.63%	7.03%
Operating Ratio			86.00%	89.00%	92.00%

Since Deal C will have 25 trucks and Deal A will only have 10 trucks, the total revenues generated by Deal C will be more than double those generated by Deal A.

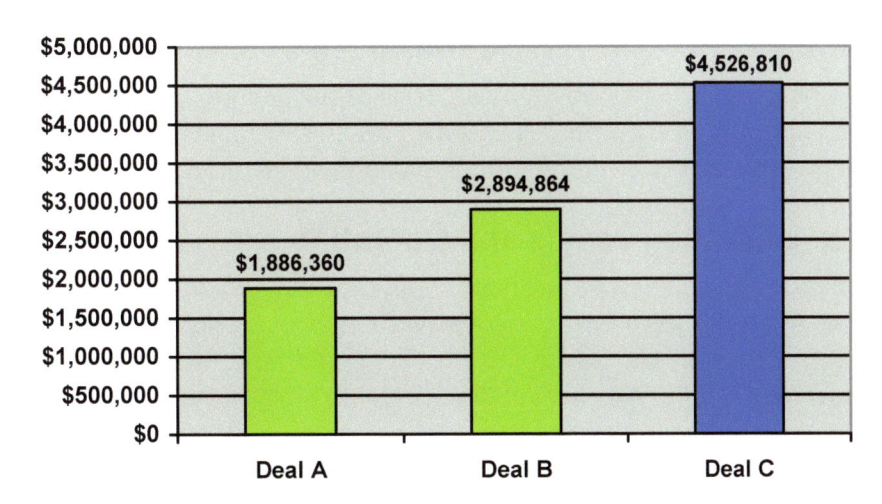

Total Gross Fleet Revenues

Deal A	$1,886,360
Deal B	$2,894,864
Deal C	$4,526,810

Even though the profit on a per-truck basis is lower in Deal C, the total fleet profit is much greater than Deal A because of the additional 15 trucks included in the fleet. Also notice that Deal C generates 3,107,000 annual fleet miles while Deal A generates only 1,066,000 annual fleet miles.

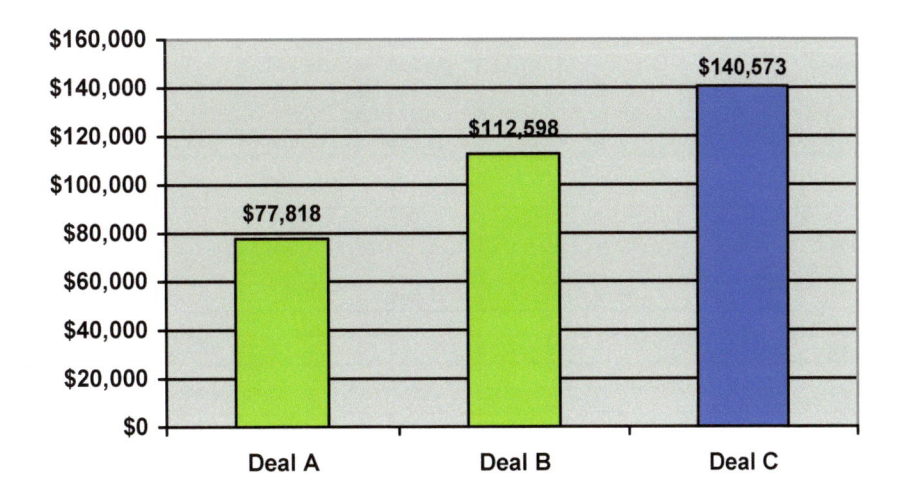

Total Fleet Earnings After Tax

Deal A	$77,818
Deal B	$112,598
Deal C	$140,573

Based on this analysis, Deal C is clearly the best fleet to choose to maximize both profits and return on investment. Deal C offers the largest fleet size, the highest total revenue and, most importantly, and the highest total earnings on the same $2,000,000 investment.

Based on this analysis, the level of investment is clearly a critical element of the fleet analysis process. Assuming one fleet is more profitable than another strictly on the basis of operating ratio is not always correct. In addition to investment levels, utilization levels also play a key role in the pricing design process as shown in the sections that follow.

Utilization and Trailer Ratio Scenario Analysis

The scenarios below provide a sensitivity analysis of the key pricing variables of utilization and trailer-to-tractor ratio. These two pricing variables can create significant gaps in pricing between the operating ratio approach and the investment-based approach.

Scenario 1: Utilization Levels and Operating Ratio Pricing

The first scenario is an analysis of profitability as expected utilization on a dedicated fleet increases from 800 miles per week to 2,800 miles per week. The example shown is based on 1 tractor and 3 trailers. The driver will earn $0.38 per mile, with a minimum weekly pay of $700 per week. The other cost assumptions are fairly straightforward.

The pricing (revenue) for each utilization level is based on an 88% operating ratio. The desired gross revenue for each utilization level is computed as total annual cost divided by the 0.88 operating ratio target.

Utilization Analysis Operating Ratio Pricing			Estimated Weekly Tractor Utilization (Miles)					
			800	1,200	1,600	2,000	2,400	2,800
Fleet Summary:			Tractors: 1			Trailers: 3		
Variable Costs	Per Mile							
Driver Pay (Min = $700)	$ 0.38	$	36,400	$ 36,400	$ 36,400	$ 39,520	$ 47,424	$ 55,328
Fringe Benefits	25.0%	$	9,100	9,100	9,100	9,880	11,856	13,832
Fuel ($2.52 per gallon)	$ 0.42	$	17,472	26,208	34,944	43,680	52,416	61,152
Maintenance	$ 0.10	$	4,160	6,240	8,320	10,400	12,480	14,560
Insurance	$ 0.10	$	4,160	6,240	8,320	10,400	12,480	14,560
Total Variable Costs		$	71,292	$ 84,188	$ 97,084	$ 113,880	$ 136,656	$ 159,432
Fixed Costs	Annual							
Tractor Depreciation	$ 13,000	$	13,000	13,000	13,000	13,000	13,000	13,000
Trailer Depreciation	$ 2,500	$	7,500	7,500	7,500	7,500	7,500	7,500
Legalization/Recruiting/Adm	$ 17,500	$	17,500	17,500	17,500	17,500	17,500	17,500
Total Fixed Costs		$	38,000	$ 38,000	$ 38,000	$ 38,000	$ 38,000	$ 38,000
Total Annual Costs		$	109,292	$ 122,188	$ 135,084	$ 151,880	$ 174,656	$ 197,432
Desired Operating Ratio			88.0%	88.0%	88.0%	88.0%	88.0%	88.0%
Desired Gross Revenue		$	124,195	$ 138,850	$ 153,505	$ 172,591	$ 198,473	$ 224,355
Less: Total Annual Costs		$	109,292	$ 122,188	$ 135,084	$ 151,880	$ 174,656	$ 197,432
Operating Income		$	14,903	$ 16,662	$ 18,421	$ 20,711	$ 23,817	$ 26,923
Operating Ratio			88.0%	88.0%	88.0%	88.0%	88.0%	88.0%

Notice that the operating ratio for each utilization level is 88%. Also notice that the operating income ranges from $14,903 at 800 miles per week to $26,923 at 2,800 miles per week. Operating income increases as utilization increases because the total variable costs are increasing as more and more mileage-based costs such as fuel, maintenance and driver pay are incurred. As costs increase, revenues and profits also increase proportionately as a result of the operating ratio, cost-plus approach.

The second half of the analysis shown below extends beyond just revenue and expenses and introduces the investment side of the deal into the evaluation.

Utilization Analysis Operating Ratio Pricing		\multicolumn{6}{c}{Estimated Weekly Tractor Utilization (Miles)}
		800	1,200	1,600	2,000	2,400	2,800
Tractors		1	1	1	1	1	1
Trailers		3	3	3	3	3	3
Tractor Cost Per Unit		$ 80,000	$ 80,000	$ 80,000	$ 80,000	$ 80,000	$ 80,000
Trailer Cost Per Unit		$ 20,000	$ 20,000	$ 20,000	$ 20,000	$ 20,000	$ 20,000
Total Tractor Investment		$ 80,000	$ 80,000	$ 80,000	$ 80,000	$ 80,000	$ 80,000
Total Trailer Investment		$ 60,000	$ 60,000	$ 60,000	$ 60,000	$ 60,000	$ 60,000
Grand Total Investment/Assets		**$ 140,000**	**$ 140,000**	**$ 140,000**	**$ 140,000**	**$ 140,000**	**$ 140,000**
Borrowing to Finance Equipment Purchase		$ 105,000	$ 105,000	$ 105,000	$ 105,000	$ 105,000	$ 105,000
Operating Income		$ 14,903	$ 16,662	$ 18,421	$ 20,711	$ 23,817	$ 26,923
Less: Interest Expense	9.50%	$ 9,975	$ 9,975	$ 9,975	$ 9,975	$ 9,975	$ 9,975
Earnings Before Tax		$ 4,928	$ 6,687	$ 8,446	$ 10,736	$ 13,842	$ 16,948
Less: Taxes	36.0%	$ 1,774	$ 2,407	$ 3,040	$ 3,865	$ 4,983	$ 6,101
Earnings After Tax		**$ 3,154**	**$ 4,280**	**$ 5,405**	**$ 6,871**	**$ 8,859**	**$ 10,846**
Return on Assets		**2.25%**	**3.06%**	**3.86%**	**4.91%**	**6.33%**	**7.75%**
Operating Ratio		**88.00%**	**88.00%**	**88.00%**	**88.00%**	**88.00%**	**88.00%**

The total investment (assets) is the same regardless of the utilization level, one truck at $80,000 and 3 trailers at $20,000 each for a total investment of $140,000. The operating income line comes directly from the operating income on the previous operating ratio portion of the analysis.

To determine return on assets, borrowing, interest expense, and taxes are also introduced to compute the earnings after tax for each utilization scenario. Return on assets for each utilization level is the earnings after tax divided by the total assets of $140,000. For example, the calculation of return on assets for the 800 mile scenario is shown below.

$$\text{Return on Assets (800)} = \frac{\text{Earnings After Tax}}{\text{Total Assets}} = \frac{\$\,3,154}{\$\,140,000} = 2.25\%$$

Notice that the return on assets ranges from 2.25% at 800 miles per week up to 7.75% at 2,800 miles per week. Since the carrier is using the operating ratio method to compute the margin, the operating ratio for each scenario is always at the desired level of 88%.

As a baseline, assume that the carrier's target level of return on assets is 5.0%, which is right around the level achieved at 2,000 miles of utilization. The 88% operating ratio pricing has failed to generate enough revenue and earnings to achieve the desired return on assets for all utilization levels less than 2,000 miles.

The graph below illustrates the performance of each scenario based on both the operating ratio and return on assets criteria.

Operating Ratio vs Return on Assets
Pricing Based on Operating Ratio

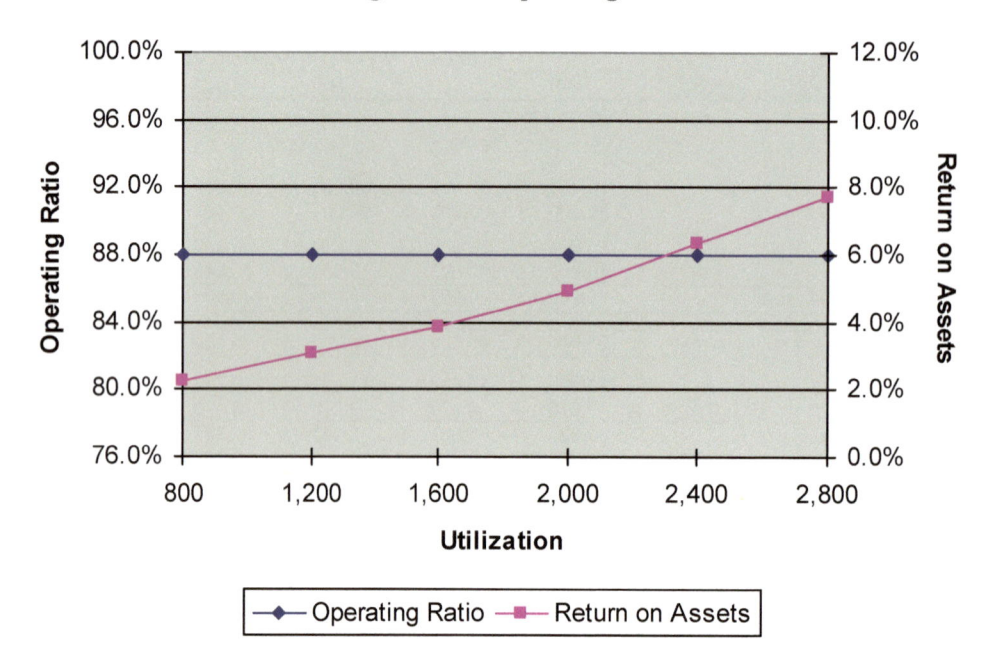

Operating ratio is based only on revenue and operating costs and does not take into account the assets (investment) associated with the project. As a result, the pricing for the low utilization levels results in an inadequate return on assets level at 800, 1,200, and 1,600 miles of utilization.

Since these opportunities are being priced too low, there is a good chance the carrier will be awarded these opportunities by the shipper. At higher utilization levels, the return on assets is excellent. Unfortunately, the carrier is likely quoting a price that is too high and may not be competitive with other carriers also quoting on the opportunity. The opportunity to secure a profitable dedicated fleet is lost, primarily due to an inaccurate pricing technique.

Scenario 1: Utilization and Return on Assets Pricing

As has been illustrated, the operating ratio pricing method fails to fully adjust pricing for extremely low or extremely high utilization levels. The pricing approach must account for both the investment level and operating costs to be completely accurate. A pricing approach where the goal is to achieve a target return on assets, regardless of operating ratio, provides the theoretical framework to correctly adjust pricing for different utilization and investment levels.

For the purposes of this illustration, assume the carrier has a target return on assets of 5%, which is very close to the return on assets that was achieved at 2,000 miles of utilization in the previous operating ratio analysis. The table below provides new pricing (desired gross revenue) based on the 5% return on assets target at all levels of tractor utilization. Operating ratio is computed based on the revenue levels determined through the return on assets approach.

Utilization Analysis Return on Assets Pricing			Estimated Weekly Tractor Utilization (Miles)					
			800	1,200	1,600	2,000	2,400	2,800
Fleet Summary:			Tractors: 1			Trailers: 3		
Variable Costs	Per Mile							
Driver Pay (Min = $700)	0.38	$	36,400	36,400	36,400	39,520	47,424	55,328
Fringe Benefits	25.0%	$	9,100	9,100	9,100	9,880	11,856	13,832
Fuel ($2.52 per gallon)	0.42	$	17,472	26,208	34,944	43,680	52,416	61,152
Maintenance	0.10	$	4,160	6,240	8,320	10,400	12,480	14,560
Insurance	0.10	$	4,160	6,240	8,320	10,400	12,480	14,560
Total Variable Costs		$	71,292	84,188	97,084	113,880	136,656	159,432
Fixed Costs	Annual							
Tractor Depreciation	13,000	$	13,000	13,000	13,000	13,000	13,000	13,000
Trailer Depreciation	2,500	$	7,500	7,500	7,500	7,500	7,500	7,500
Legalization/Recruiting/Adm	17,500	$	17,500	17,500	17,500	17,500	17,500	17,500
Total Fixed Costs		$	38,000	38,000	38,000	38,000	38,000	38,000
Total Annual Costs		$	109,292	122,188	135,084	151,880	174,656	197,432
Desired Return on Assets			5.0%	5.0%	5.0%	5.0%	5.0%	5.0%
Desired Gross Revenue		$	130,205	143,101	155,997	172,793	195,569	218,345
Less: Total Annual Costs		$	109,292	122,188	135,084	151,880	174,656	197,432
Operating Income		$	20,913	20,913	20,913	20,913	20,913	20,913
Operating Ratio			83.9%	85.4%	86.6%	87.9%	89.3%	90.4%
Tractors			1	1	1	1	1	1
Trailers			3	3	3	3	3	3
Tractor Cost Per Unit		$	80,000	80,000	80,000	80,000	80,000	80,000
Trailer Cost Per Unit		$	20,000	20,000	20,000	20,000	20,000	20,000
Total Tractor Investment		$	80,000	80,000	80,000	80,000	80,000	80,000
Total Trailer Investment		$	60,000	60,000	60,000	60,000	60,000	60,000
Grand Total Investment/Assets		$	140,000	140,000	140,000	140,000	140,000	140,000
Borrowing to Finance Equipment Purchase		$	105,000	105,000	105,000	105,000	105,000	105,000
Operating Income		$	20,913	20,913	20,913	20,913	20,913	20,913
Less: Interest Expense	9.50%	$	9,975	9,975	9,975	9,975	9,975	9,975
Earnings Before Tax		$	10,938	10,938	10,938	10,938	10,938	10,938
Less: Taxes	36.0%	$	3,938	3,938	3,938	3,938	3,938	3,938
Earnings After Tax		$	7,000	7,000	7,000	7,000	7,000	7,000
Return on Assets			5.00%	5.00%	5.00%	5.00%	5.00%	5.00%

Each utilization scenario generates an operating income of $20,913 and earnings after tax of $7,000. The revenue level is set so that the earnings after tax is exactly $7,000 for each scenario. $7,000 is exactly 5% of the asset base of $140,000. Operating ratio is computed based on the revenue streams suggested by the return on assets pricing approach.

Notice that the operating ratio levels that result from this method range from 83.9% at 800 miles per week up to 90.4% at 2,800 miles per week. The graph below compares the results of return on assets and operating ratio at each utilization level.

Operating Ratio vs Return on Assets
Pricing Based on Return on Assets

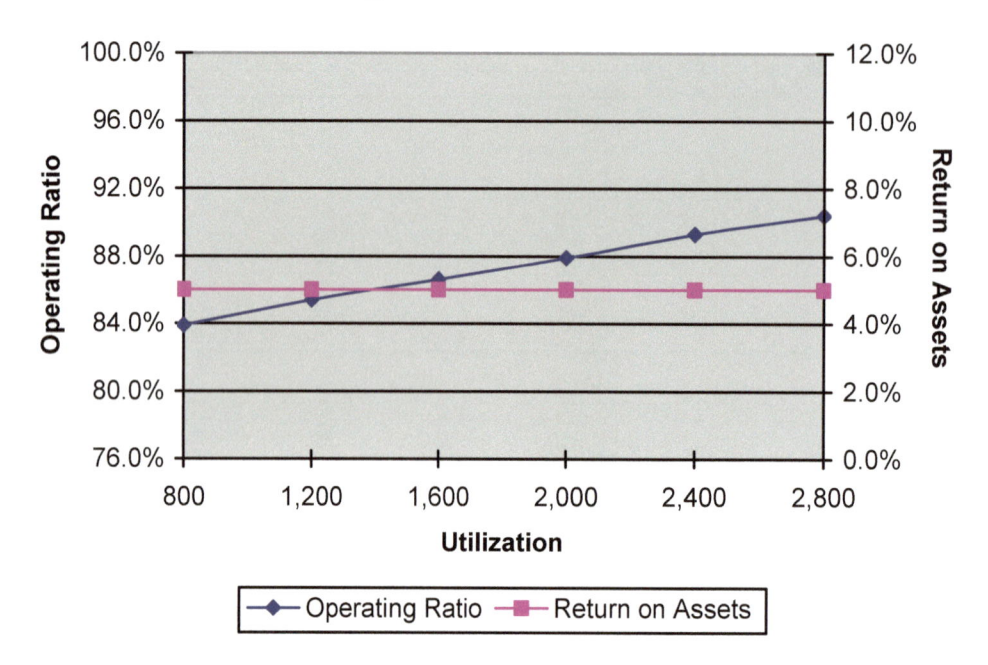

Return on assets remains constant at the planned level of 5% while the operating ratio increases as utilization increases. The operating ratio is increasing because variable expenses such as fuel, maintenance, and driver pay are also increasing. At the same time, revenues are increasing to cover these expenses, but only at a rate equal to the amount needed to cover the expenses. All the profits are set at $7,000 for each scenario to meet the target return on assets level of 5%. Operating ratio increases as utilization increases because additional incremental variable expenses are added to the total cost base.

Keep in mind that this analysis is intended only as an illustration of the weaknesses and risks of relying exclusively on operating ratio to determine dedicated pricing. The return on assets approach provides a simple framework for this illustration. The recommended investment-based approach will be presented later in this chapter.

The graph that follows provides a side-by-side comparison of the annual per-truck revenue levels (pricing) recommended by both the traditional operating ratio method and the recommended return on assets method.

Total Revenue by Pricing Method

[Bar chart showing OR Pricing and ROA Pricing across Weekly Utilization levels of 800, 1,200, 1,600, 2,000, 2,400, and 2,800]

Low Utilization (800 to 1,200). Return on assets recommends higher revenue levels than the operating ratio method in the low utilization ranges. The revenue recommended by the operating ratio method is too low because the variable costs and total cost basis are lower at these utilization levels. Since utilization is low, variable costs are also low in total. The cost-plus approach fails to generate enough revenue and margin because the underlying cost base is too low. The return on assets method, based on the level of investment instead of operating cost, is adding more margin than the operating ratio method to compensate for the very low utilization.

Average Utilization (1,600 to 2,000). Return on assets recommends around the same level of revenue in these mileage ranges, especially at the 2,000 mile level. The revenue amounts are so close because the utilization levels are right around an industry average level for all trucks. Since the traditional 88% operating ratio rule-of-thumb is based on utilization in this range, both methods yield approximately the same suggested revenue.

High Utilization (2,400 to 2,800). Return on assets recommends lower revenue levels than the operating ratio method at the higher utilization levels. Since operating ratio is fully dependent on the total cost of the operation, too much margin (profit) is added to these additional miles and the associated costs. The return on assets method recognizes that the incremental miles in these high utilization scenarios do not require as much margin because the needed level of gross margin was already earned on the first 2,000 miles. As a result, high utilization fleets can safely be priced at a higher operating ratio because the larger underlying cost basis generates a higher level of total margin.

Scenario 2: Trailer Ratio and Operating Ratio Pricing

Much like the previous scenario involving utilization, the amount of trailers on a per-tractor basis has a dramatic impact on pricing and profitability. In fact, because the investment base is changing as the trailer ratio changes, the inaccuracy of the operating ratio pricing method is even more severe at different trailer levels than at different utilization levels.

Following the same cost model and format as the utilization scenarios, the operating ratio-based pricing is shown in the table below. Instead of utilization defining the various scenarios, the trailers per tractor level defines the scenarios. The scenarios range from 0 trailers up to 9 trailers per tractor.

Trailer Investment Levels / Operating Ratio Pricing			Trailers Per Tractor (Trailer Ratio)					
			0	1	3	5	7	9
Fleet Summary:			Tractors: 1			Utilization: 2,000		
Variable Costs	Per Mile							
Driver Pay (Min = $700)	$ 0.38	$	39,520	$ 39,520	$ 39,520	$ 39,520	$ 39,520	$ 39,520
Fringe Benefits	25.0%	$	9,880	$ 9,880	$ 9,880	$ 9,880	$ 9,880	$ 9,880
Fuel ($2.52 per gallon)	$ 0.42	$	43,680	$ 43,680	$ 43,680	$ 43,680	$ 43,680	$ 43,680
Maintenance	$ 0.10	$	10,400	$ 10,400	$ 10,400	$ 10,400	$ 10,400	$ 10,400
Insurance	$ 0.10	$	10,400	$ 10,400	$ 10,400	$ 10,400	$ 10,400	$ 10,400
Total Variable Costs		$	113,880	$ 113,880	$ 113,880	$ 113,880	$ 113,880	$ 113,880
Fixed Costs	Annual							
Tractor Depreciation	$ 13,000	$	13,000	$ 13,000	$ 13,000	$ 13,000	$ 13,000	$ 13,000
Trailer Depreciation	$ 2,500	$	-	$ 2,500	$ 7,500	$ 12,500	$ 17,500	$ 22,500
Legalization/Recruiting/Adm	$ 17,500	$	17,500	$ 17,500	$ 17,500	$ 17,500	$ 17,500	$ 17,500
Total Fixed Costs		$	30,500	$ 33,000	$ 38,000	$ 43,000	$ 48,000	$ 53,000
Total Annual Costs		$	144,380	$ 146,880	$ 151,880	$ 156,880	$ 161,880	$ 166,880
Desired Operating Ratio			88.0%	88.0%	88.0%	88.0%	88.0%	88.0%
Desired Gross Revenue		$	164,068	$ 166,909	$ 172,591	$ 178,273	$ 183,955	$ 189,636
Less: Total Annual Costs		$	144,380	$ 146,880	$ 151,880	$ 156,880	$ 161,880	$ 166,880
Operating Income		$	19,688	$ 20,029	$ 20,711	$ 21,393	$ 22,075	$ 22,756
Operating Ratio			88.0%	88.0%	88.0%	88.0%	88.0%	88.0%
Tractors			1	1	1	1	1	1
Utilization			2,000	2,000	2,000	2,000	2,000	2,000
Tractor Cost Per Unit		$	80,000	$ 80,000	$ 80,000	$ 80,000	$ 80,000	$ 80,000
Trailer Cost Per Unit		$	20,000	$ 20,000	$ 20,000	$ 20,000	$ 20,000	$ 20,000
Total Tractor Investment		$	80,000	$ 80,000	$ 80,000	$ 80,000	$ 80,000	$ 80,000
Total Trailer Investment		$	-	$ 20,000	$ 60,000	$ 100,000	$ 140,000	$ 180,000
Grand Total Investment/Assets		$	80,000	$ 100,000	$ 140,000	$ 180,000	$ 220,000	$ 260,000
Borrowing to Finance Equipment Purchase		$	60,000	$ 75,000	$ 105,000	$ 135,000	$ 165,000	$ 195,000
Operating Income		$	19,688	$ 20,029	$ 20,711	$ 21,393	$ 22,075	$ 22,756
Less: Interest Expense	9.50%	$	5,700	$ 7,125	$ 9,975	$ 12,825	$ 15,675	$ 18,525
Earnings Before Tax		$	13,988	$ 12,904	$ 10,736	$ 8,568	$ 6,400	$ 4,231
Less: Taxes	36.0%	$	5,036	$ 4,645	$ 3,865	$ 3,084	$ 2,304	$ 1,523
Earnings After Tax		$	8,952	$ 8,259	$ 6,871	$ 5,483	$ 4,096	$ 2,708
Return on Assets			11.19%	8.26%	4.91%	3.05%	1.86%	1.04%
Operating Ratio			88.00%	88.00%	88.00%	88.00%	88.00%	88.00%

As the asset base increases, the return on assets declines dramatically. The return on assets is 11.19% at 0 trailers and only 1.04% at the 9 trailer level. Operating ratio remains constant at 88% for each trailer level. The graph below illustrates the dramatic decline in return on assets as the trailer level increases.

Operating Ratio vs Return on Assets
Pricing Based on Operating Ratio

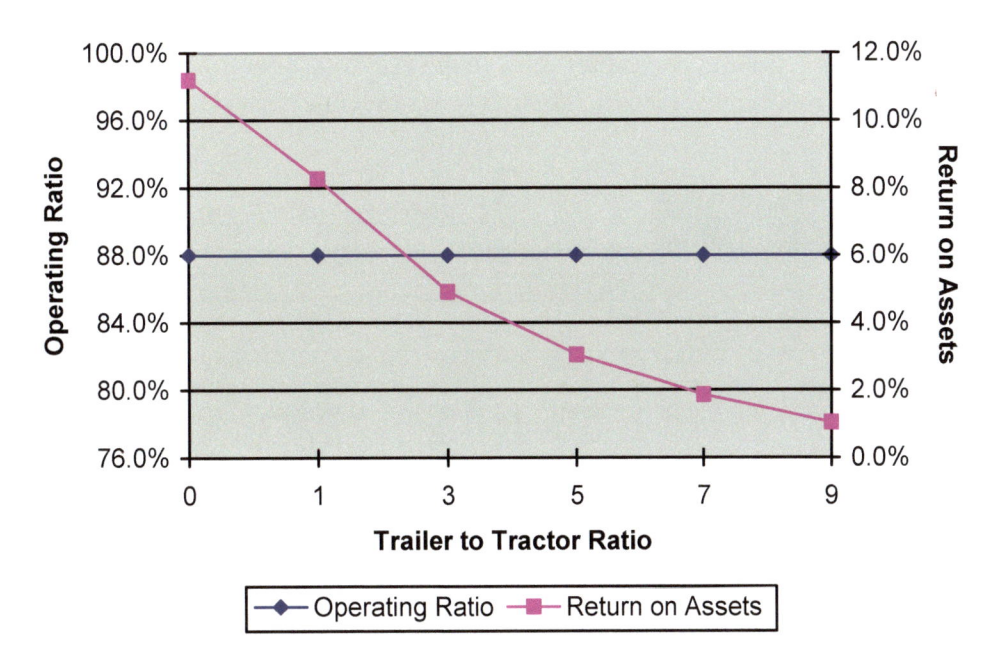

The operating ratio method accurately adjusts for the depreciation costs of each additional trailer, but fails to adjust to the increasing investment level and asset base. The operating ratio method has over-priced the 0 trailer scenario and under-priced the 9 trailer scenario. Also notice that the operating ratio line and the return on assets line cross at around the 2.7 trailer level, which is right around the industry standard trailer level.

Scenario 2: Trailer Ratio and Return on Assets Pricing

As has been illustrated, the operating ratio pricing method fails to fully adjust pricing for extremely low or extremely high trailer ratio levels because the underlying asset base is not accounted for in the approach. A pricing approach where the goal is to achieve a target return on assets, regardless of operating ratio, provides the framework to properly adjust pricing for different trailer ratio requirements. For the purposes of this illustration, assume a target return on assets of 5%, which is very close to the return on assets that was achieved at the 3 trailers per tractor ratio in the previous operating ratio analysis. The table below provides new pricing (desired gross revenue) based on the 5% return on assets target.

Trailer Investment Levels Return on Assets Pricing		0	1	3	5	7	9
Fleet Summary:		Tractors: 1			Utilization: 2,000		
Variable Costs	Per Mile						
Driver Pay (Min = $700)	$ 0.38	$ 39,520	$ 39,520	$ 39,520	$ 39,520	$ 39,520	$ 39,520
Fringe Benefits	25.0%	$ 9,880	$ 9,880	$ 9,880	$ 9,880	$ 9,880	$ 9,880
Fuel ($2.52 per gallon)	$ 0.42	$ 43,680	$ 43,680	$ 43,680	$ 43,680	$ 43,680	$ 43,680
Maintenance	$ 0.10	$ 10,400	$ 10,400	$ 10,400	$ 10,400	$ 10,400	$ 10,400
Insurance	$ 0.10	$ 10,400	$ 10,400	$ 10,400	$ 10,400	$ 10,400	$ 10,400
Total Variable Costs		$ 113,880	$ 113,880	$ 113,880	$ 113,880	$ 113,880	$ 113,880
Fixed Costs	Annual						
Tractor Depreciation	$ 13,000	$ 13,000	$ 13,000	$ 13,000	$ 13,000	$ 13,000	$ 13,000
Trailer Depreciation	$ 2,500	$ -	$ 2,500	$ 7,500	$ 12,500	$ 17,500	$ 22,500
Legalization/Recruiting/Adm	$ 17,500	$ 17,500	$ 17,500	$ 17,500	$ 17,500	$ 17,500	$ 17,500
Total Fixed Costs		$ 30,500	$ 33,000	$ 38,000	$ 43,000	$ 48,000	$ 53,000
Total Annual Costs		$ 144,380	$ 146,880	$ 151,880	$ 156,880	$ 161,880	$ 166,880
Desired Return on Assets		*5.0%*	*5.0%*	*5.0%*	*5.0%*	*5.0%*	*5.0%*
Desired Gross Revenue		$ 156,330	$ 161,818	$ 172,793	$ 183,768	$ 194,743	$ 205,718
Less: Total Annual Costs		$ 144,380	$ 146,880	$ 151,880	$ 156,880	$ 161,880	$ 166,880
Operating Income		$ 11,950	$ 14,938	$ 20,913	$ 26,888	$ 32,863	$ 38,838
Operating Ratio		*92.4%*	*90.8%*	*87.9%*	*85.4%*	*83.1%*	*81.1%*
Tractors		1	1	1	1	1	1
Utilization		2,000	2,000	2,000	2,000	2,000	2,000
Tractor Cost Per Unit		$ 80,000	$ 80,000	$ 80,000	$ 80,000	$ 80,000	$ 80,000
Trailer Cost Per Unit		$ 20,000	$ 20,000	$ 20,000	$ 20,000	$ 20,000	$ 20,000
Total Tractor Investment		$ 80,000	$ 80,000	$ 80,000	$ 80,000	$ 80,000	$ 80,000
Total Trailer Investment		$ -	$ 20,000	$ 60,000	$ 100,000	$ 140,000	$ 180,000
Grand Total Investment/Assets		$ 80,000	$ 100,000	$ 140,000	$ 180,000	$ 220,000	$ 260,000
Borrowing to Finance Equipment Purchase		$ 60,000	$ 75,000	$ 105,000	$ 135,000	$ 165,000	$ 195,000
Operating Income		$ 11,950	$ 14,938	$ 20,913	$ 26,888	$ 32,863	$ 38,838
Less: Interest Expense	9.50%	$ 5,700	$ 7,125	$ 9,975	$ 12,825	$ 15,675	$ 18,525
Earnings Before Tax		$ 6,250	$ 7,813	$ 10,938	$ 14,063	$ 17,188	$ 20,313
Less: Taxes	36.0%	$ 2,250	$ 2,813	$ 3,938	$ 5,063	$ 6,188	$ 7,313
Earnings After Tax		$ 4,000	$ 5,000	$ 7,000	$ 9,000	$ 11,000	$ 13,000
Return on Assets		**5.00%**	**5.00%**	**5.00%**	**5.00%**	**5.00%**	**5.00%**
Operating Ratio		**92.36%**	**90.77%**	**87.90%**	**85.37%**	**83.13%**	**81.12%**

As the asset base increases, the operating ratio declines dramatically. The return on assets is maintained at 5% while the operating ratio improves from 92.36% at the 0 trailer level to 81.12% the 9 trailer level. The graph below illustrates the dramatic shift in operating ratio as the trailer level increases.

Operating Ratio vs Return on Assets
Pricing Based on Return on Assets

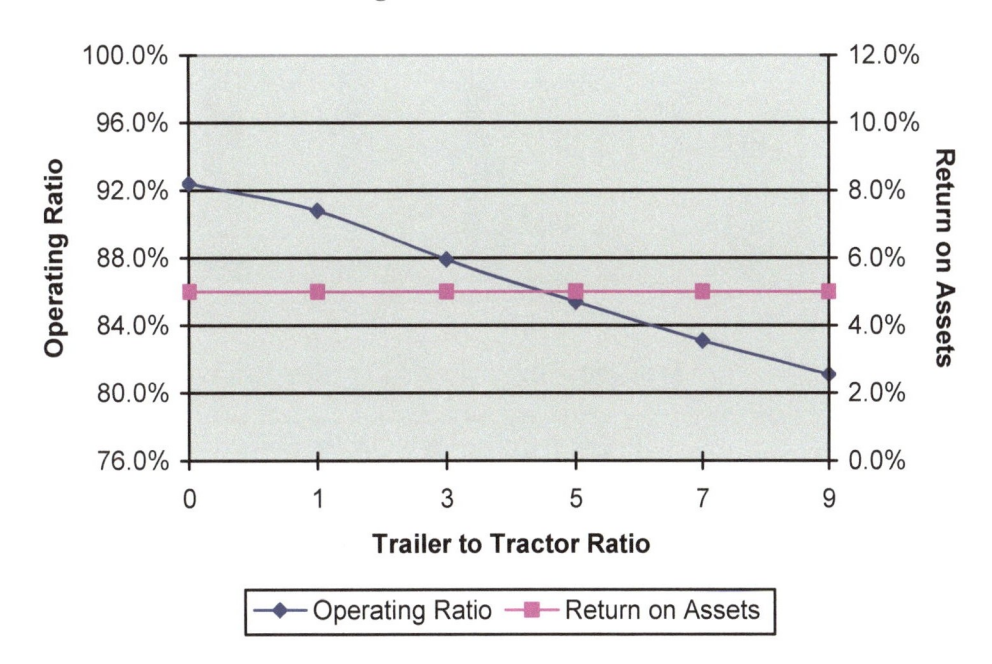

The operating ratio method accurately increases pricing for the depreciation cost of each additional trailer, but fails to adjust to the increasing investment and asset base. The return on assets method forces an even higher revenue level than operating ratio in order to generate the margin (profits) necessary to provide the required return on the increasing investment level (asset base).

An operating ratio of 88% is clearly not appropriate for all levels of the trailer to tractor ratio. The operating ratio method over-priced the highly attractive 0 trailer opportunity and under-priced the unattractive 9 trailer opportunity. If the carrier were to serve the 9 trailer per tractor fleet based on the operating ratio-based pricing, the operating profits appear attractive, but the underlying return on assets is inadequate.

The graph below provides a side-by-side comparison of the annual revenue levels (pricing) recommend by the operating ratio approach and the return on assets approach.

Total Revenue by Pricing Method

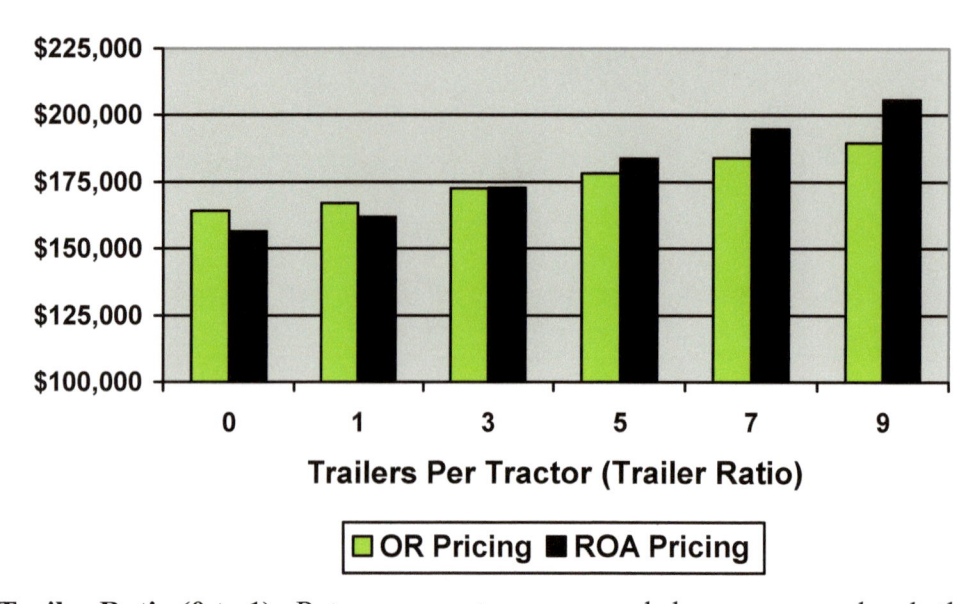

Trailers Per Tractor (Trailer Ratio)	OR Pricing	ROA Pricing
0	~$165,000	~$157,000
1	~$167,000	~$162,000
3	~$173,000	~$173,000
5	~$178,000	~$184,000
7	~$184,000	~$195,000
9	~$190,000	~$206,000

Low Trailer Ratio (0 to 1). Return on assets recommends lower revenue levels than the operating ratio method in the low trailer ratio ranges. The revenue recommended by the return on assets method is lower because the overall investment level is lower. Since the investment per tractor is lower, the fleet requires less margin and less revenue to earn an adequate return. The 88% operating ratio method only reduces the pricing for the lower depreciation cost of the trailers. The operating ratio approach does not provide the necessary adjustment for the reduction in the investment level (asset base).

Average Trailer Ratio (3). Return on assets and operating ratio recommend around the same level of revenue at the 3 trailer level. The revenue amounts are similar because the trailer levels are right around the industry average trailer level of 2.5 to 3.0 trailers per tractor. Since the traditional 88% operating ratio rule-of-thumb is based on the industry average of 2.5 to 3.0 trailers per tractor, the two methods yield approximately the same recommended revenue levels in this common trailer ratio range.

High Trailer Ratio (5 to 9). The return on assets method recommends much higher revenue levels than the operating ratio method when trailer levels are higher than normal. Since operating ratio is dependent only on the total cost of the operation, not enough margin is added to these trailer levels because the asset base is ignored by the operating ratio method. The return on assets method provides the additional revenue needed since it is directly dependent upon the size of the underlying asset base instead of only the underlying operating costs.

Investment Analysis Approach to Dedicated Pricing

Because the operating ratio method is not accurate for all situations, a more sophisticated dedicated pricing analysis approach is required. The most accurate way to establish the proper margin and pricing on dedicated fleets is to use a more sophisticated, investment analysis approach based on the criteria of Net Present Value (NPV) and Internal Rate of Return (IRR). These criteria are commonly used to evaluate incremental business investments on a cash-flow basis. The basics of these techniques will be reviewed here. A more in-depth review of these techniques can be found in the capital budgeting chapters of any basic Managerial Finance or Management Accounting textbook. After a general review, these techniques will be introduced into the dedicated pricing approach and the dedicated pricing spreadsheet model.

Review of Capital Budgeting (NPV and IRR)

Consider this simple investment example. The initial investment is $10,000, which must be paid right away. As a return, the investment will then pay $4,000 per year at the end of each year for the next four years. The chart below summarizes the cash flows associated with this investment opportunity.

Year:	0	1	2	3	4
Initial Investment	$ (10,000.00)				
Cash Inflows		$ 4,000.00	$ 4,000.00	$ 4,000.00	$ 4,000.00
Net Cash Flow	$ (10,000.00)	$ 4,000.00	$ 4,000.00	$ 4,000.00	$ 4,000.00

Now suppose a local bank has offered to loan the money for investments of this type at an annual interest rate of 10.0%. Based on this 10.0% cost of money, should the investment be made by borrowing the $10,000 from the local bank? Net present value (NPV) and internal rate of return (IRR) provide the ideal criteria for evaluating this investment opportunity.

NPV and IRR are based on the time value of money principle that a dollar today is worth more than a dollar to be received in the future. In this example, $10,000 was invested today and $16,000 will be received over the next four years, so, ignoring interest and timing, it appears that the investment yields a profit of $6,000. While this may be true, this conclusion fails to consider the "time value" of money. The analysis of the investment surely would not be the same if the investor had to wait 20 years instead of 1 year before receiving the first $4,000 payment.

To properly account for the timing of the payments, NPV and IRR can be applied to determine the true value of the investment. NPV is based on discounted cash flow techniques. Based on the interest rate (cost of funds) of 10.0%, the analysis will convert all future cash flows into present value (PV) equivalents. While this calculation can be performed a number of ways, a basic spreadsheet provides the best alternative. The table below shows the results of the NPV analysis on this investment.

Investment Analysis: Net Present Value (NPV)

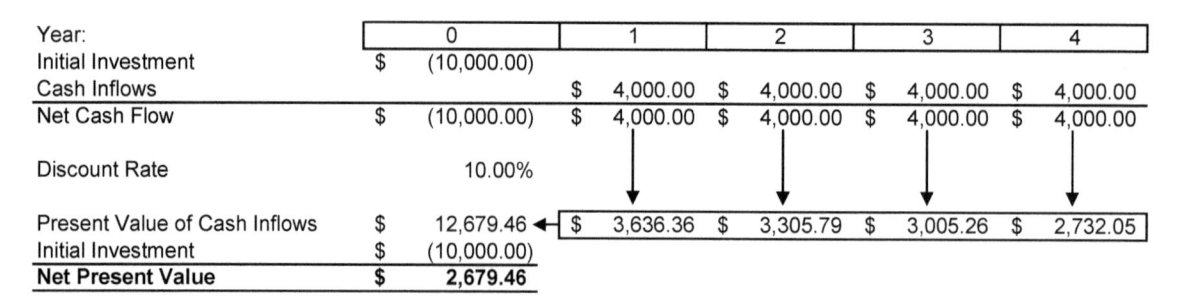

Year:	0	1	2	3	4
Initial Investment	$ (10,000.00)				
Cash Inflows		$ 4,000.00	$ 4,000.00	$ 4,000.00	$ 4,000.00
Net Cash Flow	$ (10,000.00)	$ 4,000.00	$ 4,000.00	$ 4,000.00	$ 4,000.00
Discount Rate	10.00%				
Present Value of Cash Inflows	$ 12,679.46	$ 3,636.36	$ 3,305.79	$ 3,005.26	$ 2,732.05
Initial Investment	$ (10,000.00)				
Net Present Value	$ 2,679.46				

The results show that the net present value of this investment is $2,679.46. NPV is computed as the present value of the cash inflows minus the initial investment. The rule for NPV is very simple. If the NPV is greater than or equal to $0, the investment has a positive NPV and is a favorable investment. If the NPV is less than $0, the investment has a negative NPV and is unfavorable. In this case, the positive net present value indicates that the investment yields a return in excess of the 10.0% cost of funds.

As far as the internal rate of return (IRR) criteria, the results are shown below. The spreadsheet formulas for this calculation are included in the Technical Tip at the end of this chapter.

Investment Analysis: Internal Rate of Return

Year:	0	1	2	3	4
Initial Investment	$ (10,000.00)				
Cash Inflows		$ 4,000.00	$ 4,000.00	$ 4,000.00	$ 4,000.00
Net Cash Flow	$ (10,000.00)	$ 4,000.00	$ 4,000.00	$ 4,000.00	$ 4,000.00
Discount Rate	10.00%				
Internal Rate of Return (IRR)	21.86%				

The internal rate of return is 21.86%, far greater than the 10.0% cost of funds. Therefore, based on internal rate of return, this is an excellent investment. Much like the NPV rule, if the IRR exceeds the cost of funds, the investment is considered favorable. If the IRR is less than the cost of funds, the investment is considered unfavorable. Just as was the case in this example, the NPV and IRR criteria will always lead to the same conclusion for any investment analysis.[68]

---

[68] Spreadsheet software packages provide financial functions to perform these calculations. These functions are illustrated in the Technical Tip at the end of this chapter.

Cash Flow / Investment Analysis Pricing Techniques

The Net Present Value and Internal Rate of Return investment analysis techniques provide the ideal foundation for evaluating and pricing dedicated fleet opportunities. These investment analysis tools will accurately account for the key variables of investment (tractors and trailers) and productivity (utilization). These techniques provide an analysis of both the cost and revenue of the opportunity as well as the upfront investment required to undertake the dedicated fleet.

The Steps in Investment Analysis Dedicated Fleet Pricing

The preliminary steps in investment-based pricing are the same as operating ratio pricing. The approach also requires several additional steps to facilitate the investment analysis. The primary steps in investment-based dedicated pricing are listed below.

The Steps in Investment-Based Dedicated Pricing	
Step	**Overview**
Fleet Design and Analysis	Typical fleet design including estimated utilization, number of drivers, number of tractors, and number of trailers.
Standard Operating Cost Projections	Standard fixed and variable cost projections based on the fleet design and analysis.
Total Initial Investment Projections	Compute total upfront investment including tractor costs, trailer costs, and working capital such as cash, inventory and accounts receivable.
Cash Flow Projections	Extend projections beyond operating profit to operating cash flow including taxes and non-cash expenses. Non-operating cash flows must also be estimated.
NPV and IRR Calculations	Establish preliminary pricing then compute net present value and internal rate of return for the fleet based on total investment and cash flow projections.
Set Pricing to Meet Profitability Objectives	Adjust preliminary pricing to meet or exceed minimum standards for internal rate of return and operating ratio.

The investment-based dedicated pricing approach will be explained based on the example dedicated fleet opportunity described below.

> **Example Dedicated Fleet.** A major retail shipper would like a dedicated fleet to provide weekly deliveries to each of its retail locations within a 600 mile radius of a major distribution center in Nashville, TN. After an internal analysis of historical shipment volumes, the retailer has requested dedicated pricing on a fleet of 20 trucks, 20 drivers, and 100 trailers. Each truck and driver can expect to run an average of 2,200 miles per week. However, due to seasonal business demands, actual utilization is expected to fluctuate from week to week between 1,800 and 2,500 miles. The fleet will operate 51 weeks per year after adjusting for the distribution center's scheduled holidays. The customer will have 30 day payment terms for invoices.

Each step in the investment-based pricing approach for this example fleet will be discussed in detail in the sections that follow.

Step 1: Fleet Design and Analysis

The fleet design provides estimates of the fleet size, number of trailers, and expected utilization for the dedicated fleet. For this dedicated fleet example, a fleet design is not necessary because the design was provided by the shipper.[69] The shipper in this example has requested a fleet consisting of 20 drivers, 20 tractors, and 100 trailers. Each tractor is expected to average 2,200 miles per week over 51 weeks per year. The table below shows the design entered into the dedicated pricing spreadsheet model.

Fleet Design in Pricing Model

Customer Name:	Chapter 10	Fleet Description:	Investment-Based Pricing
Fleet Parameters		**Overhead Costs**	
Number of Tractors	20.00	Tractor Legalization/Taxes	$ 2,000
Backup Tractors	0.00	Driver Recruiting Costs	$ 3,000
Number of Drivers	20.00	Administration Expenses	$ 5,000
Utilization (Miles per Tractor per Active Week)	2,200	Total Overhead (per tractor per year)	$ 10,000
Active Fleet Weeks Per Year (max = 52 weeks)	51.0		
Total Fleet Annual Miles	2,244,000	Direct Staffing (On-site CSR / Offices / Etc.)	$ -
Number of Trailers	100.00	Other Annual Expenses (Total Fleet)	$ 5,000
Trailer/Tractor Ratio	5.00	Initial Start-Up Costs (Total)	$ 10,000

The table above, from the dedicated pricing spreadsheet model, is updated to reflect the design of the fleet. The table above also includes the common overhead costs associated with the fleet, as well as other items such as on-site management and start-up costs. Each of these items is treated the same way as operating ratio-based pricing.

Step 2: Standard Operating Cost Projections

In investment-based pricing, all standard operating costs are treated exactly as they are in operating ratio-based pricing. The table below displays the primary operating cost assumptions for this example.

Standard Operating Cost Assumptions

Equipment Depreciation and Values		Other Operating Costs	
Tractors		**Fuel Costs**	
Initial Cost	$100,000	Cost Per Gallon	$1.400
Expected Salvage / Trade Value	$50,000	Miles Per Gallon	6.0
Depreciation Term (Years)	3.00	Fuel Tax	$ 0.008
Annual Depreciation Per Unit	**$16,667**	**Fuel Cost Per Mile**	**$0.241**
Monthly Depreciation Per Unit	$ 1,389		

Trailers		**Other Operating Costs**	
Initial Cost	$22,000	Insurance Cost Per Mile	$0.100
Expected Salvage / Trade Value	$13,000	Maintenance Cost Per Mile	$0.110
Depreciation Term (Years)	3.00	Fringe Benefits (% of Driver Pay)	25.0%
Annual Depreciation Per Unit	**$3,000**		
Monthly Depreciation Per Unit	$ 250		

---

[69] Future chapters provide detailed analysis methods for performing the actual fleet design process.

Each tractor is expected to cost $100,000 and each trailer is expected to cost $22,000. The base fuel cost is set at $1.40 per gallon based on the fuel peg as requested by the shipper for this example dedicated fleet. Based on an analysis of the local market and driving requirements, the carrier will set the total driver pay budget for this dedicated fleet at $44,000 per driver per year. The table below shows how other pricing parameters were entered into the dedicated pricing model spreadsheet.

Other Pricing Parameters

Other Parameters	
Driver Rate of Pay (Per Mile or Annual Gross)	$ 44,000.00
Duration of Deal/Contract (in months)	36.0
Average Collection Period (in days)	30.0

According to the customer's RFP document, the dedicated contract is expected to have a three year / 36 month term. Based on information provided by the customer, the carrier has estimated an average collection period of 30 days. These two parameters do not impact the operating cost projections. However, each of these parameters will be an important part of the investment-based pricing process that follows.

The cost projections for the example dedicated fleet are shown in the table below.

Estimated Operating Costs

Estimated Operating Costs			Fleet Totals Per Mile	Fleet Totals Annual	Per Tractor Weekly	Per Tractor Annual
Total Fleet Miles				2,244,000	2,158	112,200
Variable Costs	Assumptions					
Driver Wages	$44,000.00	$	0.39	$ 880,000	$ 846	$ 44,000
Fringe Benefits (% of wages)	25.0%	$	0.10	$ 220,000	$ 212	$ 11,000
Fuel	$0.241	$	0.24	$ 541,552	$ 521	$ 27,078
Maintenance	$0.110	$	0.11	$ 246,840	$ 237	$ 12,342
Insurance	$0.100	$	0.10	$ 224,400	$ 216	$ 11,220
Total Variable Costs		$	0.94	$ 2,112,792	$ 2,032	$ 105,640
		$	-	$ -	$ -	$ -
Fixed Costs	Assumptions	$	-	$ -	$ -	$ -
Tractor Depreciation	$ 16,667	$	0.15	$ 333,333	$ 321	$ 16,667
Trailer Depreciation	$ 3,000	$	0.13	$ 300,000	$ 288	$ 15,000
Legalization/Recruiting/Admin	$ 10,000	$	0.09	$ 200,000	$ 192	$ 10,000
On-Site Manager	$ -	$	-	$ -	$ -	$ -
Start Up /Special Equipment	$ 8,333	$	0.00	$ 8,333	$ 8	$ 417
Total Fixed Costs		$	0.38	$ 841,667	$ 809	$ 42,083
Total Cost		$	1.32	$ 2,954,459	$ 2,841	$ 147,723

The annual cost assumption of $8,333 as shown for the "Start Up/Special Equipment" line item consists of two parts. The first portion is $5,000 per year in other annual expenses. The second portion is the $10,000 in total start-up costs divided over the 3 year contract term ($10,000 ÷ 3 years = $3,333 per year).

Step 3: Total Initial Investment Projections

The determination of the total investment for the dedicated fleet is necessary for the net present value and internal rate of return calculations. For most new fleets, the total initial investment will consist of equipment, start-up costs, and working capital. The table below illustrates the calculation of the initial investment for the example dedicated fleet.

Total Investment Calculations in Pricing Model

Investment Summary	Units	Unit Cost	Total Investment	Per Truck
Tractors	20	$ 100,000	$ 2,000,000	$ 100,000
Trailers	100	$ 22,000	$ 2,200,000	$ 110,000
Start Up Costs / Other Equipment			$ 15,000	$ 750
Subtotal: Equipment			**$ 4,215,000**	**$ 210,750**
Working Capital				
Accounts Receivable	Avg. Collection Period:	30		
	Avg. Sales Per Day:	$ 9,662	$ 289,850	$ 14,493
Cash	Amount Per Truck:	$ 1,000	$ 20,000	$ 1,000
Inventory & Supplies	Amount Per Truck:	$ 450	$ 9,000	$ 450
Subtotal: Working Capital			**$ 318,850**	**$ 15,943**
Total Assets/Initial Investment			**$ 4,533,850**	**$ 226,693**

Equipment. The equipment costs are by far the largest portion of the overall investment. The total investment is simply the cost per tractor and cost per trailer multiplied by the number of tractors and trailers in the fleet. The start-up costs are a lump-sum, one-time cost item not always directly related to the size of the fleet.

Working Capital. The working capital portion of the investment is an estimate of secondary items such as accounts receivable, cash, inventory and supplies. These items are normal elements of most trucking operations. Cash will need to be on hand to support the operation of the fleet. In addition, the carrier will maintain additional inventories of tires, replacement parts, and other items needed to provide maintenance support for the fleet.

The largest and most important portion of the working capital is the estimate of accounts receivable. The two items in the calculation of accounts receivable are average sales per day and the average collection period. The average sales per day is multiplied by the average collection period (days) to compute the estimated accounts receivable balance.

When using investment-based pricing, the average collection period has an impact on the pricing decision. As a result, shippers with poor payment terms, such as 45-day payment terms, should be charged a higher rate per mile than shippers that pay invoices quickly. The difference is that a fleet for the shipper with poor payment habits will include a higher investment in accounts receivable, forcing the carrier to increase pricing to provide an adequate return on the additional investment in working capital.

Step 4: Cash Flow Projections

The net present value and internal rate of return analysis criteria are both based on operating cash flows. To determine operating cash flow, the estimated profit and loss statement must be extended well beyond the operating profit level to include taxes and operating cash flow. The new parameters for investment-based pricing analysis are listed in the table below.

Investment Pricing Analysis Parameters	
Marginal Tax Rate	36.0%
Pre-Tax Cost of Debt	7.5%
% of Project Funded by Debt	35.7%
Required Rate of Return	12.0%

Carriers should establish these assumptions annually and review them as needed. Each of these items is discussed briefly below. Please consult a CPA, financial analyst, or finance textbook for a more detailed review of these items.

Marginal Tax Rate. The marginal tax rate is applied to this analysis because, in most cases, the new dedicated fleet project will produce incremental profits above and beyond the income the carrier is already earning. The marginal tax rate is the tax rate that will be applied to the next dollar of profit above the profits that exist without the new dedicated fleet. Corporate tax rates and marginal tax rates vary based on the gross taxable income of the corporation similar to the rates shown in the table below.[70]

Example Corporate Tax Rates		
Taxable Income Range		Tax Rate
$0 - $50,000		15.0%
$50,000 - $75,000		25.0%
$75,000 - $100,000		34.0%
$100,000 - $335,000		39.0%
$335,000 - $10,000,000		34.0%
$10,000,000 - $15,000,000		35.0%
$15,000,000 - $18,333,333		38.0%
$18,333,333 - and up		35.0%

The carrier can estimate the appropriate marginal tax rate for each project based on an applicable tax rate table similar to the one shown above. The "average" or "historical" tax rate should never be used for pricing or investment analysis purposes. The tax rate for analysis purposes should always be an actual or estimated marginal tax rate.

---

[70] The rates shown here are for illustration purposes only and do not necessarily represent the current actual U.S. corporate tax rates. Tax rates vary significantly for different types of corporations and other forms of business organization.

Pre-tax Cost of Debt. The pre-tax cost of debt represents the cost of borrowing funds for the fleet project. Because the dedicated fleet represents incremental activity, the cost of borrowing should be based on the cost of the next dollar borrowed, not an average or historical cost of debt.

% of Project Funded by Debt. The capital for each new project will likely be funded through a combination of external borrowing (debt) and internal funding (equity). For a large corporation, the portion of the project funded by debt and equity should usually be based on the capital structure of the corporation. The capital structure represents how the overall corporation is financed as shown on the company's balance sheet. The percentage of debt financing according to the company balance sheet is a fair estimate of this parameter for pricing purposes. The table in the next section illustrates the calculation based on balance sheet information.

Required Rate of Return. The required rate of return should be based primarily on the company's Weighted Average Cost of Capital (WACC). The WACC is the weighted average cost of debt and cost of equity relative to the company's capital structure. The capital structure and WACC calculations are illustrated in the table below.

Capital Structure and Weighted Average Cost of Capital (WACC)

Source	Capital Structure	%	Cost	WACC
Debt	$ 25,000,000	35.7% x	4.8% =	1.7%
Equity	$ 45,000,000	64.3% x	16.0% =	10.3%
Total Company	**$ 70,000,000**		**WACC =**	**12.0%**

The cost of debt in the WACC calculation is based on the after-tax cost of debt. The formula for the after-tax cost of debt is shown below.

$$\text{After-Tax Cost of Debt} = \frac{\text{Pre-Tax Cost of Debt}}{1 - \text{Tax Rate}} = \frac{0.075}{1 - .36} = 0.048$$

While the cost of debt is relatively easy to determine, the cost of equity can be very difficult to estimate. For publicly traded firms, modern finance theory offers several models for estimating the cost of equity. Consult a CPA or finance textbook for more information on these models.

For private companies, estimating the required return on equity can be even more complex. One option for private companies is to estimate the required return for comparable publically traded firms within their own industry and assume that same required return for their company. In the absence of any specific reference information, carriers can apply a simple rule of thumb between a 12% and 18% required return on equity. This rule of thumb is roughly based on the average investor's expected return on a long-term investment in the stock market.[71]

---

[71] Carriers may also choose to estimate the required rate of return on their own without applying the WACC method shown here.

Operating Cash Flows. Based on the assumption for the tax rate, the annual operating cash flow can be estimated as shown below. The first step in determining operating cash flow is the development of the standard revenue and cost projections for the project. Operating cash flows include those items that are a part of the daily operations and included on the profit and loss statement for the fleet.

A preliminary revenue level has been established for the fleet for the purposes of this portion of the illustration. The suggested pricing will be adjusted in the next step as necessary to meet the required return of 12.0%. The annual cash flows are shown for each year of the deal in anticipation of the investment-based analysis that follows. Operating cash flow is required for the net present value and internal rate of return calculations that follow.

Operating Cash Flows

Year:		1	2	3
Total Revenue		$3,478,200	$3,478,200	$3,478,200
Variable Costs				
Driver Wages		$880,000	$880,000	$880,000
Fringe Benefits (% of wages)		220,000	220,000	220,000
Fuel		541,552	541,552	541,552
Maintenance		246,840	246,840	246,840
Insurance		224,400	224,400	224,400
Total Variable Costs		2,112,792	2,112,792	2,112,792
Fixed Costs				
Tractor Depreciation		$333,333	$333,333	$333,333
Trailer Depreciation		300,000	300,000	300,000
Legalization/Recruiting/Admin		200,000	200,000	200,000
On-Site Manager		0	0	0
Start Up /Special Equipment		8,333	8,333	8,333
Total Fixed Costs		841,667	841,667	841,667
Total Cost		2,954,459	2,954,459	2,954,459
Operating Profit		$523,741	$523,741	$523,741
Operating Ratio		84.94%	84.94%	84.94%
Less: Income Taxes	36.0%	178,072	178,072	178,072
Earnings After Tax		$345,669	$345,669	$345,669
Plus: Depreciation & Non-Cash		641,667	641,667	641,667
Operating Cash Flow		$987,336	$987,336	$987,336

After determining the operating profit, the next step in determining annual operating cash flow is to compute and deduct the estimated income taxes. The taxes are computed as the marginal tax rate multiplied by the operating income. The estimated taxes are subtracted from the operating profit to determine earnings after tax.

The second step is to add back non-cash expenses such as depreciation and start-up costs. The tractors, trailers and start-up costs are actually paid for at the beginning of the project as part of the initial investment. The equipment depreciation expense represents the "recognition" of the cost of using an asset for tax purposes, not an actual expense the carrier would write a check for each month.[72] Other expenses, such as driver wages and fuel, are paid on an ongoing basis over the life of the dedicated fleet.

The annual non-cash expenses included in the operating cash flow calculation are shown in the table below.

Non-Cash Expenses

Tractor Depreciation	$ 333,333
Trailer Depreciation	$ 300,000
Start-Up Costs / Special Equipment	$ 8,333
Total Non-Cash Items	**$ 641,667**

The two primary items that should always be "added back" as part of the operating cash flow are tractor depreciation and trailer depreciation. Other items, such as start-up costs, should be handled on a case-by-case basis. For more information on operating cash flows, consult a finance or management accounting reference source.

Non-Operating Cash Flows. In addition to operating cash flows, the non-operating cash flows must also be included in the analysis. Non-operating cash flows include any relevant items that are not a part of the profit and loss statement. The most common non-operating cash flow items are investments in equipment and working capital. The estimated non-operating cash flows for this fleet are shown below. A negative amount represents an outflow of cash and a positive amount represents incoming cash.

Non-Operating Cash Flows

Non-Operating Cash Flows	YEAR					
	0	1	2	3	4	5
Non-Operating Cash Flows						
Tractors	($2,000,000)			$1,000,000		
Trailers	(2,200,000)			1,300,000		
Other Equipment	(15,000)			0		
Accounts Receivable	(289,850)			289,850		
Other Current Assets	(29,000)			29,000		
Total Non Operating C.F.	($4,533,850)	$0	$0	$2,618,850	$0	$0

The start-up cash flows are shown at the beginning of the project in Year 0. The amounts shown here match the initial investment projections from Step 3. Year 0 is used to simply represent the beginning point of the project.

---

[72] Based on prevailing tax rules, tractors and trailers must be depreciated over a period of useful years for the asset type as specified in the tax code, not expensed as a one-time item in the year of purchase.

The amounts shown under Year 3 represent the cash flows at the end of the project. In the analysis process, the equipment values assume that the tractors and trailers are liquidated at an estimated value per unit. For simplification in this example, the tractors are sold at the year 3 book value of $50,000 each and the trailers are sold at the book value of $13,000 each.

If the equipment is to be sold at a value that is different from the book value, capital gains taxes will need to be included in the analysis. Capital gains taxes should be included even if the equipment is sold at a loss (for less than book value). The table below illustrates the tax impact of selling equipment at the end of the project.

Capital Gains Tax Example (Tractors)

	Profit	Break-Even	Loss
Purchase Price	$ 100,000	$ 100,000	$ 100,000
Book Value (End of Year 3)	$ 50,000	$ 50,000	$ 50,000
Selling Price (End of Year 3)	**$ 60,000**	**$ 50,000**	**$ 42,000**
Gain (Loss) on Sale	$ 10,000	$ -	$ (8,000)
Taxes (30%)	$ 3,000	$ -	$ (2,400)
Selling Price	$ 60,000	$ 50,000	$ 42,000
Less Taxes	$ 3,000	$ -	$ (2,400)
Net Cash Flow Per Unit	**$ 57,000**	**$ 50,000**	**$ 44,400**

The above example is only for the tractors associated with the fleet. The same process would apply to trailers as well. This example is based on traditional straight-line equipment depreciation. The book value should be adjusted as necessary when using other depreciation methods. Carriers should consult their tax advisor for more specific information on the capital gains tax process.

The working capital items such as accounts receivable, cash and inventories effectively disappear once the project is terminated, allowing the carrier to recover the capital invested in these items at the end of the project. For example, when the operation begins, the accounts receivable balance begins to accumulate. When the final invoice is paid at the end of the dedicated fleet contract, the accounts receivable balance reaches $0, effectively returning the working capital associated with accounts receivable to the carrier. Other working capital items such as cash and inventories behave in much the same manner.

Even though the working capital values are the same at the beginning and end of the project, it is still important to include these cash flows in the analysis. By including these cash flows, the pricing is forced to include an adequate return on these funds while they are associated with the project.

Step 5: Net Present Value and Internal Rate of Return Calculations

The annual operating cash flows and non-operating cash flows computed in the previous section provide the starting point for the net present value and internal rate of return calculations for the fleet. All cash flows are organized in the analysis format below.

Investment Analysis Summary

Investment Analysis Summary	YEAR					
	0	1	2	3	4	5
Cash Flows						
Tractors	($2,000,000)			$1,000,000		
Trailers	($2,200,000)			1,300,000		
Other Equipment	($15,000)			0		
Accounts Receivable	($289,850)			289,850		
Other Current Assets	($29,000)			29,000		
Total Non Operating C.F.	($4,533,850)	$0	$0	$2,618,850	$0	$0
Operating Cash Flows	----	$987,336	$987,336	$987,336	$0	$0
Present Values of Cash Flows						
Non-Operating	($4,533,850)	$0	$0	$1,864,046	$0	$0
Operating	---	925,804	821,604	729,132	0	0
Total Present Value	($4,533,850)	$925,804	$821,604	$2,593,178	$0	$0
Total Present Value	$4,340,586					
Net Present Value	($193,264)					
Internal Rate of Return	9.56%					

The cash flows come directly from the cash flow information organized in the previous sections. The investment analysis computes the net present value and internal rate of return for the proposed fleet. The present values of the non-operating and operating cash flows are computed individually then summed on the total present value line. The present values of the cash inflows are computed based on the 12.0% required rate of return determined in Step 4 of this analysis process. The present values and the internal rate of return are calculated using the financial spreadsheet functions illustrated in an upcoming Technical Tip section.

The net present value is the difference between the initial investment of $4,533,850 and the total present value of all cash inflows of $4,340,586 as shown below.

Net Present Value Calculation

Present Value of Cash Flows	$4,340,586
Initial Investment (Year 0)	- $4,533,850
Net Present Value	= ($193,264)

Notice that the net present value of the proposed fleet is a negative value based on the current proposed pricing levels. A negative net present value indicates that the project provides a return less than the required 12.0% level. The internal rate of return indicates that the actual rate of return for this project is 9.56%, far below the 12.0% requirement. The pricing must now be increased so that the required rate of return target is met.

Step 6: Set Pricing to Meet Profitability Objectives

The goal of the investment-based pricing process is to set the pricing at a level that achieves the carrier's target rate of return. For this example, the target rate of return is 12.0%. The analysis up to this point has been based on a proposed rate of $1.55 per mile. The preliminary pricing level of $1.55 per mile was established only as a starting point to facilitate the analysis process illustrated in the previous sections.

The current main sheet of the dedicated pricing model is shown below. The pricing and analysis section of the sheet displays the preliminary proposed price of $1.55 per mile and the estimated internal rate of return of 9.56%.

Dedicated Pricing Model

Customer Name:	Chapter 10	Fleet Description:	Investment-Based Pricing

Fleet Parameters

Number of Tractors	20.00
Backup Tractors	0.00
Number of Drivers	20.00
Utilization (Miles per Tractor per Active Week)	2,200
Active Fleet Weeks Per Year (max = 52 weeks)	51.0
Total Fleet Annual Miles	2,244,000
Number of Trailers	100.00
Trailer/Tractor Ratio	5.00

Overhead Costs

Tractor Legalization/Taxes	$ 2,000
Driver Recruiting Costs	$ 3,000
Administration Expenses	$ 5,000
Total Overhead (per tractor per year)	$ 10,000
Direct Staffing (On-site CSR / Offices / Etc.)	$ -
Other Annual Expenses (Total Fleet)	$ 5,000
Initial Start-Up Costs (Total)	$ 10,000

Other Parameters

Driver Rate of Pay (Per Mile or Annual Gross)	$ 44,000.00
Duration of Deal/Contract (in months)	36.0
Average Collection Period (in days)	30.0

Pricing and Analysis

Suggested Rate Per Mile (all miles)	$ 1.5500
Operating Ratio	84.94%
Internal Rate of Return	9.56%

Pro-Forma Income Statement		Fleet Totals Per Mile	Fleet Totals Annual	Per Tractor Weekly	Per Tractor Annual
Total Fleet Miles			2,244,000	2,158	112,200
Total Revenue		$1.550	$3,478,200	$3,344	$173,910
Variable Costs	Assumptions				
Driver Wages	$44,000.00	$0.392	$880,000	$846	$44,000
Fringe Benefits (% of wages)	25.0%	0.098	220,000	212	11,000
Fuel	$0.241	0.241	541,552	521	27,078
Maintenance	$0.110	0.110	246,840	237	12,342
Insurance	$0.100	0.100	224,400	216	11,220
Total Variable Costs		0.942	2,112,792	2,032	105,640
Fixed Costs	Assumptions				
Tractor Depreciation	$ 16,667	0.149	333,333	$321	$16,667
Trailer Depreciation	$ 3,000	0.134	300,000	288	15,000
Legalization/Recruiting/Admin	$ 10,000	0.089	200,000	192	10,000
On-Site Manager	$ -	0.000	0	0	0
Start Up /Special Equipment	$ 8,333	0.004	8,333	8	417
Total Fixed Costs		0.375	841,667	809	42,083
Total Cost		1.317	2,954,459	2,841	147,723
Operating Profit		$0.23	$523,741	$504	$26,187
Operating Ratio		84.94%	84.94%	84.94%	84.94%

Because of the investment-based approach, the operating ratio of 84.94% is now a secondary measure of the proposed profitability of this fleet. The carrier must consider the operating ratio in the pricing decision, but the internal rate of return target of 12.0% provides the primary measure upon which the pricing decision is based.

In order to achieve the target return of 12.0% on the proposed fleet, the preliminary rate of $1.55 per mile must be increased within the spreadsheet until an internal rate of return of 12.0% is achieved. The revised pricing model below indicates a 12.31% internal rate of return based on a suggested rate of $1.62 per mile.

Dedicated Pricing Model

Customer Name:	Chapter 10	Fleet Description:	Investment-Based Pricing

Fleet Parameters

Number of Tractors	20.00
Backup Tractors	0.00
Number of Drivers	20.00
Utilization (Miles per Tractor per Active Week)	2,200
Active Fleet Weeks Per Year (max = 52 weeks)	51.0
Total Fleet Annual Miles	2,244,000
Number of Trailers	100.00
Trailer/Tractor Ratio	5.00

Overhead Costs

Tractor Legalization/Taxes	$ 2,000
Driver Recruiting Costs	$ 3,000
Administration Expenses	$ 5,000
Total Overhead (per tractor per year)	$ 10,000
Direct Staffing (On-site CSR / Offices / Etc.)	$ -
Other Annual Expenses (Total Fleet)	$ 5,000
Initial Start-Up Costs (Total)	$ 10,000

Other Parameters

Driver Rate of Pay (Per Mile or Annual Gross)	$ 44,000.00
Duration of Deal/Contract (in months)	36.0
Average Collection Period (in days)	30.0

Pricing and Analysis

Suggested Rate Per Mile (all miles)	$ 1.6200
Operating Ratio	81.27%
Internal Rate of Return	12.31%

Pro-Forma Income Statement

		Fleet Totals Per Mile	Fleet Totals Annual	Per Tractor Weekly	Per Tractor Annual
Total Fleet Miles			2,244,000	2,158	112,200
Total Revenue		$1.620	$3,635,280	$3,495	$181,764
Variable Costs	Assumptions				
Driver Wages	$44,000.00	$0.392	$880,000	$846	$44,000
Fringe Benefits (% of wages)	25.0%	0.098	220,000	212	11,000
Fuel	$0.241	0.241	541,552	521	27,078
Maintenance	$0.110	0.110	246,840	237	12,342
Insurance	$0.100	0.100	224,400	216	11,220
Total Variable Costs		0.942	2,112,792	2,032	105,640
Fixed Costs	Assumptions				
Tractor Depreciation	$ 16,667	0.149	333,333	$321	$16,667
Trailer Depreciation	$ 3,000	0.134	300,000	288	15,000
Legalization/Recruiting/Admin	$ 10,000	0.089	200,000	192	10,000
On-Site Manager	$ -	0.000	0	0	0
Start Up /Special Equipment	$ 8,333	0.004	8,333	8	417
Total Fixed Costs		0.375	841,667	809	42,083
Total Cost		1.317	2,954,459	2,841	147,723
Operating Profit		$0.30	$680,821	$655	$34,041
Operating Ratio		81.27%	81.27%	81.27%	81.27%

The increase in the rate per mile to $1.62 increases revenues, operating profits, and operating cash flows to a level high enough to achieve the 12.0% required rate of return. The actual internal rate of return at $1.62 per mile is 12.31%. The revised net present value and cash flow calculations from within the model are shown in the next section.[73]

---

[73] The dedicated fleet pricing model spreadsheet presented throughout this book is available for purchase at www.TruckloadTransportation.com. The model includes all the various features presented in this book.

The operating cash flows for the proposed fleet based on the new rate of $1.62 per mile are shown below.

Operating Cash Flows at $1.62 Per Mile

Year:	1	2	3
Total Revenue	$3,635,280	$3,635,280	$3,635,280
Variable Costs			
Driver Wages	$880,000	$880,000	$880,000
Fringe Benefits (% of wages)	220,000	220,000	220,000
Fuel	541,552	541,552	541,552
Maintenance	246,840	246,840	246,840
Insurance	224,400	224,400	224,400
Total Variable Costs	2,112,792	2,112,792	2,112,792
Fixed Costs			
Tractor Depreciation	$333,333	$333,333	$333,333
Trailer Depreciation	300,000	300,000	300,000
Legalization/Recruiting/Admin	200,000	200,000	200,000
On-Site Manager	0	0	0
Start Up /Special Equipment	8,333	8,333	8,333
Total Fixed Costs	841,667	841,667	841,667
Total Cost	2,954,459	2,954,459	2,954,459
Operating Profit	$680,821	$680,821	$680,821
Operating Ratio	81.27%	81.27%	81.27%
Less: Income Taxes 36.0%	231,479	231,479	231,479
Earnings After Tax	$449,342	$449,342	$449,342
Plus: Depreciation & Non-Cash	641,667	641,667	641,667
Operating Cash Flow	$1,091,009	$1,091,009	$1,091,009

As a result of the new pricing, total annual revenue has increased from $3,478,200 to $3,635,280. Variable costs and fixed costs are unchanged. As a result, the annual operating cash flow has increased from $987,336 to $1,091,009 per year. These new operating cash flows are used to compute the new internal rate of return for the proposed dedicated fleet.

The table below shows the revised investment analysis for the fleet after increasing the suggested rate to $1.62 per mile.

Investment Analysis Summary at $1.62 Per Mile

Investment Analysis Summary	Year 0	Year 1	Year 2	Year 3	Year 4	Year 5
Cash Flows						
Tractors	($2,000,000)			$1,000,000		
Trailers	($2,200,000)			1,300,000		
Other Equipment	($15,000)			0		
Accounts Receivable	($302,940)			302,940		
Other Current Assets	($29,000)			29,000		
Total Non Operating C.F.	($4,546,940)	$0	$0	$2,631,940	$0	$0
Operating Cash Flows	----	$1,091,009	$1,091,009	$1,091,009	$0	$0
Present Values of Cash Flows						
Non-Operating	($4,546,940)	$0	$0	$1,873,363	$0	$0
Operating	---	1,023,016	907,875	805,693	0	0
Total Present Value	($4,546,940)	$1,023,016	$907,875	$2,679,056	$0	$0
Total Present Value	**$4,609,946**					
Net Present Value	**$63,006**					
Internal Rate of Return	**12.31%**					

Based on the new pricing, the net present value is a positive value of $63,006. A positive net present value indicates that the project is earning a rate of return higher than the 12.0% required rate of return. The internal rate of return indicates that the actual expected return for this project is 12.31%.

At the new rate of $1.62 per mile, the operating ratio for the fleet is 81.27%. The reason the operating ratio is so low is the result of the investment associated with the high trailer-to-tractor ratio of 5:1 for the proposed fleet. The investment-based pricing approach requires additional revenues in order to provide adequate returns on the unusually high trailer fleet required by this customer. Had the pricing been established based on the 88% operating ratio rule at only $1.50 per mile, the internal rate of return would have been only 7.57%. The net present value would have been negative at ($376,314). With an annual operating profit of $411,514, the fleet would have appeared to be profitable when actually it would have been highly unprofitable from an investment analysis perspective.

Additional Considerations for Investment-Based Pricing

The investment-based pricing process requires a deeper analysis and many more assumptions than the operating-ratio pricing process. As a result, the approach requires careful analysis and interpretation before finalizing a pricing decision. The topics that follow provide additional information on the interpretation and application of investment-based dedicated fleet pricing.

Dual Pricing Decision Criteria. When using investment-based pricing, the carrier should base the pricing decision on both the internal rate of return and the operating ratio. The carrier should establish minimum standards for both criteria and set the pricing at the level at which both criteria are met. For example, the carrier might establish a maximum operating ratio of 92% and a minimum internal rate of return of 12%. While both criteria are important considerations, the internal rate of return should be the primary measure for establishing pricing.

Price and Cost Inflation. The dedicated fleet pricing model presented here does not include price or cost inflation during the contract as part of the analysis process. In most cases, the shipper's pricing will remain fixed for the duration of the contract. On the cost side, the equipment depreciation should remain constant for the term of the contract. Fuel costs are effectively constant as long as a fuel surcharge agreement is in place for the fleet. However, certain operating costs will experience some inflation over the course of a multi-year contract. If necessary, the carrier's cost assumptions for maintenance, driver pay, insurance, and other items could be set to reflect the anticipated average costs over the term of the contract. As the contract length extends beyond three years, inflation considerations become increasingly relevant to the analysis.

Estimated Equipment Values. The cash flow analysis is heavily dependent on the estimated equipment values at the end of the project. Carriers must carefully estimate these values as part of the pricing process. Overstating the future equipment values will potentially result in pricing that is too low. Understating the future equipment values will potentially result in pricing that is too high. As necessary, the carrier should perform sensitivity analysis on the equipment values to determine the impact of the equipment value estimates on the overall pricing strategy.

Risk and Required Rate of Return. The weighted-average cost of capital provides the minimum required rate of return for any project. The carrier may also choose to establish business rules that dictate a higher required rate of return for fleets that involve a higher level of risk than the carrier's normal operations. Excessive risk could be based on the customer, the fleet location, driver concerns, the fleet operation, or the likelihood of achieving the operating assumptions in the pricing model. If the carrier is uncomfortable with the proposed fleet operation, the required rate of return could be increased by several percentage points to provide additional revenues and margin to compensate for the high level of risk.

Short-term Contracts. The investment-based pricing approach is highly dependent on time value of money principles. A large portion of the cash flows of any fleet project comes from the estimated equipment values at the end of the project. For projects with a contract term of two years or less, the pricing results can be skewed by the large cash flows that occur at the end of the project. The table below compares the present value calculations for the previous example fleet based on contract terms of 1, 2 and 3 years.

Present Value of Non-Operating Cash Flows at Different Contract Lengths

	Fleet Size	Year 1 Equipment Value Per Unit	Year 1 Total Cash Flow	Year 2 Equipment Value Per Unit	Year 2 Total Cash Flow	Year 3 Equipment Value Per Unit	Year 3 Total Cash Flow
Tractors	20	$ 83,333	$ 1,666,667	$ 66,667	$ 1,333,333	$ 50,000	$ 1,000,000
Trailers	100	$ 19,000	$ 1,900,000	$ 16,000	$ 1,600,000	$ 13,000	$ 1,300,000
Accounts Receivable			$ 302,940		$ 302,940		$ 302,940
Other Items			$ 29,000		$ 29,000		$ 29,000
Total Cash Flow			**$ 3,898,607**		**$ 3,265,273**		**$ 2,631,940**

Present Values:	Year 0
Year 1	$ 3,480,899
Year 2	$ 2,603,056
Year 3	$ 1,873,363

An additional consideration for the carrier is the use of the equipment at the end of the project. If the carrier is unable to utilize the equipment in other operations or sell the equipment for a fair value, the carrier is at additional risk because of the short-term dedicated fleet contract. Based on these risks, the carrier may choose to require a higher internal rate of return on short term projects.

The term of the contract and timing of non-operating cash flows can also have a significant effect on the suggested pricing based on the internal rate of return criteria. The table below summarizes the suggested pricing and key measurements for this example based on contract terms of 1, 2 and 3 years.

Pricing Analysis by Contract Length	Contract Term 1 Year	Contract Term 2 Years	Contract Term 3 Years
Suggested Rate Per Mile	$ 1.67	$ 1.64	$ 1.62
Total Annual Revenue	$ 3,747,480	$ 3,680,160	$ 3,635,280
Total Variable Costs	$ 2,112,792	$ 2,112,792	$ 2,112,792
Total Fixed Costs	$ 848,333	$ 843,333	$ 841,667
Total Operating Costs	$ 2,961,125	$ 2,956,125	$ 2,954,459
Operating Profit	$ 786,355	$ 724,035	$ 680,821
Operating Ratio	79.02%	80.33%	81.27%
Internal Rate of Return	12.06%	12.02%	12.31%

Note that the model suggests lower rates as the contract duration increases. The carrier may also choose to require a higher rate of return on projects with contract terms of only 1 or 2 years, thereby further increasing the suggested rate per mile on short-term deals.

Present Values of Operating Cash Flows. The present values of the operating cash flows in the pricing model assume that cash flows are received on a monthly basis. The table below displays the detail of the monthly cash flow analysis for Year 1.[74] The cash flows for all additional years are modeled in this same format.

Monthly Operating Cash Flow Analysis – Year 1

Monthly Cash Flow Projections	Activity	8.49%	7.67%	8.49%	8.22%	8.22%	8.49%	8.22%	8.49%	100.00%
	Days	31	28	31	30	30	31	30	31	365
	Month #	1	2	3	4	9	10	11	12	YEAR 1
	YEAR 1	JAN	FEB	MAR	APR	SEP	OCT	NOV	DEC	TOTAL
Total Revenue	$3,635,280	$308,750	$278,871	$308,750	$298,790	$298,790	$308,750	$298,790	$308,750	$3,635,280
Variable Costs										
Driver Wages	$880,000	$74,740	$67,507	$74,740	$72,329	$72,329	$74,740	$72,329	$74,740	$880,000
Fringe Benefits (% of wages)	220,000	18,685	16,877	18,685	18,082	18,082	18,685	18,082	18,685	220,000
Fuel	541,552	45,995	41,544	45,995	44,511	44,511	45,995	44,511	45,995	541,552
Maintenance	246,840	20,964	18,936	20,964	20,288	20,288	20,964	20,288	20,964	246,840
Insurance	224,400	19,059	17,214	19,059	18,444	18,444	19,059	18,444	19,059	224,400
Total Variable Costs	2,112,792	179,443	162,077	179,443	173,654	173,654	179,443	173,654	179,443	2,112,792
Fixed Costs										
Tractor Depreciation	$333,333	$28,311	$25,571	$28,311	$27,397	$27,397	$28,311	$27,397	$28,311	$333,333
Trailer Depreciation	300,000	25,479	23,014	25,479	24,658	24,658	25,479	24,658	25,479	300,000
Legalization/Recruiting/Admin	200,000	16,986	15,342	16,986	16,438	16,438	16,986	16,438	16,986	200,000
On-Site Manager	0	0	0	0	0	0	0	0	0	0
Start Up /Special Equipment	8,333	708	639	708	685	685	708	685	708	8,333
Total Fixed Costs	841,667	71,484	64,566	71,484	69,178	69,178	71,484	69,178	71,484	841,667
Total Cost	2,954,459	250,927	226,643	250,927	242,832	242,832	250,927	242,832	250,927	2,954,459
Operating Profit	$680,821	$57,823	$52,227	$57,823	$55,958	$55,958	$57,823	$55,958	$57,823	$680,821
Operating Ratio	81.27%	81.27%	81.27%	81.27%	81.27%	81.27%	81.27%	81.27%	81.27%	81.27%
Income Taxes	231,479	19,660	17,757	19,660	19,026	19,026	19,660	19,026	19,660	231,479
Earnings After Tax	$449,342	$38,163	$34,470	$38,163	$36,932	$36,932	$38,163	$36,932	$38,163	$449,342
Depreciation	641,667	54,498	49,224	54,498	52,740	52,740	54,498	52,740	54,498	641,667
Operating Cash Flow	$1,091,009	$92,661	$83,694	$92,661	$89,672	$89,672	$92,661	$89,672	$92,661	$1,091,009
Present Value of Cash Flows	------	$91,744	$82,045	$89,936	$86,173	$81,991	$83,885	$80,375	$82,232	$1,023,016

Annual revenues and costs are allocated to each month based on the percentage of activity expected to occur in each month. In this example, the activity is allocated based on the number of days in each month. The activity could also be allocated equally across 12 months without any material change to the present value results.

A basic principle of the time value of money concept is that the sooner a future cash flow is received, the higher its present value. By recognizing in the model that operating cash flows occur on a monthly basis, the monthly timing slightly increases the internal rate of return and net present value for the fleet compared to the same analysis based only on annual cash flows. As a result, the carrier is able to offer slightly lower pricing while still meeting the minimum required rate of return.

---

[74] For space considerations, the months of May, June, July and August are hidden but included in the annual totals.

Pricing for Lease Equipment or Owner-Operators

All the previous pricing analysis scenarios assumed that the carrier owned the tractor and trailer equipment associated with a dedicated fleet. Since the carrier owned the equipment, the carrier's pricing must include an adequate return on the funds invested in the equipment. In some situations, the dedicated carrier may choose to lease tractor and trailer equipment instead of owning the equipment. In these cases, the dedicated pricing approach must be adjusted to reflect the change in equipment ownership.

Since the equipment is owned by the leasing company and not the carrier, the return on investment is included in the equipment leasing company's monthly charge to the carrier. As a result, it is not necessary for the carrier to add a significant amount of margin to the pricing to provide a return on the assets associated with the fleet. Since the carrier's total investment amount is significantly reduced for these lease arrangements, the investment-based pricing calculations rarely provide the best basis for establishing pricing. Because of the low investment level, a cost-plus or operating ratio method provides the correct approach for establishing accurate pricing, especially when both the tractors and trailers are leased.

The example fleet below is the same as the previous example covering investment-based pricing. By utilizing the same fleet example, the pricing, operating profits, and operating ratio for the leasing option will be compared to the results seen when using investment-based pricing.

> **Example Dedicated Fleet.** A major retail shipper would like a dedicated fleet to provide weekly deliveries to each of its retail locations within a 600 mile radius of a major distribution center in Nashville, TN. After an internal analysis of historical shipment volumes, the retailer has requested dedicated pricing on a fleet of 20 trucks, 20 drivers, and 100 trailers. Each truck and driver can expect to run an average of 2,200 miles per week. However, due to seasonal business demands, actual utilization is expected to fluctuate from week to week between 1,800 and 2,500 miles. The fleet will operate 51 weeks per year after adjusting for the distribution center's scheduled holidays. The customer will have 30 days terms for invoices.

The carrier plans to lease the tractor and trailer equipment needed to provide this dedicated fleet. The tractors will be leased at a cost of $1,250 per month or $15,000 per year. The trailers will be leased at a cost of $375 per month or $4,500 per year. By leasing the equipment, the carrier can avoid the $4,200,000 investment in tractors and trailers as shown in the previous investment-based example. However, by leasing the equipment, the carrier will make significantly less profit on the overall fleet. A portion of the profits usually earned by the carrier will now be earned by the leasing company that provides the carrier with the tractor and trailer equipment.

The pro-forma profit and loss statement below shows the carrier's suggested pricing for the dedicated fleet opportunity based on leased tractor and trailer equipment. The pricing is established based on the operating ratio criteria.

Dedicated Pricing Model

Customer Name:	Chapter 10	Fleet Description:	Lease Equipment Example

Fleet Parameters

Number of Tractors	20.00
Backup Tractors	0.00
Number of Drivers	20.00
Utilization (Miles per Tractor per Active Week)	2,200
Active Fleet Weeks Per Year (max = 52 weeks)	51.0
Total Fleet Annual Miles	2,244,000
Number of Trailers	100.00
Trailer/Tractor Ratio	5.00

Overhead Costs

Tractor Legalization/Taxes	$ 2,000
Driver Recruiting Costs	$ 3,000
Administration Expenses	$ 5,000
Total Overhead (per tractor per year)	$ 10,000
Direct Staffing (On-site CSR / Offices / Etc.)	$ -
Other Annual Expenses (Total Fleet)	$ 5,000
Initial Start-Up Costs (Total)	$ 10,000

Other Parameters

Driver Rate of Pay (Per Mile or Annual Gross)	$ 44,000.00
Duration of Deal/Contract (in months)	36.0
Average Collection Period (in days)	30.0

Pricing and Analysis

Suggested Rate Per Mile (all miles)	$ 1.5800
Operating Ratio	86.62%
Internal Rate of Return	313.79%

Pro-Forma Income Statement		Fleet Totals Per Mile	Fleet Totals Annual	Per Tractor Weekly	Per Tractor Annual
Total Fleet Miles			2,244,000	2,158	112,200
Total Revenue		$1.580	$3,545,520	$3,409	$177,276
Variable Costs	Assumptions				
Driver Wages	$44,000.00	$0.392	$880,000	$846	$44,000
Fringe Benefits (% of wages)	25.0%	0.098	220,000	212	11,000
Fuel	$0.241	0.241	541,552	521	27,078
Maintenance	$0.110	0.110	246,840	237	12,342
Insurance	$0.100	0.100	224,400	216	11,220
Total Variable Costs		0.942	2,112,792	2,032	105,640
Fixed Costs	Assumptions				
Tractor Lease Expense	$ 15,000	0.134	300,000	$288	$15,000
Trailer Lease Expense	$ 4,500	0.201	450,000	433	22,500
Legalization/Recruiting/Admin	$ 10,000	0.089	200,000	192	10,000
On-Site Manager	$ -	0.000	0	0	0
Start Up /Special Equipment	$ 8,333	0.004	8,333	8	417
Total Fixed Costs		0.427	958,333	921	47,917
Total Cost		1.369	3,071,125	2,953	153,556
Operating Profit		$0.21	$474,395	$456	$23,720
Operating Ratio		86.62%	86.62%	86.62%	86.62%

The fixed cost portion of the pro-forma income statement now includes the tractor lease expense and trailer lease expense line items. All other costs are unchanged.[75] The pricing has been reduced from $1.64 in the investment-based example to $1.58 in this lease example. The operating ratio of 86.62% is reasonable for a deal of this type. The internal rate of return of 313.79% is not relevant to the interpretation of the analysis for this example because the carrier has no funds invested in tractor or trailer equipment. The only major investment for the carrier is in working capital in the form of an accounts receivable balance.

---

[75] Certain lease agreements may include additional costs or cover certain expenses such as a portion of equipment maintenance. For simplification, these details are excluded from this example.

The carrier's operating profit for the lease-equipment scenario is only $474,395 compared to the operating profit of $680,821 with carrier-owned equipment.

Comparison of Profits by Equipment Ownership Option

	Leased Equipment	Owned Equipment
Rate Per Mile	$ 1.58	$ 1.62
Total Revenue	$ 3,545,520	$ 3,635,280
Variable Costs	$ 2,112,792	$ 2,112,792
Fixed Costs	$ 958,333	$ 841,667
Total Cost	$ 3,071,125	$ 2,954,459
Operating Profit	**$ 474,395**	**$ 680,821**
Operating Ratio	86.62%	81.27%

The primary reason for the difference in operating profit between the two options is the equipment ownership status. Under the lease option, the leasing company earns a return on their investment in the equipment through the monthly leasing revenues from the carrier. By leasing instead of owning the equipment, the carrier gives up this portion of the potential profit from the fleet.[76]

In cases where the carrier leases equipment, the carrier should use a cost-plus or operating ratio approach to determine pricing. Since no significant investment is present, an investment-based pricing approach for this type of scenario generally does not apply. In a situation where the carrier might lease a portion of the equipment and own a portion of the equipment, the carrier should use the dual profitability rule approach and price the opportunity so that both the operating ratio and internal rate of return profitability criteria are met.

---

[76] The rate per mile in this particular example is lower with the lease arrangement than the carrier-owned equipment scenario. In other cases, the carrier-owned option will provide a lower rate per mile.

! *Technical Tip* – NPV and IRR Excel® Spreadsheet Functions

The complex calculations of net present value (NPV) and internal rate of return (IRR) can easily be performed using the built-in financial functions of spreadsheet software. The example below illustrates the use of the present value (PV) spreadsheet function to compute the present values for each cash flow.

Net Present Value Calculations

Year:	0	1	2	3	4
Initial Investment	$ (10,000.00)				
Cash Inflows		$ 4,000.00	$ 4,000.00	$ 4,000.00	$ 4,000.00
Net Cash Flow	$ (10,000.00)	$ 4,000.00	$ 4,000.00	$ 4,000.00	$ 4,000.00
Discount Rate	10.00%				
Present Value of Cash Inflows	$12,679.46 ←	$3,636.36	$3,305.79	$3,005.26	$2,732.05
Initial Investment	$ (10,000.00)				
Net Present Value	**$2,679.46**				

The table below illustrates the formulas for the net present value calculations including the PV financial function.

Net Present Value Formula Design

	B	C	D	E	F	G	H	I
2								
3		Net Present Value Design & Formulas						
4								
5								
6		Year:	0		1	2	3	4
7		Initial Investment	$ (10,000.00)					
8		Cash Inflows		$	4,000.00 $	4,000.00 $	4,000.00 $	4,000.00
9		Net Cash Flow	$ (10,000.00)	$	4,000.00 $	4,000.00 $	4,000.00 $	4,000.00
10								
11		Discount Rate	10.00%					
12								
13		PV of Cash Inflows	=SUM(F13:I13)		=PV($D$11,F6,0,F9)*-1	=PV($D$11,G6,0,G9)*-1	=PV($D$11,H6,0,H9)*-1	=PV($D$11,I6,0,I9)*-1
14		Initial Investment	=+D9					
15		Net Present Value	=SUM(D13:D14)					
16								
17								
18		Components of PV Function:		=PV(Interest Rate, Number of Periods, Payment, Future Value)				
19								

The "payment" portion of the present value function is "0" because, in this example, each yearly amount is treated as an individual event. The "payment" component is used to compute the present value of cash flows of the same amount in sequential periods.[77]

---

[77] Microsoft® product screen shots reprinted with permission from Microsoft® Corporation.

The example below illustrates the use of the internal rate of return (IRR) spreadsheet function to compute the internal rate of return for the investment.

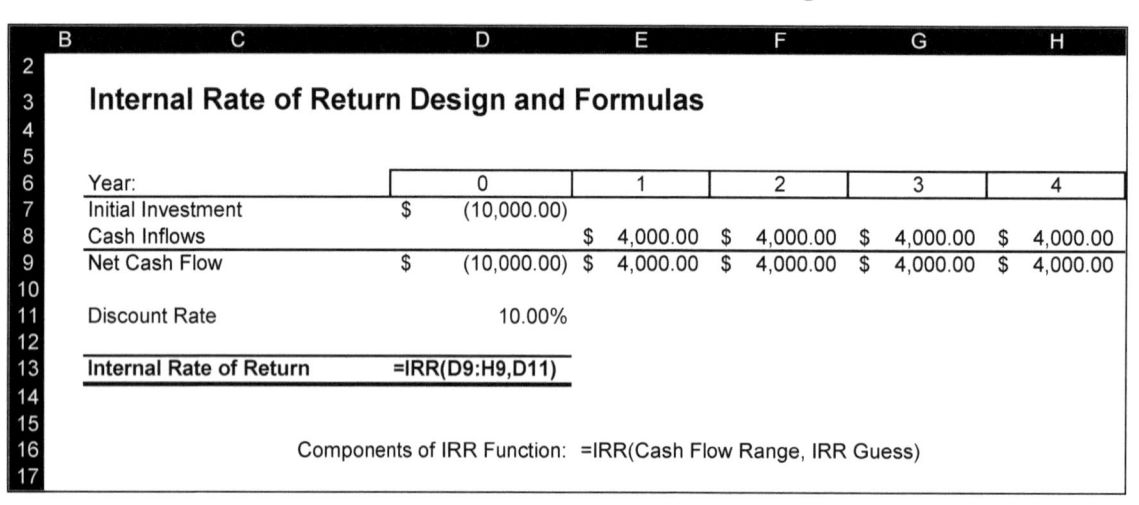

Internal Rate of Return Calculation

Year:	0	1	2	3	4
Initial Investment	$ (10,000.00)				
Cash Inflows		$ 4,000.00	$ 4,000.00	$ 4,000.00	$ 4,000.00
Net Cash Flow	$ (10,000.00)	$ 4,000.00	$ 4,000.00	$ 4,000.00	$ 4,000.00
Discount Rate	10.00%				
Internal Rate of Return	**21.86%**				

The table below demonstrates the use of the IRR spreadsheet function.

Internal Rate of Return Formula Design

	B	C	D	E	F	G	H
2							
3		Internal Rate of Return Design and Formulas					
4							
5							
6		Year:	0	1	2	3	4
7		Initial Investment	$ (10,000.00)				
8		Cash Inflows		$ 4,000.00	$ 4,000.00	$ 4,000.00	$ 4,000.00
9		Net Cash Flow	$ (10,000.00)	$ 4,000.00	$ 4,000.00	$ 4,000.00	$ 4,000.00
10							
11		Discount Rate	10.00%				
12							
13		Internal Rate of Return	=IRR(D9:H9,D11)				
14							
15							
16			Components of IRR Function: =IRR(Cash Flow Range, IRR Guess)				
17							

In order for the IRR formula to function correctly, the cash flows must be set up as shown above, with the investment (usually a negative amount) in the first column and the corresponding future cash flows (usually positive amounts) in the immediately adjacent columns in chronological order with like time periods (years in this example). Consult the spreadsheet help function for more detail on these and related financial functions.

CHAPTER 11: Special Topics in Dedicated Pricing

Because dedicated fleets are customized to the unique requirements of each shipper, carriers must often develop unique and creative approaches to the dedicated fleet design process. The next two chapters provide a variety of special situations where the dedicated pricing and design approach must be modified to meet the requirements of the dedicated shipper or solve important internal carrier issues related to the dedicated fleet solution. The special topics in this chapter include estimating and sharing backhaul revenues, structuring dedicated driver compensation programs, and evaluating the productivity and performance of dedicated fleets.

Estimating Backhaul Revenues

In a variety of dedicated pricing scenarios, the carrier will have the opportunity to generate additional revenue for the fleet by filling empty lanes with revenue from third-party customers. As the carrier determines dedicated pricing for a shipper in a bid situation, the carrier may be able to discount the dedicated shipper's pricing proposal by estimating the amount of additional revenue that can be generated on backhaul lanes through third-party shippers.

Backhaul Revenue by Destination

In most cases, the shipper's bid will include detailed information regarding the destinations of the dedicated fleet. The carrier can use this information to estimate the likelihood of securing backhaul loads and the revenue associated with each backhaul opportunity. Consider the example below of a dedicated fleet that serves the dedicated shipper's customers within a 200 mile radius of Memphis, Tennessee.

Dedicated Fleet Network

Outbound Network Summary

Outbound Dedicated Locations			
Destination City	ST	One-Way Miles	Annual Loads
Little Rock	AR	140	306
Hot Springs	AR	188	188
Conway	AR	149	135
Benton	AR	152	282
Jackson	TN	84	311
Milan	TN	96	168
Memphis	TN	1	688
Nashville	TN	200	471
Franklin	TN	208	244
Network Totals:			**2,793**

Based on this information, the carrier preparing a bid can now estimate the number of times a backhaul load can be secured with a third-party customer after a dedicated delivery is made to each destination location.

To estimate the backhaul revenues, the carrier will first review existing internal customer activity for specific backhaul opportunities. If needed, the carrier can rely on its knowledge of each destination market and further estimate a reasonable expectation for backhaul activity. If awarded the new dedicated fleet, the carrier may also deploy its sales staff to each backhaul market to solicit customers to fill very specific backhaul needs. The carrier may offer these potential customers very attractive rates in order to secure the necessary backhaul activity.

The table below illustrates a suitable format for organizing and quantifying potential backhaul revenues for a dedicated fleet network.

Estimated Backhaul Revenues by Outbound Destination

Destination City	ST	One-Way Miles	Annual Loads	% of Trips w BH Loads	Estimated BH Trips	Revenue Per Trip	Total BH Revenue	Out-of-Route Miles Per Trip	Out-of-Route Miles Total
Little Rock	AR	140	306	28.0%	85.7	$ 400	$ 34,272	10.0	857
Hot Springs	AR	188	188	25.0%	47.0	$ 425	$ 19,975	12.0	564
Conway	AR	149	135	25.0%	33.8	$ 400	$ 13,500	15.0	506
Benton	AR	152	282	25.0%	70.5	$ 400	$ 28,200	15.0	1,058
Jackson	TN	84	311	35.0%	108.9	$ 300	$ 32,655	10.0	1,089
Milan	TN	96	168	15.0%	25.2	$ 310	$ 7,812	15.0	378
Memphis	TN	1	688	10.0%	68.8	$ 175	$ 12,040	15.0	1,032
Nashville	TN	200	471	35.0%	164.9	$ 450	$ 74,183	20.0	3,297
Franklin	TN	208	244	30.0%	73.2	$ 450	$ 32,940	25.0	1,830
Network Totals:			2,793	24.3%	677.8	$ 377	$ 255,577	15.7	10,610

Out-of-Route Adjustment:
Total Out-of-Route Miles   10,610
Cost Per Out-of-Route Mile   x $ 1.25
Less: Cost of Out-of-Route Miles $ (13,263)
Net Potential Backhaul Revenue to Fleet   **$ 242,314**

The carrier must estimate two factors for each destination. First, the carrier must estimate the percentage of the time a backhaul load can be secured for each truck that delivers into the market. This estimate is shown in the "% of Trips w BH Loads" column. Second, the carrier must estimate the amount of revenue generated by each backhaul load. This estimate is shown in the "Revenue Per Trip" column.

As part of the backhaul exercise, the carrier might also choose to estimate the number of extra, out-of-route miles that will be driven while serving each backhaul load. Out-of-route miles will effectively reduce the net revenue and financial benefit of each backhaul load. The estimated out-of-route miles are shown in the "Per Trip" column under out-of-route miles. The total out-of-route miles are computed by multiplying the out-of-route miles per trip by the expected number of backhaul loads. The total out-of-route miles are then multiplied by a standard cost per mile to estimate the cost of these additional miles. The cost of the out-of-route miles is then deducted from the expected backhaul revenues to compute the net potential backhaul revenue to the fleet. The cost per mile applied to these miles should represent variable costs only. The fixed cost of the fleet is already included in the dedicated customer's pricing.

Adjusting the Dedicated Pricing. Once the potential backhaul revenues are identified, the carrier can then adjust the proposed dedicated pricing. The dedicated customer's pricing can be reduced by the estimated potential backhaul revenue as shown below.

Backhaul Revenue Adjustment to Dedicated Pricing	
Base Dedicated Fleet Cost (Pricing Model)	$ 4,953,874
Less: Estimated Net Backhaul Revenues	$ (242,314)
Net Revenue/Pricing to Dedicated Customer	**$ 4,711,560**

The adjustment as shown assumes that no backhaul revenue share agreement is in place and the carrier will retain 100% of the backhaul revenues.

If a backhaul revenue share agreement will be included in the contract, the estimated backhaul revenues can be included as part of the total cost proposal as shown below.

Backhaul Revenue Adjustment to Dedicated Cost		
Base Dedicated Fleet Cost (Pricing Model)		$ 4,953,874
Less: Backhaul Revenue Share at 75%	$ (242,314)	$ (181,735)
Net Cost to Dedicated Customer		**$ 4,772,139**

Regardless of how the credit to the dedicated customer is determined, the detailed estimate of potential backhaul revenues allows the carrier to offer the dedicated shipper a lower total transportation cost. Based on the reduced total cost, the carrier's chances of being awarded the dedicated fleet opportunity are increased significantly.

Secondary Backhaul Considerations

The carrier must also consider several other secondary factors when estimating the benefits and revenues of the backhaul activity. Several of the most common secondary backhaul considerations are described below.

Secondary Considerations with Backhauls	
Consideration	**The Risk**
Artificial Increase in the Dedicated Fleet Size	Because of the additional work time associated with backhaul loads, the dedicated fleet could become larger than what is needed by the dedicated shipper's core network. The backhaul revenues may not offset the cost of the larger fleet size. The dedicated shipper could see an increase in total cost despite the excellent backhaul performance.
Adding Trailers to the Network to Support Backhaul Customers	Based on the needs of the backhaul customers, additional trailers may be dropped at backhaul customer facilities to support the backhaul network. The revenues to cover the cost of these trailers must come from the backhaul network. The dedicated customer would not be responsible for the cost of these additional trailers.
Service Impact to Primary Dedicated Customer	Dedicated trucks and drivers may spend too much time with a backhaul load and not return to the dedicated shipper in a timely manner. The dedicated shipper's service and available dedicated fleet capacity are at risk.
Backhaul Impact on Other Carrier Fleets and Divisions	Most backhaul loads will come from the pool of available loads usually served by the carrier's existing linehaul and/or regional fleets. Carriers must monitor backhaul activity closely to determine if the available loads utilized as backhaul loads by a dedicated fleet take critically needed revenue and load activity from the intended fleet.

One the most serious risks for the carrier is the impact of dedicated backhauls on the freight availability for the carrier's other divisions. Because dedicated fleets are typically high profile, the carrier may make securing backhauls for dedicated fleets a top priority. If the carrier is unable to fill the load gap left in the carrier's other linehaul and regional divisions, those divisions will suffer at the expense of the dedicated fleets. The fact that a portion of the revenue from backhaul loads is shared with the dedicated customer further compounds the financial impact to the carrier as a whole. The carrier must exercise good judgment in balancing the needs of its core network with the backhaul needs of any dedicated fleets.

Other Backhaul Revenue Share Considerations

While the basic calculation for sharing backhaul revenue is very straightforward, other considerations can make the revenue share process more complicated. This section will describe several of the most common exceptions and a suggested method for handling each potential issue.

Linehaul Revenues

The backhaul revenue share calculation is typically very simple. The backhaul revenue share percentage is multiplied by the gross linehaul revenue for the backhaul load as shown below.

Backhaul Revenue Share Calculation

Linehaul Revenue		$ 700.00
Revenue Share %	x	80%
Backhaul Share to Shipper		**$ 560.00**

The calculation in this basic format assumes that the dedicated truck provides 100% of the transportation service for the load. A variety of other backhaul revenue share calculation issues are discussed in the sections that follow.

Accessorial Revenues

Some backhaul loads will include revenue for common accessorial items, particularly stop-offs and unloading. The bulk of the revenue for these accessorial events is specifically for driver compensation for each service. Also, the revenue for these items is independent of base linehaul charges. As a result, the carrier should retain 100% of the revenue for these items under most circumstances. The carrier should also retain 100% of the revenue for most other common accessorial items such as tolls, layovers and pass-through costs.

Fuel Surcharges

Fuel surcharge revenues for a backhaul load can be handled several ways depending on the language in the dedicated fleet contract. If the dedicated fleet contract includes a fuel surcharge provision, the carrier will collect fuel surcharge revenue from the dedicated shipper on all miles.[78] Meanwhile, the carrier may also collect fuel surcharge revenues on the third-party backhaul load. If this is the case, the carrier would be collecting double fuel surcharge revenues on the billed miles associated with the backhaul load. Because of the double fuel surcharge revenues, the dedicated shipper is entitled to participate in the benefits of the fuel surcharge revenues associated with the backhaul.

---

[78] Fuel surcharge revenues (or rebates) will not always apply. The carrier would only charge a fuel surcharge when the price of fuel exceeds the cost per gallon listed in the dedicated contract.

The sharing of fuel surcharge revenues for a backhaul load can get very complicated and confusing. In fact, any one simple approach to the fuel surcharge problem will not be fair under every possible situation. In most situations, the dedicated carrier should share the backhaul fuel surcharge revenue at the same percentage as the linehual revenue. Under this arrangement, it may appear at first glance that the carrier is benefiting by collecting double fuel surcharges on the backhaul load. However, the table below illustrates the revenue share calculations for two backhaul loads from two unique shippers with very different fuel surcharge pegs.

Sharing Fuel Surcharge Revenues for Different Customer Fuel Pegs	Backhaul Load A			Backhaul Load B		
	Backhaul Details	Revenue Share Shipper	Revenue Share Carrier	Backhaul Details	Revenue Share Shipper	Revenue Share Carrier
Revenue Share Percentages	-	75.0%	25.0%	-	75.0%	25.0%
Billed Miles	525			525		
Linehaul Rate Per Mile	$ 1.60			$ 1.78		
Fuel Peg (Cost Per Gallon)	$ 1.19			$ 2.25		
Actual Fuel Cost	$ 2.25			$ 2.25		
Fuel Surcharge Per Mile	$ 0.18			$ -		
Linehaul Revenue	$ 840.00	$ 630.00	$ 210.00	$ 934.50	$ 700.88	$ 233.63
Fuel Surcharge Revenue	$ 94.50	$ 70.88	$ 23.63	$ -	$ -	$ -
Total Revenue	$ 934.50	$ 700.88	$ 233.63	$ 934.50	$ 700.88	$ 233.63

In the above example, the carrier and shipper receive the exact same revenue share in both backhaul load scenarios. Because the rate per mile and fuel peg are much lower for backhaul load A, the carrier is entitled to a portion of the fuel surcharge revenue to compensate for the lower linehaul rate per mile. Though the carrier is collecting double fuel surcharge revenue, the shared portion of the backhaul fuel surcharge revenue only serves to normalize the carrier's revenue with the existing market price of fuel.

Out-of-Route Miles

In most cases, the carrier will incur out-of-route miles for the dedicated truck to pick up and deliver each backhaul load. The dedicated contract should specifically state which party, the dedicated shipper or the carrier, is responsible for the cost of these miles. If the dedicated shipper is responsible, the out-of-route miles associated with each backhaul load will be invoiced to the dedicated shipper. If the dedicated shipper is not required to pay the carrier for the out-of-route miles, the carrier should adjust the backhaul revenue share percentage lower (from 80% to 75% for example) to provide the necessary compensation for the out-of-route miles.

Partially Completed Backhaul Loads

Another risk for the carrier is selecting backhauls loads that don't terminate in the vicinity of the dedicated shipper's origin location. For example, suppose a carrier operates a dedicated fleet based in Dallas, TX. A dedicated truck delivers a load in Houston, TX and the carrier assigns the dedicated truck to a third-party backhaul load going from Houston, TX to St. Louis, MO. The dedicated truck will return to Dallas with the load going to St. Louis. The carrier will then assign a new driver from one of the carrier's one-way divisions to complete the trip from Dallas to St. Louis. After dropping the load in Dallas, the dedicated driver will return to the dedicated shipper for a new load.

The map below shows that the routing of the backhaul load through Dallas is actually out-of-route for the trip between Houston and St. Louis. These out-of-route miles complicate the management of the backhaul trip in several ways.

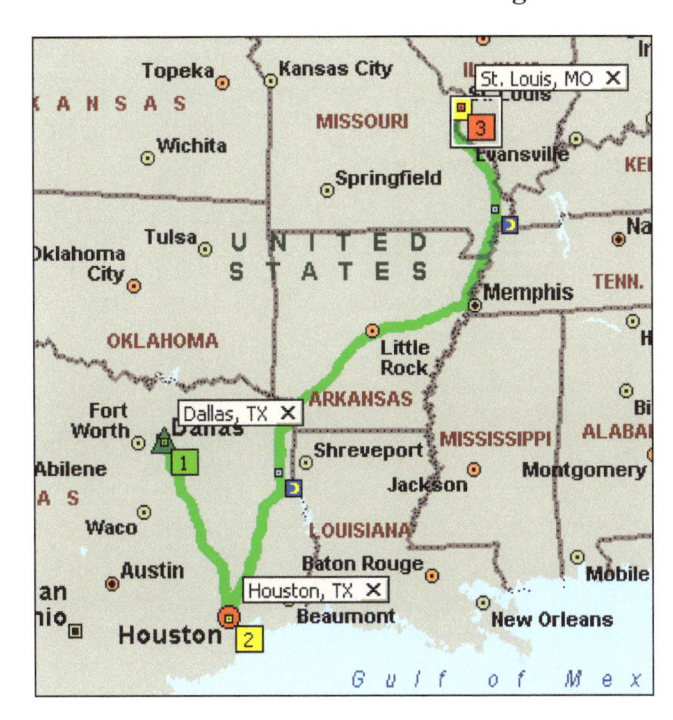

St. Louis Backhaul Routing

First, the shipper of the backhaul load pays for the trip based on the miles between Houston and St. Louis. The carrier will not be compensated for the 100 additional miles created for the trip when routed through Dallas, so net revenue per mile will deteriorate significantly as shown in the following table.

St. Louis Backhaul Net Revenue Per Mile

Backhaul Trip Revenue		$ 1,260
Routing	Loaded Miles	Revenue Per Mile
Direct Trip (Billed Miles)	840	$ 1.50
Through Dallas	940	$ 1.34
Out-of Route Miles	100	

The carrier will also incur the empty miles associated with the second truck that completes the final leg of the trip from Dallas to St. Louis. Assigning this truck to the trip also takes away an available truck from the Dallas market, which could be a positive or a negative network factor for the carrier. If the carrier already has a strong demand for truck capacity in Dallas, this relayed backhaul trip takes one available truck away from other customers in Dallas.

The carrier must also determine how to share the backhaul revenue for the trip with the dedicated customer. The carrier should only share the portion of the revenue associated with the miles driven by the dedicated truck, not the entire trip to St. Louis. The dedicated contract may or may not specify how an exception of this type is to be handled. While several approaches could be considered reasonable, a suggested method for sharing the backhaul revenue is shown below.

Revenue Share to Dedicated Customer		
Adjusted Revenue Per Mile		$ 1.34
Houston to Dallas Miles	x	241
Revenue to Dedicated Truck		$ 322.94
Backhaul Share Percentage	x	75.0%
Backhaul Credit to Customer		$ 242.21

This method bases the shared revenue on the adjusted revenue per mile of $1.34, taking into account the out-of-route miles associated with the routing through Dallas. The revenue amount eligible for sharing is $1.34 per mile times the 241 miles from Houston to Dallas served by the dedicated truck. The eligible revenue amount of $322.94 is multiplied by the 75% backhaul share percentage to determine the actual backhaul credit to the dedicated customer of $242.21.

Carriers should make certain that billing personnel are fully trained to recognize and process exceptions of this type. An inexperienced billing clerk may mistakenly share 75% of the $1,260 gross revenue for the trip instead of making the adjustment for the drop in Dallas. A mistake of this type would significantly reduce the carrier's revenue on the non-dedicated segment of the backhaul load.

The Backhaul Funnel

One approach the carrier might utilize to simplify the backhaul process is to use a "funnel" approach. Instead of attempting to locate backhaul loads in each discrete market, the carrier can select certain geographic markets and focus backhaul efforts in those areas. In the example below, the carrier has identified three major markets as possible "funnel" locations.

Dedicated Fleet Network and Backhaul "Funnel" Locations

Each funnel location represents a large market that is in-route from multiple destination locations on the return trip to the origin facility in Memphis, TN. Trucks that deliver into destination locations near each funnel can potentially secure a backhaul in the funnel market without having to wait on a backhaul in the actual destination market. If the carrier can locate one or two large backhaul accounts in the funnel market, the accounts can serve the backhaul needs of all dedicated destinations in the area.

Customizing the Driver Compensation Program

Many dedicated fleet operations contain unique network characteristics that will often dictate the need for a customized driver compensation structure. The key operating characteristics that create the need for driver pay customization include utilization levels, stop-off frequency, and driver unloading requirements. Low utilization is one of the most common reasons to customize the driver compensation structure.

Traditional driver compensation structures and pay rates simply don't provide an appropriate income for specialized dedicated drivers in many cases, especially fleets with low utilization levels. For this discussion, assume the average driver expects to earn an income of $900 per week or $46,800 per year. Consider the typical regional driver pay structure shown below.

Regional Driver Pay Program	
Pay Item	*Rate*
Mileage Pay	$ 0.37
Stops	$ 15.00
Unloading	$ 60.00

This structure will likely provide an acceptable income to a driver in a regional fleet that averages 2,200 miles per week. A driver with 2,200 miles plus one paid stop and one paid unload during a week would earn $889 for the week as shown below.

Weekly Earnings - Regional Driver			
Pay Item	*Rate*	*Activity*	*Earnings*
Mileage Pay	$ 0.37	2,200	$ 814.00
Stops	$ 15.00	1	$ 15.00
Unloading	$ 60.00	1	$ 60.00
		Total:	$ 889.00

If a carrier were to implement this same driver pay structure for a dedicated fleet that will average 1,200 miles per week with two paid stops and no unloading, the expected driver income would be extremely inadequate. Using the regional pay structure, the average driver would earn only $474 per week as shown below.

Weekly Earnings - Dedicated Driver			
Pay Item	*Rate*	*Activity*	*Earnings*
Mileage Pay	$ 0.37	1,200	$ 444.00
Stops	$ 15.00	2	$ 30.00
Unloading	$ 60.00	-	$ -
		Total:	$ 474.00

Since many pre-existing pay structures may not fit a new dedicated fleet, carriers must develop a customized pay structure appropriate to the dynamics of each dedicated fleet operation. A variety of options exist for customization such as those listed below.

Customized Dedicated Fleet Driver Pay Structures
Fixed Weekly Salary
Hourly Pay
Per Mile Pay
Activity-Based Pay (Per Load)
Modified Mileage Pay / Weekly Minimum Pay

These driver pay structures are reviewed in greater detail in the sections that follow.

Funding Driver Compensation. In order to provide adequate revenue for funding driver compensation, carriers must carefully consider contract structures and expected utilization levels when determining how dedicated revenues will be earned. Matching the revenue stream and driver compensation structure is especially critical in low utilization fleets, particularly with a fixed-variable contract structure. The examples that follow illustrate the impact of these driver pay options on a typical dedicated fleet.

Consider the following example. A shipper has requested pricing for a dedicated fleet where the expected utilization is 1,400 miles per week. The fleet will consist of 20 tractors, 20 drivers, and 60 trailers. The carrier plans to budget $850 per week for driver pay. The fuel surcharge peg is set at $1.40 per gallon. The proposed pricing from the dedicated pricing spreadsheet is shown below.

Dedicated Pricing Model

Customer Name:	Chapter 11	Fleet Description:	Driver Pay

Fleet Parameters

Number of Tractors	20.00
Backup Tractors	0.00
Number of Drivers	20.00
Utilization (Miles per Tractor per Active Week)	1,400
Active Fleet Weeks Per Year (max = 52 weeks)	52.0
Total Fleet Annual Miles	1,456,000
Number of Trailers	60.00
Trailer/Tractor Ratio	3.00

Overhead Costs

Tractor Legalization/Taxes	$	2,000
Driver Recruiting Costs	$	3,000
Administration Expenses	$	5,000
Total Overhead (per tractor per year)	$	10,000
Direct Staffing (On-site CSR / Offices / Etc.)	$	-
Other Annual Expenses (Total Fleet)	$	5,000
Initial Start-Up Costs (Total)	$	10,000

Other Parameters

Driver Rate of Pay (Per Mile or Annual Gross)	$	44,200.00
Duration of Deal/Contract (in months)		36.0
Average Collection Period (in days)		30.0

Pricing and Analysis

Suggested Rate Per Mile (all miles)	$	1.9300
Operating Ratio		86.68%
Profit Margin		13.32%

Pro-Forma Income Statement

		Fleet Totals Per Mile	Fleet Totals Annual	Per Tractor Weekly	Per Tractor Annual
Total Fleet Miles			1,456,000	1,400	72,800
Total Revenue		$1.930	$2,810,080	$2,702	$140,504
Variable Costs	Assumptions				
Driver Wages	$44,200.00	$0.607	$884,000	$850	$44,200
Fringe Benefits (% of wages)	25.0%	0.152	221,000	213	11,050
Fuel	$0.241	0.241	351,381	338	17,569
Maintenance	$0.110	0.110	160,160	154	8,008
Insurance	$0.100	0.100	145,600	140	7,280
Total Variable Costs		1.210	1,762,141	1,694	88,107
Fixed Costs	Assumptions				
Tractor Depreciation	$ 16,667	0.229	333,333	$321	$16,667
Trailer Depreciation	$ 2,200	0.091	132,000	127	6,600
Legalization/Recruiting/Admin	$ 10,000	0.137	200,000	192	10,000
On-Site Manager	$ -	0.000	0	0	0
Start Up /Special Equipment	$ 8,333	0.006	8,333	8	417
Total Fixed Costs		0.463	673,667	648	33,683
Total Cost		1.673	2,435,808	2,342	121,790
Operating Profit		$0.26	$374,272	$360	$18,714
Operating Ratio		86.68%	86.68%	86.68%	86.68%

With an expected utilization of only 1,400 miles per week, the carrier must estimate the expected potential range of the actual utilization. Based on the shipper's freight network characteristics, the range of possible actual utilization levels is determined to be between

900 and 1,900 miles. Given this relatively low utilization range, the carrier must now decide how the driver compensation package will be structured. The compensation plan must offer a satisfactory level of income to the driver without adding significant profitability risk for the carrier. If utilization is below expected levels, the carrier's revenues will decline, but the carrier must still provide satisfactory compensation to the driver. At the same time, if utilization is well above expected levels, the compensation program must not generate excessive levels of income for the driver and extra expense for the carrier.

The driver compensation plan must be reasonable for any level in the expected utilization range of 900 to 1,900 miles per week. The compensation plan must also be highly accurate within a smaller range of 1,200 to 1,600 miles per week. In this example, the pricing model calls for a budgeted driver income of $850 per week. The carrier must determine the appropriate compensation structure for the relevant range of utilization. Several potential approaches are presented and evaluated in the sections that follow.

Fixed Weekly Salary

With a fixed weekly salary pay structure, each driver is paid a flat weekly salary regardless of total miles or other productivity measures. A salary-based pay program will likely be an attractive system for many drivers because of the income security it provides. However, since drivers are paid the same fixed amount regardless of the amount of work they perform, some drivers may take advantage of the system.

A fixed salary is usually not effective because drivers have very little motivation to provide effort beyond a minimum acceptable level. A pay program of this type should have minimum productivity standards, bonus structures, and other clearly defined expectations to minimize the likelihood of drivers taking advantage of the system.

In addition, an inequitable income situation would exist as drivers that are highly productive receive the same compensation as the least productive drivers. The table below illustrates the effective per-mile pay for drivers at different utilization levels.

Since each driver earns a weekly salary of $850, drivers with low utilization earn far more per mile than drivers with above average utilization. No financial incentive exists for under-performing drivers to increase productivity and utilization. This gap could result in higher costs for the shipper since the dedicated fleet size may be larger than necessary because of the poor productivity. A compensation program with strong productivity incentives for drivers could result in a smaller fleet size and reduced costs for the dedicated shipper.

Effective Per-Mile Earnings with Fixed Salary Driver Pay Structure

Weekly Utilization	Weekly Salary	Effective Per-Mile Pay
800	$ 850.00	$ 1.06
900	$ 850.00	$ 0.94
1,000	$ 850.00	$ 0.85
1,100	$ 850.00	$ 0.77
1,200	$ 850.00	$ 0.71
1,300	$ 850.00	$ 0.65
1,400	**$ 850.00**	**$ 0.61**
1,500	$ 850.00	$ 0.57
1,600	$ 850.00	$ 0.53
1,700	$ 850.00	$ 0.50
1,800	$ 850.00	$ 0.47
1,900	$ 850.00	$ 0.45
2,000	$ 850.00	$ 0.43

Hourly Pay

Hourly pay provides a more performance-based driver pay format than a simple fixed weekly salary. Drivers must manage their availability so as to work enough hours each week to make a suitable income. Hourly pay is more equitable than a fixed weekly salary in short haul environments, especially those that may involve long unloading times, excess down time between loads, or extreme traffic issues. However, similar to a salary system, drivers may take advantage of the hourly system by taking more time than necessary to deliver each load. Carriers should establish standard times, measure driver productivity, and provide driver incentives against the standard times.

A potential risk of an hourly pay system is that the driver pay system is not consistent with the carrier's revenue stream. Consider a fixed-variable dedicated contract in which the carrier is paid a fixed amount each week for each truck and a variable rate per mile. The carrier does not have a corresponding revenue stream based on hours worked. The unmatched revenue stream and driver compensation structure could result in a serious financial gap such as the one shown in the illustration below.

Hourly Pay Gap			
Scenario	Hours Worked Per Driver Per Week	Hourly Pay Rate	Weekly Earnings
Fleet Design	50	$ 17.00	$ 850.00
Actual Implementation	55	$ 17.00	$ 935.00
Weekly Gap			$ 85.00
Annual Gap Per Driver (52 weeks)			**$ 4,420.00**

In this example, the fleet design called for each driver to work 50 hours per week and earn $17.00 per hour. After actual implementation, the average driver worked 55 hours per week instead of the planned 50 hours. Since the $17.00 per hour pay structure was already in place, each driver earned $935.00 per week instead of the budgeted amount of $850.00 per week that was included in the pricing. In this situation, the carrier will face greater driver costs than expected and the fleet will not be as profitable as projected.

The table below compares the planned financial performance of the fleet to the actual financial performance under the potential hours worked gap presented previously.

Financial Impact of Hourly Pay Gap

	\multicolumn{4}{c}{Annual Totals}			
	\multicolumn{2}{c}{Fleet Design (Pro Forma)}		\multicolumn{2}{c}{Actual Operation}		
	Per Truck		Total Fleet		Per Truck		Total Fleet
Total Fleet Miles			1,456,000				72,800
Total Revenue	$	140,504	$ 2,810,080	$	140,504	$	2,810,080
Variable Costs							
Driver Wages	$	44,200	$ 884,000	$	48,620	$	972,400
Fringe Benefits (% of wages)		11,050	221,000		12,155		243,100
Fuel		17,569	351,381		17,569		351,381
Maintenance		8,008	160,160		8,008		160,160
Insurance		7,280	145,600		7,280		145,600
Total Variable Costs	$	88,107	$ 1,762,141		93,632		1,872,641
Fixed Costs							
Tractor Depreciation	$	16,667	$ 333,333	$	16,667	$	333,333
Trailer Depreciation		6,600	132,000		6,600		132,000
Legalization/Recruiting/Admin		10,000	200,000		10,000		200,000
On-Site Manager		-	0		0		0
Start Up /Special Equipment		417	8,333		417		8,333
Total Fixed Costs	$	33,683	$ 673,667	$	33,683	$	673,667
Total Cost	$	121,790	$ 2,435,808	$	127,315	$	2,546,308
Operating Profit	$	18,714	$ 374,272	$	13,189	$	263,772
Operating Ratio			86.68%	86.68%		90.61%	90.61%

The carrier's profits fell dramatically as a result of the driver compensation gap. The carrier's annual operating profit for the total fleet declined from $374,272 to only $263,772. The operating ratio went from a planned level of 86.68% to 90.61%. Even though the drivers worked more hours than expected, the carrier's gross revenue does not change.

Per Mile Pay

Another simple compensation plan option would be to pay each driver a fixed rate per mile. The budgeted base pay of $850 per week divided by the expected utilization of 1,400 miles results in a pay rate per mile of $0.61 cents per mile (rounded). A pay rate per mile at this level would likely result in excessive driver pay for those drivers who exceed the 1,400 mile utilization expectation on a regular basis.[79] The potential earnings at various levels of utilization are shown in the table below.

Simple Rate Per Mile Pay Structure

Pay Rate Per Mile:		
Weekly Driver Income	$	850
Planned Utilization	÷	1,400
Driver Pay Rate Per Mile	$	0.61

Estimated Income Levels:		
Weekly Utilization	Pay Rate Per Mile	Weekly Income
800	$ 0.61	$ 488.00
900	$ 0.61	$ 549.00
1,000	$ 0.61	$ 610.00
1,100	$ 0.61	$ 671.00
1,200	$ 0.61	$ 732.00
1,300	$ 0.61	$ 793.00
1,400	**$ 0.61**	**$ 854.00**
1,500	$ 0.61	$ 915.00
1,600	$ 0.61	$ 976.00
1,700	$ 0.61	$ 1,037.00
1,800	$ 0.61	$ 1,098.00
1,900	$ 0.61	$ 1,159.00
2,000	$ 0.61	$ 1,220.00

Under this pay structure, the computed pay rate is $0.61 per mile. Drivers that significantly exceed the target utilization of 1,400 will earn incomes that are excessive and unreasonable. Drivers that are below the target utilization may not be earning a fair income for the work that is performed. It is possible that the lower utilization drivers are actually highly productive but have a lower than average utilization because of serving shorter length of haul loads. The carrier may be at risk of losing these productive drivers because of the inequitable pay structure present in this simple per-mile pay design.

---

[79] In most dedicated fleets, the best drivers will often exceed the average fleet utilization on a regular basis. At the same time, other individual drivers will achieve an average utilization level that is below the overall fleet average.

Activity-Based Pay

In low utilization, short haul fleets, utilization is not the only relevant measure of productivity. The number of loads served per driver per week is also a key component of productivity. A driver compensation plan based on both mileage productivity and load productivity often provides a more equitable pay structure than a simple salary or simple per-mile pay structure.

As opposed to a weekly salary, mileage pay or hourly pay, an activity-based pay system can be very effective for both driver compensation and motivation in short haul networks. The goal of the activity-based pay system is to motivate drivers to complete each load as quickly as possible in order to be available for the next load. In addition to mileage pay, the driver would also receive a flat amount of pay for each load served. A basic format for this type of pay structure is shown below.

Activity-Based Pay Program

Pay Item	Rate	Activity	Earnings
Mileage Pay	$ 0.32	1,100	$ 352.00
Per Load	$ 35.00	13	$ 455.00
Stops	$ 15.00	1	$ 15.00
Unloading	$ 60.00	1	$ 60.00
		Total:	$ 882.00

Carriers might also implement a system that adjusts the per-load amount based on the length of haul of each load. In the example below, drivers are paid 40 cents for all miles plus the per-load amounts as shown below.

Modified Activity-Based Driver Pay Structure

Driver Pay Rates		Estimated Pay Amounts			
One-Way Miles	Per-Load Pay Rate	Payroll Miles	Total Driver Pay (40¢ / mi)		
			Per-Load	Mileage	Total
0 - 10 Miles	$ 35.00	10	$ 35.00	$ 4.00	$ 39.00
11 - 20 Miles	$ 30.00	30	$ 30.00	$ 12.00	$ 42.00
21 - 30 Miles	$ 25.00	50	$ 25.00	$ 20.00	$ 45.00
31 - 40 Miles	$ 20.00	70	$ 20.00	$ 28.00	$ 48.00
41 - 50 Miles	$ 15.00	90	$ 15.00	$ 36.00	$ 51.00
51 - 60 Miles	$ 10.00	110	$ 10.00	$ 44.00	$ 54.00
61 - 70 Miles	$ 5.00	130	$ 5.00	$ 52.00	$ 57.00
71 and Up	$ -	150	$ -	$ 60.00	$ 60.00

The per-load pay declines as the length of haul increases since the driver is also earning income on the increasing number of miles. At 71 miles, a per-load pay amount is no longer applied to the trip.

Consider the activities and earnings shown below for four dedicated fleet drivers during a one week period. The fleet design was based on an average income of $800 per driver per week.

Driver Earnings Summary W/E: 10/5/08	William	Craig	Woody	David	Fleet Average
Activity:					
Loads	7	8	4	6	6
Paid Stops	3	4	2	2	3
Utilization	1,950	1,300	925	1,650	1,456
Average Length of Haul	279	163	231	275	233
Driver Pay Rates:					
Per Load	$ 25.00	$ 25.00	$ 25.00	$ 25.00	
Per Stop	$ 15.00	$ 15.00	$ 15.00	$ 15.00	
Per Mile	$ 0.40	$ 0.40	$ 0.40	$ 0.40	
Total Compensation:					
Per Load	$ 175.00	$ 200.00	$ 100.00	$ 150.00	$ 156.25
Per Stop	$ 45.00	$ 60.00	$ 30.00	$ 30.00	$ 41.25
Per Mile	$ 780.00	$ 520.00	$ 370.00	$ 660.00	$ 582.50
Total Pay	$1,000.00	$ 780.00	$ 500.00	$ 840.00	$ 780.00

The average driver income for the week was $780 per driver, consistent with the $800 per week design. The activity-based pay system has rewarded the most productive driver, William, with an income of $1,000 for the week. At the same time, the least productive driver, Woody, has earned only $500 due to low productivity. Woody must increase productivity in order to increase his income. Under a salary-based system, Woody would earn the same income as the other drivers despite his relative lack of productivity.

Under an activity-based pay system, the driver shares in the carrier's goal of maximizing utilization and productivity. The most productive drivers will make a much higher income than the least productive drivers. A program of this type might also allow the carrier to gain per-tractor productivity. As the result of improved driver motivation and productivity, the carrier may discover that a fleet designed to be a 20 driver fleet can be served with only 18 drivers. This efficiency will result in some combination of increased profits for the carrier and reduced transportation costs for the dedicated shipper.

Modified Mileage Pay

A modified mileage pay system would include a reasonable pay rate per mile and a minimum guaranteed amount of weekly pay for the driver. A sample modified mileage pay program is shown below.

Modified Driver Pay Program	
Pay Item	**Rate**
Mileage Pay	$ 0.37
Stops	$ 15.00
Unloading	$ 60.00
Weekly Minimum	$ 475.00

Under this structure, if drivers don't earn more than $475 in the week through the normal pay activities, the carrier will instead pay the driver $475 for the week. A structure like this is particularly effective during the implementation phase of new dedicated fleets. During the start-up phase, the fleet size may be larger than what is needed, so there is not enough load activity to satisfy the income requirement for all drivers.

To avoid the common problems associated with a salary pay structure, drivers should be required to meet specific standards each week in order to qualify for the minimum pay. Drivers that consistently fall into the minimum weekly pay group may need to be terminated and replaced. The pay program must provide drivers with the financial incentive to maximize productivity.

To be successful in the dedicated fleet market, carriers must develop creative methods to address these driver pay issues. Regardless of the exact pay structure, carriers must design a compensation plan that allows the carrier to attract and retain qualified drivers for the fleet. To protect profitability, the compensation plan must also fit within the driver pay budget established in the pricing process. The plan must also be flexible enough to protect both the driver's interests and the carrier's interests during periods of abnormally high or low utilization.

Matching the Driver Pay Program to Revenues

Where possible when designing a dedicated driver pay program, the driver pay structure should be consistent with the revenue components so that adequate revenue to fund driver wages is generated at any reasonable utilization level. It is not necessary for revenues and driver wages to match on a driver-by-driver basis. However, it is necessary for total revenues and gross driver wages to match on an overall basis for the fleet as a whole.

Suppose a carrier has designed a dedicated fleet based on a budgeted income of $800 per driver per week. The expected utilization for the fleet is 1,450 miles per driver per week. The pricing model for the fleet is shown below.

Dedicated Pricing Model

Customer Name:	Chapter 11	Fleet Description:	Matching Driver Pay to Revenues

Fleet Parameters

Number of Tractors	10.00
Backup Tractors	0.00
Number of Drivers	10.00
Utilization (Miles per Tractor per Active Week)	1,450
Active Fleet Weeks Per Year (max = 52 weeks)	52.0
Total Fleet Annual Miles	754,000
Number of Trailers	28.00
Trailer/Tractor Ratio	2.80

Overhead Costs

Tractor Legalization/Taxes	$	2,000
Driver Recruiting Costs	$	3,000
Administration Expenses	$	5,000
Total Overhead (per tractor per year)	$	10,000
Direct Staffing (On-site CSR / Offices / Etc.)	$	-
Other Annual Expenses (Total Fleet)	$	5,000
Initial Start-Up Costs (Total)	$	10,000

Other Parameters

Driver Rate of Pay (Per Mile or Annual Gross)	$	41,600.00
Duration of Deal/Contract (in months)		36.0
Average Collection Period (in days)		30.0

Pricing and Analysis

Suggested Rate Per Mile (all miles)	$	1.9700
Operating Ratio		80.58%
Internal Rate of Return		12.06%

Pro-Forma Income Statement

	Assumptions	Fleet Totals Per Mile	Fleet Totals Annual	Per Tractor Weekly	Per Tractor Annual
Total Fleet Miles			754,000	1,450	75,400
Total Revenue		$1.970	$1,485,380	$2,857	$148,538
Variable Costs					
Driver Wages	$41,600.00	$0.552	$416,000	$800	$41,600
Fringe Benefits (% of wages)	25.0%	0.138	104,000	200	10,400
Fuel	$0.241	0.241	181,965	350	18,197
Maintenance	$0.110	0.110	82,940	160	8,294
Insurance	$0.100	0.100	75,400	145	7,540
Total Variable Costs		1.141	860,305	1,654	86,031
Fixed Costs	Assumptions				
Tractor Depreciation	$ 16,667	0.221	166,667	$321	$16,667
Trailer Depreciation	$ 2,200	0.082	61,600	118	6,160
Legalization/Recruiting/Admin	$ 10,000	0.133	100,000	192	10,000
On-Site Manager	$ -	0.000	0	0	0
Start Up /Special Equipment	$ 8,333	0.011	8,333	16	833
Total Fixed Costs		0.446	336,600	647	33,660
Total Cost		1.587	1,196,905	2,302	119,691
Operating Profit		$0.38	$288,475	$555	$28,847
Operating Ratio		80.58%	80.58%	80.58%	80.58%

The carrier plans to pay the drivers on a per-mile basis. Based on the $800 per week income target and the utilization of 1,450 miles, drivers will be paid $0.55 per mile. Since this is a new fleet, the carrier has also guaranteed each driver that he will earn a minimum of $800 per week.

The shipper has requested pricing for the fleet in the fixed-variable format. The carrier's design of the fixed and variable rate components is shown below.

Fixed-Variable Pricing Design

Dedicated Pricing Model	Enter a percentage in the yellow cells to indicate the portion of each item to allocate to each pricing component.		
Fixed / Variable Pricing			
Chapter 11 - Matching Driver Pay to Revenues	Allocation	Variable	Fixed
	Driver Wages	100%	0%
	Operating Profit	50%	50%

		Total Revenue Allocation			Fixed / Variable Pricing		
		Fleet	Variable	Fixed	Variable	Fixed Per Truck	
Revenue/Cost Components		Totals	Rate	Rate	Per Mile	Per Year	Per Week
Driver Wages	$	416,000	$ 416,000	$ -	$ 0.552	$ -	$ -
Fringe Benefits (% of wages)	$	104,000	$ 104,000	$ -	$ 0.138	$ -	$ -
Fuel	$	181,965	$ 181,965	$ -	$ 0.241	$ -	$ -
Maintenance	$	82,940	$ 82,940	$ -	$ 0.110	$ -	$ -
Insurance (% of revenue)	$	75,400	$ 75,400	$ -	$ 0.100	$ -	$ -
Total Variable Costs	$	860,305	$ 860,305	$ -	$ 1.141	$ -	$ -
Tractor Depreciation	$	166,667	$ -	$ 166,667	$ -	$ 16,667	$ 321
Trailer Depreciation	$	61,600	$ -	$ 61,600	$ -	$ 6,160	$ 118
Legalization/Recruiting/Admin	$	100,000	$ -	$ 100,000	$ -	$ 10,000	$ 192
On-Site Manager	$	-	$ -	$ -	$ -	$ -	$ -
Start Up /Special Equipment	$	8,333	$ -	$ 8,333	$ -	$ 833	$ 16
Total Fixed Costs	$	336,600	$ -	$ 336,600	$ -	$ 33,660	$ 647
Operating Profit	$	288,475	$ 144,237	$ 144,237	$ 0.191	$ 14,424	$ 277
Total Desired Revenue	$	1,485,380	$ 1,004,543	$ 480,837	$ **1.332**	**$48,084**	**$925**

Minimum Weekly Charge		Annual	Per Truck Per Week		Final Rates:		
Base Fixed Charge			$ 925		Fixed:	$	925
Plus: Variable Driver Wages	$	520,000	$ 1,000		Variable:	$	1.332
Plus: Profit on Driver Wages	$	87,182	$ 168				
Minimum Charge Per Truck Per Week			**$ 2,092**				

Revenue Verification		Rate	Annual Units	Annual Revenue
Fixed Charge Per Tractor Per Week	$	925	520	$ 480,837
Variable Charge Per Mile	$	1.332	754,000	$ 1,004,543
Total Annual Revenue				**$ 1,485,380**

The carrier has chosen to assign 100% of the revenue needed to fund driver wages to the variable revenue component. The proposed rates include a fixed weekly charge of $925 per tractor and a rounded variable rate of $1.33 per mile.

The carrier has taken a significant risk in assigning 100% of the driver pay revenues to the variable rate component. Since the fleet is based on a relatively low utilization level of 1,450 miles per week, there is a high risk of actual utilization falling below the planned level. If the actual utilization is lower than expected, the carrier will not earn enough revenue to fund the minimum driver compensation of $800 per week.

The analysis below illustrates the driver pay funding gap that will occur at lower than expected utilization levels.

Weekly Driver Pay Revenue Gap	Rates	Actual Utilization Plan	Below Plan			
Utilization		1,450	1,350	1,250	1,150	1,050
Actual Revenues:						
Fixed Component	$ 925.00	$ 925.00	$ 925.00	$ 925.00	$ 925.00	$ 925.00
Variable Component	$ 1.33	$ 1,928.50	$ 1,795.50	$ 1,662.50	$ 1,529.50	$ 1,396.50
Total Revenue (Per Truck)		$ 2,853.50	$ 2,720.50	$ 2,587.50	$ 2,454.50	$ 2,321.50
Driver Pay Funding in Variable Rate	$ 0.550	$ 797.50	$ 742.50	$ 687.50	$ 632.50	$ 577.50
Actual Driver Pay	$ 800.00	$ 800.00	$ 800.00	$ 800.00	$ 800.00	$ 800.00
Revenue Shortfall		$ (2.50)	$ (57.50)	$ (112.50)	$ (167.50)	$ (222.50)

When utilization is less than planned, the carrier does not earn enough variable revenue to fund the minimum driver pay commitment of $800 per driver per week. As utilization falls, the driver pay revenue gap grows. The carrier's operating profits are adversely affected as a result of the revenue shortfall. To reduce the impact of the revenue gap, the carrier should adjust the allocation of revenues among the fixed and variable revenue components as shown below.

Dedicated Pricing Model
Fixed / Variable Pricing
Chapter 11 - Matching Driver Pay to Revenues

Enter a percentage in the yellow cells to indicate the portion of each item to allocate to each pricing component.

Allocation	Variable	Fixed
Driver Wages	50%	50%
Operating Profit	50%	50%

Revenue/Cost Components	Fleet Totals	Total Revenue Allocation Variable Rate	Fixed Rate	Fixed / Variable Pricing Variable Per Mile	Fixed Per Truck Per Year	Per Week
Driver Wages	$ 416,000	$ 208,000	$ 208,000	$ 0.276	$ 20,800	$ 400
Fringe Benefits (% of wages)	$ 104,000	$ 52,000	$ 52,000	$ 0.069	$ 5,200	$ 100
Fuel	$ 181,965	$ 181,965	$ -	$ 0.241	$ -	$ -
Maintenance	$ 82,940	$ 82,940	$ -	$ 0.110	$ -	$ -
Insurance	$ 75,400	$ 75,400	$ -	$ 0.100	$ -	$ -
Total Variable Costs	$ 860,305	$ 600,305	$ 260,000	$ 0.796	$ 26,000	$ 500
Tractor Depreciation	$ 166,667	$ -	$ 166,667	$ -	$ 16,667	$ 321
Trailer Depreciation	$ 61,600	$ -	$ 61,600	$ -	$ 6,160	$ 118
Legalization/Recruiting/Admin	$ 100,000	$ -	$ 100,000	$ -	$ 10,000	$ 192
On-Site Manager	$ -	$ -	$ -	$ -	$ -	$ -
Start Up /Special Equipment	$ 8,333	$ -	$ 8,333	$ -	$ 833	$ 16
Total Fixed Costs	$ 336,600	$ -	$ 336,600	$ -	$ 33,660	$ 647
Operating Profit	$ 288,475	$ 144,237	$ 144,237	$ 0.191	$ 14,424	$ 277
Total Desired Revenue	$ 1,485,380	$ 744,543	$ 740,837	$ 0.987	$74,084	$1,425

Minimum Weekly Charge	Annual	Per Truck Per Week		Final Rates:		
Base Fixed Charge		$ 1,425		Fixed:	$	1,425
Plus: Variable Driver Wages	$ 260,000	$ 500		Variable:	$	0.987
Plus: Profit on Driver Wages	$ 62,471	$ 120				
Minimum Charge Per Truck Per Week		$ 2,045				

In this design, the carrier has allocated only 50% of driver pay revenues to the variable rate component. The revised revenue gap for driver pay is shown below.

Weekly Driver Pay Revenue Gap	Rates	Actual Utilization Plan	Below Plan			
Utilization		1,450	1,350	1,250	1,150	1,050
Actual Revenues:						
Fixed Component	$ 1,425.00	$ 1,425.00	$ 1,425.00	$ 1,425.00	$ 1,425.00	$ 1,425.00
Variable Component	$ 0.99	$ 1,435.50	$ 1,336.50	$ 1,237.50	$ 1,138.50	$ 1,039.50
Total Revenue (Per Truck)		$ 2,860.50	$ 2,761.50	$ 2,662.50	$ 2,563.50	$ 2,464.50
Driver Pay Funding						
in Variable Rate	$ 0.280	$ 406.00	$ 378.00	$ 350.00	$ 322.00	$ 294.00
in Fixed Rate	$ 400.00	$ 400.00	$ 400.00	$ 400.00	$ 400.00	$ 400.00
Total Pay Funding		$ 806.00	$ 778.00	$ 750.00	$ 722.00	$ 694.00
Actual Driver Pay	$ 800.00	$ 800.00	$ 800.00	$ 800.00	$ 800.00	$ 800.00
Revenue Shortfall		$ 6.00	$ (22.00)	$ (50.00)	$ (78.00)	$ (106.00)

Under the revised pricing design, a revenue shortfall still exists. However, the revenue shortfall in the revised design is far less than the shortfall with the 100% variable allocation in the original design. The impact to the carrier's operating profits is not nearly as severe.

The second problem with the original pricing and driver pay design was in the driver pay structure. A simple pay structure of $0.55 per mile with an $800 per week minimum creates additional cost exposure for the carrier in several ways. The most common scenario is when several individual drivers exceed the planned utilization and earn incomes in excess of the $800 per week minimum. Meanwhile, several other drivers fall below the planned utilization and are paid the weekly minimum of $800. The table below illustrates this type of gap.

Utilization Spread and the Driver Pay Gap

Driver	Actual Utilization	Variable Pay $0.55	Minimum Pay	Actual Pay
1	1,700	$ 935.00	$ 800.00	$ 935.00
2	1,622	$ 892.10	$ 800.00	$ 892.10
3	1,572	$ 864.60	$ 800.00	$ 864.60
4	1,522	$ 837.10	$ 800.00	$ 837.10
5	1,472	$ 809.60	$ 800.00	$ 809.60
6	1,422	$ 782.10	$ 800.00	$ 800.00
7	1,372	$ 754.60	$ 800.00	$ 800.00
8	1,322	$ 727.10	$ 800.00	$ 800.00
9	1,272	$ 699.60	$ 800.00	$ 800.00
10	1,225	$ 673.75	$ 800.00	$ 800.00
Totals				$ 8,338.40
Averages	1,450			$ 833.84
Budget				$ 800.00
Gap Per Driver				$ 33.84

This pay system is actually rewarding and protecting drivers that under-perform relative to other drivers in the fleet. Even the best drivers can have a random low utilization week from time to time. However, a driver pay program should be designed to reward the top performers while not overprotecting the consistently poor performers.

Many of these driver pay gaps can be corrected through the design of the driver pay program. The driver pay program should provide appropriate and consistent compensation for the driver. The pay program should also provide the financial incentive for each driver to perform at a highly productive level in order to meet the revenue and profitability needs of the carrier. Several possible pay structures for the previous example are described below.

Possible Driver Pay Design Changes	
Change	**Description**
Fixed-Variable Driver Pay Program	Instead of only a mileage rate of $0.55 per mile with an $800 minimum, drivers could be paid a flat rate of $350 per week plus $0.31 per mile. A minimum weekly pay could also be included in this pay structure design.
Activity-Based Pay	Instead of only a mileage rate of $0.55 per mile with an $800 minimum, drivers could be paid on an activity-based system. For this fleet, drivers could be paid a flat rate of $40 per load and $0.35 per mile. The actual rates for a pay structure of this type should be modeled based on the shipper's unique network.
Reduce the Weekly Minimum Pay	In the previous example, the $800 weekly minimum pay was based on the pricing design. Since this minimum rewards underperforming drivers, the carrier could consider a lower minimum weekly pay level of $650 or $700 per week. A minimum pay reduction of this type will significantly reduce many of the potential driver pay gaps illustrated previously.
Extend Weekly Minimum Reconciliation Period	Instead of executing the $800 per week minimum on a weekly basis, the carrier could reconcile pay over a multi-week period such as every 4 weeks. Earnings for most drivers will balance out over several weeks, reducing the need for excessive payouts to meet the discrete minimum weekly earnings commitment.

When pricing dedicated fleet opportunities, carriers should avoid basing actual driver pay programs on the fleet's pricing design. The primary goal of the pricing is to budget an appropriate amount for driver compensation. The actual driver pay structure should be customized based on the specific driving job and the dynamics of the shipper's network while also staying within the budget established by the pricing.

In conclusion, there is no perfect solution in every case for the dedicated driver pay gap challenges. The final design of any driver pay program should be based on the unique characteristics of the shipper's network. Factors such as length of haul, seasonality, and utilization variability should all be taken into consideration. Carriers should also perform sensitivity analysis on any proposed driver pay structure to identify any potential gaps prior to the actual dedicated fleet implementation.

Measuring the Efficiency of Dedicated Fleets

Both carriers and shippers must develop key measurements to evaluate the efficiency, cost effectiveness, and profitability of dedicated fleets. Accurate cost information and internal cost allocation methodology are both essential for this effort. Two key elements of dedicated fleets that require review include the cost and revenue component and the productivity and utilization component. The sections that follow illustrate several key methods for measuring the efficiency and productivity of dedicated fleets.

Fleet Design and Actual Performance

While no dedicated fleet will operate exactly as designed, carriers should always compare the actual operation with the original pricing design. The comparison will provide explanations when fleets fail to meet profitability expectations. The analysis will also provide the carrier with valuable feedback on the design and pricing process. Prior to the actual fleet implementation, a carrier has carefully developed the dedicated fleet proposal shown below.

Dedicated Pricing Model

Customer Name:	Chapter 11	Fleet Description:	Plan vs Actual

Fleet Parameters

Number of Tractors	20.00
Backup Tractors	0.00
Number of Drivers	20.00
Utilization (Miles per Tractor per Active Week)	2,050
Active Fleet Weeks Per Year (max = 52 weeks)	51.0
Total Fleet Annual Miles	2,091,000
Number of Trailers	60.00
Trailer/Tractor Ratio	3.00

Overhead Costs

Tractor Legalization/Taxes	$ 2,000
Driver Recruiting Costs	$ 3,000
Administration Expenses	$ 5,000
Total Overhead (per tractor per year)	$ 10,000
Direct Staffing (On-site CSR / Offices / Etc.)	$ 75,000
Other Annual Expenses (Total Fleet)	$ 5,000
Initial Start-Up Costs (Total)	$ 10,000

Other Parameters

Driver Rate of Pay (Per Mile or Annual Gross)	$ 42,500.00
Duration of Deal/Contract (in months)	36.0
Average Collection Period (in days)	30.0

Pricing and Analysis

Suggested Rate Per Mile (all miles)	$ 1.6100
Operating Ratio	81.83%
Internal Rate of Return	12.22%

Pro-Forma Income Statement		Fleet Totals Per Mile	Fleet Totals Annual	Per Tractor Weekly	Per Tractor Annual
Total Fleet Miles			2,091,000	2,011	104,550
Total Revenue		$1.610	$3,366,510	$3,237	$168,326
Variable Costs	Assumptions				
Driver Wages	$42,500.00	$0.407	$850,000	$817	$42,500
Fringe Benefits (% of wages)	25.0%	0.102	212,500	204	10,625
Fuel	$0.241	0.241	504,628	485	25,231
Maintenance	$0.110	0.110	230,010	221	11,501
Insurance	$0.100	0.100	209,100	201	10,455
Total Variable Costs		0.959	2,006,238	1,929	100,312
Fixed Costs	Assumptions				
Tractor Depreciation	$ 16,667	0.159	333,333	$321	$16,667
Trailer Depreciation	$ 2,200	0.063	132,000	127	6,600
Legalization/Recruiting/Admin	$ 10,000	0.096	200,000	192	10,000
On-Site Manager	$ 75,000	0.036	75,000	72	3,750
Start Up /Special Equipment	$ 8,333	0.004	8,333	8	417
Total Fixed Costs		0.358	748,667	720	37,433
Total Cost		1.318	2,754,905	2,649	137,745
Operating Profit		$0.29	$611,605	$588	$30,580
Operating Ratio		81.83%	81.83%	81.83%	81.83%

Based on this cost proposal, the carrier is awarded the fleet and begins operations. After 12 months, the carrier performs the plan versus actual analysis shown below.

Dedicated Fleet Analysis - Plan vs Actual

Customer Name:	Chapter 11		Fleet Description:		Plan vs Actual	
Plan vs Actual	**Pricing Design**		**Actual Operation**		**Variance to Plan**	
	Per Mile	Annual	Per Mile	Annual	Per Mile	Annual
Fleet Design						
Number of Tractors		20.00		20.00		-
Number of Drivers		20.00		20.00		-
Number of Trailers		60.00		63.00		3.00
Utilization		2,050		1,942		(108.00)
Active Fleet Weeks Per Year (max = 52 weeks)		51.0		51.0		-
Rate Per Mile		$ 1.61		$ 1.61		$ -
Total Fleet Miles		2,091,000		1,980,840		(110,160)
Total Revenue	$1.610	$3,366,510	$1.610	$3,189,152	$0.000	($177,358)
Variable Costs	Assumptions					
Driver Wages	$42,500.00	$0.407 $850,000	$0.429	$850,000	$0.023	$0
Fringe Benefits (% of wages)	25.0%	$0.102 212,500	$0.107	212,500	$0.006	0
Fuel	$0.241	$0.241 504,628	$0.241	478,043	$0.000	(26,585)
Maintenance	$0.110	$0.110 230,010	$0.110	217,892	$0.000	(12,118)
Insurance	$0.100	$0.100 209,100	$0.100	198,084	$0.000	(11,016)
Total Variable Costs		$0.959 2,006,238	$0.988	1,956,519	$0.028	(49,719)
Fixed Costs	Assumptions					
Tractor Depreciation	$ 16,667	$0.159 333,333	$0.168	333,333	$0.009	0
Trailer Depreciation	$ 2,200	$0.063 132,000	$0.070	138,600	$0.007	6,600
Legalization/Recruiting/Admin	$ 10,000	$0.096 200,000	$0.101	200,000	$0.005	0
On-Site Manager	$ 75,000	$0.036 75,000	$0.038	75,000	$0.002	0
Start Up /Special Equipment	$ 8,333	$0.004 8,333	$0.004	8,333	$0.000	0
Total Fixed Costs		$0.358 748,667	$0.381	755,267	$0.023	6,600
Total Cost		$1.318 2,754,905	$1.369	2,711,786	$0.052	(43,119)
Operating Profit		$0.292 $611,605	$0.241	$477,367	($0.052)	($134,239)
Operating Ratio		81.83%		85.03%		

The expectation for the fleet was an operating ratio of 81.83%. However, the actual operation has failed to meet profitability expectations with an operating ratio of only 85.03%. The analysis shows two primary reasons for the variance to the plan, utilization and trailer counts.

Utilization has fallen below planned levels by 108 miles per week. The impact of this decline is seen in several areas. First, planned revenues are down by $177,358 as a result of the low utilization. Second, costs are spread over a lower number of miles, thereby raising the total cost per mile by 5.2 cents.[80] Also, driver incomes remain constant despite the lost utilization, further impacting total cost and cost per mile.

The number of trailers associated with the fleet is 3 more than the original design. The additional trailers add $6,600 in fixed cost to the operation. While these additional trailers may be providing efficiency benefits, the cost of the trailers is also contributing to the poor financial performance of the fleet.

---

[80] The increase in the number of trailers above plan is also contributing in part to the increase in the total cost per mile.

Tractor Utilization Charts (TUC)

Tractor utilization charts provide a visual summary of a tractor's activity over a period of the time. The charts can be used to evaluate the efficiency of an individual tractor or a fleet of tractors. The charts depict how well drivers are using available work time and reveal potential gaps and utilization opportunities within the workday and workweek.

Fleet Analysis TUC Charts

A fleet analysis TUC chart displays fleet activity over a period a time, usually one day or one week. The TUC chart below displays the one day activity for a local short haul fleet of 11 trucks. The chart reflects the time during the day that each driver was active. For simplification, time is reflected in hourly segments. Shaded areas represent active work time with green cells representing loaded driving activity and red cells representing empty driving activity.

Sample One Day TUC Chart

Driver Code	Loads	Loaded LOH	Miles	Driving Hours	12-3 am	3-6 am	6-9 am	9-12 pm	12-3 pm	3-6 pm	6-9 pm
Monday		2/11/2008									
A1017	4	30	121	9.0							
A1020	2	51	102	9.0							
A1054	2	60	119	8.0							
A1056	1	142	142	7.5							
A1067	3	59	178	9.5							
A1071	3	44	132	9.5							
A1082	1	80	80	4.5							
A1112	2	77	154	9.0							
A1142	1	142	142	8.5							
A1155	2	58	115	8.0							
B2014	2	54	108	7.0							
Totals:	23	61	1,393	89.5	0 0 0	0 4 8	9 9 9	10 10 10	9 7 6	3 2 2	2 1 0
Per Driver:	2.1	61	127	8.1		Key:	Loaded	Empty	Inactive		

The chart indicates that all drivers were reasonably productive during the workday with one possible exception. Driver A1082 only delivered one load and worked only 4.5 total driving hours of a possible 11.0 driving hours. This isolated incident does not necessarily indicate a problem. Load volume may have been down this particular day or a load planned for this driver may have been canceled. If this type of underutilization is present on a consistent basis, an opportunity to improve utilization may exist for this fleet.

The totals at the bottom of the report display how many drivers were active during each hour of the day. The maximum number of drivers active at any one time was only 10 drivers for this 11 driver fleet. If the total active drivers were to be consistently less than the fleet size, an opportunity to reduce the size of the fleet may exist.

The TUC chart below represents the same fleet on a different day. The fleet appears to be highly productive and fully utilized on this particular day.

High Productivity One Day TUC Chart

Driver Code	Loads	Loaded LOH	Miles	Driving Hours	12-3 am	3-6 am	6-9 am	9-12 pm	12-3 pm	3-6 pm	6-9 pm
Thursday		2/14/2008									
A1017	2	125	249	11.0							
A1020	2	101	201	11.0							
A1054	4	44	177	11.0							
A1056	3	40	119	9.4							
A1067	1	305	305	11.0							
A1071	2	93	186	9.0							
A1082	2	63	125	10.0							
A1112	2	71	142	10.0							
A1142	2	84	167	11.0							
A1155	3	64	191	11.0							
B2014	3	49	148	11.0							
Totals:	26	77	2,010	115.4	0 0 0	0 4 7	11 11 11	11 11 11	11 11 10	9 8 3	1 0 0
Per Driver:	2.4	77	183	10.5		Key:	Loaded	Empty	Inactive		

The chart indicates that all drivers worked a full day and most completed multiple loads during the shift. Many drivers drove the maximum of 11 total hours. The active driver totals at the bottom of the report indicate that the 11 truck fleet was fully utilized for most hours during the workday.

The TUC chart below indicates another high productivity day for this fleet during the same week.

High Productivity One Day TUC Chart

Driver Code	Loads	Loaded LOH	Miles	Driving Hours	12-3 am	3-6 am	6-9 am	9-12 pm	12-3 pm	3-6 pm	6-9 pm
Friday		2/15/2008									
A1017	2	78	155	11.0							
A1020	1	360	360	10.5							
A1054	2	69	138	7.0							
A1056	3	45	135	11.0							
A1067	4	43	170	11.0							
A1071	4	46	185	11.0							
A1082	3	60	179	11.0							
A1112	3	50	149	11.0							
A1142	2	92	184	10.0							
A1155	3	48	144	11.0							
B2014	3	55	166	11.0							
Totals:	30	66	1,965	115.5	0 0 0	0 6 10	11 11 11	11 11 10	11 11 11	10 7 4	0 0 0
Per Driver:	2.7	66	179	10.5		Key:	Loaded	Empty	Inactive		

Based on the TUC analysis, this fleet appears to be highly productive and fully utilized.

Individual Tractor Analysis TUC Charts

A TUC chart for an individual tractor provides a summary of the tractor and driver productivity over a period of time, usually one week. The TUC chart below reflects the activity of one truck from the 11 truck fleet. The chart shows each load for the week in chronological order. For further analysis, the chart also includes the departure time from each origin and the arrival time at each destination.

Individual Tractor Weekly TUC Chart

ORIGIN			DESTINATION			Loaded Miles	Empty Miles	ACTIVITY BY HOUR
City	ST	Dep Time	Arr Time	City	ST			3-6 am / 6-9 am / 9-12 pm / 12-3 pm / 3-6 pm

Driver: A1054	Loads: 12	667	636	2/10/2008 - 2/16/2008

Monday 2/11/2008 — 119 / 155
| OXFORD | TX | 06:15 | 07:35 | GREENWOOD | TX | 59 | 76 |
| OXFORD | TX | 10:25 | 11:45 | LINCOLNTON | TX | 60 | 79 |

Tuesday 2/12/2008 — 91 / 90
| OXFORD | TX | 06:10 | 07:42 | SENECA | TX | 68 | 68 |
| JACKSON | TX | 10:00 | 11:15 | GREENVILLE | TX | 23 | 22 |

Wednesday 2/13/2008 — 142 / 104
| JACKSON | TX | 04:15 | 06:00 | LINCOLNTON | TX | 68 | 68 |
| JACKSON | TX | 08:30 | 10:45 | UNION | TX | 74 | 36 |

Thursday 2/14/2008 — 177 / 158
OXFORD	TX	06:15	08:25	MONROE	TX	95	116
JACKSON	TX	12:30	13:15	CLINTON	TX	42	42
JACKSON	TX	14:45	15:15	COWPENS	TX	20	-
COWPENS	TX	15:31	16:04	WELLFORD	TX	20	-

Friday 2/15/2008 — 138 / 129
| JACKSON | TX | 06:00 | 07:45 | MONROE | TX | 105 | 105 |
| JACKSON | TX | 12:15 | 13:31 | GREENVILLE | TX | 33 | 24 |

The TUC chart indicates that this driver was reasonably productive during the week. The driver served multiple loads each day and worked a full week. Key items of emphasis at the individual driver level include missed work days, low productivity days, and long periods of inactivity during the workday. Consistent gaps of this type indicate the opportunity for productivity improvements.

The TUC charts occasionally show a driver working on more than one load during the same one hour segment. While this is often the case as the driver moves from one load to the next, certain exceptions may apply. All TUC charts shown here are based on operating data from an actual dedicated fleet. Because a carrier's time information can sometimes contain inconsistencies, TUC charts may appear unrealistic in isolated cases. Despite these occasional data inconsistencies, TUC charts still provide an excellent tool for evaluating driver and fleet productivity.

CHAPTER 12: Semi- Dedicated Pricing and Design

While many dedicated fleets fit nicely into a standard dedicated pricing format such as fixed-variable or a utilization scale, other fleets require a more sophisticated analysis and pricing approach. The most common scenario occurs when a dedicated fleet is clearly the best transportation solution for a shipper's network, but the contract structure required by the shipper is a form of one-way pricing. In these cases, carriers design a dedicated fleet solution but price the operation in a per-trip, one-way format. The one-way format does not contain any dedicated contract guarantees, so the carrier assumes the vast majority of the operating risk in the contract. The carrier must carefully balance the operating risk and financial risk to determine the appropriate revenue levels while still providing the proposal at a reasonable cost.

This chapter provides a variety of common specialized situations in dedicated fleet pricing. Each situation requires the carrier to modify the standard dedicated pricing process to conform to the shipper's pricing format and requirements. Several of the most common situations are listed below.

Specialized Semi-Dedicated Pricing Scenarios
Shorthaul Networks
Regional Distribution Networks
Mileage Band Contracts
Local Shuttles

In these situations, the carrier must balance the risks associated with the design of the operating model along with the pricing design and revenue stream. The key elements of the operating solution such as utilization and fleet size may be aggressive or conservative based on the carrier's design. If the operating solution is particularly aggressive, the carrier can balance aggressive operating assumptions with less aggressive pricing assumptions. Likewise, if the operating solution is very conservative, the carrier might consider a more aggressive approach on the pricing and cost side. The proper approach for each of these situations is discussed in greater detail in the sections that follow.

Short Haul Dedicated Fleets

Short haul fleets are commonly used to serve a shipper's needs within a specific mileage radius from the origin facility. While the exact mileage radius will be different for each individual operation, most often the short haul network will include all loads within a 200 to 250 mile radius of a facility.

The map below depicts a shipper's entire outbound network from a facility near Richmond, VA, including both short haul and long haul destinations.

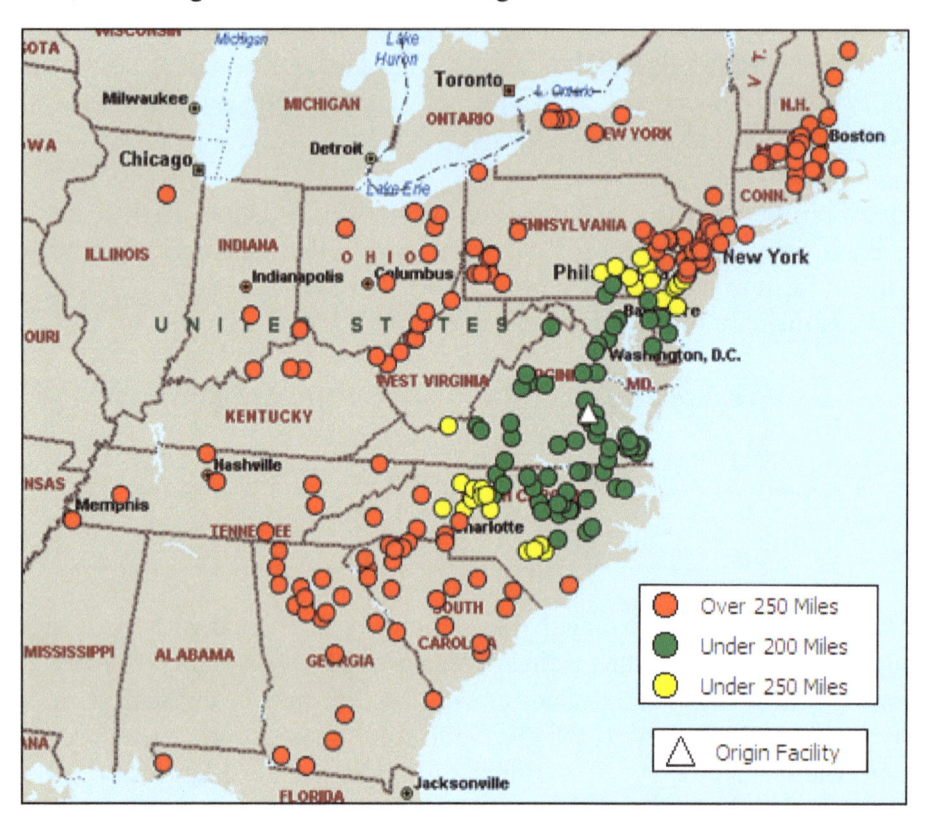

The green dots represent destination points within 200 miles of the origin facility and the yellow dots represent destination points between 201 and 250 miles from the facility. These points are the destinations that would potentially be served by a short haul dedicated fleet, especially those under 200 miles. The red dots represent all destinations beyond 250 miles. These destinations would likely be served primarily through normal one-way transportation.

Short haul loads of less than 250 miles usually don't fit into the linehaul or regional networks of most carriers and are generally unattractive to long haul truck drivers.[81] As a result, the one-way rates for these types of loads will often be very costly, especially on a

---

[81] Short loads typically don't allow carriers to achieve the goal of utilization maximization. Also, drivers earn a majority of their income from mileage pay, so longer loads are generally preferred to short loads.

per-mile basis. Given the high one-way rates and minimum charges, carriers often find it cost effective to utilize dedicated fleets in networks that contain large amounts of consistent load volumes under 250 miles.[82]

The approximate standard of a 250-mile radius is based on the amount of driving a single driver can legally achieve during a standard work day. A load traveling 250 miles from the origin point will constitute a 500 mile round trip. The 250 mile radius is a general rule of thumb for the maximum distance a driver can serve on an out-and-back basis in one day. Based on 2003 regulations, a driver is limited to 11 hours of driving time per day and 14 hours of total on-duty work time. Depending on traffic and driving speeds in the local area, the potential radius may be as low as 200 one-way miles or, in some cases, even slightly less than 200 miles.

In order for a dedicated fleet to be successful, the operating environment of the potential dedicated short haul network must meet several requirements. The most important of these requirements are listed below.

Operating Requirements for Dedicated Short Haul Fleets	
Requirement	**Description**
Sufficient Load Volumes	The network should have enough load density to allow for economies of scale in the operation.[83] The fleet must be large enough so that, on any random day, below average load volumes will not significantly impact overall efficiency and productivity. Efficiency is more difficult to achieve in very small fleets (5 trucks or fewer) than in larger fleets of 10 trucks or more. For example, one unproductive truck in a fleet of 3 trucks has a much greater efficiency impact than one unproductive truck in a 20 truck fleet.
Flexible Pick-up and Delivery Schedules	The network should have enough flexibility to allow the trucks and drivers to stay busy throughout the workday. The ideal network will allow drop trailers and allow for both morning and afternoon deliveries. Night deliveries are also desirable. If all loads in a network must deliver before 10 a.m., the fleet will not be active in the afternoon and will fail to achieve a cost-effective level of efficiency.
Balanced Load Volumes by Day of Week	In order to keep the fleet busy each day, load volumes must remain fairly consistent from day to day during the week. For example, a network with 100 loads per week would ideally ship 20 loads each day, Monday through Friday. If load volumes (or total miles) fluctuate too much from day to day, the highest level of fleet productivity will not be achieved.
Balanced Load Volumes by Week and Month	Loads volumes must remain steady and predictable from week to week and month to month throughout the year. If the network's shipping patterns are extremely seasonal or highly unpredictable, a dedicated fleet may not be the ideal solution for the network.

---

[82] The high one-way rates usually come in the form of minimum charges, a flat charge for a load regardless of the number of miles.
[83] "Economies of Scale" in this context means that there are enough loads in the network to allow for efficient, consistent and predictable operations. This might also be referred to as "Economies of Density."

Combining a network containing a large number of short loads often results in a reasonably efficient fleet operation. Loads can be efficiently scheduled so that each truck can deliver two or more loads per day, minimizing the number of trucks and drivers needed to serve the network. The resulting cost per load with the dedicated fleet solution is often far less than the cost per load based on typical one-way minimum charges.

As shown here, often the best transportation solution for a shipper's network is a dedicated fleet, but the shipper does not wish to enter into a traditional dedicated contract. Instead of a dedicated contract, the shipper will compensate the carrier on a traditional per-load basis. Despite the lack of a dedicated contract, the carrier may design a solution for the customer that includes a dedicated fleet. From the shipper's perspective, the solution is one-way transportation. However, from the carrier's perspective, the actual solution is, at least in part, a dedicated fleet. The carrier will utilize an internal dedicated fleet to meet the shipper's needs because the dedicated solution is the most cost-effective approach.

The challenge for the carrier is to achieve adequate revenue on a per-load basis to generate a profitable revenue level for the dedicated fleet. As an additional challenge in a competitive bid situation, the carrier must not only generate a profitable revenue level for the fleet, but must also provide a competitively priced bid proposal to the shipper. The sections that follow provide several examples of dedicated fleets priced in a one-way contract structure.

Shuttle / Extreme Short Haul Pricing

Many specialized shippers have networks that include shuttle operations or a very high volume of short haul lanes. The automobile manufacturing industry is a large user of short haul and shuttle transportation. Most automobile manufacturers operate in a zero inventory, just-in-time production environment. Just-in-time operations of this type put a great deal of pressure on the suppliers and transportation providers for these manufacturers. Suppliers must make continuous deliveries throughout the automaker's daily production schedule to provide component parts exactly when they are needed, allowing the automaker to operate without maintaining costly inventory.

As a result of these delivery and service requirements, suppliers for auto manufacturers often locate their production facilities in very close proximity to the automaker's facility. By establishing a location near the automaker, each supplier is able to provide excellent delivery service. The supplier's close proximity to the automaker also allows the supplier to react very quickly to changing inventory needs or service disruptions. For the carrier, the JIT production environment provides an opportunity for creative, aggressive pricing because of the consistent and predictable nature of these operations.

The map below illustrates this relationship for a typical automaker located in Detroit, Michigan. The suppliers are located in very close proximity to the automaker's production facility.

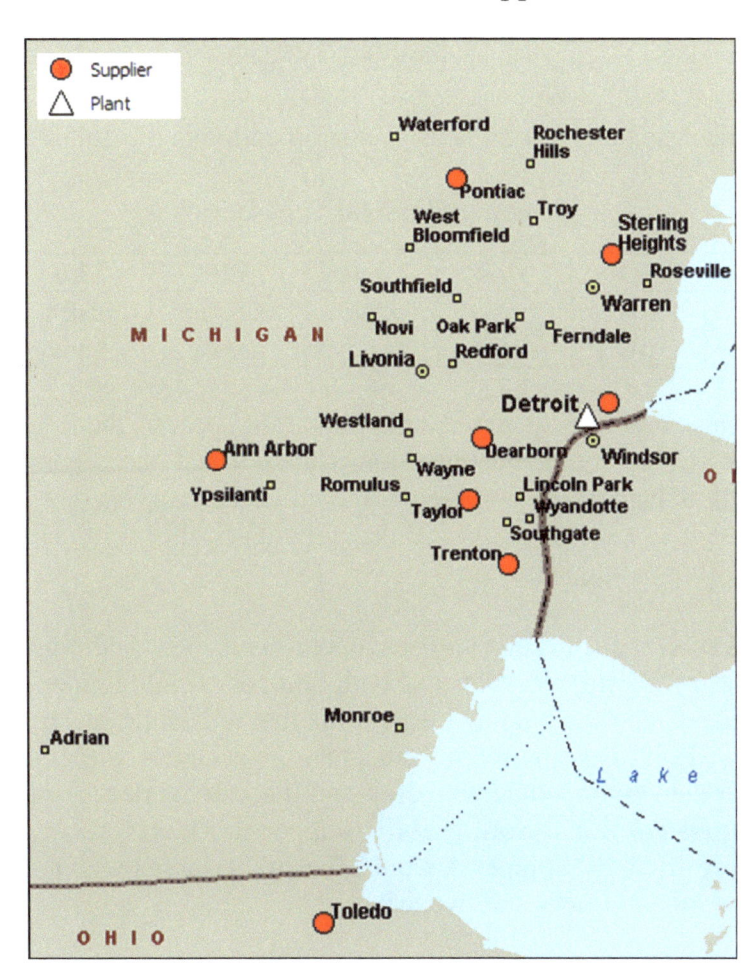

Automotive Manufacturer and Supplier Locations

These automotive short haul operations are most often priced on a per-load activity basis instead of one of the common dedicated contract types. Even though the contract is not a traditional dedicated agreement, the carrier will usually implement a dedicated fleet to serve the needs of this type of shipper. The unique nature of the operation makes a dedicated fleet the best solution because the carrier can customize the equipment, pricing, and driver compensation plan to the specifics of the operation.

Slip-Seat Fleet

A slip-seat fleet is a specialized strategy for maximizing asset utilization and reducing transportation costs. Slip-seating is the practice of utilizing one tractor in two shifts by scheduling two drivers to share one tractor. The slip-seat approach is most often utilized in short haul environments where the tractor and driver return to the origin location at the end of each shift. Slip-seating is very common in short haul and shuttle situations, such as the automotive shuttle operations discussed previously.

A simple split-seat schedule for a 24-hour shuttle operation is illustrated below.

Simple Slip-Seat Schedule

Shift	Tractor	Mon	Tue	Wed	Thu	Fri
6 am to 6 pm	101	Justin	Justin	Justin	Justin	Justin
6 pm to 6 am	101	Andy	Andy	Andy	Andy	Andy

In order to maximize productivity and the likelihood for success, the freight network served by the slip-seat operation must be a consistent out-and-back operation, usually with a short length of haul. The short length of haul is necessary so that the tractor is returned to the origin in a timely manner at the end of each shift for the second driver to begin the next shift in the same tractor.

A second critical success factor for a slip-seat operation is the scheduling of the pick-up and delivery times by the shipper. Suppose both Shipper A and Shipper B move 17 loads per day from a manufacturing plant to a warehouse that is 25 miles away. Shipper A requires that all 17 loads move between 7 am and 4 pm each day while Shipper B allows a flexible 24-hour delivery schedule with drop-and-hook deliveries. A one truck/two driver slip-seat operation would work well for Shipper B. However, because of the delivery window restrictions, Shipper A would need to be served with a more costly solution consisting of two trucks and two drivers.

In certain situations, a creative carrier might even develop a slip-seat operation involving two or more customers. The carrier might find a second customer that has night deliveries that would complement the needs of Shipper A in the previous example. By involving two complimentary customers, the carrier could generate above average revenues and profits then potentially pass a portion of the savings along to each of the two customers.

Example Inbound Automotive Parts Fleet

Suppose an automotive shipper has asked carriers to bid on a shuttle operation for a major inbound parts vendor. The vendor ships 23 loads per day Monday through Friday. Weekend shipments are extremely rare. The loads must arrive at one hour intervals throughout the day and night. The vendor is located 28 miles from the automaker's assembly plant. The assembly plant operates 50 weeks per year, so for two weeks per year, no shipments will occur. Carriers will be required to provide a total of 18 trailers to support the operation. The automotive shipper has asked carriers to provide proposals for this operation based on a simple flat rate per load for this inbound vendor lane.

Designing the Delivery Schedule

The first step for the carrier is to determine how many tractors and drivers will be needed for this operation. Because of the 24-hour operation, the carrier expects to be able to slip-seat the tractors, so the key figure is the number of drivers that will be required, not the number of trucks. The carrier has estimated the cycle time per trip at 109 minutes as shown below.

Total Trip Cycle Time					
Pick Up Dock Time	Outbound Drive Time	Delivery Dock Time	Return Drive Time	Total Cycle Minutes
20	32	25	32	109

Based on this cycle time, the carrier has established the preliminary fleet design and daily schedule shown below.

Slip-Seat Fleet Design

Shift One				Shift Two			
Load Num	Delivery Time	Round Trip Miles	Driver	Load Num	Delivery Time	Round Trip Miles	Driver
1	1:00 AM	56	A	13	1:00 PM	56	C
2	2:00 AM	56	B	14	2:00 PM	56	D
3	3:00 AM	56	A	15	3:00 PM	56	C
4	4:00 AM	56	B	16	4:00 PM	56	D
5	5:00 AM	56	A	17	5:00 PM	56	C
6	6:00 AM	56	B	18	6:00 PM	56	D
7	7:00 AM	56	A	19	7:00 PM	56	C
8	8:00 AM	56	B	20	8:00 PM	56	D
9	9:00 AM	56	A	21	9:00 PM	56	C
10	10:00 AM	56	B	22	10:00 PM	56	D
11	11:00 AM	56	A	23	11:00 PM	56	C
12	12:00 PM	56	B				
Total Miles		672				616	
Total Loads		12				11	

Design Summary	Per Day	Per Week	Per Year
Total Miles	1,288	6,440	322,000
Total Loads	23	115	5,750
Number of Drivers	4		
Number of Tractors	2		
Tractor Utilization	644	3,220	

Based on this design, the carrier is now prepared to price the shuttle operation.

Pricing the Shuttle Operation

Based on the design, the dedicated pricing for the operation is shown below. Drivers are paid $41,500 per year. The pricing is based on a required rate of return of 12.0%.

Dedicated Pricing Model

Customer Name:	Chapter 12	Fleet Description:	Slip-Seat Shuttle Fleet

Fleet Parameters

Number of Tractors	2.00
Backup Tractors	0.00
Number of Drivers	4.00
Utilization (Miles per Tractor per Active Week)	3,220
Active Fleet Weeks Per Year (max = 52 weeks)	50.0
Total Fleet Annual Miles	322,000
Number of Trailers	18.00
Trailer/Tractor Ratio	9.00

Overhead Costs

Tractor Legalization/Taxes	$ 2,000
Driver Recruiting Costs	$ 3,000
Administration Expenses	$ 5,000
Total Overhead (per tractor per year)	$ 10,000
Direct Staffing (On-site CSR / Offices / Etc.)	$ -
Other Annual Expenses (Total Fleet)	$ 5,000
Initial Start-Up Costs (Total)	$ 10,000

Other Parameters

Driver Rate of Pay (Per Mile or Annual Gross)	$ 41,500.00
Duration of Deal/Contract (in months)	36.0
Average Collection Period (in days)	30.0

Pricing and Analysis

Suggested Rate Per Mile (all miles)	$ 1.7700
Operating Ratio	79.67%
Internal Rate of Return	12.21%

Pro-Forma Income Statement		Fleet Totals Per Mile	Fleet Totals Annual	Per Tractor Weekly	Per Tractor Annual
Total Fleet Miles			322,000	3,096	161,000
Total Revenue		$1.770	$569,940	$5,480	$284,970
Variable Costs	Assumptions				
Driver Wages	$41,500.00	$0.516	$166,000	$1,596	$83,000
Fringe Benefits (% of wages)	25.0%	0.129	41,500	399	20,750
Fuel	$0.241	0.241	77,709	747	38,855
Maintenance	$0.110	0.110	35,420	341	17,710
Insurance	$0.100	0.100	32,200	310	16,100
Total Variable Costs		1.096	352,829	3,393	176,415
Fixed Costs	Assumptions				
Tractor Depreciation	$ 16,667	0.104	33,333	$321	$16,667
Trailer Depreciation	$ 2,200	0.123	39,600	381	19,800
Legalization/Recruiting/Admin	$ 10,000	0.062	20,000	192	10,000
On-Site Manager	$ -	0.000	0	0	0
Start Up /Special Equipment	$ 8,333	0.026	8,333	80	4,167
Total Fixed Costs		0.314	101,267	974	50,633
Total Cost		1.410	454,096	4,366	227,048
Operating Profit		$0.36	$115,844	$1,114	$57,922
Operating Ratio		79.67%	79.67%	79.67%	79.67%

Based on the total revenue of $569,940 per year, the carrier must now convert the annual revenue into a per-load charge as shown below.

Loads Per Day	Annual Loads	Annual Revenue	Rate Per Load
23	5,750	$569,940	$ 99.12
22	5,500	$569,940	$ 103.63
21	5,250	$569,940	$ 108.56

If the carrier expects the full annual volume of 5,750 loads to occur, a price of $99.12 per load can be offered. However, with many networks of this type, actual load volumes may fall short of expectations. If the carrier expects this to be the case, the carrier may choose to propose a slightly higher rate of $103 to $108 per load. Offering a price above $99.12 per load will also provide the carrier room to negotiate on the rate if necessary.

Mileage Band Pricing Contracts

Mileage band pricing contracts are commonly used in networks with a very high concentration of relatively short loads. Generally, these contracts extend out between 200 and 250 miles from the origin location. Mileage band contracts function as a one-way pricing structure. However, the carrier's underlying operating strategy will closely resemble that of a dedicated fleet. The table below illustrates the basic structure of a simple mileage band pricing agreement.

Example Mileage Band Pricing

Mileage Band	Annual Loads	Rate Per Load
0 - 10	752	$ 116
11 - 20	178	$ 139
21 - 30	253	$ 161
31 - 40	534	$ 182
41 - 50	56	$ 204
51 - 75	296	$ 242
76 - 100	320	$ 297
101 - 125	145	$ 351
126 - 150	432	$ 406
151 - 175	152	$ 460
176 - 200	44	$ 515
201 - 225	104	$ 569
226 - 250	4	$ 624
Total Loads:	5,380	

Utilizing the mileage band chart, a 5 mile load will cost $116. A 43 mile load will cost $204.[84] The carrier's cost is, of course, slightly more to perform a 10 mile load than a 1 mile load because of variable costs such as fuel and maintenance. Despite this fact, the carrier assumes that the actual average length of haul will be near the midpoint of each mileage band, so the costs, revenues, and average length of haul are expected to balance out over the duration of a contract involving a large number of loads.

The underlying assumption in this pricing format is that the carrier is indifferent to the relative amount of volume that actually occurs across the different bands. However, the actual pricing will fluctuate slightly based on the expected distribution of loads within the mileage bands. The fleet design and the actual pricing process will be explained in detail in the sections that follow.

One key benefit of mileage band contracts is that the carrier and shipper can avoid all the administrative issues required with other common dedicated contracts such as fixed-variable, utilization scale, and over-under agreements. The key difference is that each of

---

[84] The rates shown here are for illustration purposes only and are not intended as actual recommended rates.

those contract types requires a periodic count of dedicated tractors and an average utilization figure as part of the billing. In a mileage band agreement, carriers are not required to report on tractor counts, utilization, or empty mile measurements. Even though the carrier is effectively utilizing "dedicated" trucks, the pricing format is actually one-way pricing because no specific dedicated contract parameters or activity guarantees are included.[85]

Determining the Mileage Band Rates

In a high volume, short haul environment, carriers will often use an internal dedicated fleet to provide the majority of service for the network. A dedicated fleet is generally the best solution for high volumes of very short loads because the loads can be efficiently planned each day to maximize utilization for the dedicated fleet. Also, these short loads are generally unattractive for regional and linehaul fleets, as those fleets are designed for a higher level of utilization and a longer length of haul. Drivers in these higher utilization fleets will often become dissatisfied if assigned to extremely short loads on a regular basis.

In a mileage band contract situation, the carrier will likely choose to serve the customer's network, at least in large part, with a dedicated fleet. The fleet is "dedicated" only in terms of how the carrier manages the trucks and drivers in the customer's network. The actual mileage band pricing agreement is effectively one-way, activity-based pricing. The shipper is very likely aware of the fact that the carrier will operate much of the network on a round-trip, quasi-dedicated basis. However, the shipper has none of the obligations typically associated with a dedicated fleet agreement. The carrier assumes 100% of the operating risk for the operation. The carrier's upside for assuming this risk is in the fact that the carrier can earn above average profits on this fleet if the fleet is managed effectively and highly productive.

Along with a base dedicated fleet, the carrier may also utilize other resources, such as a nearby regional fleet, to further support the mileage band network. For example, the carrier may design the quasi-dedicated fleet to support all loads under 150 miles and plan to cover loads over 150 miles with other non-dedicated resources. This mixed approach may prove to be effective for the carrier and potentially provide an overall lower cost for the shipper. The further the mileage bands extend, the more viable this mixed solution becomes. This approach will be discussed in greater detail in the presentation of specific pricing strategies for a mileage band network that follow.

---

[85] In this case, the dedicated trucks are those trucks that the carrier has set up to work exclusively for this customer but do not operate under a specific dedicated fleet contract with the customer.

The key variable in the design of the fleet size and utilization is the cycle time for each load. The graphic below illustrates the basic cycle for these round-trip, short haul loads.

Round Trip Load Cycle

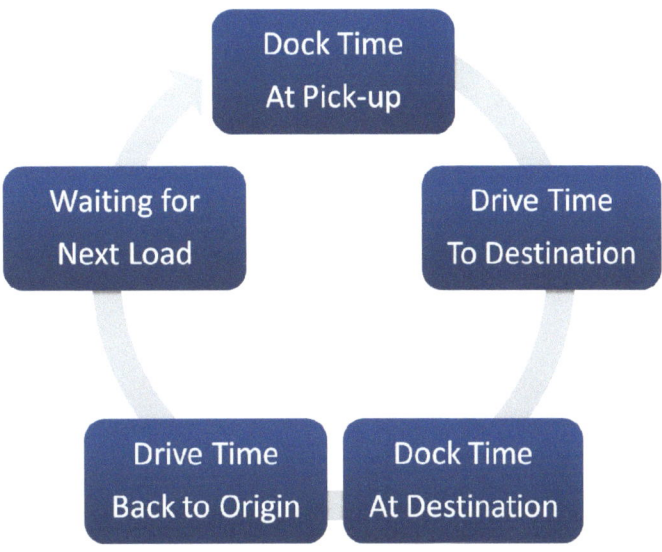

- Dock Time At Pick-up
- Drive Time To Destination
- Dock Time At Destination
- Drive Time Back to Origin
- Waiting for Next Load

The cycle shown below illustrates the cycle time for a 60 mile load. Dock time and drive time represent the primary components of the cycle time for a short haul network.

Cycle Time for 60 Mile Load

30 minutes Dock Time at Pick-up → 90 minutes Outbound Drive Time → 60 minutes Dock Time at Delivery → 90 minutes Return Drive Time → 270 minutes Total Trip Cycle Time

In order to accurately estimate drive times and dock times, the carrier must become familiar with the detailed operating characteristics of the shipper's service platform and local shipping facility. Key questions need to be answered to make accurate assumptions as to the operating characteristics of the shipper's short haul network. The purpose of these questions is to identify all the factors that contribute to the cycle time and the expected amount of time required to complete each load. Several of these key characteristics are discussed in the next section.

Shipper Network Operating Characteristics

Shipper Facility Location

The physical location of a shipper's facility can have a significant impact on the transit time, utilization and fleet size. Prior to determining estimated fleet sizes and utilization, the carrier should note the exact facility location and its relative proximity to primary roads. If the facility is located very close to major roads, trucks will move efficiently in and out of the facility. However, if the facility is located away from major roads, the fleet efficiency could be affected. For example, if the shipper's facility is located 15 miles from the closest major road and it takes 30 minutes to drive from the facility to the primary road, most outbound loads will take 20 to 40 minutes longer per trip than a well-located facility. As a result, it will likely require a larger fleet size to serve a facility with a poor location.

Road Types and Traffic

Transit times can be positively or negatively impacted by the type of roads and traffic levels throughout the delivery network. A shipping facility located in a notoriously high-traffic market will have less efficient transit times than a facility located in an area with little or no traffic. The same concept applies to the speed limits and other speed parameters associated with the primary roads in a network. The fleet size design process must account for the relative traffic and other driving conditions to accurately estimate transit times and fleet sizes.

Dock Time

Dock time represents the non-driving time spent at the shipper's pick-up and delivery locations. Dock time includes all the time from the arrival time at the customer location to the departure time. The primary activities that occur during this period include backing the trailer into position, unloading freight, and securing signatures for paperwork. Dock time usually ranges from 30 minutes to 1 hour, depending on the appointment and unloading process at each location.

Dock time is an important variable in the fleet size design process. Since dock time counts against the driver's 14 hours of available work time for the day, keeping dock time to a minimum leaves more on-duty time available for driving. The carrier should ask the shipper about their appointment scheduling and receiving process to accurately estimate average dock times for the operation. In the absence of more specific information, the carrier can generally assume 30 to 45 minutes of dock time for the pick-up and 1 hour for the delivery.

Delivery Windows

Delivery windows represent the time of day during which deliveries are allowed. For example, a dedicated fleet that serves a group of retail stores may have a delivery window at each store of 7:00 am to 4:00 pm. This window spans a 9 hour period, which fits well with the hours of service restriction of 11 driving hours per day. A large delivery window potentially allows for the maximum use of each driver's 11 hours of daily driving time. However, if the delivery window was reduced to 8:00 am to 3:00 pm, only 7 hours, the carrier will find it difficult to fully utilize each driver's 11 hours of available driving time each day and, as a result, utilization will suffer.

Delivery Method

The type of delivery and delivery process both have a significant impact on the dock time and cycle time for each trip. Typically, the least time-efficient deliveries are "live unload" deliveries. In a live unload delivery, the driver backs the trailer to the receiving door at the customer's location and waits for the trailer to be unloaded. Depending on the type of freight and the unloading method, the unloading time could range from 30 minutes to 2 hours or more. In some fleets, the driver may even be required to assist in the unloading process. Also, if the delivery location operates on a first-come, first-served basis instead of using planned delivery appointments, the driver may be required to wait in line with other drivers for the next available delivery door, further extending the total delivery dock time.

The most time-efficient deliveries occur with a "drop trailer" delivery. With a drop delivery, the driver simply drops the loaded trailer at the customer's facility and immediately picks up an available empty trailer. The entire process usually takes no longer than 30 minutes. The driver avoids most of the potential delays associated with a live delivery.

Basic Fleet Size Model Operating Assumptions

The simple fleet size model that follows provides a basic format for estimating the number of drivers required to serve a short haul network. In order to estimate the fleet size and utilization required to serve the network, the carrier must make certain assumptions to facilitate the calculations. The most important of these assumptions are discussed in detail below.

Miles Per Hour

To determine the cycle time for each load, the carrier must estimate the drive time from the origin to the destination then back to the origin. One simple method for estimating drive time is to assume a certain miles per hour for each trip. In short haul driving conditions, the driver may be able to average up to 50 miles per hour on the longer trips. However, as trip distance decreases, the average miles per hour will also decrease.

The fleet size calculation model that follows shows the miles per hour assumption for each trip distance. These assumptions are based on normal conditions. The actual physical location of the origin facility, road types, speed limits, and traffic conditions should be taken into account when making the miles per hour assumptions for any specific fleet opportunity. Notice in the shortest mileage group that the drive time is automatically set to 1 hour. This assumption keeps the solution realistic in terms of the overall fleet size calculation methodology. The 1 hour drive time prevents the very short mileage groups from having unrealistic cycle times within the fleet size model.

Dock Time Per Load

Dock time represents the time spent at the shipper's location to pick up and deliver the load. Dock time typically takes between 30 minutes and 1 hour, but certain shippers may take much longer for a variety of reasons. Since dock time counts against the driver's 14 on-duty hours per day, the dock time assumption is critical to the fleet size calculations. All other variables being equal, a fleet for a shipper with very short dock times will achieve a much higher utilization level than a shipper with longer dock times. Without more specific information from the shipper, 30 minutes to 1 hour of dock time provides a reasonable assumption.

Driver Work Hours Per Day

A driver can legally work up to 14 hours per day, including 11 hours of driving time. In short haul networks, drivers will typically average 9 to 12 hours of actual work time per day. On busy days, a driver will work very close to the 14 hour maximum. On days with below average shipping activity, a driver may work only 7 or 8 hours or less. Without more specific information, an assumption of 10 to 11 driver work hours per day is reasonable for most short haul networks.

Basic Short Haul Fleet Size Model

The model presented in this section provides a simple and straightforward approach to estimating the fleet size for most short haul networks. For this example, a fleet size will be developed for the mileage band network shown to the right.

In this example, the average loads per day are computed based on the annual load volumes over 260 active shipping days per year. The number of active shipping days and average loads per day should be based on the schedule of each shipper. Certain shippers may shut down operations for brief periods, thereby reducing the number of active shipping days. The average number of loads per day is a critical component of the fleet size model that follows, so daily estimates must be as accurate as possible.

Sample Short Haul Network		
Mileage Band	\multicolumn{2}{c	}{Load Volume}
	Annual	Per Day
0-10	966	3.72
11-20	640	2.46
21-30	1,451	5.58
31-40	716	2.75
41-50	485	1.87
51-60	232	0.89
61-70	396	1.52
71-80	329	1.27
81-90	234	0.90
91-100	136	0.52
101-110	208	0.80
111-120	144	0.55
121-130	45	0.17
131-140	28	0.11
141-150	62	0.24
151-160	110	0.42
161-170	62	0.24
171-180	32	0.12
181-190	10	0.04
191-200	48	0.18
Totals:	6,334	24.36

Fleet Size Model

Based on assumptions for the key operating parameters and the shipper's network information, the carrier can use a simple model such as the one shown below to estimate the fleet size needed to serve the network.[86]

Short Haul Fleet Size Model

Assumptions:					Cycle Time Per Trip (in hours)				Estimated Fleet Size		
Pick Up Dock Time (hrs):		0.50									
Delivery Dock Time (hrs):		0.75									
Driver Work Hours Per Day:		11.00	(max = 14 hours)		Pick-Up	Drive	Delivery	Total	Total	Drivers	Total
Mileage	Load Volume	Round Trip Miles		Miles	Dock	Drive	Dock	Time	Daily	Needed	Drivers
Band	Annual	Per Day	Per Load	Per Day	Per Hour	Time	Time	Time	Per Trip	Hours	(Band)	Needed
0-10	966	3.72	7	26	7	0.50	1.00	0.75	2.25	8.4	0.8	0.76
11-20	640	2.46	30	74	25	0.50	1.20	0.75	2.45	6.0	0.5	1.31
21-30	1,451	5.58	46	254	35	0.50	1.30	0.75	2.55	14.2	1.3	2.60
31-40	716	2.75	64	176	35	0.50	1.83	0.75	3.08	8.5	0.8	3.37
41-50	485	1.87	90	168	35	0.50	2.57	0.75	3.82	7.1	0.6	4.02
51-60	232	0.89	110	98	35	0.50	3.14	0.75	4.39	3.9	0.4	4.38
61-70	396	1.52	134	204	35	0.50	3.83	0.75	5.08	7.7	0.7	5.08
71-80	329	1.27	160	202	38	0.50	4.21	0.75	5.46	6.9	0.6	5.71
81-90	234	0.90	170	153	38	0.50	4.47	0.75	5.72	5.2	0.5	6.18
91-100	136	0.52	188	98	40	0.50	4.69	0.75	5.94	3.1	0.3	6.46
101-110	208	0.80	202	162	40	0.50	5.05	0.75	6.30	5.0	0.5	6.92
111-120	144	0.55	237	131	40	0.50	5.93	0.75	7.18	4.0	0.4	7.28
121-130	45	0.17	250	43	42	0.50	5.95	0.75	7.20	1.2	0.1	7.39
131-140	28	0.11	280	30	42	0.50	6.67	0.75	7.92	0.9	0.1	7.47
141-150	62	0.24	288	69	43	0.50	6.70	0.75	7.95	1.9	0.2	7.64
151-160	110	0.42	311	132	45	0.50	6.92	0.75	8.17	3.5	0.3	7.96
161-170	62	0.24	326	78	45	0.50	7.24	0.75	8.49	2.0	0.2	8.14
171-180	32	0.12	350	43	48	0.50	7.29	0.75	8.54	1.1	0.1	8.24
181-190	10	0.04	370	14	48	0.50	7.71	0.75	8.96	0.3	0.0	8.27
191-200	48	0.18	394	73	50	0.50	7.88	0.75	9.13	1.7	0.2	8.42
Totals:	6,334	24.36	91	2,229						92.64	8.42	
Fleet Summary:	Fleet Size (Drivers)			8.42	Miles Per Driver Per Week			1,323	Total Annual Miles:			
	Loads Per Driver Per Day			2.89	Miles Per Driver Per Day			265	579,526			

The assumptions for dock time and work hours per day are at the top of the model. The assumptions for miles per hour are in the "Miles Per Hour" column. The model is very sensitive to the miles per hour assumption, especially on the lower mileages. Carriers must use the "Total Time Per Trip" column as a check figure for the miles per hour assumptions to prevent unrealistic transit times.

The results of the model indicate that 8.42 drivers are needed to serve the network. Each driver will serve an average of 2.89 loads per day and average 1,323 miles per week. The carrier must rely on experience and expertise to validate these outputs. In this example, the fleet size and utilization level appear to be very reasonable for a network of this type.

---

[86] The complete fleet size spreadsheet model shown here, including the upcoming sensitivity analysis features, is available for purchase at www.TruckloadTransportation.com.

The table below shows the underlying spreadsheet formulas for the fleet size model.[87]

Spreadsheet Formulas for Fleet Size Model

	B	C	D	E	F	G	H	I	J	K	L	M	N
1	Assumptions:												
2	Pick-Up Dock Time (hrs):			0.50			\multicolumn{4}{c}{Cycle Time Per Trip (in hours)}		\multicolumn{3}{c}{Estimated Fleet Size}	
3	Delivery Dock Time (hrs):			0.75									
4	Driver Work Hours Per Day:			11.00	(max = 14 hours)		Pick-Up Dock Time	Drive Time	Delivery Dock Time	Total Time Per Trip	Total Daily Hours	Drivers Needed (Band)	Total Drivers Needed
5	Mileage Band	Load Volume		Round Trip Miles		Miles Per Hour							
6		Annual	Per Day	Per Load	Per Day								
7	0-10	966	C7/52/5	7	E7*D7	7	=$E$2	E7/G7	=$E$3	Sum	K7*D7	L7/$E$4	=M7
8	11-20	640	C8/52/5	30	E8*D8	25	=$E$2	E8/G8	=$E$3	Sum	K8*D8	L8/$E$4	M8+N7
9	191-200	48	C9/52/5	394	E9*D9	50	=$E$2	E9/G9	=$E$3	Sum	K9*D9	L9/$E$4	M9+N8
10	Totals:	1,654	Sum		F10/D10	Sum					Sum	Sum	
11													
12	Fleet Summary:		Fleet Size (Drivers)			=N9	Miles Per Driver Per Week			K13*5			
13			Loads Per Driver Per Day			D10/G12	Miles Per Driver Per Day			F10/G12			

For simplification, not all mileage band rows are shown. However, the formulas for the rows not shown are relatively the same as rows 8 through 10 shown above. The primary formulas in the model are shown below.

Key Fleet Size Model Formulas:

Load Volume Per Day =	Annual Loads / 52 weeks / 5 days per week
Drive Time =	Round Trip Miles Per Load / Miles Per Hour
Total Trip Time =	Pick-Up Dock Time + Drive Time + Delivery Dock Time
Total Daily Hours =	Total Time Per Trip x Load Volume Per Day
Drivers Needed =	Total Daily Hours / Driver Work Hours Per Day

These formulas work together to compute the number of drivers needed in the fleet. The carrier must review the model's assumptions and outputs closely to validate the suggested fleet size and utilization level.

The carrier may also choose to perform a sensitivity analysis of the key assumptions in the fleet size model. The primary risk for the carrier is pricing the fleet based on only 8 trucks when in reality the fleet will require 9 or 10 trucks. Since the carrier will be paid on a per-load basis, not a per-truck basis, the revenues would be inadequate and the fleet would not be profitable. The next section provides a basic sensitivity analysis approach for the key assumptions in the model.

---

[87] Microsoft® product screen shot reprinted with permission from Microsoft® Corporation.

Fleet Size Model Sensitivity Analysis

The fleet size model is very sensitive to changes in the key assumptions, particularly dock time and driver work hours per day. The adjusted model below computes the fleet size after adjusting the pick-up dock time from .50 to .75 hours and the driver work hours per day from 11.0 to 10.50 hours.

Adjusted Fleet Size
(Sensitivity Analysis)

Assumptions:					Cycle Time Per Trip (in hours)				Estimated Fleet Size		
Pick Up Dock Time (hrs):		0.75									
Delivery Dock Time (hrs):		0.75									
Driver Work Hours Per Day:		10.50	14 hour maximum		Pick-Up	Drive	Delivery	Total	Total	Drivers	Total
Mileage	Load Volume	Round Trip Miles		Miles	Dock	Drive	Dock	Time	Daily	Needed	Drivers
Band	Annual	Per Day	Per Load	Per Day	Per Hour	Time	Time	Time	Per Trip	Hours	(Band)	Needed
0-10	966	3.72	7	26	7	0.75	1.00	0.75	2.50	9.3	0.9	0.88
11-20	640	2.46	30	74	25	0.75	1.20	0.75	2.70	6.6	0.6	1.52
21-30	1,451	5.58	46	254	35	0.75	1.30	0.75	2.80	15.6	1.5	3.01
31-40	716	2.75	64	176	35	0.75	1.83	0.75	3.33	9.2	0.9	3.88
41-50	485	1.87	90	168	35	0.75	2.57	0.75	4.07	7.6	0.7	4.60
51-60	232	0.89	110	98	35	0.75	3.14	0.75	4.64	4.1	0.4	5.00
61-70	396	1.52	134	204	35	0.75	3.83	0.75	5.33	8.1	0.8	5.77
71-80	329	1.27	160	202	38	0.75	4.21	0.75	5.71	7.2	0.7	6.46
81-90	234	0.90	170	153	38	0.75	4.47	0.75	5.97	5.4	0.5	6.97
91-100	136	0.52	188	98	40	0.75	4.69	0.75	6.19	3.2	0.3	7.28
101-110	208	0.80	202	162	40	0.75	5.05	0.75	6.55	5.2	0.5	7.78
111-120	144	0.55	237	131	40	0.75	5.93	0.75	7.43	4.1	0.4	8.17
121-130	45	0.17	250	43	42	0.75	5.95	0.75	7.45	1.3	0.1	8.29
131-140	28	0.11	280	30	42	0.75	6.67	0.75	8.17	0.9	0.1	8.38
141-150	62	0.24	288	69	43	0.75	6.70	0.75	8.20	2.0	0.2	8.56
151-160	110	0.42	311	132	45	0.75	6.92	0.75	8.42	3.6	0.3	8.90
161-170	62	0.24	326	78	45	0.75	7.24	0.75	8.74	2.1	0.2	9.10
171-180	32	0.12	350	43	48	0.75	7.29	0.75	8.79	1.1	0.1	9.20
181-190	10	0.04	370	14	48	0.75	7.71	0.75	9.21	0.4	0.0	9.24
191-200	48	0.18	394	73	50	0.75	7.88	0.75	9.38	1.7	0.2	9.40
Totals:	6,334	24.36	91	2,229						98.73	9.40	

Fleet Summary:	Fleet Size (Drivers)	9.40	Miles Per Driver Per Week	1,185	Total Annual Miles:
	Loads Per Driver Per Day	2.59	Miles Per Driver Per Day	237	579,526

The table below compares the outputs from the original model with the sensitivity analysis model shown above.

Fleet Size Sensitivity Analysis	Original Model	Sensitivity Model
Assumptions:		
Pick Up Dock Time (hrs)	0.50	0.75
Delivery Dock Time (hrs)	0.75	0.75
Driver Work Hours Per Day	11.00	10.50
Model Outputs:		
Drivers Needed	8.42	9.40
Utilization	1,323	1,185
Loads Per Driver Per Day	2.89	2.59

These minor changes to pick-up dock time and driver work hours per day cause an increase in the estimated fleet size from 8.42 drivers to 9.40 drivers. The increase in the fleet size is significant enough to justify a deeper analysis. The table below shows the modeled fleet size after applying a reasonable range of assumptions for pick-up dock time and driver work hours per day.

Dock Time	\multicolumn{9}{c	}{Fleet Size Sensitivity Analysis — Driver Work Hours Per Day}
	9.50	9.75	10.00	10.25	10.50	10.75	11.00	11.25	11.50
0.40	9.50	9.25	9.02	8.80	8.59	8.39	8.20	8.02	7.84
0.45	9.62	9.38	9.14	8.92	8.71	8.50	8.31	8.13	7.95
0.50	9.75	9.50	9.26	9.04	8.82	8.62	8.42	8.23	8.06
0.55	9.88	9.63	9.39	9.16	8.94	8.73	8.53	8.34	8.16
0.60	10.01	9.75	9.51	9.28	9.05	8.84	8.64	8.45	8.27
0.65	10.14	9.88	9.63	9.39	9.17	8.96	8.75	8.56	8.37
0.70	10.26	10.00	9.75	9.51	9.29	9.07	8.86	8.67	8.48
0.75	10.39	10.13	9.87	9.63	9.40	9.18	8.98	8.78	8.59
0.80	10.52	10.25	9.99	9.75	9.52	9.30	9.09	8.88	8.69
0.85	10.65	10.38	10.12	9.87	9.64	9.41	9.20	8.99	8.80
0.90	10.78	10.50	10.24	9.99	9.75	9.52	9.31	9.10	8.90
0.95	10.91	10.63	10.36	10.11	9.87	9.64	9.42	9.21	9.01
1.00	11.03	10.75	10.48	10.23	9.98	9.75	9.53	9.32	9.11

Actual Model Output | Relevant Range

The carrier must review the sensitivity information to determine the exact number of trucks and drivers to be used in the dedicated pricing model. Carriers must rely on both experience and the available information about the shipper's network to make the final determination of the fleet size and utilization assumptions.

Fleet Size and Utilization. Based on the fleet size sensitivity analysis, the carrier has elected to price the fleet at 9.0 trucks and drivers. The utilization for the 9 truck fleet will be 1,238 miles per truck per week (579,526 annual miles / 9 trucks / 52 weeks). These are the assumptions to be entered into the dedicated pricing model.

Number of Trailers. The shipper has stated to use a 3 to 1 ratio of trailers to loads per day to estimate trailer requirements. This trailer assumption method is different from the trailer-to-tractor ratio presented previously. This type of trailer fleet size model is common for one-way environments. The 3 trailers to 1 load per day method to determine trailer requirements is a common rule of thumb. The three trailers theoretically include one trailer dropped at the origin, one trailer in transit, and one trailer dropper at the destination. The formula for determining the number of trailers is shown below.

　　Trailers Needed　=　Loads Per Day x Trailer Ratio

　　Trailers Needed　=　24.36 Loads Per Day x 3.0 = 73.08 Trailers

The 24.36 loads per day figure was previously computed in the fleet size model. Based on this trailer fleet size method, the carrier should price the fleet based on 73.08 trailers.

Applying Dedicated Pricing to the Mileage Band Rates

Dedicated Pricing and Analysis

Once the fleet size and utilization level have been determined, the carrier can use the standard dedicated pricing model to compute the cost of serving the network and the associated revenue requirements. Once the total revenue level is identified, the rates by mileage band will be established in order to generate the target total annual revenue when applied to the shipper's actual load activity.

Based on the model results of 8.42 drivers, the carrier must decide on the fleet size and utilization for cost analysis and pricing purposes. Depending on the carrier's perceived risk level of the fleet, the carrier could be aggressive and price the fleet using 8.0 trucks. If the carrier believed the operating assumptions of the fleet size model were relatively aggressive, the carrier may feel more comfortable pricing the fleet at 9.0 trucks.

To be conservative, the carrier will base the pricing on 9 trucks and a utilization level of 1,238 miles per truck per week. Based on the previous trailer model, 73 trailers will be the assumption for the trailer fleet size. The primary assumptions for the dedicated pricing model are shown below.

Dedicated Pricing Model

Customer Name:	Chapter 12	Fleet Description:	Mileage Bands

Fleet Parameters

Number of Tractors	9.00
Backup Tractors	0.00
Number of Drivers	9.00
Utilization (Miles per Tractor per Active Week)	1,238
Active Fleet Weeks Per Year (max = 52 weeks)	52.0
Total Fleet Annual Miles	579,384
Number of Trailers	73.00
Trailer/Tractor Ratio	8.11

Overhead Costs

Tractor Legalization/Taxes	$ 2,000
Driver Recruiting Costs	$ 3,000
Administration Expenses	$ 5,000
Total Overhead (per tractor per year)	$ 10,000
Direct Staffing (On-site CSR / Offices / Etc.)	$ -
Other Annual Expenses (Total Fleet)	$ 2,500
Initial Start-Up Costs (Total)	$ 15,000

Other Parameters

Driver Rate of Pay (Per Mile or Annual Gross)	$ 40,000.00
Duration of Deal/Contract (in months)	36.0
Average Collection Period (in days)	30.0

Pricing and Analysis

Suggested Rate Per Mile (all miles)	$ 2.5200
Operating Ratio	75.36%
Internal Rate of Return	10.03%

The carrier has applied the standard overhead costs to the fleet. The carrier has also budgeted $15,000 for start-up costs. Based on an analysis of both the driving job and the local market, $40,000 per year is budgeted (per driver) for driver pay.

The carrier must verify that the total annual miles in the pricing model match the total annual miles from the fleet size model. In this case, the pricing model shows 579,384 miles and the fleet size model shows 579,526 miles. This small variance is simply due to rounding and is insignificant. If the carrier should decide to price the fleet with 8 trucks instead of 9, the utilization must also be adjusted so that the miles in the pricing model match the 579,526 from the fleet size model.

The full dedicated pricing model and pro-forma income statement are shown below.

Dedicated Pricing Model

Customer Name:	Chapter 12	Fleet Description:	Mileage Bands

Fleet Parameters

Number of Tractors	9.00
Backup Tractors	0.00
Number of Drivers	9.00
Utilization (Miles per Tractor per Active Week)	1,238
Active Fleet Weeks Per Year (max = 52 weeks)	52.0
Total Fleet Annual Miles	579,384
Number of Trailers	73.00
Trailer/Tractor Ratio	8.11

Overhead Costs

Tractor Legalization/Taxes	$ 2,000
Driver Recruiting Costs	$ 3,000
Administration Expenses	$ 5,000
Total Overhead (per tractor per year)	$ 10,000
Direct Staffing (On-site CSR / Offices / Etc.)	$ -
Other Annual Expenses (Total Fleet)	$ 2,500
Initial Start-Up Costs (Total)	$ 15,000

Other Parameters

Driver Rate of Pay (Per Mile or Annual Gross)	$ 40,000.00
Duration of Deal/Contract (in months)	36.0
Average Collection Period (in days)	30.0

Pricing and Analysis

Suggested Rate Per Mile (all miles)	$ 2.5200
Operating Ratio	75.36%
Internal Rate of Return	10.03%

Pro-Forma Income Statement

		Fleet Totals Per Mile	Fleet Totals Annual	Per Tractor Weekly	Per Tractor Annual
Total Fleet Miles			579,384	1,238	64,376
Total Revenue		$2.520	$1,460,048	$3,120	$162,228
Variable Costs	Assumptions				
Driver Wages	$40,000.00	$0.621	$360,000	$769	$40,000
Fringe Benefits (% of wages)	25.0%	0.155	90,000	192	10,000
Fuel	$0.208	0.208	120,512	258	13,390
Maintenance	$0.110	0.110	63,732	136	7,081
Insurance	$0.100	0.100	57,938	124	6,438
Total Variable Costs		1.195	692,183	1,479	76,909
Fixed Costs	Assumptions				
Tractor Depreciation	$ 16,667	0.259	150,000	$321	$16,667
Trailer Depreciation	$ 2,200	0.277	160,600	343	17,844
Legalization/Recruiting/Admin	$ 10,000	0.155	90,000	192	10,000
On-Site Manager	$ -	0.000	0	0	0
Start Up /Special Equipment	$ 7,500	0.013	7,500	16	833
Total Fixed Costs		0.704	408,100	872	45,344
Total Cost		1.899	1,100,283	2,351	122,254
Operating Profit		$0.62	$359,765	$769	$39,974
Operating Ratio		75.36%	75.36%	75.36%	75.36%

The fleet is priced at $2.52 per mile with $1,460,048 in annual revenue. The fleet is expected to have an operating ratio of 75.36% and an internal rate of return of 10.03%. These profitability measures meet the carrier's criteria of an operating ratio no higher than 92% and an internal rate of return no lower than 10%.

The operating ratio may appear low at 75.36%, but this level of revenue and income is necessary to meet the internal rate of return target of 10.0%. This is a low utilization fleet with a very high trailer-to-tractor ratio. The internal rate of return requirement forces the carrier to increase revenue to insure that the 10.0% minimum return is achieved. If the carrier were to base pricing strictly on operating ratio, the fleet could have been severely underpriced.

Sensitivity Analysis – Dedicated Pricing

The most critical unknown pricing and design variable for this opportunity is the fleet size. Before determining the final pricing and revenue, the carrier may choose to evaluate the profitability of the fleet under a range of possible fleet sizes. In the analysis below, the carrier has developed pro-forma income statements for the three most likely fleet sizes of 8, 9 and 10 trucks.

Dedicated Pricing Model - Sensitivity Analysis

Customer Name:	Chapter 12	Fleet Description:	Mileage Bands

Other Parameters

Driver Rate of Pay (Per Mile or Annual Gross)	$	40,000.00
Duration of Deal/Contract (in months)		36.0
Average Collection Period (in days)		30.0
Additional assumptions shown by scenario below.		

Notes:
Adjusted fleet size to 10 in worst case and 8 in best case.
Annual revenue is the same in each scenario.

Overhead Costs

Tractor Legalization/Taxes	$	2,000
Driver Recruiting Costs	$	3,000
Administration Expenses	$	5,000
Total Overhead (per tractor per year)	$	10,000
Direct Staffing (On-site CSR / Etc.)	$	-
Other Annual Expenses (Total Fleet)	$	2,500
Initial Start-Up Costs (Total)	$	15,000

Pro-forma Income Statements	Assumptions	Worst Case Per Mile	Worst Case Annual	Expected Per Mile	Expected Annual	Best Case Per Mile	Best Case Annual
Scenario Assumptions							
Number of Tractors			10.00		9.00		8.00
Number of Drivers			10.00		9.00		8.00
Number of Trailers			80.00		73.00		73.00
Utilization			1,114		1,238		1,393
Active Fleet Weeks Per Year (max = 52 weeks)			52.0		52.0		52.0
Rate Per Mile			$ 2.52		$ 2.52		$ 2.52
Total Fleet Miles			579,384		579,384		579,384
Total Revenue		$2.520	$1,460,048	$2.520	$1,460,048	$2.520	$1,460,048
Variable Costs	Assumptions						
Driver Wages	$40,000.00	$0.690	$400,000	$0.621	$360,000	$0.552	$320,000
Fringe Benefits (% of wages)	25.0%	$0.173	100,000	$0.155	90,000	$0.138	80,000
Fuel	$0.208	$0.208	120,512	$0.208	120,512	$0.208	120,512
Maintenance	$0.110	$0.110	63,732	$0.110	63,732	$0.110	63,732
Insurance	$0.100	$0.100	57,938	$0.100	57,938	$0.100	57,938
Total Variable Costs		$1.281	742,183	$1.195	692,183	$1.108	642,183
Fixed Costs	Assumptions						
Tractor Depreciation	$ 16,667	$0.288	166,667	$0.259	150,000	$0.230	133,333
Trailer Depreciation	$ 2,200	$0.304	176,000	$0.277	160,600	$0.277	160,600
Legalization/Recruiting/Admin	$ 10,000	$0.173	100,000	$0.155	90,000	$0.138	80,000
On-Site Manager	$ -	$0.000	0	$0.000	0	$0.000	0
Start Up /Special Equipment	$ 7,500	$0.013	7,500	$0.013	7,500	$0.013	7,500
Total Fixed Costs		$0.777	450,167	$0.704	408,100	$0.658	381,433
Total Cost		$2.058	1,192,349	$1.899	1,100,283	$1.767	1,023,616
Operating Profit		$0.462	$267,699	$0.621	$359,765	$0.753	$436,432
Operating Ratio			81.67%		75.36%		70.11%

To be consistent with the fleet size model, the total annual fleet miles remain constant under each scenario. Total annual revenues also remain constant for each scenario. Since the revenues will be based on the per-load rates from the mileage bands, revenues and load volumes will be the same regardless of the number of trucks used by the carrier to serve the network. Based on the operating ratio of 81.67% in the 10 truck scenario, the carrier should feel comfortable with the planned revenue level of $1,460,048.

Allocation of Dedicated Revenues to Mileage Bands

Once the target annual revenue has been established, the carrier must convert the total annual dedicated revenue into the mileage band format. The goal is to establish a rate for each mileage band segment so that the expected total revenue from the mileage band activity equals the target annual revenue for the dedicated fleet. The allocation should also be consistent with the length of haul for each mileage band so that the carrier earns the appropriate revenue for the relative cost of serving any load in the network. A simple model for allocating the revenues by mileage band is shown below.

Allocation of Target Revenue to Mileage Bands									
				Target Annual Revenue (from pricing model)					$ 1,460,048
			Assumption:	Fixed Allocation Per Load			$ 105.00		$ 665,070
				Per Mile Allocation			$ 1.372		$ 794,978
				Total Allocated Revenue					$ 1,460,048

Mileage Band	Annual Loads	RT Miles Per Load	Annual Miles	Charge Per Load			Total Annual Revenue Validation		
				Per Load	Mileage	Total	Per Load	Mileage	Total
0-10	966	7	6,762	$ 105.00	$ 9.60	$ 114.60	$ 101,430	$ 9,276	$ 110,706
11-20	640	30	19,200	$ 105.00	$ 41.15	$ 146.15	$ 67,200	$ 26,338	$ 93,538
21-30	1,451	46	66,137	$ 105.00	$ 62.53	$ 167.53	$ 152,355	$ 90,725	$ 243,080
31-40	716	64	45,824	$ 105.00	$ 87.79	$ 192.79	$ 75,180	$ 62,860	$ 138,040
41-50	485	90	43,650	$ 105.00	$ 123.46	$ 228.46	$ 50,925	$ 59,878	$ 110,803
51-60	232	110	25,520	$ 105.00	$ 150.90	$ 255.90	$ 24,360	$ 35,008	$ 59,368
61-70	396	134	53,064	$ 105.00	$ 183.82	$ 288.82	$ 41,580	$ 72,792	$ 114,372
71-80	329	160	52,640	$ 105.00	$ 219.48	$ 324.48	$ 34,545	$ 72,210	$ 106,755
81-90	234	170	39,780	$ 105.00	$ 233.20	$ 338.20	$ 24,570	$ 54,569	$ 79,139
91-100	136	188	25,528	$ 105.00	$ 257.49	$ 362.49	$ 14,280	$ 35,019	$ 49,299
101-110	208	202	42,016	$ 105.00	$ 277.10	$ 382.10	$ 21,840	$ 57,636	$ 79,476
111-120	144	237	34,155	$ 105.00	$ 325.37	$ 430.37	$ 15,120	$ 46,853	$ 61,973
121-130	45	250	11,250	$ 105.00	$ 342.94	$ 447.94	$ 4,725	$ 15,432	$ 20,157
131-140	28	280	7,840	$ 105.00	$ 384.10	$ 489.10	$ 2,940	$ 10,755	$ 13,695
141-150	62	288	17,873	$ 105.00	$ 395.45	$ 500.45	$ 6,510	$ 24,518	$ 31,028
151-160	110	311	34,262	$ 105.00	$ 427.27	$ 532.27	$ 11,550	$ 47,000	$ 58,550
161-170	62	326	20,212	$ 105.00	$ 447.20	$ 552.20	$ 6,510	$ 27,726	$ 34,236
171-180	32	350	11,200	$ 105.00	$ 480.12	$ 585.12	$ 3,360	$ 15,364	$ 18,724
181-190	10	370	3,700	$ 105.00	$ 507.56	$ 612.56	$ 1,050	$ 5,076	$ 6,126
191-200	48	394	18,912	$ 105.00	$ 540.48	$ 645.48	$ 5,040	$ 25,943	$ 30,983
Totals:	6,334		579,526				$ 665,070	$ 794,978	$ 1,460,048

Revenues are allocated through two components, a fixed revenue amount per load and a variable rate per mile. As a first step, the carrier must establish the fixed allocation per load as an assumption. In this example, the fixed allocation is $105 per load. Once the fixed allocation is established, the remaining revenues are allocated across the total annual miles to determine the variable per-mile allocation rate. The formula for the variable per-mile allocation rate is shown below.

$$\frac{\text{Per Mile}}{\text{Allocation Rate}} = \frac{\text{Target Revenue} - \text{Revenue from Fixed}}{\text{Total Annual Miles}} = \frac{\$1{,}460{,}048 - \$665{,}070}{579{,}526 \text{ miles}} = \$1.372 \text{ per mile}$$

The fixed charge and the variable charge are added together to compute the rate per load for each mileage range. The "Total Annual Revenue Validation" columns represent the allocated rate multiplied by the number of annual loads. The sum of these columns should match the target annual revenue at the top of the model as shown.

The spreadsheet formulas for the revenue allocation model are shown below. For simplification, not all mileage bands are shown. The formulas for the rows not shown are relatively the same as rows 10 through 13.

Revenue Allocation - Spreadsheet Formulas[88]

	B	C	D	E	F	G	H	I	J	K	L
2		Allocation of Target Revenue					Target Annual Revenue (from pricing model)				$ 1,460,048
3		to Mileage Bands									
4						Assumption:	Fixed Allocation Per Load			$ 105.00	=K4*D30
5							Per Mile Allocation			=L5/F30	=L2-L4
6							Total Allocated Revenue				=SUM(L4:L5)
7											
8		Mileage	Annual	RT Miles	Annual	\multicolumn{3}{c}{Charge Per Load}	\multicolumn{3}{c}{Total Annual Revenue Validation}		
9		Band	Loads	Per Load	Miles	Per Load	Mileage	Total	Per Load	Mileage	Total
10		0-10	966	7	=E10*D10	=$K$4	=E10*$K$5	=H10+G10	=G10*D10	=H10*D10	=K10+J10
11		11-20	640	30	=E11*D11	=$K$4	=E11*$K$5	=H11+G11	=G11*D11	=H11*D11	=K11+J11
12		21-30	1,451	46	=E12*D12	=$K$4	=E12*$K$5	=H12+G12	=G12*D12	=H12*D12	=K12+J12
13		31-40	716	64	=E13*D13	=$K$4	=E13*$K$5	=H13+G13	=G13*D13	=H13*D13	=K13+J13
14		Totals:	3,773		SUM(F10:F13)				SUM(J10:J13)	SUM(K10:K13)	SUM(L10:L13)

The values in the cells L2 and K4 are the initial assumptions that drive the allocation. The values in columns D and E come directly from the fleet size model. The values in cells L6 and L14 should match the total annual revenue amount in L2.

As long as the assumption for the fixed allocation per load is reasonable, the model will allocate the revenues to each mileage band so that the rate per load for each band is equitable for the shipper and profitable for the carrier. The higher the fixed allocation per load assumption, the less the rate variance from band to band will be.

One way the carrier can perform a reasonability check on the allocated rates is to look at the suggested per load rates in the highest mileage bands. The rates in the upper mileage bands should appear reasonable and should usually be comparable to other one-way rates or minimum charges for the same mileage range. When comparing the upper mileage band rates to typical one-way rates, adjustments should be made for any special cost situations in the mileage band rates such as excess trailers, on-site managers, or special equipment. Significant variation in these factors could make the mileage band rates more difficult to compare to standard one-way rates.

If the allocated rates don't appear reasonable in either the lower or upper mileage bands, the per-load allocation assumption can be adjusted to reallocate the planned revenues. An increase in the per-load charge will increase the rates in the lower mileage bands and decrease rates in the upper mileage bands. Likewise, a decrease in the per-load charge will lower the rates in the lower mileage bands and increase rates in the upper mileage bands. If these adjustments don't correct the rates, the carrier may make manual adjustments to the allocated rates to finalize the rates in each mileage band.

---

[88] Microsoft® product screen shot reprinted with permission from Microsoft® Corporation.

Smoothing the Revenue Allocation. The process shown previously for allocating the dedicated revenues to the mileage bands is based on the shipper's current actual average length of haul for each mileage band. The risk of this approach is that the resulting rates are sometimes inconsistent from band to band. These inconsistencies create a small revenue risk for the carrier, particularly when a band is under-priced. The inconsistent rates may also be difficult for a potential shipper to understand and comprehend.

The rate inconsistencies can be easily corrected by applying a smoothing approach. The smoothing approach ignores the shipper's historical round trip distance and replaces it with the true expected round trip distance for each band as shown below.

Mileage Band	Round Trip Miles Smooth	Round Trip Miles Actual
0-10	10	7
11-20	30	30
21-30	50	46
31-40	70	64
41-50	90	90
51-60	110	110
61-70	130	134
71-80	150	160
81-90	170	170
91-100	190	188
101-110	210	202
111-120	230	237
121-130	250	250
131-140	270	280
141-150	290	288
151-160	310	311
161-170	330	326
171-180	350	350
181-190	370	370
191-200	390	394

The "smooth" round trip distance is the midpoint one-way miles of each band multiplied by 2 to complete the round trip. For example, in the 21-30 mile band, the midpoint is 25 miles. 25 one-way miles equates to a 50 mile average round trip for the band. The same calculation is applied to each band to determine the "smooth" round trip distance.

By basing the allocation on the "smooth" round trip distance, the revised rates are more accurate, especially as the shipper's network changes over time. For example, in the 101-110 band, the actual round trip distance is only 202 miles while the "smooth" distance is 210 miles. When based on the actual round trip distance of 202 miles, the allocation will not apply enough revenue to this band. As a result, the band will be under-priced for all loads over 202 round trip miles. Basing the allocation on the midpoint distance instead of the actual distance reduces the carrier's revenue risk in the likely event of future changes in the shipper's network.

To complete the "smooth" allocation, the same allocation process is applied, but the round trip miles and annual miles are based on the midpoint round trip distances instead of the actual distances as shown below in the "RT Miles Per Load" column.

Allocation of Target Revenue to Mileage Bands (Smoothed) Based on "Mid-Point" Miles				Target Annual Revenue (from pricing model)			$1,460,048		
				Assumption:	Fixed Allocation Per Load		$ 101.00	$ 639,734	
					Per Mile Allocation		$ 1.393	$ 820,314	
					Total Allocated Revenue			$1,460,048	

Mileage Band	Annual Loads	RT Miles Per Load	Annual Miles	Charge Per Load			Total Annual Revenue Validation		
				Per Load	Mileage	Total	Per Load	Mileage	Total
0-10	966	10	9,660	$ 101.00	$ 13.93	$ 114.93	$ 97,566	$ 13,456	$ 111,022
11-20	640	30	19,200	$ 101.00	$ 41.79	$ 142.79	$ 64,640	$ 26,744	$ 91,384
21-30	1,451	50	72,550	$ 101.00	$ 69.65	$ 170.65	$146,551	$ 101,056	$ 247,607
31-40	716	70	50,120	$ 101.00	$ 97.50	$ 198.50	$ 72,316	$ 69,813	$ 142,129
41-50	485	90	43,650	$ 101.00	$ 125.36	$ 226.36	$ 48,985	$ 60,801	$ 109,786
51-60	232	110	25,520	$ 101.00	$ 153.22	$ 254.22	$ 23,432	$ 35,547	$ 58,979
61-70	396	130	51,480	$ 101.00	$ 181.08	$ 282.08	$ 39,996	$ 71,707	$ 111,703
71-80	329	150	49,350	$ 101.00	$ 208.94	$ 309.94	$ 33,229	$ 68,740	$ 101,969
81-90	234	170	39,780	$ 101.00	$ 236.80	$ 337.80	$ 23,634	$ 55,410	$ 79,044
91-100	136	190	25,840	$ 101.00	$ 264.65	$ 365.65	$ 13,736	$ 35,993	$ 49,729
101-110	208	210	43,680	$ 101.00	$ 292.51	$ 393.51	$ 21,008	$ 60,842	$ 81,850
111-120	144	230	33,120	$ 101.00	$ 320.37	$ 421.37	$ 14,544	$ 46,133	$ 60,677
121-130	45	250	11,250	$ 101.00	$ 348.23	$ 449.23	$ 4,545	$ 15,670	$ 20,215
131-140	28	270	7,560	$ 101.00	$ 376.09	$ 477.09	$ 2,828	$ 10,530	$ 13,358
141-150	62	290	17,980	$ 101.00	$ 403.94	$ 504.94	$ 6,262	$ 25,045	$ 31,307
151-160	110	310	34,100	$ 101.00	$ 431.80	$ 532.80	$ 11,110	$ 47,498	$ 58,608
161-170	62	330	20,460	$ 101.00	$ 459.66	$ 560.66	$ 6,262	$ 28,499	$ 34,761
171-180	32	350	11,200	$ 101.00	$ 487.52	$ 588.52	$ 3,232	$ 15,601	$ 18,833
181-190	10	370	3,700	$ 101.00	$ 515.38	$ 616.38	$ 1,010	$ 5,154	$ 6,164
191-200	48	390	18,720	$ 101.00	$ 543.24	$ 644.24	$ 4,848	$ 26,075	$ 30,923
Totals:	6,334		588,920				$639,734	$ 820,314	$1,460,048

The computed total annual miles in the "smooth" scenario are slightly higher than the original scenario. In some cases, the total annual miles in the "smooth" scenario will be slightly lower. Either way, the difference in annual miles is very minor and insignificant in terms of the accuracy of the allocation. The fixed allocation per load in this example is adjusted slightly to compensate for the minor difference in total annual miles.

The new "smooth" rates should be very similar to the original rates but appear more consistent from band to band. The table to the right provides a side-by-side comparison of the two allocations for the first ten mileage bands. While both methods are technically correct, the "smooth" allocation protects the carrier's revenues from changes in future shipping patterns while also providing a more reasonable rate proposal for a potential shipper.

Mileage Band	Allocated Rates		
	Smooth	Actual	Variance
0-10	$ 114.93	$ 114.60	$ (0.33)
11-20	$ 142.79	$ 146.15	$ 3.37
21-30	$ 170.65	$ 167.53	$ (3.12)
31-40	$ 198.50	$ 192.79	$ (5.71)
41-50	$ 226.36	$ 228.46	$ 2.10
51-60	$ 254.22	$ 255.90	$ 1.67
61-70	$ 282.08	$ 288.82	$ 6.74
71-80	$ 309.94	$ 324.48	$ 14.55
81-90	$ 337.80	$ 338.20	$ 0.41
91-100	$ 365.65	$ 362.49	$ (3.16)

Mileage Bands with Secondary Coverage

Adjusting the Fleet Size

In cases where the shipper's facility is located in a market where the carrier has a large amount of one-way capacity for other shippers,[89] the carrier may choose to utilize this available capacity as a secondary resource to serve a small portion of the shipper's mileage band network. By introducing the secondary capacity into the previous solution, the carrier can establish the base fleet size at a level less than what is necessary to cover 100% of the mileage band load activity. With a design at a fleet size slightly smaller than the network requires, the base fleet has a higher probability of achieving an efficient utilization level. The fleet is also partially protected from the risks of the daily volume fluctuations discussed previously.

The fleet size model shown below includes several new columns. The new columns introduce a load allocation methodology where a small percentage of the loads are assigned to secondary capacity instead of the primary dedicated fleet. The dedicated fleet size is then computed using the same process, but the fleet size calculations are based on only the loads that are allocated to the dedicated fleet.

Fleet Size Model with Secondary Capacity

Mileage Band	Annual Loads	% to Fleet	Fleet Loads Annual	Fleet Loads Per Day	Loads to Backup	Round Trip Miles Per Load	Round Trip Miles Per Day	Miles Per Hr	Pick-Up Dock Time	Drive Time	Delivery Dock Time	Total Time Per Trip	Total Daily Hours	Drivers Needed (Band)	Total Drivers Needed
0-10	966	99.0%	956	3.68	10	7	26	7	0.50	1.00	0.75	2.25	8.3	0.8	0.75
11-20	640	99.0%	634	2.44	6	30	73	25	0.50	1.20	0.75	2.45	6.0	0.5	1.30
21-30	1,451	99.0%	1,436	5.52	15	46	252	35	0.50	1.30	0.75	2.55	14.1	1.3	2.58
31-40	716	99.0%	709	2.73	7	64	175	35	0.50	1.83	0.75	3.08	8.4	0.8	3.34
41-50	485	99.0%	480	1.85	5	90	166	35	0.50	2.57	0.75	3.82	7.1	0.6	3.98
51-60	232	96.0%	223	0.86	9	110	94	35	0.50	3.14	0.75	4.39	3.8	0.3	4.32
61-70	396	96.0%	380	1.46	16	134	196	35	0.50	3.83	0.75	5.08	7.4	0.7	5.00
71-80	329	95.0%	313	1.20	16	160	193	38	0.50	4.21	0.75	5.46	6.6	0.6	5.60
81-90	234	95.0%	222	0.85	12	170	145	38	0.50	4.47	0.75	5.72	4.9	0.4	6.04
91-100	136	90.0%	122	0.47	14	188	88	40	0.50	4.69	0.75	5.94	2.8	0.3	6.29
101-110	208	90.0%	187	0.72	21	202	145	40	0.50	5.05	0.75	6.30	4.5	0.4	6.71
111-120	144	90.0%	130	0.50	14	237	119	40	0.50	5.93	0.75	7.18	3.6	0.3	7.03
121-130	45	85.0%	38	0.15	7	250	37	42	0.50	5.95	0.75	7.20	1.1	0.1	7.13
131-140	28	85.0%	24	0.09	4	280	26	42	0.50	6.67	0.75	7.92	0.7	0.1	7.19
141-150	62	80.0%	50	0.19	12	288	55	43	0.50	6.70	0.75	7.95	1.5	0.1	7.33
151-160	110	75.0%	83	0.32	27	311	99	45	0.50	6.92	0.75	8.17	2.6	0.2	7.57
161-170	62	65.0%	40	0.15	22	326	50	45	0.50	7.24	0.75	8.49	1.3	0.1	7.69
171-180	32	60.0%	19	0.07	13	350	26	48	0.50	7.29	0.75	8.54	0.6	0.1	7.75
181-190	10	50.0%	5	0.02	5	370	7	48	0.50	7.71	0.75	8.96	0.2	0.0	7.76
191-200	48	40.0%	19	0.07	29	394	29	50	0.50	7.88	0.75	9.13	0.7	0.1	7.82
Totals:	**6,334**	**95.8%**	**6,070**	**23.35**	**264**	**86**	**2,000**						**86.05**	**7.82**	

Assumptions:
- Pick Up Dock Time (hrs): 0.50
- Delivery Dock Time (hrs): 0.75
- Driver Work Hours Per Day: 11.00 (max = 14 hours)

Fleet Summary:
- Fleet Size (Drivers): 7.82
- Loads Per Driver Per Day: 2.98
- Miles Per Driver Per Week: 1,278
- Miles Per Driver Per Day: 256
- Total Annual Miles: 520,032

The new "% to Fleet" column indicates the percentage of the annual loads within each mileage band to be served by the dedicated fleet. The loads not served by the fleet appear in the "Loads to Backup" column. These loads will be served by the secondary capacity. The other parts of the fleet model are unchanged. Since 264 loads are to be served by

---

[89] Secondary equipment may include trucks and drivers for other dedicated shippers as well as capacity from the carrier's irregular route linehaul and/or regional fleets.

secondary capacity, the modeled dedicated fleet size has fallen from 8.42 drivers to 7.82 drivers.

The graph below illustrates the use of dedicated fleet coverage and secondary capacity coverage for each mileage band.

Distribution of Network Coverage

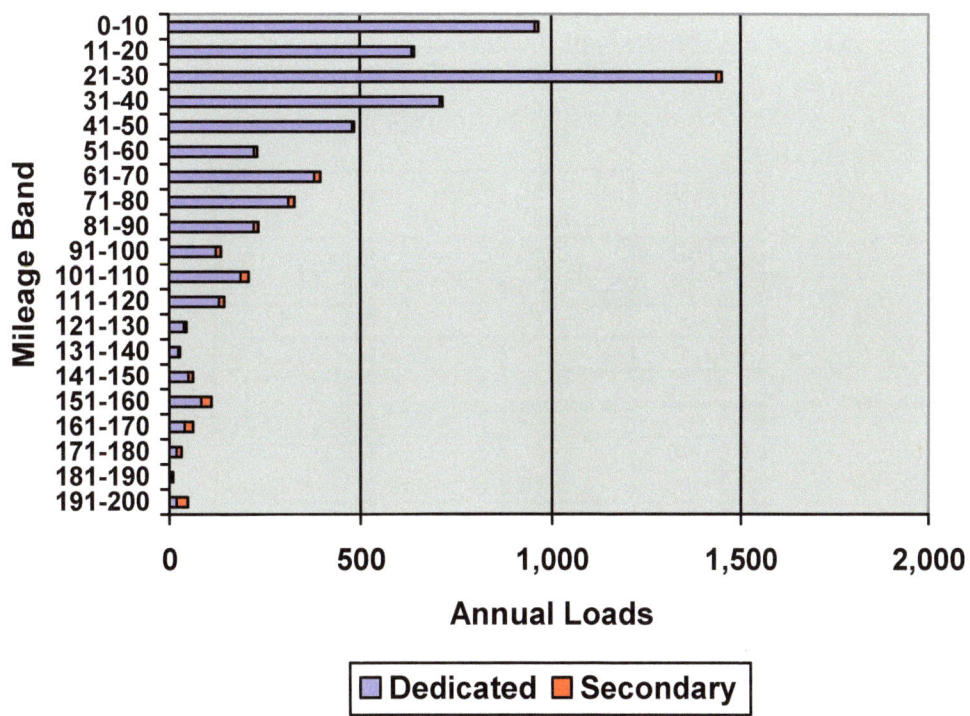

As length of haul increases, the relative proportion of service by secondary capacity increases. The carrier will follow this approach for several reasons. First, the longer loads are generally more attractive to the secondary fleets and the associated drivers. Second, assigning shorter loads to the dedicated fleet reduces total empty miles and returns the dedicated truck to the origin more quickly. By utilizing all available resources and fleets, the carrier is able to design a very efficient operation and offer the shipper excellent service at a very competitive cost.

Cost of Secondary Coverage

For the dedicated portion of the cost, the carrier can use the standard dedicated pricing model to compute the cost of serving the network and the associated revenue requirements. For the secondary coverage, the carrier can apply standard one-way pricing to determine the annual cost of the secondary activity. The per-load cost of the secondary coverage is shown in the table below. These rates will not be directly included in the customer's proposal. These rates are used only to estimate the revenue needs for the secondary load coverage portion of the network.

Annual Cost of Secondary Coverage

Mileage Band	Annual Loads	Rate Per Load	Annual Cost
0-10	10	$ 375	$ 3,750
11-20	6	$ 375	$ 2,250
21-30	15	$ 400	$ 6,000
31-40	7	$ 400	$ 2,800
41-50	5	$ 425	$ 2,125
51-60	9	$ 425	$ 3,825
61-70	16	$ 450	$ 7,200
71-80	16	$ 450	$ 7,200
81-90	12	$ 475	$ 5,700
91-100	14	$ 475	$ 6,650
101-110	21	$ 475	$ 9,975
111-120	14	$ 500	$ 7,000
121-130	7	$ 500	$ 3,500
131-140	4	$ 500	$ 2,000
141-150	12	$ 525	$ 6,300
151-160	27	$ 525	$ 14,175
161-170	22	$ 540	$ 11,880
171-180	13	$ 550	$ 7,150
181-190	5	$ 575	$ 2,875
191-200	29	$ 590	$ 17,110
Totals:	264		$ 129,465

The carrier's dedicated division will work closely with the division that will provide the secondary coverage. The secondary division will provide the dedicated division with the amount of available capacity and the desired rates by mileage band. The secondary costs will be combined with the dedicated cost to determine the final mileage band rates to be presented to the customer.

Dedicated Fleet Costs

For the dedicated portion of the cost, the carrier can use the previous dedicated pricing model and update the revised assumptions. The fleet size will be reduced from 9 trucks to 8 trucks. Utilization has increased to 1,250 miles per week. The number of trailers will remain at 73. All other cost assumptions are unchanged.

Dedicated Pricing Model

Customer Name:	Chapter 12	Fleet Description:	Mileage Bands - with Secondary

Fleet Parameters

Number of Tractors	8.00
Backup Tractors	0.00
Number of Drivers	8.00
Utilization (Miles per Tractor per Active Week)	1,250
Active Fleet Weeks Per Year (max = 52 weeks)	52.0
Total Fleet Annual Miles	520,000
Number of Trailers	73.00
Trailer/Tractor Ratio	9.13

Overhead Costs

Tractor Legalization/Taxes	$ 2,000
Driver Recruiting Costs	$ 3,000
Administration Expenses	$ 5,000
Total Overhead (per tractor per year)	$ 10,000
Direct Staffing (On-site CSR / Offices / Etc.)	$ -
Other Annual Expenses (Total Fleet)	$ 2,500
Initial Start-Up Costs (Total)	$ 15,000

Other Parameters

Driver Rate of Pay (Per Mile or Annual Gross)	$ 40,000.00
Duration of Deal/Contract (in months)	36.0
Average Collection Period (in days)	30.0

Pricing and Analysis

Suggested Rate Per Mile (all miles)	$ 2.5900
Operating Ratio	74.16%
Internal Rate of Return	10.09%

Pro-Forma Income Statement		Fleet Totals Per Mile	Fleet Totals Annual	Per Tractor Weekly	Per Tractor Annual
Total Fleet Miles			520,000	1,250	65,000
Total Revenue		$2.590	$1,346,800	$3,238	$168,350
Variable Costs	Assumptions				
Driver Wages	$40,000.00	$0.615	$320,000	$769	$40,000
Fringe Benefits (% of wages)	25.0%	0.154	80,000	192	10,000
Fuel	$0.208	0.208	108,160	260	13,520
Maintenance	$0.110	0.110	57,200	138	7,150
Insurance	$0.100	0.100	52,000	125	6,500
Total Variable Costs		1.187	617,360	1,484	77,170
Fixed Costs	Assumptions				
Tractor Depreciation	$ 16,667	0.256	133,333	$321	$16,667
Trailer Depreciation	$ 2,200	0.309	160,600	386	20,075
Legalization/Recruiting/Admin	$ 10,000	0.154	80,000	192	10,000
On-Site Manager	$ -	0.000	0	0	0
Start Up /Special Equipment	$ 7,500	0.014	7,500	18	938
Total Fixed Costs		0.734	381,433	917	47,679
Total Cost		1.921	998,793	2,401	124,849
Operating Profit		$0.67	$348,007	$837	$43,501
Operating Ratio		74.16%	74.16%	74.16%	74.16%

The rate per mile has increased slightly from $2.52 per mile to $2.59 per mile. The operating ratio and internal rate of return meet the carrier's internal requirements. Again, the total annual miles in the pricing model match the total annual miles in the fleet size model. The new target annual revenue for the dedicated portion of the service is $1,346,800. This amount, along with the cost of the secondary capacity, must now be allocated to the mileage bands.

Dedicated Allocation to Bands

Using the same process and model as before, the dedicated portion of the revenue must be allocated to the mileage bands. The table below shows the allocation of the dedicated revenue to the mileage bands based on actual miles. The "smooth" approach presented previously could also be applied to this step.

Allocation of Target Revenue to Mileage Bands
With Secondary Capacity

		Target Annual Revenue (from pricing model)	$ 1,346,800
Assumption:	Fixed Allocation Per Load	$ 105.00	$ 637,350
	Per Mile Allocation	$ 1.364	$ 709,450
	Total Allocated Revenue		$ 1,346,800

Mileage Band	Annual Loads	RT Miles Per Load	Annual Miles	Charge Per Load — Per Load	Charge Per Load — Mileage	Charge Per Load — Total	Total Annual Revenue Validation — Per Load	Total Annual Revenue Validation — Mileage	Total Annual Revenue Validation — Total
0-10	956	7	6,692	$ 105.00	$ 9.55	$ 114.55	$ 100,380	$ 9,130	$ 109,510
11-20	634	30	19,020	$ 105.00	$ 40.93	$ 145.93	$ 66,570	$ 25,948	$ 92,518
21-30	1,436	46	65,453	$ 105.00	$ 62.18	$ 167.18	$ 150,780	$ 89,294	$ 240,074
31-40	709	64	45,376	$ 105.00	$ 87.31	$ 192.31	$ 74,445	$ 61,904	$ 136,349
41-50	480	90	43,200	$ 105.00	$ 122.78	$ 227.78	$ 50,400	$ 58,935	$ 109,335
51-60	223	110	24,530	$ 105.00	$ 150.07	$ 255.07	$ 23,415	$ 33,465	$ 56,880
61-70	380	134	50,920	$ 105.00	$ 182.81	$ 287.81	$ 39,900	$ 69,467	$ 109,367
71-80	313	160	50,080	$ 105.00	$ 218.28	$ 323.28	$ 32,865	$ 68,321	$ 101,186
81-90	222	170	37,740	$ 105.00	$ 231.92	$ 336.92	$ 23,310	$ 51,487	$ 74,797
91-100	122	188	22,900	$ 105.00	$ 256.08	$ 361.08	$ 12,810	$ 31,242	$ 44,052
101-110	187	202	37,774	$ 105.00	$ 275.58	$ 380.58	$ 19,635	$ 51,533	$ 71,168
111-120	130	237	30,834	$ 105.00	$ 323.58	$ 428.58	$ 13,650	$ 42,065	$ 55,715
121-130	38	250	9,500	$ 105.00	$ 341.06	$ 446.06	$ 3,990	$ 12,960	$ 16,950
131-140	24	280	6,720	$ 105.00	$ 381.99	$ 486.99	$ 2,520	$ 9,168	$ 11,688
141-150	50	288	14,414	$ 105.00	$ 393.28	$ 498.28	$ 5,250	$ 19,664	$ 24,914
151-160	83	311	25,853	$ 105.00	$ 424.93	$ 529.93	$ 8,715	$ 35,269	$ 43,984
161-170	40	326	13,040	$ 105.00	$ 444.74	$ 549.74	$ 4,200	$ 17,790	$ 21,990
171-180	19	350	6,650	$ 105.00	$ 477.48	$ 582.48	$ 1,995	$ 9,072	$ 11,067
181-190	5	370	1,850	$ 105.00	$ 504.77	$ 609.77	$ 525	$ 2,524	$ 3,049
191-200	19	394	7,486	$ 105.00	$ 537.51	$ 642.51	$ 1,995	$ 10,213	$ 12,208
Totals:	6,070		520,032				$ 637,350	$ 709,450	$ 1,346,800

The rate-per-load amounts shown above are very similar to the rates in the original mileage band pricing prior to adding the secondary capacity option. The next step is to combine the dedicated costs and the secondary capacity costs into a "blended" rate-per-load that will become the actual rate proposal.

Combined Allocation to Mileage Bands

To determine the final rates for the customer, the carrier must blend the dedicated costs and the secondary capacity costs into a combined rate proposal. The table below illustrates the calculation of the blended mileage band rates.

Combined Mileage Band Rates

Mileage Band	Dedicated Fleet Coverage Annual Loads	Dedicated Fleet Coverage Cost Per Load	Dedicated Fleet Coverage Total Revenue	Secondary Coverage Annual Loads	Secondary Coverage Cost Per Load	Secondary Coverage Total Revenue	Total Network Annual Loads	Total Network Grand Total Revenue	Blended Rate Per Load
0-10	956	$ 114.55	$ 109,510	10	$ 375.00	$ 3,750	966	$ 113,260	$ 117.25
11-20	634	$ 145.93	$ 92,518	6	$ 375.00	$ 2,250	640	$ 94,768	$ 148.07
21-30	1,436	$ 167.18	$ 240,074	15	$ 400.00	$ 6,000	1,451	$ 246,074	$ 169.59
31-40	709	$ 192.31	$ 136,349	7	$ 400.00	$ 2,800	716	$ 139,149	$ 194.34
41-50	480	$ 227.78	$ 109,335	5	$ 425.00	$ 2,125	485	$ 111,460	$ 229.82
51-60	223	$ 255.07	$ 56,880	9	$ 425.00	$ 3,825	232	$ 60,705	$ 261.66
61-70	380	$ 287.81	$ 109,367	16	$ 450.00	$ 7,200	396	$ 116,567	$ 294.36
71-80	313	$ 323.28	$ 101,186	16	$ 450.00	$ 7,200	329	$ 108,386	$ 329.44
81-90	222	$ 336.92	$ 74,797	12	$ 475.00	$ 5,700	234	$ 80,497	$ 344.00
91-100	122	$ 361.08	$ 44,052	14	$ 475.00	$ 6,650	136	$ 50,702	$ 372.81
101-110	187	$ 380.58	$ 71,168	21	$ 475.00	$ 9,975	208	$ 81,143	$ 390.11
111-120	130	$ 428.58	$ 55,715	14	$ 500.00	$ 7,000	144	$ 62,715	$ 435.52
121-130	38	$ 446.06	$ 16,950	7	$ 500.00	$ 3,500	45	$ 20,450	$ 454.45
131-140	24	$ 486.99	$ 11,688	4	$ 500.00	$ 2,000	28	$ 13,688	$ 488.85
141-150	50	$ 498.28	$ 24,914	12	$ 525.00	$ 6,300	62	$ 31,214	$ 503.45
151-160	83	$ 529.93	$ 43,984	27	$ 525.00	$ 14,175	110	$ 58,159	$ 528.72
161-170	40	$ 549.74	$ 21,990	22	$ 540.00	$ 11,880	62	$ 33,870	$ 546.29
171-180	19	$ 582.48	$ 11,067	13	$ 550.00	$ 7,150	32	$ 18,217	$ 569.29
181-190	5	$ 609.77	$ 3,049	5	$ 575.00	$ 2,875	10	$ 5,924	$ 592.38
191-200	19	$ 642.51	$ 12,208	29	$ 590.00	$ 17,110	48	$ 29,318	$ 610.79
Totals:	6,070		$ 1,346,800	264		$ 129,465	6,334	$ 1,476,265	

The final column, Blended Rate Per Load, contains the final rates for proposal to the customer. The total revenue for this proposal, $1,476,265, is very close to the first proposal's cost of $1,460,048. The carrier could choose to slightly adjust the pricing on this second version until the total annual cost is the same or lower than the original 9 truck design.

Final Mileage Band Proposal

After all the previous pricing design and analysis, the completed mileage band proposal is ready for presentation to the potential new customer. The final mileage band rate proposal is shown below.

Mileage Band Rate Proposal

Mileage Band	Rate Per Load
0-10	$ 117.00
11-20	$ 148.00
21-30	$ 170.00
31-40	$ 194.00
41-50	$ 230.00
51-60	$ 262.00
61-70	$ 294.00
71-80	$ 329.00
81-90	$ 344.00
91-100	$ 373.00
101-110	$ 390.00
111-120	$ 436.00
121-130	$ 454.00
131-140	$ 489.00
141-150	$ 503.00
151-160	$ 529.00
161-170	$ 546.00
171-180	$ 569.00
181-190	$ 592.00
191-200	$ 611.00

These rates will be charged to the shipper on a load-by-load basis. Under the mileage band pricing format, the shipper is not concerned with whether the carrier uses a dedicated truck or some form of secondary capacity to serve the network. The shipper simply expects the carrier to provide excellent service at the per-load rates shown in the contract. There is no need for the carrier to report the number of trucks, utilization levels, or other fleet-related statistics to the shipper.

In terms of trailers, the carrier may need to report the number of trailers being used in the operation. If the shipper demands a significant increase in the number of trailers without a comparable increase in load volumes, the carrier may be entitled to invoice the shipper for the number of trailers above the planned level. The contract may actually include a provision for the carrier to invoice the shipper for additional trailers.

Though not necessary, the per-load rates have been rounded to the nearest whole dollar amount. The rounding serves to simplify the rates. The rounding of the rates will not have a material impact on the carrier's total revenue.

Advanced Simulation and Fleet Size Sensitivity Analysis

The basic fleet size model assumes that the daily load activity by band is consistent with the historical distribution of loads by band as provided by the shipper. However, on any given day, the actual load activity could vary significantly in terms of either total volume or average length of haul. When possible, carriers should incorporate these possibilities into the sensitivity analysis portion of the fleet size and design process. For the purpose of this illustration, the original mileage band activity is provided below.

Expected Mileage Band Activity

Mileage Band	Load Volume Annual	Load Volume Per Day
0-10	966	3.72
11-20	640	2.46
21-30	1,451	5.58
31-40	716	2.75
41-50	485	1.87
51-60	232	0.89
61-70	396	1.52
71-80	329	1.27
81-90	234	0.90
91-100	136	0.52
101-110	208	0.80
111-120	144	0.55
121-130	45	0.17
131-140	28	0.11
141-150	62	0.24
151-160	110	0.42
161-170	62	0.24
171-180	32	0.12
181-190	10	0.04
191-200	48	0.18
Totals:	6,334	24.36

Based on the shipper's network information shown above, the average load volume in the 0-10 mile band is 3.72 loads per day. The base fleet size model is based on this average activity level. However, on any *actual* day, the load volume for this mileage band could potentially be 0 loads or could be very high, perhaps 6 loads or more. The same is true for the actual activity in every mileage band in the network.

As day-to-day shipping activity occurs in real time, the number of trucks and drivers needed by the network will fluctuate in correlation with actual load activity. Depending on the degree of fluctuation, the carrier could face two problems. First, the carrier may not have a large enough dedicated fleet to cover all activity on certain high volume days. Second, on low activity days, the dedicated fleet could potentially fail to meet critical utilization and revenue targets.

As part of the fleet size analysis process, the carrier could perform a sensitivity analysis on the fleet size based on a variety of possible daily load activity scenarios. The two key variables in the load activity and volume analysis are the number of loads per day and the distribution of loads within the mileage bands or, in other words, the daily length of haul.

In most bid scenarios, the shipper does not provide daily shipment detail. Without actual data on daily shipments, the fluctuation in the number of daily shipments is difficult to model. However, in any short haul or mileage band scenario, the distribution of loads by mileage band is always provided and can be used for a sensitivity analysis simulation.

Simulation on Fleet Size and Mileage Band Load Distribution

Random Number Setup. The sensitivity analysis simulation will be formatted based on a technique known as Monte Carlo Simulation. The Monte Carlo method is based on the use of random numbers and a known frequency distribution. For this application, the known frequency distribution is the percentage of loads by mileage band in the shipper's information. The frequency distribution by band is shown below.

Frequency Distribution for Mileage Band Activity

Mileage Band	Load Volume Per Day	% of Loads	Simulation Ranges From	-	To
0-10	3.72	15.3%	-	-	0.153
11-20	2.46	10.1%	0.153	-	0.254
21-30	5.58	22.9%	0.254	-	0.483
31-40	2.75	11.3%	0.483	-	0.596
41-50	1.87	7.7%	0.596	-	0.672
51-60	0.89	3.7%	0.672	-	0.709
61-70	1.52	6.3%	0.709	-	0.771
71-80	1.27	5.2%	0.771	-	0.823
81-90	0.90	3.7%	0.823	-	0.860
91-100	0.52	2.1%	0.860	-	0.882
101-110	0.80	3.3%	0.882	-	0.915
111-120	0.55	2.3%	0.915	-	0.937
121-130	0.17	0.7%	0.937	-	0.944
131-140	0.11	0.4%	0.944	-	0.949
141-150	0.24	1.0%	0.949	-	0.959
151-160	0.42	1.7%	0.959	-	0.976
161-170	0.24	1.0%	0.976	-	0.986
171-180	0.12	0.5%	0.986	-	0.991
181-190	0.04	0.2%	0.991	-	0.992
191-200	0.18	0.8%	0.992	-	1.000
Totals:	24.36	100.0%			

The "% of Loads" column represents the percentage of the daily loads that historically fall within each mileage band. These values represent the known relative frequency distribution required for the simulation. The "Simulation Ranges" section represents the cumulative frequency distribution that will be used in conjunction with the random numbers to facilitate the simulation of daily load activity.

For simplification, the simulation will assume a fixed volume of 24 loads per day. Next, 24 random numbers between 0.00 and 1.00 will be generated to represent the 24 loads in a day. The table below shows a one-day simulation for exactly 24 random loads.

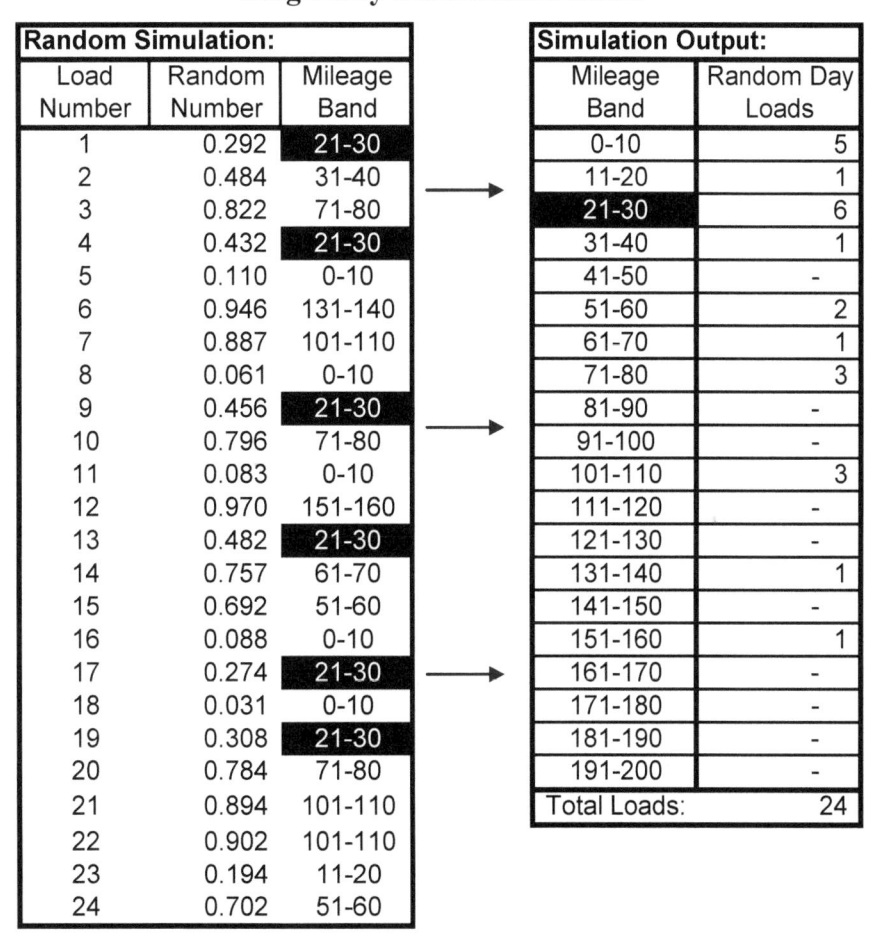

Single Day Simulation Results

Random Simulation:				Simulation Output:	
Load Number	Random Number	Mileage Band		Mileage Band	Random Day Loads
1	0.292	21-30		0-10	5
2	0.484	31-40		11-20	1
3	0.822	71-80	→	21-30	6
4	0.432	21-30		31-40	1
5	0.110	0-10		41-50	-
6	0.946	131-140		51-60	2
7	0.887	101-110		61-70	1
8	0.061	0-10		71-80	3
9	0.456	21-30	→	81-90	-
10	0.796	71-80		91-100	-
11	0.083	0-10		101-110	3
12	0.970	151-160		111-120	-
13	0.482	21-30		121-130	-
14	0.757	61-70		131-140	1
15	0.692	51-60		141-150	-
16	0.088	0-10		151-160	1
17	0.274	21-30	→	161-170	-
18	0.031	0-10		171-180	-
19	0.308	21-30		181-190	-
20	0.784	71-80		191-200	-
21	0.894	101-110		Total Loads:	24
22	0.902	101-110			
23	0.194	11-20			
24	0.702	51-60			

Each load is assigned to a corresponding mileage band based on the random number values and the simulation ranges in the previous table.[90] For example, load 9 has a random number value of 0.456. The value of 0.456 falls between 0.254 and 0.483, so this load is assigned to the 21-30 mileage band based on the "Simulation Ranges" for the mileage band load distribution.

For illustration, all 6 loads in the 21-30 mile band are highlighted to show how the load counts flow into the simulation output portion of the table. Each load and associated random number is handled this same way to randomly assign each of the 24 loads to a mileage band.

---

[90] The random numbers in this example were generated using the =RAND() Excel® spreadsheet function. The spreadsheet details for this simulation are explained in an upcoming Technical Tip section.

Fleet Size Model. The next step in the simulation is to determine the fleet size based on the daily load activity as created in the previous simulation of the 24 random loads. The standard fleet size model is used as shown below.

Fleet Size Simulation Output

Assumptions:											
Pick Up Dock Time (hrs):		0.50			Cycle Time Per Trip (in hours)				Estimated Fleet Size		
Delivery Dock Time (hrs):		0.75									
Driver Work Hours Per Day:		11.00	*(max = 14 hours)*		Pick-Up	Drive	Delivery	Total	Total	Drivers	Total
Mileage	Load Volume		Round Trip Miles	Miles	Dock	Time	Dock	Time	Daily	Needed	Drivers
Band	Annual	Per Day	Per Load	Per Day	Per Hour	Time		Time	Per Trip	Hours	(Band)	Needed
0-10	966	5.00	7	35	7	0.50	1.00	0.75	2.25	11.3	1.0	1.02
11-20	640	1.00	30	30	25	0.50	1.20	0.75	2.45	2.5	0.2	1.25
21-30	1,451	6.00	46	273	35	0.50	1.30	0.75	2.55	15.3	1.4	2.64
31-40	716	1.00	64	64	35	0.50	1.83	0.75	3.08	3.1	0.3	2.92
41-50	485	-	90	-	35	0.50	2.57	0.75	3.82	-	-	2.92
51-60	232	2.00	110	220	35	0.50	3.14	0.75	4.39	8.8	0.8	3.72
61-70	396	1.00	134	134	35	0.50	3.83	0.75	5.08	5.1	0.5	4.18
71-80	329	3.00	160	480	38	0.50	4.21	0.75	5.46	16.4	1.5	5.67
81-90	234	-	170	-	38	0.50	4.47	0.75	5.72	-	-	5.67
91-100	136	-	188	-	40	0.50	4.69	0.75	5.94	-	-	5.67
101-110	208	3.00	202	606	40	0.50	5.05	0.75	6.30	18.9	1.7	7.39
111-120	144	-	237	-	40	0.50	5.93	0.75	7.18	-	-	7.39
121-130	45	-	250	-	42	0.50	5.95	0.75	7.20	-	-	7.39
131-140	28	1.00	280	280	42	0.50	6.67	0.75	7.92	7.9	0.7	8.10
141-150	62	-	288	-	43	0.50	6.70	0.75	7.95	-	-	8.10
151-160	110	1.00	311	311	45	0.50	6.92	0.75	8.17	8.2	0.7	8.85
161-170	62	-	326	-	45	0.50	7.24	0.75	8.49	-	-	8.85
171-180	32	-	350	-	48	0.50	7.29	0.75	8.54	-	-	8.85
181-190	10	-	370	-	48	0.50	7.71	0.75	8.96	-	-	8.85
191-200	48	-	394	-	50	0.50	7.88	0.75	9.13	-	-	8.85
Totals:	**6,334**	**24.00**	**101**	**2,434**						**97.33**	**8.85**	
Fleet Summary:	Fleet Size (Drivers)			8.85	Miles Per Driver Per Week			1,375	Total Annual Miles:		
	Loads Per Driver Per Day			2.71	Miles Per Driver Per Day			275	642,362		

Because this is a "one day" simulation, the annual load volume column displays the expected annual volumes as opposed to the annualized simulation volume. Over a full year of actual load activity, the total loads by mileage band should be very close to the shipper's original base data. This simulation simply represents the possible activity in a random one day period.

This fleet size simulation iteration indicates a fleet size of 8.85 drivers, which is consistent with the 8.42 drivers from the base model. The length of haul in this iteration is 101 miles, compared to the 91 mile length of haul in the base model. The other outputs such as annual miles and utilization are shown as a reference. However, these are not the primary outputs of this simulation analysis. The primary objective and output of the simulation is the 8.85 drivers as modeled in this iteration.

Multiple Fleet Size Iterations. Now that the simulation model is in place, the carrier can run an unlimited number of scenarios and tabulate the results. The table below shows the results of 10 one-day iterations. Scenario 1 below represents the activity as shown previously in the setup of the simulation model.

10 Daily Fleet Size Simulation Iterations

Mileage Band	\multicolumn{10}{c	}{Daily Simulation Iteration Results}	Daily Average
	1	2	3	4	5	6	7	8	9	10	
0-10	5	2	2	8	3	5	2	4	4	2	3.70
11-20	1	1	2	2	2	4	3	2	0	0	1.70
21-30	6	5	7	6	3	2	4	6	6	9	5.40
31-40	1	6	4	1	3	5	3	4	3	2	3.20
41-50	0	1	2	1	3	1	1	3	0	4	1.60
51-60	2	2	1	0	1	2	1	0	1	1	1.10
61-70	1	1	1	3	0	1	1	1	2	0	1.10
71-80	3	1	1	2	2	1	2	1	1	2	1.60
81-90	0	3	1	1	1	1	3	0	1	0	1.10
91-100	0	0	0	0	0	0	0	2	1	0	0.30
101-110	3	1	1	0	0	0	1	1	1	2	1.00
111-120	0	0	1	0	0	0	0	0	1	0	0.20
121-130	0	0	0	0	0	0	1	0	0	0	0.10
131-140	1	0	0	0	1	0	1	0	0	0	0.30
141-150	0	0	0	0	1	1	0	0	0	0	0.20
151-160	1	1	0	0	2	1	0	0	2	1	0.80
161-170	0	0	0	0	1	0	0	0	0	1	0.20
171-180	0	0	0	0	1	0	0	0	1	0	0.20
181-190	0	0	0	0	0	0	1	0	0	0	0.10
191-200	0	0	1	0	0	0	0	0	0	0	0.10
Loads:	24	24	24	24	24	24	24	24	24	24	24.00
Fleet Size:	8.8	8.5	8.2	7.0	10.0	7.9	9.4	7.4	9.4	8.5	**8.51**

The 10 iterations show fleet sizes ranging from 7.0 drivers to 10.0 drivers. The average fleet size of the 10 iterations is 8.51 drivers, which is very close to the 8.42 drivers in the base model.

The table below shows the modeled fleet sizes after 50 iterations to represent a 50 day period. The first 10 iterations shown below match the 10 iterations in the table above.

\multicolumn{5}{c	}{50 Fleet Size Iterations}
8.85	7.78	7.35	8.27	8.14
8.45	8.07	9.24	7.98	8.45
8.23	9.04	7.91	8.87	7.67
7.00	8.10	8.12	9.34	8.09
10.03	7.83	9.23	7.73	8.42
7.87	9.15	7.37	6.88	8.24
9.37	7.86	9.24	8.48	8.16
7.43	7.86	7.76	8.43	8.21
9.42	8.03	9.44	9.03	7.69
8.50	8.54	8.11	8.22	9.24
\multicolumn{4}{	l	}{Average of 50 Iterations:}	8.33

The table below summarizes the 50 iterations into categories of potential fleet sizes.

50 Single-Day Iterations Summary

Fleet Size	Iterations Days	%	Average Fleet Size
6.5 - 7.5	5	10%	7.21
7.5 - 8.5	30	60%	8.09
8.5 - 9.5	14	28%	9.14
9.5 - 10.5	1	2%	10.03
All Iternations:	50		8.33

The graph below also summarizes the 50-day fleet size needs. The range containing the planned fleet size of 8.42 drivers is highlighted.

50 Single-Day Iterations Summary

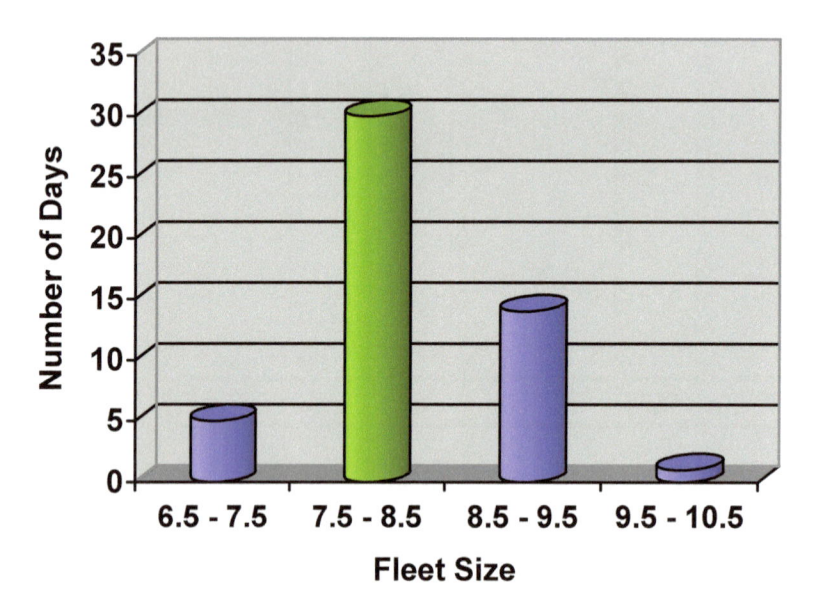

The 50-day simulation analysis provides two important pieces of information about the fleet size risk associated with this network. First, on 10% of the days, the fleet will be underutilized (5 days at 6.5 to 7.5 drivers). Second, 30% of the time the shipper's network will demand 9 trucks or more. The 30% is too high to risk setting the actual fleet size at 8 drivers, so the fleet was set at 9 drivers in the original design earlier in this chapter in the scenario without the flexible capacity. This type of analysis is also useful in determining the ideal mix of dedicated capacity and flexible capacity.

! *Technical Tip* – Monte Carlo Simulation Spreadsheet Design

The Monte Carlo simulation technique provides an excellent tool for modeling potential load activity scenarios. This technical tip provides an overview of the spreadsheet setup of the simulation model.

Step 1: Establish the Frequency Distribution
The first step is to design the frequency distribution that will be used to populate the simulation. The model in this chapter utilized the annual loads by mileage band to create the frequency distribution shown below.

Frequency Distribution for Simulation

	B	C	D	E	F	G
3	Mileage	Load Volume		Simulation Ranges		
4	Band	Per Day	% of Loads	From	-	To
5	0-10	3.72	15.3%	-	-	0.153
6	11-20	2.46	10.1%	0.153	-	0.254
7	21-30	5.58	22.9%	0.254	-	0.483
8	31-40	2.75	11.3%	0.483	-	0.596
9	41-50	1.87	7.7%	0.596	-	0.672
10	51-60	0.89	3.7%	0.672	-	0.709
11	61-70	1.52	6.3%	0.709	-	0.771
12	71-80	1.27	5.2%	0.771	-	0.823
13	81-90	0.90	3.7%	0.823	-	0.860
14	91-100	0.52	2.1%	0.860	-	0.882
15	101-110	0.80	3.3%	0.882	-	0.915
16	111-120	0.55	2.3%	0.915	-	0.937
17	121-130	0.17	0.7%	0.937	-	0.944
18	131-140	0.11	0.4%	0.944	-	0.949
19	141-150	0.24	1.0%	0.949	-	0.959
20	151-160	0.42	1.7%	0.959	-	0.976
21	161-170	0.24	1.0%	0.976	-	0.986
22	171-180	0.12	0.5%	0.986	-	0.991
23	181-190	0.04	0.2%	0.991	-	0.992
24	191-200	0.18	0.8%	0.992	-	1.000
25	Totals:	24.36	100.0%			

The load volume per day by mileage band was provided by the shipper. The % of loads and simulation ranges were added to create the frequency distribution as part of the simulation model.

The spreadsheet formulas for the frequency distribution table are shown below. The values in column C were provided by the shipper.[91]

Spreadsheet Formulas for Frequency Distribution

	B	C	D	E	F	G
2						
3	**Mileage**	**Load Volume**		**Simulation Ranges**		
4	**Band**	**Per Day**	**% of Loads**	**From**	**-**	**To**
5	0-10	3.72	=C5/$C$25	-	-	=D5
6	11-20	2.46	=C6/$C$25	=G5	-	=E6+D6
7	21-30	5.58	=C7/$C$25	=G6	-	=E7+D7
8	31-40	2.75	=C8/$C$25	=G7	-	=E8+D8
9	41-50	1.87	=C9/$C$25	=G8	-	=E9+D9
10	51-60	0.89	=C10/$C$25	=G9	-	=E10+D10
11	61-70	1.52	=C11/$C$25	=G10	-	=E11+D11
12	71-80	1.27	=C12/$C$25	=G11	-	=E12+D12
13	81-90	0.90	=C13/$C$25	=G12	-	=E13+D13
14	91-100	0.52	=C14/$C$25	=G13	-	=E14+D14
15	101-110	0.80	=C15/$C$25	=G14	-	=E15+D15
16	111-120	0.55	=C16/$C$25	=G15	-	=E16+D16
17	121-130	0.17	=C17/$C$25	=G16	-	=E17+D17
18	131-140	0.11	=C18/$C$25	=G17	-	=E18+D18
19	141-150	0.24	=C19/$C$25	=G18	-	=E19+D19
20	151-160	0.42	=C20/$C$25	=G19	-	=E20+D20
21	161-170	0.24	=C21/$C$25	=G20	-	=E21+D21
22	171-180	0.12	=C22/$C$25	=G21	-	=E22+D22
23	181-190	0.04	=C23/$C$25	=G22	-	=E23+D23
24	191-200	0.18	=C24/$C$25	=G23	-	=E24+D24
25	**Totals:**	=SUM(C5:C24)	100.0%			

The % of loads (relative frequency) is the loads for each mileage band divided into the total loads for the network. The simulation ranges begin with a "0" in cell E5. Cell G5 sets the maximum value for the band at the first band's percentage value from D5. From there, the "From" value for each new band is equal to the "To" value for the previous band. Each new "To" value for each band is equal to the "From" value from the band plus the "% of Loads" value for the same band. The "To" value for the final band should always be equal to 1.000 or 100%.

---

[91] Microsoft® product screen shot reprinted with permission from Microsoft® Corporation.

Step 2: Model a Scenario Using Random Numbers

The second step is to model a scenario using the frequency distribution table and a set of random numbers. The model shown here is based on 24 random loads per day. The 24 load level is predetermined based on the average number of loads per day. The simulation will use the frequency distribution by mileage band to model how many of the 24 loads fall into each mileage band. The completed model from earlier in the chapter is shown below.

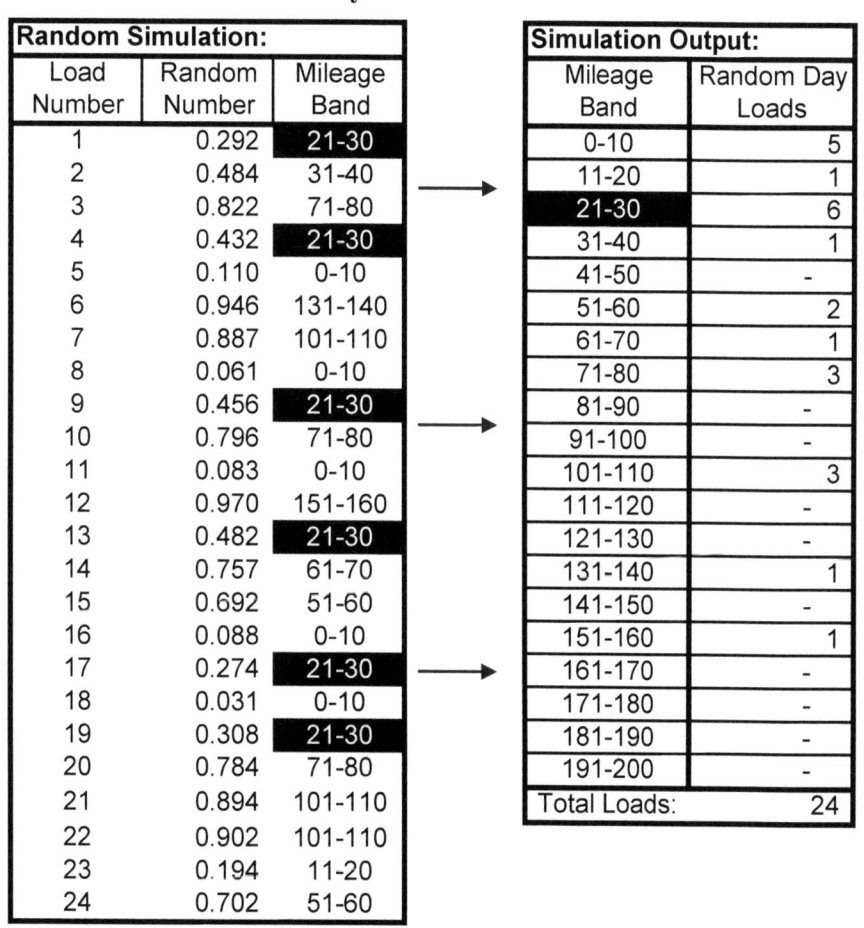

One Day Simulation Results

Random Simulation:

Load Number	Random Number	Mileage Band
1	0.292	21-30
2	0.484	31-40
3	0.822	71-80
4	0.432	21-30
5	0.110	0-10
6	0.946	131-140
7	0.887	101-110
8	0.061	0-10
9	0.456	21-30
10	0.796	71-80
11	0.083	0-10
12	0.970	151-160
13	0.482	21-30
14	0.757	61-70
15	0.692	51-60
16	0.088	0-10
17	0.274	21-30
18	0.031	0-10
19	0.308	21-30
20	0.784	71-80
21	0.894	101-110
22	0.902	101-110
23	0.194	11-20
24	0.702	51-60

Simulation Output:

Mileage Band	Random Day Loads
0-10	5
11-20	1
21-30	6
31-40	1
41-50	-
51-60	2
61-70	1
71-80	3
81-90	-
91-100	-
101-110	3
111-120	-
121-130	-
131-140	1
141-150	-
151-160	1
161-170	-
171-180	-
181-190	-
191-200	-
Total Loads:	24

The spreadsheet function =rand() is used to generate the random numbers shown in the "Random Number" column. Each random number is then associated with a corresponding mileage band using the =vlookup function with the mileage band frequency distribution as shown in the next section.

The table that follows is used to associate each random number with a mileage band and determine the final number of loads assigned to each mileage band. For space considerations, not all mileage bands are shown. In the actual spreadsheet, the columns continue to the right for each mileage band.

TRUCKLOAD TRANSPORTATION: ECONOMICS, PRICING AND ANALYSIS

Assignment of Random Numbers to Mileage Bands

	Random Simulation:								
Load Number	Random Number	Mileage Band	Band: Loads:	0-10 **5**	11-20 **1**	21-30 **6**	31-40 **1**	41-50 **0**	51-60 **2**
1	0.292	21-30		0	0	1	0	0	0
2	0.484	31-40		0	0	0	1	0	0
3	0.822	71-80		0	0	0	0	0	0
4	0.432	21-30		0	0	1	0	0	0
5	0.110	0-10		1	0	0	0	0	0
6	0.946	131-140		0	0	0	0	0	0
7	0.887	101-110		0	0	0	0	0	0
8	0.061	0-10		1	0	0	0	0	0
9	0.456	21-30		0	0	1	0	0	0
10	0.796	71-80		0	0	0	0	0	0
11	0.083	0-10		1	0	0	0	0	0
12	0.970	151-160		0	0	0	0	0	0
13	0.482	21-30		0	0	1	0	0	0
14	0.757	61-70		0	0	0	0	0	0
15	0.692	51-60		0	0	0	0	0	1
16	0.088	0-10		1	0	0	0	0	0
17	0.274	21-30		0	0	1	0	0	0
18	0.031	0-10		1	0	0	0	0	0
19	0.308	21-30		0	0	1	0	0	0
20	0.784	71-80		0	0	0	0	0	0
21	0.894	101-110		0	0	0	0	0	0
22	0.902	101-110		0	0	0	0	0	0
23	0.194	11-20		0	1	0	0	0	0
24	0.702	51-60		0	0	0	0	0	1

The formulas for the table above are shown below. For space considerations, only the first four rows and first four mileage band columns are shown. The formulas are relatively the same for the rows and columns not shown.

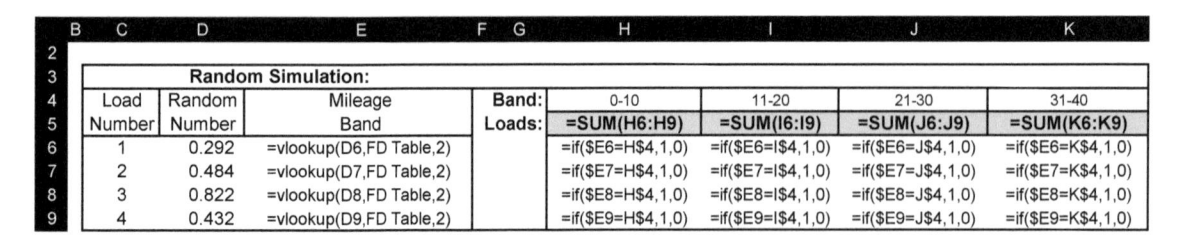

	B	C	D	E	F	G	H	I	J	K
2										
3				Random Simulation:						
4		Load Number	Random Number	Mileage Band		Band: Loads:	0-10 =SUM(H6:H9)	11-20 =SUM(I6:I9)	21-30 =SUM(J6:J9)	31-40 =SUM(K6:K9)
5										
6		1	0.292	=vlookup(D6,FD Table,2)			=if($E6=H$4,1,0)	=if($E6=I$4,1,0)	=if($E6=J$4,1,0)	=if($E6=K$4,1,0)
7		2	0.484	=vlookup(D7,FD Table,2)			=if($E7=H$4,1,0)	=if($E7=I$4,1,0)	=if($E7=J$4,1,0)	=if($E7=K$4,1,0)
8		3	0.822	=vlookup(D8,FD Table,2)			=if($E8=H$4,1,0)	=if($E8=I$4,1,0)	=if($E8=J$4,1,0)	=if($E8=K$4,1,0)
9		4	0.432	=vlookup(D9,FD Table,2)			=if($E9=H$4,1,0)	=if($E9=I$4,1,0)	=if($E9=J$4,1,0)	=if($E9=K$4,1,0)

The "FD Table" in the "vlookup" formula in column E is not shown, but looks very similar to the frequency distribution table shown previously.[92] As a final step, Row 5 from this table is used to populate the final simulation output table using either the "hlookup" spreadsheet function or a simple cell reference formula.

---

[92] A previous Technical Tip provides more information on the vlookup spreadsheet function.

Final Output. The load volume outputs from the simulation are then input into the standard fleet size model as shown below in the "Load Volume Per Day" column.

Fleet Size Simulation Output

Assumptions:											
Pick Up Dock Time (hrs):		0.50			Cycle Time Per Trip (in hours)				Estimated Fleet Size		
Delivery Dock Time (hrs):		0.75									
Driver Work Hours Per Day:		11.00	(max = 14 hours)		Pick-Up	Drive	Delivery	Total	Total	Drivers	Total
Mileage	Load Volume		Round Trip Miles	Miles	Dock	Drive	Dock	Time	Daily	Needed	Drivers
Band	Annual	Per Day	Per Load	Per Day	Per Hour	Time	Time	Time	Per Trip	Hours	(Band)	Needed

Mileage Band	Annual	Per Day	Per Load	Per Day	Miles Per Hour	Pick-Up Dock Time	Drive Time	Delivery Dock Time	Total Time Per Trip	Total Daily Hours	Drivers Needed (Band)	Total Drivers Needed
0-10	966	5.00	7	35	7	0.50	1.00	0.75	2.25	11.3	1.0	1.02
11-20	640	1.00	30	30	25	0.50	1.20	0.75	2.45	2.5	0.2	1.25
21-30	1,451	6.00	46	273	35	0.50	1.30	0.75	2.55	15.3	1.4	2.64
31-40	716	1.00	64	64	35	0.50	1.83	0.75	3.08	3.1	0.3	2.92
41-50	485	-	90	-	35	0.50	2.57	0.75	3.82	-	-	2.92
51-60	232	2.00	110	220	35	0.50	3.14	0.75	4.39	8.8	0.8	3.72
61-70	396	1.00	134	134	35	0.50	3.83	0.75	5.08	5.1	0.5	4.18
71-80	329	3.00	160	480	38	0.50	4.21	0.75	5.46	16.4	1.5	5.67
81-90	234	-	170	-	38	0.50	4.47	0.75	5.72	-	-	5.67
91-100	136	-	188	-	40	0.50	4.69	0.75	5.94	-	-	5.67
101-110	208	3.00	202	606	40	0.50	5.05	0.75	6.30	18.9	1.7	7.39
111-120	144	-	237	-	40	0.50	5.93	0.75	7.18	-	-	7.39
121-130	45	-	250	-	42	0.50	5.95	0.75	7.20	-	-	7.39
131-140	28	1.00	280	280	42	0.50	6.67	0.75	7.92	7.9	0.7	8.10
141-150	62	-	288	-	43	0.50	6.70	0.75	7.95	-	-	8.10
151-160	110	1.00	311	311	45	0.50	6.92	0.75	8.17	8.2	0.7	8.85
161-170	62	-	326	-	45	0.50	7.24	0.75	8.49	-	-	8.85
171-180	32	-	350	-	48	0.50	7.29	0.75	8.54	-	-	8.85
181-190	10	-	370	-	48	0.50	7.71	0.75	8.96	-	-	8.85
191-200	48	-	394	-	50	0.50	7.88	0.75	9.13	-	-	8.85
Totals:	6,334	24.00	101	2,434						97.33	8.85	

Fleet Summary:	Fleet Size (Drivers)	8.85	Miles Per Driver Per Week	1,375	Total Annual Miles:
	Loads Per Driver Per Day	2.71	Miles Per Driver Per Day	275	642,362

This process can be repeated to create multiple scenarios to further evaluate the potential driver needs for the network. In the previous example, the simulation process was repeated 50 times to provide the fleet size analysis shown below.

50 Single-Day Iterations Summary

Fleet Size	Iterations Days	%	Average Fleet Size
6.5 - 7.5	5	10%	7.21
7.5 - 8.5	30	60%	8.09
8.5 - 9.5	14	28%	9.14
9.5 - 10.5	1	2%	10.03
All Iternations:	50		8.33

Once the full spreadsheet model is in place, the simulation process can be repeated and the outputs saved for as many simulation iterations as desired. The simulation can be run over and over again by simply pressing the F9 key to recalculate the spreadsheet. Each time the F9 key is pressed, a new set of random numbers is generated and a fresh simulation is created.

! *Technical Tip* – Sensitivity Analysis and the "Table" Feature

Earlier in this chapter, a fleet size sensitivity analysis table was created using the handy "Table" feature available in Microsoft Excel.® The "Table" feature is fairly simple and provides an efficient method for creating sensitivity analysis information.

The fleet size sensitivity analysis table shown below was presented earlier in this chapter. The table shows the expected fleet size based on changes in two key assumptions, the dock time per load and the driver work hours her day.

Fleet Size Sensitivity Analysis

Dock Time	\multicolumn{9}{c}{Driver Work Hours Per Day}
	9.50	9.75	10.00	10.25	10.50	10.75	11.00	11.25	11.50
0.40	9.50	9.25	9.02	8.80	8.59	8.39	8.20	8.02	7.84
0.45	9.62	9.38	9.14	8.92	8.71	8.50	8.31	8.13	7.95
0.50	9.75	9.50	9.26	9.04	8.82	8.62	8.42	8.23	8.06
0.55	9.88	9.63	9.39	9.16	8.94	8.73	8.53	8.34	8.16
0.60	10.01	9.75	9.51	9.28	9.05	8.84	8.64	8.45	8.27
0.65	10.14	9.88	9.63	9.39	9.17	8.96	8.75	8.56	8.37
0.70	10.26	10.00	9.75	9.51	9.29	9.07	8.86	8.67	8.48
0.75	10.39	10.13	9.87	9.63	9.40	9.18	8.98	8.78	8.59
0.80	10.52	10.25	9.99	9.75	9.52	9.30	9.09	8.88	8.69
0.85	10.65	10.38	10.12	9.87	9.64	9.41	9.20	8.99	8.80
0.90	10.78	10.50	10.24	9.99	9.75	9.52	9.31	9.10	8.90
0.95	10.91	10.63	10.36	10.11	9.87	9.64	9.42	9.21	9.01
1.00	11.03	10.75	10.48	10.23	9.98	9.75	9.53	9.32	9.11

Actual Model Output   **Relevant Range**

The table was created quickly and easily using the "Table" spreadsheet feature. The first step in creating the table is to design the table grid in a spreadsheet exactly like the one shown below.

Fleet Size Sensitivity Analysis

Dock Time	\multicolumn{9}{c}{Driver Work Hours Per Day}
8.42	9.50	9.75	10.00	10.25	10.50	10.75	11.00	11.25	11.50
0.40									
0.45									
0.50									
0.55									
0.60									
0.65									
0.70									
0.75									
0.80									
0.85									
0.90									
0.95									
1.00									

The grid is shown below with a view of the spreadsheet columns and rows. One of the two sensitivity variables is listed across the columns and the other variable is listed down the rows. The different values represent a reasonable range of potential values for each sensitivity variable. The dock time ranges between 0.40 hours and 1.0 hours. The driver work hours per day ranges between 9.5 hours and 11.5 hours.

Spreadsheet Grid for Sensitivity Analysis

	A	B	C	D	E	F	G	H	I	J	K	L
1												
2					Fleet Size Sensitivity Analysis							
3		Dock Time				Driver Work Hours Per Day						
4		8.42	9.50	9.75	10.00	10.25	10.50	10.75	11.00	11.25	11.50	
5		0.40										
6		0.45										
7		0.50										
8		0.55										
9		0.60										
10		0.65										
11		0.70										
12		0.75										
13		0.80										
14		0.85										
15		0.90										
16		0.95										
17		1.00										
18												

The sensitivity output value, fleet size, is shown in Cell B4. The output value must be exactly in the top left corner of the grid between the rows and columns of variables as shown above. Cell B4 contains a formula that points directly to the computed fleet size from the original fleet size model. The spreadsheet must be formatted exactly as shown for the "Table" feature to work correctly.

To activate the Table feature, highlight the range for the table beginning in cell B4 down to cell K17. Next, click on Data then Table as shown to the right.[93]

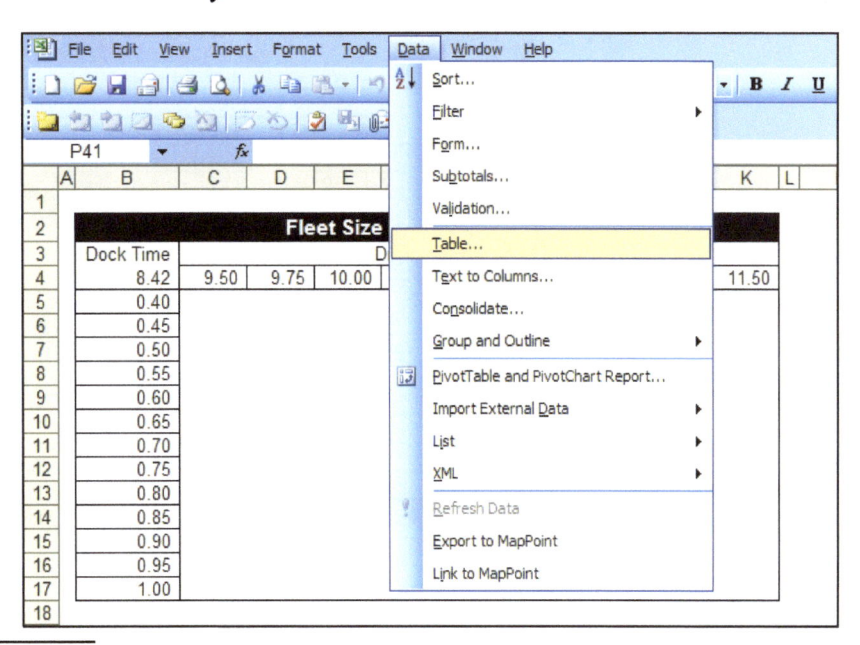

---

[93] Microsoft® product screen shots reprinted with permission from Microsoft® Corporation.

The box below will appear. This box must contain the cell address locations in the original fleet size model for the two variables.[94]

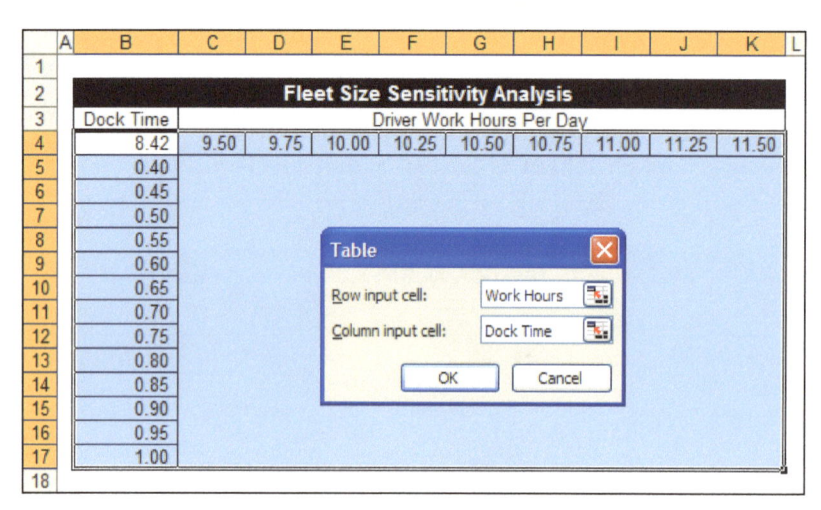

	A	B	C	D	E	F	G	H	I	J	K	L
1												
2					Fleet Size Sensitivity Analysis							
3		Dock Time			Driver Work Hours Per Day							
4		8.42	9.50	9.75	10.00	10.25	10.50	10.75	11.00	11.25	11.50	
5		0.40										
6		0.45										
7		0.50										
8		0.55										
9		0.60										
10		0.65										
11		0.70										
12		0.75										
13		0.80										
14		0.85										
15		0.90										
16		0.95										
17		1.00										
18												

Table
Row input cell: Work Hours
Column input cell: Dock Time
OK   Cancel

The row input cell and the column input cell should point to the two assumptions shown below in the original fleet size model.

Assumptions:		
Pick Up Dock Time (hrs):	0.75	Column Variable
Delivery Dock Time (hrs):	0.75	
Driver Work Hours Per Day:	10.50	Row Variable

After correctly indicating the row and column cell address locations, click OK and the completed table will appear.[95] The relevant range and actual model output were highlighted after the table was completed.

Fleet Size Sensitivity Analysis									
Dock	Driver Work Hours Per Day								
Time	9.50	9.75	10.00	10.25	10.50	10.75	11.00	11.25	11.50
0.40	9.50	9.25	9.02	8.80	8.59	8.39	8.20	8.02	7.84
0.45	9.62	9.38	9.14	8.92	8.71	8.50	8.31	8.13	7.95
0.50	9.75	9.50	9.26	9.04	8.82	8.62	8.42	8.23	8.06
0.55	9.88	9.63	9.39	9.16	8.94	8.73	8.53	8.34	8.16
0.60	10.01	9.75	9.51	9.28	9.05	8.84	8.64	8.45	8.27
0.65	10.14	9.88	9.63	9.39	9.17	8.96	8.75	8.56	8.37
0.70	10.26	10.00	9.75	9.51	9.29	9.07	8.86	8.67	8.48
0.75	10.39	10.13	9.87	9.63	9.40	9.18	8.98	8.78	8.59
0.80	10.52	10.25	9.99	9.75	9.52	9.30	9.09	8.88	8.69
0.85	10.65	10.38	10.12	9.87	9.64	9.41	9.20	8.99	8.80
0.90	10.78	10.50	10.24	9.99	9.75	9.52	9.31	9.10	8.90
0.95	10.91	10.63	10.36	10.11	9.87	9.64	9.42	9.21	9.01
1.00	11.03	10.75	10.48	10.23	9.98	9.75	9.53	9.32	9.11

Actual Model Output   Relevant Range

---

[94] Microsoft® product screen shot reprinted with permission from Microsoft® Corporation.
[95] Refer to the help feature in Microsoft Excel® for more information on this powerful feature.

CHAPTER 13: Bid Analysis and Response

Shippers typically request pricing and rate proposals from carriers in the form of an organized bid process. The primary goal of this chapter is to review the carrier methods and strategies for developing pricing proposals for potential new business. The chapter will also provide an overview of the contents of a bid and how shippers evaluate responses and select carriers. The next chapter provides detailed case studies that offer deeper insight into a carrier's bid analysis process.

Request for Proposal (RFP)

The most common method used by shippers to request pricing from carriers is through a strategic bid process. The bid documentation and supporting information is often called a Request for Proposal (RFP). The RFP will contain information, in as much detail as possible, regarding the shipper's lanes, operating platform, and other requirements and expectations.

Prior to conducting an RFP, the carrier may distribute a Request for Information (RFI). The purpose of the RFI is to gather information to understand each carrier's capabilities and to qualify carriers to participate in the shipper's transportation program. Items commonly included in an RFI are outlined below.

Common Request for Information (RFI) Items:
DOT Safety Rating[96]
Income Statement / Operating Ratio
Balance Sheet
Service Performance Records
Total Fleet Size (Tractors and Trailers)
Equipment Types
Terminal and Facility Locations / Service Area
Maintenance Programs
List of Major Customers
Awards from Other Shippers

Individual shippers may have additional items of interest that are included in their unique RFI expectations. Carriers should provide this information to shippers as accurately and completely as possible. The RFI provides carriers with the opportunity to demonstrate capabilities and potentially be invited to participate in future RFP opportunities. Shippers will have minimum standards for each of the RFI requirements. Only those carriers that meet the minimum requirements will be invited to participate in the shipper's transportation program.

---

[96] The carrier's safety rating is established by the U.S. Department of Transportation based on a detailed analysis of the carrier's accident history and other related considerations.

Shippers will evaluate the bid proposals from carriers primarily on the basis of price and total cost. However, shippers will also consider many other factors in the carrier selection process including the items listed below.

Shipper Evaluation Criteria for Carrier Selection
Financial Stability
Capacity Available to Shipper
Age and Quality of Tractors and Trailers
On-time Service Performance
Communications and Tracking Capabilities
Reporting Capabilities
Safety History and Ratings
Experience with the Specific Industry, Market, or Service Platform

Carriers must respond to the bid with competitive pricing and other information as required by the shipper. Each carrier response is unique based on the carrier's specific freight network and strategy. Large carriers may choose to provide pricing on every lane in a bid, while small carriers may bid on only certain facilities or specific lanes.

In some cases, carriers may choose to not participate in a bid. A carrier may decline to participate in the bid because of certain business requirements, lane mix, geography, or any number of shipper-related reasons. Several common reasons are listed below.

Shipper-related Reasons a Carrier May Decline a Bid Opportunity
Shipper's Lack of Financial Stability
Poor Credit History with the Shipper
Unsatisfactory Payment Terms
Excessive Insurance and Liability Requirements
Shipper has a reputation for not unloading trailers in a timely manner
Potential for trailer damage or risk of theft due to specific commodity
Existing strategic relationship with a primary competitor of the shipper

While it is rare for a carrier to decline a bid opportunity, these and related reasons are typical considerations in the carrier's decision process.

RFP and Bid Contents

While bids come in a variety of sizes and formats, the basic components of most bids are very similar. Business opportunities are presented on a lane basis, usually with an estimated annual load volume for each lane. Some shippers provide very accurate and detailed historical information on shipments while others do not. Shippers that provide carriers with accurate and detailed shipment information will receive the most accurate and potentially lowest cost pricing proposals.

The contents of each bid are based on the network offered for bid. The most common components of bids are described below.

Common Bid & RFP Components	
Component	**Description**
Bid Summary	The bid summary will include such information as bid timelines, shipper contacts, bid rules, and other items specific to the bid process.
Carrier Requirements	This section of the bid will include all carrier requirements and expectations. Common items include equipment types, service expectations, data exchange requirements, invoicing requirements, and other shipper-specific items.
Facility Profiles	Facility profiles provide critical information for each origin and destination facility in an RFP. This information might include pick-up and delivery windows, number of dock doors, trailer pool requirements, and related information.
Lane Types	Lane types provide the carrier with pricing rules and service requirements for each lane. For example, certain lane types may require a specific transit time or a certain type of trailer.
Historical Lane Data	Historical lane data provides the carrier with detailed information about the shipper's network. When available, the shipper may choose to provide the carrier with detailed load information by week, month, or time of day.
Bid Response Spreadsheet	The primary purpose of the bid response spreadsheet is to provide the carrier with a standard format for providing pricing and related information. The spreadsheet will be formatted specifically for each RFP event.

The carrier is required to respond exactly as instructed by the shipper. The shipper must evaluate each carrier's bid and compare costs among all the bids received from the participating carriers. Any deviations from the shipper's requirements by the carrier may cause the carrier's bid to be eliminated from consideration. These carrier deviations from the required process make it difficult or impossible for shippers to interpret the carrier's proposal or compare the proposal with other participating carriers.

Sample Bid Analysis

The table below provides a simple bid to illustrate the primary concepts in bid strategy and lane analysis. The demonstration bid is intentionally simplified for illustration purposes. Most bids are much larger and contain many more lanes.

Demonstration Bid							
Lane ID	Origin City	ST	Destination City	ST	Annual Loads	One-Way Miles	Rate Per Mile	Flat Charge
1	Olive Branch	MS	West Memphis	AR	600	31		
2	Olive Branch	MS	Southaven	MS	400	13		
3	Olive Branch	MS	Covington	TN	350	60		
4	Memphis	TN	Chicago	IL	100	533		
5	Memphis	TN	Dallas	TX	250	452		
6	Memphis	TN	Los Angeles	CA	420	1,795		
7	Memphis	TN	Atlanta	GA	180	389		
8	Memphis	TN	Orlando	FL	510	828		
9	Memphis	TN	Miami	FL	215	1,055		
10	Memphis	TN	Newark	NJ	390	1,084		
11	Dallas	TX	Memphis	TN	100	452		
12	Dallas	TX	Los Angeles	CA	345	1,435		
13	Dallas	TX	Orlando	FL	60	1,135		
14	Dallas	TX	Miami	FL	140	1,362		
15	Dallas	TX	Chicago	IL	355	939		
16	Dallas	TX	Atlanta	GA	175	780		
17	Chicago	IL	Los Angeles	CA	40	2,015		
18	Chicago	IL	Memphis	TN	205	533		
19	Chicago	IL	Newark	NJ	165	780		
20	Chicago	IL	Atlanta	GA	85	718		
21	Chicago	IL	Detroit	MI	210	283		
22	Newark	NJ	Memphis	TN	165	1,084		
23	Newark	NJ	Orlando	FL	110	1,075		
24	Newark	NJ	Los Angeles	CA	125	2,779		
25	Miami	FL	Memphis	TN	60	1,055		
26	Miami	FL	Atlanta	GA	85	665		
27	Atlanta	GA	Memphis	TN	400	389		
28	Atlanta	GA	Miami	FL	200	665		
29	Atlanta	GA	Orlando	FL	185	438		
30	Atlanta	GA	Columbus	OH	75	560		

The bid consists of 7 origin locations, 30 total lanes and 6,700 annual loads. The bid also offers lanes of various length of haul levels as well as a variety of different headhaul and backhaul lanes.

Carriers have the option to price each lane using either a rate per mile or a flat charge. In most cases, longer length of haul lanes will be priced on a per-mile basis and shorter length of haul lanes will be priced with a flat charge. In some cases, carriers might also be asked to provide a minimum charge.

Before Pricing the Bid

Prior to pricing the bid, carriers must closely review the origin locations and individual lanes to develop a strategy for completing the bid. For carriers that do choose to participate in a bid, several key strategic questions must be answered. Several common bid strategy questions are listed below.

Carrier Bid Strategy Questions	
Component	**Questions**
General Strategy	Will this customer and this business fit our company's strategy?
	What origin facilities should be bid on?
	What are the most attractive lanes from each origin location?
	Are there any lanes in the bid network that complement one another?
Capacity & Balance	How much total capacity is available to commit to this customer?
	How much capacity is available in each origin market?
	Is capacity needed in any of the major destination markets?
The Customer	What type of commodity(s) does this customer ship?
	Are shipments seasonal? If so, in what way?
	What are the service expectations and requirements for this business?
Driver Satisfaction	What are the driver requirements for this customer network?
	How will this business affect driver satisfaction?

After determining a general strategy for the bid response, carriers must also ask some specific questions about the characteristics of the customer's facilities and basic service platform. Sophisticated shippers will include most of this information in the supporting documentation of their bids. If the answers aren't available in the bid information, the carrier must get clarification on these items from the shipper before submitting pricing. Shippers may also allow carriers to visit each facility to ask questions and obtain a first-hand understanding of the operation. The primary lane-level, carrier-level and shipper-level questions are outlined in the sections that follow.

External Lane-Specific Questions

External, lane-specific questions relate directly to the general parameters of the lane without specifically considering the carrier or the shipper. The issues addressed include such factors as length of haul, toll costs, road conditions, and transit times.

External Lane-Specific Questions	
Component	**Questions**
General Lane Elements	What are the origin and destination points for the lane?
	What is the loaded length of haul for the lane?
Operating Costs	Will any toll costs be incurred on the lane? If so, what are the costs?
	Is reasonably-priced fuel readily available on the trip?
Transit Time	What type of roads will be traveled on the trip? Two-lane? Interstate?
	What is the average miles-per-hour and transit time for the trip?

The answers to these questions provide the carrier with a general overview of the lane. The answers will also be important as the carrier's network and the shipper's key requirements are introduced into the pricing analysis.

Internal Carrier-Related Questions

Internal carrier-related questions focus on the carrier's existing network and how the potential new customer and lane(s) will fit with current load activity. These questions help the carrier determine if a lane merits consideration for a rate proposal.

| **Internal Carrier Lane Questions** ||
Component	**Questions**
General Strategy	Do the parameters of this lane meet the existing business model?
	Does this lane offer the opportunity to profitably expand the network?
	Is the current network in need of additional freight?
	Does this lane flow through existing company maintenance facilities?
	Is this a new customer with significant future growth potential?
Capacity & Balance	How many trucks per week are currently available in the origin market?
	If capacity is not available, how will trucks be sourced to this customer?
	Is any additional capacity needed in or near the destination market?
	How will these trucks be used once they reach the destination market?
Existing Customers	What rates are being charged to current customers on this lane?
	Do any current customers have substandard rates on this lane?
	Is this lane currently profitable with existing customers?
Market Conditions	Is the origin a headhaul, backhaul or intermediate pricing market?
	Is the destination a headhaul, backhaul or intermediate pricing market?
Empty Miles	How many empty miles will be incurred to pick up these loads?
	How many empty miles will be incurred after the delivery?
Driver Satisfaction	Does this lane facilitate the need to get drivers home?
	Will this lane provide reasonable income and productivity for the driver?

A key element the carrier must always consider is a lane's fit with the carrier's general strategy and business model. If a lane does not fit the carrier's model, the carrier may decline to price the lane or may price the lane very high as a result of the poor fit. In some cases, a new lane or new customer will provide the carrier the opportunity to profitably expand the existing network and customer base. If the customer represents a major growth opportunity, the carrier may price the lane very aggressively in the hope of establishing a long-term working relationship with the new customer.

Strategic factors such as capacity and balance, market conditions, and empty miles are explained in detail throughout the chapters covering one-way pricing. These sections explain the general pricing implications of each operating variable. However, since all carriers operate unique networks, each of these factors potentially affects each carrier's pricing differently. Certain lanes and markets are a better fit for some carriers than others. If a carrier has an excellent network fit or business model for a given lane, that carrier is likely to propose much lower pricing than carriers that do not have a good network fit for the lane in question.

External Shipper-Related Questions

All pricing must be carefully adjusted based on the shipper's expectations and service platform. Shipper-related questions focus on the shipper's general requirements, service expectations, and operating model. These questions allow the carrier to identify the key issues that will dictate any customer-specific adjustments to the pricing.

External Shipper-Related Questions	
Component	**Questions**
Operating Costs	What is the fuel surcharge peg for this customer?
	What are the trailer equipment requirements for this lane?
Load Pick-Up	Are outbound trailers pre-loaded or is a live pick-up required?
	Is there an open window for pick-up or is an appointment required?
	How much dock time is typically required for the pick-up?
Load Delivery	Is there an open window for delivery or is an appointment required?
	If an appointment is required, how long is the delivery window?
	If using a drop delivery, how quickly are inbound trailers unloaded?
	How much dock time is typically required for the delivery?
Seasonality	Are load volumes reasonably consistent on a daily basis?
	Are there any end-of-month or end-of-quarter spikes in shipment levels?
Service	How does the shipper measure on-time service?
	What level of on-time service does the customer require?
	Are any special services required to meet transit time expectations?
Load Tendering	How will load information be communicated? Electronic? Phone? Fax?
	How much advance notice is provided for load pick-up times?
Driver Satisfaction	Is any driver unloading or similar labor service required on this lane?
	Does this lane ever involve multi-stop deliveries? How often?

The carrier will adjust the pricing for each lane based on the answers to these and other related questions. Many of the questions are focused on understanding the cycle times associated with each lane. If dock times or transit times create unreasonably long cycle times, the carrier will increase pricing to compensate for the longer cycle times. Specific methods for adjusting pricing are discussed in other sections.

Another area of interest for many of the questions is driver satisfaction. Because driver turnover is a critical issue for all carriers, each new business opportunity must be evaluated in terms of its impact on driver satisfaction. Carriers will sometimes pass on bid opportunities that may cause significant problems for drivers. The carrier may also provide discounted pricing for those bid opportunities that are likely to increase driver satisfaction and retention.[97]

---

[97] The various strategy questions shown here were also presented in a previous chapter covering one-way pricing strategy.

Summary Analysis of Bid Contents

Since many bids include hundreds and sometimes thousands of lanes for bid, it is important to consolidate the bid into a series of summary level reports and maps so that the carrier can quickly make a high-level, strategic evaluation of the bid opportunities. Microsoft Excel®, Microsoft Access®, and Microsoft MapPoint® provide excellent tools for organizing and summarizing the bid information. While each bid will require a customized summary analysis, some of the most common types of bid summary analysis information are described below.

Bid Summary Analysis: Map of Primary Origin Facilities

A simple map of each origin facility provides the carrier with a quick look at the scope of the bid and the geographic areas involved in the shipper's network.

Bid Summary Analysis
All Bid Origin Locations

The map above provides a quick glance at each of the origin facilities in the bid network. In large bids, the carrier might choose to color code each facility by annual volume or facility type. To keep the map simple and easy to interpret, the carrier might exclude origin locations that don't offer significant load volumes.

Bid Summary Analysis: Map of Destinations by Origin Facility

The map below provides a quick illustration of the primary destination locations for an origin facility. The shape and color of each point depicts the annual volume for each destination location.

Bid Summary Analysis
Memphis, TN Facility Outbound Destination Locations

Carriers can use maps of this type to quickly determine how each origin facility fits within the carrier's existing network of freight. The destination points can be compared to recent internal capacity and balance information to identify potential network synergies. The carrier will focus pricing strategy on the lanes and destination points that provide the greatest degree of network efficiency.

This map format would need to be created for each major origin facility in the bid. If the bid has many origin points, the carrier may only map those origin points that are of potential interest to the carrier. The carrier might perform additional mapping to further illustrate the unique characteristics of each individual bid network. The case studies in the next chapter include additional mapping and analysis examples.

Bid Summary Analysis: Pivot Tables

The carrier may also choose to use spreadsheet or database tools to further summarize the network information within the bid. For example, the table below provides a simple point-to-state summary of the overall bid contents.[98]

Loads from Origin City to Destination State

Sum of Loads		Dest ST										
Origin City	Origin ST	AR	CA	FL	GA	IL	MI	MS	NJ	OH	TN	TX	Grand Total
Atlanta	GA			385						75	400		860
Chicago	IL		40		85		210		165		205		705
Dallas	TX		345	200	175	355					100		1,175
Memphis	TN		420	725	180	100			390			250	2,065
Miami	FL				85						60		145
Newark	NJ		125	110							165		400
Olive Branch	MS	600						400			350		1,350
Grand Total		600	930	1,420	525	455	210	400	555	75	1,280	250	6,700

This information gives the carrier a quick overview of the markets involved in the bid. From this information, the carrier can identify particular lanes that may have a good fit with the carrier's existing network. Based on the lanes of interest, the carrier can then review the lane level detail and begin to develop a pricing strategy.

This information also allows the carrier to eliminate any lanes or markets that are not a good fit for the carrier's growth strategy or existing network. Eliminating undesirable lanes from consideration simplifies the bid process and reduces the amount of work associated with completing the bid.

---

[98] This table was created using the Pivot Table spreadsheet feature. The specific steps for creating Pivot Tables are included in a Technical Tip at the end of this chapter.

The table below summarizes the bid activity based on the destination state. This format allows the carrier to evaluate the origin points for all loads that deliver into a particular market. For example, the loads moving into California originate in four states, Illinois, New Jersey, Tennessee and Texas.

Loads by Destination State from Origin City, ST

Dest ST	Origin ST	Origin City	Data Sum of Loads	Sum of Total Miles
AR	MS	Olive Branch	600	18,600
AR Total			**600**	**18,600**
CA	IL	Chicago	40	80,600
	NJ	Newark	125	347,375
	TN	Memphis	420	753,900
	TX	Dallas	345	495,075
CA Total			**930**	**1,676,950**
FL	GA	Atlanta	385	214,030
	NJ	Newark	110	118,250
	TN	Memphis	725	649,105
	TX	Dallas	200	258,780
FL Total			**1,420**	**1,240,165**
GA	FL	Miami	85	56,525
	IL	Chicago	85	61,030
	TN	Memphis	180	70,020
	TX	Dallas	175	136,500
GA Total			**525**	**324,075**
IL	TN	Memphis	100	53,300
	TX	Dallas	355	333,345
IL Total			**455**	**386,645**
MI	IL	Chicago	210	59,430
MI Total			**210**	**59,430**
MS	MS	Olive Branch	400	5,200
MS Total			**400**	**5,200**
NJ	IL	Chicago	165	128,700
	TN	Memphis	390	422,760
NJ Total			**555**	**551,460**
OH	GA	Atlanta	75	42,000
OH Total			**75**	**42,000**
TN	FL	Miami	60	63,300
	GA	Atlanta	400	155,600
	IL	Chicago	205	109,265
	MS	Olive Branch	350	21,000
	NJ	Newark	165	178,860
	TX	Dallas	100	45,200
TN Total			**1,280**	**573,225**
TX	TN	Memphis	250	113,000
TX Total			**250**	**113,000**
Grand Total			6,700	4,990,750

The carrier's existing capacity and balance situation plays a key role in the evaluation of this information. If any of the destination markets are in need of additional capacity for other customers, the carrier can identify the best lanes in the bid from which to source the desired capacity. The carrier can develop a specific pricing strategy for each lane depending on the lane's relative fit with the carrier's existing network.

Developing a Strategy and Pricing the Bid

The strategy for pricing a bid will vary significantly from carrier to carrier based on individual carrier needs, areas of operation, and many other carrier-specific reasons. For the purposes of this illustration, the different strategies for three unique carrier situations will be presented. Each carrier is described in the table below.

Carrier Characteristic	Bid Strategy by Carrier		
	Carrier N **Large** **National**	**Carrier R** **Medium** **Regional**	**Carrier L** **Specialized** **Local**
Fleet Size	3,000 trucks	400 trucks	80 trucks
Service Area	National	Atlanta Region	Memphis Local
Avg. Length of Haul	782 miles	341 miles	79 miles
Average Utilization	2,482 miles	1,871 miles	1,079 miles

The general bid strategy for each of these carriers is discussed in the sections that follow.

Bid Strategy by Carrier

Carrier L – Local Carrier

Carrier L is a small carrier serving the local Memphis, TN market. This carrier will likely only have an interest in bidding on lanes around the Memphis, TN area, particularly those originating in Olive Branch, MS. Because Carrier L specializes in the local Memphis area, the carrier should be able to provide very competitive pricing on these lanes. The bid for Carrier L is shown below.

Carrier L - Local Carrier								
Lane ID	Origin		Destination		Annual Loads	One-Way Miles	Rate Per Mile	Flat Charge
	City	ST	City	ST				
1	Olive Branch	MS	West Memphis	AR	600	31		$ 150.00
2	Olive Branch	MS	Southaven	MS	400	13		$ 120.00
3	Olive Branch	MS	Covington	TN	350	60		$ 275.00

Carrier L has chosen to only bid on the three lanes out of Olive Branch, MS. These lanes fit well with the carrier's business model of serving the local Memphis, TN market. Each lane provides an excellent fit with the carrier's existing local freight and customer network. The efficiencies of these anticipated network synergies are reflected in the carrier's pricing proposal.

Carrier R – Regional Carrier

Carrier R is a medium-sized regional carrier that specializes in the Atlanta, GA regional market. This carrier will likely only have an interest in bidding on lanes that fit within the Atlanta, GA region. Carrier R will likely focus heavily on only the lanes originating and terminating in the Atlanta metro area. The table below lists only the lanes that were considered for bid by Carrier R. After a detailed internal network analysis, the carrier has provided pricing on only a small group of lanes as shown below.

	Carrier R - Regional Carrier						
	Origin		Destination		Annual	One-Way	Rate	Flat
Lane ID	City	ST	City	ST	Loads	Miles	Per Mile	Charge
7	Memphis	TN	Atlanta	GA	180	389	$ 1.88	
8	Memphis	TN	Orlando	FL	510	828		
9	Memphis	TN	Miami	FL	215	1,055		
11	Dallas	TX	Memphis	TN	100	452		
16	Dallas	TX	Atlanta	GA	175	780		
20	Chicago	IL	Atlanta	GA	85	718	$ 1.85	
26	Miami	FL	Atlanta	GA	85	665	$ 0.94	
27	Atlanta	GA	Memphis	TN	400	389	$ 1.52	
28	Atlanta	GA	Miami	FL	200	665	$ 2.65	
29	Atlanta	GA	Orlando	FL	185	438	$ 2.48	
30	Atlanta	GA	Columbus	OH	75	560	$ 1.65	

Based on the internal network analysis, Carrier R chose to supply pricing only for lanes directly related to its core Atlanta-based operation. Since the carrier has excess capacity available in Miami on a daily basis, the carrier has provided very aggressive pricing on the lane from Miami to Atlanta in an effort to secure this valuable lane. Carrier R has also provided aggressive pricing on the lane from Memphis to Atlanta.

For the lanes that move outbound from Atlanta, the carrier has provided pricing that is comparable with its existing customers. These lanes offer the carrier the opportunity to grow revenue and increase the size of the network. In addition, the carrier may also be able to use a portion of these load volumes to replace unprofitable customers in the existing network.

Carrier R has been careful to avoid bidding on any lanes that do not provide a good fit with the carrier's existing network. The carrier would not want to bid on any lanes that cannot be served successfully and profitably. At the same time, the shipper would not want the carrier to bid on lanes where it cannot be successful.

Carrier N – Large National Carrier

Carrier N is a large national carrier that serves all 48 states. This carrier could potentially have an interest in bidding on all lanes in the bid. Carrier N will most likely be interested in lanes over 500 miles that fit the needs of its high utilization business model. This carrier may also have an interest in incremental business to expand its network and increase total revenues. The carrier may bid on lanes beyond those that fit the existing network in order to grow revenues and expand operations. The table below shows the total bid and lane selections for Carrier N.

| Carrier N - National Carrier ||||||||
Lane ID	Origin City	ST	Destination City	ST	Annual Loads	One-Way Miles	Rate Per Mile	Flat Charge
1	Olive Branch	MS	West Memphis	AR	600	31		
2	Olive Branch	MS	Southaven	MS	400	13		
3	Olive Branch	MS	Covington	TN	350	60		
4	Memphis	TN	Chicago	IL	100	533	$ 1.85	
5	Memphis	TN	Dallas	TX	250	452	$ 1.95	
6	Memphis	TN	Los Angeles	CA	420	1,795	$ 1.44	
7	Memphis	TN	Atlanta	GA	180	389	$ 1.93	
8	Memphis	TN	Orlando	FL	510	828	$ 2.35	
9	Memphis	TN	Miami	FL	215	1,055	$ 2.55	
10	Memphis	TN	Newark	NJ	390	1,084	$ 1.95	
11	Dallas	TX	Memphis	TN	100	452	$ 1.25	
12	Dallas	TX	Los Angeles	CA	345	1,435	$ 1.45	
13	Dallas	TX	Orlando	FL	60	1,135	$ 2.12	
14	Dallas	TX	Miami	FL	140	1,362	$ 2.25	
15	Dallas	TX	Chicago	IL	355	939	$ 1.38	
16	Dallas	TX	Atlanta	GA	175	780	$ 1.57	
17	Chicago	IL	Los Angeles	CA	40	2,015	$ 1.42	
18	Chicago	IL	Memphis	TN	205	533	$ 1.45	
19	Chicago	IL	Newark	NJ	165	780	$ 2.10	
20	Chicago	IL	Atlanta	GA	85	718	$ 1.80	
21	Chicago	IL	Detroit	MI	210	283		
22	Newark	NJ	Memphis	TN	165	1,084	$ 1.10	
23	Newark	NJ	Orlando	FL	110	1,075	$ 1.45	
24	Newark	NJ	Los Angeles	CA	125	2,779	$ 1.40	
25	Miami	FL	Memphis	TN	60	1,055	$ 1.08	
26	Miami	FL	Atlanta	GA	85	665	$ 1.02	
27	Atlanta	GA	Memphis	TN	400	389	$ 1.55	
28	Atlanta	GA	Miami	FL	200	665	$ 2.80	
29	Atlanta	GA	Orlando	FL	185	438		
30	Atlanta	GA	Columbus	OH	75	560	$ 1.61	

Carrier N has chosen to bid on all lanes over 500 miles and other select lanes that fit existing network needs. The carrier has decided to provide aggressive pricing on several of the long haul lanes over 1,000 miles. The carrier expects these lanes to provide a significant boost to fleet utilization and driver satisfaction.

Carrier N has chosen to decline to bid on several lanes in the RFP. The very short lanes out of Olive Branch, MS were excluded because of the short length of haul. The lane from Chicago to Detroit was excluded because of the length of haul and a poor fit with existing customers. The lane from Atlanta to Orlando was excluded due to the carrier's severe capacity and balance problem in the Orlando area.

Bid Optimization Tools and Strategies

Today's sophisticated bid management and optimization tools allow the shipper to evaluate carrier bid responses and quickly identify a low cost transportation solution for a network offered for bid. These optimization tools also allow the shipper to perform sensitivity analysis on many different decision variables and scenarios during the bid evaluation and carrier selection process. Once the bids are collected from carriers, shippers can adjust various decision parameters to customize the solution to meet internal business requirements, cost objectives, and other carrier selection criteria.

The optimization tools also allow carriers to submit a highly customized bid response. As a result, carriers are able to provide very competitive pricing on the maximum number of lanes. For example, by limiting the amount of capacity offered to the shipper, the carrier can confidently submit competitive pricing across more lanes because of the load volume limitations. Instead of providing the standard pricing response without knowing specific annual load volumes, carriers can choose to make pricing contingent on capacity limitations for each lane, each location, and the entire shipper network.

As part of the bid design process, the shipper will determine the specific bid optimization variables to be included in each bid event. The optimization variables for the carrier focus primarily on the amount of capacity offered to the shipper. The optimization variables for the shipper focus on carrier selection decisions such as the number of carriers and the amount of business awarded to each participant. The most common decision variables for both the carrier and the shipper are described in detail in the sections that follow.

Decision Variables for the Carrier

The bid decision variables for carriers described below allow the carrier to limit the amount of capacity offered to the shipper. Without these capacity constraints, the carrier may not provide the lowest possible pricing on every lane. The carrier may price certain lanes higher in order to protect from being awarded load volumes in excess of what the carrier's network and available capacity can accommodate. The capacity decision variables allow the carrier to provide the best possible pricing on each lane without having to be concerned about the shipper awarding load volumes in excess of the carrier's available capacity. The carrier must formulate the bid strategy very carefully when designing a bid proposal that involves these capacity constraints. A mistake in the design could seriously limit the carrier's opportunities in the bid process.

Total Network Capacity Constraint

The total network capacity constraint allows carriers to place a limit on the total number of loads to be awarded across the entire shipper network available for bid. This constraint encourages the carrier to propose competitive pricing on as many lanes of interest as possible. The carrier is able to provide competitive pricing without the concern of being awarded an amount of business activity that would cause operational inefficiency and render the proposed pricing unprofitable.

Individual Lane Capacity Constraint

The individual lane capacity constraint allows carriers to place a maximum limit on the total number of loads to be awarded on a specific lane. Suppose a lane in a bid offers 2,000 annual loads per year from Point A to Point B. The lane opportunity is a perfect fit for a small carrier, but the carrier only has the capacity to profitably serve 500 loads per year. This carrier can provide a very aggressive price and submit a maximum capacity constraint of 500 loads on this lane. If the shipper decides to use this carrier on this lane, the shipper must identify one or more additional carriers to provide the capacity for the 1,500 remaining loads.

Origin Location Capacity Constraint

The origin location capacity constraint allows carriers to place a limit on the total number of loads to be awarded from a specific origin point across any number of available lanes. Suppose a bid offers 1,000 annual loads from an origin city to many different destination points. A carrier providing a bid response might have available capacity in the origin market and would like to provide aggressive pricing on several lanes. However, the carrier only wishes to provide capacity for a maximum of 300 loads per year. By utilizing the origin capacity constraint and providing a limit of 300 loads on the total capacity from this origin location, the carrier may bid aggressively on all lanes of interest without being concerned about being awarded an annual load volume that exceeds the available capacity of 300 annual loads.

Destination Location Volume Constraint

The destination location volume constraint allows carriers to place a limit on the total number of loads to be awarded from any number of specific lanes into a unique destination market. Suppose a carrier has provided pricing on many different lanes in a bid. The lanes involve many different origin and destination points. The carrier could use the destination volume constraint to provide protection against being awarded too many annual loads into a particular market. Most often, the carrier would use the destination volume constraint to limit the total number of loads into specific areas that are undesirable to the carrier. The example below shows a carrier's pricing, lane capacity constraints, and destination capacity constraints for all loads to Atlanta, GA.

Lane				Carrier X Bid Response		
Lane ID	Origin	Destination	Annual Loads	Rate Per Mile	Lane Capacity	Destination Capacity
L1	Little Rock, AR	Atlanta, GA	150	$ 1.90	150	275
D1	Dallas, TX	Atlanta, GA	100	$ 2.20	100	
C5	Columbus, OH	Atlanta, GA	100	$ 1.70	50	
M3	Memphis, TN	Atlanta, GA	250	$ 1.55	125	

Based on this response, the carrier is only willing to provide service for 275 loads into Atlanta, GA. The shipper must determine which lanes, if any, to award to this carrier.

The example bid response below illustrates how the total network, origin, and lane capacity constraints all work together to reflect the carrier's strategy. In this example, the carrier is willing to serve a total of 400 annual loads across the available lanes.

Lane				Carrier X Bid Response			
Lane ID	Origin	Destination	Annual Loads	Rate Per Mile	Lane Capacity	Origin Capacity	Network Capacity
L1	Little Rock, AR	Atlanta, GA	150	$ 1.90	150		
L2	Little Rock, AR	Denver, CO	80	$ 2.20	50	200	
L3	Little Rock, AR	Chicago, IL	200	$ 1.70	100		
L4	Little Rock, AR	Columbus, OH	60	$ 1.65	60		400
D1	Dallas, TX	Atlanta, GA	100	$ 1.45	100		
D2	Dallas, TX	Chicago, IL	300	$ 1.68	100		
D3	Dallas, TX	Columbus, OH	50	$ 1.42	50	250	
D4	Dallas, TX	Memphis, TN	125	$ 1.38	125		
D5	Dallas, TX	Mobile, AL	140	$ 1.55	70		

Carrier Capacity Optimization Constraints

As part of the shipper's analysis, the optimization process will convert each carrier's response into optimization constraints. Based on the carrier's response in the above example, the capacity optimization constraints for the shipper's carrier selection process can be defined as shown below.

Decision Variables:
```
L1ₓ = Number of loads awarded to Carrier X on Lane L1
L2ₓ = Number of loads awarded to Carrier X on Lane L2
L3ₓ = Number of loads awarded to Carrier X on Lane L3
L4ₓ = Number of loads awarded to Carrier X on Lane L4
D1ₓ = Number of loads awarded to Carrier X on lane D1
D2ₓ = Number of loads awarded to Carrier X on Lane D2
D3ₓ = Number of loads awarded to Carrier X on Lane D3
D4ₓ = Number of loads awarded to Carrier X on Lane D4
D5ₓ = Number of loads awarded to Carrier X on Lane D5
```

Total Network Capacity Constraint:
```
Total Capacity:    L1ₓ + L2ₓ + L3ₓ + L4ₓ + D1ₓ + D2ₓ + D3ₓ + D4ₓ + D5ₓ ≤ 400
```

Origin Constraints:
```
Origin Capacity - Little Rock, AR:   L1ₓ + L2ₓ + L3ₓ + L4ₓ ≤ 200
Origin Capacity - Dallas, TX:        D1ₓ + D2ₓ + D3ₓ + D4ₓ + D5ₓ ≤ 250
```

Lane Constraints:
```
L1 Lane Capacity:   L1ₓ ≤ 150        L2 Lane Capacity:   L2ₓ ≤ 50
L3 Lane Capacity:   L3ₓ ≤ 100        L4 Lane Capacity:   L4ₓ ≤ 60
D1 Lane Capacity:   D1ₓ ≤ 100        D2 Lane Capacity:   D2ₓ ≤ 100
D3 Lane Capacity:   D3ₓ ≤ 50         D4 Lane Capacity:   D4ₓ ≤ 125
D5 Lane Capacity:   D5ₓ ≤ 70
```

The constraints shown represent only the constraints for Carrier X. Similar constraints would be created for each carrier and each lane involved in the RFP.

The graphic below further illustrates the relationships between the total network capacity constraint, the origin capacity constraints, and the lane capacity constraints for the carrier in the previous example.

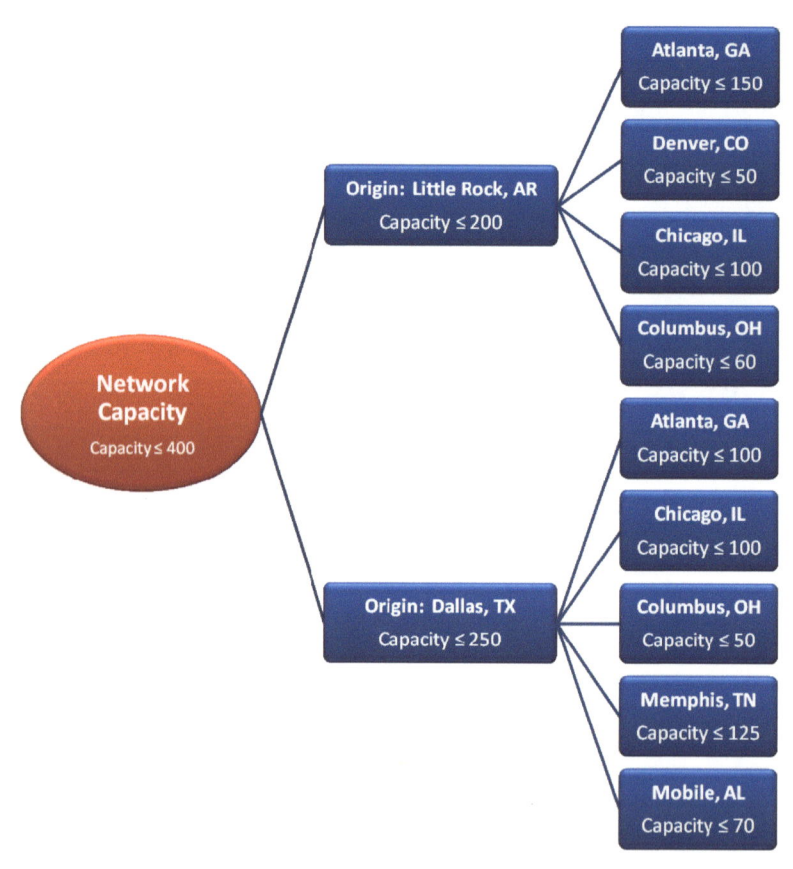

Bid Response Constraints from Carrier X

```
Network Capacity (Capacity ≤ 400)
├── Origin: Little Rock, AR (Capacity ≤ 200)
│   ├── Atlanta, GA (Capacity ≤ 150)
│   ├── Denver, CO (Capacity ≤ 50)
│   ├── Chicago, IL (Capacity ≤ 100)
│   └── Columbus, OH (Capacity ≤ 60)
└── Origin: Dallas, TX (Capacity ≤ 250)
    ├── Atlanta, GA (Capacity ≤ 100)
    ├── Chicago, IL (Capacity ≤ 100)
    ├── Columbus, OH (Capacity ≤ 50)
    ├── Memphis, TN (Capacity ≤ 125)
    └── Mobile, AL (Capacity ≤ 70)
```

Based on the response from Carrier X, the shipper could award the load volumes as shown below while meeting all the carrier's capacity requests.

	Lane			Carrier X Business Award			
Lane ID	Origin	Destination	Annual Loads	Loads Awarded	Lane Capacity	Origin Capacity	Network Capacity
L1	Little Rock, AR	Atlanta, GA	150	100	150		
L2	Little Rock, AR	Denver, CO	80	40	50	200	
L3	Little Rock, AR	Chicago, IL	200	0	100		
L4	Little Rock, AR	Columbus, OH	60	60	60		
	Origin Subtotal			200			400
D1	Dallas, TX	Atlanta, GA	100	100	100		
D2	Dallas, TX	Chicago, IL	300	50	100		
D3	Dallas, TX	Columbus, OH	50	0	50	250	
D4	Dallas, TX	Memphis, TN	125	0	125		
D5	Dallas, TX	Mobile, AL	140	50	70		
	Origin Subtotal			200			
	Network Grand Total			400			

Decision Variables for the Shipper

The primary purpose of the decision variables and constraints for the shipper is to manage the final award of business to a group of carriers. The shipper's carrier selection decision will involve tradeoffs between cost, service, and administrative requirements. For example, the "low-cost" solution for a bid may be to award lanes and load volumes to 30 different carriers. However, the shipper may wish to limit the number of carriers serving the network to only 10 in order to set the carrier base at a manageable level. The "maximum number of carriers" constraint allows the shipper to see the additional cost associated with the solution using only 10 carriers. This and several of the most common shipper decision variables and constraints are described below. The table below provides a sample bid as a frame of reference for the various constraints and decision variables.

Lane ID	Lane Origin	Destination	Annual Loads
L1	Little Rock, AR	Atlanta, GA	150
L2	Little Rock, AR	Denver, CO	80
L3	Little Rock, AR	Chicago, IL	200
L4	Little Rock, AR	Columbus, OH	60
D1	Dallas, TX	Atlanta, GA	100
D2	Dallas, TX	Chicago, IL	300
D3	Dallas, TX	Columbus, OH	50
D4	Dallas, TX	Memphis, TN	125
D5	Dallas, TX	Mobile, AL	140
Total Annual Loads			1,205

Minimum Carrier Volume or Revenue

For many reasons, shippers may choose to require the bid solution to award a minimum number of loads or minimum annual revenue to specific carriers. The shipper might do this to protect a relationship with an incumbent carrier that has successfully served the shipper in the past. The incumbent carrier likely has a deep understanding of the shipper's network and the shipper does not want to jeopardize this valuable business relationship. For example, Carrier Z has worked with the shipper for many years and currently performs about 400 loads per year. In order to maintain the network volume for Carrier Z, the shipper might apply the constraint below to the business award optimization so that Carrier Z is awarded a minimum of 300 loads per year.

Carrier Z Minimum Business Volume Constraint:

Total Volume: $L1_z + L2_z + L3_z + L4_z + D1_z + D2_z + D3_z + D4_z + D5_z \geq 300$

The shipper could apply similar constraints for any other carrier participating in the RFP. The total minimum business volume constraints could not exceed the 1,205 total loads available in the shipper's network.

Maximum Carrier Volume or Revenue

For many reasons, shippers may elect to limit the total amount of revenue or load volume awarded to a specific carrier. A limitation on the amount of volume awarded to a specific carrier may be for the protection of the carrier, the shipper, or both. Usually, the shipper does not want their business revenue to represent too large of a proportion of the carrier's total network. Along the same lines, the shipper may limit the maximum volume for all carriers so that any one carrier does not control too large a proportion of the shipper's activity. If a major carrier for the shipper were to suddenly not be available, the shipper's ability to ship and deliver products could be seriously compromised.

Suppose Carrier S is a small but effective carrier. The shipper would like for Carrier S to be involved in the network, but wishes to limit total annual volume to 200 loads. The shipper could introduce the constraint below into the business award optimization to achieve this objective.

Carrier S Maximum Business Volume Constraint:
```
Total Volume:   L1_S + L2_S + L3_S + L4_S + D1_S + D2_S + D3_S + D4_S + D5_S ≤ 200
```

The carrier could apply similar constraints for any other carrier participating in the RFP. The constraint could also be based on total dollars instead of total load volume.

Maximum Number of Carriers

Shippers may place a limit on the number of carriers that are included in the award of business. Limiting the number of carriers will almost always cause the shipper's total network cost to increase. However, the shipper's administrative costs will likely be reduced by having a smaller group of carriers to manage. At the individual facility level, minimizing the number of carriers may potentially reduce the total number of drop trailers staged at each origin facility and simplify certain daily procedures. The table below illustrates a summary of the carrier base sensitivity analysis.

Lane Award Alternatives	Lowest Cost 8 Carriers	Fixed Carrier Base Scenarios 4 Carriers	3 Carriers	2 Carriers
Total Annual Cost	$ 1,432,000	$ 1,447,200	$ 1,464,700	$ 1,502,900
Premium to Lowest Cost		$ 15,200	$ 32,700	$ 70,900
% Premium		1.1%	2.3%	5.0%
Number of Carriers	7	4	3	2
Highest Revenue Carrier	$ 525,500	$ 525,500	$ 665,500	$ 842,500

This analysis provides the shipper with a summary of the cost tradeoffs associated with the number of carriers included in the lane awards.

Other Carrier Selection Criteria

While the shipper's primary goal in almost any RFP is to minimize total cost, the shipper must also take other important factors into account when selecting carriers. Other key selection factors include service capabilities, financial strength, technological capabilities, and overall experience with the shipper. Each of these factors can also be quantified and included in the carrier selection optimization model along with carrier cost information. In the final carrier selection, the shipper may be willing to endure slightly higher transportation costs with a carrier that provides significantly better on-time service relative to other low-cost alternatives.

"Packaged" Bid Responses

Many of the modern bid optimization tools used by shippers allow carriers the option of grouping two or more bid lanes together to form a "packaged" or "bundled" bid. The key provision of a packaged bid is that the carrier's pricing for the packaged bid is contingent upon being awarded all lanes included in the package. Packaged bids allow shippers to realize additional transportation cost savings by allowing carriers to bid confidently on multi-lane solutions that offer efficiencies such as maximum equipment utilization or reduced empty miles. As a result of the packaged bid format, the carrier can offer lower rates in the packaged bid as compared to each individual stand-alone lane bid.

While carriers can create a packaged bid involving any group of lanes, a packaged bid should generally involve some type of strategic grouping of related lanes. The packaged bid must also offer some level of cost savings from the total cost of the independent lane bids. Without offering any savings, the packaged bid adds no value to the bid response above and beyond each stand-alone bid submission. A simple packaged bid solution is shown below.

Two Lane Packaged Bid

Lane Number	Origin	Destination	Annual Loads	Stand-Alone Bid Rate / Load	Stand-Alone Bid Annual Cost	Packaged Bid Rate / Load	Packaged Bid Annual Cost
1001	Chicago, IL	Milwaukee, WI	500	$ 475.00	$ 237,500	$ 450.00	$ 225,000
1008	Milwaukee, WI	Chicago, IL	800	$ 425.00	$ 340,000	$ 395.00	$ 316,000
Totals:			1,300		$ 577,500		$ 541,000
					Savings from Packaged Bid:		$ 36,500
					% Savings:		6.32%

In the above example, a carrier has packaged the two complimentary lanes between Chicago and Milwaukee. The carrier offers a discount on both lanes in the packaged bid because the carrier is guaranteed to be awarded both lanes in the proposed bundle. In the proposed scenario, the carrier is able to assemble an efficient network of loads traveling back and forth between Chicago and Milwaukee.

Several of the most common types of strategic packages are listed below.

Common Packaged Bid Strategies for Carriers	
Strategy	**Summary**
Complementary Lanes	Complementary lane packages group two or more lanes together that move in complementary directions. For example, in the previous demonstration bid, a carrier might package the 390 loads per year from Memphis, TN to Newark, NJ with the 165 loads from Newark, NJ back to Memphis, TN.
Lane Density	Lane density packages involve groups of similar lanes with relatively low volume bundled together to create a package with a significant level of load volumes. The package may also serve to meet a unique freight need for the carrier. For example, in the demonstration bid, a carrier based in Los Angeles, CA that needs loads back to Los Angeles might package the lanes from Memphis, Dallas, and Chicago that go back into Los Angeles, giving the carrier a total of 805 loads per year back into the Los Angeles market.
Dedicated Short Haul Fleets	Though low-volume, short haul lanes are generally unattractive for most carriers, creating a package of related short haul lanes can create an attractive dedicated fleet opportunity. A nice dedicated fleet package could be created for the demonstration bid by grouping all three Olive Branch, MS lanes together into a short haul package of 1,350 loads.

These and other packaged bid strategies are discussed in detail in the next section and in a case study in the next chapter.

Bid Strategy and Package Bids

Each new bid presents carriers with unique opportunities to creatively package lanes and build complementary solutions. While the basic lane-packaging strategies are always the same, carriers that develop creative solutions for each individual shipper network will have the greatest success with lane packaging. This section provides several examples of packaged bid strategies and lane bundling techniques. Each example represents a package for one of the carriers in the previous bid example.

Package Bid Strategy: Complementary Lanes

A complementary lane package usually involves lanes moving in opposite directions between two markets. The primary efficiency for this type of package is a reduction in the total empty miles required to serve the lanes involved. For example, suppose in the example bid that Carrier N would like to package the two lanes that move between Dallas, TX and Memphis, TN as shown below.

Lanes Selected for a Memphis – Dallas Complementary Package

Carrier N - National Carrier								
	Origin		Destination		Annual	One-Way	Rate	Flat
Lane ID	City	ST	City	ST	Loads	Miles	Per Mile	Charge
5	Memphis	TN	Dallas	TX	250	452	$ 1.95	
11	Dallas	TX	Memphis	TN	100	452	$ 1.25	

The primary efficiencies from this package will come in the form of reduced empty miles. The analysis below indicates the estimated mileage savings as a result of packaging these complementary lanes into an efficient bundle.

Estimated Mileage Savings as a Result of the Packaged Bid

Origin		Destination		Miles Per Trip: Stand-Alone Bid			Miles Per Trip: Package Bid			Mileage
City	ST	City	ST	Loaded	Empty	Total	Loaded	Empty	Total	Reduction
Memphis	TN	Dallas	TX	452	95	547	452	80	532	(15)
Dallas	TX	Memphis	TN	452	60	512	452	46	498	(14)

Based on the above analysis, Carrier N expects to reduce empty miles by 15 miles per trip from Memphis and 14 miles per trip from Dallas. These expected efficiencies allow Carrier N to provide reduced pricing in the packaged bid as shown below.

Revised Pricing for the Packaged Bid

Stand-Alone Lane Bids:								Stand Alone Network:					
Origin		Destination		Annual	One-Way	Rate	Total	Estimated Miles Per Trip			Annual	Cost	Net Rev
City	ST	City	ST	Loads	Miles	Per Mile	Cost	Loaded	Empty	Total	Miles	Per Trip	Per Mile
Memphis	TN	Dallas	TX	250	452	$ 1.95	$ 220,350	452	95	547	136,750	$ 881	$ 1.61
Dallas	TX	Memphis	TN	100	452	$ 1.25	$ 56,500	452	60	512	51,200	$ 565	$ 1.10
Totals:				350			$ 276,850	Network Totals:			187,950		$ 1.47

Packaged Bid Based on Empty Mile Savings								Package Bid Network:					
Origin		Destination		Original	Package	Package	Total	Estimated Miles Per Trip			Annual	Cost	Net Rev
City	ST	City	ST	Cost	Savings	Bid Rates	Cost	Loaded	Empty	Total	Miles	Per Trip	Per Mile
Memphis	TN	Dallas	TX	$220,350	$ (6,043)	$ 1.90	$ 214,307	452	80	532	133,000	$ 857	$ 1.61
Dallas	TX	Memphis	TN	$ 56,500	$ (1,545)	$ 1.22	$ 54,955	452	46	498	49,800	$ 550	$ 1.10
Totals:				$276,850	$ (7,587)		$ 269,263	Network Totals:			182,800		$ 1.47

As a result of the packaged bid efficiencies, the carrier is able to reduce the Memphis to Dallas rate from $1.95 per mile to $1.90 per mile. The new rate is based on the same net revenue per mile of $1.61 applied to the new total trip of 532 miles as shown below.

$$\text{Revised Rate} = \frac{\$1.61 \times 532 \text{ miles}}{452 \text{ billed miles}} = \frac{\$857}{452 \text{ billed miles}} = \$1.90 \text{ per mile}$$

The same process is applied to the Dallas to Memphis lane to determine the packaged bid rate for this lane.

$$\text{Revised Rate} = \frac{\$1.10 \times 498 \text{ miles}}{452 \text{ billed miles}} = \frac{\$550}{452 \text{ billed miles}} = \$1.22 \text{ per mile}$$

Compared to the carrier's original bid, the packaged bid offers the shipper a potential savings of $7,587 per year. The shipper will compare this bid offer to other stand-alone and packaged bid responses from other participating carriers to determine the low-cost solution for these lanes.

Packaged Bid Strategy: Short Haul Dedicated Fleets

Generally speaking, extremely short lanes are undesirable for most over-the-road carriers. However, a group of short haul lanes bundled together to assemble a large volume of short haul business can create a profitable dedicated fleet opportunity. The larger the volume of activity in a short haul network, the more stable and productive a dedicated fleet becomes. Packaging these type lanes together provides carriers with a method for quantifying the value of the synergies through reduced pricing for the shipper.

In the sample bid, Carrier L has recognized a dedicated fleet opportunity involving the three lanes out of Olive Branch, Mississippi. The lanes, when bundled together, include 1,350 annual loads. The lanes selected for the package are listed in the table below.

Lanes Selected for a Short Haul Dedicated Fleet Package

	Carrier L - Local Carrier							
Lane ID	Origin City	ST	Destination City	ST	Annual Loads	One-Way Miles	Rate Per Mile	Flat Charge
1	Olive Branch	MS	West Memphis	AR	600	31		$ 150.00
2	Olive Branch	MS	Southaven	MS	400	13		$ 120.00
3	Olive Branch	MS	Covington	TN	350	60		$ 275.00

The pricing shown above was proposed by Carrier L assuming each lane is awarded individually, so the efficiencies of a dedicated fleet package involving all three lanes are not reflected. The carrier can use a fleet size and pricing model to determine the fleet size, utilization and pricing for the lane package. Based on this analysis (not shown), the carrier can propose the packaged bid pricing shown below.

Revised Pricing for Packaged Bid

Stand-Alone Lane Bids:							
Origin City	ST	Destination City	ST	Annual Loads	One-Way Miles	Flat Rate Per Load	Total Cost
Olive Branch	MS	West Memphis	AR	600	31	$ 150.00	$ 90,000
Olive Branch	MS	Southaven	MS	400	13	$ 120.00	$ 48,000
Olive Branch	MS	Covington	TN	350	60	$ 275.00	$ 96,250
Totals:				1,350			$ 234,250

Packaged Bid Based on Network Density:							
Origin City	ST	Destination City	ST	Original Cost	Package Savings	Flat Rate Per Load	Total Cost
Olive Branch	MS	West Memphis	AR	$ 90,000	$ (4,800)	$ 142.00	$ 85,200
Olive Branch	MS	Southaven	MS	$ 48,000	$ (2,000)	$ 115.00	$ 46,000
Olive Branch	MS	Covington	TN	$ 96,250	$ (5,250)	$ 260.00	$ 91,000
Totals:				$ 234,250	$ (12,050)		$ 222,200

By creating efficiencies through packaging the related lanes together, Carrier L is able to offer the shipper an annual savings of $12,050 compared to the carrier's stand-alone bid.

Packaged Bid: Lane Density

Carrier N has an internal goal to increase business in the Chicago market. The sample bid has several lanes into and out of Chicago. Carrier N has decided to package the desirable inbound and outbound Chicago lanes into a package to create a large bundle of business. The carrier plans to package the lanes shown below.

Lanes Selected for a Chicago Lane Density Package

	Carrier N - National Carrier						
	Origin		Destination		Annual	One-Way	Rate	Flat
Lane ID	City	ST	City	ST	Loads	Miles	Per Mile	Charge
4	Memphis	TN	Chicago	IL	100	533	$ 1.85	
15	Dallas	TX	Chicago	IL	355	939	$ 1.38	
17	Chicago	IL	Los Angeles	CA	40	2,015	$ 1.42	
18	Chicago	IL	Memphis	TN	205	533	$ 1.45	
19	Chicago	IL	Newark	NJ	165	780	$ 2.10	
20	Chicago	IL	Atlanta	GA	85	718	$ 1.80	

The lanes selected for the package provide a well-balanced flow of load activity in and out of the Chicago Market. The inbound and outbound lane balance is summarized in the table below.

Inbound and Outbound Lane Balance for Chicago Package

	Origin		Destination		Inbound	Outbound
Lane ID	City	ST	City	ST	Loads	Loads
4	Memphis	TN	Chicago	IL	100	
15	Dallas	TX	Chicago	IL	355	
17	Chicago	IL	Los Angeles	CA		40
18	Chicago	IL	Memphis	TN		205
19	Chicago	IL	Newark	NJ		165
20	Chicago	IL	Atlanta	GA		85
Total Loads:					455	495

This well-balanced package provides two key benefits for the carrier. First, the carrier will gain some empty mile efficiencies by moving trucks into and out of the same facility. Second, the carrier will gain some operating efficiencies by using the same pool of trailers for inbound and outbound loads. In addition, the balanced network flow allows the carrier to grow revenues without creating any capacity and balance problems in the Chicago market.

The package will also benefit the capacity and balance situation for the carrier in other markets. First, the carrier has excess capacity in the Dallas market. The Dallas lane allows the carrier to move trucks out of the Dallas market. Second, the carrier needs additional capacity in the Memphis market. The net balance of the lanes into and out of Memphis gives the carrier an additional 105 trucks of capacity in the Memphis market.

After an analysis of the operating efficiencies for this package of lanes, the carrier plans to offer the reduced pricing as shown in the table below.

Revised Pricing for Packaged Bid

Lane ID	Origin City	ST	Destination City	ST	Inbound Loads	Outbound Loads	Lane Pricing Original	Lane Pricing Package	Annual Cost Original	Annual Cost Package	Savings
4	Memphis	TN	Chicago	IL	100		$1.85	$1.82	$98,605	$97,006	$1,599
15	Dallas	TX	Chicago	IL	355		$1.38	$1.34	$460,016	$446,682	$13,334
17	Chicago	IL	Los Angeles	CA		40	$1.42	$1.39	$114,452	$112,034	$2,418
18	Chicago	IL	Memphis	TN		205	$1.45	$1.38	$158,434	$150,786	$7,649
19	Chicago	IL	Newark	NJ		165	$2.10	$2.08	$270,270	$267,696	$2,574
20	Chicago	IL	Atlanta	GA		85	$1.80	$1.76	$109,854	$107,413	$2,441
Total Loads:					455	495			$1,211,631	$1,181,617	$30,015

The package offers the shipper a savings of $30,015 over the carrier's original stand-alone lane bids. The shipper will compare the costs of this full package with the stand-alone bids and packaged bids of other carriers. If this package is the low-cost proposal, Carrier N will have an excellent chance of being awarded these lanes.

Multiple Packaged Bid Strategy. Since the package includes six different lanes, the carrier must consider offering additional packages that include only subsets of the full package. The risk of this package is that competing carriers may offer very aggressive pricing on certain lanes included in the package. If this is the case, the packaged bid may not offer the lowest cost solution for the shipper.

Competing Carriers Provide a Lower Cost Solution than Packaged Bid

Lane ID	Origin City	ST	Destination City	ST	Low Cost Carrier	Annual Loads	Lane Pricing Low Cost	Lane Pricing Package	Annual Cost Low Cost	Annual Cost Package	Savings
4	Memphis	TN	Chicago	IL	Carrier N	100	$1.85	$1.82	$98,605	$97,006	$1,599
15	Dallas	TX	Chicago	IL	**Carrier Z**	355	$1.27	$1.34	$423,348	$446,682	$(23,334)
17	Chicago	IL	Los Angeles	CA	**Carrier X**	40	$1.38	$1.39	$111,228	$112,034	$(806)
18	Chicago	IL	Memphis	TN	Carrier N	205	$1.45	$1.38	$158,434	$150,786	$7,649
19	Chicago	IL	Newark	NJ	**Carrier X**	165	$1.95	$2.08	$250,965	$267,696	$(16,731)
20	Chicago	IL	Atlanta	GA	Carrier N	85	$1.80	$1.76	$109,854	$107,413	$2,441
Total Loads:						950			$1,152,434	$1,181,617	$(29,182)

Suppose both Carrier Z and Carrier X have provided very favorable pricing on several of the lanes included in Carrier N's packaged bid. As a result, the shipper can minimize costs by awarding these lanes on a lane-by-lane basis. In much the same way, Carrier N is also at risk of a competing carrier including one or all of the package lanes in a competing packaged bid. If the competing packaged bid provides the shipper with a lower total cost, Carrier N's packaged bid will not be successful.

To provide some protection against these packaged bid risks, the carrier can use a multiple packaged bid strategy involving the lanes included in the primary package. While Carrier N is unaware of the pricing and packages of competing carriers, Carrier N can still estimate which lanes provide the greatest risk and design additional subset packages to protect the overall packaged bid strategy.

As part of the multiple package strategy, Carrier N has identified two lanes that could provide a potential risk to the overall Chicago packaged bid strategy. The first lane is Memphis inbound to Chicago. The second lane is Chicago outbound to Newark, NJ. To hedge against the risk of low pricing on the high risk lanes, the carrier will propose three additional packaged bids for this network. The new packages will exclude some or all of the high risk lanes while still retaining a reasonable level of network balance from the original package. Each alternate Chicago packaged bid is summarized below.

Alternate Chicago Bid Package 1 – Exclude Newark, NJ Outbound Lane

Lane ID	Origin City	ST	Destination City	ST	Inbound Loads	Outbound Loads	Lane Pricing Original	Lane Pricing Package	Annual Cost Original	Annual Cost Package	Savings
4	Memphis	TN	Chicago	IL	100		$1.85	$1.82	$98,605	$97,006	$1,599
15	Dallas	TX	Chicago	IL	355		$1.38	$1.34	$460,016	$446,682	$13,334
17	Chicago	IL	Los Angeles	CA		40	$1.42	$1.39	$114,452	$112,034	$2,418
18	Chicago	IL	Memphis	TN		205	$1.45	$1.38	$158,434	$150,786	$7,649
20	Chicago	IL	Atlanta	GA		85	$1.80	$1.76	$109,854	$107,413	$2,441
Total Loads:					455	330			$941,361	$913,921	$27,441

Alternate Chicago Bid Package 2 – Exclude Memphis to Chicago

Lane ID	Origin City	ST	Destination City	ST	Inbound Loads	Outbound Loads	Lane Pricing Original	Lane Pricing Package	Annual Cost Original	Annual Cost Package	Savings
15	Dallas	TX	Chicago	IL	355		$1.38	$1.34	$460,016	$446,682	$13,334
17	Chicago	IL	Los Angeles	CA		40	$1.42	$1.39	$114,452	$112,034	$2,418
18	Chicago	IL	Memphis	TN		205	$1.45	$1.38	$158,434	$150,786	$7,649
19	Chicago	IL	Newark	NJ		165	$2.10	$2.08	$270,270	$267,696	$2,574
20	Chicago	IL	Atlanta	GA		85	$1.80	$1.76	$109,854	$107,413	$2,441
Total Loads:					355	495			$1,113,026	$1,084,611	$28,416

Alternate Chicago Bid Package 3 – Exclude Memphis to Chicago and Newark, NJ

Lane ID	Origin City	ST	Destination City	ST	Inbound Loads	Outbound Loads	Lane Pricing Original	Lane Pricing Package	Annual Cost Original	Annual Cost Package	Savings
15	Dallas	TX	Chicago	IL	355		$1.38	$1.34	$460,016	$446,682	$13,334
17	Chicago	IL	Los Angeles	CA		40	$1.42	$1.39	$114,452	$112,034	$2,418
18	Chicago	IL	Memphis	TN		205	$1.45	$1.38	$158,434	$150,786	$7,649
20	Chicago	IL	Atlanta	GA		85	$1.80	$1.76	$109,854	$107,413	$2,441
Total Loads:					355	330			$842,756	$816,915	$25,842

These three alternate packages offer the shipper savings comparable to the original Chicago package. Each package also offers the carrier a reasonable level of network balance for the Chicago market. Also notice that the lane pricing in each of these packages is the same as the original package. Maintaining the same pricing prevents these packages from competing with the original package. However, the carrier may choose to raise or lower pricing from package to package as necessary to properly reflect the specific efficiencies of each package.

The carrier could also consider packages that exclude the Chicago to Los Angeles lane. This is a low volume lane that does not fit well geographically with other lanes in the packaged bid. Given that this lane is such a minor portion of the overall package, the carrier could provide the same packages as shown previously but exclude the Los Angeles lane.

Packaged Bid Strategy: Additional Considerations

Packaged bids provide carriers with a variety of options for introducing a sophisticated bid response strategy. However, if not used properly, the optimization and lane packaging tools can cause a variety of problems and complications. This section covers several potential packaged bid issues and how to avoid package-related problems.

Potential Savings. When a carrier designs a packaged bid, the shipper's total cost in the packaged bid should always be less than the total cost of the carrier's stand-alone lane bids. At least one lane in the packaged bid must be priced lower than in the stand-alone lane bids. A packaged bid with a cost greater than or equal to the cost of the individual stand-alone lane bids is meaningless and a waste of time for the shipper to evaluate.

Stand-Alone Bid Requirement. In many bid optimizations, the bid process requires the carrier to provide a stand-alone lane bid on any lane that will be included in a packaged bid. In certain cases, a carrier may only have an interest in a package of lanes and does not wish to be awarded any individual lanes included in a packaged bid. In these cases, the proper strategy is to provide a very high rate on the stand-alone bids then offer the actual competitive rates only in the packaged bids. The carrier could price the undesirable stand-alone lanes at a coded price of $99.99 per mile or $9,999 per load. This coded approach will allow the carrier to avoid any undesirable stand-alone lanes while also providing the shipper with a clear indication of the carrier's lane and packaged bid strategy.

Build Packaged Bids for a Reason. A bid package should always represent a reasonable strategy that includes some measurable level of lane synergies. Carriers should never make bid packages consisting of unrelated lanes or packages that don't offer savings to the shipper. Unnecessary packages add no value to the bid process and do not increase the carrier's chances of being awarded a particular group of lanes.

Mutually Exclusive Packaged Bids. When designing multiple packaged bids, carriers must carefully review the contents of each package to avoid mutually exclusive packaged bids. When two packages have at least one lane in common, the packages are mutually exclusive so that the carrier can only be awarded one of the two packages. Since a lane can only be awarded one time, only one package containing that lane can be awarded. To manage this problem, carriers can design a series of related packages similar to the approach shown previously for the Chicago network.

The next chapter includes a detailed case study that involves extensive packaged bid analysis. This case study provides additional insight into the packaged bid design and analysis process.

Shipper Network Data in RFPs

As part of the bid development process, shippers will provide carriers with shipment history to allow the carrier to develop a detailed understanding of the shipper's network and traffic patterns. When available, the shipper may include more detailed information above and beyond what is included in the basic lane information for pricing purposes. This additional information allows the carrier to evaluate key elements of the shipper's network such as monthly seasonality, day of week activity, and other network variables.

Shippers generally elect to share only the most relevant and useful information with carriers in order to maintain a reasonable level of confidentially regarding sensitive shipment information. The determination of relevant data should be based on the nature of the operation, the format of the bid, and the structure of the pricing and contract. For example, a short haul, mileage band bid would dictate the need for different information than a bid consisting of only long haul lanes over 500 miles.

Summary Load Volumes

In most cases, shippers will provide carriers with some form of summary load information by lane. The summary information typically contains estimated or actual annual load volumes for each lane. In some cases, the load data may represent a period other than one year. A typical format for summary lane information is shown below.

	Sample Bid Lane Information					
	Origin		Destination		Annual Loads	One-Way Miles
Lane ID	City	ST	City	ST		
1	Olive Branch	MS	West Memphis	AR	600	31
2	Olive Branch	MS	Southaven	MS	400	13
3	Olive Branch	MS	Covington	TN	350	60
4	Memphis	TN	Chicago	IL	100	533
5	Memphis	TN	Dallas	TX	250	452
6	Memphis	TN	Los Angeles	CA	420	1,795
7	Memphis	TN	Atlanta	GA	180	389
8	Memphis	TN	Orlando	FL	510	828
9	Memphis	TN	Miami	FL	215	1,055
10	Memphis	TN	Newark	NJ	390	1,084

The information shown also includes the standard miles for each lane. While not all RFP's include the miles, shippers will often include the miles to provide mileage consistency for the bid responses. Providing the miles also saves the carrier some time by not having to look up the miles. However, carriers will often compare the shipper's miles with the carrier's internal standard miles and make any necessary pricing adjustments if the two mileage standards do not match. A case study in the next chapter provides an example of this type of mileage adjustment.

The risk to the carrier of the basic annual summary information shown above is that the information does not reflect any seasonal shipping patterns. The data implies that the shipments move in a steady pattern over the course of one year. However, if the shipments are highly seasonal, the carrier's pricing strategy must be adjusted.

For example, suppose the shipper for this RFP is a major home improvement retailer that sells highly seasonal products such as lawnmowers and Christmas trees. If the Memphis origin location ships only lawnmowers, most of the shipments will actually occur over a three to four month period from February to May. Whenever possible, the shipper should share this type of seasonal information with potential carriers. In most cases, the carrier will charge more for seasonal shipping patterns. However, if a seasonal pattern provides a fit within the carrier's network, the carrier may actually offer very favorable pricing for the seasonal business.

To enhance the annual information, the shipper may choose to expand the data format to reflect seasonal patterns. In the table below, the shipper has included the high and low weeks for each lane, providing the carrier with a clearer picture of the shipping patterns at the lane level.

Lane ID	Origin City	ST	Destination City	ST	Annual Loads	One-Way Miles	Load Volumes by Week Average	High	Low
1	Olive Branch	MS	West Memphis	AR	600	31	11.5	21.0	6.0
2	Olive Branch	MS	Southaven	MS	400	13	7.7	14.0	2.0
3	Olive Branch	MS	Covington	TN	350	60	6.7	11.0	3.0
4	Memphis	TN	Chicago	IL	100	533	1.9	5.0	0.0
5	Memphis	TN	Dallas	TX	250	452	4.8	8.0	2.0
6	Memphis	TN	Los Angeles	CA	420	1,795	8.1	18.0	3.0
7	Memphis	TN	Atlanta	GA	180	389	3.5	8.0	0.0
8	Memphis	TN	Orlando	FL	510	828	9.8	35.0	0.0
9	Memphis	TN	Miami	FL	215	1,055	4.1	11.0	1.0
10	Memphis	TN	Newark	NJ	390	1,084	7.5	19.0	2.0

Sample Bid Lane Information

Shippers may also include 52 weeks of information reflecting the number of loads shipped by week. Usually the exact choice of data to be included in the RFP is based on the availability of accurate data and the relevance of the detailed data to the RFP strategy.

Discrete Shipment History

In many bid formats, shippers will provide carriers with discrete load detail information. The data should provide as much information about each shipment as possible. Typically the most important discrete data items include date and time information for the pick-up and delivery of each load. The carrier can use the date and time information to closely analyze seasonal load volumes and shipping patterns by time of day.

Sample Discrete Shipment History Data

PU Date	Del Date	Origin	Destination	Dest Name	Miles
1/4/2009	1/5/2009	Memphis, TN	Atlanta, GA	Store 503	380
1/6/2009	1/7/2009	Memphis, TN	Dallas, TX	Store 460	453
1/8/2009	1/9/2009	Memphis, TN	New Orleans, LA	Store 375	393
1/11/2009	1/12/2009	Memphis, TN	Dallas, TX	Store 460	453
1/13/2009	1/14/2009	Memphis, TN	Atlanta, GA	Store 503	380
1/15/2009	1/16/2009	Memphis, TN	Mobile, AL	Store 251	392
1/18/2009	1/19/2009	Memphis, TN	New Orleans, LA	Store 375	393
1/20/2009	1/21/2009	Memphis, TN	Dallas, TX	Store 460	453
1/22/2009	1/23/2009	Memphis, TN	Mobile, AL	Store 251	392
1/25/2009	1/26/2009	Memphis, TN	Mobile, AL	Store 251	392
1/27/2009	1/28/2009	Memphis, TN	Atlanta, GA	Store 503	380
1/29/2009	1/30/2009	Memphis, TN	Dallas, TX	Store 460	453
1/4/2009	1/5/2009	Memphis, TN	Dallas, TX	Store 460	453
1/6/2009	1/7/2009	Memphis, TN	Atlanta, GA	Store 503	380
1/8/2009	1/9/2009	Memphis, TN	Mobile, AL	Store 251	392
1/11/2009	1/12/2009	Memphis, TN	Mobile, AL	Store 251	392
1/13/2009	1/14/2009	Memphis, TN	Atlanta, GA	Store 503	380
1/15/2009	1/16/2009	Memphis, TN	Dallas, TX	Store 460	453
1/18/2009	1/19/2009	Memphis, TN	New Orleans, LA	Store 375	393

The data shown above is a sample format. Actual RFP data may include additional fields of information for thousands of historical shipments. The data may also include pick-up times, delivery times, trailers types, and other information relevant to the network included in the RFP.

Discrete shipment history with date and time information gives the carrier the unlimited ability to model and analyze the shipper's network. Carriers can identify inbound and outbound lanes and match load activity by date and time to identify any network efficiencies that may exist. However, the detailed historical data may not always be truly representative of future shipping patterns. Carriers must carefully consider the detailed shipment history in terms of the future expectations for the network. While the shipment history is likely the best information available, the carrier should never assume the history is a perfect representation of future shipments.

Shipment Data for Multi-Stop Designs

For certain networks and RFP's, shippers may request that carriers design multi-stop delivery routes as part of the solution design and pricing process. To facilitate the load-building and design process, the shipper will provide carriers with shipment volumes by delivery location. The shipment data will include average or detailed shipment volumes by location as shown in the example table below.

Multi-Stop Delivery Data – Average Only

Destination Store	Location	Annual Deliveries	Average Pieces
Store 251	Mobile, AL	52	680
Store 252	Birmingham, AL	52	512
Store 375	New Orleans, LA	52	1,044
Store 385	Baton Rouge, LA	52	652
Store 503	Atlanta, GA	52	1,158
Store 810	Jackson, MS	52	890
Store 841	Memphis, TN	52	944
Store 843	Collierville, TN	52	814

The shipper must also provide carriers with the maximum amount of volume that can fit on each shipment. In this example, assume the shipper can fit up to 2,800 pieces on each trailer. Based on this rule, the carrier will design routes to minimize total loads and minimize the total miles to serve the shipper's network each week. An example set of delivery routes is shown below.

Sample Multi-Stop Delivery Routes

Destination Store	Location	Annual Deliveries	Average Pieces	Total Pieces
Route 1:				
Store 375	New Orleans, LA	52	1,044	
Store 385	Baton Rouge, LA	52	652	1,696
Route 2:				
Store 841	Memphis, TN	52	944	
Store 810	Jackson, MS	52	890	
Store 251	Mobile, AL	52	680	2,514
Route 3:				
Store 843	Collierville, TN	52	814	
Store 252	Birmingham, AL	52	512	
Store 503	Atlanta, GA	52	1,158	2,484

The example above is just one possible set of feasible delivery routes for this network. Each different carrier may create a slightly different set of routes based on transit times, availability of backhauls, and many other factors.

While a simple shipment average can be used to develop the route design, the average fails to indicate seasonal patterns and fluctuations in shipment size. Random increases in shipment volume will occasionally cause planned routes to exceed the capacity of 2,800 pieces per trailer. When this occurs, planned routes will split into two routes or other existing routes must be modified to accommodate the increase in volume.

To allow for better route design, shippers might elect to provide carriers with detailed shipment history. The detailed information allows carriers to perform a deeper statistical analysis on shipment volumes to anticipate and minimize changes to the planned delivery routes. A sample of the detailed weekly shipment data is shown below.

Multi-Stop Delivery Data with Weekly Detail

Destination		Annual Deliveries	Average Pieces	Actual Pieces by Week (2008)					
Store	Location			1	2	3	4	5	6
Store 251	Mobile, AL	52	680	588	721	699	654	744	563
Store 252	Birmingham, AL	52	512	553	420	531	514	576	395
Store 375	New Orleans, LA	52	1,044	1,068	1,085	984	1,018	1,108	927
Store 385	Baton Rouge, LA	52	652	560	693	671	626	716	535
Store 503	Atlanta, GA	52	1,158	1,066	986	1,177	1,132	1,222	1,041
Store 810	Jackson, MS	52	890	798	931	909	961	954	773
Store 841	Memphis, TN	52	944	882	1,035	1,148	918	1,008	927
Store 843	Collierville, TN	52	814	722	955	843	788	878	697

The actual data would include information for a full 52 weeks or other reasonable period. With this information, the carrier can extend the analysis beyond a simple average and use different statistical values for the load-building design. The table below shows revised load-building data based on increasing the average by one standard deviation.

Revised Data for Load-Building: +1 Standard Deviation

Destination		Annual Deliveries	Average Pieces	Standard Deviation	Avg + 1 St. Dev
Store	Location				
Store 251	Mobile, AL	52	680	73	**753**
Store 252	Birmingham, AL	52	512	74	**586**
Store 375	New Orleans, LA	52	1,044	68	**1,112**
Store 385	Baton Rouge, LA	52	652	73	**725**
Store 503	Atlanta, GA	52	1,158	89	**1,247**
Store 810	Jackson, MS	52	890	82	**972**
Store 841	Memphis, TN	52	944	98	**1,042**
Store 843	Collierville, TN	52	814	98	**912**

The carrier can develop the routes based on the revised volume level of the average plus one standard deviation. The standard deviation calculation requires discrete data to be computed accurately.[99] When computing averages and other statistics on transportation data, extreme outliers in the data set should be excluded from the calculations.

---

[99] Consult any statistics textbook or similar reference source for more information on averages, the standard deviation, and the normal distribution.

Designing the routes based on the adjusted shipment volumes significantly reduces the likelihood of route disruptions during high volume shipping periods. The routes shown below are based on the adjusted shipment volumes.

Routes Based on Adjusted Volumes

Destination		Annual Deliveries	Planned Pieces	Total Pieces
Store	Location			
Route 1:				
Store 375	New Orleans, LA	52	1,112	
Store 385	Baton Rouge, LA	52	725	1,838
Route 2:				
Store 841	Memphis, TN	52	1,042	
Store 810	Jackson, MS	52	972	
Store 251	Mobile, AL	52	753	2,767
Route 3:				
Store 843	Collierville, TN	52	912	
Store 252	Birmingham, AL	52	586	
Store 503	Atlanta, GA	52	1,247	2,744

The original routes did not require any adjustments with the new load volume data. However, both Route 2 and Route 3 are very close to exceeding the 2,800 piece trailer capacity. Carriers may choose to adjust the routes from this design to create some additional buffer between the route design and the 2,800 piece trailer capacity.

Route 2 and Route 3 do offer some clever protection against shipment volumes exceeding the 2,800 piece capacity. The first stop on both routes is located in the Memphis metropolitan area. If either route should split into two loads, the first load can be a local Memphis delivery and the second load can be the longer haul delivery to the longer distance locations. Even though the route would split into two loads, the carrier would not incur a large number of additional miles to make the two deliveries.

The detailed shipment history can also be used to test the routes to identify how often each route will exceed the 2,800 piece limit. Using actual weekly history, the carrier could test several different routing scenarios and identify the scenario with the least likelihood of routes that exceed the 2,800 piece limit.

! *Technical Tip* – Using Excel® Spreadsheet Pivot Tables

The "Pivot Table" feature, available in most spreadsheets, provides a quick and easy method for summarizing bid contents and analyzing proposals. As a reference, a portion of the "demonstration bid" lane table is shown below. The column headings in the table have been reformatted to provide unique column headings for each field of information. The "Total Miles" field was added by multiplying miles by annual loads.

Demonstration Bid						
Lane ID	Origin City	Origin ST	Dest City	Dest ST	Loads	Miles	Total Miles
1	Olive Branch	MS	West Memphis	AR	600	31	18,600
2	Olive Branch	MS	Southaven	MS	400	13	5,200
3	Olive Branch	MS	Covington	TN	350	60	21,000
4	Memphis	TN	Chicago	IL	100	533	53,300
5	Memphis	TN	Dallas	TX	250	452	113,000
6	Memphis	TN	Los Angeles	CA	420	1,795	753,900
7	Memphis	TN	Atlanta	GA	180	389	70,020
8	Memphis	TN	Orlando	FL	510	828	422,280
9	Memphis	TN	Miami	FL	215	1,055	226,825
10	Memphis	TN	Newark	NJ	390	1,084	422,760

To begin a new pivot table using Microsoft Excel,® open the spreadsheet file that contains the data table such as the bid information table shown above. Create an empty spreadsheet tab where the new pivot table will be stored. To begin creating a pivot table, click Data then select "PivotTable and PivotChart Report" as shown below.[100]

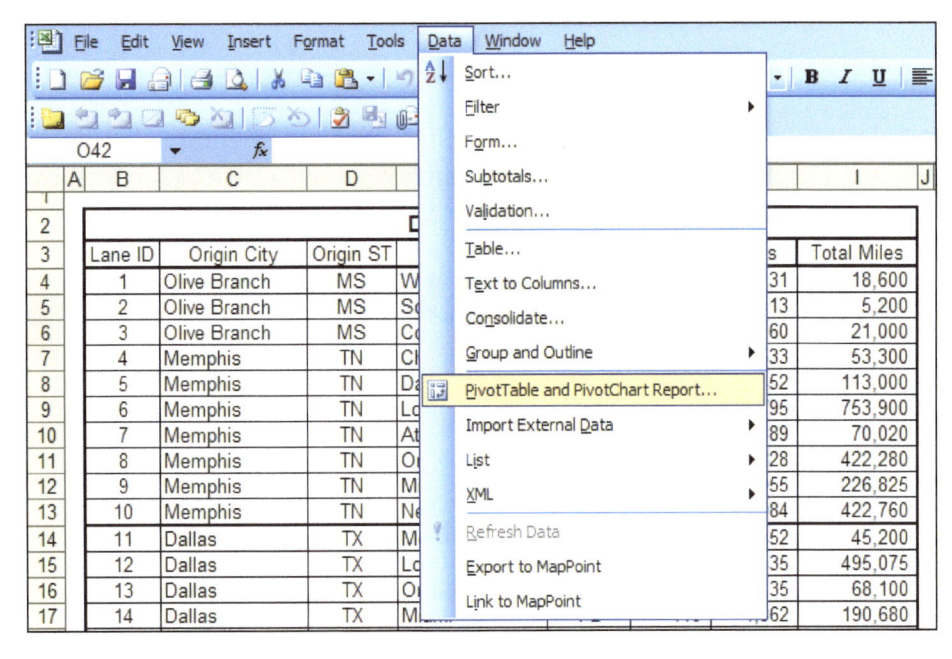

From here, the PivotTable wizard will guide the rest of the process.

---

[100] Microsoft® product screen shot reprinted with permission from Microsoft® Corporation. Instructions are based on Microsoft Excel® 2003.

The PivotTable Wizard box shown below will appear in Step 1.

Step 1:
For most common pivot table applications, select "Microsoft Office Excel® list or database" as shown to the right then click Next. Step 2 of the PivotTable wizard will then appear as shown below.

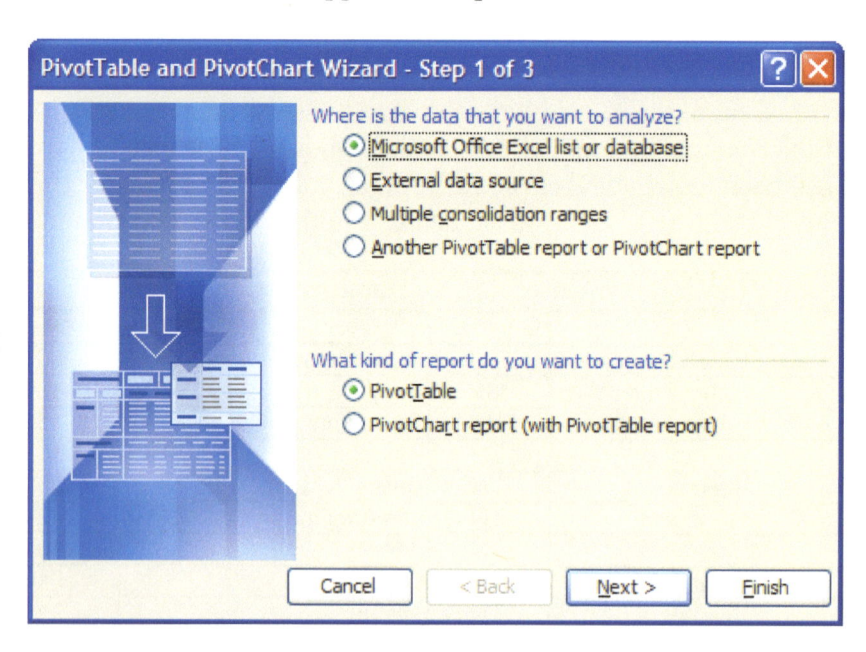

Step 2:
Step 2 asks the user to identify the data table that will feed the information to the new pivot table.

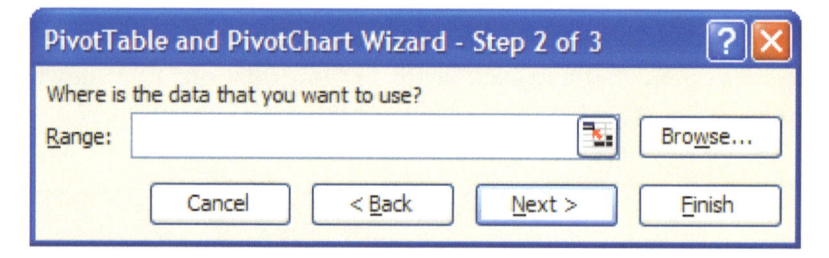

Click the cell range selector shown to the left of the "Browse" button. Highlight the desired data table including the first row of column headings down to the last row of data. Click Next and Step 3 of the wizard will appear as shown below.

Step 3:
Select "Existing worksheet" and indicate the cell address where the top left corner of the new pivot table will be located.[101] Click finish.

---

[101] Microsoft® product screen shots reprinted with permission from Microsoft® Corporation.

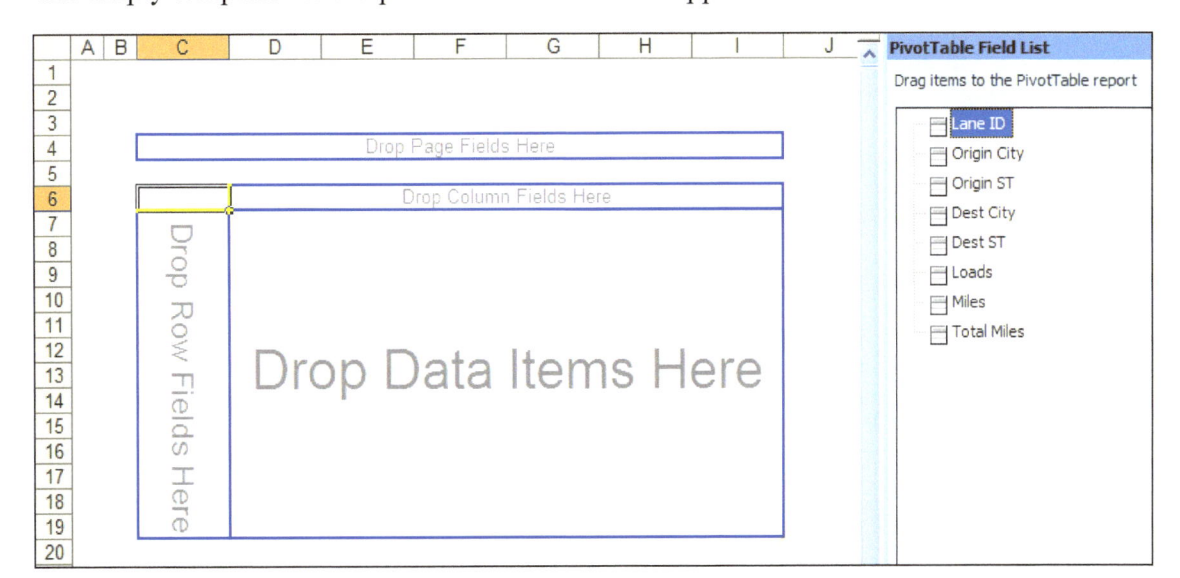

The empty template for the pivot table should now appear as shown below.[102]

The pivot table will consolidate information based on unique values for the "Row Fields" down the left and the "Column Fields" across the top. The "Data Items" are usually numeric fields that can be summed, averaged or counted.[103]

For this example, a pivot table will be created to sum the number of loads from each origin city to each destination state. To create the table, click on a field from the field list on the right and drop it into the desired box within the pivot table. Origin City and Origin ST should be dropped in the "Row Field" section. Origin ST should be dropped to the right of Origin City for this example. Dest ST should be dropped in the "Column Field" section and Loads should be dropped in the "Data Items" section.[104]

Pivot Table: Loads from Origin City to Destination State

Sum of Loads		Dest ST									
Origin City	Origin ST	AR	CA	FL	GA	IL	MI	MS	NJ	OH	TN	TX	Grand Total
Atlanta	GA			385						75	400		860
Chicago	IL		40		85		210		165		205		705
Dallas	TX		345	200	175	355					100		1,175
Memphis	TN		420	725	180	100			390			250	2,065
Miami	FL				85						60		145
Newark	NJ		125	110							165		400
Olive Branch	MS	600						400			350		1,350
Grand Total		600	930	1,420	525	455	210	400	555	75	1,280	250	6,700

The pivot table gives a quick summary of the activity in the demonstration bid. The bid contains 6,700 total loads. Empty cells in the pivot table indicate a value of zero.

---

[102] Microsoft® product screen shot reprinted with permission from Microsoft® Corporation.
[103] In addition to summing, averaging and counting, there are many other calculations available for summarizing both numerical and text information.
[104] When first using pivot tables, the exact clicking, dropping and dragging process takes some practice. Many pivot table users develop their own unique style and process for designing pivot tables.

Pivot tables can be designed to summarize and organize information in many different ways based on the needs and creativity of the user and the business problem at hand. Another example pivot table for the bid data is shown below. This table summarizes the bid information by destination state then by the origin point.

Pivot Table: Loads by Destination State from Origin City, ST

Dest ST	Origin ST	Origin City	Data Sum of Loads	Sum of Total Miles
AR	MS	Olive Branch	600	18,600
AR Total			**600**	**18,600**
CA	IL	Chicago	40	80,600
	NJ	Newark	125	347,375
	TN	Memphis	420	753,900
	TX	Dallas	345	495,075
CA Total			**930**	**1,676,950**
FL	GA	Atlanta	385	214,030
	NJ	Newark	110	118,250
	TN	Memphis	725	649,105
	TX	Dallas	200	258,780
FL Total			**1,420**	**1,240,165**
GA	FL	Miami	85	56,525
	IL	Chicago	85	61,030
	TN	Memphis	180	70,020
	TX	Dallas	175	136,500
GA Total			**525**	**324,075**
IL	TN	Memphis	100	53,300
	TX	Dallas	355	333,345
IL Total			**455**	**386,645**
MI	IL	Chicago	210	59,430
MI Total			**210**	**59,430**
MS	MS	Olive Branch	400	5,200
MS Total			**400**	**5,200**
NJ	IL	Chicago	165	128,700
	TN	Memphis	390	422,760
NJ Total			**555**	**551,460**
OH	GA	Atlanta	75	42,000
OH Total			**75**	**42,000**
TN	FL	Miami	60	63,300
	GA	Atlanta	400	155,600
	IL	Chicago	205	109,265
	MS	Olive Branch	350	21,000
	NJ	Newark	165	178,860
	TX	Dallas	100	45,200
TN Total			**1,280**	**573,225**
TX	TN	Memphis	250	113,000
TX Total			**250**	**113,000**
Grand Total			6,700	4,990,750

This format allows the manager to view the lane activity by destination state. The manager can quickly see the number of loads into any given state and the origin points for the load activity. The average length of haul could also be computed based on the total annual miles column.

Pivot tables take practice and experimentation. To become proficient at pivot tables, users must try various methods and develop their own personal style for designing tables.

! *Technical Tip* – Spreadsheet Text Tricks and Techniques

Often in bid analysis, data provided by shippers must be edited or manipulated by carriers to meet different internal analysis needs. The quick tricks shown here are handy for modifying data to meet specific formatting and organizational needs.

Separating Multiple Pieces of Information Combined in a Single Cell

Suppose a bid contains a single cell with both the city and state combined as shown in cell B4 below. The example shows how to use spreadsheet text functions to isolate only the state in a single cell and only the city name in a single cell.

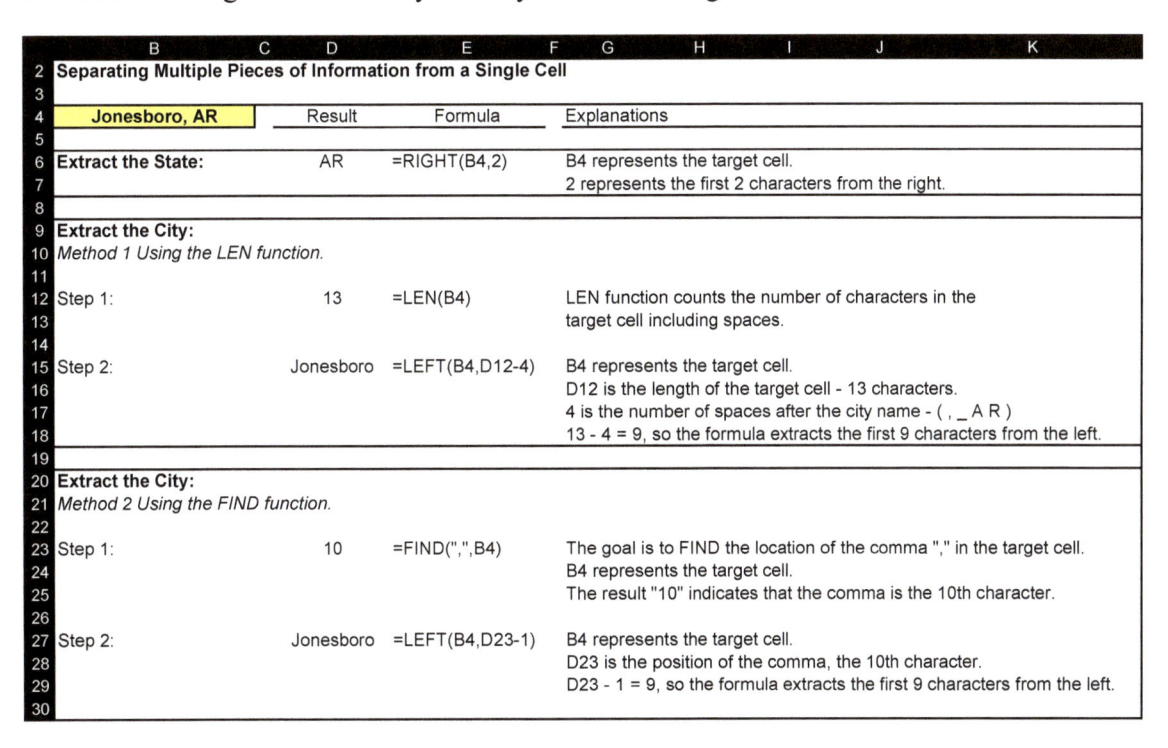

	B	C	D	E	F	G	H	I	J	K
2	Separating Multiple Pieces of Information from a Single Cell									
3										
4	**Jonesboro, AR**		Result		Formula		Explanations			
5										
6	**Extract the State:**		AR		=RIGHT(B4,2)		B4 represents the target cell.			
7							2 represents the first 2 characters from the right.			
8										
9	**Extract the City:**									
10	*Method 1 Using the LEN function.*									
11										
12	Step 1:		13		=LEN(B4)		LEN function counts the number of characters in the			
13							target cell including spaces.			
14										
15	Step 2:		Jonesboro		=LEFT(B4,D12-4)		B4 represents the target cell.			
16							D12 is the length of the target cell - 13 characters.			
17							4 is the number of spaces after the city name - (, _ A R)			
18							13 - 4 = 9, so the formula extracts the first 9 characters from the left.			
19										
20	**Extract the City:**									
21	*Method 2 Using the FIND function.*									
22										
23	Step 1:		10		=FIND(",",B4)		The goal is to FIND the location of the comma "," in the target cell.			
24							B4 represents the target cell.			
25							The result "10" indicates that the comma is the 10th character.			
26										
27	Step 2:		Jonesboro		=LEFT(B4,D23-1)		B4 represents the target cell.			
28							D23 is the position of the comma, the 10th character.			
29							D23 - 1 = 9, so the formula extracts the first 9 characters from the left.			
30										

The process to extract the state is only one step because the state abbreviation is usually at the end of the cell and always exactly 2 characters. The "Right" function isolates the state quickly and easily.[105]

Because the city name could be any number of characters in length, the city name requires two steps. The first step is to create a reference point for the entire cell using either the "Find" or "Len" function. The second step is a "left" function with the reference point used to calculate the appropriate number of characters to isolate beginning with the first character from the left.[106]

---

[105] If the target cell contains extraneous blank spaces, apply the =trim(target cell) function to remove the unnecessary spaces before applying the techniques shown here.
[106] Microsoft® product screen shot reprinted with permission from Microsoft® Corporation.

The example below shows that if the formulas are set up correctly, the text functions can be copied to isolate the information for a large set of data regardless of the different lengths of the city names. After copying the formulas, the final results should be closely reviewed for errors. The source data may not be formatted consistently across all the target cells.

	B	C	D	E	F	G	H	I	J	K
31										
32	Copying Formulas for Large Data Sets									
33										
34	Target Cells		Result	Formula			Explanations:			
35	Jonesboro, AR		Jonesboro	=LEFT(B35,FIND(",",B35)-1)			Here the two steps are combined into one formula.			
36	Atlanta, GA		Atlanta	=LEFT(B36,FIND(",",B36)-1)						
37	Dallas, TX		Dallas	=LEFT(B37,FIND(",",B37)-1)			Using the formulas correctly allows the formulas			
38	East Point, GA		East Point	=LEFT(B38,FIND(",",B38)-1)			to be copied easily for large sets of data.			
39										

Combining Text Information from Two or More Cells (Concatenation)
Suppose information in two cells such as city and state needs to be combined. Many spreadsheet mileage programs require the city and state information to be in one cell in a "Mobile, AL" format. The example below demonstrates two methods for combining the city and state cells and also adding the "comma + space" between the city and state.

	B	C	D	E	F
2	Combining Two or More Cells (Concatenation)				
3					
4	City	ST		Result	Formula
5	Mobile	AL		Mobile, AL	=B5&", "&C5
6	Birmingham	AL		Birmingham, AL	=B6&", "&C6
7	Dunwoody	GA		Dunwoody, GA	=B7&", "&C7
8	Jacksonville	FL		Jacksonville, FL	=B8&", "&C8
9					
10					
11	Optional Method			Mobile, AL	=CONCATENATE(B5,", ",C5)
12	Using "Concatenate"			Birmingham, AL	=CONCATENATE(B6,", ",C6)
13	Function			Dunwoody, GA	=CONCATENATE(B7,", ",C7)
14				Jacksonville, FL	=CONCATENATE(B8,", ",C8)
15					

The example shows two different methods for combining the information. The "&" symbol can be used much like the "+" is used for addition in numeric formulas. The "&" must be used between each cell reference or other text element. Similarly, the "concatenate" function can be used to combine multiple cells of information as well as freeform text.[107]

---

[107] Microsoft® product screen shots reprinted with permission from Microsoft® Corporation.

CHAPTER 14: Case Studies in Bid Response Analysis

The focus of this chapter is on the application of the one-way and dedicated pricing techniques presented throughout this book. Each case study will present a variety of challenges for the carrier in the design of a competitive and accurate bid response. While every carrier participating in a bid will have a unique strategy, these case studies provide a basic overview of the general thought process and analysis an average carrier might use in each bid response design. The cases cover a variety of common topics including one-way bids, packaged bids, and dedicated bids.[108]

Case 1: Traditional One-Way Bid

The Case

A small industrial parts manufacturer operates a production facility in Atlanta, GA. The facility ships industrial parts to a network of distribution centers across the county. Shipments to some customers are seasonal due to product types or customer demand patterns. All loads are drop-and-hook pick-ups and deliveries, so no delivery appointments are required. The shipper considers loads to be on-time as long as shipments are delivered on or before the scheduled delivery date. The shipper will operate under the fuel surcharge agreement for each carrier. Therefore, no adjustments to the proposed rates are necessary to accommodate any fuel surcharge differences.

The bid includes the shipper's high volume lanes to major customers. These lanes are shown in the table below. The shipper has also provided a breakdown of shipments by quarter to quantify the seasonality associated with each customer destination. The miles as shown are based on the shipper's internal mileage system. All per-mile loads will be paid based on these miles as defined by the shipper.

Primary Bid Lanes

Destination City	ST	Annual Loads	One-Way Miles	Q1	Q2	Q3	Q4
Miami	FL	194	665	42	51	53	48
Memphis	TN	453	385	88	109	125	131
Los Angeles	CA	217	2,184	41	35	58	83
Abilene	TX	313	971	70	85	90	68
Denver	CO	126	1,406	42	16	47	21
Chicago	IL	209	721	51	53	48	57
Newark	NJ	337	868	75	93	81	88

---

[108] All costs, rates and prices shown are fictional and do not represent actual pricing recommendations.

In addition to these primary lanes, the shipper has asked each carrier to provide a backup pricing matrix from Atlanta, GA to the states of GA, FL, TN, OH, LA, WV, TX, WI and MI. The shipper has additional customers in these states that receive occasional random shipments. Also, the majority of the manufacturer's inbound materials are delivered by rail, so no inbound truckload shipments are included in the shipper's network.

The carrier in this case is a medium-size carrier based in Nashville, TN. The carrier only serves the eastern two-thirds of the United States. The carrier operates a 400 truck linehaul fleet with an average utilization of 2,350 miles per week and an empty mile percentage of approximately 11.0%. The most common length of haul for the carrier is between 500 and 800 miles.

Carrier Analysis

Lane Review

The first step in the carrier analysis process is to determine which lanes provide a fit with the carrier's network. The map below shows each destination point in the bid by annual load volume, along with the carrier's current area of service.

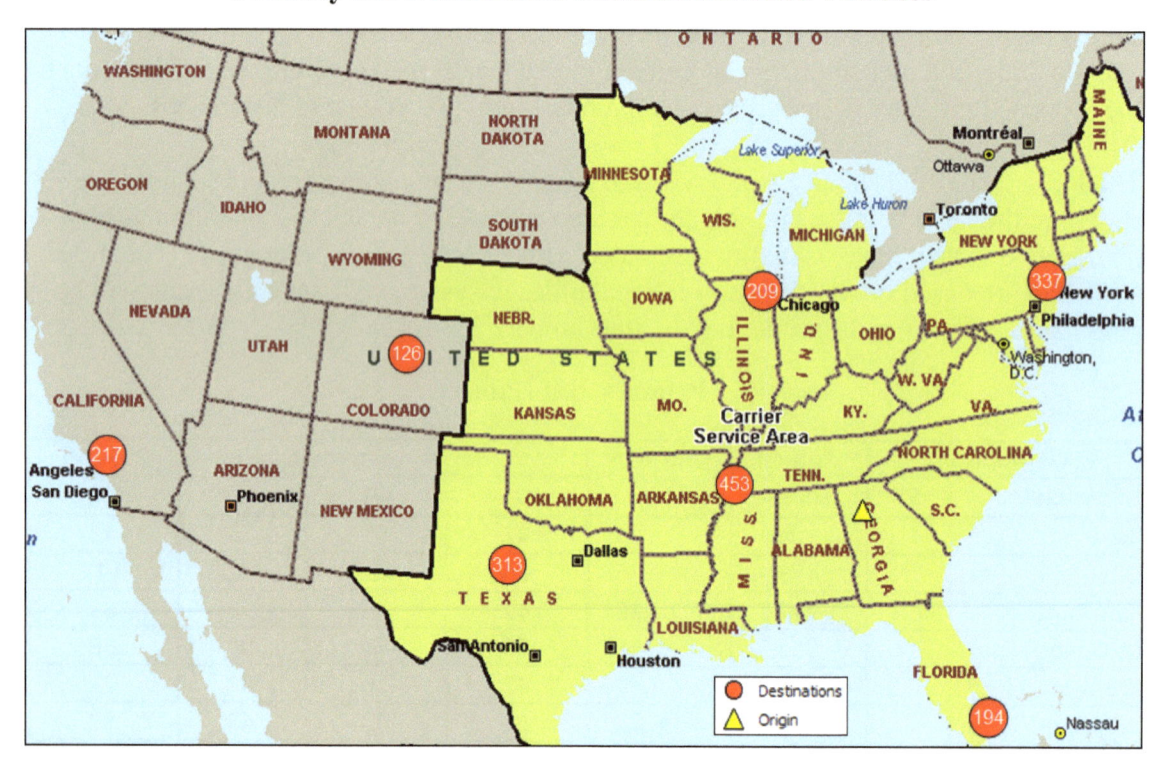

Primary Bid Destinations and Annual Load Volumes

The shaded area of the map represents the carrier's primary service area. Since the lanes to Denver, CO and Los Angeles, CA fall outside the service area, the carrier will decline to provide a bid on these destinations. The remaining destinations fall within the carrier's service area, so each of these lanes will be reviewed closely for potential pricing.

Mileage Verification

Since the shipper is requesting pricing based on a mileage standard that differs from the carrier's internal standard, the carrier must compare the shipper's miles with the carrier's standard miles on each lane.

Comparison of Shipper Miles and Carrier Miles

| Destination | | Annual | Shipper | Carrier | Mileage |
City	ST	Loads	Miles	Miles	Difference
Miami	FL	194	665	651	14
Memphis	TN	453	385	377	8
Los Angeles	CA	217	2,184	2,128	56
Abilene	TX	313	971	959	12
Denver	CO	126	1,406	1,401	5
Chicago	IL	209	721	710	11
Newark	NJ	337	868	844	24

The mileage difference is significant on several of the lanes. In the final proposal, the carrier must adjust pricing to meet the shipper's mileage standard to avoid any revenue discrepancies as a result of the differences in mileage.

Follow-Up Questions

After reviewing the bid and the network, the carrier submitted several follow-up questions to the shipper in an effort to better understand the service requirements and operating characteristics of the network. The carrier's questions and the shipper's responses are listed below.

Carrier Follow-Up Questions	
Carrier Question	**Shipper's Response**
How long does it typically take for trailers to be unloaded at the receiving location?	All inbound trailers will be unloaded within three days of the delivery day, excluding weekends. Trailer detention charges are allowed.
How many drop trailers will the carrier be required to maintain at the origin facility?	Carriers should maintain a pool of drop trailers equal to the carrier's average daily load volume. Drop Trailers = Annual Loads / 240 days
Do shipment volumes increase significantly at the end of the month or the end of the quarter?	Shipment volumes are typically steady throughout each month. Any spikes in volume will be communicated to carriers in a timely manner.

Before pricing the bid, the carrier must have a clear understanding of the shipper's requirements and expectations. Follow-up questions also demonstrate the carrier's interest in the business opportunity. Where appropriate, shippers should share the answers to one carrier's questions with all other carriers participating in the RFP. The sharing of questions and answers prevents any one carrier from have an informational advantage when responding to the RFP.

Carrier Solution Design

Based on the preliminary lane review, the carrier has chosen to consider rates proposals on the lanes to Chicago, Miami, Memphis, Abilene and Newark. The carrier will analyze each lane independently for network fit, capacity and balance considerations, and estimated empty miles. Based on the results of each individual lane analysis, the carrier will adjust pricing as needed on lanes of interest or decline to bid on lanes that do not fit the current needs of the carrier's network.

Internal Capacity and Balance

The first critical factor in the lane analysis is capacity and balance. Prior to the lane analysis, the carrier has gathered the information for the capacity and balance status of each market over the past three months. Capacity and balance information should not go too far back in time because the carrier's network will gradually evolve as customers and lanes change within the network. Existing customer load volumes can also change dramatically over time. Evaluating capacity and balance on a one to three month period will usually provide the most accurate reflection of the carrier's current network.

Capacity and Balance by Market

Analysis Zone	Inbound Loads	Outbound Loads	Net Balance	Avg Weekly Balance
GA - N	304	267	37	2.8
FL - C	188	116	72	5.5
FL - S	297	125	172	13.2
IL - N	188	277	(89)	(6.8)
NJ	87	49	38	2.9
TN - W	247	358	(111)	(8.5)
TX - E	122	108	14	1.1
TX - S	145	167	(22)	(1.7)
TX - W	36	18	18	1.4

Capacity and Balance — Three Months Ending May 30th

The capacity and balance information provides a clear indication of which markets have available trucks and which markets are in need of trucks. The origin for this bid, Atlanta, GA, is located in the GA–N zone, representing north Georgia. The origin zone has approximately 2.8 trucks per week of availability, so this bid is a good opportunity to secure loads for the market's existing capacity.

The capacity and balance report also includes several additional markets that are near the actual destination markets. The South, East and West zones in Texas have been included for the analysis of the Abilene, TX lane. The central Florida market (FL–C) and the south Florida market (FL–S) have been included for the analysis of the Miami lane. Including nearby markets allows the carrier to consider the capacity situations in contiguous zones as part of the bid strategy.

Guideline Pricing

As a starting point, the carrier will base pricing on its internal guideline rates for each lane. Since the carrier does not serve California or Colorado, guideline pricing is not available for those destinations. The guideline pricing shown below is based on the carrier's internal mileage standards. Any adjustments to the rates to meet the shipper's mileage standard will be performed prior to the final proposal.

Guideline Pricing for Bid Lanes

Guideline Rates		
From: Atlanta, GA		
Destination Pricing Zone	Rate Per Mile	Minimum Charge
CA - S	- NA -	- NA -
CO	- NA -	- NA -
FL - S	$ 2.45	$ 750.00
IL - N	$ 1.42	$ 600.00
NJ	$ 2.05	$ 700.00
TN - W	$ 1.35	$ 400.00
TX - E	$ 1.75	$ 600.00
TX - S	$ 1.65	$ 600.00
TX - W	$ 1.85	$ 650.00

Based on the results of the lane analysis, the carrier will adjust pricing up or down from the guideline standards as needed. The sections that follow provide an overview of the detailed pricing analysis for each individual lane.

Individual Lane Analysis

Each individual lane will be considered for pricing on a case-by-case basis. Each individual lane analysis is summarized in the sections below.

Atlanta, GA (GA–N) to Miami, FL (FL–S). The capacity and balance analysis indicates that the carrier currently has a severe surplus of trucks in the south and central Florida area. The existing unbalanced situation requires the carrier to move trucks empty from central Florida to Atlanta on a regular basis. As a result, the carrier has decided to decline to bid on the Miami, FL lane.

Atlanta, GA (GA–N) to Newark, NJ (NJ). The capacity and balance analysis indicates that the New Jersey area currently has a surplus of capacity. The carrier conducted a careful internal analysis of the existing customers that ship on the Atlanta to New Jersey lane. The carrier identified an underperforming customer that currently ships approximately 240 loads per year on the lane. The underperforming customer has a rate of $1.82 per mile compared to the carrier's average rate on this lane of $1.97 per mile. The carrier would like to submit an aggressive price for this lane. If the carrier is awarded the lane, the carrier can potentially discontinue service for the underperforming customer and replace those loads with the new customer's activity.

The pricing strategy for this lane is very straightforward. The carrier's expertise in current market pricing will come into play, making this pricing decision more of an art than a science. The key quantifiable variable is that the carrier must charge a rate higher than the existing customer's rate of $1.82 per mile. After considerable debate, the carrier has decided to submit a bid on this lane at a rate of $1.92 per mile.

Atlanta, GA (GA–N) to Chicago, IL (IL–N). The Atlanta to Chicago lane is very attractive because the carrier has available capacity in Atlanta and needs more capacity in Chicago. A win-win situation of this type is ideal, so the carrier should price this lane aggressively. The lane volume to Chicago is approximately 4 loads per week, so this lane would help balance the capacity situation in Chicago.

The primary quantifiable benefit of this win-win lane synergy is a potential reduction in empty miles. The guideline rate of $1.42 per mile can be reduced slightly to reflect these synergies. The analysis to adjust the rate for empty miles is shown below.

	Atlanta to Chicago Empty Mile Efficiencies	
Standard Charges	Length of Haul	710
	Guideline Rate Per Mile	x $ 1.42
	Guideline Flat Charge	$ 1,008.20
Standard Net Rev. Per Mile	Typical Empty Mile %	12.3%
	Typical Lane Empty Miles	100
	Total Trip Miles	810
	Net Revenue Per Mile	$ 1.245
Rate Adjustment for Empty Miles	Expected Empty Miles	65
	Total Trip Miles	775
	Net Revenue Per Mile	$ 1.245
	Revised Flat Charge	$ 964.64
	Revised Rate Per Mile	**$ 1.36**

The above analysis indicates an expected reduction in empty miles from 100 miles per load to 65 miles per load. The first box computes the standard rate per load of $1,008.20. The second box computes the standard net revenue per mile of $1.245 based on 100 empty miles per trip. The rate adjustment box computes the revised flat charge as the new total miles per trip multiplied by the standard net revenue per mile of $1.245. The revised rate per mile of $1.36 is the new flat charge of $964.64 divided by the billed miles of 710. The entire analysis is based on the carrier's standard mileage for this lane of 710 miles. The carrier's final decision is to price this lane at $1.36 per mile.

Atlanta, GA (GA–N) to Memphis, TN (TN–W). Much like the Atlanta to Chicago lane, the Atlanta to Memphis lane is also an ideal match with existing capacity and balance needs in both markets. As a result, the carrier will also price this lane aggressively. The empty miles pricing analysis for this lane is shown below.

	Atlanta to Memphis Empty Mile Efficiencies	
Standard Charges	Length of Haul	377
	Guideline Rate Per Mile	x $ 1.35
	Guideline Flat Charge	$ 508.95
Standard Net Rev. Per Mile	Typical Empty Mile %	20.1%
	Typical Lane Empty Miles	95
	Total Trip Miles	472
	Net Revenue Per Mile	$ 1.078
Rate Adjustment for Empty Miles	Expected Empty Miles	70
	Total Trip Miles	447
	Net Revenue Per Mile	$ 1.078
	Revised Flat Charge	$ 481.99
	Revised Rate Per Mile	**$ 1.28**

The analysis on this lane indicates a flat charge of $481.99 and a mileage rate of $1.28 per mile. Based on feedback from other recent bids and sales activity, the carrier's sales team believes a rate of $475 per will be required to secure this lane. The empty mile analysis serves to validate the proposed rate of $475 per trip. As a result, the carrier's final decision is to price this lane at a flat rate of $475 per trip.

Atlanta, GA (GA–N) to Abilene, TX (TX–W). The key variable in the pricing analysis for this lane is the location of Abilene in relation to the major cities in Texas. The carrier does not have any significant customers in the Abilene area. As a result, the carrier will likely relocate the trucks that land in Abilene to the closest major city. The major city of Dallas is about 185 miles from Abilene as shown in the map below.

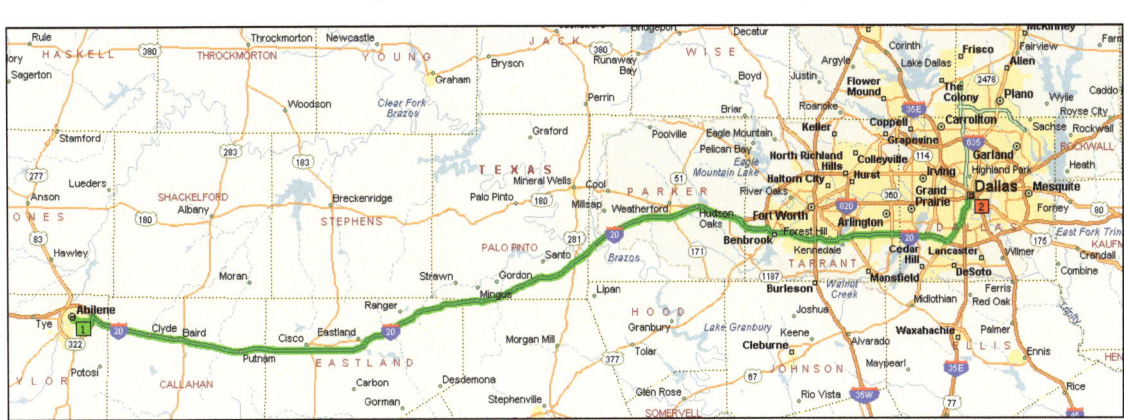

Abilene, TX Location Relative to Dallas, TX

Because of Abilene's remote location, the carrier should expect to incur an above average empty mile level to serve this destination. Despite Abilene's location, the carrier would still like to submit a bid on this lane. The need for loads out of the Atlanta market and the long length of haul make this lane attractive for the carrier even with the potential empty miles issue.

The guideline rate on this lane is $1.75 per mile. The carrier must adjust the rate higher to compensate for the anticipated excess empty miles. Based on the capacity and balance information for TX–E, the Dallas market is currently balanced, so serving this new lane may create balance issues in the Dallas area. For both reasons, the carrier must not be overly aggressive in pricing the lane. In fact, the carrier should price the lane slightly higher than the recommended guideline rate. The analysis below adjusts the rate upward based on the anticipated empty miles.

	Atlanta to Abilene Empty Mile Adjustment		
Standard Charges	Length of Haul		959
	Guideline Rate Per Mile	x $	1.75
	Guideline Flat Charge	$	1,678.25
Additional Empty Mile Costs	Typical Lane Empty Miles		110
	Expected Empty Miles		165
	Additional Empty Miles		55
	Cost Per Mile	x $	1.25
	Additional Charges	$	68.75
Rate Adjustment for Empty Miles	Guideline Charges	$	1,678.25
	Additional Charges	$	68.75
	Total Charges	$	1,747.00
	Revised Rate Per Mile	$	**1.82**

The above analysis adds $68.75 to the guideline rate per load. The additional cost is computed based on a cost per mile of $1.25 and 55 additional empty miles. This approach increases the guideline rate by 7 cents to $1.82 per mile. The carrier's final decision is to price the lane at the adjusted rate of $1.82 per mile.

Much of the lane analysis shown here is based on quantifiable information. However, the carrier will also use market expertise and experience to adjust final rates. Every carrier approaches this pricing analysis in a unique way. The objective of the various lane analysis examples shown here is to demonstrate several of the different approaches a carrier might utilize to determine appropriate one-way rates on individual lanes.

Carrier Pricing and Proposal

After completing the lane analysis, the carrier is ready to prepare the final bid proposal for the shipper. Prior to finalizing the proposal, the carrier must convert the per-mile pricing to be consistent with the shipper's lane mileages. The rate conversion is shown in the table below.

Mileage Rate Conversions

Destination City	ST	Carrier Miles		Carrier Rate		Flat Charge		Shipper's Miles		Converted Rate
Miami	FL	651	x	No bid	=		÷	665	=	
Memphis	TN	377	x	$ 1.26	=	$ 475.00	÷	385	=	$ 1.23
Los Angeles	CA	2,128	x	No bid	=		÷	2,184	=	
Abilene	TX	959	x	$ 1.82	=	$ 1,745.38	÷	971	=	$ 1.80
Denver	CO	1,401	x	No bid	=		÷	1,406	=	
Chicago	IL	710	x	$ 1.36	=	$ 965.60	÷	721	=	$ 1.34
Newark	NJ	844	x	$ 1.92	=	$ 1,620.48	÷	868	=	$ 1.87

To determine the converted rate, the carrier's flat charge is divided by the shipper's miles. The converted rates will be submitted as the carrier's bid. The final proposal, including backup point-to-state rates, is shown below.

Carrier Pricing Proposal
September 14, 2008

Lane Rates		
Origin: Atlanta, GA		
Destination		Rate
City	ST	Per Mile
Miami	FL	
Memphis	TN	$ 1.23
Los Angeles	CA	
Abilene	TX	$ 1.80
Denver	CO	
Chicago	IL	$ 1.34
Newark	NJ	$ 1.87

Backup Rates		
Origin: Atlanta, GA		
Destination	Rate	Minimum
State	Per Mile	Charge
FL	$ 2.55	$ 700.00
GA	$ 1.95	$ 475.00
LA	$ 1.67	$ 650.00
MI	$ 1.85	$ 650.00
OH	$ 1.45	$ 600.00
TN	$ 2.05	$ 500.00
TX	$ 1.85	$ 600.00
WI	$ 1.65	$ 650.00
WV	$ 1.95	$ 700.00

The carrier must also be sure that no rate conflicts exist between the point-to-point lane rates and the backup point-to-state rates. The per-mile lane rates to TN and TX are lower than the backup rates, so no conflicts exist. The carrier's proposal is ready to be submitted to the shipper.

Case 2: One-Way Bid with Packaging and Optimization

The Case

A major beverage manufacturer operates four production and distribution facilities across the United States. The facilities are located in Columbus, OH, Jacksonville, FL, Shreveport, LA, and Kansas City, KS. In addition to customer outbound shipments, each facility ships certain finished goods to other company facilities. Each location makes a specific mix of beverage products with some low demand products produced only at certain locations. These low demand products must be produced at one facility then shipped to other locations for distribution to the final customer.

The manufacturer is currently conducting an RFP for these interplant shipments. The RFP includes the 12 lanes shown below.

Lanes Included in RFP

Lane Number	Origin City	ST	Destination City	ST	Annual Loads
1001	Columbus	OH	Shreveport	LA	252
1002	Columbus	OH	Jacksonville	FL	180
1003	Columbus	OH	Kansas City	KS	130
2001	Shreveport	LA	Jacksonville	FL	410
2002	Shreveport	LA	Columbus	OH	352
2003	Shreveport	LA	Kansas City	KS	290
3001	Jacksonville	FL	Columbus	OH	179
3002	Jacksonville	FL	Shreveport	LA	159
3003	Jacksonville	FL	Kansas City	KS	122
4001	Kansas City	KS	Columbus	OH	80
4002	Kansas City	KS	Shreveport	LA	62
4003	Kansas City	KS	Jacksonville	FL	120

Shreveport, LA is the only facility that produces several specialized products, so outbound interplant volumes are much heavier out of this facility. For the most part, shipment volumes are fairly steady throughout the year, so seasonality is not a significant factor in this network.

The interplant network in this bid is the ideal environment for the use of packaged bids. Carriers will benefit greatly by delivering into a facility and often reloading with an outbound load from the same location, avoiding empty miles. Given these inherent efficiencies, the shipper will allow carriers to submit packaged bids as part of the RFP design. The shipper expects to enjoy significant cost savings as a result of the packaged bid proposals submitted by participating carriers.

The shipper has also established certain restrictions on how the network and individual lanes will be awarded to carriers. The primary business award restrictions are listed in the table below.

Shipper's Lane Award Rules	
Shipper Restriction	**Reasons for Restriction**
Single Source Lane Award. Each lane will be single-sourced by only one carrier.	By having only one carrier per lane, the process of managing and loading outbound trailers at the origin facility is simplified.
Maximum of 3 Network Carriers. The total network will be served by 3 or fewer carriers.	This restriction simplifies the management of carriers for the shipper. It also simplifies the management of the trailer pools at each facility.
Minimum of 2 Carriers Per Facility No one carrier will be awarded all outbound lanes from a facility.	The shipper does not want any one facility to be 100% dependent on a single carrier for all outbound transportation.

Carriers must keep these restrictions in mind when designing packaged bids. Any packaged bid that includes all three outbound lanes from a facility will not be valid.

The service requirements for these interplant lanes are very flexible. All lanes are a drop-and-hook pick-up and drop-and-hook delivery. All facilities are open 24 hours a day, so loads can be picked up and delivered at any time. To be considered on-time, loads must be delivered on or before the scheduled delivery day. The shipper's service platform provides the carrier with tremendous flexibility for planning loads and maximizing asset utilization. A typical pick-up and delivery timeline for the Shreveport to Columbus lane is shown below.

Shreveport to Columbus Lane	
Trailer Ready Time:	Monday at 10 am
Delivery Day:	Friday by 11:59 pm
Loaded Miles:	940 miles
Transit Time:	Appoximately 48 hours

Based on the trailer ready time, transit time, and delivery day, the carrier has maximum flexibility in managing the load. The carrier can choose to pick up the load as late as Wednesday and still make the delivery on time. The carrier could also choose to pick up the load on Monday or Tuesday and make delivery on Wednesday, Thursday or Friday. This type of flexibility will also allow the carrier to maximize the number of inbound and outbound load matches at each of the shipper's facilities.

All fuel surcharges will be based on the fuel surcharge requirements as defined by the carrier's standard contract. The miles for the fuel surcharge calculation will be based on the carrier's standard mileages. As a result of the heavy use of drop trailers in the network, the carrier can expect the number of trailers committed to the shipper to be equal to the 3 trailers per load per day model.

Carrier Analysis

Lane Mileages

As with all bids, the carrier must determine the miles for each lane based on the carrier's standard miles. The carrier's miles for this bid are shown below.

Bid Lanes with Miles

Lane Number	Origin City	ST	Destination City	ST	Annual Loads	Carrier Miles
1001	Columbus	OH	Shreveport	LA	252	940
1002	Columbus	OH	Jacksonville	FL	180	805
1003	Columbus	OH	Kansas City	KS	130	658
2001	Shreveport	LA	Jacksonville	FL	210	858
2002	Shreveport	LA	Columbus	OH	352	940
2003	Shreveport	LA	Kansas City	KS	290	552
3001	Jacksonville	FL	Columbus	OH	179	805
3002	Jacksonville	FL	Shreveport	LA	159	858
3003	Jacksonville	FL	Kansas City	KS	122	1,132
4001	Kansas City	KS	Columbus	OH	80	658
4002	Kansas City	KS	Shreveport	LA	62	552
4003	Kansas City	KS	Jacksonville	FL	120	1,132

All the lanes included in the bid have a fairly long length of haul. The shortest lane is 552 miles and the longest is 1,132 miles. This length of haul range is a perfect fit for the carrier's business model in this case.

Carrier Capacity and Balance Analysis

The carrier must closely review each origin and destination market in the bid and determine how much, if any, capacity the carrier has available for this shipper. The carrier's current capacity and balance for each market over the most recent 10-week period is shown below.

Capacity and Balance				
10 weeks ending October 24				
Analysis Zone	Inbound Loads	Outbound Loads	Net Balance	Avg Weekly Balance
OH - C	310	370	(60)	(6.0)
LA - N	195	110	85	8.5
FL - N	208	140	68	6.8
FL - C	277	136	141	14.1
MO - W	163	121	42	4.2

The carrier has available capacity in each origin market other than Columbus, OH. The central Florida region, FL – C, is also included to identify the amount of additional nearby capacity that may be available to support the Jacksonville, FL location.

Bid Network Analysis

As always, the carrier's capacity and balance situation is an important factor for the bid strategy. Because of the unique nature of this bid, the shipper's network balance is also important. Each facility in the bid has both inbound and outbound load volumes, so the shipper's network balance is also a very important consideration. Further, since the RFP allows for lane packaging, packaged bids can be used to strategically leverage the expected balance for each location. The shipper's inbound and outbound lane analysis by location is shown below.

RFP Inbound-Outbound Lane Summary

| Annual Loads | Destination | | | | Total |
Origin	Columbus	Jacksonville	Kansas City	Shreveport	Network
Columbus		180	130	252	562
Jacksonville	179		122	159	460
Kansas City	80	120		62	262
Shreveport	352	210	290		852
Total	611	510	542	473	2,136

The above analysis summarizes the bid lanes in a clear format that allows the carrier to better understand the network flows. The table below summarizes the inbound and outbound flows to determine the balance situation within the shipper's network.

| Customer Network Analysis | | | | |
| Annual Loads | | | | |
Customer Location	Inbound Loads	Outbound Loads	Net Balance	Avg Weekly Balance
Columbus, OH	611	562	49	0.9
Jacksonville, FL	510	460	50	1.0
Kansas City, KS	542	262	280	5.4
Shreveport, LA	473	852	(379)	(7.3)
Total Network	2,136	2,136	-	-

Overall, the Columbus and Jacksonville locations are well-balanced. As expected, the Shreveport location has many more outbound shipments than inbound shipments. Kansas City is unbalanced, with 280 more inbound shipments than outbound shipments. The shipper's network situation, combined with the carrier's capacity and balance, will play a key role in determining the bid strategy and lane packaging approach for the carrier.

Network Map

The simple nature of this network provides an excellent opportunity to map the network flows on a lane-by-lane basis. The full network map is shown below.

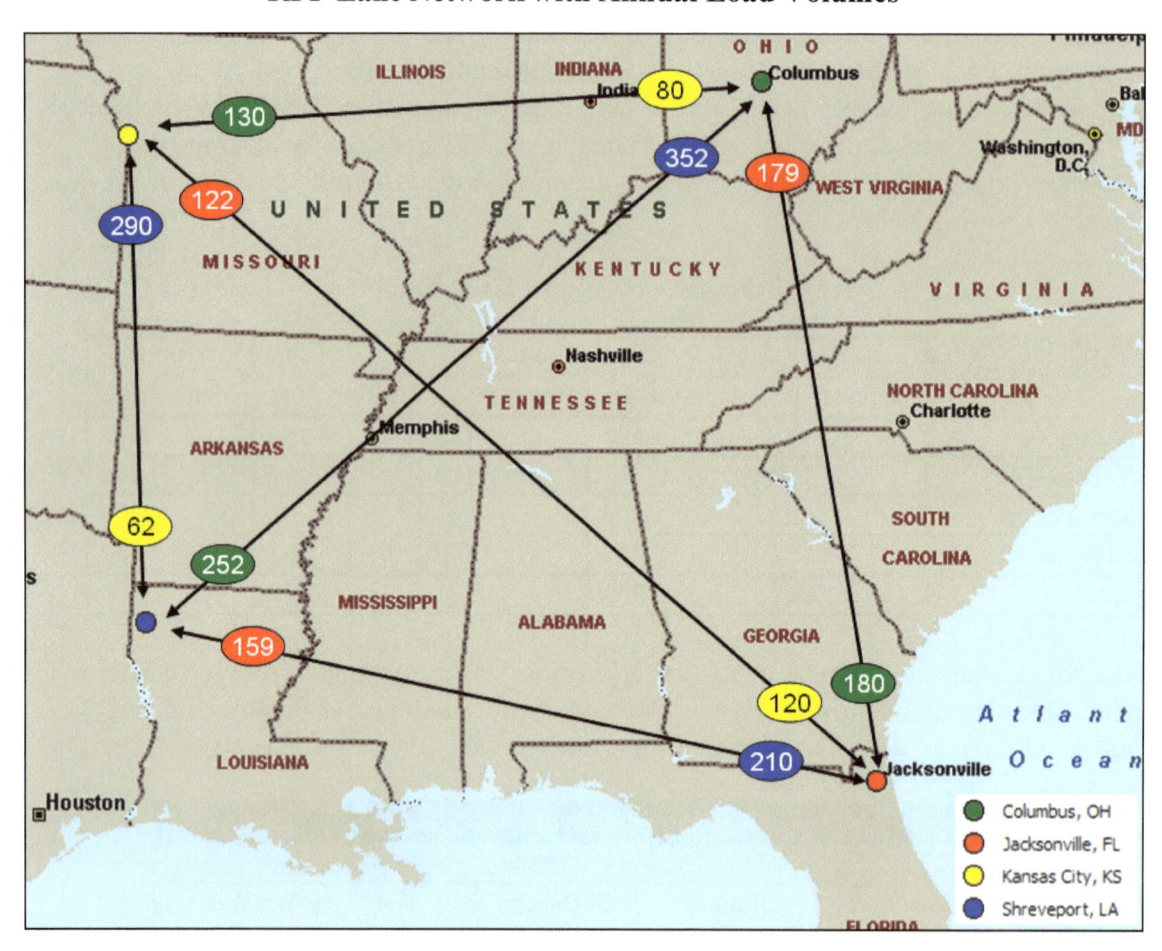

RFP Lane Network with Annual Load Volumes

A map of this type provides the carrier with a perfect view of the network for evaluating the general network flow and identifying packaged bid opportunities. The color of each circle represents the origin location. The number inside each circle represents the annual load volume on the lane. For example, the lane from Columbus to Jacksonville contains 180 annual loads.

The carrier can quickly see the inbound and outbound balance on shipments between any two facilities. For example, the lanes between Columbus and Jacksonville are very balanced. On the other hand, the lanes between Kansas City and Shreveport are highly unbalanced. The net impact of the shipper's network on the carrier's overall capacity and balance in each market is a primary consideration for the packaged bid designs.

Carrier Solution Design

Bid Strategy

The carrier for the bid in this case is a large national carrier. The carrier views this bid primarily as an excellent opportunity to expand the existing network and increase revenues. While certain lanes may fill a specific network need, the primary strategy is to submit competitive pricing on all lanes. The bid proposal will include several creative packaged bids as well as stand-alone pricing on each lane.

Stand-Alone Lane Pricing

Prior to designing any packaged bids, the carrier must first establish stand-alone pricing for each lane of interest. The carrier will begin the pricing with standard guideline rates then discount those rates based on the expected efficiencies inherent in the shipper's service platform and requirements. The preliminary guideline pricing is shown below.

Carrier Guideline Rates Prior to Discounts

	\multicolumn{4}{c}{Guideline Rates}
	\multicolumn{4}{c}{Destination}
Origin	Columbus	Jacksonville	Kansas City	Shreveport
Columbus		$ 2.05	$ 1.85	$ 1.75
Jacksonville	$ 1.10		$ 1.25	$ 1.15
Kansas City	$ 1.22	$ 1.78		$ 1.45
Shreveport	$ 1.33	$ 1.90	$ 1.55	

Because of the shipper's flexible service requirements, the carrier will discount the guideline pricing significantly. The shipper's flexibility provides the carrier with two quantifiable benefits. First, the flexibility in pick-up days and times allows the carrier to minimize empty miles by waiting until an available truck is very close to the shipper to pick up the load. Second, the 24-hour drop-and-hook option will reduce cycle times by eliminating buffer time and minimizing dock times on each end of the trip. Using activity-based costing, the estimated savings per load are shown below.

Estimated Savings	Savings Activity	Savings Per Load
Drop-and Hook		
Hours Saved	1.25	
Cost Per Hour	$ 10.00	$ 12.50
Reduced Empty Miles		
Miles Saved	25	
Cost Per Mile	$ 1.10	$ 27.50
Total Savings Per Load		$ 40.00

Based on this analysis, the shipper's efficiencies are worth an estimated $40 per load. The estimated discount is a flat amount of $40 per load because all of the efficiencies are related primarily to the load pick-up and delivery events, so length of haul is not a factor in the estimated savings. The carrier can discount each load by $40 to incorporate these efficiencies into the rates. The adjusted stand-alone lane rates are shown below.

Stand-Alone Lane Rates								
Lane Number	Origin City	ST	Destination City	ST	Annual Loads	Carrier Miles	Guideline Rate	Per Mile Discount	Adjusted Rate
1001	Columbus	OH	Shreveport	LA	252	940	$ 1.75	$ 0.04	$ 1.71
1002	Columbus	OH	Jacksonville	FL	180	805	$ 2.05	$ 0.05	$ 2.00
1003	Columbus	OH	Kansas City	KS	130	658	$ 1.85	$ 0.06	$ 1.79
2001	Shreveport	LA	Jacksonville	FL	210	858	$ 1.90	$ 0.05	$ 1.85
2002	Shreveport	LA	Columbus	OH	352	940	$ 1.33	$ 0.04	$ 1.29
2003	Shreveport	LA	Kansas City	KS	290	552	$ 1.55	$ 0.07	$ 1.48
3001	Jacksonville	FL	Columbus	OH	179	805	$ 1.10	$ 0.05	$ 1.05
3002	Jacksonville	FL	Shreveport	LA	159	858	$ 1.15	$ 0.05	$ 1.10
3003	Jacksonville	FL	Kansas City	KS	122	1,132	$ 1.25	$ 0.04	$ 1.21
4001	Kansas City	KS	Columbus	OH	80	658	$ 1.22	$ 0.06	$ 1.16
4002	Kansas City	KS	Shreveport	LA	62	552	$ 1.45	$ 0.07	$ 1.38
4003	Kansas City	KS	Jacksonville	FL	120	1,132	$ 1.78	$ 0.04	$ 1.74

The adjusted rates above will provide the proposed pricing for each lane on a stand-alone basis. These rates will also establish the starting rates for any discounts offered as part of any packaged bid proposals.

Packaged Bid Analysis

The carrier is now ready to carefully analyze the shipper's network to identify potential efficiencies and design packaged bid proposals. The carrier must keep the shipper's bid restrictions in mind when designing packaged bids. Most importantly, the shipper has a restriction that one carrier can only be awarded a maximum of two of the three outbound lanes for a facility. Therefore, the carrier should not create any packaged bids that include more than two outbound lanes from any one facility.

The carrier has decided to follow the three general strategies described below for developing package bids.

Potential Packaged Bid Strategies	
Strategy	**Summary**
Out-and-Back	Package the two lanes out and back between two facilities. For example, package Jacksonville to Columbus with Columbus to Jacksonville.
Balanced Tours	Package three or four lanes together that tour the shipper's network. Packages should maintain reasonable balance or fill an existing capacity and balance need for the carrier.
High Volume Networks	Package bundles of lanes involving multiple locations that result in a reasonable balance of inbound and outbound activity at each location.

Out-and-Back Packages

Out-and-back packages are relatively easy to identify and price since only two facilities are involved. The most attractive packages are typically those that are well balanced. However, unbalanced packages may also be attractive when the load volume imbalance actually serves to fill an existing network need for the carrier. The carrier has identified the three out-and-back package opportunities listed below.

Out-and-Back Package Bid Opportunties						
Package	Lane			Annual Loads	One-Way Miles	Origin Balance
	Number	Origin	Destination			
A	3001	Jacksonville, FL	Columbus, OH	179	805	1
	1002	Columbus, OH	Jacksonville, FL	180	805	(1)
B	3003	Jacksonville, FL	Kansas City, KS	122	1,132	(2)
	4003	Kansas City, KS	Jacksonville, FL	120	1,132	2
C	1001	Columbus, OH	Shreveport, LA	252	940	100
	2002	Shreveport, LA	Columbus, OH	352	940	(100)

Packages A and B are very well balanced. Package C provides the Columbus, OH market with an inflow of 100 additional trucks per year, or about 2 trucks per week. This inflow of capacity benefits the carrier's current capacity and balance situation in Columbus. The carrier is currently out of balance in Columbus by 6 trucks per week, so Package C would provide additional capacity in the Columbus market.

The primary benefit of the out-and-back packaged bids is the potential for reduced empty miles when a match occurs between an inbound load and an available outbound load. In this shipper's network, the chances of a match are especially high because of the flexible pick-up and delivery times. The chances of a load match also increase as the overall load volume increases. For example, if the out-and-back lane only had 20 loads in each direction per year, the chances of getting a match are very low. On the other hand, a lane with 200 annual loads in each direction would enjoy frequent matches.

In networks where the inbound and outbound load volumes are highly out of balance, the number of matches can become easier to estimate. For example, if a location has 500 inbound loads and 100 outbound loads per year, it is safe to assume that the location will match nearly all of the 100 outbound loads with a corresponding inbound load. The matching assumes the inbound and outbound loads flow in a complementary seasonal pattern. If the seasonal shipping patterns of the inbound and outbound loads are not complementary, the probability of matching loads is reduced.

While several statistical models could be developed to estimate the number of potential matches, the best method for estimating matches is often basic trucking experience. If the carrier has past experience with this network, the historical information and general knowledge of the network provide the carrier with the information needed to estimate potential matches. The carrier's estimates for inbound and outbound load matches for the out-and-back packaged bids are shown below.

		Estimated Inbound-Outbound Load Matches				
		Lane		Annual	Percent	Matching
Package	Number	Origin	Destination	Loads	Matching	Loads
A	3001	Jacksonville, FL	Columbus, OH	179	50%	90
A	1002	Columbus, OH	Jacksonville, FL	180	50%	90
B	3003	Jacksonville, FL	Kansas City, KS	122	40%	49
B	4003	Kansas City, KS	Jacksonville, FL	120	40%	48
C	1001	Columbus, OH	Shreveport, LA	252	75%	189
C	2002	Shreveport, LA	Columbus, OH	352	35%	123

The carrier is now ready to discount the stand-alone lane pricing to create the packaged bid pricing. The total cost of the packaged bid must be lower than the total cost of the lanes on a stand-alone basis. Without offering savings, packaged bids are meaningless.

The potential savings will be achieved through reduced empty miles on the matching inbound and outbound loads. The savings will occur only on the matching loads. Empty miles are expected to be normal on the remaining loads. The carrier has estimated the empty mile savings at $50 per load based on the analysis shown below.

Estimated Savings Per Matching Load	
Typical Empty Miles	61
Expected Empty Miles on Matching Loads	0
Empty Miles Reduction Per Match	61
Empty Miles Cost Per Mile	x $ 0.82
Savings Per Matching Load	**$ 50.02**

For simplification and consistency, the carrier will discount all matching loads by $50. In reality, individual carriers may use a variety of different variables and approaches to estimate the savings associated with a packaged bid. The $50 savings will apply only to the matching loads and not all loads for the lane as shown below for Package C.

	Estimated Savings Per Load					
	Lane		Annual	Matching	Savings	Savings
Package	Origin	Destination	Loads	Loads	$50/ Ld	Per Load
C	Columbus, OH	Shreveport, LA	252	189	$ 9,450	$ 37.50
C	Shreveport, LA	Columbus, OH	352	123	$ 6,150	$ 17.47

The savings of $50 per matching load is spread over all loads on a lane to determine the final savings per load. For the Columbus to Shreveport lane, the net savings is $37.50 per load across all loads on the lane. For the Shreveport to Columbus lane, the net savings of $50 per matching load is $17.47 across all loads.

The carrier is now ready to compute the final pricing for each of the packaged bids. All matching loads will be discounted by $50 per load. The savings will then be reflected in the final rate per mile for each lane in each packaged bid proposal. The rate adjustment calculations are shown below.

Packaged Lane Pricing Calculations

Out-and-Back Package Bids - Stand-Alone Cost

Pkg	Lane Origin	Lane Destination	One-Way Miles	Annual Loads	Annual Miles	Stand-Alone Rate	Cost Per Load	Lane Cost	Stand-Alone Total Cost
A	Jacksonville, FL	Columbus, OH	805	179	144,095	$1.05	$845.50	$151,345	
A	Columbus, OH	Jacksonville, FL	805	180	144,900	$2.00	$1,610.25	$289,845	$441,190
B	Jacksonville, FL	Kansas City, KS	1,132	122	138,104	$1.21	$1,375.00	$167,750	
B	Kansas City, KS	Jacksonville, FL	1,132	120	135,840	$1.74	$1,974.96	$236,995	$404,745
C	Columbus, OH	Shreveport, LA	940	252	236,880	$1.71	$1,605.00	$404,460	
C	Shreveport, LA	Columbus, OH	940	352	330,880	$1.29	$1,210.20	$425,990	$830,450

Out-and-Back Package Bids - Package Rate Adjustments

Pkg	Lane Origin	Lane Destination	Matching Loads	Savings $50 / Ld	Saving Per Mile	Package Rate	Pkg Cost Per Load	Lane Cost	Package Total Cost
A	Jacksonville, FL	Columbus, OH	90	$4,500	$0.031	$1.02	$821.10	$146,977	-2.0%
A	Columbus, OH	Jacksonville, FL	90	$4,500	$0.031	$1.97	$1,585.85	$285,453	$432,430
B	Jacksonville, FL	Kansas City, KS	49	$2,450	$0.018	$1.20	$1,358.40	$165,725	-1.0%
B	Kansas City, KS	Jacksonville, FL	48	$2,400	$0.018	$1.73	$1,958.36	$235,003	$400,728
C	Columbus, OH	Shreveport, LA	189	$9,450	$0.040	$1.67	$1,569.80	$395,590	-1.8%
C	Shreveport, LA	Columbus, OH	123	$6,150	$0.019	$1.27	$1,193.80	$420,218	$815,807

The first section of the analysis computes the stand-alone cost of each packaged bid. The packaged bid will then be discounted from the stand-alone cost. The bottom section of the analysis computes the annual package savings at $50 per matching load. The total annual savings is spread over the total annual miles to determine a net savings per mile. The stand-alone rate is then discounted by the rounded net savings per mile to determine the final rate.

The final column displays the total cost of the packaged bid and displays the percentage discount from the stand-alone cost. The savings from the packaged bid efficiencies ranges from 1.0% to 2.0%. Carriers must always evaluate the percentage savings and per mile savings to insure that the packaged bids provide only a reasonable discount.

Since rates are customarily quoted in cents per mile, each final package rate per mile is rounded to two decimal places. As a result of the rounding, the final savings of the package may be slightly different than the computed savings at $50 per load. The effect of rounding on the revenue to the carrier and savings to the shipper is immaterial.

The benefit of the packaged bid opportunity to the carrier is the guarantee of being awarded all lanes in the package. With stand-alone lane pricing, the carrier may be awarded several stand-alone lanes. However, without knowing the exact lane awards, the carrier cannot discount pricing for the network efficiencies. With packaged bids, the carrier's pricing is based on a specific group of lanes, so appropriate pricing discounts can be extended since the award of the lanes is guaranteed by the packaged bid process.

Balanced Tours

Balanced tours involve three or more facilities and are more complex than simple out-and-back packages. For this bid, balanced tour packages will involve complementary inbound and outbound lanes for either three or four facilities. The inbound and outbound load volumes do not need to be perfectly balanced for each facility. However, each facility should be reasonably balanced in most package designs. Any packaged bid imbalance at a facility should serve to improve an existing capacity and balance issue for the carrier in the local market of the unbalanced facility.

The carrier's first balanced tour package is illustrated in the map below.

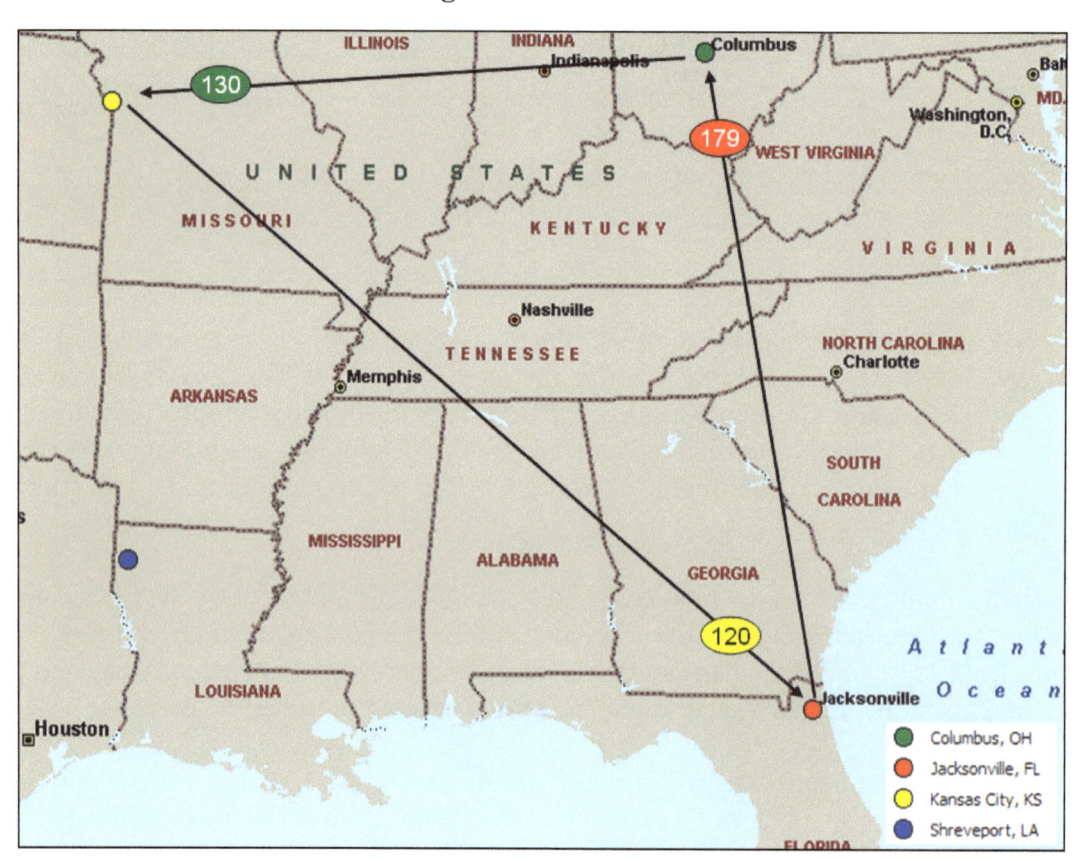

Package D - Balanced Tour

The package involves a simple three-leg tour between Jacksonville, Columbus, and Kansas City. In this package, trucks move in a triangle-pattern tour of the facilities. The package also meets the carrier's existing network capacity and balance needs in two locations. In Jacksonville, where the carrier has excess capacity, the package includes more outbound loads than inbound loads. In Columbus, where the carrier is in need of additional capacity, the package includes more inbound loads than outbound loads. While these two network needs are being met, Kansas City remains relatively balanced with 120 outbound loads compared to 130 inbound loads.

The two balanced tour packages for the carrier are outlined in the table below.

		Balanced Tour Packages				
		Lane		Annual	One-Way	Origin
Package	Number	Origin	Destination	Loads	Miles	Balance
D	4003	Kansas City, KS	Jacksonville, FL	120	1,132	10
	3001	Jacksonville, FL	Columbus, OH	179	805	(59)
	1003	Columbus, OH	Kansas City, KS	130	658	49
E	3002	Jacksonville, FL	Shreveport, LA	159	858	21
	2002	Shreveport, LA	Columbus, OH	352	940	(193)
	1002	Columbus, OH	Jacksonville, FL	180	805	172

Package E also provides the carrier with some improvements in the existing network capacity and balance situation. In Shreveport, where the carrier has excess capacity, the package includes more outbound loads than inbound loads. In Columbus, where the carrier is in need of additional capacity, the package includes more inbound loads than outbound loads. While these two network needs are being met, Jacksonville remains relatively balanced with 159 outbound loads compared to 180 inbound loads.

The carrier is now ready to determine the pricing for each packaged bid. The carrier has decided to apply the same savings of $50 per load that was used in the previous packaged bids. The pricing for Package D and Package E is shown below.

Balanced Tour Packaged Bid Pricing

	Balanced Tour Package Bids - Stand-Alone Cost								
	Lane		One-Way	Annual	Annual	Stand-	Cost	Lane	Stand-Alone
Pkg	Origin	Destination	Miles	Loads	Miles	Alone Rate	Per Load	Cost	Total Cost
D	Kansas City, KS	Jacksonville, FL	1,132	120	135,840	$ 1.74	$ 1,974.96	$ 236,995	
	Jacksonville, FL	Columbus, OH	805	179	144,095	$ 1.05	$ 845.50	$ 151,345	
	Columbus, OH	Kansas City, KS	658	130	85,540	$ 1.79	$ 1,177.30	$ 153,049	$ 541,389
E	Jacksonville, FL	Shreveport, LA	858	159	136,422	$ 1.10	$ 946.70	$ 150,525	
	Shreveport, LA	Columbus, OH	940	352	330,880	$ 1.29	$ 1,210.20	$ 425,990	
	Columbus, OH	Jacksonville, FL	805	180	144,900	$ 2.00	$ 1,610.25	$ 289,845	$ 866,361

	Balanced Tour Package Bids - Package Rate Adjustments								
	Lane		Matching	Savings	Saving	Package	Pkg Cost	Lane	Package
Pkg	Origin	Destination	Loads	$50 / Ld	Per Mile	Rate	Per Load	Cost	Total Cost
D	Kansas City, KS	Jacksonville, FL	36	$ 1,800	$ 0.013	1.73	$ 1,958.36	$ 235,003	-1.4%
	Jacksonville, FL	Columbus, OH	54	$ 2,700	$ 0.019	1.03	$ 829.15	$ 148,418	
	Columbus, OH	Kansas City, KS	52	$ 2,600	$ 0.030	1.76	$ 1,158.08	$ 150,550	$ 533,971
E	Jacksonville, FL	Shreveport, LA	64	$ 3,200	$ 0.023	1.08	$ 926.64	$ 147,336	-2.0%
	Shreveport, LA	Columbus, OH	148	$ 7,400	$ 0.022	1.27	$ 1,193.80	$ 420,218	
	Columbus, OH	Jacksonville, FL	180	$ 9,000	$ 0.062	1.94	$ 1,561.70	$ 281,106	$ 848,659

The two balanced tour packages offer savings of 1.4% and 2.0% compared to the stand-alone lane pricing. In reality, the carrier might submit several different versions of these packaged bids. The carrier might also consider combining Package D and Package E to make one large package with an additional discount.

Balanced Networks

Balanced network packages may include lanes from any facility traveling in any direction. The goal of each package is to create a balanced network of inbound and outbound lanes for each facility. If the package is not fully balanced, any imbalance in the package should improve an existing imbalance in the carrier's current network.

Balanced network packages will often be an extension of smaller packages. The balanced network package below is an extension of Package D from the balanced tour packages. The package design includes two lanes that were also included in Package D.

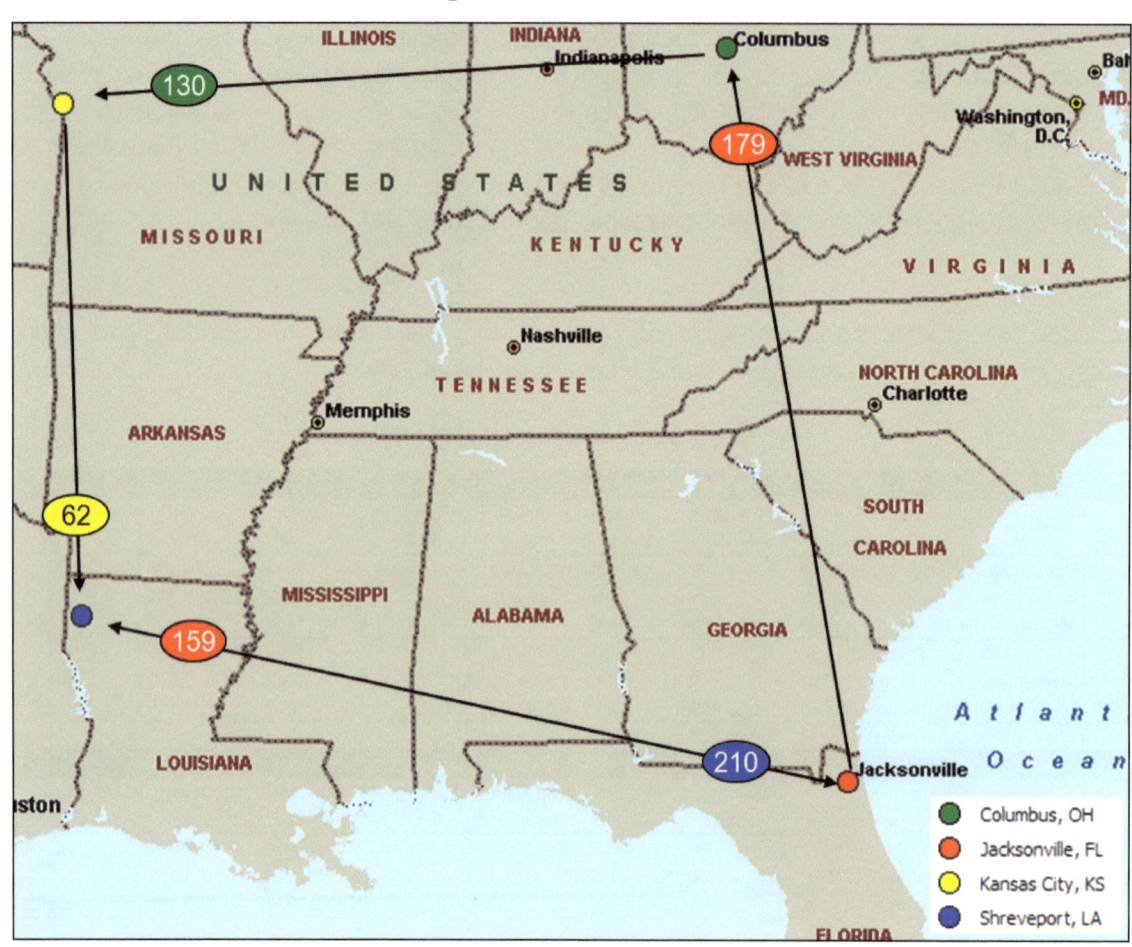

Package F - Balanced Network

The balanced network package incorporates two lanes from Package D and extends the package to include lanes into and out of Shreveport. The total package includes 740 annual loads or about one-third of the customer's total network. In reality, the carrier will likely create several different balanced network packages. For the purpose of this case study, the carrier will only submit this single balanced network package.

There are a number of potentially suitable lane combinations that could be combined to create balanced network packages. For larger networks, the carrier might choose to utilize optimization software to identify efficient tours and balanced networks. For a relatively simple network like the one in this case, a simple trial-and-error process is often more effective. The model below provides a simple format for quickly evaluating potential network scenarios.

Balanced Network Spreadsheet Model

Full Network

Annual Loads	Destination				Total
Origin	Columbus	Jacksonville	Kansas City	Shreveport	Network
Columbus		180	130	252	562
Jacksonville	179		122	159	460
Kansas City	80	120		62	262
Shreveport	352	210	290		852
Total	611	510	542	473	2,136

This table represents the full network of lanes. The carrier must select lanes to create potential packaged bid scenarios. Scenarios are evaluated in the final table.

Lane Selections

1 = Selected	Destination				Total
Origin	Columbus	Jacksonville	Kansas City	Shreveport	Network
Columbus		-	1	-	1
Jacksonville	1		-	1	2
Kansas City	-	-		1	1
Shreveport	-	1	-		1
Total	1	1	1	2	5

This section of the table is used to select lanes for inclusion in the package. A "1" is entered into the lane cell to add the lane to the package. A total of 5 lanes are included.

Selected Network

Annual Loads	Destination				Total
Origin	Columbus	Jacksonville	Kansas City	Shreveport	Network
Columbus		-	130	-	130
Jacksonville	179		-	159	338
Kansas City	-	-		62	62
Shreveport	-	210	-		210
Inbound Loads	179	210	130	221	740
Outbound Loads	130	338	62	210	740
Available Trucks	49	(128)	68	11	

This table displays the load volumes for each of the selected lanes. Network capacity and balance is computed in the bottom section. Lane selections can be adjusted until an efficient and balanced network package is created.

This model allows the carrier to quickly perform "what-if" analysis on different lane combinations. In the "Lane Selections" portion of the model, the totals indicate how many lanes are selected for each facility. The totals allow the carrier to track lane selections so that the shipper's rule limiting the number of outbound lanes to two per carrier per facility is met. Once an efficient network package is created, the results can be saved for packaging and pricing as part of the bid response.

The proposed network package is reasonably balanced at three of the four facilities. The Jacksonville location has more outbound loads than inbound loads. However, since the carrier has excess capacity available in Jacksonville, this imbalance in the package will improve the carrier's existing network balance. The package also adds 49 trucks per year to the Columbus market, further improving the carrier's existing balance situation. The finalized capacity and balance for Package F is summarized below.

Balanced Network Package					
Package	Lane Number	Origin	Destination	Annual Loads	One-Way Miles	Origin Balance
F	3001	Jacksonville, FL	Columbus, OH	179	805	(128)
	1003	Columbus, OH	Kansas City, KS	130	658	49
	4002	Kansas City, KS	Shreveport, LA	62	552	68
	2001	Shreveport, LA	Jacksonville, FL	210	858	11
	3002	Jacksonville, FL	Shreveport, LA	159	858	(128)

Just as in the other packages, the carrier must estimate the percentage of inbound and outbound load matches at each origin location. The load-match estimates for this package are shown below.

Balanced Network Package					
Package	Lane Number	Origin	Destination	Annual Loads	Percent Matching	Matching Loads
F	3001	Jacksonville, FL	Columbus, OH	179	60%	107
	1003	Columbus, OH	Kansas City, KS	130	40%	52
	4002	Kansas City, KS	Shreveport, LA	62	75%	47
	2001	Shreveport, LA	Jacksonville, FL	210	25%	53
	3002	Jacksonville, FL	Shreveport, LA	159	60%	95

The percentage of matches can be based on optimization results, statistical analysis, or carrier experience. Regardless of the technical approach, the carrier should adjust the final matches based on the existing network capacity and balance for the carrier. For example, the Jacksonville matching percentage may appear to be too high when considering only the bid network. However, since the carrier has a large amount of capacity already available in Jacksonville, the effective load matches and empty miles savings will be very high.

One other strategic consideration for the carrier is the existence of competing packages within the carrier's overall proposal. For example, the Jacksonville to Columbus lane is included in Package A, Package D, and Package F. As a result, the three packages are mutually exclusive so that one and only one of these three packages can be awarded to the carrier. When lanes are shared among several packages, the carrier should consider lowering rates in the most desirable package in order increase the likelihood of being awarded the most beneficial package bid.

The carrier is now ready to determine the pricing for the balanced network packaged bid. The carrier has decided to apply the same savings of $50 per load that was used in the previous packaged bids. The pricing for Package F is shown below.

Balanced Network Packaged Bid Pricing

Pkg	Lane Origin	Lane Destination	One-Way Miles	Annual Loads	Annual Miles	Stand-Alone Rate	Cost Per Load	Lane Cost	Stand-Alone Total Cost
	Jacksonville, FL	Columbus, OH	805	179	144,095	$ 1.05	$ 845.50	$ 151,345	
	Columbus, OH	Kansas City, KS	658	130	85,540	$ 1.79	$ 1,177.30	$ 153,049	
F	Kansas City, KS	Shreveport, LA	552	62	34,224	$ 1.38	$ 760.40	$ 47,145	
	Shreveport, LA	Jacksonville, FL	858	210	180,180	$ 1.85	$ 1,590.20	$ 333,942	
	Jacksonville, FL	Shreveport, LA	858	159	136,422	$ 1.10	$ 946.70	$ 150,525	$ 836,006

Pkg	Lane Origin	Lane Destination	Matching Loads	Savings $50/Ld	Saving Per Mile	Package Rate	Pkg Cost Per Load	Lane Cost	Package Total Cost
	Jacksonville, FL	Columbus, OH	107	$ 5,350	$ 0.037	$ 1.01	$ 813.05	$ 145,536	
	Columbus, OH	Kansas City, KS	52	$ 2,600	$ 0.030	$ 1.76	$ 1,158.08	$ 150,550	
F	Kansas City, KS	Shreveport, LA	47	$ 2,350	$ 0.069	$ 1.31	$ 723.12	$ 44,833	-2.1%
	Shreveport, LA	Jacksonville, FL	53	$ 2,650	$ 0.015	$ 1.84	$ 1,578.72	$ 331,531	
	Jacksonville, FL	Shreveport, LA	95	$ 4,750	$ 0.035	$ 1.07	$ 918.06	$ 145,972	$ 818,423

Package F offers the shipper a 2.1% savings compared to the stand-alone lane pricing. Since this is a major package, the carrier may consider an additional discount to increase the likelihood of being awarded the bundle of business. After some consideration, the carrier has decided to reduce the total cost of this package slightly as shown below.

Final Adjusted Pricing for Package F

Pkg	Lane Origin	Lane Destination	Annual Loads	Preliminary Design Rate	Preliminary Design Total Cost	Final Package Rate	Final Package Total Cost	Savings Total	Savings %
	Jacksonville, FL	Columbus, OH	179	$ 1.01	$ 145,536	$ 1.00	$ 144,095	$ 1,441	1.0%
	Columbus, OH	Kansas City, KS	130	$ 1.76	$ 150,550	$ 1.73	$ 147,984.20	$ 2,566	1.7%
F	Kansas City, KS	Shreveport, LA	62	$ 1.31	$ 44,833	$ 1.29	$ 44,148.96	$ 684	1.6%
	Shreveport, LA	Jacksonville, FL	210	$ 1.84	$ 331,531	$ 1.82	$ 327,927.60	$ 3,604	1.1%
	Jacksonville, FL	Shreveport, LA	159	$ 1.07	$ 145,972	$ 1.05	$ 143,243.10	$ 2,728	1.9%
	Package Totals		740		$ 818,423		$ 807,399	$ 11,024	1.4%

The carrier has reduced the total cost of the package by an additional 1.4%. The pricing for each lane has been reduced slightly based on the carrier's market pricing expertise and bid design experience. Even if a competing carrier has lower pricing on one or two lanes in this package, if the overall package provides the shipper with a lower total cost, the carrier will have a good chance of being awarded this package.

Packaged Bid Review and Validation

All packaged bids should be reviewed carefully before submission to the shipper. When multiple packages include the same lane, the carrier can only be awarded one of the proposed packages that include the common lane. The table below provides a simple format for visually evaluating the contents of all packaged bids in a proposal. All lanes in the bid are listed in the rows. A column is included in the table for each unique packaged bid scenario.

Packaged Bid Contents Summary

Lane Number	Origin City	ST	Destination City	ST	A	B	C	D	E	F
1001	Columbus	OH	Shreveport	LA			252			
1002	Columbus	OH	Jacksonville	FL	180				180	
1003	Columbus	OH	Kansas City	KS				130		130
2001	Shreveport	LA	Jacksonville	FL						210
2002	Shreveport	LA	Columbus	OH			352		352	
2003	Shreveport	LA	Kansas City	KS						
3001	Jacksonville	FL	Columbus	OH	179			179		179
3002	Jacksonville	FL	Shreveport	LA					159	159
3003	Jacksonville	FL	Kansas City	KS		122				
4001	Kansas City	KS	Columbus	OH						
4002	Kansas City	KS	Shreveport	LA						62
4003	Kansas City	KS	Jacksonville	FL		120		120		
Annual Loads Included in Package:					359	242	604	429	691	740

Using this summary format, the carrier can see how frequently each lane is used across all the proposed packaged bid scenarios. For example, lane 3001 is used in three different packaged bids. Lanes 2003 and 4001 were not included in any packaged bids. Several other lanes are included in multiple packaged bids.

After a review of the packaged bid scenarios, the carrier may choose to remove or modify certain packaged bids before submitting the final proposal. The carrier might also identify additional packaged bid opportunities during the review process. By carefully reviewing all packaged bid designs, the carrier can avoid potential strategy errors and provide the shipper with an accurate, feasible packaged bid proposal.[109]

---

[109] The packaged bid review format as shown may need to be modified to accommodate bids with a large number of lanes or a large number of packaged bids.

Carrier Pricing and Proposal

The carrier is now ready to organize the stand-alone lane pricing and packaged bids into the final proposal for submission to the shipper. The carrier must review the bid lane detail carefully for potential pricing errors before submitting the bid to the shipper. With large bids including many lanes, data entry and formatting errors can easily occur.

Stand-Alone Lane Pricing

The stand-alone pricing provides the base of the carrier's overall proposal. While the carrier will offer the most attractive rates in the packaged bids, accurate stand-alone lane pricing is still a critical component of the overall proposal. The carrier's stand-alone proposal is shown below.

Carrier Pricing Proposal
Stand-Alone Lane Rates
February 24, 2009

Lane Number	Origin City	ST	Destination City	ST	Annual Loads	Carrier Miles	Rate Per Mile
1001	Columbus	OH	Shreveport	LA	252	940	$ 1.71
1002	Columbus	OH	Jacksonville	FL	180	805	$ 2.00
1003	Columbus	OH	Kansas City	KS	130	658	$ 1.79
2001	Shreveport	LA	Jacksonville	FL	210	858	$ 1.85
2002	Shreveport	LA	Columbus	OH	352	940	$ 1.29
2003	Shreveport	LA	Kansas City	KS	290	552	$ 1.48
3001	Jacksonville	FL	Columbus	OH	179	805	$ 1.05
3002	Jacksonville	FL	Shreveport	LA	159	858	$ 1.10
3003	Jacksonville	FL	Kansas City	KS	122	1,132	$ 1.21
4001	Kansas City	KS	Columbus	OH	80	658	$ 1.16
4002	Kansas City	KS	Shreveport	LA	62	552	$ 1.38
4003	Kansas City	KS	Jacksonville	FL	120	1,132	$ 1.74

In most bids, the shipper will provide a standardized format for submitting pricing proposals. The carrier must follow the shipper's format exactly to avoid being eliminated from consideration or having bids misinterpreted by the shipper. The pre-defined format also facilitates the bid analysis process for the shipper.

Packaged Bid Proposal

In most bids, carriers provide the most attractive rates in the form of packaged bids. Carriers must review packaged bids carefully before submitting proposals to shippers. The various packaged bid scenarios can become complex, so a careful review is necessary to avoid errors, confusion, or infeasible bid results. After careful review, the carrier has developed the packaged bid proposal shown below.

Carrier Pricing Proposal
Packaged Bids
February 24, 2009

Package	Lane Number	Origin	Destination	Annual Loads	Rate Per Mile
A	3001	Jacksonville, FL	Columbus, OH	179	$ 1.02
	1002	Columbus, OH	Jacksonville, FL	180	$ 1.97
B	3003	Jacksonville, FL	Kansas City, KS	122	$ 1.20
	4003	Kansas City, KS	Jacksonville, FL	120	$ 1.73
C	1001	Columbus, OH	Shreveport, LA	252	$ 1.67
	2002	Shreveport, LA	Columbus, OH	352	$ 1.27
D	4003	Kansas City, KS	Jacksonville, FL	120	$ 1.73
	3001	Jacksonville, FL	Columbus, OH	179	$ 1.03
	1003	Columbus, OH	Kansas City, KS	130	$ 1.76
E	3002	Jacksonville, FL	Shreveport, LA	159	$ 1.08
	2002	Shreveport, LA	Columbus, OH	352	$ 1.27
	1002	Columbus, OH	Jacksonville, FL	180	$ 1.94
F	3001	Jacksonville, FL	Columbus, OH	179	$ 1.00
	1003	Columbus, OH	Kansas City, KS	130	$ 1.73
	4002	Kansas City, KS	Shreveport, LA	62	$ 1.29
	2001	Shreveport, LA	Jacksonville, FL	210	$ 1.82
	3002	Jacksonville, FL	Shreveport, LA	159	$ 1.05

The carrier has provided the shipper with several attractive packaged bid alternatives. The carrier has priced Package F aggressively and hopes to be awarded this bundle of business. Since the carrier's overall goal in the bid is to increase revenues and expand the freight network, the carrier will also be pleased to be awarded any combination of packaged bids and stand-alone lanes.

Case 3: Regional Distribution Bid

The Case

A major retailer operates a regional distribution center in Philadelphia, PA. The distribution facility serves 20 retail stores within a 350 mile radius. Each retail store receives either 2 or 3 scheduled deliveries each week. During busy periods, stores may receive additional deliveries as needed. The carrier is required to maintain a trailer pool of 15 trailers at the distribution facility at all times. The carrier will have additional trailers in transit and dropped at some retail store locations.

Due to space limitations, some stores receive live deliveries. The remaining stores receive drop deliveries. The carrier's drivers are not required to assist in the unloading process at the receiving store location. Carriers are expected to consistently achieve 99.0% on-time delivery service. Each store and the planned number of scheduled weekly deliveries are shown below.

Destination Stores Included in RFP

Store	City	ST	Deliveries	Live/Drop	Store	City	ST	Deliveries	Live/Drop
1001	Philadelphia	PA	2	Live	1011	Drexel Hill	PA	3	Live
1002	Elizabeth	NJ	2	Live	1012	Camden	NJ	2	Drop
1003	Allentown	PA	3	Drop	1013	Brooklyn	NY	2	Drop
1004	Cherry Hill	NJ	3	Live	1014	Bronx	NY	3	Drop
1005	Reading	PA	2	Drop	1015	Syracuse	NY	2	Drop
1006	Lancaster	PA	3	Drop	1016	Manchester	NH	2	Drop
1007	Upper Darby	PA	2	Live	1017	Worcester	MA	2	Drop
1008	Vineland	NJ	3	LIve	1018	Boston	MA	3	Drop
1009	Baltimore	MD	2	Drop	1019	Providence	RI	3	Drop
1010	Newark	NJ	3	Drop	1020	Bridgeport	CT	3	Drop

As part of the bid response, carriers must develop and submit a weekly delivery schedule for the store network based on the rules listed below.

Delivery Schedule Design Parameters

- 2 delivery per week stores must skip a day between deliveries
- 2 delivery per week stores cannot have a Monday and Friday delivery schedule
- 3 delivery per week stores cannot deliver on three consecutive days
- All deliveries must be made between 6 am and 4 pm, Monday through Friday
- The daily delivery count should be reasonably balanced on a daily basis

Carriers are required to submit one-way, flat-rate pricing on a store-by-store basis. Carriers should base pricing on a fuel surcharge peg of $1.60 per gallon. Carriers can expect 7 day payment terms from this shipper. The shipper intends to have one carrier serve the entire outbound delivery network for the facility.

Carrier Analysis

As a preliminary analysis, the carrier must run the miles to each store and map the store network. The map and mileage information will give the carrier a preliminary understanding of the network in preparation for the solution design. The miles to each store are shown below.

Miles to Each Destination Store

\multicolumn{5}{c	}{Destination Store}
Store	City	ST	Miles	Freq
1001	Philadelphia	PA	4	2
1002	Elizabeth	NJ	80	2
1003	Allentown	PA	63	3
1004	Cherry Hill	NJ	12	3
1005	Reading	PA	64	2
1006	Lancaster	PA	79	3
1007	Upper Darby	PA	8	2
1008	Vineland	NJ	41	3
1009	Baltimore	MD	102	2
1010	Newark	NJ	92	3
1011	Drexel Hill	PA	9	3
1012	Camden	NJ	18	2
1013	Brooklyn	NY	95	2
1014	Bronx	NY	107	3
1015	Syracuse	NY	255	2
1016	Manchester	NH	351	2
1017	Worcester	MA	273	2
1018	Boston	MA	312	3
1019	Providence	RI	277	3
1020	Bridgeport	CT	156	3
				50

The miles indicate two distinct store groupings by length of haul. The majority of stores are no more than 107 miles from the distribution center, with 5 stores less than 20 miles from the facility. Six stores are 150 or more miles from the distribution center.

The network has a total of 50 weekly deliveries across all stores. At 50 total deliveries, the ideal delivery schedule will have exactly 10 loads per day across a five day delivery schedule. A balanced schedule is usually ideal for workflow processes in the shipper's distribution center and may also provide some utilization efficiencies for the carrier.

The map of the store network is shown below. Stores are highlighted based on whether the store receives two or three scheduled deliveries per week.

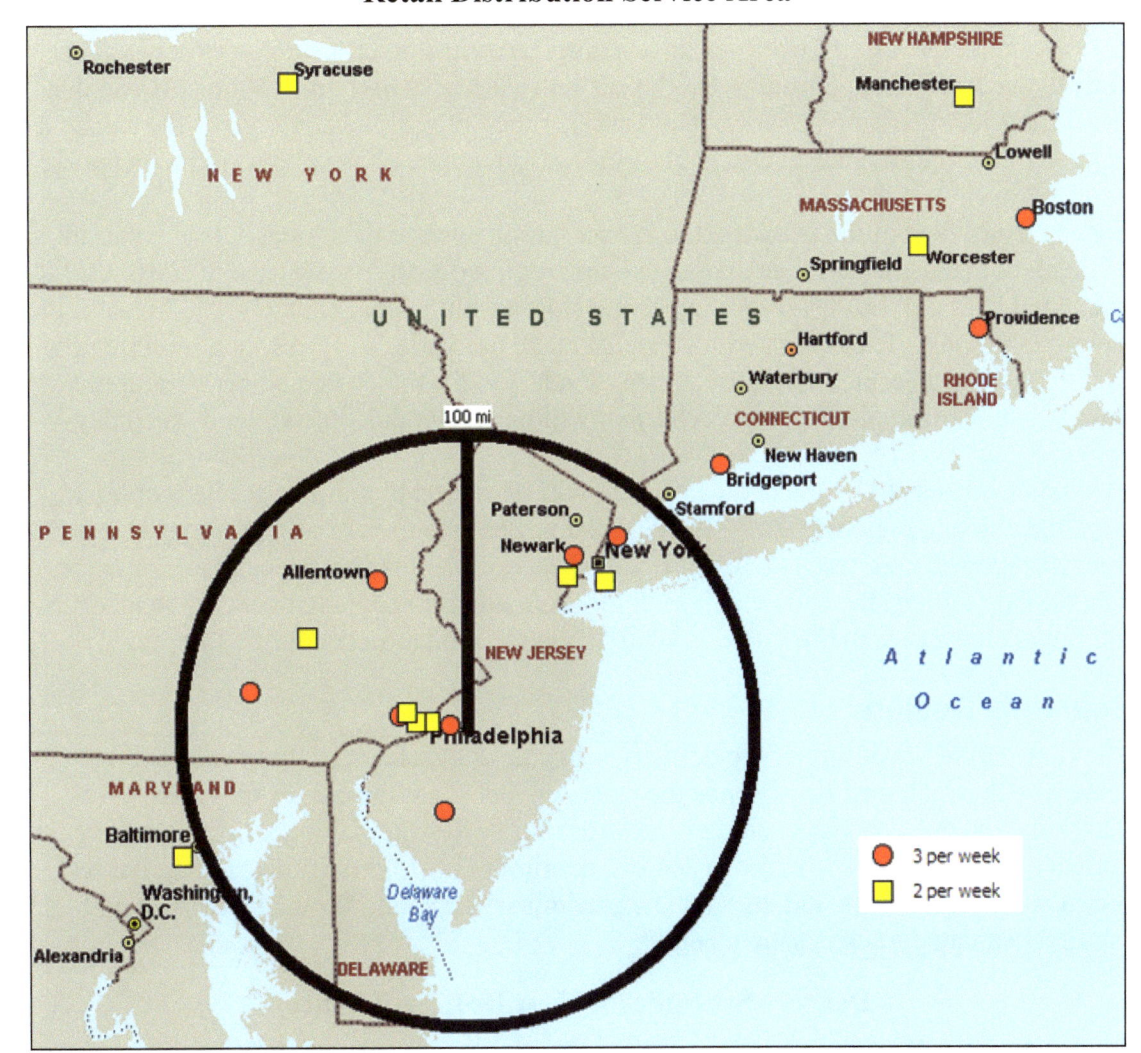

Retail Distribution Service Area

As a general reference, a 100-mile radius circle has been added to the map. The majority of stores are located within 100 miles of the distribution center. Several stores are located relatively far away in such places as Boston, MA and Syracuse, NY. The map gives the carrier a preliminary indication of what type of resources will be needed to serve the facility.

The stores located within 100 miles will likely be served with out-and-back service without any concern for backhauls. However, the longer distance stores are too far away for any carrier to return empty to the distribution facility while still remaining cost competitive. The carrier can quickly see which markets will require backhauls and begin estimating what backhaul opportunities might be available, along with the revenue associated with those backhaul loads.

Carrier Solution Design

In this bid opportunity, the carrier must not only price each lane, but must also develop the weekly delivery schedule for all the stores in the network. While developing the delivery schedule is extra work for the carrier, the control over the delivery schedule is actually an excellent opportunity for the carrier to design a high utilization solution that fits the carrier's existing network. Customizing the delivery schedule gives the carrier a high degree of confidence in the level of utilization that can be expected in the network.

Based on a review of the network, the carrier has decided to develop a hybrid solution utilizing both a dedicated fleet and an existing regional fleet that serves the Northeast. A dedicated fleet will be designed to serve the stores within approximately 100 miles of the shipper's facility. The dedicated trucks will make deliveries to stores then return empty to the distribution center. Because all stores selected for the dedicated network are less than 100 miles from the facility, each truck will be able to deliver two loads each day.

The stores not served by the dedicated fleet will be served by random trucks available from the existing regional fleet. The service for these stores will be basic one-way transportation. These trucks will not return empty to the distribution center. For some destination markets, the carrier will seek to locate other shippers with available loads into the Philadelphia area in order to efficiently source regional trucks to this shipper.

Schedule Design

The first step in the design of the delivery schedule is to select the stores that will be served by the dedicated fleet. Once the stores are selected, the carrier must also determine the delivery days and delivery times for each store. The goal is to set the delivery days and times in order to achieve maximum utilization (miles and deliveries) for each dedicated truck and driver. The preliminary schedule for the stores selected for the first dedicated truck is shown below.

Delivery Schedule for First Dedicated Truck

Destination Store					DELIVERY DAY					Delivery
Store	City	ST	Miles	L/D	Freq	MON	TUE	WED	THU	FRI	Time
1001	Philadelphia	PA	4	Live	2		X		X		7:00
1002	Elizabeth	NJ	80	Live	2		X		X		13:30
1003	Allentown	PA	63	Drop	3	X		X		X	13:00
1004	Cherry Hill	NJ	12	Live	3	X		X		X	6:30

Based on the schedule, the driver will deliver two loads each day. To fill the driver's five day work week, two stores with two deliveries per week and two stores with three deliveries per week were selected. The delivery days for each store were then set to meet the shipper's restrictions and fill the truck's weekly schedule. The delivery times for each store were also set to meet the shipper's delivery window requirement and optimize the truck's daily schedule. The truck will make one morning delivery and one afternoon delivery each day.

The stores were also selected based on length of haul. Each day, the driver has one short delivery and one longer delivery. The complementary length of haul levels balance the workload between days and also provide some level of service protection. When possible, the longer length of haul deliveries are scheduled for later in the day. This approach minimizes the potential service disruptions of traffic, maintenance, and other issues by having the longer return trip scheduled for the end of the workday.

Based on this approach, the carrier continues to develop the schedule for additional dedicated trucks and drivers as shown below.

Delivery Schedule for Dedicated Trucks and Drivers

	Destination Store					DELIVERY DAY					Delivery
	Store	City	ST	Miles	L/D	Freq	MON	TUE	WED	THU	FRI	Time
Truck 1	1001	Philadelphia	PA	4	Live	2		X		X		7:00
	1002	Elizabeth	NJ	80	Live	2		X		X		13:30
	1003	Allentown	PA	63	Drop	3	X		X		X	13:00
	1004	Cherry Hill	NJ	12	Live	3	X		X		X	6:30
Truck 2	1005	Reading	PA	64	Drop	2		X		X		14:00
	1006	Lancaster	PA	79	Drop	3	X		X		X	13:45
	1007	Upper Darby	PA	8	Live	2		X		X		7:00
	1008	Vineland	NJ	41	Live	3	X		X		X	6:00
Truck 3	1009	Baltimore	MD	102	Drop	2		X		X		14:00
	1010	Newark	NJ	92	Drop	3	X		X		X	13:30
	1011	Drexel Hill	PA	9	Live	3	X		X		X	6:00
	1012	Camden	NJ	18	Drop	2		X		X		7:00

The final solution will include three dedicated trucks serving the stores in the schedule shown above. The carrier must now develop the schedule for the remaining stores to be served with one-way regional transportation. The daily delivery schedule for the one-way stores is shown below.

Delivery Schedule for One-Way Stores

Destination Store						DELIVERY DAY					Delivery
Store	City	ST	Miles	L/D	Freq	MON	TUE	WED	THU	FRI	Time
1013	Brooklyn	NY	95	Drop	2		X		X		6:00
1014	Bronx	NY	107	Drop	3	X		X		X	6:00
1015	Syracuse	NY	255	Drop	2		X			X	10:00
1016	Manchester	NH	351	Drop	2	X		X			8:30
1017	Worcester	MA	273	Drop	2		X		X		13:00
1018	Boston	MA	312	Drop	3	X		X	X		10:00
1019	Providence	RI	277	Drop	3	X		X		X	9:30
1020	Bridgeport	CT	156	Drop	3		X		X	X	13:00

The main priorities for scheduling these stores include balancing the facility's schedule and meeting the shipper's delivery day restrictions. The delivery times for each store are then set on a store-by-store basis based on traffic, backhaul availability, and other unique factors. For example, the Brooklyn, NY and Bronx, NY deliveries are scheduled for 6 am. Since these stores are located in a very high traffic area, scheduling the deliveries for

6 am should minimize the amount of traffic delays associated with these stores. The delivery times for the one-way stores in MA, NH, RI and CT are set during mid-morning in order to have the trucks available for other customers immediately after delivery.

Once all considerations have been met, the delivery schedule can be finalized. The full weekly delivery schedule is shown below.

Weekly Delivery Schedule – All Stores

Store	City	ST	Miles	L/D	Freq	MON	TUE	WED	THU	FRI	Delivery Time
1001	Philadelphia	PA	4	Live	2		X		X		7:00
1002	Elizabeth	NJ	80	Live	2		X		X		13:30
1003	Allentown	PA	63	Drop	3	X		X		X	13:00
1004	Cherry Hill	NJ	12	Live	3	X		X		X	6:30
1005	Reading	PA	64	Drop	2		X		X		14:00
1006	Lancaster	PA	79	Drop	3	X		X		X	13:45
1007	Upper Darby	PA	8	Live	2		X		X		7:00
1008	Vineland	NJ	41	Live	3	X		X		X	6:00
1009	Baltimore	MD	102	Drop	2		X		X		14:00
1010	Newark	NJ	92	Drop	3	X		X		X	13:30
1011	Drexel Hill	PA	9	Live	3	X		X		X	6:00
1012	Camden	NJ	18	Drop	2		X		X		7:00
1013	Brooklyn	NY	95	Drop	2		X		X		6:00
1014	Bronx	NY	107	Drop	3	X		X		X	6:00
1015	Syracuse	NY	255	Drop	2		X			X	10:00
1016	Manchester	NH	351	Drop	2	X		X			8:30
1017	Worcester	MA	273	Drop	2		X		X		13:00
1018	Boston	MA	312	Drop	3	X		X	X		10:00
1019	Providence	RI	277	Drop	3	X		X		X	9:30
1020	Bridgeport	CT	156	Drop	3		X		X	X	13:00
Totals					50	10	10	10	10	10	

The delivery schedule is perfectly balanced with 10 deliveries scheduled for each day. The daily schedule for store 1018 in Boston, MA consists of a Monday, Wednesday and Thursday delivery schedule. This small delivery day adjustment allows for the daily schedule to be perfectly balanced. If the business is awarded to the carrier, the shipper and carrier may negotiate minor changes to the schedule to satisfy individual store needs.

The actual development of the delivery schedule may require the carrier to go through a number of different iterations and schedule designs. Even this small schedule for 20 stores could have many different suitable designs. Each carrier will approach the schedule design in a way that meets the carrier's needs while also providing a solution to the shipper with the lowest possible cost.

The last part of the design process is to determine the utilization and other parameters for the three dedicated trucks. The estimated utilization for the dedicated trucks is computed in the table below.

Estimated Dedicated Fleet Utilization

Truck	Store	City	ST	Miles	L/D	Freq	MON	TUE	WED	THU	FRI	Per Store	Total
1	1001	Philadelphia	PA	4	Live	2		X		X		16	
1	1002	Elizabeth	NJ	80	Live	2		X		X		320	
1	1003	Allentown	PA	63	Drop	3	X		X		X	378	
1	1004	Cherry Hill	NJ	12	Live	3	X		X		X	72	786
2	1005	Reading	PA	64	Drop	2		X		X		256	
2	1006	Lancaster	PA	79	Drop	3	X		X		X	474	
2	1007	Upper Darby	PA	8	Live	2		X		X		32	
2	1008	Vineland	NJ	41	Live	3	X		X		X	246	1,008
3	1009	Baltimore	MD	102	Drop	2		X		X		408	
3	1010	Newark	NJ	92	Drop	3	X		X		X	552	
3	1011	Drexel Hill	PA	9	Live	3	X		X		X	54	
3	1012	Camden	NJ	18	Drop	2		X		X		72	1,086

Total Loads: 30   Summary Statistics: Total Weekly Miles: 2,880
Average Fleet Utilization: 960
Estimated Annual Miles: 149,760

The estimated utilization for the fleet is 960 miles per tractor per week. Because of this shipper's needs, the fleet is expected to operate 52 weeks per year. As a result, the total annual miles for the fleet are expected to be 149,760. Substitute drivers will be brought in as needed to provide the regular dedicated drivers with vacation time.

Based on an analysis of the work requirements for this fleet and the local driver market, the carrier plans to budget approximately $850 per week for driver pay. Based on the utilization and pay budget, the carrier has developed a driver pay structure of $50 per load and $0.37 per mile. The expected earnings are shown in the table below.

Driver Pay Design and Cost

Driver / Truck	Loads	Miles	Load	Mile	Loads	Miles	Total
1	10	786	$ 50.00	$ 0.37	$ 500.00	$ 290.82	$ 790.82
2	10	1,008	$ 50.00	$ 0.37	$ 500.00	$ 372.96	$ 872.96
3	10	1,086	$ 50.00	$ 0.37	$ 500.00	$ 401.82	$ 901.82
Totals	30	2,880			$ 1,500.00	$ 1,065.60	$ 2,565.60

Average Weekly Pay Per Driver: $ 855.20

The driver pay system is designed to provide drivers with reasonable financial incentive on both long and short loads. The per-mile rate of pay must be kept at a reasonable level so that driver pay is not excessive should these drivers serve longer loads outside of the core dedicated stores. To balance the workload and income among the drivers, the carrier will also rotate the stores and routes served by each driver on a weekly basis.

Trailer Requirements

The carrier must also estimate the number of trailers required to serve the network. The shipper requires that 15 trailers be dropped at the distribution center at all times. There will also be trailers in transit and trailers dropped at the stores that allow drop deliveries. The estimated total trailer requirement is shown below.

Estimated Trailer Requirements

Location	Trailers
Dropped at Distribution Center	15
In-Transit	7
Dropped at Stores	14
Total Trailers	**36**

The in-transit trailer estimate of 7 units is based on 10 loads per day less the 3 double-turns performed by the dedicated trucks. The figure of 14 units dropped at stores is based on the number of individual stores that allow drop trailers.

As a check figure, the carrier can compute the ratio of total trailers to the average number of loads per day. The calculation of the trailer-to-load ratio is shown below.

$$\frac{\text{Trailer to}}{\text{Load Ratio}} = \frac{\text{Total Trailers}}{\text{Avg. Loads Per Day}} = \frac{36 \text{ trailers}}{10 \text{ loads per day}} = 3.6 \text{ trailers per load}$$

Based on past experience with this shipper, the carrier believes the 3.6 trailers per daily load to be reasonable and consistent with expectations. To provide a small buffer, the carrier will base the pricing on a total requirement of 40 trailers or a 4-to-1 ratio.

Trailer Allocation. Because of the hybrid solution, the carrier must allocate the cost of the trailers to the costs associated with the dedicated fleet and one-way service. For simplification, the carrier has chosen to allocate trailer costs based on the percentage of loads served by each service type as shown below.

Trailer Assignments for Pricing Purposes

Service Type	Loads	% of Loads	Trailers
Dedicated Fleet	30	60%	24
One-Way Service	20	40%	16
Totals	**50**		**40**

The allocation provides the information necessary for including trailer costs in the dedicated pricing model for the three dedicated trucks.

Carrier Pricing and Proposal

Based on the solution design, the carrier must develop a competitive and accurate cost proposal. Because of the hybrid approach, the final pricing will come from two different sources. The dedicated pricing model will be used to determine the cost and pricing for the dedicated stores. For the one-way stores, general guideline pricing for the region will be used to determine the preliminary rates.

Pricing for Dedicated Stores

The dedicated pricing model is used to compute the total revenue needs for the dedicated portion of the network. The design phase of the bid analysis process identified all the key dedicated pricing variables such as tractor counts, trailer counts, utilization, and driver wages. The dedicated pricing model for the three truck fleet is shown below.

Dedicated Pricing Model

Customer Name:	Chapter 14	Fleet Description:	Case Study 3

Fleet Parameters

Number of Tractors	3.00
Backup Tractors	0.00
Number of Drivers	3.00
Utilization (Miles per Tractor per Active Week)	960
Active Fleet Weeks Per Year (max = 52 weeks)	52.0
Total Fleet Annual Miles	149,760
Number of Trailers	24.00
Trailer/Tractor Ratio	8.00

Overhead Costs

Tractor Legalization/Taxes	$ 2,000
Driver Recruiting Costs	$ 3,000
Administration Expenses	$ 5,000
Total Overhead (per tractor per year)	$ 10,000
Direct Staffing (On-site CSR / Offices / Etc.)	$ -
Other Annual Expenses (Total Fleet)	$ 5,000
Initial Start-Up Costs (Total)	$ 7,500

Other Parameters

Driver Rate of Pay (Per Mile or Annual Gross)	$ 44,460.00
Duration of Deal/Contract (in months)	36.0
Average Collection Period (in days)	7.0

Pricing and Analysis

Suggested Rate Per Mile (all miles)	$ 3.4600
Operating Ratio	73.26%
Internal Rate of Return	11.09%

Pro-Forma Income Statement		Fleet Totals Per Mile	Fleet Totals Annual	Per Tractor Weekly	Per Tractor Annual
Total Fleet Miles			149,760	960	49,920
Total Revenue		$3.460	$518,170	$3,322	$172,723
Variable Costs	Assumptions				
Driver Wages	$44,460.00	$0.891	$133,380	$855	$44,460
Fringe Benefits (% of wages)	25.0%	0.223	33,345	214	11,115
Fuel	$0.275	0.275	41,134	264	13,711
Maintenance	$0.110	0.110	16,474	106	5,491
Insurance	$0.100	0.100	14,976	96	4,992
Total Variable Costs		1.598	239,309	1,534	79,770
Fixed Costs	Assumptions				
Tractor Depreciation	$ 16,667	0.334	50,000	$321	$16,667
Trailer Depreciation	$ 2,200	0.353	52,800	338	17,600
Legalization/Recruiting/Admin	$ 10,000	0.200	30,000	192	10,000
On-Site Manager	$ -	0.000	0	0	0
Start Up /Special Equipment	$ 7,500	0.050	7,500	48	2,500
Total Fixed Costs		0.937	140,300	899	46,767
Total Cost		2.535	379,609	2,433	126,536
Operating Profit		$0.93	$138,561	$888	$46,187
Operating Ratio		73.26%	73.26%	73.26%	73.26%

The dedicated pricing model was adjusted for several variables specific to this potential customer. First, the fuel cost was set at $1.60 per gallon to match the shipper's fuel peg.

Also, the average collection period was set to 7 days to reflect the shipper's excellent payment terms. All other costs are based on the carrier's standard costing system. The suggested annual revenue for the fleet is $518,170.

Since this is not an actual dedicated fleet with a typical dedicated fleet contract, pricing must be structured on a per-load or "one-way" basis. The next step is to assign a rate per load to each store served by the dedicated fleet. The dedicated revenues are allocated to each store using the model shown below.

Allocation of Dedicated Revenues to Each Lane

Allocation of Target Revenue to Each Dedicated Lane										

Target Annual Revenue (from pricing model): $ 518,170
Assumption: Fixed Allocation Per Load $ 190.00 $ 296,400
Per Mile Allocation $ 1.481 $ 221,770
Total Allocated Revenue $ 518,170

Store Number	Location	Annual Loads	RT Miles Per Load	Annual Miles	Charge Per Load - Per Load	Charge Per Load - Mileage	Charge Per Load - Total	Total Annual Revenue Validation - Per Load	Total Annual Revenue Validation - Mileage	Total Annual Revenue Validation - Total
1001	Philadelphia, PA	104	8	832	$ 190.00	$ 11.85	$ 201.85	$ 19,760	$ 1,232	$ 20,992
1002	Elizabeth, NJ	104	160	16,640	$ 190.00	$ 236.93	$ 426.93	$ 19,760	$ 24,641	$ 44,401
1003	Allentown, PA	156	126	19,656	$ 190.00	$ 186.59	$ 376.59	$ 29,640	$ 29,107	$ 58,747
1004	Cherry Hill, NJ	156	24	3,744	$ 190.00	$ 35.54	$ 225.54	$ 29,640	$ 5,544	$ 35,184
1005	Reading, PA	104	128	13,312	$ 190.00	$ 189.55	$ 379.55	$ 19,760	$ 19,713	$ 39,473
1006	Lancaster, PA	156	158	24,648	$ 190.00	$ 233.97	$ 423.97	$ 29,640	$ 36,500	$ 66,140
1007	Upper Darby, PA	104	16	1,664	$ 190.00	$ 23.69	$ 213.69	$ 19,760	$ 2,464	$ 22,224
1008	Vineland, NJ	156	82	12,792	$ 190.00	$ 121.43	$ 311.43	$ 29,640	$ 18,943	$ 48,583
1009	Baltimore, MD	104	204	21,216	$ 190.00	$ 302.09	$ 492.09	$ 19,760	$ 31,417	$ 51,177
1010	Newark, NJ	156	184	28,704	$ 190.00	$ 272.47	$ 462.47	$ 29,640	$ 42,506	$ 72,146
1011	Drexel Hill, PA	156	18	2,808	$ 190.00	$ 26.66	$ 216.66	$ 29,640	$ 4,158	$ 33,798
1012	Camden, NJ	104	36	3,744	$ 190.00	$ 53.31	$ 243.31	$ 19,760	$ 5,544	$ 25,304
Totals:		1,560		149,760				$ 296,400	$ 221,770	$ 518,170

This allocation model, explained in greater detail in an earlier chapter, distributes the total required revenue to each store to establish an appropriate per-load rate. The model allocates a flat amount of $190 of cost to each load then allocates the remaining costs on a per-mile basis. In the spreadsheet model, the $190 per load figure can be adjusted up or down until the allocated rate per load amounts achieve the best revenue fit with each different length of haul. The "Total Revenue Validation" section serves to verify that the allocation is accurate and matches the original target revenue before allocation.

Pricing for One-Way Stores

The pricing for the remaining one-way stores can be established through the use of a guideline pricing matrix. The guideline pricing matrix is simply an internal carrier schedule of suggested rates for any origin or destination point. The applicable guideline rate table for the lanes in this bid is shown below.

Guideline Rates		
From: Philadelphia, PA		
Destination State	Rate Per Mile	Minimum Charge
CT	$ 2.60	$ 600.00
MA	$ 2.65	$ 700.00
MD	$ 2.10	$ 500.00
ME	$ 1.55	$ 650.00
NH	$ 2.55	$ 700.00
NJ	$ 1.55	$ 450.00
NY	$ 2.25	$ 500.00
PA	$ 1.85	$ 400.00
RI	$ 2.58	$ 700.00
VA	$ 1.65	$ 500.00

The guideline rates can be applied to the lanes in the bid to determine preliminary rates for each store as shown below.

Application of Guideline Rates to Each Store

Destination Store				Guideline Rates		Effective
Store	City	ST	Miles	Per Mile	Minimum	Rate
1013	Brooklyn	NY	95	$ 2.25	$ 213.75	$ 500.00	$ 500.00
1014	Bronx	NY	107	$ 2.25	$ 240.75	$ 500.00	$ 500.00
1015	Syracuse	NY	255	$ 2.25	$ 573.75	$ 500.00	$ 573.75
1016	Manchester	NH	351	$ 2.55	$ 895.05	$ 700.00	$ 895.05
1017	Worcester	MA	273	$ 2.65	$ 723.45	$ 700.00	$ 723.45
1018	Boston	MA	312	$ 2.65	$ 826.80	$ 700.00	$ 826.80
1019	Providence	RI	277	$ 2.58	$ 714.66	$ 700.00	$ 714.66
1020	Bridgeport	CT	156	$ 2.60	$ 405.60	$ 600.00	$ 600.00

To apply the guideline rates, the first step is to apply the rate per mile and compute the flat charge at the rate per mile. For the first store, 1013 Brooklyn, the rate of $2.25 per mile on 95 miles is a charge of $213.75. The next step is to compare the mileage rate with the minimum charge. For store 1013, the minimum charge is $500. The effective rate is then the higher of the mileage rate or the minimum charge. In the case of store 1013, the minimum of $500 will apply. This same guideline pricing process is repeated for each store in the bid. In many cases, the carrier may choose to adjust the guideline rates up or down slightly based on the operating characteristics of the customer's network. In the case of this bid, the carrier believes the guideline rates are consistent with the requirements of the customer network, so no adjustments are necessary.

Final Pricing Proposal for the Customer

The carrier is now ready to prepare the final pricing document for submission to the potential customer. The finalized proposal is shown below. Rates are rounded to the nearest whole dollar to simplify the contract.

Carrier Rate Proposal
Effective: 10/1/2008
Origin: Philadelphia, PA

Store	City	ST	Miles	Freq	Annual Loads	Rate Per Load	Annual Cost
1001	Philadelphia	PA	4	2	104	$ 202.00	$ 21,008
1002	Elizabeth	NJ	80	2	104	$ 427.00	$ 44,408
1003	Allentown	PA	63	3	156	$ 377.00	$ 58,812
1004	Cherry Hill	NJ	12	3	156	$ 226.00	$ 35,256
1005	Reading	PA	64	2	104	$ 380.00	$ 39,520
1006	Lancaster	PA	79	3	156	$ 424.00	$ 66,144
1007	Upper Darby	PA	8	2	104	$ 214.00	$ 22,256
1008	Vineland	NJ	41	3	156	$ 311.00	$ 48,516
1009	Baltimore	MD	102	2	104	$ 492.00	$ 51,168
1010	Newark	NJ	92	3	156	$ 462.00	$ 72,072
1011	Drexel Hill	PA	9	3	156	$ 217.00	$ 33,852
1012	Camden	NJ	18	2	104	$ 243.00	$ 25,272
1013	Brooklyn **	NY	95	2	104	$ 500.00	$ 52,000
1014	Bronx **	NY	107	3	156	$ 500.00	$ 78,000
1015	Syracuse	NY	255	2	104	$ 574.00	$ 59,696
1016	Manchester	NH	351	2	104	$ 895.00	$ 93,080
1017	Worcester	MA	273	2	104	$ 723.00	$ 75,192
1018	Boston	MA	312	3	156	$ 827.00	$ 129,012
1019	Providence	RI	277	3	156	$ 715.00	$ 111,540
1020	Bridgeport	CT	156	3	156	$ 600.00	$ 93,600
Totals				50	2,600		$ 1,210,404

** NYC Borroughs charge of $250 will also apply.

The pricing design was based on a combination of dedicated pricing for the short haul lanes and guideline pricing for the longer length of haul lanes. Since the pricing is based on two different methods, the carrier must verify that pricing is reasonably consistent between the two methods. The best checkpoint for validation in this case is between stores 1009 Baltimore and 1014 Bronx. These stores have a similar length of haul, so the rates for the two stores should be similar. Baltimore has a rate of $492 and Bronx has a rate of $500, so the rates appear to be consistent across the different pricing methods. The pricing proposal and delivery schedule are now complete and ready to be submitted to the potential customer.

Case 4: Dedicated Fleet with Fixed-Variable Pricing

The Case

A manufacturing company currently operates a 23 truck private fleet used primarily to deliver outbound finished goods to customers within a 200 mile radius of its Chattanooga, TN facility. The company believes the private fleet offers superior service while also providing the shipper with guaranteed capacity to serve this critical transportation segment. In order to focus the management team and other internal resources on core business areas, the company is conducting a dedicated fleet bid to outsource the private fleet to a for-hire carrier. The fleet's current area of service and primary destinations are shown on the map below.

Chattanooga, TN Private Fleet Service Area

The shipper currently owns a fleet of trailers that will continue to be used in this operation. As a result, the carrier will not be required to provide any trailers for the fleet. However, the shipper will ask the carrier to provide a weekly rate for carrier trailers should the need arise for additional equipment. The carrier will be required to provide the tractors and drivers for the fleet. The shipper's existing fleet of trucks is under a lease agreement that expires concurrent with the planned start-up date for the new dedicated fleet contract.

The shipper has gathered the historical shipment information and other operating statistics shown below to provide carriers with an overview of the fleet operation.

Activity	2008 Fleet Activity by Quarter				2008 Totals
	Qrt 1	Qrt 2	Qrt 3	Qrt 4	
Total Miles	416,240	443,680	414,692	451,360	1,725,872
Total Loads	2,365	2,360	2,411	2.480	9,616
Average LOH	88	94	86	91	90
Fleet Size	22	22	23	23	22.5
Utilization	1,455	1,551	1,387	1,510	1,475

Based on a recent internal network analysis and experience with similar fleets at other company facilities, the shipper believes that the fleet is likely to be more productive if managed by an efficient dedicated carrier. As a result, the shipper has asked the carrier to provide fixed-variable dedicated pricing based on the revised fleet size and utilization expectations shown below.

Operating Statistics for Bid Design	
Annual Miles	1,725,972
Annual Loads	9,616
Bid Fleet Size	20
Bid Utilization	1,660

Carriers should provide pricing based on a fleet size of 20 trucks and drivers with a 52 week utilization level of 1,660 miles per tractor per week. The carrier's pricing proposal should be based on a fuel peg of $1.90 per gallon. The carrier will also be required to provide an on-site manager at the facility. The carrier's proposal should include the pricing components outlined below.

Carrier Rate Proposal

Cost Component	Weekly Units	Proposed Rate	Weekly Cost
Fixed Tractor Charge Per Week	20		$ -
Variable Mileage Charge	33,192		$ -
On-Site Manager	1		$ -
Stop-offs	10		$ -
Additional Trailers	0		$ -
Total Weekly Cost			$ -

The carrier must provide the rates as requested. The weekly cost of the proposal will be computed based on the carrier's proposed pricing. The shipper will evaluate proposals primarily on the basis of the total weekly cost. Carriers must also submit a detailed start-up plan in addition to the pricing proposal.

Carrier Analysis

Follow-Up Questions

Since the shipper has provided the fleet size and utilization for the fleet, the carrier is not required to perform any significant design analysis. However, the carrier has submitted a short list of follow-up questions to the shipper. The carrier's questions and the shipper's responses are listed in the table below.

Carrier Follow-Up Questions	
Carrier Question	**Shipper's Response**
Who is responsible for the ongoing maintenance of the shipper's existing trailer fleet?	The carrier is responsible for all normal trailer maintenance costs. The cost of trailer maintenance should be included in the pricing proposal.
What happens if the estimated fleet size of 20 trucks is too low and utilization fails to meet targets?	Since the pricing is in the fixed-variable format, the carrier should be indifferent to reasonable changes in actual utilization. No pricing adjustments will be allowed unless the utilization falls below 1,300 miles.
Do carriers have the option of hiring the existing drivers? Do the drivers currently belong to a union?	Hiring the existing drivers would be ideal. The drivers do not belong to a union. Drivers currently earn between $36,000 and $50,000 per year depending on productivity and experience.
What is the proposed length of the dedicated contract?	The contract will be for 3 years. No rate increases will be considered until after the 3 year term.

Based on the shipper's responses, the carrier has a better understanding of the requirements and expectations. The carrier considers the three year contract term to be reasonable and fair. The carrier must carefully evaluate the impact of the actual fleet size being greater than the planned level of 20 tractors. If the shipper's fleet size target of 20 tractors is not achieved, utilization will not be as high as expected. Regardless of utilization, the carrier's fixed-variable pricing must still provide adequate revenues to achieve profit expectations and fund driver compensation.

The ability to hire the existing drivers will allow the carrier to hire from an experienced pool of drivers. The existing drivers will be familiar with the shipper's requirements and expectations. However, the existing drivers may not be comfortable working under the carrier's work rules and processes. Though not always the case, the carrier will likely hire most of the needed drivers from the shipper's existing drivers. The carrier may also need to hire additional drivers to fill all the driving positions for the fleet.

The carrier cannot automatically assume that the cost of maintaining the shipper's trailers will be the same as maintaining the carrier's normal trailers. The carrier must inspect the shipper's existing trailer fleet to determine the current condition and the expected maintenance requirements. The carrier can then estimate the costs of trailer maintenance and adjust costs and revenues accordingly if necessary.

Utilization and Fleet Size

Although the shipper has provided an estimated fleet size and utilization level, the carrier should still perform some independent analysis to identify the range of potential fleet sizes and utilization levels. The carrier must perform pricing sensitivity analysis to determine the financial impact of different fleet size and utilization scenarios. In the analysis table below, the carrier has expanded the shipper's preliminary information to compute the average loads per driver per day.

Loads Per Driver Per Day Analysis

Activity	Qrt 1	Qrt 2	Qrt 3	Qrt 4	2008 Totals
Total Miles	416,240	443,680	414,692	451,360	1,725,972
Total Loads	2,365	2,360	2,411	2,480	9,616
Average LOH	88	94	86	91	90
Fleet Size	22	22	23	23	22.5
Weekly Utilization	1,455	1,551	1,387	1,510	1,475
Work Days	61	61	61	58	241
Loads Per Driver Per Day	1.76	1.76	1.72	1.86	1.77

The "Loads Per Day" statistic gives the carrier a frame of reference for the amount of productivity that can be expected from each driver. Since this is a short haul, out-and-back fleet, the "Loads Per Day" statistic provides an additional measure of productivity in addition to utilization. The carrier can balance the two productivity statistics to identify reasonable productivity expectations for the fleet. The table below reflects the productivity measures at different potential fleet sizes.

Productivity Across Potential Fleet Size Scenarios

Activity	19.0	20.0	21.0	22.0	22.5	23.0
Total Loads	9,616	9,616	9,616	9,616	9,616	9,616
Total Miles	1,725,972	1,725,972	1,725,972	1,725,972	1,725,972	1,725,972
Utilization	1,747	1,660	1,581	1,509	1,475	1,443
Loads Per Driver Per Day	2.10	2.00	1.90	1.81	1.77	1.73
Miles Per Driver Per Day	377	358	341	326	318	311

The carrier has also added the "Miles Per Driver Per Day" statistic to the analysis. This new statistic is simply the weekly utilization viewed on a daily basis (5 days). Breaking the utilization down to a daily basis is easier to interpret, especially for a short haul fleet of this type. Based on experience with similar operations, the carrier expects the actual fleet size to be between 20 and 23 tractors. The carrier feels that the fleet cannot average more than 2.0 loads per driver per day or 360 miles per day given the length of haul of 90 one-way miles per trip.

Carrier Solution Design

The carrier's solution must be designed in several separate components based on the shipper's required pricing format. Outside of the typical dedicated pricing process, the carrier must determine the rates for stops, the on-site manager, and the extra trailers. The fixed and variable rates for the fleet will be determined using the standard dedicated pricing spreadsheet.

On-Site Manager

As part of the fleet, the carrier is required to provide a full-time fleet manager at the shipper's facility. The carrier has estimated the annual cost and suggested pricing for the fleet manager in the table below.

On-Site Manager Charge		
Base Annual Salary	$	65,000
Fringe Benefits (28%)	$	18,200
Office / Phone / Computer	$	2,450
Contingency	$	1,250
Total Cost	$	86,900
Markup at 7.5%	$	6,518
Suggested Cost to Customer	$	93,418
Weekly Charge to Customer	**$**	**1,796**

The carrier estimates the total annual cost of providing the on-site manager to be $86,900. The final charge to the customer will be $1,796 per week for the on-site manager. The carrier marks up the actual costs by 7.5% to add a small profit. A large markup on a secondary item such as an on-site manager is not necessary. The carrier should earn substantial margins on the core fleet operation, so secondary items such as an on-site manager can safely include smaller margins than direct trucking operations.

Stop Charge

The carrier has an existing contract with the shipper that includes a stop charge of $75 per stop for typical one-way shipments. A portion of this stop charge includes revenues to cover the fixed costs associated with the driving time that is lost during stop-offs. Since the proposed dedicated fleet will be based on a fixed-variable rate structure, the carrier will already be charging the shipper for all of the tractor's work time in the fixed charge per tractor per week. In addition, the shipper's utilization estimates already reflect the impact of the expected stop-offs on utilization, so the base dedicated pricing will automatically provide the appropriate revenue level. As a result, the carrier can discount the existing $75 charge and provide a more attractive cost proposal. Without performing any specific analysis, the carrier has decided to charge $45 per stop for this dedicated fleet proposal to be consistent with other recent proposals for this shipper.[110]

---

[110] Carriers may apply activity-based costing assumptions to adjust the stop charge. In this example, the carrier has reduced the stop charge based on experience and estimates of competitor stop charges.

Extra Trailer Charge

The carrier must also determine an independent charge for extra trailers. The carrier plans to source extra trailers as needed from either a local leasing company or its existing fleet of company-owned trailers. To determine the stand-alone monthly trailer charge, the carrier can apply a cash flow model similar to the model used for dedicated pricing. A simple model for determining the monthly trailer charge based on a required return of 10.0% is shown below.

Cash Flow Model for Monthly Trailer Pricing		0	1	2	3	4	5
Initial Investment (Trailer Cost)		$ (22,000)					
Cash Flows:							
Operating Cash Flow	$ 307		$ 3,678	$ 3,678	$ 3,678	$ 3,678	$ 3,678
Salvage Value of Trailer							$ 13,000
Total Cash Flow		$ (22,000)	$ 3,678	$ 3,678	$ 3,678	$ 3,678	$ 16,678
Present Value of Cash Flows (10%)			$ 3,344	$ 3,040	$ 2,764	$ 2,512	$ 10,356
Total Present Value		$ 22,016					
Net Present Value		$ 16					
Internal Rate of Return		10.0%					

Operating Cash Flow	
Monthly Trailer Charge	$ 370
Depreciation Expense	$ 183
Operating Income	$ 187
Income Tax (34%)	$ 63
Earnings After Tax	$ 123
Plus: Depreciation	$ 183
Operating Cash Flow	**$ 307**

← Calculation of operating cash flow from trailer revenues.

The three assumptions for the model include the initial cost of the trailer, the future salvage value of the trailer, and the number of years of service for the trailer. The carrier can then set a monthly charge for the trailer and convert the monthly rate into annual cash flows. The cash flows from the monthly rate, along with the salvage value of the trailer, are discounted based on a required return of 10.0%. The model then computes the net present value and internal rate of return based on the monthly trailer charge revenues. The carrier can adjust the proposed monthly trailer charge until the target rate of return of 10% is achieved. Because of the very low risk and infrequent activity for this revenue stream, the carrier reduced the required return for this item from 11.0% to 10.0%.

The carrier also checked with two local trailer rental vendors in Chattanooga regarding trailer rental charges. One vendor charged a rate of $355 per month and the second charged $375 per month. Based on these rental rates and the carrier's cash flow analysis, the carrier has decided to propose an extra trailer rate of $364 per month or $84 per trailer per week. The conversion of the monthly rate to a weekly rate is shown below.

Weekly Trailer Rate		
Monthly Rate	$	364.00
Months	x	12
Annual Rate	$	4,368.00
Weeks	÷	52
Weekly Rate	**$**	**84.00**

Fixed-Variable Fleet Pricing

The fixed-variable fleet pricing represents the most important component of the cost proposal. The dedicated fleet will comprise the majority of the shipper's total transportation cost. In addition to the standard cost projections, the carrier must determine the appropriate level of driver pay and estimate the cost of maintaining the shipper's trailers.

The shipper's private fleet drivers currently earn between $36,000 and $50,000 per year based on productivity and experience. The carrier also has a similar dedicated fleet in the area where the drivers earn $40,000 to $45,000 annually based on productivity. Based on these two benchmarks, the carrier will budget $44,000 in annual earnings for each driver. The actual driver pay structure will be designed later in the process.

To determine the estimated cost of maintaining the shipper's trailers, the carrier's maintenance team conducted a thorough inspection of the trailer fleet. The maintenance team concluded that the trailers were in good condition for their age, so maintenance costs should not be much higher than the carrier's existing cost per mile. The carrier will need to maintain certain additional parts in inventory specifically for these trailers. After completing the trailer review, the carrier has decided to add 2 cents to the standard maintenance cost per mile. The carrier's primary operating cost assumptions are shown below. Other overhead cost assumptions are shown in the pricing model that follows.

Base Operating Cost Assumptions

Equipment Depreciation and Values	
Tractors	
Initial Cost	$100,000
Expected Salvage / Trade Value	$50,000
Depreciation Term (Years)	3.00
Annual Depreciation Per Unit	**$16,667**
Monthly Depreciation Per Unit	$ 1,389

Other Operating Costs		
Fuel Costs		
Cost Per Gallon		$1.900
Miles Per Gallon		6.0
Fuel Tax	$	0.008
Fuel Cost Per Mile		**$0.325**

Trailers	
Initial Cost	$22,000
Expected Salvage / Trade Value	$11,000
Depreciation Term (Years)	5.00
Annual Depreciation Per Unit	**$2,200**
Monthly Depreciation Per Unit	$ 183

Other Operating Costs	
Insurance Cost Per Mile	$0.100
Maintenance Cost Per Mile	$0.130
Fringe Benefits (% of Driver Pay)	25.0%

The maintenance cost of $0.13 per mile reflects the additional cost to maintain the shipper's trailers. The fuel cost is set at $1.90 per gallon based on the shipper's fuel peg. All other costs are standard for this carrier.

Preliminary Fixed-Variable Pricing. The preliminary dedicated fleet cost forecast and pricing is shown below. The pricing is based on the shipper's fleet size of 20 drivers and utilization of 1,660 miles per tractor per week. The carrier has a minimum required return on investment of 11.0%. However, because of the potential utilization risk, the carrier has chosen to apply a required return of 14.0% to this particular fleet.

Dedicated Pricing Model

Customer Name:	Chapter 14	Fleet Description:	Case Study 4

Fleet Parameters

Number of Tractors	20.00
Backup Tractors	0.00
Number of Drivers	20.00
Utilization (Miles per Tractor per Active Week)	1,660
Active Fleet Weeks Per Year (max = 52 weeks)	52.0
Total Fleet Annual Miles	1,726,400
Number of Trailers	0.00
Trailer/Tractor Ratio	0.00

Overhead Costs

Tractor Legalization/Taxes	$ 2,000
Driver Recruiting Costs	$ 3,000
Administration Expenses	$ 5,000
Total Overhead (per tractor per year)	$ 10,000
Direct Staffing (On-site CSR / Offices / Etc.)	$ -
Other Annual Expenses (Total Fleet)	$ 5,000
Initial Start-Up Costs (Total)	$ 7,500

Other Parameters

Driver Rate of Pay (Per Mile or Annual Gross)	$ 44,000.00
Duration of Deal/Contract (in months)	36.0
Average Collection Period (in days)	30.0

Pricing and Analysis

Suggested Rate Per Mile (all miles)	$ 1.7300
Operating Ratio	87.00%
Internal Rate of Return	14.15%

Pro-Forma Income Statement		Fleet Totals Per Mile	Fleet Totals Annual	Per Tractor Weekly	Per Tractor Annual
Total Fleet Miles			1,726,400	1,660	86,320
Total Revenue		$1.730	$2,986,672	$2,872	$149,334
Variable Costs	Assumptions				
Driver Wages	$44,000.00	$0.510	$880,000	$846	$44,000
Fringe Benefits (% of wages)	25.0%	0.127	220,000	212	11,000
Fuel	$0.325	0.325	560,505	539	28,025
Maintenance	$0.130	0.130	224,432	216	11,222
Insurance	$0.100	0.100	172,640	166	8,632
Total Variable Costs		1.192	2,057,577	1,978	102,879
Fixed Costs	Assumptions				
Tractor Depreciation	$ 16,667	0.193	333,333	$321	$16,667
Trailer Depreciation	$ 2,200	0.000	0	0	0
Legalization/Recruiting/Admin	$ 10,000	0.116	200,000	192	10,000
On-Site Manager	$ -	0.000	0	0	0
Start Up /Special Equipment	$ 7,500	0.004	7,500	7	375
Total Fixed Costs		0.313	540,833	520	27,042
Total Cost		1.505	2,598,410	2,498	129,920
Operating Profit		$0.22	$388,262	$373	$19,413
Operating Ratio		87.00%	87.00%	87.00%	87.00%

The carrier has priced the fleet at $1.73 per mile or $2,986,672 in annual revenue. No trailer costs are included since the trailers are provided by the shipper. The next step for the carrier is to allocate this revenue to the fixed and variable pricing components.

The table below shows the allocation of the total annual revenue into the fixed and variable pricing components. The carrier has chosen to allocate 85% of driver wages and 60% of operating profits to the variable rate. The remaining balance of these revenues is allocated to the weekly fixed charge.

Determination of Fixed and Variable Rate Components

Dedicated Pricing Model
Fixed / Variable Pricing
Chapter 14 - Case Study 4

Enter a percentage in the yellow cells to indicate the portion of each item to allocate to each pricing component.

Allocation	Variable	Fixed
Driver Wages	85%	15%
Operating Profit	60%	40%

	Total Revenue Allocation			Fixed / Variable Pricing		
	Fleet	Variable	Fixed	Variable	Fixed Per Truck	
Revenue/Cost Components	Totals	Rate	Rate	Per Mile	Per Year	Per Week
Driver Wages	$ 880,000	$ 748,000	$ 132,000	$ 0.433	$ 6,600	$ 127
Fringe Benefits (% of wages)	$ 220,000	$ 187,000	$ 33,000	$ 0.108	$ 1,650	$ 32
Fuel	$ 560,505	$ 560,505	$ -	$ 0.325	$ -	$ -
Maintenance	$ 224,432	$ 224,432	$ -	$ 0.130	$ -	$ -
Insurance	$ 172,640	$ 172,640	$ -	$ 0.100	$ -	$ -
Total Variable Costs	$ 2,057,577	$ 1,892,577	$ 165,000	1.096	$ 8,250	$ 159
Tractor Depreciation	$ 333,333	$ -	$ 333,333	$ -	$ 16,667	$ 321
Trailer Depreciation	$ -	$ -	$ -	$ -	$ -	$ -
Legalization/Recruiting/Admin	$ 200,000	$ -	$ 200,000	$ -	$ 10,000	$ 192
On-Site Manager	$ -	$ -	$ -	$ -	$ -	$ -
Start Up /Special Equipment	$ 7,500	$ -	$ 7,500	$ -	$ 375	$ 7
Total Fixed Costs	$ 540,833	$ -	$ 540,833	$ -	$ 27,042	$ 520
Operating Profit	$ 388,262	$ 232,957	$ 155,305	$ 0.135	$ 7,765	$ 149
Total Desired Revenue	$ 2,986,672	$ 2,125,534	$ 861,138	**$ 1.231**	**$43,057**	**$828**

Minimum Weekly Charge	Annual	Per Truck Per Week		Final Rates:	
Base Fixed Charge		$ 828		Fixed:	$ 828
Plus: Variable Driver Wages	$ 935,000	$ 899		Variable:	$ 1.231
Plus: Profit on Driver Wages	$ 115,089	$ 111			
Minimum Charge Per Truck Per Week		**$ 1,838**			

Revenue Verification	Rate	Annual Units	Annual Revenue
Fixed Charge Per Tractor Per Week	$ 828	1,040	$ 861,138
Variable Charge Per Mile	$ 1.231	1,726,400	$ 2,125,534
Total Annual Revenue			**$ 2,986,672**

The current model reflects a variable rate of $1.23 per mile and a fixed charge per tractor per week of $828. Because the carrier is relatively uncertain about the fleet size and utilization, the carrier must validate that the pricing is profitable across a variety of fleet size scenarios. The fleet size sensitive analysis is presented in the next section.

Based on the proposed fixed-variable pricing, the table below illustrates the financial impact of different fleet sizes and utilization levels. The worst case scenario is based on a fleet size of 23 units and a utilization level of 1,250 miles per week.

Dedicated Pricing Model - Sensitivity Analysis

Customer Name:	Chapter 14	Fleet Description:	Case Study 4

Other Parameters

Driver Rate of Pay (Per Mile or Annual Gross)	$ 44,000.00
Duration of Deal/Contract (in months)	36.0
Average Collection Period (in days)	30.0
Additional assumtions shown by scenario below.	

Notes:
Same annual miles in each scenario. Number of trucks is adjusted based on expectations.

Overhead Costs

Tractor Legalization/Taxes	$ 2,000
Driver Recruiting Costs	$ 3,000
Administration Expenses	$ 5,000
Total Overhead (per tractor per year)	$ 10,000
Direct Staffing (On-site CSR / Etc.)	$ -
Other Annual Expenses (Total Fleet)	$ 5,000
Initial Start-Up Costs (Total)	$ 7,500

Pro-forma Income Statements		Worst Case Per Mile	Worst Case Annual	Expected Per Mile	Expected Annual	Best Case Per Mile	Best Case Annual
Scenario Assumptions							
Number of Tractors			23.00		21.00		20.00
Number of Drivers			23.00		21.00		20.00
Number of Trailers			0.00		0.00		0.00
Utilization			1,250		1,581		1,660
Active Fleet Weeks Per Year (max = 52 weeks)			52.0		52.0		52.0
Total Fleet Miles			1,495,000		1,726,400		1,726,400
Fixed Rate	$ 828.00		$ 990,288		$ 904,176		$ 861,120
Variable Rate	$ 1.23		$ 1,838,850		$ 2,123,472		$ 2,123,472
Total Revenue		$1.892	$ 2,829,138	$1.754	$ 3,027,648	$1.729	$ 2,984,592
Variable Costs	Assumptions						
Driver Wages	$44,000.00	$0.677	$1,012,000	$0.535	$924,000	$0.510	$880,000
Fringe Benefits (% of wages)	25.0%	$0.169	253,000	$0.134	231,000	$0.127	220,000
Fuel	$0.325	$0.325	485,377	$0.325	560,505	$0.325	560,505
Maintenance	$0.130	$0.130	194,350	$0.130	224,432	$0.130	224,432
Insurance	$0.100	$0.100	149,500	$0.100	172,640	$0.100	172,640
Total Variable Costs		$1.401	2,094,227	$1.224	2,112,577	$1.192	2,057,577
Fixed Costs	Assumptions						
Tractor Depreciation	$ 16,667	$0.256	383,333	$0.203	350,000	$0.193	333,333
Trailer Depreciation	$ 2,200	$0.000	0	$0.000	0	$0.000	0
Legalization/Recruiting/Admin	$ 10,000	$0.154	230,000	$0.122	210,000	$0.116	200,000
On-Site Manager	$ -	$0.000	0	$0.000	0	$0.000	0
Start Up /Special Equipment	$ 7,500	$0.005	7,500	$0.004	7,500	$0.004	7,500
Total Fixed Costs		$0.415	620,833	$0.329	567,500	$0.313	540,833
Total Cost		$1.816	2,715,060	$1.552	2,680,077	$1.505	2,598,410
Operating Profit		$0.076	$114,078	$0.201	$347,571	$0.224	$386,182
Operating Ratio			95.97%		88.52%		87.06%

Each scenario is based on the proposed rates of $1.23 per mile and $828 per tractor per week. The expected scenario is based on 21 tractors instead of the shipper's fleet size of 20 units. The shipper's design of 20 tractors and a 1,660 utilization level is actually reflected in the best case scenario. The worst case scenario shows an expected operating ratio of 95.97%. Since this operating ratio is unsatisfactory, the carrier must adjust the fixed-variable pricing design to protect against poor profitability under the worst case scenario.

Final Fixed-Variable Pricing. The carrier must revise the allocation of revenue between the fixed and variable pricing components to protect profitability in low utilization scenarios. The proposed reallocation of revenues among the two pricing components is shown below.

Revised Determination of Fixed and Variable Rate Components

Dedicated Pricing Model *Fixed / Variable Pricing* Chapter 14 - Case Study 4	Enter a percentage in the yellow cells to indicate the portion of each item to allocate to each pricing component.		
	Allocation	Variable	Fixed
	Driver Wages	30%	70%
	Operating Profit	30%	70%

	Total Revenue Allocation			Fixed / Variable Pricing		
	Fleet	Variable	Fixed	Variable	Fixed Per Truck	
Revenue/Cost Components	Totals	Rate	Rate	Per Mile	Per Year	Per Week
Driver Wages	$ 880,000	$ 264,000	$ 616,000	$ 0.153	$ 30,800	$ 592
Fringe Benefits (% of wages)	$ 220,000	$ 66,000	$ 154,000	$ 0.038	$ 7,700	$ 148
Fuel	$ 560,505	$ 560,505	$ -	$ 0.325	$ -	$ -
Maintenance	$ 224,432	$ 224,432	$ -	$ 0.130	$ -	$ -
Insurance	$ 172,640	$ 172,640	$ -	$ 0.100	$ -	$ -
Total Variable Costs	$ 2,057,577	$ 1,287,577	$ 770,000	$ 0.746	$ 38,500	$ 740
Tractor Depreciation	$ 333,333	$ -	$ 333,333	$ -	$ 16,667	$ 321
Trailer Depreciation	$ -	$ -	$ -	$ -	$ -	$ -
Legalization/Recruiting/Admin	$ 200,000	$ -	$ 200,000	$ -	$ 10,000	$ 192
On-Site Manager	$ -	$ -	$ -	$ -	$ -	$ -
Start Up /Special Equipment	$ 7,500	$ -	$ 7,500	$ -	$ 375	$ 7
Total Fixed Costs	$ 540,833	$ -	$ 540,833	$ -	$ 27,042	$ 520
Operating Profit	$ 388,262	$ 116,479	$ 271,783	$ 0.067	$ 13,589	$ 261
Total Desired Revenue	$ 2,986,672	$ 1,404,055	$ 1,582,617	**$ 0.813**	**$79,131**	**$1,522**

Minimum Weekly Charge	Annual	Per Truck Per Week		**Final Rates:**	
Base Fixed Charge		$ 1,522		Fixed:	$ 1,522
Plus: Variable Driver Wages	$ 330,000	$ 317		Variable:	$ 0.813
Plus: Profit on Driver Wages	$ 29,853	$ 29			
Minimum Charge Per Truck Per Week		**$ 1,868**			

Revenue Verification	Rate	Annual Units	Annual Revenue
Fixed Charge Per Tractor Per Week	$ 1,522	1,040	$ 1,582,617
Variable Charge Per Mile	$ 0.813	1,726,400	$ 1,404,055
Total Annual Revenue			**$ 2,986,672**

In the revised pricing design, only 30% of driver wages and profits are allocated to the variable rate per mile. The revised allocation of revenues results in a reduced rate per mile and an increased fixed charge per week. The fixed charge is increased from $828 per week to $1,522 per week. The variable charge is reduced from $1.23 per mile to $0.81 per mile. These changes make the carrier's revenue far more consistent across different utilization levels. The carrier can now apply these rates to the sensitivity analysis to estimate profitability across the potential scenarios.

The updated sensitivity analysis based on the new fixed-variable pricing structure is shown below.

Dedicated Pricing Model - Sensitivity Analysis

Customer Name:	Chapter 14	Fleet Description:	Case Study 4

Other Parameters

Driver Rate of Pay (Per Mile or Annual Gross)	$ 44,000.00
Duration of Deal/Contract (in months)	36.0
Average Collection Period (in days)	30.0
Additional assumtions shown by scenario below.	

Notes: Same annual miles in each scenario. Number of trucks is adjusted based on expectations.

Overhead Costs

Tractor Legalization/Taxes	$ 2,000
Driver Recruiting Costs	$ 3,000
Administration Expenses	$ 5,000
Total Overhead (per tractor per year)	$ 10,000
Direct Staffing (On-site CSR / Etc.)	$ -
Other Annual Expenses (Total Fleet)	$ 5,000
Initial Start-Up Costs (Total)	$ 7,500

Pro-forma Income Statements		Worst Case Per Mile	Worst Case Annual	Expected Per Mile	Expected Annual	Best Case Per Mile	Best Case Annual
Scenario Assumptions							
Number of Tractors			23.00		21.00		20.00
Number of Drivers			23.00		21.00		20.00
Number of Trailers			0.00		0.00		0.00
Utilization			1,250		1,581		1,660
Active Fleet Weeks Per Year (max = 52 weeks)			52.0		52.0		52.0
Total Fleet Miles			1,495,000		1,726,400		1,726,400
Fixed Rate	$ 1,522.00		$ 1,820,312		$ 1,662,024		$ 1,582,880
Variable Rate	$ 0.81		$ 1,210,950		$ 1,398,384		$ 1,398,384
Total Revenue		$2.028	$ 3,031,262	$1.773	$ 3,060,408	$1.727	$ 2,981,264
Variable Costs	Assumptions						
Driver Wages	$44,000.00	$0.677	$1,012,000	$0.535	$924,000	$0.510	$880,000
Fringe Benefits (% of wages)	25.0%	$0.169	253,000	$0.134	231,000	$0.127	220,000
Fuel	$0.325	$0.325	485,377	$0.325	560,505	$0.325	560,505
Maintenance	$0.130	$0.130	194,350	$0.130	224,432	$0.130	224,432
Insurance	$0.100	$0.100	149,500	$0.100	172,640	$0.100	172,640
Total Variable Costs		$1.401	2,094,227	$1.224	2,112,577	$1.192	2,057,577
Fixed Costs	Assumptions						
Tractor Depreciation	$ 16,667	$0.256	383,333	$0.203	350,000	$0.193	333,333
Trailer Depreciation	$ 2,200	$0.000	0	$0.000	0	$0.000	0
Legalization/Recruiting/Admin	$ 10,000	$0.154	230,000	$0.122	210,000	$0.116	200,000
On-Site Manager	$ -	$0.000	0	$0.000	0	$0.000	0
Start Up /Special Equipment	$ 7,500	$0.005	7,500	$0.004	7,500	$0.004	7,500
Total Fixed Costs		$0.415	620,833	$0.329	567,500	$0.313	540,833
Total Cost		$1.816	2,715,060	$1.552	2,680,077	$1.505	2,598,410
Operating Profit		$0.212	$316,202	$0.220	$380,331	$0.222	$382,854
Operating Ratio			89.57%		87.57%		87.16%

Based on the revised fixed-variable rate structure, the financial results are far more consistent across each potential fleet size scenario. The revenues in the previous pricing structure were highly dependent upon utilization levels to achieve profitability. By increasing the fixed weekly charge, the carrier's revenues become more consistent across different utilization levels. Based on these results, the carrier's final decision is to price the fleet at $1,522 per tractor per week and $0.81 per mile.

Carrier Pricing and Proposal

Pricing Proposal

Based on the solution design and detailed pricing analysis, the carrier's final rate proposal is shown below. In the final proposal, the fixed and variable rates are rounded for simplification. The overall revenue effects of the rounding are immaterial to both the carrier and the shipper.

Dedicated Fleet Proposal
December 10, 2009

Carrier Rate Proposal

Cost Component	Weekly Units	Proposed Rate	Weekly Cost
Fixed Tractor Charge Per Week	20	$ 1,522.00	$ 30,440.00
Variable Mileage Charge	33,192	$ 0.81	$ 26,885.52
On-Site Manager	1	$ 1,796.49	$ 1,796.49
Stop-offs	10	$ 45.00	$ 450.00
Additional Trailers (Weekly Rate)	0	$ 84.00	$ 0.00
Total Weekly Cost			**$ 59,572.01**

The total weekly cost is based on the shipper's format and operating assumptions. If the fleet size and utilization change from the shipper's assumptions, the carrier's revenues will also change. The on-site manager revenue remains constant regardless of the fleet size. Separating the on-site manager charge from the fixed and variable rates protects both the shipper and the carrier from cost and revenue gaps when the actual fleet size differs from the original pricing design.[111]

The majority of the carrier's revenue is generated by the fixed and variable rates for the fleet. While the accessorial rates for the secondary activities are important, the most important pricing consideration by far is the direct fixed-variable rates for the fleet. The carrier has intentionally kept the rates for the secondary items as low as possible to increase the attractiveness of the proposal. Since these items will comprise a very small percentage of the total revenue, the rates on these items include minimal profit margins.

---

[111] A previous chapter provides a detailed breakdown of the risks of including on-site management costs within the dedicated rate components.

Start-Up Implementation Plan

As part of the proposal, the carrier must also provide a detailed start-up plan. The highlights of the carrier's start-up plan are shown in the implementation schedule below. For space considerations, the timeline as shown is condensed compared to an actual schedule. The scheduled start date for the fleet is Monday, February 22nd.

Implementation Schedule

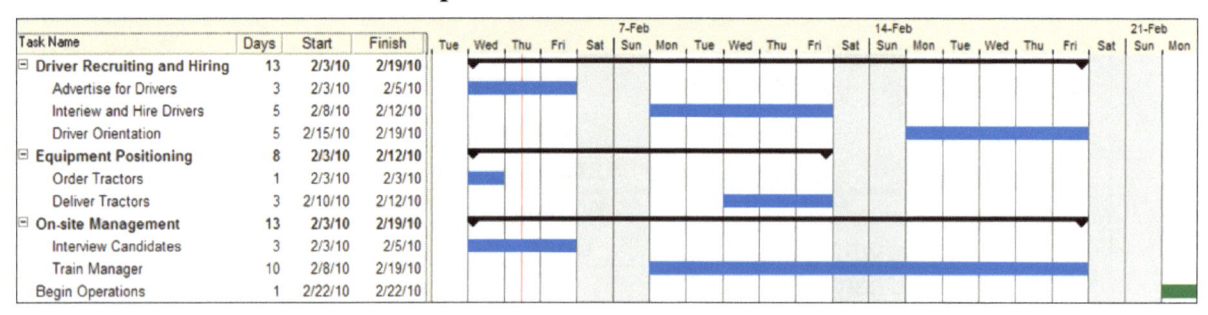

Task Name	Days	Start	Finish
Driver Recruiting and Hiring	13	2/3/10	2/19/10
Advertise for Drivers	3	2/3/10	2/5/10
Interview and Hire Drivers	5	2/8/10	2/12/10
Driver Orientation	5	2/15/10	2/19/10
Equipment Positioning	8	2/3/10	2/12/10
Order Tractors	1	2/3/10	2/3/10
Deliver Tractors	3	2/10/10	2/12/10
On-site Management	13	2/3/10	2/19/10
Interview Candidates	3	2/3/10	2/5/10
Train Manager	10	2/8/10	2/19/10
Begin Operations	1	2/22/10	2/22/10

The implementation schedule includes several common steps for implementing a dedicated fleet or other transportation solution. In reality, an actual dedicated fleet start-up plan would have more detailed steps and take place over a period longer than three weeks. Each individual fleet start-up plan will have unique tasks and events specific to the requirements of the fleet.

CHAPTER 15: Key Concepts for Shippers

The focus of this chapter is on truckload transportation concepts that apply specifically to shippers. The concepts will assist the shipper in the process of effectively managing truckload transportation operations and costs. The greater the shipper is able to understand the carrier business model, the more effective the shipper will be at negotiating with carriers, complying with the needs of carriers, and managing overall transportation costs. This chapter will introduce a number of concepts that combine carrier expertise with common shipper challenges and decisions.[112]

Shipper Transportation Cost Measurements

Every shipper has a unique network of distribution centers, products, customers, and service platforms. Many shippers also have very specific transportation requirements and unique network characteristics. Most shippers also have internal methods by which truckload transportation costs are measured, benchmarked and allocated. The goal of these internal transportation cost tracking methods is to measure costs, explain variances in costs, and identify opportunities to reduce costs.

Because transportation networks are extremely dynamic and complex, shippers sometimes develop cost measurements that don't accurately reflect the true cost dynamics of the network, or even worse, that provide misleading cost information. Several common shipper transportation cost measurements are listed below.

| Common Shipper Transportation Cost Metrics ||||
Transportation Cost Measurement	Calculation	Strength	Weakness
Cost Per Mile	Total Cost ÷ Total Miles	Simplicity Easy to Understand	Ignores Many Critical Factors
Cost Per Unit of Product	Total Cost ÷ Units of Product	Simplicity Relates Easily to Core Business	Ignores Distance and Volume of Product Per Load
Cost Per Unit of Product Per Mile	Total Cost ÷ Units of Product ÷ Total Miles	Considers Relative Distance in Cost Metric	Difficult to Interpret and Compare

Shippers often use metrics of this type to measure cost performance, set transportation cost goals, and make critical business decisions. While each measure provides useful information, the shipper must keep many other operating factors in mind before reaching any final conclusions about the cost performance of the transportation network. When these measures are used to compare shipper facilities in different locations with different products and networks, the relative results can be particularly misleading and inaccurate.

---
[112] Readers will get much greater value from the concepts in this chapter after first reviewing all other chapters in this book.

In most cases, the shipper's goal should be to minimize total transportation costs and not to minimize a particular measurement of transportation costs. Shipping managers that make decisions and design solutions based strictly on a discrete goal for a certain measurement are at risk of making decisions that will only *appear* to reduce transportation costs. Certain initiatives intended to decrease transportation costs may actually result in increased costs. Those decisions and network changes may not be in the best interest of the organization as a whole and may actually reduce the shipper's overall profits. The examples and illustrations that follow will show how these cost measurements can be misleading and lead to poor decisions.

Cost Per Mile

Cost per mile is a useful measure when applied and interpreted correctly. However, when other network operating factors are not also considered, comparing cost per mile trends and relative costs among facilities can be very misleading. The measurement program must be designed and interpreted carefully in order to avoid inaccurate conclusions. Cost per mile is particularly sensitive to average length of haul levels and market pricing conditions.

Length of Haul. In the majority of cases, the most critical consideration with respect to cost per mile analysis is length of haul. A facility with a longer length of haul will typically have a lower cost per mile than a facility with a much shorter length of haul. The example below compares the transportation costs of two facilities with significantly different average length of haul levels.

Cost Per Mile Comparison by Facility

Transportation Cost Per Mile by Facility	Facility A	Facility B
Total Shipments	1,000	1,000
Average Length of Haul	300	500
Total Miles	300,000	500,000
Total Transportation Cost	$ 750,000	$ 1,000,000
Average Cost Per Shipment	$ 750	$ 1,000
Average Cost Per Mile	**$ 2.50**	**$ 2.00**

The table shows that Facility B has a much lower cost per mile than Facility A. If cost per mile was the only factor considered by management in evaluating cost performance, Facility B would be considered more cost efficient than Facility A. However, Facility A has a lower total transportation cost than Facility B, mainly because of the lower average length of haul and fewer total miles.

The only meaningful conclusion that the shipper's management can reach from this information is that the difference in cost per mile for the two facilities is, at least in large part, a function of the length of haul difference between the facilities. There is no specific information to indicate that one facility has outperformed the other in terms of transportation cost efficiency as measured by the cost per mile metric. Facility B may be in a poor location relative to its customer base, which increases length of haul. The longer length of haul results in a higher total transportation cost but a lower cost per mile.

Market Conditions. A second factor that should be considered in comparing cost per mile for multiple facilities is each facility's general market type. If Facility A is located in a strong headhaul market and Facility B is located in a severe backhaul market, the cost per mile measurements for each facility will be difficult to compare.[113] Consider the example for the two facilities shown below.

Cost Per Mile Comparison by Facility

Transportation Cost Per Mile by Facility	Facility B	Facility H
Total Shipments	1,000	1,000
Average Length of Haul	700	700
Total Miles	700,000	700,000
Total Transportation Cost	$ 1,225,000	$ 1,715,000
Average Cost Per Shipment	$ 1,225	$ 1,715
Average Cost Per Mile	**$ 1.75**	**$ 2.45**

In this example, Facility B has a much lower cost per mile than Facility H. However, both facilities have the exact same length of haul. The primary reason for the difference in cost per mile is that Facility B is located in a backhaul market and Facility H is located in a headhaul market. The difference in cost per mile is related primarily to the prevailing markets rates in each market, not any particular efficiency created by Facility B's management or transportation providers.

While the origin market is a key factor influencing cost per mile, the market characteristics of the various destination markets could also influence a facility's cost per mile. For example, a facility that ships often into backhaul markets will likely have a higher cost per mile than a facility that ships more often into headhaul markets. Management should take market type into account when interpreting per-mile cost performance for a facility or group of facilities.

---

[113] One-way headhaul markets typically have higher than average rate per mile levels across all distances while one-way backhaul markets typically have lower than average rate per mile levels across all distances.

Trend Analysis. Another important consideration for evaluating the cost per mile measurement is trend analysis. Consider the example below.

Quarterly Transportation Costs – Facility A

Transportation Cost Per Mile Facility A	Q1	Q2	Q3	Q4	YTD Totals
Total Shipments	1,000	1,000	1,000	1,000	4,000
Average Length of Haul	300	340	380	420	360
Total Miles	300,000	340,000	380,000	420,000	1,440,000
Total Transportation Cost	$ 750,000	$ 816,000	$ 874,000	$ 924,000	$ 3,364,000
Average Cost Per Shipment	$ 750	$ 816	$ 874	$ 924	$ 841
Average Cost Per Mile	**$ 2.50**	**$ 2.40**	**$ 2.30**	**$ 2.20**	**$ 2.34**

Notice that the cost per mile for Facility A declines steadily from Quarter 1 through Quarter 4. If the evaluation of transportation cost performance is based exclusively on cost per mile, this facility appears to be making significant improvements in cost. However, the facility's total transportation costs have increased each quarter without any increase in the number of total shipments (1,000 shipments in each quarter). The increase in length of haul has caused total transportation costs to increase while causing a corresponding decrease in cost per mile. All other things being equal, this facility's costs have increased despite the significant decrease in transportation cost per mile.

Quarterly Cost Per Mile and Length of Haul – Facility A

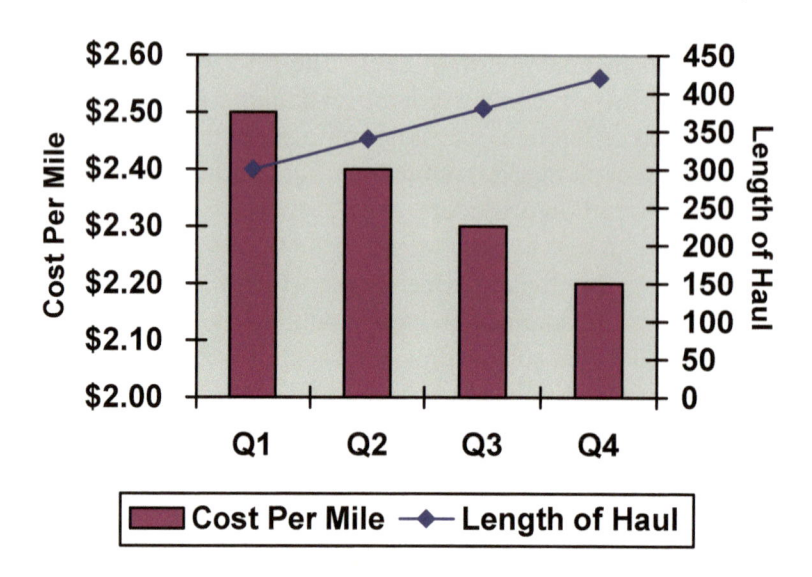

The graph above clearly indicates that as length of haul has increased, cost per mile has declined. When evaluating and comparing transportation costs and per-mile costs, shippers must be certain that key transportation variables such as length of haul have not changed before reaching any conclusions about cost per mile performance.

Cost Per Unit of Product

Cost per unit of product is a critical internal measure for many shippers, especially manufacturing companies. Each shipper will utilize a cost-per-unit measure that is appropriate for their operation. These cost-per-unit measures are very effective when measuring the actual costs of producing a product such as direct materials, direct labor, and manufacturing overhead. Shippers will use these cost-per-unit measurements to compare cost performance and measure efficiency between different facilities or manufacturing plants. Shippers will often use this cost-per-unit concept to measure transportation costs in much the same way.

Because of the dynamics of a transportation network, a cost-per-unit approach is inherently risky when comparing and planning transportation costs. The transportation cost per unit, based on periodic accounting statements, is important product-related information for the manufacturer. However, the transportation cost per unit, particularly when based purely on accounting information, is not always an accurate indication of the cost effectiveness of transportation management. Listed below are several common factors that impact the transportation cost per unit that must be evaluated along with accounting information.

Transportation Cost Per Unit Variables			
Network Variable	**Transportation Cost Impact**		
	Variable Behavior:	Increases	Decreases
Length of Haul	Influenced by customer locations and shipment activity.	Costs Increase	Costs Decrease
Equipment Requirements	Dictated by shipper and/or customer needs.	Costs Increase	Costs Decrease
Fuel Surcharges	Beyond the control of the shipper or the carrier.	Costs Increase	Costs Decrease
Accessorial Charges	Dictated by shipper or facility requirements.	Costs Increase	Costs Decrease
Trailer Load Factor	Controlled by shipper processes and influenced by customer demand and sales.	Costs Decrease	Costs Increase
Accounting Processes	Accounting processes can significantly impact cost per unit measurements generated exclusively from accounting information. Timing of invoices and transportation cost accruals can skew information from period to period. Also, the units sold or produced used in accounting information may not match the number of units actually shipped.		

Before reaching any significant conclusions regarding transportation cost performance and efficiency, shippers must be aware of any changes in these critical variables. When evaluating cost trends and comparing cost performance among similar facilities, shippers must be aware of these key factors over time or among the different facilities. For the examples in this chapter, "Cost Per Ton" will be used to represent cost per unit as this measure could easily apply to any shipper.[114]

---

[114] Most shippers regularly measure weight per shipment as an indicator of general productivity and proper trailer capacity utilization.

The example below shows the cost per ton (unit) for a manufacturer with three production facilities in the Atlanta, Georgia metro area.

Cost Per Ton (Unit) Analysis	Facility		
	Atlanta	Marietta	Tucker
Total Transportation Cost	$ 646,183	$ 788,588	$ 977,172
Total Tons Shipped (Units)	24,000	24,000	24,000
Cost Per Ton (Unit)	$ 26.92	$ 32.86	$ 40.72

Based on this information alone, Atlanta appears to be extremely efficient in managing transportation costs while Tucker appears to be relatively inefficient. However, each facility utilizes the same carrier and operates under the same mileage band rating and cost agreement. The table below breaks down the shipment and cost detail by facility by mileage band.

Facility Cost Detail		Number of Shipments			Total Cost		
Miles	Rate	Atlanta	Marietta	Tucker	Atlanta	Marietta	Tucker
0-10	$165.00	1,745	360	75	$ 287,925	$ 59,400	$ 12,375
11-20	$230.00	140	205	81	$ 32,200	$ 47,150	$ 18,630
21-30	$260.00	450	162	73	$ 117,000	$ 42,120	$ 18,980
31-40	$265.00	116	1,125	65	$ 30,740	$ 298,125	$ 17,225
41-50	$281.00	15	542	45	$ 4,215	$ 152,302	$ 12,645
51-60	$291.00	232	345	365	$ 67,512	$ 100,395	$ 106,215
61-70	$313.00	86	108	124	$ 26,918	$ 33,804	$ 38,812
71-80	$328.00	29	11	854	$ 9,512	$ 3,608	$ 280,112
81-90	$343.00	34	46	745	$ 11,662	$ 15,778	$ 255,535
91-100	$360.00	36	19	251	$ 12,960	$ 6,840	$ 90,360
101-110	$372.00	4	54	60	$ 1,488	$ 20,088	$ 22,320
111-120	$385.00	78	14	105	$ 30,030	$ 5,390	$ 40,425
121-130	$394.00	24	7	77	$ 9,456	$ 2,758	$ 30,338
131-140	$415.00	11	2	80	$ 4,565	$ 830	$ 33,200
Totals		3,000	3,000	3,000	$ 646,183	$ 788,588	$ 977,172

	Atlanta	Marietta	Tucker
Total Tons Shipped	24,000	24,000	24,000
Tons Per Shipment	8.00	8.00	8.00
Cost Per Ton (Unit)	$ 26.92	$ 32.86	$ 40.72
Total Miles (one-way)	67,520	113,650	225,870
Average Length of Haul	23	38	75

Because each facility operates under the same pricing structure, the difference in cost per ton from facility to facility is directly related to the average length of haul and no other factor. Also note that each facility has an average of 8.0 tons per shipment, so trailer load factor does not skew the cost per ton figures.[115]

---

[115] Trailer load factor represents the degree to which the available space in the trailer is fully utilized.

Changes in Trailer Load Factor

Trailer load factor represents the degree to which the storage capacity of the trailer is fully utilized. Load factor is often measured as weight per trailer or cubic space utilization per trailer.[116] The transportation cost per unit can fluctuate dramatically with variability in the trailer load factor. In most cases, the load factor is controlled and managed by the shipper, not the carrier. A shipper's load factor is primarily influenced by customer order quantities and the load-building and planning process. The load factor is only rarely controlled or managed by the carrier or the transportation solution.[117]

The monthly table below illustrates a shipper's cost per ton as the trailer load factor declines. The number of shipments, length of haul, and fuel surcharge amounts all remain constant each month across the period shown.

Cost Per Ton (Unit) as Trailer Load Factor Decreases

Transportation Cost Per Ton Trend Analysis	JAN	FEB	MAR	APR	MAY	JUN	YTD Totals
Number of Shipments	1,000	1,000	1,000	1,000	1,000	1,000	6,000
Avg. Length of Haul	125	125	125	125	125	125	125
Total Tons Shipped	10,000	9,500	9,000	8,500	8,000	7,500	52,500
Tons Per Shipment	**10.00**	**9.50**	**9.00**	**8.50**	**8.00**	**7.50**	**8.75**
Linehaul Transportation Cost	$ 250,000	$ 247,000	$ 244,000	$ 241,000	$ 238,000	$ 235,000	$ 1,455,000
Fuel Surcharges	$ 15,000	$ 15,000	$ 15,000	$ 15,000	$ 15,000	$ 15,000	$ 90,000
Total Transportation Cost	$ 265,000	$ 262,000	$ 259,000	$ 256,000	$ 253,000	$ 250,000	$ 1,545,000
Cost Per Ton:							
Linehaul Transportation	$ 25.00	$ 26.00	$ 27.11	$ 28.35	$ 29.75	$ 31.33	$ 27.71
Fuel Surcharges	$ 1.50	$ 1.58	$ 1.67	$ 1.76	$ 1.88	$ 2.00	$ 1.71
Total Transportation	$ 26.50	$ 27.58	$ 28.78	$ 30.12	$ 31.63	$ 33.33	$ 29.43

In this example, total cost per ton increases from $26.50 in January to $33.33 in June. This increase in cost per ton is a direct result of the decline in load factor, not the result of any transportation inefficiencies. Trailer load factor declines from 10.0 tons per shipment in January to only 7.5 tons per shipment in June. Also notice, during this same period, the actual transportation solution has become more cost effective as total linehaul costs decline each month in the period while total shipments and average length of haul remain constant.

Despite the fact that total cost per ton has increased, the transportation solution itself has actually become more cost effective. It is critical for the shipper to identify the root

---

[116] Shippers will typically focus on either weight or cube, depending on the product. For heavy products, the focus is more often on weight. For lighter products, the focus is more often on cube.
[117] Certain specialized transportation solutions will assign the load-building and scheduling responsibility to the carrier, making the carrier responsible for maximizing the trailer load factor. Factors beyond the carrier's control such as customer demand and shipment quantities will still play a significant role in the trailer load factor.

cause of the increase in cost per ton and not prematurely assume that the increase in cost per ton is the result of an inefficient transportation solution.

Fuel Surcharges

The price of fuel and subsequent fuel surcharges will, at certain times, have a significant impact on a shipper's transportation cost. All other factors being equal, an increase in the price of fuel will eventually cause a corresponding increase in transportation costs for virtually all shippers.[118] Before reaching conclusions about an increase in cost per unit figures, the shipper should determine what impact the cost of fuel is having on the transportation cost measurements. Consider the monthly cost breakdown shown below.

Cost Per Ton (Unit) as Fuel Costs Increase

Transportation Cost Per Ton Trend Analysis	JAN	FEB	MAR	APR	MAY	JUN	YTD Totals
Number of Shipments	1,000	1,000	1,000	1,000	1,000	1,000	6,000
Avg. Length of Haul	125	125	125	125	125	125	125
Total Tons Shipped	8,000	8,000	8,000	8,000	8,000	8,000	48,000
Tons Per Shipment	8.00	8.00	8.00	8.00	8.00	8.00	8.00
Linehaul Transportation Cost	$ 250,000	$ 247,000	$ 244,000	$ 241,000	$ 238,000	$ 235,000	$ 1,455,000
Fuel Surcharges	$ 15,000	$ 22,000	$ 29,000	$ 36,000	$ 43,000	$ 50,000	$ 195,000
Total Transportation Cost	$ 265,000	$ 269,000	$ 273,000	$ 277,000	$ 281,000	$ 285,000	$ 1,650,000
Cost Per Ton:							
Linehaul Transportation	$ 31.25	$ 30.88	$ 30.50	$ 30.13	$ 29.75	$ 29.38	$ 30.31
Fuel Surcharges	**$ 1.88**	**$ 2.75**	**$ 3.63**	**$ 4.50**	**$ 5.38**	**$ 6.25**	**$ 4.06**
Total Transportation	$ 33.13	$ 33.63	$ 34.13	$ 34.63	$ 35.13	$ 35.63	$ 34.38

In the above example, total transportation cost per ton has increased, which will likely lead the shipper to conclude that transportation costs are being poorly managed. However, a closer review of the monthly information indicates that linehaul transportation cost has declined from $31.25 per ton in January to $29.38 per ton in June. When excluding fuel, this trend actually indicates a possible improvement in transportation cost efficiency.

The increase in cost per unit was actually caused by a dramatic increase in fuel surcharge costs over the six month period, not deterioration in transportation efficiency. Fuel surcharge cost per ton increased from $1.88 per ton in January to $6.25 per ton in June. This increase in fuel cost was much greater than the cost reductions in linehaul costs. Also notice that tons shipped, number of shipments, and length of haul remained constant from month to month during this period, eliminating these variables as possible factors influencing the cost per ton (unit) trend.

---

[118] Transportation costs will only increase for contracts that include a fuel surcharge provision. Shippers without fuel surcharge agreements with carriers will not immediately see increased costs as a result of an increase in the price of fuel.

The graph below illustrates the per-ton trends in linehaul costs, fuel costs, and total costs over the six month period.

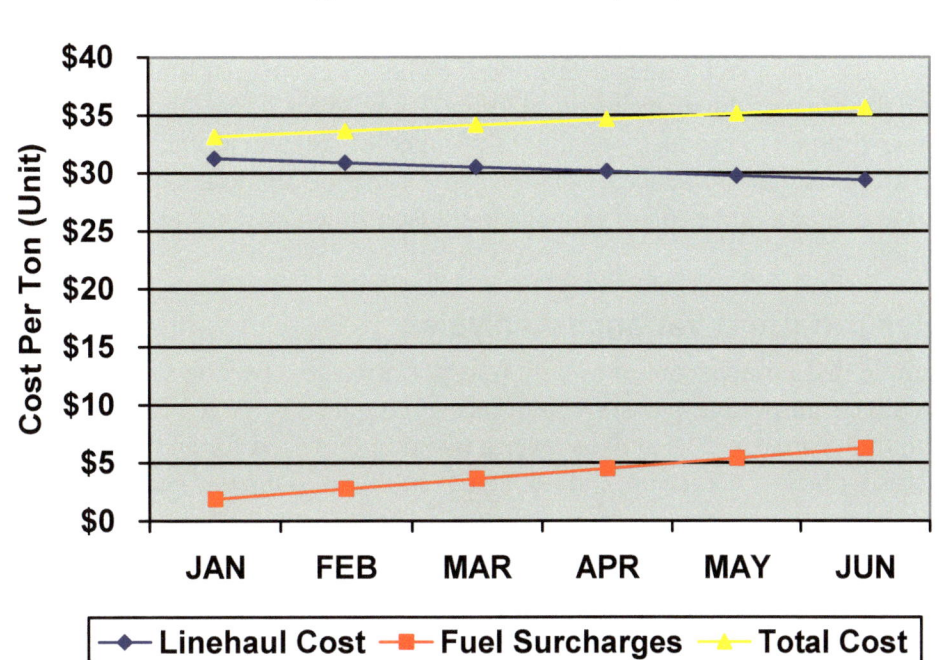

Fuel Surcharges and Cost Per Ton (Unit) Trends

The graph clearly shows the downward trend in linehaul cost and the upward trend in fuel surcharge costs. In the short run, the linehaul cost portion is the only portion of transportation cost within the control of the shipper's management team. Shippers must be certain to identify the root causes of any significant change in costs before reaching conclusions regarding the cost effectiveness of transportation management or any particular transportation solution.

Flexible Budgeting and Transportation Cost Analysis

Manufacturers often use management accounting and variance analysis techniques to identify the underlying causes of period-to-period changes in the cost per unit to manufacture a product. Based on predetermined standards for the price and quantity of input materials, these techniques determine if a change in cost per unit was the result of a change in the price of the materials used to make a product, a change in the quantity of materials consumed to produce one unit of product, or some combination of both a price variance and a quantity variance.[119] These same variance analysis techniques can be modified to evaluate and explain changes in transportation cost per unit as shown in the next section.

Cost Per Ton (Unit) Variance Analysis

The example that follows continues with transportation cost per ton serving as a representative transportation cost per unit measurement. The table below shows the change in transportation cost activity over a two month period for an individual manufacturing facility. Take special notice of each item in the variance column.

Transportation Cost Activity for Variance Analysis

Transportation Cost Per Ton Variance Analysis	JAN	FEB	Variance
Number of Shipments	1,000	1,000	-
Avg. Length of Haul	125	125	-
Total Tons Shipped	10,000	9,500	(500)
Tons Per Shipment	**10.00**	**9.50**	**(0.50)**
Linehaul Transportation Cost	$ 250,000	$ 245,000	$ (5,000)
Fuel Surcharges	$ 15,000	$ 17,000	$ 2,000
Total Transportation Cost	$ 265,000	$ 262,000	$ (3,000)
Cost Per Shipment:			
Linehaul Transportation	$ 250.00	$ 245.00	(5.00)
Fuel Surcharges	$ 15.00	$ 17.00	2.00
Total Transportation	$ 265.00	$ 262.00	(3.00)
Cost Per Ton:			
Linehaul Transportation	$ 25.00	$ 25.79	$ 0.79
Fuel Surcharges	$ 1.50	$ 1.79	$ 0.29
Total Transportation	$ 26.50	$ 27.58	$ **1.08**

---

[119] Refer to a book on Management Accounting for a detailed review of these variance analysis techniques as they apply to general cost accounting.

Based on this table, total transportation cost per ton has increased by $1.08 per ton from January to February. The shipper should now seek to identify the underlying causes of the variance and determine what portion of the variance was caused by a change in load factor and what portion of the variance was caused by a change in pure transportation costs and transportation efficiency.

A variance analysis approach, similar to that for manufacturing costs, will break down the $1.08 per ton variance into a load factor variance and a transportation cost variance. The variance analysis approach shown here utilizes the prior period tons per shipment (tons per load) as the "standard quantity" for computing variances.

Transportation Cost Per Ton (CPT) Variance Analysis	Calculations	Total CPT Variance
Load Factor Variance:		
Current Period Cost Per Shipment	$ 262.00	
Prior Period Tons Per Load	10.00	
CPT at Prior Period Tons Per Load	$ 26.20	
Current Period Tons Per Load	9.50	
CPT at Current Period Tons Per Load	$ 27.58	
Tons Per Load (Load Factor) Variance		$ 1.38
Transportation Cost Variance:		
Linehaul		
Change in Linehaul Cost Per Load	$ (5.00)	
Prior Period Tons Per Load (Standard)	10.00	
Linehaul Cost Variance Per Ton		$ (0.50)
Fuel		
Change in Fuel Cost Per Load	$ 2.00	
Prior Period Tons Per Load (Standard)	10.00	
Fuel Surcharge Cost Variance Per Ton		$ 0.20
Total Transportation Cost Variance		$ (0.30)
Variance Summary:		
Tons Per Load (Load Factor) Variance		$ 1.38
Direct Transportation Cost Variance		$ (0.30)
Total Cost Per Ton Variance		$ 1.08

The variance analysis above breaks the $1.08 cost per ton variance into a transportation cost variance (price variance) and a load factor variance (quantity variance). In this example, the load factor, with an unfavorable variance of $1.38, was the main factor that caused the cost per ton to increase, not transportation costs. In fact, the transportation cost variance was a favorable variance, indicating that transportation cost efficiency actually improved during the period and helped to offset a portion of the unfavorable variance in the load factor. The information indicates that the carrier and transportation solution have performed well while the shipper and facility have not.

Now consider a situation where the trailer load factor improves from one period to the next. The table below is very similar to the previous example, but tons per shipment increases from 10.0 in January to 11.0 in February.

Transportation Cost Activity for Variance Analysis

Transportation Cost Per Ton Variance Analysis	Month 2009 JAN	FEB	Variance
Number of Shipments	1,000	1,000	-
Avg. Length of Haul	125	125	-
Total Tons Shipped	10,000	11,000	1,000
Tons Per Shipment	**10.00**	**11.00**	1.00
Linehaul Transportation Cost	$ 250,000	$ 245,000	$ (5,000)
Fuel Surcharges	$ 15,000	$ 17,000	$ 2,000
Total Transportation Cost	$ 265,000	$ 262,000	$ (3,000)
Cost Per Shipment:			
Linehaul Transportation	$ 250.00	$ 245.00	(5.00)
Fuel Surcharges	$ 15.00	$ 17.00	2.00
Total Transportation	$ 265.00	$ 262.00	(3.00)
Cost Per Ton:			
Linehaul Transportation	$ 25.00	$ 22.27	$ (2.73)
Fuel Surcharges	$ 1.50	$ 1.55	$ 0.05
Total Transportation	$ 26.50	$ 23.82	**$ (2.68)**

As a result of load factor changes and transportation cost changes, the total transportation cost declined by $2.68 per ton in February. The variance analysis that follows demonstrates the degree to which this reduction in cost is related to both load factor improvements and transportation cost efficiencies.

The table below provides the detailed cost per ton variance analysis for the two month comparison period.

Transportation Cost Per Ton (CPT) Variance Analysis	Calculations	Total CPT Variance
Load Factor Variance:		
Current Period Cost Per Shipment	$ 262.00	
Prior Period Tons Per Load	10.00	
CPT at Prior Period Tons Per Load	$ 26.20	
Current Period Tons Per Load	11.00	
CPT at Current Period Tons Per Load	$ 23.82	
Tons Per Load (Load Factor) Variance		**$ (2.38)**
Transportation Cost Variance:		
Linehaul		
Change in Linehaul Cost Per Load	$ (5.00)	
Prior Period Tons Per Load (Standard)	10.00	
Linehaul Cost Variance Per Ton		$ (0.50)
Fuel		
Change in Fuel Cost Per Load	$ 2.00	
Prior Period Tons Per Load (Standard)	10.00	
Fuel Surcharge Cost Variance Per Ton		$ 0.20
Total Transportation Cost Variance		**$ (0.30)**
Variance Summary:		
Tons Per Load (Load Factor) Variance		$ (2.38)
Direct Transportation Cost Variance		$ (0.30)
Total Cost Per Ton Variance		**$ (2.68)**

The variance analysis indicates that the vast majority of the cost per ton improvement is the result of the load factor variance. A $2.38 improvement in cost per ton is the result of load factor improvements while the improvement from true transportation efficiency is only $0.30 per ton.

The shipper must consider the impact of the load factor before reaching any conclusion regarding the cost efficiency of the actual transportation solution. In this example, the shipper could incorrectly conclude that the carrier and transportation solution have performed exceptionally well during this period. However, while the transportation solution is performing reasonably well, the bulk of the improvement in cost per ton is related to the improvement in load factor, not the actual transportation solution.

The formulas used in the previous variance analysis are listed below.

$$\text{Load Factor Variance} = \frac{\text{Current Period Cost Per Load}}{\text{Prior Period Units Per Load}} - \frac{\text{Current Period Cost Per Load}}{\text{Current Period Units Per Load}}$$

$$\text{Linehaul Variance} = \frac{\text{Change in Linehaul Cost Per Load}}{\text{Prior Period Units Per Load}}$$

$$\text{Fuel Variance} = \frac{\text{Change in Fuel Surcharge Cost Per Load}}{\text{Prior Period Units Per Load}}$$

This variance analysis format provides a simple example for shippers to follow. Each shipper can use this format as a guideline for developing a variance analysis approach that is appropriate for each individual network or cost center.

With the appropriate information, the transportation cost variance could be extended and broken down even further to include variance analysis on other transportation variables such as pricing changes, accessorial costs, fuel surcharges, equipment requirements, and length of haul. This information could be reflected in a deeper variance analysis directly on the transportation cost per load before introducing load factor into the final cost per ton (unit) analysis. This detailed variance breakdown will give the shipper additional insight into the cost effectiveness of the transportation solution and the key cost-driving variables within their transportation network.

Transportation Cost Allocations

Many shippers have the need to allocate truckload transportation costs, especially dedicated fleet costs, to individual business units or profit centers such as plants, retail stores, or other discrete locations within the company. These transportation cost allocations play a major role in the profitability of each business unit, so accurate allocations are very important to the shipper.

Because of the billing structure of most dedicated contracts, the cost of each individual load is not as clearly defined as it is with one-way, load-based pricing. To properly evaluate costs, shippers will often find it necessary to allocate dedicated fleet costs to the individual load level. After evaluating two common but inaccurate methods, this section will provide a simple and accurate model for properly allocating lump-sum dedicated fleet costs to the individual load level. This section will also provide some incremental cost analysis techniques for evaluating special situations and decisions.

Cost Allocation Models

A variety of simple methods can be developed for allocating truckload transportation costs. Some shippers may use a very simple cost per mile or cost per load approach. In almost all networks, these methods will not provide an accurate allocation of truckload transportation costs. The table below shows the load activity and transportation costs for a shipper's group of retail stores.

Dedicated Fleet Cost Summary Report

Store Number	City	ST	One-Way Miles	4-week Activity Loads	4-week Activity Miles
1055	Columbus	OH	4	42	336
1098	Columbus	OH	6	38	456
1016	Dayton	OH	68	32	4,352
1451	Toledo	OH	141	41	11,562
1260	Lima	OH	80	11	1,760
1874	Lancaster	OH	26	35	1,820
Month Totals				**199**	**20,286**

Dedicated Fleet Costs:

Item	Rate	Units	Weeks	Total
Trucks	$ 1,700.00	5	4	$ 34,000.00
Miles	$ 0.88	20,286		$ 17,851.68
Total Cost				$ 51,851.68

Network Statistics: Cost Per Mile: $ 2.56
Cost Per Load: $ 260.56

The cost and load information indicates an average cost per mile of $2.56 and an average cost per load of $260.56. These simple statistics could be used to allocate transportation costs to each individual store location.

Cost Per Mile Allocation

Using the information from the previous table, a simple cost per mile allocation is shown in the table below. The cost per mile of $2.56 is multiplied by total miles to determine the total cost and cost per load for each store.

\multicolumn{8}{c	}{Simple Cost Per Mile Allocation}
\multicolumn{3}{c	}{Store}	One-Way	\multicolumn{2}{c	}{4-week Activity}	Cost Per	\multicolumn{2}{c	}{Allocated}
Number	City	ST	Miles	Loads	Miles	Mile	Total Cost	Cost Per Load
1055	Columbus	OH	4	42	336	$ 2.56	$ 858.83	$ 20.45
1098	Columbus	OH	6	38	456	$ 2.56	$ 1,165.55	$ 30.67
1016	Dayton	OH	68	32	4,352	$ 2.56	$ 11,123.85	$ 347.62
1451	Toledo	OH	141	41	11,562	$ 2.56	$ 29,552.85	$ 720.80
1260	Lima	OH	80	11	1,760	$ 2.56	$ 4,498.62	$ 408.97
1874	Lancaster	OH	26	35	1,820	$ 2.56	$ 4,651.98	$ 132.91
Totals				199	20,286	$ 2.56	$ 51,851.68	$ 260.56

The simple allocation approach as shown does not accurately reflect true costs at the load level. Cost allocations to the shorter length of haul locations are far too low. Likewise, cost allocations to the longer length of haul stores are much too high. This cost per mile approach does not properly account for fixed costs, dock times, and other variables that are not directly related to mileage activity and length of haul.

A good rule of thumb for evaluating allocations is to compare the allocated cost per load to comparable one-way rates for each destination. The allocated cost per load amounts for the two Columbus, OH stores are far too low when compared to one-way pricing expectations. Based on these results, the cost per mile approach clearly does not provide an accurate cost allocation method for this network.

Cost Per Load Allocation

Also using the information from the original table, a simple cost per load allocation is shown in the table below. The average cost per load of $260.56 is multiplied by total loads to determine the total cost for each store.

\multicolumn{8}{c	}{Simple Cost Per Load Allocation}
\multicolumn{3}{c	}{Store}	One-Way	\multicolumn{2}{c	}{4-week Activity}	Cost Per	\multicolumn{2}{c	}{Allocated}
Number	City	ST	Miles	Loads	Miles	Load	Total Cost	Cost Per Mile
1055	Columbus	OH	4	42	336	$ 260.56	$ 10,943.57	$ 32.57
1098	Columbus	OH	6	38	456	$ 260.56	$ 9,901.33	$ 21.71
1016	Dayton	OH	68	32	4,352	$ 260.56	$ 8,337.96	$ 1.92
1451	Toledo	OH	141	41	11,562	$ 260.56	$ 10,683.01	$ 0.92
1260	Lima	OH	80	11	1,760	$ 260.56	$ 2,866.17	$ 1.63
1874	Lancaster	OH	26	35	1,820	$ 260.56	$ 9,119.64	$ 5.01
Totals				199	20,286	$ 260.56	$ 51,851.68	$ 2.56

The cost per mile for each store is computed by dividing total cost by total miles. The cost per mile provides an excellent indication of the inaccuracy of this allocation method. For example, the allocated cost per mile for the Toledo, OH store is only $0.92 per mile. Since the dedicated contract includes a variable rate of $0.88 per mile, this store is being allocated almost none of the fixed costs associated with the dedicated fleet. At the same time, the shorter distance stores are being allocated an unreasonable portion of the fleet's fixed costs.

Suggested Allocation Method

The table below provides a suggested allocation method that combines the cost per mile and cost per load approaches. The first step in the approach is to assume a flat fixed cost per load for all loads in the network.[120] In this example, the base assumption is a fixed rate of $100 per load. The remaining costs not accounted for in the per-load allocation are allocated based on total miles.

Suggested Allocation Method

Allocation Method	Rate	Units	Total Cost
Per Load Allocation Amount:	$ 100.00	199	$ 19,900.00
Per Mile Allocation Amount:	$ 1.58	20,286	$ 31,951.68
Total Cost to Be Allocated:			$ 51,851.68

Store Number	City	ST	One-Way Miles	4-week Activity Loads	4-week Activity Miles	Per Load Allocation Per Load	Per Load Allocation Per Mile	Total Allocation Per Load	Total Allocation Per Mile	Total Cost	Cost Per Load
1055	Columbus	OH	4	42	336	$ 100.00	$ 12.60	$ 4,200.00	$ 529.22	$ 4,729.22	$ 112.60
1098	Columbus	OH	6	38	456	$ 100.00	$ 18.90	$ 3,800.00	$ 718.23	$ 4,518.23	$ 118.90
1016	Dayton	OH	68	32	4,352	$ 100.00	$ 214.21	$ 3,200.00	$ 6,854.66	$ 10,054.66	$ 314.21
1451	Toledo	OH	141	41	11,562	$ 100.00	$ 444.17	$ 4,100.00	$ 18,210.85	$ 22,310.85	$ 544.17
1260	Lima	OH	80	11	1,760	$ 100.00	$ 252.01	$ 1,100.00	$ 2,772.11	$ 3,872.11	$ 352.01
1874	Lancaster	OH	26	35	1,820	$ 100.00	$ 81.90	$ 3,500.00	$ 2,866.61	$ 6,366.61	$ 181.90
Totals				199	20,286			$ 19,900.00	$ 31,951.68	$ 51,851.68	$ 260.56

By combining the fixed per-load amount with a variable per-mile rate, this method provides a very reasonable allocation of total costs. The resulting cost per load for each store is in approximately the same range as typical one-way costs for each destination. Length of haul is also properly taken into account.

Comparison of Allocation Methods

The table below provides a comparison of the three cost allocation methods.

Comparison of Allocation Methods

Store Number	City	ST	One-Way Miles	4-week Activity Loads	4-week Activity Miles	Per Mile Method Per Load	Per Mile Method Total Cost	Per Load Method Per Load	Per Load Method Total Cost	Suggested Method Per Load	Suggested Method Total Cost
1055	Columbus	OH	4	42	336	$ 20.45	$ 858.83	$ 260.56	$ 10,943.57	$ 112.60	$ 4,729.22
1098	Columbus	OH	6	38	456	$ 30.67	$ 1,165.55	$ 260.56	$ 9,901.33	$ 118.90	$ 4,518.23
1016	Dayton	OH	68	32	4,352	$ 347.62	$ 11,123.85	$ 260.56	$ 8,337.96	$ 314.21	$ 10,054.66
1451	Toledo	OH	141	41	11,562	$ 720.80	$ 29,552.85	$ 260.56	$ 10,683.01	$ 544.17	$ 22,310.85
1260	Lima	OH	80	11	1,760	$ 408.97	$ 4,498.62	$ 260.56	$ 2,866.17	$ 352.01	$ 3,872.11
1874	Lancaster	OH	26	35	1,820	$ 132.91	$ 4,651.98	$ 260.56	$ 9,119.64	$ 181.90	$ 6,366.61
Totals				199	20,286	$ 260.56	$ 51,851.68	$ 260.56	$ 51,851.68	$ 260.56	$ 51,851.68

The suggested method provides an excellent balance between the other two approaches. The cost per load results with the suggested method are much more reasonable relative to length of haul than the simple cost per mile or cost per load techniques. The suggested

---

[120] The flat rate per load allocation amount is intended to reflect the approximate cost of a zero mile load. The rate represents fixed per-load activity such as dock times, trailer needs, and other fixed costs.

approach properly accounts for both fixed and variable costs, especially in terms of length of haul.

Applying Cost Allocations

Shippers can apply accurate transportation cost allocation information to avoid mistakes related to incremental network decisions such as closing a store location. In most cases, closing a store will not eliminate 100 percent of the store's allocated transportation costs when using a dedicated fleet. The shipper could easily assume that the transportation cost savings from closing the store will be equal to the allocated transportation costs as shown below if the shipper were to close the Lima, OH store location.

Incorrect Lima, OH Savings	
Total Loads	11
Allocated Cost Per Load x $	352.01
Total Allocated Cost	$ 3,872.11

The actual cost impact depends on many network factors such as dedicated fleet size, length of haul, utilization, and fleet-specific overhead costs. The shipper must utilize an incremental analysis approach to determine the anticipated transportation cost savings from closing the store.

Suppose the retail shipper in the previous example chose to close the store located in Lima, OH. The revised dedicated fleet activity and cost summary are shown below.

Revised Fleet Activity Summary Following Lima, OH Store Closing

Store			One-Way	4-week Activity	
Number	City	ST	Miles	Loads	Miles
1055	Columbus	OH	4	42	336
1098	Columbus	OH	6	38	456
1016	Dayton	OH	68	32	4,352
1451	Toledo	OH	141	41	11,562
1260	Lima	OH	80	-	-
1874	Lancaster	OH	26	35	1,820
Month Totals				188	18,526

Dedicated Fleet Costs:

Item	Rate	Units	Weeks	Total
Trucks	$ 1,700.00	5	4	$ 34,000.00
Miles	$ 0.88	18,526		$ 16,302.88
Total Cost				$ 50,302.88

Network Statistics: Cost Per Mile: $ 2.72
 Cost Per Load: $ 267.57

Since the Lima, OH store received only 11 loads during the period, the reduction in load activity and miles was not large enough to reduce the fleet size from 5 trucks to 4 trucks. Therefore, fixed tractor costs remain the same. The store closing does result in a reduction of 1,760 miles, for a total network savings of $1,548.80.

Lima, OH Store Closing

Expected Savings

Total Loads	11
Allocated Cost Per Load x $	352.01
Expected Savings	$ 3,872.11

Actual Savings

Miles	1,760
Cost Per Mile x $	0.88
Actual Savings	$ 1,548.80

Since the fleet size was not reduced, the remaining stores must now absorb the fixed fleet cost that was previously being allocated to the Lima, OH store. The reallocated costs are shown in the table below.

Cost Allocations After Lima, OH Closing (Suggested Allocation Method)

Allocation Method	Rate	Units	Total Cost
Per Load Allocation Amount:	$ 100.00	188	$ 18,800.00
Per Mile Allocation Amount:	$ 1.70	18,526	$ 31,502.88
Total Cost to Be Allocated:			$ 50,302.88

Store Number	City	ST	One-Way Miles	4-week Loads	Activity Miles	Per Load Allocation Per Load	Per Load Allocation Per Mile	Total Allocation Per Load	Total Allocation Per Mile	Total Cost	Cost Per Load
1055	Columbus	OH	4	42	336	$ 100.00	$ 13.60	$ 4,200.00	$ 571.36	$ 4,771.36	$ 113.60
1098	Columbus	OH	6	38	456	$ 100.00	$ 20.41	$ 3,800.00	$ 775.41	$ 4,575.41	$ 120.41
1016	Dayton	OH	68	32	4,352	$ 100.00	$ 231.26	$ 3,200.00	$ 7,400.44	$ 10,600.44	$ 331.26
1451	Toledo	OH	141	41	11,562	$ 100.00	$ 479.53	$ 4,100.00	$ 19,660.82	$ 23,760.82	$ 579.53
1260	Lima	OH	80	-	-	$ -	$ -	$ -	$ -	$ -	$ -
1874	Lancaster	OH	26	35	1,820	$ 100.00	$ 88.42	$ 3,500.00	$ 3,094.85	$ 6,594.85	$ 188.42
Totals				188	18,526			$ 18,800.00	$ 31,502.88	$ 50,302.88	$ 267.57

Since the remaining stores absorb additional fixed costs, the allocated cost per load of each remaining store has increased. The overall network cost per load has also increased.

Comparison of Allocated Costs After Store Closing

Store Number	City	ST	One-Way Miles	Before Closing Loads	Miles	Per Load	Total Cost	After Closing Loads	Miles	Per Load	Total Cost
1055	Columbus	OH	4	42	336	$ 112.60	$ 4,729.22	42	336	$ 113.60	$ 4,771.36
1098	Columbus	OH	6	38	456	$ 118.90	$ 4,518.23	38	456	$ 120.41	$ 4,575.41
1016	Dayton	OH	68	32	4,352	$ 314.21	$ 10,054.66	32	4,352	$ 331.26	$ 10,600.44
1451	Toledo	OH	141	41	11,562	$ 544.17	$ 22,310.85	41	11,562	$ 579.53	$ 23,760.82
1260	Lima	OH	80	11	1,760	$ 352.01	$ 3,872.11	-	-	$ -	$ -
1874	Lancaster	OH	26	35	1,820	$ 181.90	$ 6,366.61	35	1,820	$ 188.42	$ 6,594.85
Totals				199	20,286	$ 260.56	$ 51,851.68	188	18,526	$ 267.57	$ 50,302.88

Each remaining store experiences a slight increase in allocated cost as a result of the Lima, OH store closing.

Dedicated Fleets and Marginal Cost Analysis

A major benefit of a fixed-variable dedicated fleet for shippers is the potential cost savings in the efficient use of the fleet. As fleet productivity increases, the shipper's costs fall significantly. Consider the example below.

Fixed-Variable Rate Structure

- **Fixed Charge:** $1,600 per truck per week
- **Variable Charge:** $0.62 per mile

Because the fixed weekly charge per truck is paid regardless of the number of miles driven, the shipper is in a unique position to minimize per-load costs by maximizing the utilization of the dedicated fleet. Consider a simple network where the shipper has only one customer that is located 40 miles away. The shipper contracts for a one truck dedicated fleet at the rates shown above, a $1,600 per truck per week charge and a variable rate of $0.62 per mile.

The truck/driver is capable of delivering up to 5 round trip customer loads each day based on DOT hours of service restrictions and expected cycle times. The actual number of loads will fluctuate each day based on customer demand. The table below summarizes the shipper's cost per load depending on the average number of loads delivered each day.

Fixed-Variable Pricing Cost Per Load Analysis	Rates:	Utilization Scenarios (Loads Per Day)				
Number of Loads Per Day		1	2	3	4	5
Number of Loads Per Week (5 days)		5	10	15	20	25
Round Trip Miles Per Load		80	80	80	80	80
Total Daily Miles		80	160	240	320	400
Total Weekly Miles		400	800	1,200	1,600	2,000
Total Weekly Costs:						
Fixed Tractor Charge	$1,600.00	$1,600.00	$1,600.00	$1,600.00	$1,600.00	$1,600.00
Variable Mileage Charge	$0.62	$248.00	$496.00	$744.00	$992.00	$1,240.00
Total Weekly Costs		$1,848.00	$2,096.00	$2,344.00	$2,592.00	$2,840.00
Average Cost Per Load		$369.60	$209.60	$156.27	$129.60	$113.60

The fixed-variable pricing structure creates a dynamic where, as more loads are served by the dedicated truck, the lower and lower the shipper's cost per load becomes. If the shipper only averages one load per day, the cost per load is $369.60. However, if the shipper is able to average 4 loads per day, the cost drops to $129.60 per load.

Another method of approaching the average cost per load breakdown is through an incremental or marginal analysis. The table that follows breaks the costs down into an incremental cost per load format. The cost of the truck per day is $1,600 divided by 5 days or $320 per day. The variable cost of each trip is $0.62 per mile times the 80 round trip miles or $49.60 per trip. Therefore, in effect, the first load per day costs $320 plus $49.60 or $369.60 per load. Since the weekly fixed tractor charge is paid for by the first load, the effective incremental cost of each additional daily load is only the variable cost of $49.60 per trip.

Incremental Cost Per Load Analysis	Utilization Scenarios (Loads Per Day)				
Number of Loads Per Day	1	2	3	4	5
Load 1	$ 369.60	$ 369.60	$ 369.60	$ 369.60	$ 369.60
Load 2		$ 49.60	$ 49.60	$ 49.60	$ 49.60
Load 3			$ 49.60	$ 49.60	$ 49.60
Load 4				$ 49.60	$ 49.60
Load 5					$ 49.60
Total Daily Cost	$ 369.60	$ 419.20	$ 468.80	$ 518.40	$ 568.00
Average Cost Per Load	$ 369.60	$ 209.60	$ 156.27	$ 129.60	$ 113.60

This incremental approach to the cost per load is very important for the shipper to understand when operating under a fixed-variable dedicated pricing contract. Suppose the shipper is consistently averaging 3 loads per day so that the average cost is $156.27 per load. The shipper is then approached by an outside carrier with an offer to serve exactly one load per day at a cost of $100 per load. The outside carrier has a special network need to fill and can only provide one truck per day at the $100 rate per load.

At first glance, the shipper would appear to save $56.27 per load by utilizing the third-party carrier for one load per day. However, the detailed incremental analysis below clearly shows that the shipper will actually *increase* total costs and cost per load by accepting the carrier's offer of $100 per load.

Incremental Analysis of Outside Carrier Offer

Incremental Cost Per Load Analysis	Dedicated Only	Outside Carrier
Load 1 - Dedicated	$ 369.60	$ 369.60
Load 2 - Dedicated	$ 49.60	$ 49.60
Load 3 - Dedicated or Outside Carrier	$ 49.60	$ 100.00
Total Daily Cost	$ 468.80	$ 519.20
Average Cost Per Load	$ 156.27	$ 173.07

The analysis above shows that the shipper's cost will actually increase if the $100 per load offer is accepted. Even though the average cost per load was initially $156.27, the incremental or marginal cost for the third load each day was only $49.60 per load, much less than the $100 per load offer. By accepting the $100 per load offer, the shipper's average cost per load would actually increase from $156.27 to $173.07 in the three loads per day scenario. Without a clear understanding of the incremental nature of the fixed-variable dedicated pricing structure, the shipper could make a costly mistake by accepting the $100 per load offer.

Shipper Cost Strategies for Short Haul Pricing

Short haul pricing, usually under 250 miles, can be a challenge to manage for many shippers. One common format for managing short haul pricing is mileage bands. Mileage bands provide a simple and consistent format for organizing short haul pricing. However, the simplistic nature of the format requires carriers to make certain operating assumptions that influence the final pricing. Several key pricing strategy variables include time-of-day information, seasonal shipping patterns, and actual lane-level destinations. By providing this detailed information to carriers, shippers can expect the pricing provided by carriers to fully reflect the key variables of the shipper's unique network requirements.

Time-of-Day Information

Whenever available, the shipper should provide potential carriers with ship times and delivery times for the load volumes included in the mileage bands. The time information will allow the carrier to model the network and identify any utilization synergies within the shipper's mileage band network. The time of day information could be provided on a load-by-load basis or in a summary format such as the one shown below. This table shows the frequency of departure times from the origin in three hour segments.

Annual Load Summary by Time of Day - Origin Facility										
Day of Week	Loads Per Day	Annual Loads	\multicolumn{8}{c}{Load Count by Origin Departure Time}								
			12 am to 3 am	3 am to 6 am	6 am to 9 am	9 am to 12 pm	12 pm to 3 pm	3 pm to 6 pm	6 pm to 9 pm	9 pm to 12 am
Sunday	0.06	3	-	-	1	1	-	1	-	-
Monday	16.04	834	15	123	286	232	149	22	6	1
Tuesday	15.96	830	12	133	291	254	97	31	8	4
Wednesday	18.71	973	19	124	311	280	188	44	5	2
Thursday	18.08	940	20	155	328	294	122	17	3	1
Friday	17.88	930	11	169	337	287	101	22	3	-
Saturday	1.02	53	4	11	21	15	1	-	-	1
Totals	17.55	4,563	81	715	1,575	1,363	658	137	25	9

Day of Week		% of Total Loads	12 am to 3 am	3 am to 6 am	6 am to 9 am	9 am to 12 pm	12 pm to 3 pm	3 pm to 6 pm	6 pm to 9 pm	9 pm to 12 am
Sunday		0%	0.0%	0.0%	33.3%	33.3%	0.0%	33.3%	0.0%	0.0%
Monday		18%	1.8%	14.7%	34.3%	27.8%	17.9%	2.6%	0.7%	0.1%
Tuesday		18%	1.4%	16.0%	35.1%	30.6%	11.7%	3.7%	1.0%	0.5%
Wednesday		21%	2.0%	12.7%	32.0%	28.8%	19.3%	4.5%	0.5%	0.2%
Thursday		21%	2.1%	16.5%	34.9%	31.3%	13.0%	1.8%	0.3%	0.1%
Friday		20%	1.2%	18.2%	36.2%	30.9%	10.9%	2.4%	0.3%	0.0%
Saturday		1%	7.5%	20.8%	39.6%	28.3%	1.9%	0.0%	0.0%	1.9%
Totals		100%	1.8%	15.7%	34.5%	29.9%	14.4%	3.0%	0.5%	0.2%

When the time-of-day information indicates that the shipment activity is evenly spread throughout the workday, the carrier can assume a high level of utilization (loads per day) for the trucks and drivers associated with the shipper's network. The carrier is able to price the network aggressively based on the expected level of scheduling productivity. However, if no time of day information is provided, the carrier will not be able to make any aggressive productivity assumptions and will price the network high enough to provide protection against scheduling risk and low tractor utilization scenarios.

The time of day analysis should also be applied to delivery times. The table below provides the same analysis for delivery times across all deliveries.

Annual Load Summary by Time of Day - Delivery Times										
Day of Week	Loads Per Day	Annual Loads	\multicolumn{8}{c	}{Load Count by Delivery Time}
			12 am to 3 am	3 am to 6 am	6 am to 9 am	9 am to 12 pm	12 pm to 3 pm	3 pm to 6 pm	6 pm to 9 pm	9 pm to 12 am
Sunday	0.02	1	-	-	-	-	-	-	1	-
Monday	23.71	1,233		16	393	389	328	82	17	8
Tuesday	24.79	1,289	4	30	400	381	355	85	20	14
Wednesday	27.48	1,429	2	25	453	395	422	111	15	6
Thursday	24.77	1,288	7	32	419	372	346	93	15	4
Friday	25.02	1,301	4	24	410	365	359	116	10	13
Saturday	2.02	105	3	6	34	19	34	7		2
Totals	25.56	6,646	20	133	2,109	1,921	1,844	494	78	47

Day of Week		% of Total Loads	\multicolumn{8}{c	}{Load Count by Delivery Time}
			12 am to 3 am	3 am to 6 am	6 am to 9 am	9 am to 12 pm	12 pm to 3 pm	3 pm to 6 pm	6 pm to 9 pm	9 pm to 12 am
Sunday		0%	0.0%	0.0%	0.0%	0.0%	0.0%	0.0%	100.0%	0.0%
Monday		27%	0.0%	1.3%	31.9%	31.5%	26.6%	6.7%	1.4%	0.6%
Tuesday		28%	0.3%	2.3%	31.0%	29.6%	27.5%	6.6%	1.6%	1.1%
Wednesday		31%	0.1%	1.7%	31.7%	27.6%	29.5%	7.8%	1.0%	0.4%
Thursday		28%	0.5%	2.5%	32.5%	28.9%	26.9%	7.2%	1.2%	0.3%
Friday		29%	0.3%	1.8%	31.5%	28.1%	27.6%	8.9%	0.8%	1.0%
Saturday		2%	2.9%	5.7%	32.4%	18.1%	32.4%	6.7%	0.0%	1.9%
Totals		146%	0.3%	2.0%	31.7%	28.9%	27.7%	7.4%	1.2%	0.7%

Based on this information, the carrier can see that about 90% of the deliveries each day occur between 6 am and 3 pm. The carrier will also notice that the deliveries between 6 am and 3 pm are spread evenly throughout the 9 hour period, allowing for a reasonable level of utilization and multiple trips per day for each driver. Only about 4% of deliveries occur from 6 pm to 6 am, so potential slip-seat efficiencies do not exist within this particular network.

Seasonal Shipping Patterns

Whenever available, the shipper should provide potential carriers with seasonal shipping patterns for the load volumes included in the mileage bands. The seasonality information will allow the carrier to accurately model the network and determine the correct amount of resources needed to serve the network.

Potential seasonal shipping patterns appear most often in two forms. The first is day-to-day fluctuation in load activity. The second is fluctuation from week-to-week or month-to-month over a longer period. Generally, steady load activity from day to day will allow the carrier to use less tractor and driver resources and manage the fleet more efficiently on a daily basis. These efficiencies will then allow the carrier to potentially offer the lowest possible cost.

Week-to-week or month-to-month fluctuations in volume are also significant, but are usually easier for the carrier to manage. The carrier can adjust the resources used to serve the shipper's changing volumes as needed. The more extreme the fluctuations in shipping patterns, the greater the cost impact in the carrier's pricing. Consider the table below depicting the monthly load volumes for two seasonal shippers.

Shipper	Item	Jan	Feb	Mar	Apr	May	Jun	Jul	Aug	Sep	Oct	Nov	Dec	Total
A	Loads	200	200	210	210	210	240	240	240	280	290	290	290	2,900
	% of Loads	6.9%	6.9%	7.2%	7.2%	7.2%	8.3%	8.3%	8.3%	9.7%	10.0%	10.0%	10.0%	
B	Loads	150	150	300	175	175	175	345	345	190	195	350	350	2,900
	% of Loads	5.2%	5.2%	10.3%	6.0%	6.0%	6.0%	11.9%	11.9%	6.6%	6.7%	12.1%	12.1%	

Both shippers shown in the table have seasonal shipping patterns. Shipper A has a consistent growth in shipment volumes from month to month, peaking at the end of the year. Without too much difficulty, the carrier can continue to add resources to the network as volume increases. The carrier can reduce the resource level in January when the volume returns to the lower level.

Shipper B has dramatic changes in volume over several periods during the year. Shipment volumes spike up in March, July, August, November and December. In a short haul network, volume swings of this proportion create a major challenge for the carrier. The carrier must constantly add and remove trucks and drivers, incurring significant costs as resources move into and out of the network.

In the case of seasonal shipments, the shipper should provide this information so that potential carriers can design and price accordingly. Shippers should not intentionally hide undesirable shipment patterns in order to obtain favorable pricing. Over time, carriers will likely request rate increases as a result of the undisclosed network requirements. Likewise, shippers with steady shipping patterns could realize a potential savings by providing shipment data to validate the lack of seasonal shipping fluctuations.

Mileage Band Destinations

Whenever possible in a bid situation, the shipper should provide potential carriers with actual lane-level information for the load volumes included in the mileage bands. The lane information will allow the carrier to identify any destinations that fit well with the carrier's existing network. The carrier can then provide applicable pricing discounts as a result of any potential shipper or carrier network synergies.

In pure mileage band pricing, the destination for pricing purposes is defined only in terms of one-way miles from the origin and is not dependent on the actual destination. As a result, the shipper may forgo certain opportunities for reducing costs. When designing a bid or rate agreement based on a mileage band format, the shipper might consider utilizing point-to-point pricing on certain strategic, high volume lanes, especially those in the upper ranges of the mileage bands.

The map below shows several major destinations for a shipper based in Indianapolis, IN considering a bid based on a mileage band format. Each of the four destinations shown below has significant annual load volumes and falls within the 151-160 mile band.

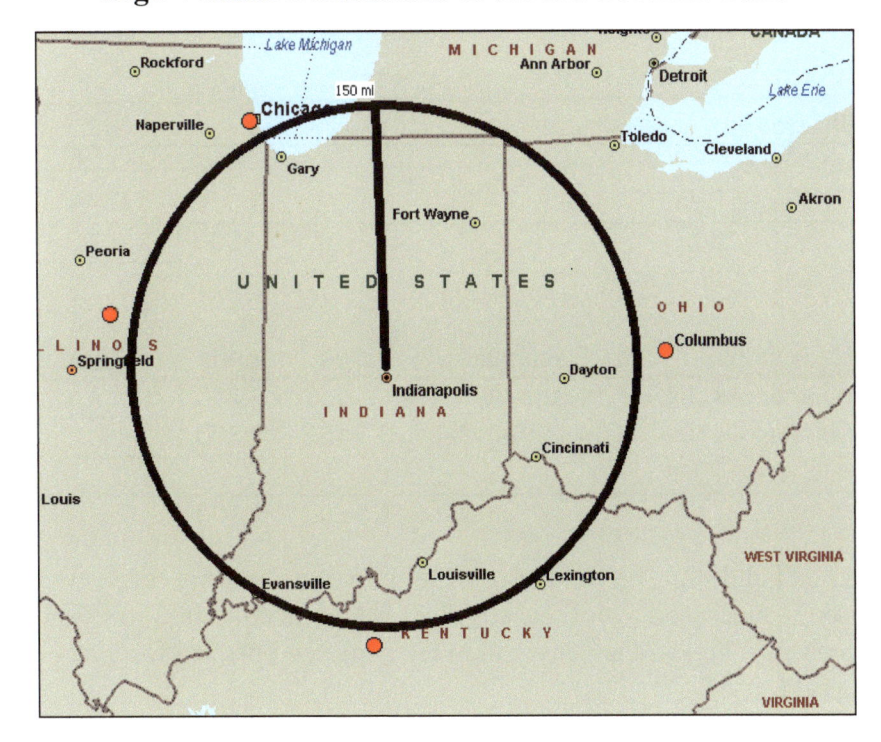

High Volume Destinations in the 151-160 Mile Band

Under normal circumstances, the shipper would include the total load volume in the mileage band format for pricing. However, this particular network offers two opportunities for exceptions to the pure mileage band format. Two destinations, Chicago, IL and Columbus, OH, are major headhaul markets. As a result, some carriers may be willing to offer aggressive, low-cost pricing on these specific lanes. Because Chicago and Columbus are major markets, certain carriers will be able to match a portion of this shipper's loads with the loads of other customers and create an efficient network. At the same time, the two other destinations in the 151-160 mile band do not offer the same opportunity. The destinations in central Kentucky and central Illinois are more likely to be typical out-and-back destinations and must be priced accordingly.

The shipper can take advantage of the lane-specific cost efficiencies through the bid design and lane design process. The Chicago lane and the Columbus lane could each be removed from the mileage bands and priced on a lane-specific, point-to-point basis. The basic bid design is shown below.

Bid Design for High-Volume Exception Lanes

Lanes in 151-160 Mileage Band

Origin	Destination	Miles	Loads	Lane Type
Indianapolis, IN	Chicago, IL	152	300	Pt. to Pt.
Indianapolis, IN	Columbus, OH	152	200	Pt. to Pt.
Indianapolis, IN	Clarkson, KY	152	250	Band
Indianapolis, IN	Lincoln, IL	152	350	Band
		Total Loads:	1,100	

↓

Bid Design:

Mileage Band	Loads	Rate
151-160	600	?

Origin	Destination	Miles	Loads	Rate
Indianapolis, IN	Chicago, IL	152	300	?
Indianapolis, IN	Columbus, OH	152	200	?

Total Loads: 1,100

With this revised bid design, carriers have the option of submitting reduced pricing on the two point-to-point lanes. To avoid rate conflicts, the point-to-point rates for the two individual lanes must be less than or equal to the suggested pricing for the corresponding mileage band rate.

For simplification, the practice of removing certain lanes from the mileage band format should only be used on relatively high volume lanes. Also, the practice should only rarely be used on extremely short lanes where out-and-back service is highly likely. Each shipper network will have unique criteria for what load volume levels and what distances would justify establishing a point-to-point lane.

Diseconomies of Scale in One Way Pricing

In certain cases, shippers will attempt to negotiate quantity discounts with carriers in exchange for awarding additional large quantities of linehaul business from a single shipping location to a single carrier. While quantity discounts have a sound financial basis when these shippers purchase raw materials or other goods from suppliers, the same cost theory does not always apply to trucking operations. For example, suppose a major home improvement retailer has historically ordered 100,000 hammers per year from its primary supplier at a cost of $10.00 per hammer. Then, when negotiating the purchase of hammers for the next year, the retailer offers to purchase 200,000 hammers from the supplier if the supplier will lower the price of the hammers to $9.00 per unit. The general expectation is that, because of the significant increase in units, the supplier should be able to produce the additional hammers at a lower cost per unit.

In trucking, the same economies of scale theory holds true only for a single truck. As the single truck produces more and more miles (units), the cost per mile (cost per unit of production) continues to decline. As discussed previously, this is one of the main reasons trucking companies seek to maximize miles per week (production) on each truck.

Unlike the single truck scenario, the economies of scale principle generally does not hold true for an increasing amount of one-way load volume from a single customer shipping location. For example, suppose this same home improvement retailer has a single carrier serving a distribution center located in Savannah, GA. The carrier currently provides truckload service for 10 loads per day from the location. The 10 loads show an average billed revenue per mile of $1.50 and an average length of haul of 1,000 miles.

On any given day, the carrier will dispatch the 10 closest, available trucks into Savannah to provide the service. The map below illustrates where these 10 trucks might be sourced from under normal conditions.

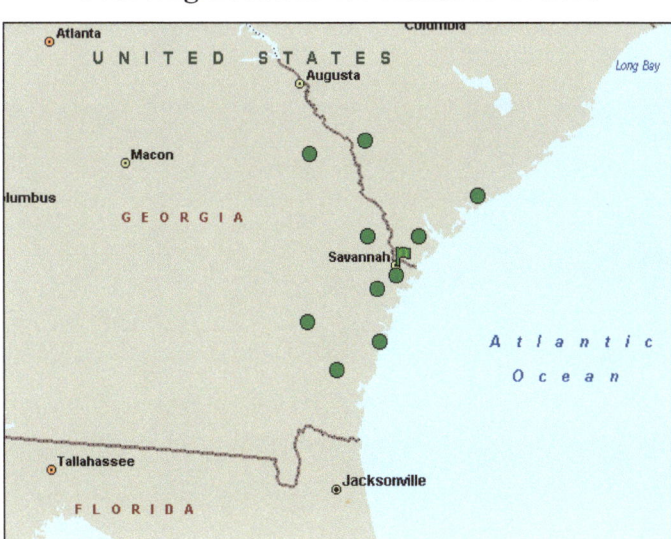

Sourcing Location for Initial 10 Trucks

Suppose these 10 trucks come from an average of 45 empty miles away and that the carrier's average cost per mile is $1.25. Based on these assumptions, the chart below details the approximate profit the carrier will earn on each of the 10 loads.

Load Number	Miles Loaded	Miles Empty	Miles Total	Empty Miles %	Revenue Per Mile Loaded	Revenue Per Mile Net	Total Revenue	Cost Per Mile	Cost Per Load	Profit Per Load
1	1,000	0	1,000	0.0%	$ 1.50	$ 1.50	$ 1,500	$ 1.25	$ 1,250	$ 250
2	1,000	10	1,010	1.0%	$ 1.50	$ 1.49	$ 1,500	$ 1.25	$ 1,263	$ 237
3	1,000	20	1,020	2.0%	$ 1.50	$ 1.47	$ 1,500	$ 1.25	$ 1,275	$ 225
4	1,000	30	1,030	2.9%	$ 1.50	$ 1.46	$ 1,500	$ 1.25	$ 1,288	$ 212
5	1,000	40	1,040	3.8%	$ 1.50	$ 1.44	$ 1,500	$ 1.25	$ 1,300	$ 200
6	1,000	50	1,050	4.8%	$ 1.50	$ 1.43	$ 1,500	$ 1.25	$ 1,313	$ 187
7	1,000	60	1,060	5.7%	$ 1.50	$ 1.42	$ 1,500	$ 1.25	$ 1,325	$ 175
8	1,000	70	1,070	6.5%	$ 1.50	$ 1.40	$ 1,500	$ 1.25	$ 1,338	$ 162
9	1,000	80	1,080	7.4%	$ 1.50	$ 1.39	$ 1,500	$ 1.25	$ 1,350	$ 150
10	1,000	90	1,090	8.3%	$ 1.50	$ 1.38	$ 1,500	$ 1.25	$ 1,363	$ 137

Notice that each additional truck must come from further and further away from the customer location. As a result, the carrier's net revenue per mile and profit per load both decline with each additional load.

Now suppose the carrier agrees to haul an additional 20 loads per day under these same assumptions. The map below illustrates the fact the each additional truck will continue to come from further and further away from the customer's shipping location.

Sourcing Locations for 20 Additional Trucks

Even though the shipper has asked for a discount for this additional volume, for this analysis the rate is kept constant at $1.50 per mile for easier comparisons. The chart below shows the estimated profitability of the next 20 loads.

Load Number	Loaded (Miles)	Empty (Miles)	Total (Miles)	Empty Miles %	Revenue Per Mile Loaded	Revenue Per Mile Net	Total Revenue	Cost Per Mile	Cost Per Load	Profit Per Load
11	1,000	100	1,100	9.1%	$ 1.50	$ 1.36	$ 1,500	$ 1.25	$ 1,375	$ 125
12	1,000	110	1,110	9.9%	$ 1.50	$ 1.35	$ 1,500	$ 1.25	$ 1,388	$ 113
13	1,000	120	1,120	10.7%	$ 1.50	$ 1.34	$ 1,500	$ 1.25	$ 1,400	$ 100
14	1,000	130	1,130	11.5%	$ 1.50	$ 1.33	$ 1,500	$ 1.25	$ 1,413	$ 88
15	1,000	140	1,140	12.3%	$ 1.50	$ 1.32	$ 1,500	$ 1.25	$ 1,425	$ 75
16	1,000	150	1,150	13.0%	$ 1.50	$ 1.30	$ 1,500	$ 1.25	$ 1,438	$ 63
17	1,000	160	1,160	13.8%	$ 1.50	$ 1.29	$ 1,500	$ 1.25	$ 1,450	$ 50
18	1,000	170	1,170	14.5%	$ 1.50	$ 1.28	$ 1,500	$ 1.25	$ 1,463	$ 38
19	1,000	180	1,180	15.3%	$ 1.50	$ 1.27	$ 1,500	$ 1.25	$ 1,475	$ 25
20	1,000	190	1,190	16.0%	$ 1.50	$ 1.26	$ 1,500	$ 1.25	$ 1,488	$ 13
21	1,000	200	1,200	16.7%	$ 1.50	$ 1.25	$ 1,500	$ 1.25	$ 1,500	$ -
22	1,000	210	1,210	17.4%	$ 1.50	$ 1.24	$ 1,500	$ 1.25	$ 1,513	$ (13)
23	1,000	220	1,220	18.0%	$ 1.50	$ 1.23	$ 1,500	$ 1.25	$ 1,525	$ (25)
24	1,000	230	1,230	18.7%	$ 1.50	$ 1.22	$ 1,500	$ 1.25	$ 1,538	$ (38)
25	1,000	240	1,240	19.4%	$ 1.50	$ 1.21	$ 1,500	$ 1.25	$ 1,550	$ (50)
26	1,000	250	1,250	20.0%	$ 1.50	$ 1.20	$ 1,500	$ 1.25	$ 1,563	$ (63)
27	1,000	260	1,260	20.6%	$ 1.50	$ 1.19	$ 1,500	$ 1.25	$ 1,575	$ (75)
28	1,000	270	1,270	21.3%	$ 1.50	$ 1.18	$ 1,500	$ 1.25	$ 1,588	$ (88)
29	1,000	280	1,280	21.9%	$ 1.50	$ 1.17	$ 1,500	$ 1.25	$ 1,600	$ (100)
30	1,000	290	1,290	22.5%	$ 1.50	$ 1.16	$ 1,500	$ 1.25	$ 1,613	$ (113)

Estimated Profit Per Load (Loads 11 to 30)

Notice that the carrier begins to lose money on the 22nd load and that the loss per load continues to increase. Had the carrier agreed to a lower rate with the customer, the amount of money lost would have been even greater.

For the average carrier, increases in load volume from a single location cause the carrier's cost per load to increase with each additional load. All other things being equal, the carrier cannot justify a reduction in the rate per mile for this customer. In fact, the carrier actually needs a rate increase to financially justify a commitment to the additional 20 loads.

In certain situations, the estimated profitability in the analysis presented previously may change. Several potential situations are discussed below.

- **Load Alternatives**: If the carrier has no other nearby load options with customers that pay competitive rates, the retailer's additional loads may actually be the carrier's most profitable alternative, even if the carrier actually loses money by serving some loads. On the other hand, if the carrier has many profitable load options in this market, the carrier may be much more profitable by continuing to provide trucks to these customers rather than to provide extra trucks to the retailer, especially if the retailer demands a reduced rate.

- **Inbound Loads**: The retailer may be able to offer the carrier some additional loads inbound to the distribution center to complement the additional outbound loads. With the introduction of the inbound loads, the carrier's empty miles will be reduced and a reduction in the pricing might then be justified.

- **Destination Volumes**: Suppose the retailer's loads from this location always go to a single location, Chicago, IL, for example. If this were the case, the carrier would now have two potential problems. In addition to the empty miles problem at the origin, the carrier may now also have too many trucks in the destination market. The additional trucks at the destination may have to incur above average empty miles to reach their next load. However, if the carrier has a major customer in the destination that needs extra capacity, the additional volume may be beneficial to the carrier. The carrier may benefit by reducing empty miles to serve a customer in the destination market more than the additional empty miles incurred to serve the retailer in the origin market.

- **Origin Location**: Savannah, GA in this example is in a relatively isolated location on the Atlantic Ocean, making it even more difficult to position trucks into the location. All trucks coming into this location must come from the west, northwest, and southwest. If the origin location were more accessible, the empty miles problem may not be as severe.

While in some cases the additional volume will be beneficial to the carrier, as a rule, providing service to increasing long haul volume from a single location will eventually cause the carrier's profits to deteriorate. This deterioration will be more significant if the carrier's network is not adjusted to serve the volume in a profitable manner. If the carrier simply continues to incur additional empty miles to position available trucks to the shipper from further and further away, the carrier will not be profitable on the incremental load volumes.

Carriers cannot be expected to reduce rates just because a shipper provides additional outbound load volume from a location. A carrier providing service for 4 loads per day may reduce rates in order increase total volume to 10 loads because the carrier has an additional 6 trucks available in the local market each day. However, that same carrier cannot reduce rates again to increase volume to 20 loads per day because the carrier will now have to bring the incremental trucks in from outside the local market, thus reducing the profit per load. Shippers must understand that a carrier's cost structure is complex and that additional loads do not necessarily create increased efficiencies for the carrier, especially in a dynamic one-way network.

Volume-based One-Way Pricing

Because of the diseconomies of scale in one-way networks that eventually result from increasing load volumes on a lane or origin, the shipper may choose to deploy a pricing mechanism to account for the carrier's network model. One method is to develop a rating system with volume-based pricing levels or tiers. The table below provides an example of a tiered pricing structure.

Tiered Pricing		
Tier Level	Weekly Load Volumes	Rate Per Mile
Tier 1	1 to 15	$ 1.45
Tier 2	16 to 24	$ 1.52
Tier 3	25 and up	$ 1.58

Under this structure, the first 15 loads each week would be charged at $1.45 per mile. Loads 16 through 24 would be charged at $1.52 per mile. Beyond the 24th load, any additional loads would be charged at $1.58 per mile.

The tiers for each lane would be defined in the shipper's bid information. The carrier would then provide pricing for each tier based on the carrier's available capacity and overall ability to serve the lane. The shipper would then evaluate the total cost of the carrier's pricing proposal based on the expected number of loads to fall within each tier. The low cost carrier would be the one with the lowest total cost as shown in the bid analysis example below.

Tiered Pricing and Bid Analysis (720 billed miles)					
Tier Level	Annual Loads	Rate Per Mile Carrier A	Rate Per Mile Carrier B	Annual Cost Carrier A	Annual Cost Carrier B
Tier 1	375	$ 1.45	$ 1.43	$ 391,500	$ 386,100
Tier 2	125	$ 1.52	$ 1.58	$ 136,800	$ 142,200
Tier 3	50	$ 1.58	$ 1.66	$ 56,880	$ 59,760
Totals	550	$ 1.4777	$ 1.4850	$ 585,180	$ 588,060

Based on the above analysis, Carrier A provides the lowest total annual cost. Carrier A has proposed the higher Tier 1 rate at $1.45 per mile. However, Carrier A has much lower rates for Tier 2 and Tier 3 activity. The shipper should base the carrier selection decision on the lowest total cost, not simply the carrier with the lowest Tier 1 rate.

A pricing structure of this type benefits both the shipper and the carrier. In Tier 1, the carrier is able to offer the best possible rate on the first group of shipments without being concerned about the cost of serving load activity above this level at the lower Tier 1 rate. The carrier is protected from volume surges by the higher rates in the upper tiers. The shipper is able to enjoy lower costs in Tier 1 as a result of the volume protection provided to the carrier by the tiered rate structure.

One downside of a system of this type is the administration of the pricing and the determination of which loads qualify for each tier. Shippers that utilize tiered pricing should have a system in place to manage the process and insure that the carrier is paid correctly according to the tiered pricing agreement.

Outsourcing Private Fleets to Dedicated Carriers

A large number of shippers operate private fleets that function in much the same manner as a dedicated fleet. A private fleet is an arrangement where a shipper owns and manages a fleet of trucks, trailers and drivers. Private fleets can be any size, though most range in size from 1 to 50 trucks. However, one well-known U.S. retailer has a private fleet consisting of several thousand trucks and drivers.

Operating a private fleet gives the shipper a great deal of control over the transportation program. However, the shipper must also manage common trucking challenges such as safety, driver turnover, and equipment maintenance. While some shippers do an excellent job of managing a private fleet, most private fleet operators do not have the same level of internal expertise to manage these trucking-related challenges as do experienced truckload carriers.

At some point, most private fleet operators face the question of whether to retain the private fleet or outsource the fleet operation to a dedicated carrier. The ultimate decision is usually based on many factors including cost, customer service, liability, and focus. While every shipper's thought process will be unique, the table below lists some common arguments for outsourcing a private fleet.

Arguments for Outsourcing a Private Fleet
Focus on Core Competencies. Private fleet operators are, in effect, managing a trucking company. These management responsibilities require the company to focus on activities outside of their core business and primary areas of expertise.
Trucking Expertise. Private fleet operators often lack the trucking expertise of experienced carriers. Trucking expertise may include management experience, computer systems, maintenance networks, driver training programs, sales networks, and general operating efficiencies.
Insurance Cost and Liability. Operators of small private fleets have tremendous exposure to accidents and liability. The significant cost of insurance may make small private fleets cost prohibitive. Shipper logos displayed on tractors and trailers can increase liability and litigation exposure.
Flexible Fleet Sizing. Carriers can adjust most dedicated fleet sizes to meet peak seasonal needs. Carriers can also reduce the size of the fleet during slower shipping periods. Private fleet operators are not able to react to changing fleet size needs, especially in the short run.
Balance Sheet. Private fleet operators that own tractor and trailer equipment have company assets tied up in items not directly related to their core business operation. Outsourcing the private fleet allows the shipper to free up capital for use in other areas of their business.
Access to Backhauls. The majority of private fleet operators do not have access to a well-developed backhaul network like those of established for-hire carriers. Carrier-provided backhauls will also likely be at higher revenue levels than the backhauls that can be obtained by most private fleet operators.

For many reasons, shippers are often very reluctant to outsource a private fleet. The table below describes several common reasons for retaining a private fleet.

Arguments for Retaining a Private Fleet
Customer Service. Many private fleet operators believe the private fleet allows for greater control over customer service as well as the ability to consistently provide outstanding on-time service.
Control Over Capacity. Private fleet operators feel more in control of capacity by maintaining a private fleet. Shippers can rely on their own fleet during periods of limited capacity and not be at the risk of relying heavily on outside carriers with limited capacity.
Driver Turnover. Private fleet operators often have less driver turnover than most dedicated carriers. Reduced driver turnover should also result in better customer service levels.
Image and Marketing. Many shippers have operated private fleets for many years and believe the fleet plays a positive role in the company's image and marketing. Company logos and product images are often featured prominently on both tractors and trailers.

When considering outsourcing a private fleet to a dedicated carrier, the private fleet operator must identify the costs of the private fleet for comparison with carrier cost proposals. The standard fleet costs such as trucks, trailers, driver wages, maintenance, insurance and fuel are typically very easy for private fleet operators to identify. However, private fleet operators may fail to include certain less visible costs in the comparison such as those listed below.

Potential Hidden Costs of a Private Fleet
Equipment Legalization. Cost of permits and other forms of legal registration for tractors and trailers.
Insurance and Liability. Direct insurance costs as well as liability and exposure to accidents and legal problems.
Driver Fringe Benefits. Private fleet drivers are often company employees and receive a full benefits package including health insurance, retirement plans, and other benefits.
Administration. The cost of the management team associated with the day-to-day management of the fleet is significant in many cases. The administrative team handles such items as leases, maintenance, driver recruiting, DOT compliance, safety, customer service, and many other trucking-related administrative duties.
Equipment Replacement. If the private fleet is using outdated equipment that must soon be replaced with newer equipment, the "comparison" cost may need to be adjusted to reflect the cost of the new equipment instead of the historically less-costly and outdated equipment.
Cost of Capital. The capital cost of company resources invested in tractor and trailer equipment and related assets must be included. Capital invested in transportation equipment could be reallocated to core business activities if the fleet is outsourced to a dedicated carrier.

Perhaps the most overlooked item on the previous list is the cost of capital. Suppose a private fleet operator owns $2,000,000 in equipment as part of the private fleet. Assuming the shipper has a cost of capital of 9%, there is a significant hidden cost here. The table below illustrates the cost of capital for this private fleet.

Annual Cost of Capital for Private Fleet		
Investment in Equipment	$	2,000,000
Cost of Capital	x	9.0%
Cost of Capital Expense	$	180,000

When comparing private fleet costs to the proposed dedicated fleet costs from carriers, the omission of the cost of capital, when applicable, could make a significant difference in the comparison. On the carrier cost side, the cost of capital is included in the carrier's pricing proposal. A major portion of the carrier's operating profit represents the required return on investment for the equipment used in the fleet.

When evaluating proposals, the private fleet operator must be certain that all relevant costs are included in the analysis and any irrelevant costs are excluded. Without proper comparison costs, the shipper could easily reach a poor decision and miss an opportunity to reduce costs by outsourcing the private fleet operation to a dedicated carrier.

Summary

The goal of this chapter is to provide shippers with accurate tools and techniques for measuring and analyzing truckload costs and operations. The better the shipper is able to understand the trucking business model and cost behaviors, the better the shipper will be able to manage transportation costs and negotiate rates. By understanding the carrier's needs, the shipper will make a better business partner for truckload carriers and enjoy the benefits of that enhanced relationship in the long run.